The History
of the Religion of Israel

The History of the Religion of Israel

An Old Testament Theology

John Howard Raven

BAKER BOOK HOUSE
Grand Rapids, Michigan

Hardcover edition issued 1933
by the New Brunswick Theological Seminary

Paperback edition issued 1979
by Baker Book House Company
ISBN: 0-8010-7691-9

PHOTOLITHOPRINTED BY CUSHING - MALLOY, INC.
ANN ARBOR, MICHIGAN, UNITED STATES OF AMERICA
1979

FOREWORD

With the reissuance of John Howard Raven's *History of the Religion of Israel*, readers may once again enter into the thought of a man who was one of the stalwarts of the faith. For many, this will be a totally new experience, because the book's initial release in 1933 was through private printing at his own seminary, accompanied by only limited publicity and circulation. Yet Raven was one of a generation of great Reformed and Presbyterian scholars of the Old Testament. They drew their inspiration from Princeton's William Henry Green in the 1890s; and their roster included such masters of orthodoxy as Robert Dick Wilson, John D. Davis, Geerhardus Vos, and Oswald T. Allis. How appreciative I was for the characteristic graciousness of Dr. Raven when in 1946 he sent me, a struggling graduate at Princeton, a gift copy of *Religion of Israel*, autographed, and with his engraved card attached to the flyleaf.

John Howard Raven (1870–1949) was a lifelong champion of conservative theology within the Reformed Church of America. After graduating from its New Brunswick Seminary in 1894 and then serving as a pastor, he was called back to his alma mater to teach Old Testament; he retired in 1939, forty-one years later. He was honored by elevation to the presidency of the faculty and, from 1923 to 1925, of the seminary as a whole. He lectured in Old Testament at Princeton Seminary from 1926 to 1931 and published volumes on biblical interpretation and the Hebrew language. He is best remembered for his *Old Testament Introduction*. It was *the* standard text for Bible-believing Americans from its publication in 1906, through that period of theological drought that followed upon Princeton's reorganization in 1929, and down into the 1940s, when a reviving evangelical scholarship at last incited the works of E. J. Young and Merrill Unger, among the next generation.

What then is Raven's *History of the Religion of Israel?* Do not judge a book by its title. Confessedly, many similarly entitled works of this period advocated a godless historicism; they were lifeless, rationalistic studies on how Old Testament ideas evolved out of primitive Hebrew beliefs, works that for almost half a century (following the posthumous appearance in 1873 of Oehler's *Theology of the Old Testament*) effectively banished true biblical doctrine from Germany. But Raven's is a genuine theology of the Old Testament—not just what men thought, but what God taught, authoritatively preserved in inspired Scripture. In how many other publications of this sort, for example, even today, can we find a serious discussion of what God revealed to Adam? We find it in Raven. Not that his book is complete: he was never able to carry it beyond the time of Manasseh (697–642 B.C.), during whose evil reign Raven believed the Book of

Job to have been written. But then it is in just the
earlier periods of Israel's history that the evangelical
view stands in the sharpest contrast to the reconstruc-
tion of liberalism.

A final word of caution. As do all pioneers, Raven
may have sometimes allowed his creative interaction
with the problems of biblical interpretation that were
current in his day to lead him into utterances that
our more practiced ears find unguarded. Do we take
issue with his theories on prophetic emotionalism (pp.
189–91)? On traces of Davidic polytheism (pp. 206–
7)? On the condition of the righteous after death
(p. 247)? Good: we are exercising the same sort of
consecrated "criticism" that Raven himself exemplified
so beautifully in his treatment of circumcision and the
removal of guilt (pp. 175–76) or of the nature of
faith (pp. 468–74). To John Howard Raven, then,
may be applied that admonition of old:

Inquire, I pray thee, of the former age;
and consider the things searched out by their fathers.

(Job 8:8)

J. BARTON PAYNE
Professor of Old Testament
Covenant Theological Seminary

CONTENTS

INTRODUCTION

I. Definition. This subject was formerly treated under the title of Old Testament Theology. Old Testament Theology is that part of Biblical Theology which is derived from the Old Testament. Biblical Theology has been defined as "the theology of the Bible in its historical formation" (Briggs, General Introduction to the Study of Holy Scripture p. 569) and similarly Old Testament Theology has been defined as the "historico-genetic delineation of the religion contained in the canonical writings of the Old Testament" (Ochler Theology of the Old Testament, Vol. I, p. 7.). Thus Old Testament Theology presents the religion of Israel in its origin and historical development. In the strict sense there is no theology in the Old Testament, although it presupposes certain conceptions which may be presented in theological form. Since its method is essentially historical it is better to call the subject the History of the Religion of Israel.

II. Relation to Other Studies. While Systematic Theology is based upon the Bible as truly as Biblical Theology, its method and arrangement are different. Systematic Theology presents the teachings of scripture in a logical and philosophical system. Its arrangement of its subject matter is not historical but logical. Furthermore, Biblical Theology inquires merely, What were the conceptions of the religion of the Bible at various stages of its development? What was the teaching of the differ-

5

ent books and authors of scripture? Biblical Theology as such has nothing to do with the question whether these teachings are true or false and of present validity. These are questions for Systematic Theology.

Inasmuch as the religion of the Bible is essentially historical and not merely didactic or doctrinal, the logical position of Biblical Theology is before that of Systematic Theology. Systematic Theology should not derive its material directly from scripture without regarding the historical development of its religion. Upon the other hand, Biblical Theology is dependent upon exegesis. It takes the material furnished by exegesis and arranges it in historical order, showing the influence of one idea upon another and how the religion developed. This intermediate position of Biblical Theology between exegesis and Systematic Theology is an honorable one. Since Judaism and Christianity are historic religions, they can never be understood except by the historic method of inquiry.

Old Testament Theology, or rather the History of the Religion of Israel, is also dependent upon the Higher Criticism, which seeks to determine the authorship, date and composition of the books of the Old Testament. This dependence, however, is different in the narrative or historical parts of the Hebrew scriptures from what it is in the prophetic or poetic parts as well as the so-called Wisdom literature. In the historical books the sole inquiry necessary for the historian of Israel's religion is whether these books present an accurate picture of the religion of the time. Are they really historical? If so, the date when the history was written and the author who wrote it become secondary in importance. The only bearing they have lies in the fact that, if the history was written long after the events recorded, it may not present those events accurately. In this case its value may be chiefly in the light it sheds on the religion of the time it was written. The case is entirely different with the books which do not record history, such as the prophetical books, the Psalms and the Proverbs. It is essential to know when these books were written so that the religious ideas which they set forth may be placed in the true stage of the progress of Israel's religion.

It is in its relation to the Higher Criticism that the greatest difficulty arises in tracing the history of the religion of Israel. Several of the books are anonymous and some of them give scarcely any indication of their date. This is particularly true of many of the Psalms. Certain writers on the history of the religion depend upon the religious ideas expressed to determine the date of the writing. They often use this criterion to overthrow an ancient tradition concerning the authorship and, therefore, the date of a book or a part of a book. While such considerations may have some force, they should be employed with caution. It is by no means sure that a book or a writing which exhibits a certain conception of God or of the ritual dates from the same period as another writing which expresses similar ideas. At least this test is not safely used to overthrow other surer indications of date. It should be employed only when other signs are lacking.

III. Critical Standpoint. The higher critical standpoint of this book is in the main the older traditional one.
Its author regards the divisive theories of the Pentateuch
and other books as unproven and the dates to which its
alleged documents are assigned as highly conjectural.
He finds no sufficient reason to doubt that David wrote
most of the Psalms which are assigned to him and that
Solomon was the author of a large part of the Proverbs.
He does not regard the books of Chronicles as of very
little historical value. In general he does not believe
that the prophets came before the law and that a large
part of the Old Testament was composed in the late
Persian period or the Greek or Maccabean periods. On
the other hand he does not believe that Solomon wrote
Ecclesiastes and that David wrote all the Psalms which
bear his name. He doubts whether the prophet Jonah
wrote the book of Jonah. He finds good reasons for
regarding the speeches of Elihu (chapters 32-37) in the
book of Job as a later addition. This is not the place to
state the reasons for these critical opinions. They are
mentioned only to give a general idea of the critical standpoint from which this book is written.

IV. Other Preliminary Considerations. (1) This
book attempts to distinguish between the divinely
appointed revealed religion of the Old Testament and
Israel's adherence to that religion. Just as Christianity
cannot be judged fairly by the religious life of many
Christians—or rather lack of it—so the religion of the
Old Testament should not be judged by the conduct of
Israel. The actual religious conditions of the time were
often far below the standards of the authoritative teach-

ers. From the very fact that the religion was so exalted and so spiritual it was all the harder to understand it and to put it into practice. The number of those who understood it and who lived it was always small. The religion of the prophets was one thing and the religion of the people was another. There were times of apostasy, like the period of the Judges, when scarcely any of the people retained even a nominal adherence to the religion of their fathers. The prophets and other inspired men were always ahead of their times. Yet their teaching was never so far in advance but that a few choice souls understood and followed them. So step by step through frail human instruments God was leading Israel and preparing them for the revelation of his Son.

(2) The revelation of the Old Testament was progressive, and the ideas revealed were suited to the times in which they were given. What Jesus said to his disciples was true also of every stage of God's revelation to Israel, "I have yet many things to say unto you but ye cannot bear them now" (John 16:12). This progress, however, was not entirely natural. It had its natural side. The great spiritual leaders of Israel felt deeply and brooded long over the religious condition of the people. They did not speculate concerning the nature of God or his dealings with men in an abstract way. They sought God through the heart rather than the head. And at the very same time that they were seeking him, Jehovah was seeking them. So God and man met and the result was revelation. Thus on the one hand the Old Testament presents a progressive revelation of the Eternal God, and on the other hand a progressive discovery of God by chosen men.

CHAPTER I.

The Religion of the Patriarchs.

Genesis 12-50.

I. Sources. Strictly speaking, our only source of information concerning the religion of the patriarchs, Abraham, Isaac and Jacob, and their families is found in chapters twelve to fifty of the book of Genesis. The comparative fulness of the narrative in these chapters seems to indicate that they were based upon traditions handed down from the patriarchs themselves through Joseph to Moses. It is possible that these traditions were in written form, but of this we cannot be certain. Chapters one to eleven, on the other hand, contain introductory material. There is no reason to believe that the account of creation in chapter one rests upon material which was handed down to the patriarchs and so to Moses. At least the form in which it has come to us agrees better with the theory that Moses was its author and that he placed it where it is as an appropriate introduction to the following history. The case is different with chapters two to eleven. Their primitive character, their brevity, except in the stories of Adam and Eve, Cain and Abel, and Noah, and the genealogies which intervene, suggest they they contain material which was handed down orally till the time of Abraham. We may, therefore, discover in these chapters evidences of the beginnings of religion among the ancestors of Abraham and to some degree among those peoples with whom they came in contact. In doing so, however, it is necessary to take account of the fact that these chapters were not committed to writing until ages after most of the events recorded and hence they may reflect religious conceptions of the time of the patriarchs. Furthermore, the whole of Genesis may reflect to some degree the religious conceptions of Moses and his time.

II. Religion Before Abraham. Chapters two to eleven of Genesis do not give us a religious history of mankind to the time of Abraham in the manner of modern historians. The information they furnish concerning the other religions is very meager. There are here, however, priceless indications concerning that primitive religion which prepared for the religion of the patriarchs as the religion of the patriarchs prepared for the religion of Israel. This primitive religion—true as far as the imperfect knowledge of those remote ages would permit—was the religion of the ancestors of Abraham in the godly line of Seth and of Shem. There were, however, many defections from it even in the godly line. We may be sure that the religion made progress during the ages before Abraham, although our sources are too scant to trace this progress.

The following general features may be distinguished in the religion of Abraham's ancestors.

(1) THE IDEA OF GOD. Their idea of God was very primitive and anthropomorphic. They believed that God formed man from the dust of the ground and breathed

into his nostrils the breath of life in the most realistic fashion (Gen. 2:7). He planted a garden in Eden and put man there (Gen. 2:8, 15). He talked with man with audible voice (Gen. 2:16, 18; 3:8, 9-19; 4:6-7, 9-15; 6:3, 13-22; 7:1-5; 8:15-17; 9:1-17). He brought the animals to man to see what he would call them (Gen. 2:19). He formed woman from one of man's ribs (Gen. 2:21-22). He walked in the garden (Gen. 3:8). He spoke to the serpent (Gen. 3:14). He made coats of skins for Adam and Eve (Gen. 3:21). He drove them out of the garden (Gen. 3:24). He put a mark on Cain (Gen. 4:15). He repented that he had made man (Gen. 6:6-7). When Noah and his family were safely in the ark God shut him in (Gen. 7:16). When Noah offered a sacrifice God smelled a sweet savor (Gen. 8:21). He came down to see the city and the tower which man built (Gen. 11:5).

While we recognize that these statements, taken symbolically and figuratively, present very profound truth, it is not at all probable that primitive men so understood them. The conception of God as an infinite being unconditioned by space and time, without parts and passions, was as much beyond them as the ideas of a grown man are beyond those of a child. While there are anthropomorphisms throughout the Old Testament and to some degree they are essential to a theistic conception of God, the anthropmorphisms of the early chapters of Genesis are more primitive than those of later times. (See article on Anthropomorphisms, by James Lindsay, in the International Standard Bible Encyclopedia.)

There is no light in these chapters themselves on the question whether the Sethite line were monotheists. However, arguing back from the faith of the patriarchs and of early Israel, it is safe to say that while they worshipped only one God and believed him greater and truer than all others, they did not deny the existence of other Gods or believe that their God was the only God. Thus they should be called henotheists rather than monotheists.

It is also impossible to tell under what name they worshipped him. The statement immediately after the record of the birth of Enosh, the son of Seth, "Then began men to call upon the name of Jehovah" (Gen. 4:26) may indicate that this name is exceedingly ancient. Indeed, as Ryle points out, "it is not unreasonable to suppose that the name belongs to prehistoric antiquity" (Cambridge Bible on Gen. 4:26). It is certain that the noble conceptions which were later associated with the name were unknown to these primitive men. It is also possible that the name was introduced into these early records at a later time.

The Sethite line believed that God cared for man. This is reflected in the statements that he put man in the garden (Gen. 2:8, 15), that he made woman to help him (Gen. 2:18), that he made coats of skins for them (Gen. 3:21), and that he provided a way to save Noah and his family from the waters of the flood (Gen. 6:8, 18).

On the other hand, they believed that God punished those who disobeyed him. Thus he drove Adam and Eve out of the garden (Gen. 3:24), he made Cain a fugitive (Gen. 4:12), he destroyed mankind by the flood (Gen.

6:7), and he scattered those who built the tower of Babel (Gen. 11:8).

Although their attitude toward God was mostly one of fear, there are some indications that they had a slight conception of God's mercy. These are the promise that the seed of the woman should bruise the serpent's head (Gen 3:15), Lamech's expectation that Noah would mitigate the curse of God because of man's sin (Gen. 5:29), and the covenant with Noah that God would not again destroy mankind by a flood (Gen. 8:21-22).

(2) WORSHIP.

The two universal elements of worship, prayer and sacrifice, were found in this early period. While the expression "to call upon the name of Jehovah" (Gen. 4:26) suggests prayer rather than sacrifice, it is used where the two are associated in the story of Abraham (Gen. 12:8) and Isaac (Gen. 26:25). Possibly prayer accompanied sacrifice from the earliest times. We should not read back into the story of Cain and Abel the distinctions of the Mosaic ritual and think that Cain's offering was not acceptable because, being from the fruit of the ground, it contained no blood and thus could not atone for sin. The suggestion of Patrick Fairbairn (The Typology of Scripture, Vol. I, pp. 249-50) that the clothing with coats of skins rather than fig leaves may have indicated animal rather than vegetable offerings as acceptable to God, is ingenious but not convincing. The story of Cain itself seems to show that his offering was not acceptable because he took no pains to select the best that he had while Abel brought of the firstlings of his flock and of the fat thereof (Gen. 4:3-4).

The differences between the offerings of Cain and Abel on the one hand (Gen. 4:3-5) and that of Noah on the other (Gen. 8:20-21) are suggestive. Nothing is said of an altar in the former account. How Cain and Abel brought their offerings to God we do not know. Nothing is said of fire as if they thought the flames could send up the offerings to God. There is no hint of any distinction between clean and unclean animals. Noah, however, began by building an altar. He took of every clean beast and bird and offered burnt offerings on the altar. It was the flames which wafted the sacrifice to God. This shows a more highly developed conception of sacrifice than the older story. While the distinction of clean and unclean animals existed, it was not the highly developed distinction of Mosaic times.

There are no indications that worship was confined to any one place or that it was carried on by any one set of persons. Sacred places and an official priesthood were later developments, at least so far as the ancestors of Abraham are concerned. According to tradition, Terah, the father of Abraham, worshipped other Gods (Josh. 24:2). He probably did so under the idolatrous forms which were common in Babylonia in his day. With this exception, there is no evidence in scripture that the ancestors of Abraham worshipped idols, although it is probable that many of them did.

There are two instances from these prehistoric times of a more spiritual type of religion. It is recorded of

Enoch that he "walked with God and he was not for God took him" (Gen. 5:24). It was also said of Noah that he walked with God (Gen. 6:9) and Abraham was commanded to walk before him (Gen. 17:1). Although we should not read into this expression a spiritual content which was impossible in those days, it exhibits a certain conscientiousness, a sense of the reality of God which is superior to mere ceremonialism.

(3) THE IDEA OF MAN.

The sense of the unity of the human race is the more remarkable in these chapters because they are so primitive. Whether Adam be the name of an individual or a designation of the human race, it is clear that mankind is represented as one stock from whom all are descended.

As to his nature, man is represented as two fold. God formed him from the dust of the ground (Gen. 2:7) as he formed the beasts and the birds (Gen. 2:19), but the preeminence of man above the beasts is shown in the further statement that God "breathed into his nostrils the breath of life." This imparting of the breath or spirit of God to man made him in some sense like God and brought him into special relation to God. It agrees with the Mosaic representation of man as made in the image of God, after his likeness (Gen. 1:26-27).

This special relation to God, showed itself in the position of dominion which man held in the earth. The animals were subject to him. The process of naming them, putting his estimate upon them (Gen. 2:19-20) revealed to man his vast superiority to them. Woman was made to be his helper (Gen. 2:21-23). Man was responsible only to God and bound to obey God (Gen. 2:16-17; 3:2, 3, 11; 4:9-15; 6:3, 14, etc.). If he disobeyed, God punished him in this life (Gen. 3:16-19; 4:10-12). By disobedience to God he lost dominion over the earth and became subject to it (Gen. 3:23).

Although the human race was one, the free choice of obedience or disobedience to God divided them into two lines from the beginning—those descended from the murderer Cain and those descended from Seth, who took the place of righteous Abel (Gen. 4:25). Within the righteous Sethite line there is a similar free process of selection. Sin had corrupted this righteous line almost completely before the flood. "Jehovah saw that the wickedness of man was great in the earth and that every imagination of the thoughts of his heart was only evil continually" (Gen. 6:5). After the flood the free process of selection continued. Ham, Noah's youngest son, was rejected because he dishonored his father (Gen. 9:22, 24-25). Shem, the oldest son, with his descendants remained under the favor of God, while Japheth and his descendants received their knowledge of God from the Semites (Gen. 9:26-27).

(4) SALVATION AND THE MESSIANIC HOPE.

The only hope primitive man had for deliverance from the evil effects of sin was in the future. It was hidden in the words of God to the serpent: "I will put enmity between thee and the woman and between thy seed and her seed: he shall bruise thy head and thou shalt bruise his heel" (Gen. 3:15). Although primitive man had no conception of the length of human history and certainly did not understand these words as a promise of an individual Saviour, he saw in a vague way the perpetual warfare between man and the tempter and he never lost the hope that some descendant of his—or perhaps all his descendants together—would destroy the tempter and thus free man from the curse due to sin. This hope is reflected in the enigmatic words of Eve at the birth of her first son, "I have gotten a man with the help of Jehovah" (Gen. 4:1), which may be rendered literally, "I have gotten man, even Jehovah." It is reflected more clearly in the words of Lamech at the birth of Noah, "This same shall comfort us in our work and in the toil of our hands which cometh because of the ground which Jehovah hath cursed" (Gen. 5:29).

This hope of deliverance through the seed of the woman is the root out of which long ages afterward the Messianic hope sprang. Strictly speaking, it should not be called the Messianic hope until the time of David. It did not attain a personal form until long after the patriarchal age. Nevertheless, throughout the book of Genesis the free process of selection was focussing the hope more and more definitely upon the line from which at last the Messiah came. Hence in the broader sense we may speak of the promise that the seed of the woman should bruise the serpent's head (Gen. 3:15) and Lamech's words at the birth of Noah (Gen. 5:29) as Messianic predictions. Noah's blessing upon Shem and indirectly upon Japheth (Gen. 9:25-27), also marks an important development in the Messianic idea.

(5) The Covenant with Noah.

The idea of a covenant between God and man, which later was the basis of the conception of the chosen people Israel, has its beginning in this early time. It is intimately related to the development of the Messianic hope. The conditions of the covenant as in all later covenants were prescribed by God. Man could obtain the blessings of the covenant only by obedience to the conditions which God laid down. In foretelling the flood God said to Noah, "I will establish my covenant with thee; and thou shalt come into the ark, thou and thy sons and thy wife and thy sons' wives with thee" (Gen. 6:18). In recollection of this promise and in thanksgiving for his deliverance, after the flood, "Noah builded an altar unto Jehovah, and took of every clean beast and of every clean bird, and offered burnt-offerings on the altar, and Jehovah smelled the sweet savor, and Jehovah said in his heart, I will not again curse the ground any more for man's sake, for that the imagination of man's heart is evil from his youth, neither will I again smite any more everything living, as I have done. While the earth remaineth, seedtime and harvest, and cold and heat, and summer and winter and day and night shall not cease" (Gen. 8:20-22). While this covenant was made with Noah, it is later spoken of as being also with his seed and with every living creature, the birds and the cattle and every beast of the earth (Gen. 9:9-10, 15-16). The rainbow was taken as its token or pledge.

All mankind share in the blessings of this covenant. It is the divine guarantee that the earth, the theater of human history, shall not itself be destroyed until God has wrought out upon it all that is hidden in his eternal purpose. Although negative in form it amounts to a promise of a continuance of the human race, the seed of the woman, through which the hope of deliverance was to be fulfilled. It is the broad foundation upon which the covenant with Abraham and all later covenants rest.

(6) SIN AND THE TEMPTER.

Although we may not speak of a doctrine of sin and certainly not of a doctrine of Satan in this early time, the story of the temptation displays a marvellous insight into the working of evil in human nature. It is represented as coming to Eve in a suggestion from the serpent (Gen. 3:1-4). Nevertheless it was not until Eve yielded to the suggestion and looking upon the tree "saw that it was good for food and that it was a delight to the eyes and that the tree was to be desired to make one wise" that "she took of the fruit thereof and did eat" (Gen. 3:6). She was "drawn away by her own lust and enticed" (Jas. 1:14). Although primitive man had no conception of a personal devil and the idea of a literal serpent and of the serpent as a mere name of the Evil One are both objectionable, the temptation came to Eve from without and was directed by an evil intelligence hostile to God which ever works for the enslavement and destruction of mankind. Such is the rudimentary beginning of the doctrine of Satan whom the Revelation calls "the old serpent" (Rev. 12:9; 20:2).

The effects of sin in estrangement from God, the desire to hide from him, suspicion and hostility between man and man are clearly set forth in this great story. The inevitable result was that man was driven from God's presence, driven not merely by the act of a holy God but by his own rebellious will. Sin is more developed in the story of Cain and Abel (Gen. 4:1-15). The unreasoning anger, the fallen countenance, the treacherous deed of hatred, the spurning of the suggestion that Cain was his brother's keeper, the complaint at his punishment without appreciation of his guilt, are characteristic of sin in all ages. The searching inquiry "Why art thou wroth and why is thy countenance fallen? If thou doest well, shall it not be lifted up, and if thou doest not well, sin coucheth at the door and unto thee shall be its desire and thou shall rule over it" (Gen. 4:6-7), displays an insight into the way sin works within us which is as true now as it was then.

The beginnings of civilization are represented as coming in the godless Cainite line. Cain built the first city (Gen. 4:17). Jabal, a descendant of Cain, was the originator of nomadic pastoral life (Gen. 4:20). His brother Jubal was the first to use musical instruments (Gen. 4:21). A half-brother, Tubal-Cain, forged cutting instruments of brass and iron (Gen. 4:22). The proud exultation of the Cainite Lamech (Gen. 4:23-24) as he rejoiced in his sword, breathes the spirit of wicked self-reliance, hatred of God and defiance of his fellow-men which in every age has provoked war and ruthlessly destroyed those who dared to oppose themselves. If the chief aspect of sin in the story of Adam and Eve is disobediance to God, and its chief aspect in the story of Cain and Abel selfish hatred of one's fellow-men, if later it showed itself as defiant pride, by the time of the flood it is presented as a corruption which permeated the minds of almost the entire human race. "Jehovah saw that the wickedness of man was great in the earth, and that every imagination of the thoughts of his heart was only evil continually" (Gen. 6:5). This suggestive verse represents sin as having its origin in the heart of man and is in agreement with the saying of Christ, "Out of the heart come forth evil thoughts, murders, adulteries, fornications, thefts, false witness, railings" (Mt. 15:19).

After the flood sin showed itself in the proud attempt to build a tower whose top should reach to heaven (Gen. 11:1-9). The avowed purpose of the tower and the city was to exalt man's name and to unify mankind on the basis of self-interest. Like every other such attempt to gain civilization and peace without God, it defeated itself. It reminds us of Our Lord's saying, "He that gathereth not with me scattereth" (Mt. 12:30).

The development of the arts of civilization in the Cainite line does not mean that the ancestors of Abraham regarded these arts as sinful in themselves. Genesis represents Abraham as living at Shechem, Hebron and other cities. He lived in tents and had cattle like Jubal. Laban used musical instruments like Jabal (Gen. 31:27). In adopting the arts of civilization the patriarchs did not sin against God. The fruit of the tree of the knowledge of good and evil is calculated to make one wise (Gen. 3:6). Civilization may develop to a high degree without God; but if so, it contains within itself the germs of its own destruction. True civilization must have religion as its moving principle. "The fear of Jehovah is the beginning of wisdom" (Ps. 111:10; Prov. 9:10).

III. The Religion of the Patriarchs. The great advances in the history of religion always came through some great personality, such as Abraham, Moses, David and Isaiah, who was willing to make a new start and whose spirit was open to the revelations of God. Man's discovery of God and God's revelation of himself were opposite sides of the same event. The first of these great pioneers of religion was Abraham who spiritually as well as physically, left his father's house and went to a land that God showed him. He was the father of the faithful (Gal. 3:9), the friend of God (Isa. 41:8; Jas. 2:23). He is honored alike by Jews, Christians and Moslems, all of whom derive their knowledge of God from him. The religion of the patriarchs was preeminently the religion of Abraham. Isaac and Jacob inherited that religion and passed it on. While the experiences of Isaac, Jacob and the sons of Jacob enlarged their conception of religion, it was Abraham who gave the greatest contribution. After him there was no great forward movement in religion until the time of Moses.

(1) The Idea of God.

The names of God in patriarchal times were Elohim, Jehovah, Adonai, El, El Shaddai and El Elyon. The ideas which were associated with these names may be judged more accurately from their usage than from their etymology, even if the etymology were not doubtful. Elohim, like the English word God, is not a proper name but a common noun and may be used of heathen deities as well as of the true God.   In reference to the true God it was commonly used where there was no thought of special revelation or intimate fellowship with man.   Jehovah is the proper name of God by which the patriarchs and later the chosen people knew him.   Jehovah is the God of revelation and grace, who made himself known to the patriarchs, the God of the covenant.   Adonai means My Lord or My Master.   It is a title of honor which may be used in reference to a man of distinction as well as to God.   El emphasizes the power of God and may be rendered the Almighty.   It is sometimes used of mighty men, angels and heathen deities.   In Genesis it occurs only a few times, chiefly in combination with Shaddai and Elyon.   El Shaddai (Gen. 17:1; 28:3; 35:11; 43:14; 48:3) is properly rendered God Almighty and El Elyon (Gen. 14:18, 19, 20, 22) God Most High.   Although the names Elohim, Jehovah, Adonai and El are the same which were used in later times we should not conclude that the patriarchs appreciated their full significance as did those of later periods in history.

The patriarchal conception of God was primitive and anthropomorphic.   He appeared to Abraham (Gen. 12:7; 17:1, 3, 22; 18:1), to Isaac (Gen. 26:2, 24) and to Jacob (Gen. 28:10-22).   He spoke to Abraham (Gen. 12:1-3, 7; 17:1).   His word came in a vision (Gen. 15:1).   He went up from Abraham (Gen. 17:22).   He went down to see Sodom (Gen. 18:21).   He went his way (Gen. 18:33). He went up from Jacob (Gen. 35:13).   Sometimes the appearance of God was in a dream (Gen. 20:3; 28:10-

22; 31:24). Indeed dreams have quite a prominent place in Genesis (Gen. 15:1; 20:3; 26:24; 28:10-22; 31:11-13, 24; 37:5-10; 40:8, 21-22; 41:25, 28, 32, 39) and were regarded as a means of divine revelation.

A special form of the divine appearance was the Angel of Jehovah. This angel appeared to Hagar (Gen. 16:7-14). He spoke as Jehovah himself (verse 10) and was identified with Jehovah (verse 13). Three men appeared to Abraham (Gen. 18:2). One of them spoke as God (Gen. 18:10, 14) and was spoken of as Jehovah (Gen. 18:1, 13, 22). The other two were called angels (Gen. 19:1). The angel of God called out of heaven to Hagar (Gen. 21:17) and to Abraham (Gen. 22:11, 15). The man who wrestled with Jacob (Gen. 32:24-32) was evidently a manifestation of God, for in striving with him, Jacob is said to have striven with God (verse 28) and Jacob called the place Peniel, the face of God, saying, "I have seen God face to face and my life is preserved" (verse 30). Hosea speaks of him as "the angel" (Hos. 12:4). The Angel of Jehovah was in fact Jehovah himself, temporarily manifest in human form. It is to him that the aged Jacob referred as "the angel who hath redeemed me from all evil" (Gen. 48:16).

Other angels are mentioned in the patriarchal stories who were inferior to the Angel of Jehovah, mere messengers of God. Thus after the three men visited Abraham we read, "The men turned from thence and went toward Sodom; but Abraham stood yet before Jehovah" (Gen. 18:22). If this verse is interpreted in the light of chapter 19, it is clear that two of the three were inferior angels. They went away to carry out God's bidding on Sodom (Gen. 19:1). The third angel who was the spokesman was the Angel of Jehovah, God himself. He remained with Abraham or rather "Abraham stood yet before Jehovah." Inferior angels are mentioned also in Gen. 28:12 and 32:1-2. Thus although the doctrine of angels was not fully developed in the days of the patriarchs, there was the beginning of the distinction between the Angel of Jehovah and other angels which appeared in later times.

The patriarchs were henotheists rather than monotheists. They worshipped only one God, Jehovah. Nevertheless some of the expressions, particularly in the story of Abraham, show that he was so far in advance of his age that he conceived of Jehovah as the God not of Israel merely but of all mankind. He spoke of God as the possessor of heaven and earth (Gen. 14:22), as the God of heaven and the God of the earth (Gen. 24:3), and most significant of all, as the judge of all the earth (Gen. 18:25). Concerning the last title, Ryle remarks, "Whether or not the writer admitted the existence of other gods in other lands, he here asserts the complete sovereignty of Jehovah. This is not monotheism but it is the stage next before it" (Commentary on Genesis). Accordingly the power of Jehovah extended beyond the bounds of Israel. He rained fire and brimstone on Sodom and Gomorrah (Gen. 19:24). He "healed Abimelech and his wife and his maid servants" (Gen. 20:17). He "plagued Pharaoh and his house because of Sarai, Abram's wife" (Gen. 12:17). He was with Joseph in Egypt and made him prosper (Gen. 39:2-3) as he did Joseph's Egyptian master (Gen. 39:5). He was with Joseph in the Egyptian prison (Gen. 39:21-23). Joseph at least believed that Jehovah's providential guidance was not merely for his own sake or that of his brethren but for Egypt (Gen. 45:5-9; 50:20). Similarly Abraham believed in the divine providence (Gen. 24:7) as did also his servant (Gen. 24:14, 27), Laban (Gen. 24:50), and Jacob (Gen. 28:15; 43:14; 48:15, 21). This divine providence will have its greatest manifestation in the fact that all the nations of the earth shall be blessed in Abraham (Gen. 18:18) and in his seed (Gen. 22:18), as well as in the seed of Jacob (Gen. 26:4).

The most prominent attribute of God in the patriarchal conception was his power as he said to Moses, "I appeared unto Abraham, unto Isaac and unto Jacob as God Almighty; but by my name Jehovah I was not known to them" (Exod. 6.3). This does not mean that the patriarchs had not known the name Jehovah but that God was to them chiefly a God of power and not Jehovah the God of revelation, the covenant God. Five times he is called God Almighty (Gen. 17:1; 28:3; 35:11; 43:14; 48:3). God said to Abraham, "Is anything too hard for Jehovah?" (Gen. 18:14). He is also called the Everlasting God (Gen. 21:33). He is righteous in his dealings with men (Gen. 18:25). He will judge Egypt (Gen. 15:14). He judges between men (Gen. 16:5; 31:42, 53) and punishes wickedness (Gen. 44:16). Abraham exclaimed, "That be far from thee to do after this manner, to slay the righteous with the wicked, that so the righteous should be as the wicked; that be far from thee; shall not the Judge of all the earth do right?" (Gen. 18:25). The ethical conception of God is especially prominent in the confession of Judah to Joseph, "What shall we say unto my lord? What shall we speak? How shall we clear ourselves? God hath found out the iniquity of thy servants" (Gen. 44:16). The mercy and faithfulness of God are expressed in the words of the servant of Abraham: "Blessed be Jehovah the God of my master Abraham who hath not forsaken his lovingkindness and his truth toward my master" (Gen. 24:27).

(2)   CEREMONIES OF RELIGION.

There are no traces of polytheism among the patriarchs. Jacob commanded his household to put away the foreign gods (Gen. 35:2-4). Judah apparently thought that Tamar was a temple prostitute such as were connected with the shrines of the Canaanites (Gen. 38:21-22). There were teraphim, small household idols, in the house of Laban (Gen. 31:19, 30, 34). The oak of Moreh (Gen. 12:6), the oak of Mamre (Gen. 13:18; 14:13; 18:1), the tamarisk in Beersheba (Gen. 21:33) and the oaks at Shechem (Gen 35:4) and Bethel (Gen. 35:8) may have been sacred trees. Enmishpat (Gen. 14:7), Beer-la-hai-roi (Gen. 16:14) and Beersheba (Gen. 21:30-31) seem to have been named from sacred wells. Joseph used a divining cup (Gen. 44:5, 15). Nevertheless when we remember that the whole life of the patriarchs was lived among idolaters, it is surprising that they yielded to these heathen practices so seldom.

Sacrifices are mentioned several times in the patriarchal

period. Abraham built an altar at Shechem (Gen. 12:7) and at Bethel (Gen. 12:8; 13:4). The mysterious ceremony described in Gen. 15:9-11 should probably be regarded as a sacrifice. The division of the animals and birds into two parts indicated the two parties to the covenant, the birds of prey which tried to devour the carcasses represent the hostile powers like Egypt which would try to thwart it (Gen. 15:13-14), and the flaming torch which passed between the pieces represented Jehovah who confirmed the covenant (Gen. 15:17). The extraordinary occasion on which Abraham prepared to offer his son Isaac as a sacrifice but was prevented by Jehovah's command to substitute a ram (Gen. 22:1-13) may indicate that animal sacrifice now took the place of human sacrifice. This sacrifice was made on one of the mountains in the land of Moriah (Gen. 22:2). Jacob's pouring oil upon the top of his pillar was symbolic of an offering (Gen. 28:18; 35:14).

There are many places of sacrifice mentioned in Genesis. The patriarchs may have been influenced by the old Canaanite shrines but there is no evidence that they corrupted the worship of Jehovah with idolatry. "Jacob said unto his household and to all that were with him, Put away the foreign gods that are among you and purify yourselves and change your garments and let us arise and go up to Bethel and make there an altar unto God who answered me in the day of my stress and was with me in the way which I went" (Gen. 35:2-3). So Isaac built an altar at Beersheba (Gen. 26:25) and Jacob one at Shechem (Gen. 33:20). Jacob before he left his native land for the last time, offered sacrifices at Beersheba (Gen. 46:1).

There are no traces in patriarchal times of a priestly order or tribe. As the head of the family the father was also its priest. He offered sacrifices and carried on the other ceremonies of religion. Melchizedek is spoken of as a priest of God Most High (Gen. 14:18).

There are several instances of prayer in Genesis. The most remarkable is the intercession of Abraham for Sodom (Gen. 18:22-33). Its unselfishness, its importunity, and its sublime faith are not exceeded by any prayer in scripture. Abraham's prayer for Abimelech (Gen. 20:17), the prayer of Abraham's servant for success in his enterprise (Gen. 24:12-14), Isaac's prayer that Rebekah should have a son (Gen. 25:21), and Jacob's prayer for deliverance from Esau (Gen. 32:9-12) show how large a place prayer had in the life of the patriarchs. There are no signs of formalism in these prayers. In one instance prayer is described as speaking in the heart (Gen. 24:45). Althought the ceremonies of religion in patriarchal times were very primitive, the genuineness of the heart's approach to God in prayer was as marked as at any later period of the history of religion.

There are two references to tithing in Genesis. After Abraham's success in his expedition against the four kings he gave to Melchizedek a tenth of all the spoil (Gen. 14:20). At Bethel Jacob made a vow that he would give a tenth to God (Gen. 28:22). Both of these are exceptional. Since tithing existed among the ancient Assyrians and other peoples its mention in Genesis need not surprise us. There is no evidence that it was performed regularly as it was after the time of Moses (Lev. 27:30-33).

There is only one reference to a vow in Genesis. At Bethel "Jacob vowed a vow, saying, If God will be with me and will keep me in this way that I go and will give me bread to eat and raiment to put on so that I come again to my father's house in peace and Jehovah will be my God, then this stone which I have set up for a pillar shall be God's house; and of all that thou shalt give me I will surely give the tenth unto thee" (Gen. 28:20-22).

An ancient symbolic ceremony was observed in the taking of an oath. Abraham's servant put his hand under Abraham's thigh when he swore that he would not take a wife for Isaac from the daughters of the Canaanites (Gen. 24:2, 9). Joseph likewise put his hand under Jacob's thigh when he swore that Jacob would not be buried in Egypt but in Canaan (Gen. 47:29). By placing his hand upon the generative organs the appeal was made to those yet to be born to attest the oath and avenge its violation.

Closely related to this idea was the rite of circumcision. It was practiced in Egypt and probably in Arabia before the time of Abraham. Connected with the promise of Isaac, it took a new meaning, the consecration of the generative function to Jehovah (Gen. 17:9-27). Thus the seed of Abraham in which all the nations of the earth should be blessed was set apart to God. The same rite was forced upon the men of Shechem as the condition of marriage between them and the children of Israel (Gen. 34 :13-24).

(3) THE COVENANT WITH ABRAHAM.

This covenant is based upon God's command that Abraham should leave his native land and go to a country that God would show him. The conditions of the covenant as always were appointed by God. On man's part it required implicit obedience to God's commands. Upon this condition God promised two things: (a) the increase of his seed into a great nation and (b) their possession of the promised land (Gen. 12 :1-3). The first of these promises was an enlargement of the primitive promise concerning the seed of the woman (Gen. 3 :15). Nearly all the remainder of Genesis is concerned with the carrying out of this promise. It was renewed to Abraham four times, each time after some signal manifestation of his worthiness. Thus after his unselfishness in allowing Lot to take the best of the land, Jehovah said to him, "Lift up now thine eyes and look from the place where thou art, northward and southward and eastward and westward for all the land which thou seest, to thee will I give it and to thy seed forever. And I will make thy seed as the dust of the earth; so that if a man can number the dust of the earth, then may thy seed also be numbered" (Gen. 13 :14-16). After his rescue of Lot God "brought him forth abroad, and said, Look now toward heaven, and number the stars, if thou be able to number them: and he said unto him, So shall thy seed be" (Gen. 15 :5). "In that day Jehovah made a covenant with Abram saying, Unto thy seed have I given this land from the river of Egypt unto the great river, the river Euphrates, the Kenite and the Kenizzite and the Kadmonite and the Hittite and the Perizzite and the Rephaim and the Amorite and the Canaanite and the Girgashite and the Jebusite" (Gen. 15:18-21). After the expulsion of Hagar, God took circumcision as the pledge or token of the covenant and changed his name to Abraham saying, "The father of a multitude of nations have I made thee" (Gen. 17:1-21). Finally after Abraham stood the great test of faith in his willingness to offer Isaac as a sacrifice, God said, "By myself have I sworn, saith Jehovah, because thou hast done this thing and hast not withheld thy son, thine only son, that in blessing I will bless thee and in multiplying I will multiply thy seed as the stars of the heaven and as the sand which is upon the seashore; and thy seed shall possess the gate of his enemies; and in thy seed shall all the nations of the earth be blessed, because thou hast obeyed my voice" (Gen. 22:15-18).

This promise was renewed to Isaac for Abraham's sake (Gen. 26:2-5, 24) as well as to Jacob (Gen. 28:13-15; 35:11-12; 46:3). The Messianic hope was hidden in the promise that in the seed of Abraham all nations of the earth should be blessed. When, therefore, Jacob was blessing his sons he indicated which of them should be the custodian of this priceless heritage. He passed by Reuben, Simeon and Levi because of their sin, but to Judah he said, "The sceptre shall not depart from Judah, nor the ruler's staff from between his feet until he come whose it is and unto him shall the obedience of the peoples be" (Gen. 49:10). When Joseph was dying he recalled the

promise and said to his brethren "God will surely visit you
and bring you up out of this land unto the land which he
swore to Abraham, to Isaac and to Jacob" (Gen. 50:24).
This covenant with Abraham was the most important element in the religion of the patriarchs. It was out of it
that the religion of Israel developed.

(4) THE FUTURE LIFE.

Information on the patriarchal belief in the future life
is very scanty. What little there is shows three things:
(a) that they believed in a future life, (b) that it was not
a prominent part of their belief and (c) that they looked
upon the passage to the future life as something to be
dreaded. The hope of the patriarchs was not in a life
after death but in coming generations.

God told Abraham "Thou shalt go to thy fathers in
peace; thou shalt be buried in a good old age" (Gen.
15:15). His death is described in these words, "Abraham
gave up the ghost, and died in a good old age, an old man
and full of years, and was gathered to his people. And
Isaac and Ishmael, his sons, buried him in the cave of
Machpelah" (Gen. 25:8-9). It is noteworthy that his
being gathered to his people is mentioned as though it
were a different thing from his being buried. That they
were regarded as different things is evident, for Abraham's ancestors were buried in Mesopotamia while he was
buried in the cave of Machpelah at Hebron. Yet he was
said to go to his fathers, to be gathered to his people when
he died. Evidently he was thought to be with them in
some conscious or semi-conscious existence.

The death of Isaac is described in similar language,

"Isaac gave up the ghost and died, and was gathered unto his people, old and full of days: and Esau and Jacob, his sons, buried him" (Gen. 35:29). More significant is the statement of Jacob when his wicked sons showed him Joseph's coat dipped in blood. He thought Joseph was dead, that some evil beast had devoured him. Joseph was not buried at all, as he thought. Yet he said, "I will go down to Sheol to my son mourning" (Gen. 37:35). He was going to Sheol to his son. The distinction between Sheol and the grave is clear. The body would be in the grave but the spirit would be in Sheol. Three other times Sheol is mentioned in Genesis. When he refused to let Benjamin go down to Egypt Jacob said that if any harm befell him "then will ye bring down my gray hairs with sorrow to Sheol" (Gen. 42:38). Judah quoted these words of Jacob when he pleaded with Joseph for Benjamin (Gen. 44:29), and he said that if Benjamin did not return to Canaan with his brethren "thy servants will bring down the gray hairs of thy servant our father with sorrow to Sheol" (Gen. 44:31).

In speaking of his death Jacob called it sleeping with his fathers (Gen. 47:30) and being gathered to his people (Gen. 49:29). When he died it is said that he "was gathered unto his people" (Gen. 49:33). This happened in Egypt but he was not buried there. In chapter 50 it is recorded that Jacob's sons according to his request took his body to Canaan for burial. It is true that he was buried in the cave of Machpelah with Abraham (Gen. 50:12-13); but he was gathered to his people when he died in the land of Egypt.

(5) MORALITY OF THE PATRIARCHAL PERIOD.

The morality of this period, as of every later period, should be judged according to the degree of moral attainment in the time. It was largely a matter of custom rather than of a sense of ethical values. Thus Abimlech said to Abraham, "Thou hast done deeds unto me that ought not to be done" (Gen. 20:9). Laban said to Jacob, "It is not so done in our place" (Gen. 29:26). The wickedness of Shechem is described as a thing which "ought not to be done" (Gen. 34:7). Nevertheless righteousness was required. God said to Abraham, "Walk before me and be thou perfect" (Gen. 17:1). In the story of Sodom and Gomorrah there is a clear distinction between right and wrong. The wickedness of Sodom is condemned (Gen. 18:20, 23; 19:7, 15) and is represented as the cause of its ruin. On the other hand the righteousness of Abraham is commended (Gen. 18:19).

The polygamy of the patriarchs is frankly told but not divinely approved. Indeed the evil results of polygamy in their families present a strong argument against it. It gave rise to the jealousy between Sarah and Hagar and the expulsion of Hagar and Ishmael from Abraham's house. The Angel of Jehovah told Hagar to return and be subject to Sarah (Gen. 16:9). Abraham did not wish to cast them out (Gen. 21:11). God accommodated himself to the lower standard while he was teaching Abraham the greater lesson (Gen. 21:12-13). The polygamous wives of Isaac were a grief of mind to him and to Rebekah (Gen. 26:34-35). The polygamy of Jacob was the source of most of the evils in his family

(Gen. 29:21-30; 30:1-9). The rivalry and hatred between his sons, and the later divisions between the tribes, were due in part to the fact that they had different mothers. Thus the principal tribe of the Southern Kingdom was descended from Judah, a son of Leah, while the leading tribe of the Northern Kingdom was Ephraim, who was descended from Joseph, a son of Rachel.

There are instances of low as well as high standards in sexual relations. Lot's offering of his daughters to the men of Sodom shows a low standard (Gen. 19:8). He regarded his daughters as his property and exalted the law of hospitality above his duty to them. Nevertheless Lot's conduct is so vastly superior to that of the Sodomites that it seems almost virtuous. Genesis tells the story of Lot's incest without comment (Gen. 19:30-38). Yet the fact that the Israelites despised the Moabites and Ammonites who came from such an incestuous origin shows that incest was condemned. Reuben lay with Bilhah, his father's concubine (Gen. 35:22), and for this sin he forfeited his birthright (Gen. 49:3-4). Judah was guilty of lewdness with Shua (Gen. 38:1-7) and with Tamar (Gen. 38:13-18). On the other hand, God commended the innocence of Abinelech (Gen. 20:6). The indignation of Jacob's sons when Shechem lay with Dinah was not altogether due to the fact that the Shechemites were uncircumcised (Gen. 34:7). Joseph's refusal to lie with Potiphar's wife, even though such an alliance might have brought him great advantage in Potiphar's house, shows a lofty sense of sexual morality. He said, "How then can I do this great wickedness and sin against God?"

(Gen. 39:9). To him the wrong would have been not merely against Potiphar but against God. The story of Isaac and Rebekah shows an ideal regard for courtesy and fine feeling (Gen. 24). Such courtesy, however, was not always given to those of alien tribes.

Although Abraham's life exhibits virtue of a high order, he was guilty of lying concerning Sarah both in Egypt (Gen. 12:10-20) and at Gerar (Gen. 20). Isaac was guilty of the same offense (Gen. 26:6-11). Even more contemptible was Jacob's deception of his aged father (Gen. 27:1-40). His shameless lies (verses 19 and 24) are made even worse by his claim that Jehovah was his helper (verse 20). Jacob's trickery with Laban (Gen. 30:37-43) is another blot on his record. It is not surprising that the sons of such a man were guilty of trickery against the men of Shechem (Gen. 34:25-29). Jacob disapproved of what they had done (Gen. 34:30-31) and on account of it he passed by Simeon and Levi, the chief offenders in giving the blessing (Gen. 49:5-7). Jacob suffered similar treatment at the hands of his own sons to that which he had given to his father (Gen. 37:31-35).

The family life of the patriarchs was marred by hatred between brothers. So bitter was the hatred of Esau against Jacob that he had to leave his father's house for fear of death (Gen. 27:41-46). Joseph's brethren hated him and plotted to kill him (Gen. 37:18-20). Reuben interfered to save his life (Gen. 37:21-24, 29-30). Judah did not wish to kill his brother (Gen. 37:25-28) but was willing to profit by selling him to the Ishmaelites.

The magnanimity of Abraham in yielding the best of

the land to his nephew Lot (Gen. 13) calls forth our highest praise. The character of Joseph also presents many virtues. His faithfulness to Potiphar (Gen. 39:5-6), to the keeper of the prison (Gen. 39:22-23) and to Pharaoh (Gen. 41:41-44) is worthy of the emulation of all young men who wish to succeed. His unconquerable optimism under adverse conditions was another secret of success. His intense love for his own brother Benjamin (Gen. 43:29) and for his father (Gen. 43:27) is very pathetic. The extraordinary combination of harshness and love in his dealing with his brethren (Gen. 42-45) reminds us of the conflict between the justice and the love of God. As if to punish them, he spoke roughly to them (Gen. 42:7) called them spies (Gen. 42:9, 12), demanded that Benjamin be brought (Gen. 42:15), bound Simeon (Gen. 42:24), put the cup in Benjamin's sack (Gen. 44:2) and sent his steward after them (Gen. 44:4-13). Yet all his severity was tempered with love. At last it brought them to their knees (Gen. 44:16-17) and awakened in Judah's heart that brother love which they had all forgotten in Joseph's youth (Gen. 44:18-34). The gradual triumph of love over severity in Joseph's conduct presents an interesting study. At first he kept all his brethren in prison, then only Simeon (Gen. 42:15, 17, 19). He wept at the sight of their trouble (Gen. 42:24). He filled their sacks with grain (Gen. 42:25). He put their money in their sacks (Gen. 42:25, 28, 35; 43:21; 44:1). At last he could not restrain himself and without any sign of vindictiveness he made himself known to them (Gen. 45:1). It would be hard to find a nobler

example of magnanimity in life or literature than that of
Joseph when he said to his brethren, "And now be not
grieved nor angry with yourselves that ye sold me hither:
for God did send me before you to preserve life" (Gen.
45:5). Through all the years he never took advantage
of his position to punish them. When they feared that
he would do so after Jacob's death, he reassured them,
saying, "Fear not: for am I in the place of God? And
as for you, ye meant evil against me; but God meant it
for good, to bring to pass as it is this day, to save much
people alive" (Gen. 50:20).

CHAPTER II.

The Religion of Moses.

Genesis I, Exodus, Leviticus, Numbers, Deuteronomy, Psalm 90.

Scripture gives no direct evidence concerning the religion of the descendants of Jacob while they were in Egypt. The fact that the religion of Moses was based upon that of the patriarchs and that his God was repeatedly called the God of the patriarchs (Exod. 3:6, 15, 16; 4:5; 6:3) suggests that the Israelites continued to worship Jehovah while they were in Egypt. On the other hand, it is scarcely possible that they were not influenced by the religion of the Egyptians. A people who were so prone to forsake Jehovah for Baal and other heathen deities in later times must have had the same characteristics between the time of Joseph and that of Moses. The worship of the golden calf in the wilderness (Exod. 32) was probably suggested by that of Apis, the sacred bull of Egypt. It may have been a reversion to a worship in which some of them engaged before they left that land.

Whatever was the history of Israel's religion during this period of silence, it is certain that the religion of Moses was not a new religion. He was not its founder. He took the primitive religion of the patriarchs and by divine inspiration breathed into it a new and vastly higher spirit. The advance in religious conceptions, both in matters of ritual and of doctrine, which God accomplished through Moses was so great that for the first time it became a well-developed and articulated organism. From his time throughout Old Testament history he was regarded as the organizer of the religion of Jehovah, if not its founder. God "made known his ways unto Moses, his doings unto the children of Israel" (Ps. 103:7). The Jews of Christ's time protested; "We are disciples of Moses" (Jno. 9:28). Moses and the prophets were the authoritative exponents of Israel's religion (Luke 16:29, 31). Moses as the lawgiver and Elijah as the founder of prophecy appeared with Christ on the mount of transfiguration (Matt. 17:3-4, etc.). Yet neither Elijah nor any other character of the Old Testament made so great a contribution to Israel's religion as Moses. The remark which the editor of the book of Moses made was true until the time of Our Lord, "There hath not arisen a prophet since in Israel like unto Moses whom Jehovah knew face to face" (Deut. 34:10). He was the greatest representative of the Old Covenant. "The law was given through Moses; grace and truth came through Jesus Christ" (Jno. 1:17).

I. Sources.

The sources for our knowledge of the religion of Moses are found in the first chapter of Genesis, the last four books of the Pentateuch and the ninetieth Psalm. It is impossible to state with certainty whether the opening chapter of Genesis was based upon a revelation given

first to Moses or had been handed down to him from
an older revelation. In either case its present form was
probably Mosaic, for its conception of God seems much
more advanced than that of the patriarchs and agrees
admirably with that of Moses. While the inscription
of the ninetieth Psalm as "A Prayer of Moses the man
of God" was not an original part of the Psalm, it represents an ancient tradition which there is no good reason
to deny. There is nothing in it impossible to Moses. The
points of resemblance to Deuteronomy do not confirm
the Mosaic authorship if Moses was not the author of
Deuteronomy; but if Moses was the author of Deuteronomy, as the book itself affirms (Deut. 1:1, 3, 5; 4:44-
45; 5:1; 27:1, 9, 11; 29:1, 2; 31:1, 2, 9, 10, 22, 24-26,
30; 32:44-46; 33:1, 2, 4), and as was almost universally
believed until modern times, the resemblances of the
Psalm to that book make the ancient tradition that Moses
wrote it reasonable.

The reasons for adhering to the traditional view that
Moses was the author of the Pentateuch, except for the
last chapter of Deuteronomy which gives the account of
his death and burial, cannot be given here. Strictly speaking, the question of authorship is not essential to our
present purpose, provided it is admitted that we have
in the Pentateuch a true picture of the religion of Moses.
The picture might be true if the books were written by
Joshua, Eleazar or some other writer soon after Moses'
time; but if, as most modern critics believe, they contain
nothing certainly from that time but were compiled by
late redactors from documents written in Palestine cen-

turies after Moses, we can gain from these books no true picture of Moses' religion, however valuable the documents may be, as indicating the religion of Israel when they were written.

In designating our subject the religion of Moses, we should not think of him as an individual merely but as the great leader of Israel. The subject, therefore, includes the religion of all the people and not only of Moses. It may be entitled more fully the Religion of Moses and of Israel in his Time. Hence the last chapter of Deuteronomy should be included as one of our sources of information, since, although Moses did not write it, there is no good reason to doubt that it was added soon after his day and thus presents contemporary evidence concerning the subjects with which it deals. Moses, like all other great religious leaders, was in advance of his times. He was not entirely a child of his age. Otherwise he could not have been Israel's greatest religious teacher in the old dispensation. Hence we should not think of his religion as identical with the religion of Israel in his time. Most of his people did not rise to his lofty ideas and it took centuries for Israel even to approximate the religion which this great man of God realized.

II. The Religion of Moses and of Israel in his Time.

(1) THE IDEA OF GOD.

Although, as we have seen, Jehovah was the proper name of God in the time of the patriarchs, it received a new and much deeper significance in the time of Moses. We do not know whether the patriarchs associated any etymology with the name; but, if they did, this etymology does not seem to have influenced their conception of the divine being. The important question for our present purpose is not whether the etymology given in Exodus (3:14) is scientifically correct. It is the etymology which Moses accepted and therefore is of great assistance as indicating the ideas which he associated with the name. He regarded this etymology as significant and it is evident in his later usage of the name that he meant it in this sense.

The manner of the introduction of the etymology is most important. "Moses said unto God (at the burning bush), Behold, when I come unto the children of Israel, and shall say unto them, The God of your fathers hath sent me unto you; and they shall say to me, What is his name? what shall I say unto them? And God said unto Moses, I Am That I Am: and he said, Thus shalt thou say unto the children of Israel, I Am hath sent me unto you. And God said moreover unto Moses, Thus shalt thou say unto the children of Israel, Jehovah, the God of your fathers, the God of Abraham, the God of Isaac, and the God of Jacob hath sent me unto you: this is my name forever and this is my memorial unto all generations" (Exod. 3:13-15). We should not read into this statement a meaning which could not have been understood by Moses or his contemporaries. There are, however, a few facts which must have been appreciated by them.

(a) The name as given in verse 14 is in the first person and is rendered I Am in the English version. The Hebrew word rendered I Am differs in its first letter from the name Jehovah, because it is first person singular. The account presupposes that the name Jehovah was the third person singular of the same verb. If I Am is the correct rendering of the former word, Jehovah should be rendered He Is. The reason it takes the form I Am is because God is the speaker. Speaking of himself he says I Am. Israel, however, speaking of him used the third person and said Jehovah, He Is.

(b) The rendering I Am does not express the meaning of the Hebrew adequately. The verb is in the imperfect tense which in Hebrew ordinarily expresses future time. Hence it should be translated "I Shall Be", and in the fuller form "I Shall Be That Which I Shall Be." Similarly Jehovah should be rendered, "He Shall Be".

(c) The verb used here does not mean to be essentially but to be phenomenally. It does not affirm mere existence but refers to the process of becoming, coming to be, showing oneself to be. It is a rare form of the common verb rendered to come to pass many times in the Old Testament (Gen. 4:8; 11:2; 12:14; 19:17, etc.). It is translated to become only twice in the Authorized Version (Deut. 27:9; II. Sam. 7:24), but many other times this rendering would bring out the force of the original (Gen. 2:7; 3:5, 20; 4:2; 15:5; 24:51, etc.). Sometimes it is rendered to come as in Gen. 15:1 and I Sam. 4:1. Thus we may translate the divine name "I Shall Become" and in its fuller form "I Shall Become that which I Shall Become" More fully paraphrased it is "I shall show myself to be that which I shall show myself to be", and Jehovah means "He Shall show himself to be that which he shall show himself to be".

The thought is not of the Independent, Self-existent One, The Absolute who exists without dependence upon any other. It is rather that of the Self-revealing One who holds the future in his omnipotent control. He did not show to Moses that which he would come to be to Israel in later times, but he said, "I shall be that which I shall be." God's revelation of himself is an unfolding progressive revelation. As Jehovah meant more to Moses than to the patriarchs, so would he mean more still to each succeeding generation. Although we must guard against reading too much into the name, it certainly contained the idea of a progressive revelation of God.

It is because of this meaning of Jehovah that it is preeminently the covenant name of God. The God who reveals himself to each succeeding generation as each generation has need and as each generation is able to receive the revelation, is the God who can never fail to keep every promise he has made. There are infinite resources in his nature which no emergency can exhaust. He is "able to do exceeding abundantly above all that we ask or think" (Eph. 3:20). Some such thoughts as these must have been suggested to Moses by the name Jehovah. Through him these ideas passed to the Israel of his day.

The peculiar usage of the name is explained by its meaning. When God begins an announcement by the statement, "I am Jehovah", it is not to distinguish him from other deities but to suggest that he is about to give a new revelation of himself. So, for example, "God spake unto Moses and said unto him, I am Jehovah and I appeared unto Abraham, unto Isaac and unto Jacob as God Almighty but by my name Jehovah I was not known to them" (Exod. 6:3). When we examine the usage of the expression to know God and to know the name of God, it is evident that this verse does not mean that the patriarchs never heard the name Jehovah. It means that though they used the name, they had no such deep appreciation of its meaning as God was about to reveal to Moses. To know the name of God means to appreciate by experience the ideas connected with the name, to receive the revelation of God suggested by it, to accept God as he is revealed in it. So Solomon asked that God would answer the foreigner who prayed toward the temple at Jerusalem "that all the peoples of the earth may know thy name, to fear thee as doth thy people Israel" (I. Kgs. 8:43). So David sang, "They that know thy name will put their trust in thee, for thou Jehovah hast not forsaken them that seek thee" (Ps. 9:10), and God speaking through another Psalmist, said, "Because he hath set his love upon me, therefore will I deliver him. I will set him on high because he hath known my, name" (Ps. 91:14). Other examples of this usage are found in Isa. 52:6; 64:2; Jer. 16:21 and Ezek. 39:6-7.

It is on this account that so often it is said in connection with some manifestation of the divine power, or wisdom or love, "And they shall know that I am Jehovah". For example, soon after the statement that God was not known to the patriarchs by his name Jehovah, we read

"Wherefore say unto the children of Israel I am Jehovah and I will bring you out from under the burdens of the Egyptians and I will rid you out of their bondage and I will redeem you with an outstretched arm and with great judgments, and I will make you to me for a people and I will be to you a God, and ye shall know that I am Jehovah your God, who bringeth you out from under the burdens of the Egyptians" (Exod. 6:6-7). The deliverance of Israel from Egypt with all its accompanying wonders was in order to make Israel know that he was Jehovah. Similarly, "The Egyptians shall know that I am Jehovah when I stretch forth my hand upon Egypt and bring out the children of Israel from among them" (Exod. 7:5). This expression is common not only in the Pentateuch (Exod. 7:17; 8:22; 10:2; 14:4, 18; 16:12; 29:46; 31:13; Deut. 29:6), but elsewhere, particularly in Ezekiel (6:7, 10, 13, 14; 7:4, 9, 27; 11:10, 12; 12:15, 16, 20, etc.).

The idea of God in Moses' religion is preeminently the idea which he associated with the name Jehovah. This idea finds its fullest expression in the wonderful revelation which God gave to Moses on Mount Sinai. "Jehovah passed by before him and proclaimed, Jehovah, Jehovah, a God merciful and gracious, slow to anger and abundant in lovingkindness and truth, keeping lovingkindness for thousands, forgiving iniquity and transgression and sin, and that will by no means clear the guilty, visiting the iniquity of the fathers upon the children, and upon the children's children, upon the third and upon the fourth generation" (Exod. 34:6-7). This is called a proclamation of the name of Jehovah (Exod. 34:5), that is, of his nature as expressed in his name. All its elements are mentioned elsewhere in the Mosaic revelation. Yet nowhere else in the Old Testament is there so comprehensive a statement of the divine nature. It says nothing of the power, wisdom, eternity and unchangeableness of God, attributes which would rather suggest the name Elohim. It reveals him in his moral nature as a God of love, justice and truth. The significant fact is not that these attributes are mentioned but that they are mentioned together. The love and justice of God are seen in harmonious relations. The same God who forgives iniquity and transgression and sin will not completely clear the guilty. He keeps lovingkindness for thousands but he visits the iniquity of the fathers upon the children upon the third and upon the fourth generation. In the light of the New Testament revelation, we discover a way to harmonize these apparently conflicting attributes. Moses could not do so. Yet he had no doubt either of the love or of the justice of God.

The same conception of the moral nature of Jehovah is found in the Ten Commandments. The God who commanded his people to obey these ethical precepts must have been an ethical God. He did not require ethical standards in Israel which were not the laws of his own being. While there are some traces of the temporary in the Ten Commandments, they are amazingly timeless. Jehovah is "a jealous God visiting the iniquity of the fathers upon the children upon the third and upon the fourth generation of them that hate me and showing lovingkindness unto thousands of them that love me and keep my commandments" (Exod. 20:5-6). Here Jehovah's punitive justice is manifested to those who hate him as far as the fourth generation, but his lovingkindness is manifested to thousands of those who love him and keep his commandments. The love of Jehovah is evidently more powerful than his justice.

Moses believed that God was the Creator of the heavens and the earth. Indeed, he placed the grand account of that creation at the beginning of his book. The orderly and progressive arrangement of the first chapter of Genesis culminating in the creation of man represents God as a God of law who has made all things, who rules all things, and whose eternal purpose controls both creation and history.

There is no direct reference to the method of creation, whether by the divine fiat bringing things into existence fully developed or by the slow process of evolution. Although Moses doubtless understood the revelation as indicating creation by fiat, we can see that the record agrees better with the idea of a progressive evolutionary creation. The divine fiats went forth as described in the chapter but the carrying out of the fiats took vastly long periods of time. Nothing is ever finished. Each creative decree goes on through all the remaining creative days and, indeed, to the end of time. This is evident in the command to the fishes, the birds, and to man to be fruitful and multiply (Gen. 1:22, 28). The decree making man in God's image finds its fulfilment throughout all history and will not be completely fulfilled until all things are brought in subjection to him (Gen. 1:26, 28; Ps. 8:3-8; Heb. 2:5-9). Of this, however, Moses had no conception. It is only in the light of the fulfilment that we can see these ideas hidden in his inspired words.

Although in one sense the chapter before us contains an account of the creation, it is all from the standpoint of the earth and man. This explains the statements that light was brought into being on the first day and the sun, moon and stars on the fourth day. Strictly speaking, the thing which happened on the fourth day was not the creation of the sun but its being seen in the firmament of heaven. From the beginning the sun was there. The diffused light of the first day came from it; but the thick cloud which enveloped the earth obscured the firmament so that the source of the light could not be seen. The condition is beautifully described in the words of Jehovah to Job, "When I made clouds the garment thereof and thick darkness a swaddling-band for it" (Job. 38:9). At last on the fourth day the sun's rays broke through the clouds and the sun itself appeared. The terrestrial human standpoint is seen in the whole record, "And God said, Let there be lights in the firmament of heaven to divide the day from the night; and let them be for signs, and for seasons, and for days and years, and let them be for lights in the firmament of heaven to give light upon the earth; and it was so" (Gen. 1:14-15). So far as the earth was concerned this was the function of the heavenly bodies, their divine purpose. Moses knew nothing of any other purpose; but even if he had known as much as we do about the sun, moon and stars, he might still have written as he did, for he was not writing a book on astronomy or on geology but on religion. The appropriate thing was to show the function of the heavenly bodies in relation to man.

Several of the divine attributes appear in the time of Moses. He is eternal. Moses sings, "The eternal God is thy dwelling place and underneath are the everlasting arms" (Deut. 33:27). "Before the mountains were brought forth or ever thou hadst formed the earth and the world, even from everlasting to everlasting thou art God" (Ps. 90:2). He is all-powerful for he created all things and he says: "There is none that can deliver out of my hand" (Deut. 32:39). As we have seen he is a God of justice, love and truth (Exod. 34:6-7).

It is somewhat difficult to determine whether Moses understood the spirituality of God. When he said, "Show me, I pray thee, thy glory", Jehovah answered, "I will make all my goodness pass before thee and will proclaim the name of Jehovah before thee. . . . Thou canst not see my face; for man shall not see me and live. . . . Behold there is a place by me and thou shalt stand upon the rock, and it shall come to pass, while my glory passeth by, that I will put thee in a cleft of the rock and will cover thee with my hand until I have passed by: and I will take away my hand, and thou shalt see my back; but my face shall not be seen" (Exod. 33:18-23). Later Jehovah, speaking of his intimate revelation to Moses, said, "The form of Jehovah shall he behold" (Num. 12:8). Taken by themselves these verses seem to indicate some physical or bodily presence of God which Moses saw. He saw the back of Jehovah when he passed by. He saw God's form. Possibly these expressions refer to Moses' experience of a thunderstorm in Mount Sinai which he regarded as a manifestation of God. He saw God in the storm as Job heard God speak out of the storm (Job. 38:1). Whatever was the experience to which Moses referred, the revelation of God was not external but within the heart and mind of Moses. This is shown by the added promise that Jehovah would proclaim his name before him (Exod. 33:19). Moses' belief in the spirituality of God is seen in the second commandment, "Thou shalt not make unto thee a graven image, nor any likeness of any thing that is in heaven above, or that is in the earth beneath, or that is in the water under the earth" (Exod. 20:4). The God who forbade Israel to make any representation of himself could not have been thought of by Moses as confined to a physical body. Indeed, the absence of a clear description of any physical thing which Moses saw, leads us to infer that the revelation was a spiritual one. The physical eyes of Moses may have seen a great storm pass by; but his spiritual eyes saw the goodliness of Jehovah. Moses came to believe that God was specially present in the ark. When it moved he said, "Rise up, O Jehovah, let thine enemies be scattered; and let them that hate thee flee before thee. And when it rested, he said, Return, O Jehovah, unto the ten thousands of the thousands of Israel" (Num. 10:35-36). Yet the ark was not regarded as an idol to be worshipped. In it were the two tables of stone on which were written the ten commandments (Exod. 25:21). These stone tables were not worshipped.

The presence of Jehovah was a spiritual presence. The only symbol of God's presence was the cloud that covered the mercy-seat (Lev. 16:2) which was probably a part of the pillar of cloud and fire which was over the tabernacle (Exod. 40:34-38; Num. 9:15-23; 10:11-12, 33-34, etc.).

The anthropomorphisms of Moses' time were fewer and less primitive than those of the patriarchal age. God said to Moses, "I will come and talk with thee there" (Num. 11:17). "Jehovah came down in the cloud and spake unto him" (Num. 11:25). "Jehovah came down in a pillar of cloud, and stood at the door of the tent and called Aaron and Miriam; and they both came forth" (Num. 12:5). It is repeatedly said that God was angry (Num. 11:1, 10, 33; 12:9; Deut. 1:34, 37; 3:26, etc.).

The Angel of Jehovah appeared to Moses in the flame from the burning bush (Exod. 3:2). That the Angel of Jehovah is God himself becomes evident when he is spoken of as God (Exod. 3:4, 6) and Jehovah (Exod. 3:7). In the account of the Exodus, we read, "The Angel of God, who went before the camp of Israel, removed and went behind them; and the pillar of cloud removed from before them and stood behind them" (Exod. 14:19). From this passage it seems that the Angel of God appeared in the pillar of cloud. This is evident from later passages in which it was promised that the Angel would guide them precisely as the pillar of cloud guided them (Exod. 23:20; 32:34; 33:2). This angel was a manifestation of God, for God said, "My presence shall go with thee and I will give thee rest" (Exod. 33:14). In reference to it,

Moses said years afterward that God "brought thee out with his presence" (Deut. 4:37). Isaiah called him the Angel of his Presence (Isa. 63:9). The Angel of Jehovah appeared also to Balaam (Num. 22:22-35).

The Spirit of God is spoken of not as a distinct person in the godhead but as the influence of God. Thus the Spirit of God came upon Balaam inciting him to prophesy (Num. 24:2). So God put the Spirit which was upon Moses upon the seventy elders (Num. 11:17, 25, 26). Similarly, "Jehovah said unto Moses, Take thee Joshua, the son of Nun, a man in whom is the Spirit, and lay thy hand upon him" (Num. 27:18). "And Joshua, the son of Nun, was full of the spirit of wisdom, for Moses had laid his hands upon him" (Deut. 34:9).

The awful experience at Sinai was calculated to give Moses and Israel a sense of the majesty and glory of God. "There were thunders and lightnings and a thick cloud upon the mount and the voice of a trumpet exceeding loud; and all the people that were in the camp trembled. And Moses brought forth the people out of the camp to meet God; and they stood at the nether part of the mount. And Mount Sinai, the whole of it, smoked, because Jehovah descended upon it in fire; and the smoke thereof ascended as the smoke of a furnace, and the whole mountain quaked greatly" (Exod. 19:16-18). "And all the people perceived the thunderings, and the lightnings, and the voice of the trumpet, and the mountain smoking: and when the people saw it, they trembled and stood afar off" (Exod. 20:18). "And Moses drew near unto the thick darkness where God was" (Exod. 20:21).

While Moses' conception of God approaches very close to monotheism, it does not quite reach it. He believed in the God who said, "Thou shalt have no other gods before me" (Exod. 20:3), "Make no mention of the name of other gods, neither let it be heard out of thy mouth" (Exod. 23:13). He believed that his God was the Creator of the heavens and the earth (Gen. 1). He was no mere national deity. Jehovah said, "Against all the gods of Egypt I will execute judgments. I am Jehovah" (Exod. 12:12, compare Num. 33:4). Moses sang, "Who is like unto thee, O Jehovah, among the Gods?" (Exod. 15:11), and Jethro said to Moses, "Now I know that Jehovah is greater than all Gods" (Exod. 18:11). Moses said that Israel in the wilderness "sacrificed unto demons which were no God" (Deut. 32:17). The word for demons used here is found elsewhere only once (Ps. 106:37). It probably means protective spirits. Thus while Moses believed that Jehovah was vastly greater than all other deities and in a contest with them he would certainly conquer, he never came to the point of denying the existence of other gods. The Egyptian gods are referred to as existing and the demons that Israel worshipped are referred to in the same way.

Although Moses was not quite a monotheist, he was practically so. He believed in the God who said, "There is none like me in all the earth" (Exod. 9:14), who chose Israel as his people, saying, "All the earth is mine" (Exod. 19:5). He wished Israel to know that Jehovah is God, "There is none else besides him" (Deut. 4:35, 39). The power which Moses conceded to other deities was so small in comparison with that of Jehovah as to be practically negligible. In comparison with him they did not deserve to be called gods at all.

In saying this, we should not imagine that the whole nation came as near to monotheism as Moses did. Although there is not much evidence on this subject, we may be sure that most Israelites regarded Jehovah as merely the greatest among the gods and for Israel the only God. That was certainly the idea that Balaam had. When Balak sent for him to curse Israel he realized that in matters affecting Israel he had to do with the God of Israel. Therefore he said to the messengers, "If Balak would give me his house full of silver and gold, I cannot go beyond the word of Jehovah, my God, to do less or more" (Num. 22:18) and to Balak himself, "Have I now any power at all to speak anything? The word that God putteth in my mouth, that shall I speak" (Num. 22:38). Balaam recognized the superiority of Jehovah, but there is no reason to believe that he thought of Jehovah as the Creator and Ruler of the whole world, as Moses did.

(2) Jehovah's Covenant with Israel at Sinai.

Jehovah was the God of the covenant. His name from the Exodus and onward was indissolubly connected with the covenant which he made at Sinai with Moses and Israel. The very mention of his name recalled this covenant to every faithful Israelite. Since the Mosaic covenant was the charter of all Israel's religious rights and duties throughout their history, since its place in their national life was superior even to that of the constitution

in the life of our nation, it deserves consideration even
before the moral and the ceremonial law.

The Mosaic covenant was not new. It was a carrying
out and enlargement of the covenant with Abraham (Gen.
12:1-3) as the covenant with Abraham was a carrying
out and enlargement of the earlier covenant with Noah
(Gen. 9:8-17) and the primitive promise concerning the
seed of the woman (Gen. 3:15). God had promised to
multiply Abraham's seed, to give to them the land of
Canaan and to bless through them all the nations of the
earth (Gen. 12:1-3; 13:14-17; 17:1-8; 22:15-18). When
the Israelites were oppressed in Egypt, apparently there
was danger that this covenant with the patriarchs should
be broken. They might have been exterminated and with
them the promise of eternal blessing to mankind; but "God
heard their groaning, and God remembered his covenant
with Abraham, with Isaac, and with Jacob, and God saw
the children of Israel, and God took knowledge of them"
(Exod. 2:24-25). Later God said to Moses, "I have also
established my covenant with them (the patriarchs), to
give them the land of Canaan" (Exod. 6:4). Even after
the covenant with Israel at Sinai, the older covenant with
the patriarchs was still in force and was frequently referred to (Exod. 32:13; 33:1; Lev. 26:42; Num. 32:11;
Deut. 1:8; 6:10; 9:5, 27; 29:13; 30:20; 34:4). The
covenant with the patriarchs and that with Moses were
mentioned together as essentially the same (Deut. 29:13).

As in every divine covenant, God dictated the terms.
On his part he promised to deliver Israel from the bondage of Egypt and to give them the land of Canaan for

a perpetual possession. Israel's part was to obey Jehovah's law, particularly the Ten Commandments. Jehovah commanded Moses to say to Israel, "I am Jehovah, and I will bring you out from under the burdens of the Egyptians and I will rid you out of their bondage, and I will redeem you with an outstretched arm and with great judgments, and I will take you to me for a people and I will be to you a God; and ye shall know that I am Jehovah your God, who bringeth you out from under the burdens of the Egyptian. And I will bring you in unto the land which I sware to give to Abraham, to Isaac, and to Jacob; and I will give it to you for a heritage. I am Jehovah" (Exod. 6:6-8).

The essence of this promise was the choice of Israel as the heir of the promises to Abraham, Isaac and Jacob. This conception of Israel became clearer still when Jehovah had delivered them from Egypt and brought them to Sinai. There he said to them, "Now therefore if ye will obey my voice indeed and keep my covenant, then ye shall be mine own possession from among all peoples: for all the earth is mine; and ye shall be unto me a kingdom of priests and a holy nation" (Exod. 19:5-6). Here it is evident that Jehovah chose the nation Israel, as he had chosen their ancestor Abraham, not for their own sake, but for the sake of all mankind. They were to be Jehovah's special possession from all peoples, not that other peoples were to be rejected, but because of the fact that Jehovah owned all nations and cared for them. The choice of Israel was God's method of revealing himself to all mankind. His making them a kingdom of priests and a holy nation implies the same idea, for their priestly function was to be in relation to all the nations of the earth. Thus on the plains of Moab, Moses said to them, "Thou art a holy people unto Jehovah thy God: Jehovah thy God hath chosen thee to be a people for his own possession above all peoples that are upon the face of the earth. Jehovah did not set his love upon you, nor choose you, because ye were more in number than any people; for ye were the fewest of all peoples, but because Jehovah loveth you and because he would keep the oath which he sware unto your fathers" (Deut. 7:6-8, compare also Deut. 4:37; 10:15; 14:2). When they disobeyed Jehovah and regarded themselves as the chosen people of God for their own sake and forgot that the choice of them was one of sovereign love, Amos and Isaiah showed them that they had no preeminence above other peoples (Amos 9:7; Isa. 19:25). When they rejected their Messiah, Jehovah rejected them and they will not be restored until they repent (Rom. 11:1-32).

The Messiamic hope is hidden in the choice of Israel and their priestly function. When they broke the covenant and were driven into exile, the faithful remnant of the nation realized the prophetic conception of the Servant of Jehovah and suffered not only for their own sins but for those of their fathers (Lam. 5:7; Isa. 53:4-6). Thus Israel foreshadowed that true Servant of Jehovah who is both priest and sacrifice, the Lamb of God that taketh away the sin of the world. All this was hidden in the promise to Moses but Moses had little or no conception of its fulness.

The central position of the covenant at Sinai in the religion of Moses appears from the use of the word. The two tables of the law were the most sacred possession of Israel. They were called the tables of the covenant (Deut. 9:9, 11, 15, compare Exod. 34:10, 27-28; Deut. 4:13). The ark was called the ark of the covenant because it contained those tables (I Kgs. 8:21). The part of Exodus which contains the ten commandments was called the book of the covenant (Exod. 24:7) because these commandments were regarded as its most important contents. Later a larger section of the Pentateuch received this name for the same reason (II Kgs. 23:2, 21; II Chron. 34:30).

The extreme importance of the choice of Israel at Sinai, which was the divine side of the covenant, appears also from the frequent allusions to it by later writers (I Kgs. 3:8; Ps. 33:12; 135:4; Isa. 14:1; 41:8-9; 44:1-2; 49:7; Jer. 33:24; Ezk. 20:5). The deliverance from Egypt which preceded the covenant is referred to more than forty times (Exod. 20:2; Deut. 5:6; 7:8; Josh. 24:6, 17; Judges 2:1, 12; 6:13; I Sam. 8:8; 10:18; 12:6, 8; II Sam. 7:6, 23; I Kgs. 8:16, 21, 51, 53; 9:9; 12:28; II Kgs. 17:7, 36; II Chron. 6:5; 7:22; Neh. 9:18; Ps. 81:10; Jer. 2:6; 7:22; 11:4, 7; 16:14; 23:7; 32:21; 34:13; Ezek. 20:6, 9, 10; Dan. 9:15; Hos. 11:1; 12:13; Am. 2:10; 3:1; 9:7; Mic. 6:4). This great event which could not be separated in Israel's thought from the covenant itself, was the foundation of their national existence. The introduction to the ten commandments mentions it as Jehovah's warrant for giving those commandments (Exod. 20:2; Deut. 5:6). Joshua recalled it in his farewell address (Josh. 24:6, 17). Gideon appealed to it (Judges 6:13). David referred to it as the greatest evidence of Jehovah's favor (II Sam. 7:23). Solomon mentioned it repeatedly in his prayer at the dedication of the temple (I Kgs. 8:16, 21, 51, 53).

The frequency of the references to it in the time of the Exile was to remind Israel that the God who had delivered them from Egypt would not completely cast them off. Indeed, Jeremiah twice foretold that Jehovah by the restoration of Israel from the Exile would give them an evidence of his grace even greater than the deliverance with which their national life began. "Behold the days come, saith Jehovah, That it shall no more be said, As Jehovah liveth, that brought up the children of Israel out of the land of Egypt; but As Jehovah liveth, that brought up the children of Israel from the land of the north and from all the countries whither he had driven them" (Jer. 16:14-15, compare 23:7-8). Jeremiah recognized the covenant at Sinai as the Magna Charta of the religion of Israel, the old covenant or testament by which we name the Hebrew scriptures. Yet he looked forward to a new and better covenant. "Behold the days come, saith Jehovah, that I will make a new covenant with the house of Israel, and with the house of Judah, not according to the covenant that I made with their fathers in the day that I took them by the hand to bring them out of the land of Egypt; which my covenant they broke although I was a husband unto them, saith Jehovah. But this is the covenant that I will make with the house of Israel after those days, saith

Jehovah, I will put my law in their inward parts and in
their heart will I write it; and I will be their God and
they shall be my people" (Jer. 31:31-33). Thus the covenant at Sinai is the basis of the old dispensation as the gift
of the Holy Spirit is the basis of the new. In the old
covenant the law was external, written upon tables of
stone, while in the new covenant it would be internal,
written upon the fleshy tables of the heart.

Before leaving the covenant another important feature
of it needs to be observed. It was between Jehovah and
the nation Israel and the religion which was based upon
it was the religion of the nation. The covenant was not
with individuals as such. The members of the nation
obtained the benefits of the covenant only by membership
in the nation. Circumcision was the outward sign of this
membership and thus it was the sign or token of the
covenant. It is difficult for us with our strong emphasis
upon individualism in religion to realize that the religion of
Israel in the time of Moses was national and not individual. Yet so it was. The whole religious life of the
individual was bound up in the life of the nation. This
continued to be true of the religion of Israel so long as
the nation stood. It was only when the nation was carried
into Exile and its national life disappeared that religion
became an individual matter. Nevertheless, even in the
times of Moses there were beginnings of individualism.
The ten commandments could not be obeyed by the nation
except as the individuals obeyed them. Many of the
offerings were made by individuals. As time went on,
individualism became more and more prominent. It is

specially so in many of the Psalms which speak of the individual in direct relation to God. Yet it remained for the New Testament to give the individual his true place in religion. The Old Testament was for the most part national.

(3) THE MORAL LAW.

The moral law, as found in the ten commandments, presents Israel's part in the covenant with Jehovah at Sinai (Exod. 20:1-17; Deut. 5:6-21). Jehovah announced that he had already fulfilled an important part of his obligation under the covenant. "I am Jehovah thy God who brought thee out of the land of Egypt, out of the house of bondage" (Exod. 20:2; Deut. 5:6). Having done this much he had a right to demand of Israel a fulfilment of their part which consisted chiefly in obedience to the moral law.

We cannot tell how deep an appreciation Moses had of the full meaning of these commandments. He certainly did not understand them in the spiritual sense which Our Lord gave to them. Nevertheless he must have had a much deeper appreciation of their true meaning than the people of his day.

Certain outstanding features of these commandments deserve our attention:

(a) Religion and morality are not distinguished. If the first four commandments present Israel's duty to God, the last six present their duty to each other. Nevertheless the last six are presented not merely as Israel's duty to other men but as Israel's duty to Jehovah. Behind the men and women to whom in the first instance the duty is

performed, is God who demands obedience. This makes
morality religious and so it is viewed throughout the Old
Testament. So after Our Lord had summarized man's
duty to God which he regarded as the first and great commandment, he said that the second commandment was
like unto it (Matt. 22:37-40). True human relations
grow out of true relations to God. Morality without religion has lost its deepest meaning and its highest impulse.
Human conduct in all its relations was viewed by the Old
Testament as in God's sight (Gen. 38:7; Exod. 15:26;
Num. 32:13; Deut. 6:18; 21:9; 31:29, etc.). To mention
only one example, when David had committed his great
sin against Bathsheba and Uriah, he said "Against thee,
thee only have I sinned, and done that which is evil in
thy sight" (Ps. 51:4).

(b) The commandments are timeless, equally appropriate in any age and land. There are, however, two
incidental allusions to Israel's situation. The reason for
observance of the Sabbath as given in Deuteronomy is
"Thou shalt remember that thou wast a servant in the
land of Egypt and Jehovah thy God brought thee out
thence by a mighty hand and by an outstretched arm.
Therefore Jehovah thy God commanded thee to keep
the sabbath day" (Deut. 5:15). While this reason
applied only to Israel it cannot be said that it touches the
timelessness of the command itself. The motive for
honoring father and mother is "that thy days may be long
in the land which Jehovah thy God giveth thee" (Exod.
20:12), or in the other version, "that thy days may be
long and that it may go well with thee in the land which

Jehovah thy God giveth thee" (Deut. 5:16). This is a reference to Israel's coming into the land of Canaan. It does not, however, make the commandment temporary. The prohibition against bearing false witness and that against coveting seem to refer only to fellow Israelites (Exod. 20:16-17; Deut. 5:20-21). We should not, however, infer that the Israelites were free to bear false witness against foreigners and to covet their property. The ten commandments presented the law of conduct in the theocracy. Foreign relations are not mentioned. When, however, a foreigner came to live within the gates of Israel, he was required to keep the sabbath (Exod. 20:10; Deut. 5:14).

(c) The spirituality of the ten commandments appears at certain points. While a merely formal obedience to some of them might seem possible, in other cases obedience must spring from an attitude of the heart. Taking the name of Jehovah in vain might refer either to perjury or to profanity. In the latter case obedience depends not merely upon the words spoken but the manner of saying them, the reverent or irreverent attitude. Honoring father and mother is clearly a case of the same sort. No external conduct, however correct, would suffice to obey this commandment unless it proceeded from a true attitude of heart. The same is preeminently true of the tenth commandment, for coveting is altogether a matter of the heart. These three examples justify us in the conclusion that while the great mass of Israelites in all ages were satisfied with an external obedience, there was always a small number of more spiritual men and women who

:19). Moses had at least some
thought that "love is the fulfil-
13:10).

L LAW

or a complete presentation of the
s details. We present therefore
atures.

WORSHIP

vorship mentioned in Moses' time
Mount Sinai, which was called the
od. 3:1; 4:27). "Now Moses was
ethro, his father-in-law, the priest of
e flock to the back of the wilderness,
untain of God unto Horeb" (Exod.
appeared to him in the burning bush
nly I will be with thee; and this shall
hee, that I have sent thee: when thou
the people out of Egypt, ye shall serve
untain" (Exod. 3:12). In accordance
e God commanded Moses to say to
, the God of the Hebrews hath met with
s go, we pray thee, three days' journey
ss that we may sacrifice to Jehovah our
:18). In obedience to this command,
ron came and said unto Pharaoh, thus
the God of Israel, let my people go that
feast unto me in the wilderness" (Exod.
haraoh refused, the command was repeated
ou shalt say unto him, Jehovah the God of
hath sent me unto thee, saying, Let my
t they may serve me in the wilderness: and

recognized that all these commandments required the obedience of the heart.

(d) The comprehensiveness of the decalogue is most remarkable. Scarcely a duty of man can be mentioned which is not either stated or implied. While originally intended for a small nation living in the simple social and political conditions of ancient times, they need very little adaptation and enlargement to fit the complex relations of modern civilization. Even now this code has never been surpassed. Here is one of the greatest evidences of inspiration in scripture. Great as Moses was, we cannot believe that he could have produced this wonderful codification of moral principles without divine inspiration.

(e) The negative form of all the commandments except the fourth and fifth implies a strong affirmative. The first commandment required more than the mere putting away of strange gods. Nothing less than individual allegiance to Jehovah would suffice. The second commandment not only prohibited idolatry but by so doing required a spiritual conception of Jehovah. The third commandment not merely forbade profanity but enjoined reverence. The sixth commandment, while in form it merely prohibited murder, by implication required such conduct as would preserve life. The seventh commandment was not satisfied with mere abstinence from adultery. It enjoined purity in all sexual relations. The eighth commandment meant more than not to steal. It commanded a due regard for all the property rights of others. The ninth commandment enjoined telling the truth as well as abstaining from falsehood. Finally the tenth commandment not merely forbade coveting but required a man to be satisfied with the things which he had.

Aside from the ten commandments, there are other direct precepts which belong to the moral rather than the ceremonial law. The most comprehensive of these is the summary of the law which Moses gave shortly before his death. "And, now, Israel, what doth Jehovah thy God require of thee, but to fear Jehovah thy God, to walk in all his ways and to love him and to serve Jehovah thy God with all thy heart and with all thy soul, to keep the commandments of Jehovah and his statutes which I command thee this day for thy good?" (Deut. 10:12-13). In form this resembles the familiar summary which Micah gave, "What doth Jehovah require of thee but to do justly and to love kindness and to walk humbly with thy God?" (Mic. 6:8). The chief difference is that Moses' summary contains no direct command for justice and kindness toward others. On the face of it, it relates only to Israel's duty to Jehovah. This difference, however, is apparent rather than real. Fearing Jehovah, walking in his ways, loving him, serving him with all the heart and with all the soul, keeping his commandments and his statutes surely include the performance of every duty that an Israelite owed to his fellows. Even the duty of man to man was conceived of as a duty to God. The moral and religious significance of an act of man could not be seen so long as it was thought of as terminating upon his fellow. Moses and the prophets saw every act of man as done in the sight of Jehovah, as in some sense done to Jehovah. The spirit of Our Lord's word, "Inasmuch as ye did it unto one of these, my brethren,

land of Egypt" (Deut. 10 appreciation of the great ment of the law" (Rom.

(4) THE CEREMONI Space will not suffice ceremonial law in all i only the outstanding fe

A. THE PLACE OF The first place of was Mount Horeb or mountain of God (E keeping the flock of J Midian; and he led th and came to the mo 3:1). There God "and he said, Certa be the token unto hast brought forth God upon this mo with this promis Pharaoh, "Jehova us: and now let into the wilderne God" (Exod. "Moses and A saith Jehovah, they may hold 5:1). When to Moses, "Th the Hebrews, people go, th behold, hitherto, thou hast not hearkened" (Exod. 7:16). Accordingly Moses and Aaron said to Pharaoh, "We will go three days' journey into the wilderness and sacrifice to Jehovah our God, as he shall command us, and Pharaoh said I will let you go, that ye may sacrifice to Jehovah your God in the wilderness; only ye shall not go very far away: entreat for me" (Exod. 8:27-28). It was Moses' evident intention to bring Israel to the mountain of God, Mount Horeb or Sinai. This intention was carried out and at last "Israel encamped before the mount and Moses went up unto God, and Jehovah called unto him out of the mountain saying, Thus shalt thou say to the house of Jacob, and tell the children of Israel: Ye have seen what I did unto the Egyptians and how I bore you on eagles' wings and brought you unto myself" (Exod. 19:2-4).

It is clear from these passages that Jehovah was thought of as being present at Mount Sinai. It was the mountain of God (Exod. 3:1; 4:27). There he appeared to Moses and in bringing Israel there he brought them unto himself (Exod. 19:4). There Israel tarried many months. There Moses communed with God. There he received the ten commandments (Exod. 24:12; 31:18) and the legislation contained in the latter part of Exodus, the whole of Leviticus (Lev. 25:1; 26:46; 27:34) and the early chapters of Numbers (Num. 1:1; 9:1). Yet in spite of all this there is no evidence that Mount Sinai was regarded as a permanent place for the worship of Jehovah. Indeed all the evidence is against it. In his song of triumph after the crossing of the Red Sea Moses did not look forward to Mount Sinai but to the promised land for he sang, "Thou wilt bring them in and plant them in the mountain of thine inheritance, the place, O Jehovah, which thou hast made for thee to dwell in, the sanctuary, O Lord, which thy hands have established" (Exod. 15:17). Although Israel wandered nearly forty years in the wilderness, they never, so far as the record shows, came back to Mount Sinai to worship Jehovah. Having brought them to himself at Mount Sinai, he went with them in their wanderings guiding them by the pillar of cloud and fire until they should come to the land of Canaan. During this period the place of worship was not Mount Sinai but the tabernacle or tent of meeting which moved from place to place under the guidance of God. Even after Israel came into Canaan, Mount Sinai was not regarded as a place of worship. There is no record of pilgrimages thither with the single exception of Elijah. He went from Beersheba "forty days and forty nights unto Horeb, the mount of God" (I Kgs. 19:8). It is surprising in view of the fact that the constitution of the theocracy was given at Mount Sinai that it is mentioned only nine times in the entire Old Testament outside of the Pentateuch and that all but one of these passages refers to the experiences of Israel there in the past (Judges 5:5; I Kgs. 8:9; 19:8; II Chron. 5:10; Neh. 9:13; Ps. 68:8, 17; 106:19; Mal. 4:4).

In the farewell addresses of Moses on the plains of Moab he looked forward to the time when Jehovah would choose a place in the land of Canaan to set his name there. This was to be the permanent place for the worship of Jehovah. "Unto the place which Jehovah your God shall choose out of all your tribes, to put his name there, even unto his habitation shall ye seek, and thither thou shalt come and thither ye shall bring your burnt offerings and your sacrifices and your tithes and the heave-offering of your hand, and your vows, and your freewill-offerings and the firstlings of your herd and of your flock, and there ye shall eat before Jehovah your God, and ye shall rejoice in all that ye put your hand unto, ye and your households, wherein Jehovah thy God hath blessed thee." (Deut. 12:5-7). Moses referred to this place no less than twenty times (Deut. 12:5, 11, 14, 18, 21, 26; 14:23, 24, 25; 15:20; 16:2, 6, 7, 11, 15, 16; 17:8, 10; 26:2; 31:11) always calling it the place that Jehovah would choose. He never mentions the name of the place and it seems probable that he did not know what place it would be. Joshua referred to the place in the same way, probably meaning the tabernacle at Shiloh (Josh. 9:27, compare Josh. 18:1). Solomon at the dedication of the temple recalled Moses' prediction and quoted God's words to his father, David, "Since the day that I brought forth my people Israel out of Egypt, I chose no city out of all the tribes of Israel to build a house that my name might be there" (I Kgs. 8:16 compare II Sam. 7:4-5). The Chronicler adds, "But I have chosen Jerusalem that my name might be there" (II Chron. 6:6). In his prayer on that occasion Solomon referred twice to God's choice of Jerusalem as the place of his sanctuary (I Kgs. 8:44, 48; II Chron. 6:34, 38) and it is mentioned several times elsewhere (I Kgs. 11:13, 32, 36; 14:21; II Kgs. 21:7; 23:27; II Chron. 7:12, 16; 12:13; 33:7; Ps. 78:68; 132:13). After the exile Zechariah looked forward to another choice of Jerusalem which was fulfilled when the temple was rebuilt (Zech. 1:17; 2:12; 3:2)..

B.   THE TABERNACLE

At Mount Sinai Israel built their first sanctuary for the worship of Jehovah in obedience to his command, "Let them make me a sanctuary that I may dwell among them. According to all that I show thee the pattern of the tabernacle, and the pattern of all the furniture thereof, even so shall ye make it" (Exod. 25:8-9). The reason for the great strictness in making the tabernacle and its furniture according to the pattern was because each thing had a symbolic significance. The building was divided into two compartments. The western one, called the holy of holies, was a perfect cube, ten cubits in each direction, to symbolize the perfection of the God who dwelt there. This compartment contained only one article of furniture, the ark of covenant which was a chest of acacia wood covered within and without with pure gold (Exod. 25:10-22). Inside the ark were kept the two tables of stone on which were written the ten commandments. The lid of the ark which was of solid gold was called the mercy seat. Two cherubim of gold were part of the mercy seat. They faced each other at opposite ends of the mercy seat with wings outspread. The cherubim stood for the presence of God and God was thought of as dwelling between them over the mercy seat, for he said to Moses, "There I will meet with thee, and I will commune with thee from above the mercy seat, from between the two cherubim which are upon the ark of the testimony, of all things which I will give thee in commandment unto the children of Israel" (Exod. 25:22, compare also Exod. 30:6 and Num. 7:89). The ark of the covenant was the most precious possession of the Israelites. When it was taken away the tabernacle lost its significance. Indeed, we may speak of the tabernacle as built to house the ark of the covenant as the symbol of the presence of Jehovah.

Next to the holy of holies was the holy place which was ten cubits broad and twenty cubits long. It was separated from the holy of holies by a curtain or veil. The holy place contained three things. Near the curtain separating the holy place from the holy of holies stood the altar of incense. This was made of acacia wood covered with gold (Exod. 30:1-10). Incense was burned on it morning and evening and the smoke of the incense passed through the curtain into the presence of God. The incense symbolized the adoration of Israel. In reference to it, David said, "Thou art holy O thou that inhabitest the praises of Israel" (Ps. 22:3). "Let my prayer be set forth as incense before thee, the lifting up of my hand as the evening sacrifice" (Ps. 141:2). When the angel appeared to Zacharias to announce the birth of John the Baptist, "the whole multitude of the people were praying without at the hour of incense" (Luke 1:10). So the four living creatures and the twenty-four elders of the Revelation carried "golden bowls full of incense, which are the prayers of the saints" (Rev. 5:8, compare 8:3-4).

On the south side of the holy place stood the golden candlestick, or rather lamp-stand, which had one shaft and six branches supporting seven lamps. It was of solid gold (Exod. 25:31-40). The lamps were filled with olive oil and were kept burning from evening till morning. This was the lamp of God which was burning in the tabernacle at Shiloh on the night when God spoke to the boy Samuel (I Sam. 3:3). The constant shining of the lamps probably symbolized the constant worship of Israel (Zech. 4:1-6) and the candlestick itself probably represented Israel, the people of God. So the Lord said to John, "The seven candlesticks are the seven churches" (Rev. 1:20). On the arch of Titus in Rome is a representation of the candlestick carried by captives in the triumph after his victory in the Jewish war.

On the north side of the holy place stood the table of showbread. The table was made of acacia wood covered with gold (Exod. 25:23-29). On it were constantly kept twelve loaves of bread, representing the twelve tribes of Israel. The loaves were renewed every Sabbath. The term showbread might be better rendered "bread of the face or presence." It probably signified the constant presentation of the tribes of Israel before God, an idea similar to that of Paul's injunction to "present your bodies a living sacrifice, holy, acceptable to God, which is your spiritual service" (Rom. 12:1). A representation of the table of showbread is also seen on the arch of Titus at Rome.

The tabernacle stood in a court, fifty cubits from north to south and one hundred cubits from east to west. This court was surrounded by a fence five cubits high. The entrance to the court was at the eastern end. The tabernacle was in the western part of the court and its door was toward the entrance to the court. Between the tabernacle and the entrance stood the altar of burnt-offering, on which all the sacrifices were offered. It was made of acacia wood covered with brass. Its upper corners had projections which were called horns (Exod. 38:1-7). Standing between the entrance to the court and the door of the tabernacle, this altar was a constant reminder to Israel that they could not approach God unless their sins were atoned for by the blood of sacrifice. A fugitive might flee for refuge and lay hold of the horns of the altar, thus appealing to the atoning blood (I Kgs. 1:50-51; 2:28). Amos foretold that even this refuge would be taken away. "In the day that I shall visit the transgressions of Israel upon him I will also visit the altars of Bethel, and the horns of the altar shall be cut off and fall to the ground" (Am. 3:14). A laver of brass or copper stood in the court between the altar of burnt-offering and the door of the tabernacle (Exod. 38:8). There the priests were required to wash their hands and their feet before offering sacrifice at the altar of burnt-offering and before entering the tabernacle. The meaning of this was that they must be sanctified before approaching God (Exod. 30:17-21).

Over the tabernacle stood the pillar of cloud by day and of fire by night as the symbol of Jehovah's presence. When this pillar was lifted up it was a sign that Israel should break camp and move under the guidance of the pillar (Exod. 40:34-38). Then the Levites took the tabernacle apart and carried it to the next place of encampment setting it up there. Some of the furniture was carried by Aaron and his sons (Num. 18:3). The ark of the covenant was carried at the head of the procession. "And it came to pass, when the ark set forward that Moses said, 'Rise up, O Jehovah, and let thine enemies be scattered; and let them that hate thee flee before thee.' And when it rested, he said, 'Return, O Jehovah, unto the ten thousands of the thousands of Israel'" (Num. 10:35-36, compare Ps. 132:8).

The names by which the tabernacle was called show how it was regarded. The word rendered tabernacle in the Revised Version means literally a dwelling. It was conceived of as the dwelling-place of God as he commanded, "Let them make me a sanctuary that I may dwell among them" (Exod. 25:8). When the tabernacle moved, God moved with it, as Nathan said to David, "Thus saith Jehovah, Shalt thou build me a house for me to dwell in? For I have not dwelt in a house since the day that I brought up the children of Israel out of Egypt, even to this day, but have walked in a tent and in a tabernacle" (II Sam. 7:5-6). The tabernacle was the moving dwelling-place of Jehovah. A second very common name for the sanctuary was "the tent of meeting." The word for meeting does not refer to the act of meeting nor to the assembly but means the sacred seasons of the religious year. It was at the tabernacle that Israel was to keep their sacred appointments with God at the various feasts and fasts, as well as the sabbaths and new moons. It was the trysting-place of Jehovah and his people. The third name was the tabernacle of the testimony (Exod. 38:21) or tent of the testimony (Num. 9:15), a name which was suggested by the fact that the tables of the law, which are called the tables of the testimony (Exod. 31:18), were in the tabernacle. As the ten commandments testified to the righteous will of God, so did the tabernacle testify to his presence with Israel.

C. THE PRIESTS AND LEVITES

When Israel became the chosen people of Jehovah he

said to them, "Ye shall be unto me a kingdom of priests and a holy nation" (Exod. 19:6). This conception of the priesthood superseded the old patriarchal conception in which the head of the family was its priest. Obviously the priestly function could not be exercised by all the people. Hence God commanded Moses, "bring thou near unto thee Aaron thy brother, and his sons with him, from among the children of Israel, that he may minister unto me in the priest's office, even Aaron, Nadah and Abihu, Eleazar and Ithamar, Aaron's sons" (Exod. 28:1). When the priestly garments were made for them they were anointed in a solemn ceremony at the door of the tent of meeting (Exod. 40:12-16). Their anointing was to be to them for an everlasting priesthood throughout their generations (Exod. 40:15). All the descendants of Aaron were to be hereditary priests. If any of them, however, had a physical blemish, he was not allowed to exercise the priestly function (Lev. 21:16-24) because only the best could perform the service of Jehovah. When Aaron died, "Eleazar his son ministered in the priest's office in his stead" (Deut. 10:6).

The priesthood in the strict sense was confined to Aaron and his sons (Num. 16:40). No one else was allowed to perform the service of the sanctuary. However, the task of caring for the tabernacle and moving it when Israel migrated required a larger number than Aaron and his four sons. This service might have been performed by the first-born in all the tribes, who were set apart to Jehovah (Exod. 13:11-12). Another arrangement, however, was made because of the faithfulness of the tribe of Levi to which Aaron belonged. When Moses saw the

wickedness of the people in worshipping the golden calf
he "stood in the gate of the camp and said, Whoso is
on Jehovah's side, let him come unto me. And all the
sons of Levi gathered themselves together unto him. And
he said unto them, Thus saith Jehovah the God of Israel,
Put ye every man his sword upon his thigh, and go to
and fro from gate to gate throughout the camp and slay
every man his brother, and every man his companion, and
every man his neighbor. And the sons of Levi did according
to the word of Moses: and there fell of the people that
day about three thousand men. And Moses said, Consecrate yourselves to Jehovah, yea every man against his
son and against his brother, that he may bestow upon you
a blessing this day" (Exod. 32:26-29). It was on account
of their loyalty to Jehovah, even though it was shown
in this bloody way, that the Levites were made the priestly
tribe. Their relation to Aaron and his sons, their relation to the first-born and their duties are indicated in the
following passage: "Jehovah spake unto Moses, saying,
Bring the tribe of Levi near, and set them before Aaron
the priest, that they may minister unto him. And they
shall keep his charge, and the charge of the whole congregation before the tent of meeting, to do the service of
the tabernacle. And they shall keep all the furniture of
the tent of meeting, and the charge of the children of
Israel, to do the service of the tabernacle. And thou shalt
give the Levites unto Aaron and to his sons; they are
wholly given unto him on the behalf of the children of
Israel. And thou shalt appoint Aaron and his sons, and
they shall keep their priesthood: and the stranger that
cometh nigh shall be put to death. And Jehovah spoke

unto Moses, saying, And I, behold, I have taken the Levites from among the children of Israel instead of all the first-born that openeth the womb among the children of Israel; and the Levites shall be mine" (Num. 3:5-12). The substitution of the Levites for the first-born is mentioned repeatedly (Num. 3:40-41, 45; 8:16-18). The distinction of the duties of the sons of Aaron from those of the other Levites appears more fully in the words of Jehovah to Aaron, "Thou and thy sons and thy fathers' house with thee shall bear the iniquity of the sanctuary; and thou and thy sons with thee shall bear the iniquity of the priesthood. And thy brethren also, the tribe of Levi, the tribe of thy father, bring thou near with thee, that they may be joined unto thee and minister unto thee; but thou and thy sons with thee shall be before the tent of the testimony. And they shall keep thy charge and the charge of all the tent; only they shall not come nigh unto the vessels of the sanctuary and unto the altar, that they die not, neither they nor ye" (Num. 18:1-3). When the camp moved the Levites took the tabernacle down, carried the parts to the next place and set it up again (Num. 1:50-53). Different parts of the tabernacle were in charge of different divisions of the tribe of Levi (Num. 3:25-26, 29-31, 36-37; 4:1-49). The other Levites were subject to Aaron and his sons and in general it was their duty to assist the priests in the performance of the less sacred parts of their office. This relation between the priests and the Levites persisted through all the history of the children of Israel. When the tabernacle came into the land of Canaan and was set up at Shiloh an important part of the duty of the Levites ceased; but when David brought up the ark from Kirjath-jearim to Jerusalem and established the sanctuary there, new duties came to them. Accordingly they were divided into four classes, (1) those who assisted the priests in the work of the sanctuary, (2) those who judged legal cases and kept the record as scribes, (3) the gate-keepers of the sanctuary, and (4) the musicians (I Chron. 24-26). It is an evidence of the antiquity of the Pentateuchal ceremonial law that these distinctions are not mentioned in it. There seems to have been no musical service in connection with the worship of the sanctuary until the time of David.

Aaron was supreme over all the priests and Levites and was called the high priest (Lev. 21:10; Num. 35:25). Like the other priests he might marry (Lev. 21:7, 9, 13-14) and the high-priesthood was hereditary in his family. Certain priestly duties were performed only by him, the most important of which were officiating on the day of atonement (Lev. 16) and consulting the Urim and Thummim. The garments of the high priest were important because of their symbolic significance. He wore suspended about his neck and hanging over his chest the breastplate which was rectangular, having four rows of precious stones each containing three stones in settings of gold. Upon each of these twelve stones was the name of one of the tribes of the children of Israel. The back of the breastplate was a pocket in which were the Urim and Thummim. On account of them the breast-plate was called the breastplate of judgment and it was commanded, "Aaron shall bear the names of the children of Israel in the breastplate of judgment upon his heart, when he goeth in unto the holy place, for a memorial for Jehovah continually. And thou shalt put in the breast-plate of judgment the Urim and the Thummim and they shall be upon Aaron's heart, when he goeth in before Jehovah; and Aaron shall bear the judgment of the children of Israel upon his heart before Jehovah continually" (Exod. 28:29-30). Thus the high priest came before Jehovah as the representative of the children of Israel. He was to keep them and their interests, collectively and severally, in his affectionate memory and to bring them to the remembrance of Jehovah.

The details concerning the Urim and Thummim are very difficult of interpretation. The meaning of the words is probably "lights and perfections." These two words occur together (Lev. 8:8; Ezra. 2:63; Neh. 7:65) although the order is sometimes reversed (Deut. 33:8) and Urim sometimes occurs alone (Num. 27:21; I Sam. 28:6). The Urim and Thummim were kept in the ephod, inside of the breastplate which was attached to the ephod (Lev. 8:8). It seems probable that they were precious stones, but if so they were distinct from the twelve stones of the breastplate. It is certain that the high priest consulted the Urim and Thummim on behalf of the nation but in what manner we do not know. Thus it was said that Joshua "shall stand before Eleazar the priest, who shall inquire for him by the judgment of the Urim before Jehovah; at his word shall they go out, and at his word shall they come in, both he and all the children of Israel with him, even all the congregation" (Num. 27:21). There were several instances of consulting Jehovah which were probably by this means, although the Urim and Thummim are usually not mentioned (Judges 1:1; 20:18,

23, 27-28; I Sam. 10:22; 14:36-42; 23:9-12; 30:7-8; II
Sam. 2:1; 5:19, 23-24). The answer was generally very
simple, consisting either of yes or no (Judges 20:23, 27-
28; I Sam. 23:11-12; 30:7-8; II Sam. 2:1; 5:19, 23) or
the selection of a tribe (Judges 1:2; 20:18). Some have
supposed from this that the light flashed out from the
Urim and Thummim if the answer was affirmative, but
did not flash if it was negative. This can hardly account
for the facts, for sometimes the answer was refused (I
Sam. 14:37; 28:6) and sometimes it was more than could
be indicated by such means (I Sam. 10:22; II Sam.
5:24). The most illuminating reference to the subject is
found in the Septuagint rendering of I Sam. 14:41, "And
Saul said, O Jehovah, the God of Israel, why hast thou
not answered thy servant this day? If the iniquity be in
me or in Jonathan my son, give Urim; and if it be in thy
people Israel, give Thummim. And Jonathan and Saul
were taken by lot, but the people escaped" (See Driver
Exodus in Cambridge Bible pp. 313-314). It is by no
means certain that any outward manifestation was given
from the Urim and Thummim. As a part of the vesture
of the high priest they may have merely symbolized his
authority to receive light and truth from Jehovah. Consulting the Urim and Thummim may have been by
prayer and the answer merely an assurance in the heart
of the high priest—an assurance which he confidently
believed came from Jehovah.

The ephod was the upper garment of the high priest
to which the breastplate was attached. It was composed
of two parts, one hanging in front, and one behind.
These two parts were attached by shoulder pieces on each

of which was an onyx stone. The names of the tribes of Israel were engraved on these stones, six on one stone and six on the other (Exod. 28:9-10). They were called stones of memorial for the children of Israel and we read "Aaron shall bear their names before Jehovah upon his two shoulders for a memorial" (Exod. 28:12). The ephod was made of "gold, blue, purple, scarlet, and fine twined linen, the work of the skilful workman" (Exod. 28:6). "They did beat the gold into thin plates and cut it into wires, to work it in the blue, and in the purple, and in the scarlet and in the fine linen" (Exod. 39:3). On account of its containing the Urim and Thummim, the ephod was regarded as a very sacred thing and later it was sometimes an object of worship. Gideon took golden ear-rings from the men of Israel and "made an ephod thereof, and put it in his city, even in Ophrah; and all Israel played the harlot after it there; and it became a snare unto Gideon and to his house" (Judges 8:27). Micah also had a house of gods and he made an ephod and teraphim and consecrated one of his sons who became his priest" (Judges 17:5). Likewise Hosea spoke of the ephod in connection with the pillar and teraphim as an object of worship (Hos. 3:4). The ephod is mentioned in connection with consulting Jehovah (I Sam. 23:9-12; 30:7-8) and some have supposed that it was consulted. It is more probable that the consultation was not with the ephod itself but with the Urim and Thummim which it contained. Samuel when he was a boy in the tabernacle at Shiloh wore a linen ephod but this was different from the high-priestly garment (I Sam. 2:18).

The common priests also wore linen ephods (I Sam. 22:18) as did David (II Sam. 6:14; I Chron. 15:27).

The robe of the ephod was distinct from it. It was worn underneath and was longer than the ephod. It was all of blue. Upon the skirts of it were pomegranates of blue, purple, scarlet and twined linen (Exod. 28:33) and bells of gold alternating. The purpose of the bells is explained by the statement that "the sound thereof shall be heard when he goeth in unto the holy place before Jehovah, and when he cometh out, that he die not" (Exod. 28:35).

Upon his head the high priest wore a mitre or turban which was made of fine linen (Exod. 28:39). Over it on the forehead was a plate of gold bearing the inscription "Holy to Jehovah" (Exod. 28:36-37). "It shall be upon Aaron's forehead and Aaron shall bear the iniquity of the holy things, which the children of Israel shall hallow in all their holy gifts; and it shall be always upon his forehead, that they may be accepted before Jehovah" (Exod. 28:38). This was to emphasize the importance of holiness in approaching God.

The high priest wore these sacred garments whenever he ministered in the tabernacle with one important exception. On the day of atonement when he went into the holy of holies to atone for himself and the people, he laid these garments aside (Lev. 16:23-24).

D.　HOLY TIMES

The sabbath is not mentioned in the time of the patriarchs. There are, however, indications in the story of the flood that time was divided into periods of seven days (Gen. 7:4; 8:10, 12). The periods of seven years that

Jacob served Laban for Leah and Rachel are called weeks (Gen. 29:20, 27-28). Although the word sabbath was used in ancient Babylonia, and every seventh day from the beginning of the month (also the nineteenth day, which was the forty-ninth from the beginning of the preceding month) was regarded as inauspicious for any enterprise, the idea was quite different from that of the sabbath among the children of Israel. There was a recognition of the sabbath in the giving of the manna, which was before the giving of the decalogue. Twice as much manna was collected on the sixth day so as to suffice also for the sabbath (Exod. 16:5, 22). In this connection Moses said to the people, "This is that which Jehovah hath spoken. Tomorrow is a solemn rest, a holy sabbath unto Jehovah" (Exod. 16:23, compare verse 25). Jehovah commanded, "Let no man go out of his place on the seventh day" (Exod. 16:29).

The form of the fourth commandment suggests that the sabbath was not new, for Israel was commanded to "remember the sabbath day, to keep it holy" (Exod. 20:8). The reason for the sabbath connects it with the account of creation, "for in six days Jehovah made heaven and earth, the sea and all that in them is, and rested the seventh day: wherefore Jehovah blessed the sabbath day, and hallowed it" (Exod. 20:11). This corresponds to the statement of Genesis, "On the seventh day God finished his work which he had made; and he rested on the seventh day from all his work which he had made. And God blessed the seventh day, and hallowed it; because that in it he rested from all his work which God had created and made" (Gen. 2:2-3). The Hebrew word rendered "rested" in these verses is the verb from the same stem as the noun sabbath. The fourth commandment as given by Moses on the plains of Moab differs slightly from the form as given on Mount Sinai. The man-servant and maid-servant were to keep the sabbath "that thy man-servant and thy maid-servant may rest as well as thou. And thou shalt remember that thou wast a servant in the land of Egypt, and Jehovah thy God brought thee out thence by a mighty hand and by an out-stretched arm: therefore Jehovah thy God commanded thee to keep the sabbath day" (Deut. 5:14-15). This is not a variant form of the commandment. Moses before his death gave Israel an additional reason for keeping the sabbath.

While the sabbath was a day of rest from ordinary work it also had its special worship. So Jehovah said, "Six days shall work be done; but on the seventh day is a sabbath of solemn rest, a holy convocation, ye shall do no manner of work; it is a sabbath unto Jehovah in all your dwellings" (Lev. 23:3). This holy convocation may be referred to in the prediction of Ezekiel, "The people of the land shall worship at the door of that gate (the gate of the inner court of the temple) before Jehovah on the sabbath and on the new moons" (Ezek. 46:3). There were two other ritual distinctions of the sabbath in the Mosaic law. On each sabbath the priest renewed the twelve loaves of showbread on the table in the holy place (Lev. 24:5-8). Thus symbolically the twelve tribes of Israel presented themselves anew before Jehovah on every sabbath day. Later it was provided that the burnt offering of the sabbath should be twice as great as that on the other days (Num. 28:6).

The presence of the fourth commandment in the decalogue seems to contradict the statement that the decalogue presents the moral law for it is apparently ceremonial rather than moral. When, however, the profound meaning of the sabbath is understood, we see that the fourth commandment is in fact moral and not merely ceremonial. The idea of rest is wrought into the very structure of the creation and of man. Those who ignore it suffer a reduction in their producing power. It is profoundly true that God sanctified the day of rest. "The sabbath was made for man" (Mk. 2:27). Although Moses did not understand this deeper meaning of the sabbath, we can see in it the reason that this commandment was placed in the midst of the moral law.

As the people rested every seventh day so the land rested every seventh year. In that sabbatical year the land was not to be cultivated but to lie fallow "that the poor of thy people may eat" (Exod. 23:10-11; Lev. 25:1-7). In that year also every Hebrew must cancel the debts owed him by fellow Israelites and Hebrew slaves must go free (Deut. 15:1-18). When seven periods of seven years each had passed by, there was an additional year called the year of jubilee. On the day of atonement in that year men went through the land blowing on the trumpets to "proclaim liberty throughout the land unto all the inhabitants thereof" (Lev. 25:10). The people went back to their original possessions, and those in bondage were freed (Lev. 25:13-55; 27:17-18; Num. 36:4). These wise provisions were calculated to prevent those extremes of wealth and poverty which produce so many social evils. The announcement of the year of jubilee on the day of atonement was to suggest that the release and liberty of that year had their origin in the atoning sacrifice of that day, a sacrifice which looked forward to the great sacrifice of Calvary. It is therefore appropriate that the inscription on the liberty bell in Philadelphia should have the inscription "to proclaim liberty throughout the land, unto all the inhabitants thereof" (Lev. 25:10).

The first day of the month had a distinction beyond other days. On that day trumpets were blown over the burnt-offerings and peace-offerings (Num. 10:10). The special sacrifices of the day are described in detail (Num. 28:11-15). It does not appear that in Mosaic times the new moon was a time of rest as was the case later (Amos 8:5). However, the first of the seventh month was a day of rest and a holy convocation (Lev. 23:24-25; Num. 29:1-6).

The law of Moses prescribed four festivals in each year, (1) the passover on the fourteenth day of the first month, (2) the feast of unleavened bread beginning the day after the passover, (3) the feast of weeks celebrated fifty days after the passover, and (4) the feast of tabernacles beginning on the fifteenth of the seventh month (Lev. 23; Deut. 16:16). The first two of these, however, were regarded as one and thus Jehovah commanded, "Three times thou shalt keep a feast unto me in a year" (Exod. 23:14), and Moses said, "Three times in a year shall all thy males appear before Jehovah thy God in the place which he shall choose; in the feast of unleavened bread and in the feast of weeks and in the feast of tabernacles" (Deut. 16:16). In this statement the passover was regarded as a part of the feast of unleavened bread.

The passover and the feast of unleavened bread were not established at Mount Sinai, but grew out of the momentous events of the deliverance of Israel from Egypt. The last and most terrible plague which Jehovah visited upon Egypt was the slaughter of the first-born, "from the first-born of Pharaoh that sitteth upon his throne, even unto the first-born of the maid-servant that is behind the mill; and all the first-born of cattle" (Exod. 11:5). From this destruction the children of Israel were exempt (Exod. 11:7). The method of their exemption is told in connection with the establishment of the passover. "Jehovah spake unto Moses and unto Aaron in the land of Egypt, saying, This month shall be unto you the beginning of months: it shall be the first month of the year to you. Speak ye unto all the congregation of Israel, saying, In the tenth day of this month they shall take to them every man a lamb, according to their father's houses, a lamb for a household: and if the household be too little for a lamb, then shall he and his neighbor next unto his house take one according to the number of the souls; according to every man's eating ye shall make your count for the lamb. Your lamb shall be without blemish, a male a year old; ye shall take it from the sheep or from the goats; and ye shall keep it until the fourteenth day of the same month; and the whole assembly of the congregation of Israel shall kill it at even. And they shall take of the blood and put it on the two side-posts and on the lintel, upon the houses wherein they shall eat it. And they shall eat the flesh in that night roast with fire, and unleavened bread; with bitter herbs they shall eat it. Eat not of it raw, nor boiled at all with water, but roast with fire; its head with its legs and with the inwards thereof. And ye shall let nothing of it remain until the morning; but that which remaineth of it until the morning ye shall burn with fire. And thus ye shall eat it: with your loins girded, your shoes on your feet, and your staff in your hand; and ye shall eat it in haste: it is Jehovah's passover. For I will go through the land of Egypt in that night, and will smite all the first-born in the land of Egypt, both man and beast; and against all the gods of Egypt I will execute judgments: I am Jehovah. And the blood shall be to you for a token upon the houses where ye are: and when I see the blood, I will pass over you, and there shall no plague be upon you to destroy you when I smite the land of Egypt. And this day shall be unto you for a memorial and ye shall keep it a feast to Jehovah: throughout your generations ye shall keep it a feast by an ordinance forever" (Exod. 12:1-14).

Such was the institution of the passover. Israel was commanded to begin their year with this month in order to suggest that their deliverance from the smiting of the first-born marked a new beginning in their national life. Having as yet no sacrificial system, no tabernacle or priesthood, the paschal lamb was an exceptional kind of sacrifice. It was a family sacrifice, in some cases two families joining in it to emphasize the communion of the family. Putting the blood of the lamb on the side-posts and on the lintel of the houses suggested that only by a sacrifice for their sin could the first-born of Israel be saved from death. Eating the flesh of the lamb meant that the household partook of the advantages of the sacrifice. The unleavened bread eaten with the lamb symbolized purity and the bitter herbs the bitter bondage under which they had suffered. Eating the lamb with their loins girded, their shoes on their feet and their staves in their hands was to emphasize their readiness to leave Egypt in haste. Such was the first celebration of the passover. Its later celebrations throughout the history of Israel were intended to keep their national birthday in the memory of the people. It was a feast to Jehovah who saved their first-born by the blood of the lamb and delivered them from the bondage of Egypt.

The close relation of the feast of unleavened bread to the passover appears from the fact that the paschal lamb was to be eaten with unleavened bread (Exod. 12:8). Indeed, the feast of unleavened bread was but a continuation of the passover and its record follows immediately after that of the passover. "Seven days shall ye eat unleavened bread; even the first day ye shall put away leaven out of your houses: for whosoever eateth leavened bread from the first day until the seventh day, that soul shall be cut off from Israel. And in the first day there shall be to you a holy convocation, and in the seventh day a holy convocation; no manner of work shall be done in them, save that which every man must eat, that only may be done by you. And ye shall observe the feast of unleavened bread; for in this self-same day have I brought your hosts out of the land of Egypt: therefore shall ye observe this day throughout your generations by an ordinance forever" (Exod. 12:15-17). The holy convocation with which the feast began was the passover. The idea was that the people who had been saved by the blood of the lamb should put away all corruption from their houses and remain a pure people. "In the first month, on the fourteenth day of the month (the day of the passover, see Exod. 12:6) at even, ye shall eat unleavened bread, until the one and twentieth day of the month at even" (Exod. 12:18). This commandment was renewed to Israel when they fled from Egypt (Exod. 13:6-7). It was renewed to them again at Mount Sinai (Lev. 23:5-8). Years afterwards Moses spoke of it once more shortly before his death. "Thou shalt sacrifice the passover unto Jehovah thy God, of the flock and the herd, in the place which Jehovah shall choose, to cause his name to dwell there. Thou shalt eat no leavened bread with it; seven days shalt thou eat unleavened bread therewith, even the bread of affliction; for thou camest forth out of the land of Egypt in haste: that thou mayest remember the day when thou camest forth out of the land of Egypt all the days of thy life" (Deut. 16:2-3). The second celebration of the passover was at Mount Sinai, one year after Israel left Egypt (Num. 9:1-14). It was celebrated again at Gilgal after they had entered the promised land (Josh. 5:10-11).

The second of the three feasts was the feast of weeks. Its name came from the fact that it was celebrated seven weeks after the beginning of the harvest. "Ye shall count unto you from the morrow after the sabbath from the day that ye brought the sheaf of the wave-offering: seven sabbaths shall there be complete: even unto the morrow after the seventh sabbath shall ye number fifty days; and ye shall offer a new meal-offering unto Jehovah" (Lev. 23:15-16). The commandment takes a slightly different form in Deuteronomy, "Seven weeks shalt thou number unto thee: from the time thou begin- nest to put the sickle to the standing grain shalt thou begin to number seven weeks. And thou shalt keep the feast of weeks unto Jehovah thy God with a tribute of a free- will-offering of thy hand, which thou shalt give according as Jehovah thy God blesseth thee" (Deut. 16:9-10). The sabbath from which the law of Leviticus dates the feast of weeks was probably not the weekly sabbath but the first day of the feast of unleavened bread on which all servile work was forbidden (Lev. 23:7-8). This seems probable from the fact that the ceremony of waving the sheaf before Jehovah is described directly after the account of the feast of unleavened bread (Lev. 23:9-11). Simi- larly the day of atonement was called a sabbath (Lev. 23:32).

The feast of weeks was also called the feast of harvest, "the first-fruits of thy labors which thou sowest in the field" (Exod. 23:16), because on that day the first-fruits of the wheat harvest were presented before Jehovah (Exod. 34:22) and once it is called "the day of the first fruits" (Num. 28:26). In later times it was called the day of Pentecost (Acts 2:1). The idea of the feast of weeks was the consecration of the first- fruits of the land to God as the idea of the feast of ingathering in the seventh month was thanksgiving. No work was done on that day. There was a holy convoca- tion (Lev. 23:21). Besides the usual sacrifice two wave- loaves of leavened bread were presented before Jehovah, together with a special burnt-offering and a special sin-offering (Lev. 23:17-20).

Before considering the third and last feast of the religious year, it is appropriate to examine the ceremonies which led up to it and in particular those of the day of atonement which were so closely related to the feast of tabernacles. The seventh month of the year was a holy month because the number seven was a symbol of holiness. On the first day of this month there were a solemn rest and a holy convocation (Lev. 23:23-25; Num. 29:1). A special burnt-offering, meal-offering and sin-offering were offered on that day (Num. 29:2-6). The tenth day of the same month was the day of atonement, the only fast day prescribed by the Mosaic law and the most significant day in the religious year. So far as the people were concerned, it was described as follows: "On the tenth day of this seventh month is the day of atonement: it shall be a holy convocation unto you, and ye shall afflict your souls: and ye shall offer an offering made by fire unto Jehovah. And ye shall do no manner of work in that same day; for it is a day of atonement, to make atonement for you before Jehovah your God. For whatsoever soul it be that shall not be afflicted in that same day; he shall be cut off from his people. And whatsoever soul it be that doeth any manner of work in that same day, that soul will I destroy from among his people. Ye shall do no manner of work: it is a statute forever throughout your generations in all your dwellings. It shall be unto you a sabbath of solemn rest, and ye shall afflict your souls: in the ninth day of the month at even, from even unto even, shall ye keep your sabbath" (Lev. 23:26-32).

The sacrifices of the day of atonement are mentioned briefly in Numbers (29:7-10).

The priestly ceremonies of the day of atonement are described at considerable length. After the death of Nadab and Abihu (Lev. 10:1-2; 16:1; Num. 26:61), Jehovah commanded that Aaron should not come at all times into the holy place within the veil (Lev. 16:2). He was to come only with a young bullock for a sin-offering and a ram for a burnt-offering (Lev. 16:3). He was to wash himself and put on the linen coat, breeches, girdle and mitre (Lev. 16:4). He should also take from the people two he-goats for a sin-offering and a ram for a burnt-offering (Lev. 16:5). The bullock was to be presented as a sin-offering for himself and his family (Lev. 16:6). The ceremony connected with the two goats was significant. Aaron brought them to the door of the tent of meeting and cast lots upon them to determine which should be for Jehovah and which for Azazel (Lev. 16:7-8). Azazel is not mentioned outside of this chapter. While its meaning is not surely known, the most probable suggestion is that it was a demon or spirit which was thought of as inhabiting the solitary parts of the desert (Lev. 16:22). After presenting the bullock as a sin-offering for himself and his family (Lev. 16:11-14), he killed the goat upon which the lot fell for Jehovah and returning with its blood into the holy of holies, sprinkled it upon the mercy-seat to make atonement for the holy place and for the tent of meeting (Lev. 16:15-16). No one was to be in the tent of meeting while the high-priest performed this ceremony (Lev. 16:17). After he had finished he went out to the altar of burnt-offering and put some of the blood of the goat on the horns of the altar, sprinkling it seven times (Lev. 16:18-19). "And when he hath made an end of atoning for the holy place, and the tent of meeting, and the altar, he shall present the live goat: and Aaron shall lay both his hands upon the head of the live goat, and confess over him all the iniquities of the children of Israel, and all their transgressions, even all their sins; and he shall put them upon the head of the goat, and shall send him away by the hand of a man that is in readiness into the wilderness: and the goat shall bear upon him all their iniquities unto a solitary land: and he shall let go the goat in the wilderness" (Lev. 16:20-22). After this the priest shall put off his linen garments and wash himself.

This solemn ceremony was to be performed every year on the day of atonement. The high-priest performed it on behalf of the whole people of Israel. He, and he only, could go into the very presence of Jehovah in the holy of holies, and he only on this one day in the year. No ceremony could possibly indicate more clearly that all the sins of the people were atoned for and taken away. The sins were transferred to the goat from the people and the goat was taken away into the wilderness to be seen no more. This ceremony of atonement was in addition to all the other atoning sacrifices of the year. It was a complete amnesty from sin. Whatever sins attached to the people or any of them before the day of atonement were now completely removed. Well might they rejoice in the thought that their transgressions were forgiven and their sins covered.

It was five days after the day of atonement, on the

fifteenth day of the seventh month that the feast of tabernacles began, and it lasted seven days (Lev. 23:34).
After the seven days there was an eighth day on which
there was a holy convocation (Lev. 23:35-36). The ceremonies are describèd as follows: "On the fifteenth day
of the seventh month, when ye have gathered in the fruits
of the land, ye shall keep the feast of Jehovah seven days:
on the first day shall be a solemn rest and on the eighth
day shall be a solemn rest. And ye shall take you on the
first day the fruit of goodly trees, branches of palm-trees,
and boughs of thick trees, and willows of the brook; and
ye shall rejoice before Jehovah your God seven days.
And ye shall keep it a feast unto Jehovah seven days in
the year: it is a statute forever throughout your generations; ye shall keep it in the seventh month. Ye shall
dwell in booths seven days; all that are home-born in
Israel shall dwell in booths; that your generations may
know that I made the children of Israel to dwell in booths
when I brought them out of the land of Egypt: I am
Jehovah your God" (Lev. 23:39-43). The sacrifices of
the feast are also told: "Seven days ye shall offer an
offering made by fire unto Jehovah: on the eighth day
shall be a holy convocation unto you; and ye shall offer
an offering made by fire unto Jehovah: it is a solemn
assembly; ye shall do no servile work" (Lev. 23:36, compare also Num. 29:12-34).

This third feast of the year had a two-fold aspect. It
was called the feast of tabernacles, or rather booths, to
recall that the children of Israel lived in booths while they
were wandering in the wilderness on the way to the
promised land. The word rendered tabernacles in the

name of the feast (Lev. 23:34) is the same which is
rendered booths elsewhere (Lev. 23:42-43). After the
people came into the land it was intended to remind them
of the gracious providence of God in bringing them safely
through the wilderness, from the humble condition in
which they dwelt in booths to the prosperous condition
in which they dwelt in houses. To remind them of this
they left their houses and dwelt in booths again during
the days of the feast (Neh. 8:13-17). Thus it was a time
of glad thanksgiving for God's care. It was also a feast
of thanksgiving for all the harvests of the year which
were now gathered in. On this account it was also called
the feast of ingathering (Exod. 23:16; 34:22). As the
first-fruits of the land were given to God at the beginning
of the harvest in the feast of weeks, so now God was
praised for the completed harvest. It was a time of great
joy, and this joy was shown in feasting in which the poor
shared. Thus Moses said, "Thou shalt rejoice in thy
feast, thou, and thy son, and thy daughter, and thy man-
servant and thy maid-servant, and the Levite and the
sojourner, and the fatherless and the widow that are
within thy gates" (Deut. 16:14). It was also the time
for the public reading of the law every seven years, that
is, the sabbatical year. "Moses commanded them, saying,
At the end of every seven years, in the set time of the
year of release, in the feast of tabernacles, when all Israel
is come to appear before Jehovah thy God in the place
which he shall choose, thou shalt read this law before all
Israel in their hearing. Assemble the people, the men and
the women and the little ones, and thy sojourner that is
within thy gates, that they may hear and that they may

learn, and fear Jehovah their God and observe to do all the words of this law; and that their children, who have not known may hear, and learn to fear Jehovah your God, as long as ye live in the land whither ye go over the Jordan to possess it" (Deut. 31:10-13). This feature had a prominent part in the celebration of the feast, in the time of Nehemiah (Neh. 8:1-18). Being the gladdest feast of the year, it was the feast of tabernacles which Jeroboam, the first king of the Northern Kingdom, established at Bethel. He celebrated it, however, in the eighth month (I Kgs. 12:32-33). After the exile, Zechariah foretold that in the last days all nations shall come to Jerusalem to keep the feast of tabernacles (Zech. 14:16).

E. SACRIFICES AND OFFERINGS

An elaborate system of sacrifices and offerings was established by Moses at Mount Sinai, which was to be observed in the wilderness and after Israel came into the promised land. While this system included the few primitive sacrifices of patriarchal times, its immense advance beyond primitive custom in such an early stage of the development of Israel's religion is not surprising when we recall that Israel had lived for generations in a country with a highly developed ritual of sacrifice. This does not mean that the sacrificial system of Israel in Mosaic times was borrowed in whole, or perhaps even in part, from the Egyptians, but that Israel's life in Egypt made it for them a natural thing that from the beginning of their national existence they should have an elaborate system of sacrifices and offerings. Thus the long course of development of the system which many modern critics trace from the time of Moses until after the exile was unnecessary. It was altogether a natural thing when Moses pleaded with Pharoah to let Israel go and serve Jehovah in the wilderness and Pharoah answered, "Go ye, serve Jehovah; only let your flocks and your herds be stayed; let your little ones also go with you," that Moses replied, "Thou must also give into our hand sacrifices and burnt-offerings, that we may sacrifice unto Jehovah our God. Our cattle also shall go with us; there shall not a hoof be left behind; for thereof must we take to serve Jehovah our God; and we know not with what we must serve Jehovah until we come thither" (Exod. 10:24-26). Pharoah was willing to release Israel provided their cattle did not go with them; but Moses, although he did not know the full form of the sacrificial service until he reached Mount Sinai, recognized even in Egypt that the natural way of serving Jehovah was by animal sacrifice. Therefore the cattle must go with them.

The offerings of the Mosaic ritual may be classified as public and private, i. e., those which were offered by the people as a whole and those which were offered by individuals. A more useful classification is according to the nature of the offering: (1) drink-offerings, (2) meal-offerings and (3) animal offerings. While the term offerings includes all three of these, only the last may be termed sacrifices. The chief description of the offerings and their conditions is found in chapters one to seven of Leviticus, although there are many other references to the subject. It seems best to follow the order of Leviticus.

The first offering mentioned in Leviticus is the burnt-offering. The Hebrew word so rendered means literally "a thing going up." The reference is to the idea that the flame of the sacrifice went up to Jehovah. Accordingly the verb to go up is often used in the causative conjugation with the noun in the expression to offer a burnt-offering, literally to cause the burnt-offering to go up (Exod. 24:5; 32:6; Lev. 17:8; Deut. 12:13-14, etc.). So it is said to be "an offering made by fire (literally a fire-offering) of a sweet savor unto Jehovah" (Lev. 1:9, 13, 17). Noah offered a burnt-offering (Gen. 8:20) as did Abraham (Gen. 22:2-3, 6-8, 13) and Jethro (Exod. 18:12). The burnt-offering must consist of a bullock, a sheep, a goat, turtle-doves or young pigeons (Lev. 1:5, 10, 14). In each case it must be a male without blemish (Lev. 1:3, 10). The offerer must bring it to the door of the tent of meeting (Lev. 1:3). Of the bullock it is said, "He shall lay his hand upon the head of the burnt-offering and it shall be accepted for him to make atonement for him" (Lev. 1:4). This act signified that the animal was the man's own sacrifice, the substitute for himself (Compare Lev. 16:21-22). Sometimes the offerer and sometimes the priest killed the burnt-offering (Lev. 1:5, 11, 15), but in either case it was the priest who burned the entire animal, with the exception of the blood and the impure parts, upon the altar (Lev. 1:6-9, 12-13, 15-17). The blood of the animals was sprinkled by the priest round about the altar (Lev. 1:5, 11) and the blood of the birds was drained out on the side of the altar (Lev. 1:15). Sometimes this sacrifice was called a whole burnt-offering (Deut. 33:10; Ps. 51:19) from the fact that it was all offered to God. It signified the complete consecration of the offerer to God. Burnt-offerings were presented on many occasions in the Mosaic ritual. Perhaps the most important was the continual burnt-offering which was made every morning and every evening and which consisted of a lamb a year old (Exod. 29:38-42; Num. 28:3-8). Thus the children of Israel presented their sacrifice to Jehovah every morning and evening.

The second offering is called in the Revised Version the meal-offering. The word means a gift and is sometimes used in this broader sense (Gen. 32:13, 18, 20, 21, etc.). The offering consisted of (1) fine flour on which the offerer poured oil and put frankincense (Lev. 2:1), (2) unleavened cakes of fine flour mingled with oil, (3) unleavened wafers anointed with oil (Lev. 2:4-5), or (4) grain in the ear parched with fire having oil and frankincense upon it (Lev. 2:14-15). It was forbidden to have any leaven in a meal-offering, for leaven was a symbol of corruption (Lev. 2:11). Honey also was prohibited (Lev. 2:11). On the other hand, salt with its preserving power was required in every meal-offering (Lev. 2:13). The priest took a part or the whole of the meal-offering and burned it as a memorial upon the altar (Lev. 2:2-3, 9-10, 16). Like the burnt-offering it was called "an offering made by fire of a sweet savor unto Jehovah" (Lev. 2:2, 9, 11, 15).

Since the meal-offering was a mere gift to God and not containing blood it could not atone for sin, it could be offered only by one who had obtained acceptance with God through some previous animal sacrifice. Hence it was often not an independent offering but a mere accompaniment of an animal sacrifice. Every burnt-offering was accompanied with a meal-offering (Exod. 29:40-42; Num. 15:4, 9; 28:5). An exception to the law requiring an animal sacrifice to atone for sin was made in the case of the poor (Lev. 5:11-13). The significance of the meal-offering was the expression of gratitude to God.

The third offering was called the peace-offering. It resembled the burnt-offering in consisting of an animal, but the ritual and its significance were quite different. It might be any animal without blemish, either male or female, but not a bird (Lev. 3:1, 6, 7, 12). The offerer laid his hand upon its head and killed it before the tent of meeting (Lev. 3:2, 8, 13). The priest sprinkled the blood upon the altar round about, burned the fat upon the altar and threw away the entrails (Lev. 3:3-5, 7-11, 13-16). The breast and the thight went to the priests, but they did not eat them until they had been offered to God, the breast as a wave-offering and the thigh as a heave-offering (Lev. 7:31-34). The offerer took the remainder and had a glad feast with his friends (Lev. 7:15-18) to which the poor were invited (Ps. 22:26). It was a feast of communion with God and he was the host (Zeph. 1:7). The peace-offering was one of the fire-offerings (Lev. 3:5, 11, 16).

There were several kinds of peace-offerings according to their occasion. Thus a thank-offering was the free expression of gratitude to God for some signal blessing (Lev. 7:11-14). A freewill-offering was a similar expression of gratitude to God (Lev. 22:18-25), but apparently was not occasioned by any special mark of the divine mercy. Hence it was more spontaneous. Offerings were also made in fulfilment of vows and may be called votive-offerings (Lev. 7:16; 22:18, 21, 23; Num. 15:8).

All these were different kinds of peace-offerings. The idea of them all was glad· and peaceful communion with God and one's fellow-men.

The fourth offering was the sin-offering. It must be an animal, either a young bullock without blemish, a goat or a lamb (Lev. 4:3, 14, 23, 32). If the offerer was an individual, whether the king or one of the common people (Lev. 4:2, 22, 27), he brought the animal to the tent of meeting, laid his hand upon its head and killed it (Lev. 4:4, 24, 33). The priest then put some of the blood upon the horns of the altar of incense or the altar of burnt-offering and poured out the rest of the blood at the base of the altar of burnt-offering (Lev. 4:7, 25, 30, 34). If the whole congregation offended, the elders acted for them in relation to the sin-offering (Lev. 4:15). In any case there was no feast by the offerers because their sacrifice was in order to secure good standing before God. The fat was burned on the altar (Lev. 4:10, 19, 26, 31, 35). In some cases the remainder of the animal was burned outside the camp (Lev. 4:11-12, 21), while in others it belonged to the priests. The sin-offering was to atone for known but unintentional offenses. There was no atonement for him who sinned deliberately, with a high hand (Num. 15:27-31).

The fifth offering in the Levitical order was the trespass or guilt-offering. It was required when a man failed to respond when adjured to testify (Lev. 5:1), when he touched an unclean animal or man (Lev. 5:2-3), or when he swore rashly (Lev. 5:4). In these cases he must confess his sin and bring his trespass-offering to Jehovah, a female from the flock, a lamb or a goat (Lev. 5:5-6).

If he could not afford a lamb, he might bring two turtle-doves or two young pigeons, one for a sin-offering and the other for a burnt-offering (Lev. 5:7). If he could not afford even this, he might offer the tenth part of an ephah of fine flour for a sin-offering, without oil or frankincense (Lev. 5:11-12). The priest burned a handful. of it on the altar as a memorial and the remainder belonged to the priest (Lev. 5:13). In case of a trespass in the holy things, i. e., withholding part of an offering, the guilty one was required to make restitution, adding one-fifth thereto, and to offer a ram without blemish (Lev. 5:14-19). The same law applied to any false dealing with another Israelite (Lev. 6:1-7). The blood of the trespass-offering was sprinkled on the altar round about, the fat was burned and the remainder was eaten by the priest (Lev. 7:1-7).

The portions of the animal sacrifices which belonged to the priests were consecrated to Jehovah before they were eaten. The breast was waved before Jehovah and so was called a wave-offering. The thigh was heaved and was called a heave-offering (Lev. 7:28-34). Similarly, the first ripe sheaf of the harvest was offered as a wave-offering at the passover (Lev. 23:10-11). Fifty days later at the feast of weeks, two wave-loaves of two-tenth parts of an ephah of fine flour baked with leaven were offered in the same manner (Lev. 7:15-17).

The drink-offering was never independent. It consisted of wine and was presented in connection with the meal-offering which accompanied animal sacrifices (Ex. 29:40-41; Lev. 23:13, 18; Num. 6:15, 17; 15:5, 7, 10, 24; 28:7-10, 14, 15, 24, 31; 29:6). Blood was never used as a drink-offering. So the Psalmist declares of the wicked, "their drink-offerings of blood will I not offer" (**Ps.** 16:4).

While the great majority of Israelites performed their sacrificial duties as a matter of custom without considering the spiritual meaning of the sacrifices, Moses and with him a few others had a deeper conception of the matter. This comés out in the significant statement which accompanies the prohibition of the drinking of blood. Speaking in Jehovah's name, Moses said, "The life of the flesh is in the blood; and I have given it to you upon the altar to make atonement for your souls, for it is the **blood** that maketh atonement by reason of the life" (Lev. 17:11). The word rendered life at the beginning and the end of this verse is the same which is rendered souls in the middle of the verse. According to the Hebrew conception the life or soul resided in the blood (Deut. 12:23). The life or soul was also the seat of the passions, which in a sinful man were against God (Jer. 6:8). Hence, in order that a sinful man should become acceptable to God, it was necessary that his blood and with it his sinful soul should be poured out. Since this could not be done without his death, God graciously accepted an animal in his stead. The pouring out of the blood of the **animal** was instead of the pouring out of man's blood. The virtue of the animal's blood consisted in the fact that the life or soul was in it. It was life for life, soul for soul. This was further emphasized by placing the hand upon the animal's head (Lev. 1:4; 3:2, 8, 13; 4:4, 15, 24, 29, 33; 8:14, 18, 22; Num. 8:12). There is no indication that Moses realized the imperfection of animal sacrifices as a means of atonement. The idea that these imperfect sacrifices were accepted only because they pointed forward to a perfect sacrifice to come was quite behind him. Nevertheless, the multiplicity of sacrifices indicated his deep sense of the sin of man and his corresponding sense of the holiness of God. It may be that in his time of meditation the elaborateness of the sacrificial system gave him a feeling of dissatisfaction with it, but he could not realize that "it is impossible that the blood of bulls and goats should take away sins" (Heb. 10:4). For this noble conception the prophets prepared (Isa. 1:11; 66:3; Jer. 6:20; Amos 5:22; Mic. 6:6-7, etc.).

F. CLEAN AND UNCLEAN ANIMALS

It is possible that the distinction between clean and unclean animals, which was common among ancient peoples, had its origin in primitive taboos, which are now imperfectly understood. If this is true, however, of the distinction in the Mosaic legislation, we have here another instance in which the religion of the Old Testament took an element from other peoples and gave it a new and higher meaning. The distinction between clean and unclean animals is recognized in the story of the flood (Gen. 7:2; 8:20), but the list of such animals is not given.

Certain principles are mentioned in Leviticus by which the two classes may be distinguished and lists are given. Clean animals are those which part the hoof and also chew the cud (Lev. 11:2; Deut. 14:6). One of these qualifications without the other is not sufficient (Lev. 11:4-7; Deut. 14:7-8). Clean fishes are those which have fins and scales (Lev. 11:9-12; Deut. 14:9-10).

This applies not only to those which are fishes zoologically, but to all creatures that live in the water. No principle is given concerning the birds, but a list of twenty unclean birds is found, all of them carnivorous, eating blood or carrion (Lev. 11:13-18; Deut. 14:12-18). All winged creeping things that go upon all fours are unclean, with the exception of locusts in their various forms (Lev. 11:20-23). All creeping things, such as the mouse and the lizard, are unclean (Lev. 11:29-30), as well as those with many feet (Lev. 11:41-42). It was forbidden to eat any unclean thing (Lev. 11:46-47). In some cases animals, fishes, birds, and creeping things may have been regarded as unclean because of a natural abhorrence for them. In other cases it was probably for symbolic reasons. Since the Israelites were forbidden to drink blood, any creature that did so was unclean. This ruled out all carnivorous birds. The distinction, however, had its main purpose in the conception that Israel was a holy people and therefore must keep free from all contamination. This is evident in the command, "I am Jehovah your God: sanctify yourselves therefore, and be ye holy; for I am holy: neither shall ye defile yourselves with any manner of creeping things that moveth upon the earth. For I am Jehovah that brought you up out of the land of Egypt, to be your God: ye shall therefore be holy, for I am holy" (Lev. 11:44-45).

G. CEREMONIAL UNCLEANNESS

Some of the conceptions of ceremonial uncleanness in the Mosaic legislation may have had their origin before the beginnings of Israel's national life. Indeed, similar ideas have existed among many primitive peoples. If so, their meaning as found in the religion of Moses should not be understood in the superstitious sense which prevailed among other peoples.   They were a part of the conception that Israel was a holy people and thus to keep free from all uncleanness.   Nevertheless, we should not confound ceremonial with moral uncleanness.   The distinction between the holy and the common, or as we should say, between the sacred and the secular, was not the same as that between the unclean and the clean (Lev. 10:10). Nor was ceremonial uncleanness identical with physical uncleanness, although the two sometimes coincided. Ceremonial uncleanness meant unfitness for intercourse with Jehovah and his people Israel.

There were several different causes of ceremonial uncleanness.   The first was contact with the carcass of an unclean animal, fish, or creeping thing (Lev. 11:8, 11, 28, 31-32, 35-38) or even with the carcass of a clean animal under some circumstances (Lev. 11:39-40).   In such cases, a man was unclean until the evening and he must wash his clothes (Lev. 11:24-28, 31, 39-40).   Any vessel which the carcass touched was unclean, as well as any food or seed (Lev. 11:34-38).

The second cause of uncleanness was that of a woman in childbirth.   In the case of a boy the mother was unclean seven days and even after that she must not touch a hallowed thing or come into the sanctuary for thirty-three days more (Lev. 12:1-4).   If the child was a girl, the mother was unclean for fourteen days and was excluded from the sanctuary thirty-six days afterward (Lev. 12:5).   At the end of this period of purifying she must bring a lamb as a burnt-offering, and a young pigeon or a turtle-dove as a sin-offering. If she could not afford a lamb, two turtle-doves or two young pigeons were accepted, one for a burnt-offering and the other for a sin-offering (Lev. 12:6-8). It was not meant by these provisions that childbirth was sinful in itself. On the contrary man was told to multiply (Gen. 1:28). Yet in those functions which he had in common with other animals he needed purifying before he could approach God.

The third cause of ceremonial uncleanness was leprosy. This dreadful disease was more abhorrent than any other and was regarded as a special judgment of God. The leper was required to cover his upper lip and to cry, "Unclean, unclean." So long as he had the disease he must dwell alone outside the camp (Lev. 13:45-46). If there were apparent indications of leprosy in a man's skin, he must go to one of the priests for examination. If the priest pronounced it leprosy, the afflicted man must go outside the camp. If the priest was doubtful, he shut him up seven days. On the seventh day he was examined again. If the plague had not spread, he was pronounced clean. He could wash his clothes and go free. If, however, the plague had spread, he was unclean as a leper (Lev. 13:1-44). If there was the stain of leprosy in a garment, it must be burned (Lev. 13:47-53). Otherwise the garment could be washed or the stained part torn out (Lev. 13:53-58). Careful directions are given for the ceremonial purifying of a man who was cured, including the presenting of a sin-offering (Lev. 14:1-32). Provision was also made for the inspection and cleansing of a house in which there were marks of leprosy (Lev. 14:33-53).

The fourth cause of uncleanness was a discharge from the generative organs. Not only the man himself, but the bed on which he lay and anything on which he sat was unclean. Anyone who touches them must "wash his clothes and bathe himself in water and be unclean until the even" (Lev. 15:1-12). The man who had the discharge must wait seven days after it ceased. Then he shall wash his clothes and wash himself in running water. On the eighth day he shall offer two turtle-doves or two young pigeons, one for a sin-offering and the other for a burnt-offering (Lev. 15:13-15). The same law applied to women in their usual menstrual discharges of blood and in any unusual discharges of blood (Lev. 15:19-30). The purpose of the law is revealed in the words, "Thus shall ye separate the children of Israel from their uncleanness, that they die not in their uncleanness, when they defile my tabernacle that is in the midst of them" (Lev. 15:31).

The fifth and last cause of ceremonial uncleanness was touching the dead body of any man. This was a much more serious matter than touching the carcass of an animal, even an unclean animal Anyone who touched the dead body of a man was unclean seven days. He must perform certain rites of purification on the third and seventh days (Num. 19:11-13). If a person died in a tent, everyone in the tent or who came into it was unclean seven days (Num. 19:14). Anyone who touched one slain in the field or a bone of a man or a grave was unclean seven days (Num. 19:16). The ashes of the sin-offering were put in a vessel with running water, hyssop was dipped into it, and the water sprinkled upon the tent and its vessels as well as upon the persons there. This was done on the third and on the seventh day (Num. 19:17-19). The reason for this law is similar to that for the other laws. "The man that shall be unclean, and shall not purify himself, that soul shall be cut off from the midst of the assembly, because he hath defiled the sanctuary of Jehovah" (Num. 19:20). All these laws were calculated to impress upon the people a profound sense of the purity and holiness of God.

H. CIRCUMCISION

It is somewhat surprising that circumcision has such a small place in the Mosaic ceremonial law and indeed in the history of Moses' time. As the sign or sacrament of the covenant with Abraham (Gen. 17:9-27) it was practiced by the Israelites in Egypt (Josh. 5:5). There is a somewhat mysterious reference to circumcision in the life of Moses when he was returning with his Midanite wife, Zipporah, and his two sons from the wilderness to Egypt. "It came to pass on the way at the lodging place, that Jehovah met him and sought to kill him. Then Zipporah took a flint and cut off the foreskin of her son and cast it at his feet; and she said, Surely a bridegroom of blood art thou to me. So he let him alone. Then she said, A bridegroom of blood art thou, because of the circumcision" (Exod. 5:24-26). Some authorities interpret this incident as a relic of the primitive conception according to which circumcision was a rite of initiation into manhood and must be performed before marriage. They think that Moses was uncircumcised and that when Jehovah showed his disapproval of this omission by bringing him nigh to death, Zipporah circumcised the younger son and cast the foreskin at Moses' feet, thus bringing Moses the virtue of circumcision. Then Jehovah permitted him to recover and Zipporah thinking that she was bound to him by the bloody rite, said, "A bridegroom of blood are thou." It is, however, quite improbable that Moses was uncircumcised. The story is better explained by supposing that Zipporah objected to circumcising her son, but when Moses was very sick as a mark of Jehovah's displeasure for this omission, she performed the rite and in her anger said to Moses, "A bridegroom of blood art thou because of the circumcision."

In connection with the establishment of the passover it was provided that a foreigner could not partake of it unless he was circumcised. "When a stranger shall sojourn with thee and will keep the passover to Jehovah, let all his males be circumcised, and then let him come near and keep it; and he shall be as one that is born in the land: but no uncircumcised person shall eat thereof" (Exod. 12:48). This clearly implies that the Israelites were circumcised.

The only reference to circumcision in Leviticus is an incidental one in the law concerning the ceremonial uncleanness of a woman at childbirth. If a boy is born "in the eighth day the flesh of his foreskin shall be circumcised" (Lev. 12:3). This is in agreement with the covenant with Abraham, which said, "he that is eight days old shall be circumcised among you" (Gen. 17:12). It is surprising that the Israelites did not obey this commandment in the wilderness. While those who came from Egypt were circumcised before they left there, the children born in the wilderness were not circumcised until they came into Canaan (Josh. 5:5, 7). The command of Moses "circumcise therefore the foreskin of your heart" (Deut. 10:16) and his promise, "Jehovah thy God will circumcise thy heart and the heart of thy seed, to love Jehovah thy God with all thy heart and with all thy soul, that thou mayest live" (Deut. 30:6), show that he at least appreciated somewhat the true meaning of circumcision. To him it was the symbol of a change of character. This reminds us of Paul's teaching, "circumcision is that of the heart, in the spirit not in the letter" (Rom. 2:29), and in Christ "ye were also circumcised with a circumcision not made with hands, in the putting off of the body of the flesh in the circumcision of Christ" (Col. 2:11).

I. TITHES

Tithing did not originate among the Israelites, but was practiced by the ancient Egyptians, Phenicians and other peoples. During the famine, Joseph required the Egyptians to give a fifth of their produce to Pharaoh (Gen. 47:24). Abraham paid a tithe of his spoil to Melchizedek (Gen. 14:20) and Jacob at Bethel made a vow that if God would care for him, he would give him a tenth of all he had (Gen. 28:20-22). Thus in the Mosaic legislation tithing was not a new requirement but rather a systematizing of a custom which had long existed. The chief statement on the subject is found in Lev. 27:30-33. "All the tithe of the land, whether of the seed of the land, or of the fruit of the tree, is Jehovah's: it is holy unto Jehovah. And if a man will redeem aught of his tithe, he shall add unto it the fifth part thereof. And all the tithe of the herd or of the flock, whatsoever passeth under the rod, the tenth shall be holy unto Jehovah. He shall not search whether it be good or bad, neither shall he change it; and if he change it at all, then both it and that for which it is changed shall be holy; it shall not be redeemed." The theory of the Mosaic law was that on account of the covenant between Jehovah and Israel, everything which Israel had belonged to Jehovah. Jehovah graciously permitted them to retain nine-tenths, provided they recognized his ownership by the payment of one-tenth.

The Mosaic legislation made a new provision in giving all the tithes to the Levites in payment for their services in connection with the sanctuary and in lieu of the fact that they were to receive no portion in the land (Num. 18:21, 24). The Levites, however, were required to present a tithe of their tithes as a heave-offering to Jehovah (Num. 18:25-32). Moses commanded Israel that when they came into the land of Canaan they should bring their tithes to the place which Jehovah would choose to set his name there, i. e., the central sanctuary (Deut. 12:5-6). Bringing tithes to a distant place would be a very burdensome requirement after the people were scattered all over the land. Accordingly while they must tithe their produce every year (Deut. 14:22), it was permissible for those who lived at a distance to sell the tenth and with the money purchase at the central sanctuary that which they could offer (Deut. 14:24-26). Furthermore, every three years the tithe might be put in store in the place where a man lived (Deut. 14:28). "When thou hast made an end of tithing all the tithe of thine increase in the third year, the year of tithing, then thou shalt give it unto the Levite, to the sojourner, to the fatherless and to the widow, that they may eat within thy gates and be filled" (Deut. 26:12). Ordinarily, however, this feasting was at the central sanctuary (Deut. 12:17-18). Hence if the exception was availed of, the Israelite made a solemn declaration. "I have put away the hallowed things out of my house and also have given them unto the Levite, and unto the sojourner, to the fatherless and to the widow, according to all thy commandment which thou hast commanded me" (Deut. 26:13). All the tithe except the part used in the glad feast went to the Levites and was their principal means of support. In this connection Moses gave special warning to care for the Levites. "The Levite that is within thy gates, thou shalt not forsake him; for he hath no portion nor inheritance with thee" (Deut. 14:27). It was also on account of their need that the sojourner, the fatherless and the widow were to share in the glad feast at the payment of the tithes (Deut. 14:29).

J. Vows

Vows like tithes are much more ancient than the beginnings of Israel's national life. They are indeed so ancient that we may almost consider them a necessary part of religion. In this respect they resemble prayer and sacrifice to which they are so closely related. A typical vow was that of Jacob at Bethel, "If God will be with me and will keep me in this way that I go, and will give me bread to eat and raiment to put on so that I come again to my father's house in peace, and Jehovah will be my God, then this stone which I have set up for a pillar, shall be God's house: and of all that thou shalt give me I will surely give the tenth unto thee" (Gen. 28:20-22). The worshipper promised to do something for God upon condition that God did something for him. Thus when the king of Arad made war on Israel, "Israel vowed a vow unto Jehovah and said, If thou wilt indeed deliver this people into my hand, then I will utterly destroy their cities" (Num. 21:2). The word to destroy used here means to devote, consecrate, set apart to God. That which was so set apart became a kind of sacrifice and as such it must be completely consumed.

In the nature of the case a vow was voluntary. No one was bound to make a vow and he suffered no disability if he failed to do so. But if he made one he could not withdraw from it except under unusual conditions. Thus Moses said, "When thou shalt vow a vow unto Jehovah thy God, thou shalt not be slack to pay it: for Jehovah thy God will surely require it of thee; and it will be sin in thee. But if thou shalt forbear to vow, it shall be no sin in thee. That which is gone out of thy lips, thou shalt observe and do; according as thou hast vowed unto Jehovah thy God, a freewill-offering, which thou hast promised with thy mouth" (Deut. 23:21-23, compare Num. 30:2). If, however, a woman in her father's house made a vow and her father heard it, the validity of the vow depended upon him. If he·said nothing against it, it stood; but if he objected, the vow was void and his daughter was free from it (Num. 30:3-5). A man had the same veto power concerning the vows of his wife (Num. 30:6-8). The vow of a widow or of a divorced woman, however, was binding (Num. 30:9).

If a man made a vow devoting a person, possibly a member of his family or slave, to Jehovah, he could redeem his vow by the payment of an amount which was graded according to the sex, age and strength of the person devoted. Thus a man between twenty and sixty years of age was estimated at fifty silver shekels, a woman of the same age at thirty shekels, a boy between five and twenty years old, twenty shekels, and a girl, ten shekels, a boy from a month old to five years old, five shekels, and a girl, three shekels, a man over sixty years old, fifteen shekels, and a woman, ten shekels (Lev. 27:1-7). In some cases the priests could reduce these figures (Lev. 27:8). If a beast was redeemed, a fifth must be added to the appraised value (Lev. 27:13). So if a house or land was devoted to Jehovah by vow, it could be redeemed on the estimation of the priest (Lev. 27:14-25). The firstlings of cattle could not be devoted to God because they were his already (Lev. 27:26, compare Exod. 13:1). If an unclean beast was given to God by vow, it must be redeemed at the priest's appraisal with one-fifth added (Lev. 27:27). The whole tendency of these regulations was to teach Israel that all their life was lived in God's sight and that therefore they should be very careful in making vows and very strict in carrying them out.

K. Nazirites

A special vow was that by which a person consecrated himself as a Nazirite, either for a given period or for life. Samson was a Nazirite from his birth by special divine command (Judges 13:5). Hannah also seems to have consecrated Samuel as a Nazirite before his birth, although the word does not occur (I Sam. 1:11). The

meaning of the word is "separated." A man vowed to
separate himself from others in certain respects. He
was not, however, a hermit and except in a few particulars, he was not an ascetic. He must abstain from wine
and strong drink as well as from eating anything that
comes from the grape-vine (Num. 6:1-4). He must not
cut the hair of his head (Num. 6:5). He must not come
near a dead body, even that of a near relative (Num.
6:6-8). If by accident his hair touched a dead body,
it must be cut off after seven days and he must offer two
turtle-doves or two young pigeons, one for a sin-offering
and the other for a burnt-offering. He must also begin
the period of his vow again and offer a he-lamb a year
old for a trespass-offering (Num. 6:9-12). When the
period of his separation is finished, the Nazirite must
offer a he-lamb a year old for a burnt-offering, a ewe-
lamb a year old for a sin-offering, a ram for a peace-
offering, also a basket of unleavened bread, cakes of fine
flour mingled with oil, and unleavened wafers anointed
with oil with the customary drink-offering (Num. 6:13-
17). Then he must shave his head at the door of the
tent of meeting and put the hair on the altar with the
peace-offering. The priest takes the boiled shoulder of
the ram, one unleavened cake and one unleavened wafer
and puts them in the hand of the Nazirite after which
he waves them as a wave-offering before Jehovah. Then
the Nazirite is free from his vow. The meaning of the
Nazirite vow seems to have been devotion to the simple
life, such as the Israelites lived in the wilderness, in contrast with the luxury which they would find among the
Canaanites.

L. SIGNIFICANCE OF THE CEREMONIAL LAW IN THE HISTORY OF RELIGION

As we look back upon the elaborate ceremonial of the Mosaic period we are led to wonder whether on the whole it was a blessing or a curse. The inevitable tendency of ceremonial in religion is to lead to formalism. The great masses of the people being unspiritual fix their attention upon the external rite and fancy that it has some magic virtue in itself. For them it brings almost no knowledge of God or of man's relation to God. That this came about among the Israelites is attested by many passages of the prophetic writings (Isa. 1:10-17; 29:13; Jer. 7:21-23; Hos. 6:6; Am. 6:21-25; Mic. 6:6-8). On the other hand, there was undoubtedly a small number in every age of Israel's history who, being more spiritual, felt, even if they could not express, something of the symbolic meaning of the ceremonies. For them they were an incalculable blessing. It was by these choice souls that religion in its purity was handed on to later generations. And, what is most important, without the ceremonies they could never have known the truth. If even now abstract truth is difficult of apprehension, then it would have been impossible. In ancient times God graciously condescended to reveal himself through visible symbols, object lessons easy of apprehension. When this imperfect method of instruction, suited to the childhood of the race, had served its purpose, the amount of the ceremonial was reduced so as to lead men to those spiritual realities for which the symbols stood. The whole history of religion has been a gradual emancipation from the bondage of symbolism to the pure religion of the spirit. While we thank

God for the degree in which we have attained this religion of the spirit, let us not despise the long and pain-
ful process through which this has been accomplished.

Although the forms of the Mosaic ceremonial had but
a temporary value, certain outstanding characteristics or
emphases of it are eternal. It was calculated by its constant repetition to impress upon its worshippers a profound sense (1) of the holiness of God and (2) of the
sin of man. These two basal conceptions are so often
repeated in it that we need not mention any passages.
Age after age as the people observed these ceremonies,
these two ideas were impressed forcibly upon them. God
was to them no weak ruler whose law could be broken
with impunity. Sin was to them no superficial imperfection, lightly committed and easily cured. The tremendous
sanctions of the divine law were borne in upon the Israelites through the ritual in a way which they could never
forget.

There is another aspect of the Mosaic religion which is
sometimes overlooked. With all its emphasis upon the
holiness of God and the sin of man, with all its emphasis
upon the fear of Jehovah, it was in many parts a religion
of joy. In speaking of the place which God would choose
after they entered Canaan, Moses said, "There ye shall
eat before Jehovah your God, and ye shall rejoice in all
that ye put your hand unto, ye and your households,
wherein Jehovah thy God hath blessed thee" (Deut. 12:7).
Moses repeatedly emphasized the element of joy in their
worship (Deut. 12:12, 18; 14:26; 16:11, 15; 26:11;
27:7; 28:47). "Thou shalt be altogether joyful" (Deut.
26:15). Indeed, he foretold that if Israel should fail

and be rejected it would be because of their neglect of the duty and privilege of joy. "Because thou servedst not Jehovah thy God with joyfulness, and with gladness of heart, by reason of the abundance of all things, therefore shalt thou serve thine enemies that Jehovah shall send against thee" (Deut. 28:47-48).

(5) THE IDEA OF MAN

The idea of man which underlies the religion of the Mosaic period is a distinct advance beyond that of the patriarchs. If we are right in regarding the first chapter of Genesis as a new work of Moses rather than a re-editing of an older tradition, the brief statement of the creation of man becomes significant. "And God said, Let us make man in our image, after our likeness: and let them have dominion over the fish of the sea, and over the birds of the heavens, and over the cattle and over all the earth, and over every creeping thing that creepeth upon the earth. And God created man in his own image, in the image of God created he him; male and female created he them. And God blessed them; and God said unto them, Be fruitful and multiply and replenish the earth and subdue it; and have dominion over the fish of the sea and over the birds of the heavens and over every living thing that moveth upon the earth" (Gen. 1:26-28).

This noble statement agrees admirably with the primitive one that "Jehovah God formed man of the dust of the ground and breathed into his nostrils the breath of life; and man became a living soul" (Gen. 2:7). The primitive anthropomorphic character of the latter statement, however, is now entirely gone. The profound suggestion that God made man in his own image, after his likeness, appears to be an inspired interpretation of the old idea that God made man from the dust and breathed into his nostrils his own divine life. Moses could not have understood this in a realistic way. Since nowhere in his writings does he represent God as having a form like man's, since, indeed, he knew that God forbade the making of any form of himself (Exod. 20:4), the image and likeness of God in which man was made could not refer primarily or chiefly to his body. While Moses may have recognized that there is something godlike even about the body of man—its erect position, its marvellous adaptation as the instrument of man's spirit—we dare not presume to think that he had much of this idea. What he meant by the image and likeness of God was precisely those things in which man is distinguished from other animals. Even primitive man recognized his superiority to the brutes. Among them all he did not find a help meet for him (Gen. 2:20). They, too, were formed from the ground as he was (Gen. 2:19), but he and he only was made in the image and likeness of God.

"In what," says Dr. James Orr, "did this divine image or likeness to God consist? Not in bodily form, for God is Spirit, nor yet simply, as the Socinians would have it, in dominion over the creatures; but in those features of man's rational and moral constitution in which the peculiar dignity of man, as distinguished from the animal world below him, is recognized. Man, as a spiritual nature, is self-conscious, personal, rational, free, capable of rising to the apprehension of general truths and laws, of setting ends of conduct before him, of apprehending right and wrong, good and evil, of framing ideas of God, infinity, eternity, immortality, and of shaping his life in the light of such conceptions. In this he shows himself akin to God; is able to know, love, serve and obey God. The germ of sonship lies in the idea of the image" (Hastings' One Volume Dictionary of the Bible). All this is true of man and we can see all this in the designation, the image of God; but we should not imagine that Moses saw all this in the expression. As a man of profound spiritual insight, he saw that man was like God, particularly in the mental and spiritual parts of his nature. He may have felt, as a late Psalmist did, that man was "terribly distinguished" above the brutes (Ps. 139:14); but he could not sound the almost infinite depths of meaning in his own inspired words. Even now we can realize only a little of what the inspiring spirit meant by the image of God in man. In this, as in many other things, human history is a progressive interpretation of scripture.

There are in the Mosaic writings indications of that consistent system of psychology which underlies the Old Testament. There is no comprehensive statement of the different parts of man's nature such as is found in other parts of scripture and particularly in the New Testament (I Thess. 5:23). The distinction of body, soul and spirit seems to have been not yet understood. The nearest approach to it is in the expression "all thy heart and all thy soul" (Deut. 4:29; 10:12; 11:13; 13:3; 30:2, 6, 10). Once it is "with all thy heart and with all thy soul and with all thy might" (Deut. 6:5); but Moses certainly did not regard the might as a part of man coordinate with his heart and his soul. Indeed, we may question whether he meant to distinguish the heart from the soul. He used popular, not technical or scientific language. However, he distinguished the immaterial part of man from his body.

The most illuminating passage concerning the soul is that of Leviticus, "The life of the flesh is in the blood; and I have given it to you upon the altar to make atonement for your souls: for it is the blood that maketh atonement by reason of the life" (Lev. 17:11). The word for life and the word for soul in this verse are the same. It is that which differentiates a living man or animal from a dead one. It was thought of as residing in the blood, since the shedding of blood meant death. It was the seat of the passions. Hence the soul was said to abhor (Lev. 26:15, 43), to loathe (Num. 21:5), to desire (Deut. 12:15, 20, 21; 14:26) as well as to love (Deut. 6:5; 10:12; 13:3; 30:6). In the passages just referred to, the heart also is said to love. Hence the heart is equally with the soul the seat of the affections. It is used elsewhere, however, in quite a different sense, viz., as the seat of the intellect. A man lays a thing to his heart (Deut. 4:39), considers in his heart (Deut. 8:5), lays up words in his heart (Deut. 11:18) and has a thought in his heart (Deut. 15:9). In his Psalm Moses speaks of getting a heart of wisdom (Ps. 90:12). So while the soul and the heart have the affections in common, the soul has its own part as the seat of the life and the heart its part as the abode of the intellect, the mind. The spirit is not spoken of so often in the Pentateuch as a part of man's nature. The word is the common one for wind. Hence, as the soul resided in the blood, the spirit resided in the breath. Apparently the spirit and the heart are in part synonymous, for if it is said that Pharaoh hardened his heart (Exod.

8:15, 32; 9:34), it is also said of Sihon that God hardened his spirit (Deut. 2:30). The spirit had its relation to the emotions as the soul and the heart, for mention is made of anguish of spirit (Exod. 6:9) and of the spirit of jealousy (Num. 5:14, 30). Just as Moses speaks of the life or soul of the flesh˺ (Lev. 17:11), he also speaks of the spirits of all flesh (Num. 16:22; 27:16). All things considered, we conclude that there is no clear conception in the writings of Moses of the inner nature of man.

(6) THE IDEA OF SIN

While the consciousness of sin is universal among men and in the most primitive stories of Genesis it is clearly manifest (Gen. 3 and 4), a great advance in the understanding of it was the inevitable result of the awful revelations at Mount Sinai. When the people trembled because of the thunderings, and the lightnings, and the voice of the trumpet and the mountain smoking, Moses said, "Fear not: for God is come to prove you, and that his fear may be before you, that ye sin not" (Exod. 20:20). The purpose of the law was to keep the people from sin. Yet the revelation of the Mosaic law meant a great increase in the consciousness of sin. Deeds which hitherto seemed harmless were now seen in their true sinfulness, as Paul said, "Until the law sin was in the world, but sin is not imputed when there is no law" (Rom. 5:13), "by the works of the law shall no flesh be justified in his sight; for through the law cometh the knowledge of sin" (Rom. 3:20).

It is therefore natural that in connection with the revelation of the moral and the ceremonial law there should be a new revelation of the awfulness of sin in the sight of God. This revelation also went side by side with the unfolding of the holiness of God. The more holy, righteous, pure God was seen to be, the blacker was sin which was rebellion against him. Furthermore, the love and condescension of God in entering into covenant with Israel made any breach of the covenant more heinous. Before men had sinned in part through ignorance. Now they sinned against light, against love, against holiness. Their responsibility was increased with their knowledge and their opportunity.

The distinction between wilfull and unintentional sins is clearly marked. The sin-offering was intended only for those who sinned unwittingly (Lev. 4:2, 22, 27; 5:17; Num. 15:27-29). One who sinned unwittingly was nevertheless guilty; but his guilt could be removed by the sacrifice. It was very different with wilfull sins. "The soul that doeth aught with a high hand, whether he be home-born or a sojourner, the same blasphemeth Jehovah; and that soul shall be cut off from among his people" (Num. 15:30).

Another principle of great importance emerges in this period. It is that the effect of sin and the punishment for it cannot be confined to the person who commits it. God visits the iniquity of the fathers upon the children upon the third and fourth generation of them that hate him (Exod. 20:5; Deut. 5:9). This principle finds repeated expression (Exod. 34:7; Lev. 26:39; Num. 14:18). The sense of individual responsibility is so highly developed among us that this seems unjust. Yet it is not a principle of the Mosaic law merely, but of all human life. It is as true today as it was three thousand years ago that the iniquities of the fathers are visited upon the children unto the third and fourth generation. Many of the ills we suffer are due to the sins of our ancestors and the ills which our descendants shall suffer will be due in part to our sins. This is a necessary result of the unity of the race and the fact of heredity. Although Moses knew little of the method of it, the fact was clearly revealed to him. It should be understood that this principle does not refer to guilt. It does not mean that the third and fourth generation are morally accountable for the sins of their fathers. It is merely that they suffer for them. Israel had much to learn before they could come to the individualism of Ezekiel, "The soul that sinneth, it shall die: the son shall not bear the iniquity of the father, neither shall the father bear the iniquity of the son; the righteousness of the righteous shall be upon him, and the wickedness of the wicked shall be upon him" (Ezek. 18:20). The older principle had to be learned through centuries of suffering before they could appreciate this new truth. And this older principle was appropriate in the time when God was dealing with the nation. By it the individual in Israel could learn his responsibility for the welfare of the nation, that his acts had their bearing not merely upon their present, but their future welfare. This thought was calculated to increase the sense of individual responsibility.

There is one remarkable incident in the life of Moses which seems to contradict the idea that one person may suffer for the sin of another. When Israel worshipped the golden calf, Moses prayed that God would forgive them and he added, "If not, blot me, I pray thee, out of

the book which thou hast written." God was not willing
to take Moses as a substitute for Israel's sin, for he
answered "Whosoever hath sinned against me, him will
I blot out of my book" (Exod. 32:32-33). Here we have
the germ of the individualism of Ezekiel.

The multiplicity of terms by which sin was called
showed its varied aspects. The general word for sin
means etymologically failure, missing the mark. It is,
however, rarely found in this sense (Judges 20:16) and
it is not probable that the etymological meaning was in
the thought of those who used it (Lev. 4:3, 14, 23, 26,
28, etc.). The usual Hebrew word for iniquity is from a
stem which means to bend or twist (Exod. 20:5; 28:38,
43, etc.). Hence the noun would refer to the crooked-
ness of sin; but here again the etymology should not be
pressed. The word for transgression means literally rebellion (Exod. 23:21; Lev. 16:16, 21, etc.). It is a wilfull violation of the commandment of God. These three
words are found together in the revelation of Jehovah to
Moses as the God who forgives iniquity and transgression
and sin (Exod. 34:7). The word rendered trespass in
English means literally guilt or offence (Lev. 5:15; Num.
5:7-8). It refers to the condition of a person by which
he is deserving of punishment. The word for wicked has
the opposite meaning to righteous (Exod. 9:27; 23:1,
7; Deut. 25:1-2). Such are the principal words for sin
in its various aspects.

It is a significant fact that the common word for sin
and that for a sin-offering are identical (Lev. 4) that the
word for trespass also means a trespass-offering (Lev. 5)
and that the word for iniquity also means punishment

(Gen. 4:13; Lev. 16:22; 26:41, 43). The first two of these three facts emphasizes the thought that the sin or the trespass passed upon the animal of the sacrifice. Thus the animal became identified with the sin or the trespass so that it was called by these words. This reminds us of the statement of Paul, "Him who knew no sin he made to be sin on our behalf that we might become the righteousness of God in him" (II Cor. 5:21). The identity of the word for iniquity and that for punishment shows that in the thought of Israel the two could never be separated. Iniquity contained within itself the germs of its own punishment. Bearing the iniquity meant bearing the punishment (Lev. 5:1, 17, 18; 10:17 etc.). Moses expressed this thought to the two and a half tribes whose inheritance was east of the Jordan. When he urged them to cross the river and assist their brethren in the conquest of the land, he added, "If ye will not do so, behold ye have sinned against Jehovah; and be sure your sin will find you out" (Num. 32:23).

The Mosaic literature, as indeed the entire old Testament, deals with sin for the most part as conduct rather than character. Yet indications are not lacking that Moses recognized the origin of sin in the heart. The tenth commandment forbids a sin which is not an overt act, but a sinful attitude of heart. The command, "Thou shalt not hate thy brother in thy heart" (Lev. 19:17), is in the same class. The origin of sin in the heart appears even more clearly in the provision that "if any man hate his neighbor, and lie in wait for him, and rise up against him, and smite him mortally so that he dieth," he cannot hide in one of the cities of refuge (Deut. 19:11-12). On the other hand the frequent command to love one's fellow-men (Lev. 19:18, 34; Deut. 10:19) and to love God (Deut. 6:5; 10:12; 11:1, 13, 22; 13:3; 19:9; 30:6, 20) implies that good conduct as well as bad has its source in the heart.

(7) SALVATION AND THE MESSIANIC HOPE

Words like salvation and redemption have become so firmly fixed in our Christian thought as being related to sin that it is difficult for us to put ourselves back into a time when they had no such meaning. Yet such was the case in Moses' day. A typical use of the word salvation is found in the story of the exodus when Israel was pursued by the Egyptians. "Moses said unto the people, Fear ye not, stand still, and see the salvation of Jehovah, which he will work for you today; for the Egyptians whom ye have seen today, ye shall see them again no more forever. Jehovah will fight for you, and ye shall hold your peace" (Exod. 14:13-14). Commemorating this deliverance Moses sang, "Jehovah is my strength and song, and he is become my salvation" (Exod. 15:2). This was salvation from the Egyptians, not salvation from sin. The word is never used in the time of Moses in any other than this external sense (Exod. 14:13, 30; 15:2; Num. 10:9; Deut. 20:4; 22:27; 28:29; 32:15; 33:29). The same is true of the word to deliver (Exod. 3:8; 12:27; 18:4, 8-10; Deut. 23:14). Even the word to redeem is never used in relation to sin. It refers either to deliverance from one's enemies (Exod. 6:6; 15:13), the redemption of land (Lev. 25:25-26), of a slave (Lev. 25:48-49) or of something devoted to God (Lev. 27:13, 15, 19, 20, 31).

The individual Israelite of Moses' time considered himself safe so long as he was in good standing as a member of the chosen nation. This gave him the advantages of the covenant which Jehovah made with the nation at Mount Sinai. Apart from the nation and its religious ordinances, the individual was out of relation to Jehovah and therefore not safe. If he committed a wilfull sin he had no hope. He was "cut off from among his people" (Num. 15:30) and lost the advantages of the covenant. But if he sinned unwittingly he could bring his sacrifice and be forgiven (Lev. 4:20, 26, 31, 35; Num. 15:27-28). This reinstated him as a member of the nation in good standing, who received all the advantages which the daily sacrifices and those of the day of atonement brought to the nation and its members. It was necessary also for the individual to obey the ten commandments and to observe all the manifold requirements of the ceremonial law which touched his life at so many points. In the solemn ceremony at Ebal and Gerizim after pronouncing curses upon those who broke various moral laws, those on Mount Ebal would say, "Cursed be he that confirmeth not the words of this law to do them. And all the people shall say, Amen" (Deut. 27:26).

It scarcely needs to be said that the idea of a future salvation from the penalty of sin after death, is entirely absent from the Mosaic writings and with a few possible exceptions from the entire Old Testament. Heaven and hell were absolutely unknown to Moses. Religion had to do with this life. Salvation must be now and here and consisted in external matters. It is true that the life of the nation was conceived of as going on generation after generation. The death of the individual did not affect it. Hence the nation had its hope in the future, which we call the Messianic hope.

At first thought it is surprising that the great hope which dominated the religion of the patriarchs and which had so large a part in the religion of David and of the writing prophets has such a small place in the religion of Moses and his time. Our surprise is increased when we remember that the writings of Moses present the fullest picture in the Old Testament of the constitution of Israel's national life and of Israel's religion, particularly on its ceremonial side. We would expect that this hope would express itself in some way in the ceremonies of Israel's religion or in the story of their migration from Egypt to the promised land. Further meditation, however, shows that there were two principal reasons for the small place it had in the writings and the time of Moses. The first, and perhaps the principal reason was that the time of Moses was a time of fulfilment, of realization rather than of expectation. God had said to Abraham that his seed should inherit the land in which he lived (Gen. 12:7; 13:14-17), but he also said, "Know of a surety that thy seed shall be sojourners in a land that is not theirs, and shall serve them; and they shall afflict them four hundred years; and also that nation whom they shall serve, will I judge; and afterward shall they come out with great substance. And in the fourth generation they shall come hither again; for the iniquity of the Amorite is not yet full" (Gen. 15:13-14, 16). In fulfilment of this prediction Joseph, his brethren and his father were brought providentially to Egypt. Their descendants were delivered from the bondage of Egypt in Moses' day and were on their way to possess the land which Jehovah had promised to Abraham, Isaac and Jacob. It was natural that the attention of Moses and of Israel should be absorbed by the great experience of the exodus, by the tremendous revelations at Mount Sinai and by the expectation of their early possession of the promised land. The fruition of their national hopes in the possession of that land was so near that they did not look beyond it to that great Figure who was the goal of their history. It doubtless seemed to them that if only they could have the promised land as their very own, they could not ask or hope for more.

The other reason for the small element of Messianic prophecy in the time of Moses was the rudimentary nature of the hope which was handed down to them. That hope was found in the promise to Abraham that in his seed should all the families of the earth be blessed and that his seed should possess the land of Canaan (See section on The Covenant with Abraham, pp. 33-35). This promise, renewed to Isaac and Jacob, was now apparently to receive its fulfilment in Israel's conquest of the land. It was natural that Moses and Israel should see in this conquest the fulfilment of the promise to Abraham and not look beyond it for any other fulfilment. For the promise was not yet centered on a person. It is true that Jacob, with prophetic insight, had given the birthright particularly to Judah, saying, "The sceptre shall not depart from Judah, nor the ruler's staff from between his feet until he come whose it is and unto him shall the obedience of the peoples be" (Gen. 49:10). While we can see in these words a prediction of the Messiah to whom the sceptre of right belongs and Ezekiel centuries later seems to have understood them in this sense (Ezek. 21:27), Moses and the people of his time did not so understand them. To them they meant nothing more than that Judah was to be the ruling tribe and that the sceptre would remain with that tribe until the coming of a mysterious person to whom the sceptre of right belonged. Here was the germ of the promise of the Ideal King in David's line; but it was too rudimentary for Moses and the people to understand it. Their thoughts were fixed upon the nation, the seed of Abraham. History had not yet unfolded sufficiently for them to see how in that seed all the families of the earth should be blessed. To them the seed of Abraham was the whole people of Israel. To the nation Israel the promise belonged and in the nation the promise would be fulfilled. As the river Jordan rises on the slopes of Mount Herman and, after flowing many miles, empties itself into the Sea of Galilee, so the Messianic hope passed down by the patriarchs emptied itself into the national life of Israel. As the traveler standing by that sea could not perceive that the river would flow out of it, so Moses and the people of his time could not see that out from the seed of Abraham, out from the nation Israel, would eventually come a King of the tribe of Judah in whom the promise to Abraham would find its highest fulfilment.

In view of these facts, it is quite natural that the earliest Messianic allusions, using the term in the broader sense, in the time of Moses were hidden in statements concerning the nation. God commanded Moses to say to Pharaoh, "Thus saith Jehovah, Israel is my son, my first-born:

and I have said unto thee, Let my son go that he may serve me" (Exod. 4:22-23). Although Moses could not see in this designation of Israel as Jehovah's son, his first-born, anything more than the adoption of the nation, in the light of the fulfilment, we can see here a hint that in Israel was hidden the King to whom Jehovah said, "Thou art my son; this day have I begotten thee. Ask of me and I shall give thee the nations for thine inheritance and the uttermost parts of the earth for thy possession" (Ps. 2:7-8). Israel, the first-born son of God included the only begotten and well-beloved Son. Indeed, the far-off purpose of the adoption of Israel was the revelation of the Son of God (Hos. 11:1, compare Mt. 2:15).

Another hint of the great hope of Israel is hidden in the words which God on Mount Sinai commanded Moses to say to the children of Israel, "Now therefore, if ye will obey my voice indeed, and keep my covenant, then ye shall be mine own possession from among all peoples: for all the earth is mine: and ye shall be unto me a kingdom of priests and a holy nation" (Exod. 19:5-6). Moses could not appreciate the fulness of meaning in these great words. They can be understood only in the light of the divine purpose in the choice of Israel as his special possession, a purpose which has unfolded in the history of that people and found its realization in Jesus Christ. It was not for Israel's sake that God chose them, but because all the earth was his. God's choice of Israel was related to his world-purpose (compare Deut. 4:37; 7:6-8; 10:15; 14:2). The very idea of a kingdom of priests and a holy nation is vain and narrow except as a means of bringing salvation and the knowledge of God to all the nations of the earth. This was the purpose of the choice of Israel and this purpose was not accomplished until the coming of him who was both king and priest, the priest forever after the order of Melchizedek (Ps. 110:4). He was the reason for the choice of Israel.

The relation of Israel to the world-purpose of God is specially prominent in the statement of the song of Moses just before his death, "When the Most High gave to the nations their inheritance, when he separated the children of men, he set the bounds of the peoples according to the number of the children of Israel" (Deut. 32:8). The underlying thought of this statement is that in the world-plan of God each nation has its part to play, but that the most important part was that of Israel. So in allotting to each nation its territory, God was mindful to reserve a special place for Israel according to their number. This did not mean injustice to any people. God promised the land of Canaan to the seed of Abraham, but he would not fulfill that promise in Abraham's day because "the iniquity of the Amorite was not yet full" (Gen. 15:16). The Amorites would have abundant opportunity to repent while Israel was growing up into a nation. The reason for this special treatment of Israel was that through them God was to reveal himself to all mankind. In matters of religion Japheth dwells in the tents of Shem (Gen. 9:27). "Salvation is from the Jews" (Jno. 4:22). In the progress of human history God is not unmindful of other elements of civilization, such as government, art, literature and science. But the dominant element in human history to which all others must pay tribute is religion. This is the supreme contribution of Israel to the world. In making place for Israel in Canaan, God was preparing the scene for the incarnation of his Son.

The prophecy of Balaam is one of the most remarkable in the Old Testament. Urged by Balak, king of Moab, to curse Israel that he might conquer them more easily, Balaam replied that he could speak only what Jehovah told him. Instead of cursing Israel, this seer of Pethor in Mesopotamia blessed them three times. In the last prophecy under the divine guidance he perceived the Messiah hidden in Israel and he said: "I see him, but not now; I behold him but not nigh: there shall come forth a star out of Jacob, and a sceptre shall rise out of Israel, and shall smite through the corners of Moab, and break down all the sons of tumult. . . . Out of Jacob shall one have dominion and shall destroy the remnant from the city" (Num. 24:17, 19). The star out of Jacob refers to a king as the parallel reference to a sceptre shows. This prediction is based in part upon the blessing on Judah (Gen. 49:10), but it goes beyond it in the definiteness of its personal statement. Indeed, it is the first definite prediction of a personal Messiah in Old Testament history. As such it helped to prepare for the still more definite prediction of the Messiah in David's day. The Jews in ancient times regarded this prophecy of Balaam as referring to the Messiah and the Targum so interpreted it. From it the false Messiah of the reign of Hadrian was called Barcochba, which means "son of the star."

Near the end of his life Moses revealed to Israel a promise which God had given him on Mount Sinai almost forty years before. It is in these words, "I will raise them up a prophet from among their brethren, like unto thee; and I will put my words in his mouth, and he shall speak unto them all that I shall command him. And it shall come to pass that whosoever will not hearken unto my words which he shall speak in my name, I will require it of him" (Deut. 18:18-19). Many commentators regard this as a prediction of the prophetic office, of the line of prophets who would follow Moses. While this interpretation need not be excluded, the proper understanding of the Old Testament prophets recognizes that they anticipated a prophet greater than they, the Prophet of Nazareth. This passage seems to have been understood in New Testament times as predicting a great prophet. Although they did not identify this prophet with the Messiah, the Jews spoke of the two together. When John the Baptist denied that he was the Christ and that he was Elijah they still asked him, "Art thou the prophet? (Jno. 1:21, compare verse 25). Some seem to have thought that Jesus was the prophet (Jno. 7:40-41). Peter (Acts 3:22-23) and Stephen (Acts 7:37) quoted Moses' words as fulfilled in Jesus Christ. Moses was the greatest prophet of the old dispensation in his intimacy of fellowship with God (Deut. 34:10). In this respect he was not eclipsed until Jesus came. Jesus was the prophet like unto Moses. When Moses and Elijah appeared in glory with him it was not appropriate as Peter suggested to erect a tabernacle for each of them. Moses and Elijah vanished while Jesus alone remained. Their purpose and work were temporary. He alone was eternal (Mt. 17:1-?, etc.).

(8) THE FUTURE LIFE.

The few slight indications of a belief in the future life

which come from the time of Moses are identical with those we have already found in the patriarchal period. Just as it was said of Abraham (Gen. 25:8), Isaac (Gen. 35:29) and Jacob (Gen. 49:29,33) that they were gathered to their people, so it was said of Aaron (Num. 20:24, 26) and Moses (Num. 27:13; 31:2; Deut. 32:50). In fact, while in Genesis the expression varies somewhat, taking the form, to go to one's fathers (Gen. 15:15) or to sleep with one's fathers (Gen. 47:30), there is no variation whatever in the last four books of the Pentateuch. The death of Moses is directly compared with that of Aaron. Jehovah told Moses that when he had viewed the land of Canaan from the mountain he would be gathered to his people as Aaron, his brother, was gathered (Num. 27:13, compare Deut. 32:50).

There can be no reasonable doubt that this expression meant the same thing in Moses' day which it had meant in patriarchal times. Death was one thing and being gathered to one's people was another (Deut. 32:50). The latter referred to a reunion with one's ancestors in Sheol. There are no indications as to their conception of the condition of life in Sheol except that Jacob regarded it as a calamity to go there (Gen. 37:35; 42:38; 44:29, 31). Aaron and Moses doubtless felt the same way. They had no hope of a future life, but a dread of going into that dark and unknown region.

There is only one reference to Sheol in the last four books of the Pentateuch. It is in Moses' farewell song: "For a fire is kindled in mine anger and burneth unto the lowest Sheol, and devoureth the earth with its increase and setteth on fire the foundations of the mountains"

(Deut. 32:22). The parallelism places Sheol in the same general region as the foundations of the mountains, i. e., under the earth. The expression, the lowest Sheol, does not indicate that in their opinion Sheol was divided into several parts. It is merely a poetic way of referring to the lowest part of Sheol (Ps. 86:13). The anger of Jehovah against the wicked is represented as so great that, not satisfied with showing itself among the living, it burns to the lowest part of the abode of the dead.

We have so long used Moses' great Psalm in the funeral service that we overlook its entire lack of any reference to the future life. There is a tone of sadness about it. God brings man back to the dust from which he was made (Ps. 90:3, compare Gen. 3:19). God is eternal, but man is a creature of a day (Ps. 90:2, 4-7). Life is a time of sorrow and it comes to an end as a sigh (Ps. 90:9-10). The part of wisdom is to make the most of life while we have it, to number our days so as to get a heart of wisdom (Ps. 90:12). Grand as this Psalm is, it could not have been written by a man who had any hope beyond death. In this respect as well as others it agrees well with the time of Moses.

(9) INSPIRATION.

A few words should be said about the idea of inspiration because the beginnings of scripture date from this period. Many times it is said that God spoke to Moses (Exod. 7:8, 19; 8:15; 12:1; 31:12, etc.). God commanded Moses to write down what he told him and he did so (Exod. 17:14; 24:4; 34:27-28; Deut. 31:9). The literal understanding of these expressions would imply that God's revelation to Moses was in the exact words which he wrote down. Yet the language which is attributed to God is in the familiar style of Moses. It is evident, therefore, that God's revelation was not in words, but in thoughts which God put into his mind while he thought deeply on the things of God and of Israel. It was not dictation but inspiration. The book of the covenant is referred to (Exod. 24:7) and the book of law (Deut. 28:58, 61; 29:20, 21, 27; 30:10; 31:24, 26). The latter book was evidently regarded as sacred, for it was kept in the holy of holies beside the ark of the covenant (Deut. 31:26).

Inside the ark were the two tables of the law which are said to have been written with the finger of God (Exod. 31:18; Deut. 9:10). It is said elsewhere that these tables were written on both their sides. "The tables were the work of God, and the writing was the writing of God, graven upon the tables" (Exod. 32:15-16, compare Exod. 24:12; 34:1; Deut. 4:13; 5:22; 10:2, 4). If these expressions be taken literally, they have no bearing on the inspiration of Moses, for Moses was not in that case the author of the ten commandments. He did not even write them down at the dictation of God. God wrote them and all that Moses did was to carry the written tablets down Mount Sinai and put them in the ark of the covenant. It is plain, however, that these expressions were meant figuratively. Moses did not believe that God had a body. Therefore he could not believe that he had a literal finger. When at God's command Moses stretched out his rod and smote the dust of the earth so that it became lice, the Egyptian magicians tried to imitate him, but failed. Then they said, "This is the finger of God" (Exod. 8:19), i. e., "This is supernatural," beyond the

power of man. So Our Lord said, "If I by the finger of
God cast out demons, by whom do your sons cast them
out?" (Luke 11:20). The finger of God meant the power
of God. So David spoke of the heavens as the work of
God's fingers (Ps. 8:3). The statement that the two tables
of the law were written with the finger of God might be,
then, a figurative way of saying that they were divine in
their origin. So Driver writes, "That the tables on which
the decalogue was written are said to have been inscribed
by the finger of God (cf. 34:1) is an expression of the
sanctity and venerable antiquity attributed to them" (Commentary on Exodus 31:18).

While this interpretation may satisfy the expression
"written with the finger of God," it scarcely accounts for
the statement that the writing was the writing of God,
graven upon the tables (Exod. 32:16). The tables were
literal tables of stone. If Moses, or some one else at
his direction, engraved the ten commandments on the
tables, it is difficult to understand what he meant when
he said that the writing was the writing of God. This
seems to refer to some physical event. The most reasonable suggestion is that the lightning on Mount Sinai made
its mark on the rocks and that Moses under the guidance
of the Spirit interpreted these marks in the ten commandments. We do not mean that the marks had any meaning
apart from the fact that they were a terrific display of
God's power. To Moses they meant "I am Jehovah thy
God who brought thee out of the land of Egypt, out of
the house of bondage. Thou shalt have no other gods
before me, etc." Many another man has seen the marks

of God's lightning on the rocks; but only to Moses did they mean the moral law. This was inspiration indeed.

That some such interpretation is correct seems necessary from the fact that the ten commandments are said elsewhere to have been written by Moses. Jehovah commanded him, "Write thou these words, for after the tenor of these words I have made a covenant with thee and with Israel. . . . And he wrote upon the tables the words of the covenant, the ten commandments" (Exod. 34:27-28). What was the purpose of Moses writing the decalogue on the tables if God had already written the same Hebrew letters there? If, however, the only marks on the tables were the marks of the lightning, put there by the finger of God, it was quite appropriate that Moses should inscribe upon them his inspired interpretation of those marks. Furthermore, the ten commandments in other places are said to have been spoken rather than written: "God spake all these words, saying," etc. (Exod. 20:1). "These words [the decalogue which immediately precedes] Jehovah spake unto all your assembly in the mount out of the midst of the fire, of the cloud and of the thick darkness with a great voice" (Deut. 5:22, compare Deut. 9:10). If the writing of God on the tables of stone was the mark of God's lightning, the great voice with which he spoke was the thunder. In both cases it required inspiration for Moses to interpret it. The writing was the writing of God and the voice was the voice of God. God neither writes nor speaks the language of men. It requires an inspired man to interpret the handwriting of God on the rocks and his majestic voice in the thunder. Moses was such an inspired man.

(10)   THE MORALITY OF THE MOSAIC PERIOD.

There are two distinct subjects which deserve study in
this connection, the morality of the Mosaic legislation and
the morality of the Israelites in this time.   The exalted
moral ideas of the ten commandments have already been
considered.

A.   THE MORALITY OF THE MOSAIC LEGISLATION.

Besides the direct evidence of high moral standards in
the decalogue, there are many other indications that Moses
meant the people to be pure, holy, set apart to God.   This
was symbolized by the prohibition of the eating of unclean animals (Lev. 11:43-44), the purification from ceremonial uncleanness (Lev. 13-15) and the ceremonial clean-
ness of the priests (Lev. 21:15; 22:9, 16).   The repeated
emphasis upon the idea that Israel must be holy because
Jehovah was holy (Lev. 19:2; 20:7, 26; 22:32-33) cannot
be deprived of its moral note.   Holiness was a moral idea
and not a mere consecration to Jehovah.   This moral idea
of holiness extended even to the land.   It was the holy
land.   Therefore it must keep its sabbath every seventh
year (Lev. 25:1-7) and the tithe of its produce must be
set apart to Jehovah (Lev. 27:30-33).

In addition to these general signs of idealism in the legislation, there are many others of a definite sort.   Such
were the mitigation of the requirements concerning trespass-offerings for the poor (Lev. 5:11), the command to
leave some of the gleanings for them (Lev. 19:9-10;
23:22), the law against oppression (Lev. 19:13), equal
justice for rich and poor (Lev. 19:15), equal punishment
for the adulterer and the adulteress (Lev. 20:10-12), the
requirement to help the poor (Lev. 25:35), the prohibition

of collecting interest from Israelites (Lev. 25.36-38), the law against making them slaves (Lev. 25:39), the provision for freedom in the year of jubilee (Lev. 25:40-43, 47-55), the provision of a city of refuge for anyone who killed another by accident (Num. 35:9-28), that the Israelites should be generous to the poor (Deut. 15:7-11), that a gift should be made to a slave when he was freed (Deut. 15:12-14), that judges should decide justly and shun bribes (Deut. 16:18-20), that two or more witnesses were required to condemn a man (Deut. 17:6; 19:15), that the king should avoid extravagance and rule in the fear of God (Deut. 17:14-20), that in war a city be offered peace before it was attacked (Deut. 20:10-11), that a strayed animal be returned to its owner (Deut. 22:1-4), and that a garment should not be kept as a pledge from a poor man (Deut. 24:12-13). The restoration of land to its original owner in the year of jubilee tended to prevent the extremes of wealth and poverty which produce so many of the evils of modern society (Lev. 25:13-17, 23-28). The law that no inheritance could be transferred from one tribe to another tended to keep any tribe from becoming much more powerful than the others and dominating them (Num. 36:7, 9). Although the sin of one man or a few sometimes brought punishment on the innocent (Num. 16:20-22), the ideal was presented that only the guilty should suffer (Deut. 24:16). Unwitting sins could be atoned for but high-handed sins could not (Num. 15:27-31). The religious aspect of morality was emphasized by the provision that in a case of fraud, not only must the guilty man restore what he had taken with one-fifth added thereto, but he must also present a trespass-offering to God (Lev. 6:1-7).

On the other hand, there are examples of extreme severity in penalties. Death was the penalty for the worship of false gods (Ex. 22:20; Lev. 20:2; Deut. 13:6-18), for sorcery or wizardry (Exod. 22:18; Lev. 20:27), for breaking the sabbath (Exod. 31:14-15; 35:2), and for false prophecy (Deut. 13:1-5; 18:20). Such severe penalties were necessary to maintain faithfulness to the worship of Jehovah. Until quite recent times there have been many capital offences in the laws of modern states.

B.   MORALITY OF ISRAEL IN THE TIME OF MOSES.

Corresponding to the extreme penalties of the legislation there were examples of extreme severity in conduct. Those who worshipped the golden calf were slaughtered, and the tribe of Levi seem to have been honored because they did this bloody work (Exod. 32:25-29; Num. 3:9). Fire came forth from Jehovah and destroyed Nadab and Abihu who offered strange fire before Jehovah (Lev. 10:1-5). The whole congregation stoned a man who cursed and Jehovah is said to have commanded this penalty (Lev. 24:10-14, 23). Korah, Dathan and Abiram were swallowed up by the earth because they rebelled against Moses and Aaron (Num. 16). In this case the people complained that the punishment was too severe (Num. 16:41). All the chiefs of the people were hung at the command of Jehovah because Israel worshipped Baal-peor (Num. 25:1-5). These severe penalties may be excused because of the crude character of the times and the necessity of preventing apostasy. The command of Jehovah to drive out the Canaanites (Num. 33:52) and the extermination of the Amorites, including women and children by Jehovah's act (Deut. 2:34, 36; 3:2-3, 6), may be justified by their wickedness (Deut. 9:4-5), for Jehovah gave them abundant opportunity to repent (Gen. 15:16). The commendation of Phinehas by Jehovah for killing an Israelite and the Midianitish woman whom the Israelite brought unto his brethren (Num. 25:6-13) was for his zeal for the purity of Israel (note verse 11).

The most difficult case was the war against the Midianites. The record states that Jehovah commanded it as a war of vengeance (Num. 31:1-3), that it was led by Phinehas the priest taking the holy vessels of the sanctuary (Num. 31:6), that they slew every male (Num. 31:7), that Moses was angry because they spared the women and children (Num. 31:14-18), that afterwards the soldiers purged themselves by religious ceremonies (Num. 31:19-20) and that a portion of the spoil was consecrated to Jehovah (Num. 31:28-31). The moral difficulty of this story is not in the fact that Israel and Moses did these things. They were children of their age and acted accordingly. While justice to them requires us to judge them according to their imperfect knowledge, there is no moral or religious necessity to vindicate them. The only difficulty in this story lies in the fact that this bloody war is represented as commanded by Jehovah: "Jehovah spake unto Moses, saying, Avenge the children of Israel of the Midianites" (Num. 31:1-2). Moses summoned the army "to execute Jehovah's vengeance on Midian" (Num. 31:3). We are free to condemn Moses, Phinehas and Israel if the evidence shows that they did wrong according to their light. But we cannot condemn Jehovah. We may be sure that whatever part he had in the matter was absolutely just and right. Now Jehovah's part in the matter according to the story, consisted in commanding Moses to make a war of vengeance on the Midianites. Whatever wickedness there was in the way this command was carried out rests on the men who committed the wickedness. Was the command to make a war of vengeance wicked? If so we we may be sure that Jehovah never issued such a command, even though Moses may have honestly believed that he did. The question cannot be settled by the simple affirmation that a war of vengeance is contrary to the spirit of the New Testament, although that is absolutely true. The matter at issue in this war was not a personal or a national one. It was not a case of Jehovah commanding Israel to let loose the fires of their wrath against a people who had wronged them. The main point of the story is that there was real danger lest the Midianites would so corrupt Israel with idolatry and licentiousness that the pure religion of Jehovah would perish from the earth. That was the reason for the holy war. The Midianites had joined with the Moabites to hire Balaam to curse Israel (Num. 22:4-6). When this attempt failed, a far more insidious attack upon Israel's national life began. "The people began to play the harlot with the daughters of Moab, for they called the people unto the sacrifices of their gods; and the people did eat and bowed down to their gods. And Israel joined himself unto Baal-peor: and the anger of Jehovah was kindled against Israel" (Num. 25:1-3). A particular instance along the same line is mentioned. A certain Israelite named Zimri brought a Midianitish woman named Cozbi unto his brethren for impure purposes (Num. 25:6, 14-15). If something very drastic was not done without delay, the whole people of Israel would be corrupted. Phinehas with zeal for Jehovah thrust the Israelite and the Midianitsh woman through with a spear (Num. 25:7-8). When we recognize the situation, we are not surprised that Jehovah commended Phinehas (Num. 25:10-12).

The reason for the war against the Midianites was the necessity of protecting Israel against their insidious influence. "Jehovah spake unto Moses, saying, Vex the Midianites and smite them, for they vex you with their wiles wherewith they have beguiled you in the matter of Peor, and in the matter of Cozbi, the daughter of the prince of Midian, their sister, who was slain on the day of the plague in the matter of Peor" (Num. 25:16-18). It was Jehovah's war against Midian more than it was Israel's. It was to execute Jehovah's vengeance upon Midian. If some of the Israelites realizing this went too far in their cruelty, the guilt rests upon them. When we consider the character of the time, however, there is nothing in the story which should trouble us.

The statement that Jehovah commanded Israel to borrow from the Egyptians not intending to repay and thus to despoil the Egyptians, should be understood in the light of Oriental custom (Exod. 3:22; 11:2; 12:35-36). Probably the Egyptians understood that these were gifts for the feast to Jehovah in the wilderness. Moses regarded them as legitimate spoil in the contest of Jehovah against Egypt. They can be justified only as an act of war.

The expression "sons of Belial," or as the Revised Version has it, "base fellows," occurs only once in the

Pentateuch (Deut. 13:13) but it is quite common in later books (Judges 19:22; 20:13; I Sam. 1:16; 2:12; 10:27; 25:17, 25; 30:22; II Sam. 16:7; 20:1; 23:6; I Kgs. 21:10, 13; II Chron. 13:7). It means godless, worthless men. Israel had such as every other nation has. Unless the people were warned against them there was danger that they would lead them to wickedness (Deut. 13:13).

It is not necessary to justify Moses for murdering the Egyptian who strove with the Israelite (Exod. 2:12). His sympathy for his people was commendable, but his brutal way of showing it need not be defended.

Over against this rather black record of human sin may be placed a few fine things. The friendly cooperation of Jethro with Moses is one of them. Moses invited him to go with Israel to the promised land. "Come thou with us," said he, "and we will do thee good" (Num. 10:29). When Jethro refused, Moses urged him again, saying that he would be instead of eyes to Israel, i. e., he would guide them, "And it shall be, if thou go with us, yea it shall be, that what good soever Jehovah shall do unto us, the same will we do unto thee" (Num. 10:31-32). The broad-minded justice of Moses in allowing the daughters of Zelophehad to receive their father's inheritance (Num. 27:1-11) excites our admiration. The proposal of the tribes of Reuben and Gad, and half the tribe of Manasseh to assist the other tribes in their conquests west of the Jordan and Moses' insistence that they do so showed a strong sense of national unity and patriotism (Num. 32:16-27). These are but a few of the beautiful incidents in the story of Moses' time. There were doubtless many others which were not recorded.

CHAPTER III.

The Religion from Moses to David.

Joshua, Judges, Ruth, I Samuel.

The sources of information for the history of the religion of this period are the four books named above. The history which they contain, however, is a continuation of that in the Pentateuch. Hence we cannot understand it nor appreciate the religious conditions of this period without considering the history and the religion of the Mosaic period. The history recorded in the entire first book of Samuel is included in this chapter, thus bringing the story to the death of Saul. Although Samuel was the moving force in that religious and political revival which led up to the establishment of the kingdom and the building of the temple, he was not a writer and he belongs in the period of the judges rather than that of the kings (I Sam. 7:6, 15-17). Although, furthermore, the early life of David is recounted in I Samuel, our interest is not primarily in the religious life of individuals but in that of the nation. It is, therefore, best to include in this period the life of David until his accession as king. The beautiful little book of Ruth is a valuable source of information because it presents a story from the time of the judges (Ruth 1:1).

The effect of coming into the promised land was very damaging to the religious life of Israel for three principal reasons, (1) because the people were widely separated from each other instead of living in one large camp as they had done in the wilderness, (2) because they exchanged the hardships and privations of the wilderness life for the plenty and luxury of Canaan and (3) because they came in contact with the idolatry and wickedness of the Canaanites. Hence it is not surprising that for about two centuries after the conquest, not only was there no advance beyond the religious ideas of the Mosaic period, but those noble ideas, and that matchless moral law and elaborate ceremonial law were well-nigh submerged. "The people served Jehovah all the days of Joshua, and all the days of the elders that outlived Joshua, who had seen all the great work of Jehovah that he had wrought for Israel. . . . And also all that generation were gathered unto their fathers: and there arose another generation after them that knew not Jehovah, nor yet the work which he had wrought for Israel. And the children of Israel did that which was evil in the sight of Jehovah and served the Baalim, and they forsook Jehovah the God of their fathers, who brought them out of the land of Egypt, and followed other gods, of the gods of the peoples that were round about them, and bowed themselves down unto them: and they provoked Jehovah to anger. And they forsook Jehovah, and served Baal and Ashtaroth" (Judges 2:7, 10-13). Such is the summary of the whole period. With monotonous regularity it is said that the children of Israel did evil in the sight of Jehovah and he delivered them into bondage to some one of their enemies (Judges 3:7-8, 12-

14; 4:1-2; 6:1; 10:6-7; 13:1), that in their distress they cried unto Jehovah who sent them a judge who delivered them (Judges 3:9-11, 15-30; 4:3-24; 6:7, etc.; 10:10, etc.; 13:2, etc.). So long as the judge lived, all went well with them so far as their political condition was concerned; but as soon as he died they forsook Jehovah again (Judges 2:18-19; 8:33-34). One of the greatest causes of Israel's apostasy was their intermarriage with the people of the land. "The children of Israel dwelt among the Canaanites, the Hittites and the Amorites and the Perizzites and the Hivites and the Jebusites and they took of their daughters to be their wives and gave their own daughters to their sons and served other gods" (Judges 3:5-6).

Almost the only relief to this evil condition was at the beginning and the end of the period. While the generation lived who remembered the guidance of God in the wilderness the people were comparatively faithful to Jehovah. On the other hand, it is a wonderful evidence of the divine power in the religion of Israel that after two centuries of almost continuous idolatry Samuel was able to accomplish a great reformation (I Sam. 7:3-4). The religion of Israel would have died and no reformation would have been possible, had there not been multitudes in obscure places who did not yield to the popular idolatry but remained true to Jehovah. A beautiful example of such faithfulness is given in the book of Ruth.

(1) THE IDEA OF GOD.

The Mosaic conceptions emerge in a few passages. The story of the passage of the Jordan shows that the people regarded Jehovah as present in the ark. The ark went ahead to symbolize Jehovah's guidance (Josh. 3:3-4).

The walls of Jericho fell down when the people guided by the ark went around the city seven times (Josh. 6:6-16). It was a superstitious reverence for the ark which led the elders to suggest bringing it into the battle against the Philistines (I Sam. 4:3-4). The statement that "all Israel shouted with a great shout so that the earth rang again" when the ark was brought into the camp, (I Sam. 4:5) makes a very unfavorable impression. It seems to suggest an unspiritual faith in some magical power of the ark. Even after the sad experiences which followed when the ark of Jehovah was taken, the people did not learn their lesson, for Saul suggested bringing it into the war once more (I Sam. 14:18).

There are only a few indications of their conception of the nature of God. His anger against the people for their sins is spoken of many times (Josh. 7:1, 26; 23:16; Judges 2:14, 20; 3:8; 6:39; 10:7; I Sam. 28:18). So far was this anger from being regarded as unworthy of Jehovah that Saul was rejected because he did not execute the fierce wrath of Jehovah upon the Amalekites (I Sam. 28:18). The love of God is not mentioned in the literature of this period and his mercy only in Ruth (2:20) and I Samuel (20:14). The holiness of God is referred to only in Joshua (5:15; 24:19) and I Samuel (2:2; 6:20).

The title, Jehovah of hosts, which does not occur in the Pentateuch but is so common in the later literature, is found toward the end of this period (I Sam.. 1:3, 11; 4:4; 15:2; 17:45). It conceives of God as the Commander of the armies of heaven, which may be the angels or the stars. He is indeed "the God of the armies of

Israel" (I Sam. 17:45), but the stars are also his host (Neh. 9:6; Isa. 40:26; 45:12) as are the angels (Ps. 103:21). The angel that appeared to Joshua announced himself as the prince of the host of Jehovah (Josh. 5:14-15). These titles show that Jehovah was thought of as a God of great resources and power, if not omnipotent. The ark was once described as "the ark of the covenant of the Lord of all the earth" (Josh. 3:11). The children of Reuben, the children of Gad and half the tribe of Manasseh, said, "The Mighty One, God, Jehovah, the Mighty One, God, Jehovah, he knoweth" (Josh. 22:22). Naomi, Ruth, Boaz and the people of Bethlehem in simple faith thought of Jehovah as controlling their whole lives (Ruth 1:6, 8, 9, 13, 21; 2:12; 4:11-14).

Another divine title of great importance originated in the beginning of this time. "Joshua said, Hereby ye shall know that the living God is among you and that he will without fail drive out from before you the Canaanite, and the Hittite, and the Hivite and the Perizzite and the Girgashite and the Amorite and the Jebusite" (Josh. 3:10). The expression "the living God" means the God who is active in the affairs of the world and in human history, the immanent God. David used this title with great force when he charged Goliath with defying the armies of the living God (I Sam. 17:26, 36). Jehovah was the living God in contrast with idols. Hence when the ark which symbolized his presence was brought into the temple of Dagon at Ashdod, the idol fell down before it and was broken (I Sam. 5:3-4). Indeed, so long as the ark remained in Philistia, Jehovah visited judgments upon the Philistines (I Sam. 5:6-12) as he had done to

the Egyptians. The Philistines regarded Jehovah as merely the God of Israel (I Sam. 5:7, 8, 10, 11) but were
glad to be rid of his ark, because he fought against them.
There were several theophanies in this time. "It came
to pass, when Joshua was by Jericho, that he lifted up
his eyes and looked, and behold there stood a man over
against him with his sword drawn in his hand: and
Joshua went unto him, and said unto him, Art thou for
us, or for our adversaries? And he said, Nay; but as
prince of the host of Jehovah am I now come. And
Joshua fell on his face to the earth, and did worship and
said unto him, What saith my lord unto his servant? And
the prince of Jehovah's host said unto Joshua, Put off
thy shoe from off thy foot; for the place whereon thou
standest is holy. And Joshua did so" (Josh. 5:13-15).
Although this prince of Jehovah's host is called merely a
man and not the Angel of Jehovah, there can be no doubt
that he was the same angel who appeared in patriarchal
times (p. 26) and to Moses (pp. 56-57), the Angel of
the Presence of Jehovah who guided Israel through the
wilderness. Joshua recognized this by falling on his
face before him and worshipping him. The Angel of
Jehovah indicated it by commanding Joshua to put off
his shoe because he stood on holy ground. In the same
language God had addressed Moses from the burning
bush (Exod. 3:5). The answer of the Angel to Joshua
when he asked whether he was for Israel or their
enemies is suggestive. He was neither for Israel nor
for their enemies, but came as prince or commander
of the army of Jehovah. At the very beginning of the
conquest of Canaan he came with drawn sword to see

that perfect justice was done both to Israel and to their
enemies. If Israel obeyed God they could count on his
aid, but if they disobeyed him the prince of the army of
Jehovah would fight for their enemies.

Accordingly at the beginning of the period of the
judges "the angel of Jehovah came up from Gilgal to
Bochim. And he said, I made you to go up out of Egypt,
and have brought you unto the land which I sware unto
your fathers; and I said, I will never break my covenant
with you: and ye shall make no covenant with the inhabitants of the land; ye shall break down their altars.
But ye have not hearkened unto my voice: why have ye
done this? Wherefore I also said, I will not drive them
out from before you; but they shall be as thorns in your
sides and their gods shall be a snare unto you. And it
came to pass, when the angel of Jehovah spake these
words unto all the children of Israel, that the people
lifted up their voice and wept" (Judges 2:1-4).

The Angel of Jehovah appeared to Gideon to equip
him for the task of delivering Israel from the Midia-
mites (Judges 6:11-24). He is called the Angel of
Jehovah six times and once the Angel of God. It is
apparently the same person who is spoken of as Jehovàh.
"Jehovah looked upon him and said, Go in this thy might
and save Israel from the hand of Midian: have not I sent
thee?" (verse 14). Gideon was a mighty man of valor
(verse 12). Jehovah would have him use this native
strength but he added to it by the consciousness that
Jehovah's eyes were upon him. Gideon recognized that
he had seen the Angel of Jehovah and feared that he
would die. It was Jehovah who reassured him saying.

"Peace be unto thee; fear not: thou shalt not die" (verse 23). This shows that Gideon knew that the Angel of Jehovah was in fact Jehovah himself.

The appearance of the Angel of Jehovah to the wife of Manoah and later to Manoah himself, foretelling the birth of Samson (Judges 13:2-23) is even more·varied in its phenomena. The record speaks of him as the Angel of Jehovah ten times. Manoah's wife, however, called him a man of God saying "A man of God came unto me and his countenance was like the countenance of the angel of God, very terrible; and I asked him not whence he was, neither told he me his name" (verse 6). When he appeared again she called him a man and Manoah asked him whether he was the man who had spoken with his wife (verse 10-11). When Manoah urged him to remain and eat he answered, "Though thou detain me, I will not eat of thy bread; and if thou wilt make ready a burnt-offering, thou must offer it unto Jehovah" (verse 16). This refusal to eat food is surprising since the three angels who appeared to Abraham ate the food which was prepared for them (Gen. 18:8). Whatever be the true explanation of this divergence, the idea here is that the Angel of Jehovah being divine, did not need and would not take human food. Hence the explanation is offered that "Manoah knew not that he was the angel of Jehovah" (verse 16). When Manoah asked his name, the angel answered "Wherefore askest thou after my name seeing it is wonderful" (verse 18). Manoah understood this answer to mean that the man was God himself; for he offered a sacrifice to Jehovah and the angel went up in the flame. The reaction of Manoah and his wife to this theophany was the same as that of Gideon. He said to his wife, "We shall surely die because we have seen God" (verse 22) but his wife did not believe so (verse 23).

While the Old Testament characters regarded these theophanies as temporary manifestations of God in human form, they did not realize that in fact they were fore-gleams of the incarnation. The writer to the Hebrews regarded angels as the special mediators of the old dispensation and the Son of God as the Mediator of the new dispensation. (Heb. 2:2-4).

The Spirit of Jehovah is said to have come upon Othniel (Judges 3:10), Gideon (Judges 6:34) and Jephthah (Judges 11:29). The same Spirit moved Samson (Judges 13:25) and came mightily upon him (Judges 14:6, 19; 15:14). So the Spirit of Jehovah came mightly upon Saul causing him to prophesy (I Sam. 10:6, 10) and upon David (I Sam. 16:13). The Spirit of God came upon Saul's messengers so that they prophesied (I Sam. 19:20-24). Although these expressions resemble what it said about the Holy Spirit in the New Testament, there is here no distinction of persons in the Godhead. The Spirit of God in the Old Testament is God himself exercising active influence and imparting divine life.

(2) THE CEREMONIES OF RELIGION.

It is very difficult to determine how much the Mosaic ceremonial law was observed during the period between Moses and David, particularly in the time of the judges. The statement that "the people served Jehovah all the days of Joshua, and all the days of the elders that out-lived Joshua" (Judges 2:7) implies that in the main they observed the moral and ceremonial laws of the Mosaic period while Joshua lived and for a short time thereafter. There were many of the ceremonial laws, however, which could not be observed during the conquest of the land because of the unsettled conditions. For the full performance of the ceremonies it was necessary that the ark of the covenant be established in a permanent sanctuary. The religious fortunes of Israel in large measure went with the ark. The priests carried this precious possession in solemn procession through the Jordan (Josh. 3:3-17; 4:5-18). It is not stated where they placed it but since the people encamped at Gilgal (Josh. 4:19) it must have been there. The priests carried it around Jericho and returned into the camp, repeating this procession once a day for six days and seven times on the seventh day (Josh. 6:4-15). When Israel was defeated in their first attack upon Ai, "Joshua rent his clothes, and fell to the earth upon his face before the ark of Jehovah until the evening, he and the elders of Israel" (Josh. 7:6). In the solemn ceremony between Mount Ebal and Mount Gerizim the ark was the central feature (Josh. 8:33). It was not until the conquest of the greater part of the land that the tabernacle was set up at Shiloh (Josh. 18:1). The ark is not mentioned in this connection, but it was undoubtedly there. It must have remained there during all the time of the judges for the record states "the ark of the covenant of God was there in those days, and Phinehas, the son of Eleazar, the son of Aaron, stood before it in those days" (Judges 20:27-28). On that occasion it was brought eight miles from Shiloh to Bethel and then returned to the tabernacle (verse 26). It was in the tabernacle at

Shiloh and the service was carried on there by Eli and his sons (I Sam 1:3; 3:3). At the suggestion of the elders it was taken from the tabernacle into the battle (I Sam. 4:3-6). At the terrible news that it was captured by the Philistines all the city cried out, the aged Eli fell dead and the wife of Phinehas gave premature birth to a child, whom she named Ichabod (no glory) saying "The glory is departed from Israel" because the ark of God was taken (I Sam. 4:11-22). After bringing calamity to the Philistines the ark was sent back into the territory of Israel (I Sam. 6:10-16). It was at the village of Beth-shemesh a short time and a much longer time at Kirjath-jearim, but no general worship was carried on there (I Sam. 7:1-2). In the reign of Saul it seems to have been at Gibeah and Ahijah the priest was there (I Sam. 14:18-19), but there was no regular ritual of the sanctuary until David brought it up to the tent which he pitched for it at Jerusalem (II Sam. 6:1-18). While it was in the tabernacle at Shiloh the tribes east of the Jordan as well as the other tribes recognized it as the only legitimate place for the sacrifices to Jehovah (Josh. 22:19, 29).

The infrequency of references to sacrifices in the time of Joshua is due to the unsettled condition of the sanctuary. When the ark was there Joshua built an altar of unhewn stones at Mount Ebal and offered thereon burnt-offerings and sacrificed peace-offerings (Josh. 8:30-31). The tribes living east of the Jordan built a great altar by the river, but when the other tribes started to make war against them on account of it, they declared that they did not mean it for sacrifice as a rival to the altar at Shiloh, but only as a witness or memorial to future generations that they had a part in the sacrifices at the central sanctuary (Josh. 22:10-34).

The altar which Gideon built at Ophrah where the Angel of Jehovah appeared to him could be justified by that unusual event (Judges 6:24-28). The place was sanctified by the theophany. This altar was to replace an altar of Saul. It was built in the orderly manner and sacrifices were offered on it (verse 26). Similarly Manoah was justified in building an altar and offering a sacrifice in the place where the Angel of Jehovah appeared to him (Judges 13:16, 19-20). The altar which the people built at Bethel on which they offered burnt-offerings and peace-offerings (Judges 21:4) was quite irregular, unless, as seems possible (Judges 20:27-28), the ark was there at the time.

The first book of Samuel represents the sacrificial service as carried on regularly at Shiloh, but how long it had been so before that time we do not know. Elkanah "went up out of his city from year to year to worship and to sacrifice unto Jehovah of hosts in Shiloh, and the two sons of Eli, Hophni and Phinehas, priests unto Jehovah, were there" (I Sam. 1:3, 7, 21). Although the Mosaic law required every male to make the pilgrimage to the central sanctuary three times a year (Deut. 16:16), this seems to have been commuted to once a year later. Even in the time of the judges there was a feast of Jehovah every year at Shiloh (Judges 21:19). The tabernacle at Shiloh is called the temple of Jehovah (I Sam. 1:9). When the child Samuel was weaned, his mother Hannah brought him up to Shiloh, offered her sacrifice and consecrated the child to the service of Jehovah (I Sam. 1:24-28). As a boy Samuel ministered to Jehovah before Eli the priest (I Sam. 2:11, 18). Evidently there were many who brought sacrifices to Shiloh for "the custom of the priests with the people was that, when any man offered sacrifice, the priest's servant came, while the flesh was boiling, with a flesh-hook of three teeth in his hand; and he struck it into the pan or kettle or caldron or pot; all that the flesh-hook brought up the priest took therewith. So they did in Shiloh unto all the Israelites that came thither. Yea before they burnt the fat, the priest's servant came, and said to the man that sacrificed, Give flesh to roast for the priest; for he will not have boiled flesh of thee, but raw. And if the man said unto him, They will surely burn the fat first, and then take as much as thy soul desireth; then he would say, Nay, but thou shalt give it me now; and if not, I will take it by force. And the sin of the young men was very great before Jehovah, for the men despised the offering of Jehovah" (I Sam. 2:13-17). The law provided that the breast and thigh of the sacrificial animal belonged to the priests (Lev. 7:29-34), while the fat was to be burned upon the altar (Lev. 3:3-5). The wicked sons of Eli not satisfied with this portion sent their servant to demand more and even to take it by force. They also were guilty of sacrilege by demanding their share before the share of Jehovah was burnt upon the altar. Shocking as their impiety was, it presupposes the requirements of the sacrificial law. These wicked men were also.guilty of impurity with the women who served at the door of the tabernacle (I Sam. 2:22-25).

The beautiful story of Jehovah's speaking to the boy
Samuel incidentally shows that the ark and the golden
candlestick were in the tabernacle at Shiloh and that the
light was kept burning during part of the night (I Sam.
3:3). When the ark was sent back by the Philistines "the
Levites took down the ark of Jehovah, and the coffer
that was with it, wherein the jewels of gold were, and
put them on the great stone; and the men of Beth-shemesh offered burnt-offerings and sacrified sacrifices the
same day unto Jehovah" (I Sam. 6:15). These offerings
were made legitimate by the presence of the ark. They
expressed the gratitude of the men of Beth-shemesh for
its restoration. While the ark was absent from the tabernacle there was no proper and regular place for sacrifice.
Accordingly Samuel built an altar unto Jehovah at Ramah
where he lived (I Sam. 7:17). There he offered sacrifice
on the high place and as was customary, the people partook of the feast with him (I Sam. 9:11-14). He also
offered sacrifices at Gilgal (I Sam. 10:8) and it was at
that place that Saul was made king with sacrifices of
peace-offerings (I Sam. 11:14-15). There also the people
sacrificed after Saul's victory over the Amalekites (I Sam.
15:21). Saul built still another altar after he defeated
the Philistines (I Sam. 14:35). Samuel sacrificed to
Jehovah at Bethlehem (I Sam. 16:1-5). In fact, there
was an annual sacrifice there (I Sam. 20:6, 29). The
saying of Samuel to Saul, "to obey is better than sacrifice and to hearken than the fat of rams" (I Sam. 15:22)
displays a spiritual conception of sacrifice in which he
anticipated the great prophets (Amos 5:22; Mic. 6:6-8;
Isa. I:11-13).

It was customary through all this period to seek Jehovah's will by casting lots (Josh. 7:14-18; 14:1-2; 18:6,
8, 10; 19:51). Sometimes, however, the inquiry was at
the ark or by means of the Urim and Thummim which
were in the ephod. The principal instances of such consultation in this period have already been mentioned
(Judges 1:1-2; 20:18, 23, 27-28; I Sam. 10:22; 14:36-
42; 23:9-12; 30:7-8). Gideon asked golden ear-rings
from the people and with them made an ephod which he
put in Ophrah. "All Israel played the harlot after it
there; and it became a snare unto Gideon and to his
house" (Judges 8:27). Apparently this ephod was not
used as a garment for the high priest, but was an object
of idolatrous worship, for it is mentioned with the graven
image, the teraphim and the molten image (Judges 18:17).

The high-priesthood followed by inheritance according
to the Mosaic law during the life-time of Joshua and
from the time of the birth of Samuel until the accession
of David. Eleazar, the son of Aaron, who succeeded his
father as high priest, held that office during the remainder
of Moses' life (Num. 20:25-28; Deut. 10:6; Josh. 14:1;
17:4; 19:51; 21:1; 24:33). He was followed by Phinehas
(Judges 20:28). It is not known how Eli secured the
high-priesthood (I Sam. 1:3). He seems to have been a
descendant of Ithamar, the youngest son of Aaron. In the
time of Solomon there were rival claimants to the office,
Abiathar of the house of Eli descended from Ithamar
(I Kgs. 2:27; I Chron. 24:3, 6) and Zadok, who was descended from Eleazar (I Chron. 24: 3, 6). However,
Eli got his office, it followed in his line as far as Abiathar.
The wicked sons of Eli, Hophni and Phinehas, died be-

fore their father (I Sam. 4:11). Apparently Eli was succeeded by Ahitub, a son of Phinehas (I Sam. 14:3). At
any rate in Saul's reign Ahijah, one of Ahitub's sons, was
high priest for a time (I Sam. 14:3) and then Ahimelech,
another son of Ahitub (I Sam. 21:1; 22:11). Ahimelech
lived at Nob, which was called the city of the priests
(I Sam. 22:11, 19). Later still Abiathar, the son of
Ahimelech, had the sacred office (I Sam. 23:9; 30:7).

Priests of lesser rank and Levites are mentioned frequently in this period (Josh. 3:3, 6, 8, 13-17; 4:3, etc.).
The priests, the Levites, carried the ark through the Jordan (Josh. 3:3). The Levites received no inheritance
in the land as Moses had commanded (Josh. 14:3-4; 18:7;
compare Deut. 18:1-2) except forty-eight cities with their
suburbs (Josh. 21:1-42 compare Lev. 25:32 and Num.
35:1-8). Appropriate to their office it was the Levites
who took the ark down from the cart which brought it
from Philistia to Beth-shemesh (I Sam. 6:15).

There are two strange stories about Levites in the period
of the judges. In the hill-country of Ephraim lived a man
named Micah, of whom it is said that he "had a house of
gods, and he made an ephod, and teraphim and consecrated
one of his sons, who became his priest" (Judges 17:5). Later a wandering Levite from Bethlehem-judah came that
way and Micah hired him as his priest (Judges 17:8-13).
Later still some wandering Danites stole the idols and
hired the Levite to go with them, making him their priest
at Laish, which they called Dan. (Judges 18:14-29).
This became the centre of worship for the tribe of Dan.
"The children of Dan set up for themselves the graven
image; and Jonathan, the son of Gershom, the son of

Moses, he and his sons were priests to the tribe of the
Danites until the day of the captivity of the land. So
they set them up Micah's graven image which he made,
all the time that the house of God was in Shiloh" (Judges
18:30-31).

The other story tells of a Levite "sojourning on the
farther side of the hill-country of Ephraim" who took a
concubine from Bethlehem-judah (Judges 19:1). She
ran away from him, returning to her father's house. The
Levite went there and brought her back with him. At
Gibeah she was shamefully abused by the men of the
town. There the Levite told the old man who entertained him that he was going to the house of Jehovah
(Judges 19:18). If this reading is correct, it doubtless
refers to Shiloh. The outrage of the men of Gibeah so
incensed the other tribes of Israel that they made war
upon the tribe of Benjamin (Judges 20).

These two stories give an accurate picture of the social
and religious conditions in that time. The Levites who
according to the Mosaic law were to be supported by the
tithes of the people (Num. 18:21-24) were mostly poor in
the time of the judges because the tithes were not paid.
As the record states "in those days there was no king in
Israel; every man did that which was right in his own
eyes" (Judges 17:6 compare 18:1). While those Levites
who lived near the sanctuary at Shiloh or the sanctuary at
Dan may have had a tolerable living, others in remote
parts such as the hill-country of Ephraim were the objects of charity or wandered from place to place seeking
employment. Thus the Levite of the first story was glad
to attach himself to the sanctuary at Micah's house. Its

idolatrous character did not trouble him. Furthermore he had no scruples about leaving Micah when he had an opportunity for better pay from the Danites (Judges 18:19-20). The other Levite was apparently in better circumstances, for he was able to have a concubine. His moral condition, however, was equally bad. Since the Levites of this time were such disgraceful members of society, we may be sure that the great majority of the people had no respect for the religion which they represented. Indeed there is every reason to believe that with a few exceptions the people were on the same moral plane.

There are very few references to the various holy times in the period between Moses and David. The sabbath is not mentioned once. Nevertheless there seems to have been a recognition of it when the people went around the walls of Jericho seven times on the seventh day, while on the other days they did so only once (Josh. 6:15). There are also several allusions to a period of seven days (Judges 14:12, 17; I Sam. 10:8; 11:3; 13:8). The sabbatical year and the year of jubilee are not mentioned. David spoke of the new moon as the time when he should sit at meat with the king (I Sam. 20:5, 18, 24). The only one of the annual feasts which is named is the passover. It was on the tenth day of the first month that the children of Israel came up out of the Jordan and encamped at Gilgal (Josh. 4:19). This was the very day when each family was to take the lamb for the passover (Exod. 12:3). The lamb was kept until the fourteenth day of the month when the passover was celebrated (Exod. 12:6). Accordingly after the Israelites had encamped at Gilgal "they kept the passover on the fourteenth day of the month at even in the plains of Jericho. And they did eat of the produce of the land on the morrow after the passover, unleavened cakes and parched grain in the selfsame day" (Josh. 5:10-11). The record does not state whether they kept the feast of unleavened bread which followed immediately after the passover; but the passover at least was observed according to the Mosaic law. Even in the wicked time of the judges there was a feast of Jehovah in Shiloh from year to year (Judges 21:19). Although the name of this feast is not stated, it is likely that it was the passover. It was probably for the same feast that Elkanah went to Shiloh every year. He went "to worship and to sacrifice unto Jehovah of hosts" (I Sam. 1:3, 7, 21). It was a glad time of feasting (I Sam. 1:4, 8, 9) and Eli thought that Hannah was drunk (I Sam. 1:13-15). There was also a yearly sacrifice at Bethlehem (I Sam. 20:6) but whether it was connected with one of the three festivals we do not know.

The distinction between clean and unclean animals was understood and perhaps observed by some of the people. The Angel of Jehovah who appeared to Manoah and his wife to announce the birth of Samson forbade the woman to drink wine or strong drink or to eat any unclean thing (Judges 13:4, 7, 14). The idea of ceremonial uncleanness was also not entirely forgotten. Phinehas and the princes, who were sent by the tribes west of the Jordan to remonstrate with the east-Jordanic tribes for building an altar, said to them, "If the land of your possession be unclean, then pass ye over unto the land of the possession of Jehovah, wherein Jehovah's tabernacle dwelleth, and take possession among us" (Josh. 22:19). This statement shows a true conception of the nature of ceremonial purity. The tabernacle at Shiloh sanctified the land and made it ceremonially clean. When the new moon came and David did not appear to eat with the king Saul thought "Something hath befallen him, he is not clean; surely he is not clean" (I Sam. 20:26). This thought shows that Saul was acquainted with the Levitical law according to which a person who had touched a dead body or was otherwise ceremonially unclean was excluded from all religious festivals (Lev. 7:19-21). It was necessary for everyone to be sanctified before partaking of the sacrificial meal (I Sam. 16:5).

The only reference to circumcision is at the beginning of the period. At Gilgal immediately after the crossing of the Jordan all the males who had been born after Israel left Egypt were circumcised (Josh. 5:2-9). For some unknown reason they were not circumcised in the wilderness but when this rite was performed, "Jehovah said unto Joshua, this day have I rolled away the reproach of Egypt from off you. Wherefore the name of that place was called Gilgal unto this day" (Josh. 5:9). Although there is no reference to circumcision after this in this period, it is overwhelmingly probable that many if not all the Hebrews were circumcised. When Samson wished to marry a Philistine woman his father and mother said to him, "Is there never a woman among the daughters of thy brethren, or among all my people, that thou goest to take a wife of the uncircumcised Philistines" (Judges 14:3). On another occasion Samson prayed that Jehovah would keep him from falling into the hand of the uncircumcised (Judges 15:18). Jonathan also referred to the

Philistines as uncircumcised (I Sam. 14:6). David spoke
with the utmost contempt of Goliath as "this uncircumcised Philistine" (I Sam. 17:26, 36) and Saul asked his
armor-bearer to thrust him through lest the uncircumcised
Philistines come and do it (I Sam. 31:4). They would
not have spoken so unless this rite was generally observed
among the Israelites.

Two vows are mentioned in this time. "Jephthah vowed
a vow unto Jehovah and said, If thou wilt indeed deliver
the children of Ammon into my hand, then it shall be that
whatsoever cometh forth from the doors of my house to
meet me, when I return in peace from the children of
Ammon, it shall be Jehovah's and I will offer it up for a
burnt-offering" (Judges 11:30-31). It was a rash and
foolish vow and Jephthah lived to regret it bitterly, for
on his victorious return from the war his only child, a
daughter, came out to meet him with timbrels and dances.
Nevertheless obedient to the Mosaic law Jephthah fulfilled
all that he had said (Num. 30:2). Very different was
Hannah's vow. Praying in the bitterness of her soul she
said, "O Jehovah of hosts, if thou wilt indeed look on the
affliction of thy handmaid, and remember me and not forget thy handmaid, but wilt give unto thy handmaid a man-
child, then I will give him unto Jehovah all the days of his
life, and there shall no razor come upon his head" (I Sam.
1:11). In fulfillment of this vow Hannah consecrated the
boy Samuel as a Nazirite to Jehovah and he grew up to
be one of the greatest and most influential men in the
whole history of Israel.

There is not the slightest allusion to tithing in the literature of this period and it seems probable that the law

requiring the people to give one-tenth of their increase to
Jehovah (Lev. 27:30-33) was disregarded.   There is an
incidental confirmation of this in the apparent poverty of
the Levites during the time of the judges.   By the Mosaic
law the tithes should go to them (Num. 18:21, 24) and if
they had actually received them they would have been as
well off as the rest of the people.   Moses had warned the
people not to forsake the Levites (Deut. 12:19; 14:27).
By classing them with the sojourner, the fatherless and
the widow he apparently realized that they would be regarded as objects of charity (Deut. 16:11, 14; 26:11, 12).
There is another evidence of the neglect of the law of
tithes in the words of Samuel when Israel asked for a
king like the nations around them.   He warned them that a
king would take the tenth of their seed and of their vineyards and give it to his officers and servants (I Sam.
8:15, 17).   Apparently the people were free from taxation
before the establishment of the kingdom.   In the dis-
ordered conditions they made no regular payments to support the government or the religion.

There were at least two Nazirities in this time.   Samson was a Nazirite not by his own vow or that of his
mother, but by the command of Jehovah before his birth.
The Angel of Jehovah said to his mother, "Thou shalt conceive and bear a son and no razor shall come upon his
head; for the child shall be a Nazirite unto God from
the womb" (Judges 13:5).   There were two principal
marks of the Nazirite according to the Mosaic law, (1)
that he drank no wine or strong drink and (2) that he
allowed his hair to grow (Num. 6:1-21).   Samson had
one of these marks.   The other was transferred to his

mother. She was to drink no wine nor strong drink and to eat no unclean thing because her child was to be a Nazirite (Judges 13:4, 7). Probably Samson also abstained from the fruit of the vine. So long as he obeyed the Nazirite vows he was able to perform great deeds through the strength which God gave him; but when through his moral weakness he allowed his hair to be cut off, (Judges 16:4-17) his "strength went from him" (Judges 16:19) for "Jehovah was departed from him" (Judges 16:20). By the vow of his mother Samuel was a Nazirite from his birth (I Sam. 1:11, 28; 2:18, 26; 3:1, 19-20). He differed greatly from Samson since he was consecrated to Jehovah. If Samson delivered Israel from their political foes, Samuel delivered them from their moral and religious foes. In him we see the relation between the true Nazirite and the developing office of the prophet which in a later age would be Israel's greatest glory (I Sam. 3:20).

The unusual method of taking Jericho (Josh. 6) was intended to show Israel that the conquest of the land was Jehovah's work and that therefore the first-fruits of that conquest should be devoted or set apart to him. The Levitical law had said, "No devoted thing that a man shall devote unto Jehovah of all that he hath, whether of man or beast, or of the field of his possession, shall be sold or redeemed: every devoted thing is most holy until Jehovah. No one devoted, that shall be devoted from among men, shall be ransomed; he shall surely be put to death" (Lev. 27:28-29). Jericho having been devoted with all that was in it except Rahab and her family, Joshua charged the people strictly not to take anything for themselves (Josh. 6:17-19, 21, 24, 26). When Achan violated this solemn charge, he brought the curse on the whole people and they could not regain their standing before Jehovah until they were sanctified by executing him (Josh. 7).

A very solemn ceremony was performed by all the people in the valley between Mount Ebal and Mount Gerizim, a ceremony which Moses had commanded. At first he said briefly, "It shall come to pass when Jehovah thy God shall bring thee into the land whither thou goest to possess it, that thou shalt set the blessing upon Mount Gerizim and the curse upon Mount Ebal" (Deut. 11:29). Later he explained this more fully telling them to set up great stones, to cover them with plaster and to write on them the words of the law. They were also to build an altar of unhewn stones and offer thereon burnt-offerings and peace-offerings. Half the tribes were to stand on Mount Ebal and the other half on Mount Gerizim while the Levites pronounced the curses on those who disobeyed the law. After each curse all the people should say Amen. (Deut. 27). This ceremony was carried out exactly. The ark of the covenant stood in the midst and all Israel on either side of it. There Joshua "read all the words of the law, the blessing and the curse, according to all that is written in the book of the law" (Josh. 8:30-35). This solemn ceremony was intended to initiate the whole people of Israel into their national status. They became a nation when Jehovah adopted them at Mount Sinai (Exod. 19:5-6). Yet they could not enter into the fullness of their national heritage until they entered the land which Jehovah had promised to Abraham, Isaac and Jacob. Their national

life depended upon the covenant with Jehovah whose conditions were stated in the law. Therefore as soon as they
came to the center of the land, to those mountains which
command the greatest view of it, to that place where Abraham first entered the land (Gen. 12:6), in this solemn
manner they renewed their allegiance to Jehovah. The
key to the understanding of this ceremony is in the statement which is connected with Moses' command to do it.
"Moses and the priests the Levites spake unto all Israel
saying, Keep silence and hearken, O Israel: This day
thou art become the people of Jehovah, thy God. Thou
shalt therefore obey the voice of Jehovah thy God and
do his commandments and his statutes, which I command
thee this day" (Deut. 27:9-10). Now indeed were they
the people of Jehovah in the fullest sense. The issues
of life and death, of blessing and cursing, were before
them. Shortly before his death Joshua gathered all the
people to Shechem between Mount Ebal and Gerizim and
after he had addressed them, they renewed their covenant
with Jehovah (Josh. 24:1-28).

A common method of the development of religious
ceremonies is illustrated in connection with the story of
Jephthah's daughter. After it tells of the fulfillment of
Jephthah's vow by sacrificing his daughter it says, "It was
a custom in Israel that the daughters of Israel went yearly
to celebrate the daughter of Jephthah the Gileadite four
days in a year" (Judges 11:39-40). The Hebrew word to
celebrate used here occurs elsewhere only in the song of
Deborah as she sang, "Far from the noise of archers, in
the places of drawing water, there shall they rehearse the
righteous acts of Jehovah, even the righteous acts of his

rule in Israel" (Judges 5:11). So the tomb of Jephthah's daughter became a place of annual pilgrimage for the daughters of Israel. There they mourned her death as they rehearsed the story of her father's vow. There is no trace of this pilgrimage in the later history of the Old Testament, but the Samaritans worshipped Jephthah's daughter as the heavenly virgin (See Cooke in Cambridge Bible on Judges and Ruth).

When the children of Israel entered the promised land they came in contact with religions which were new to them. Many of them yielded entirely to these foreign cults, forsaking Jehovah, while others worshipped the gods of the land side by side with Jehovah. Since these heathen religions had such an important influence not upon the religion of Jehovah but upon the religion of Israel, a history of the religion of Israel is not complete without some account of them. The most important so far as Israel was concerned was the worship of the Baalim. The frequency of the mention of this worship in the period of the judges shows that during a large part of that time Israel worshipped Baal rather than Jehovah. They served the Baalim (Judges 2:11-13) forsaking Jehovah. "They forgot Jehovah their God and served the Baalim" (Judges 3:7). The men of Ophrah were indignant against Gideon and wished to kill him because he broke down the altar of Baal (Judges 6:30). Joash, Gideon's father, called his son Jerub-baal (let Baal contend) because he had said, "Let Baal contend for himself" (Judges 6:31-32). When Gideon was dead Israel "turned again and played the harlot after the Baalim and made Baal-berith their god" (Judges 8:33). Later still their religious practices became more varied. They "served the Baalim and the Ashtaroth, and the gods of Syria and the gods of Sidon, and the gods of Moab, and the gods of the children of Ammon, and the gods of the Philistines and they forsook J e h o v a h and served him not" (Judges 10:6).

The name Baal means lord or owner. The deity of each place in Canaan was called its Baal and together they are called the Baalim. Probably Baal was originally a sun-god and Ashtoreth whose worship often accompanied his was a moon-goddess. Yet the particular forms of the worship differed according to the physical features of the different places. Since the fertility of the soil depends largely upon the sun, Baal was thought of as giving the fruits of the earth. Although the Baal religion was not speculative, the worship was in effect an adoration of the reproductive power of nature as conditioned by the particular locality. That is the reason for the licentious rites which accompanied it (I Kgs. 14:24). It was usually carried on at a high place or hill. Although not many aspects of the religion are seen in the book of Judges, it is probable that it did not differ greatly from the Baal worship of later times. Beside the altar of Baal was an Asherah which was probably the trunk of a tree (Judges 3:7; 6:25, 26, 28, 30). Many think that it was a substitute for a sacred grove, but it is more probable that it was the symbol of a goddess named Asherah who may have been identical with Ashtoreth. In the worship of Baal human sacrifices were offered. A father made his son to pass through the fire (Jer. 19:5). The worshipper also kissed the image of Baal (I Kgs. 19:18) and the

prophets of Baal cut themselves in their worship thinking
to please the deity (I Kgs 18:28). Names of places like
Baal-gad (Josh. 11:17) and Baal-hermon (Judges 3:3)
were originally the names of the particular Baals of those
places. Baal-peor (Num. 25:1-3) was the Baal of Mount
Peor. Baal-zebub the deity of Ekron (II Kgs. 1:6, 16)
was the lord of flies who was supposed to be able to protect against them. Baal-berith (Judges 8:33; 9:4) means
"lord of the covenant" and seems to suggest that this Baal
of Shechem made a covenant with his worshippers. Although the name of the Canaanite deity is not mentioned
in Genesis, it is probable that it was the religion of the
Canaanites in the time of the patriarchs. Certain trees
(Gen. 12:6; 13:18; 14:13; 18:1; 21:33; 35:4, 8) and
certain perennial fountains (Gen. 14:7; 16:14; 21:30-31)
seem to have been regarded as sacred because they displayed the life-giving energy of the Baalim. The palm-
tree under which the prophetess Deborah dwelt (Judges
4:5), the oak at Shechem where the men of that place
assembled (Judges 9:6) and the oak of Meonenim (the
augurs) (Judges 9:37) were probably such sacred trees.
While there were long periods in the times of the judges
when the Israelites went over to the worship of the Baalim,
the judges themselves, who were the great religious
leaders of Israel, were all champions of the worship of
Jehovah and as long as the judge lived the people worshipped Jehovah alone (Judges 2:19). Throughout all
the centuries down to the exile Baal worship was the
greatest foe of the religion of Jehovah. When Ahab
married Jezebel, the daughter of Ethbaal, king of the
Sidonians, there was a life and death struggle between the

two religions. The spectacular contest between Elijah and the prophets of Baal (I Kgs. 18:20-40) gave the religion of Jehovah only a temporary victory. Even the furious zeal of Jehu for Jehovah did not permanently exterminate the Baal worship (II Kgs. 10:18-28) for the eighth-century prophets had still to inveigh against it (Hos. 2:8, 13, 17; 11:2; 13:1).

The inclusive statement of the book of Judges (10:6) says that Israel served the gods of Syria, Sidon, Moab, Ammon and the Philistines although the names of the deities are not mentioned. The supreme god of Syria was Hadad, whose name occurs in the names of Ben-hadad (son of Hadad, I Kgs. 20:1-34) and Hadad-ezer (Hadad is a help, II Sam. 8:3-12) kings of Syria. Rimmon was another Syrian deity (II Kgs. 5:18) or possibly another aspect of the same detity, for the names were combined into Hadad-rimmon (Zech. 12:11) as the names of Amon and Re were combined into Amon-re in Egypt. Rimmon was originally a weather god, the deity of storm and rain, thunder and lightning. Hadad had the same functions. The god of the Phenician city of Sidon was the local Baal with whom Ashtoreth was associated (I Kgs. 11:5, 33). Indeed the worship of the Baalim is thought to have originated in Phenicia and to have spread from there throughout the land of Canaan.

The god of Moab was Chemosh (Num. 21:29; Judges 11:24; I Kgs. 11:7, 33; II Kgs. 23:13; Jer. 48:7, 13, 46). This deity was a form of Baal and his worship included the sacrifice of children as burnt-offerings (II Kgs. 3:27). Ruth the Moabitess forsook this abominable worship for that of Jehovah (Ruth 1:16). Molech the god of the Am-

monites seems to have been but another name for Chemosh
and his worship did not differ from that of Chemosh.
Even at Mount Sinai the Israelites knew about the corrupt
worship of Molech and they were specially forbidden to
offer their sons to him on pain of death (Lev. 18:21;
20:2-5). Nevertheless Solomon built a high place for
Chemosh and Molech near Jerusalem (I Kgs. 11:7) and
in later times the Israelites made their sons and daughters
to pass through the fire to him (II Kgs. 23:10; Jer.
32:35). Molech means king and the names Milcom (I
Kgs. 11:5, 33; II Kgs. 23:13) and Malcam (Zeph. 1:5)
are variant forms with the same meaning. The name
Melcarth (king of the city) under which the Sidonians
worshipped Baal has the same origin. Dagon was the
national god of the Philistines. They offered a great
sacrifice of joy to him when they captured Samson (Judges
16:23). They brought the ark of Jehovah into the temple
of Dagon at Ashdod and before it the image fell down
and was broken (I Sam. 5:1-5). There they also fastened
the head of Saul (I Chron. 10:10). From the resemblance of the name to the Hebrew word for fish, some
have supposed that Dagon was a fish god, while others
think he was an agricultural deity. The place Beth-
dagon (house of Dagon) in the territory of Judah near
Philistia got its name from this god (Josh. 15:41).

The Israelites made graven and molten images of these
various deities and bowed down to them (Judges 17:3;
18:14, 17, 20, 30). There were diviners in Philistia (I
Sam. 6:2) and in adopting the Philistine gods the children
of Israel doubtless had their diviners. There were in
Israel also wizards and those that had familiar spirits,

for Saul put them out of the land (I Sam. 28:3). Nevertheless Saul was able to find a woman that had a familiar spirit at Endor (I Sam. 28:7) and he consulted her. The pillar at Shechem where the people made Abimelech king (Judges 9:6) was probably a memorial stone which marked a heathen shrine. Such pillars were forbidden by the Mosaic law (Exod. 23:24; 34:13). Some of the people in the time of the judges had teraphim, small household gods (Judges 17:5; 18:14, 17, 18, 20) such as Rachel stole from her father Laban (Gen. 31:19, 30, 34).

(3) THE BEGINNINGS OF PROPHECY.

During the time between Moses and the eighth-century prophets, prophecy underwent a transformation until it became distinct and extraordinary. Moses was a prophet and Jehovah promised to raise up from Israel another prophet like him (Deut. 18:15-19). The work of the great prophets of Israel was founded upon his work. Nevertheless prophecy did not attain its distinctive character in Moses since he was also in some sense a priest and performed the functions of a king. The true conception of prophecy is suggested by the word of God to Moses, "See I have made thee as God to Pharaoh and Aaron thy brother shall by thy prophet. Thou shalt speak all that I command thee; and Aaron thy brother shall speak unto Pharaoh" (Exod. 7:1-2). The prophet was therefore the spokesman and messenger of God, his mouthpiece and interpreter.

The glimpses of prophecy which we gain from the book of Judges and the first book of Samuel are not very reassuring. Deborah, the prophetess, dwelling under the palm-tree between Ramah and Bethel with all Israel coming up to her for judgment is a wholly different figure from Amos or Isaiah (Judges 4:4-5). She incited the people to war and went with them. (Judges 4:6-10, 14). She rejoiced in the treachery of Jael and sang a song of triumph in which she gloried in the downfall of the Canaanites and glorified the wickedness of Israel (Judges 5). Yet in her fiery zeal for Jehovah's cause as she saw it, she was very like Amos and Isaiah. The difference lay in the fact that her interest was political and military, while that of the writing prophets was religious. Jehovah took this mighty stream of prophecy, so capable of good or ill and turned it into the greatest power for moral and spiritual good before the time of Christ.

The only other prophet mentioned in the book of Judges was of a different kind from Deborah. When the Israelites cried to Jehovah because of the oppression of the Midianites, Jehovah sent this unnamed prophet who reproached them for their idolatry (Judges 6:7-10). Samuel combined in himself both ideas. Like Deborah he judged Israel (I Sam. 7:6, 15-16) but like the unnamed prophet he reproved them for their sins. Samuel did not obtain his prophetic office by inheritance, as the priestly office was obtained, but by a special divine call. He lived in evil times. "The word of Jehovah," which was given so fully to the writing prophets of later centuries, "was rare in those days. There was no widely spread vision" (I Sam. 3:1). The first revelation to Samuel came in his boyhood. It required him to tell Eli of the fall of his high-priestly house because of the wickedness of his sons (I Sam. 3:2-18). Faithful in this important and difficult task, he "grew and Jehovah was with him and did let none of his words fall to the ground. And all Israel from Dan even to Beer-sheba knew that Samuel was established to be a prophet of Jehovah" (I Sam. 3:19-20).

The prophetic activity of Samuel did not have to do with predictions or even for the most part with addresses of any sort. He was a great religious and social reformer in Israel. When the ark was captured by the Philistines and the high priest Eli died, the religious life of Israel suffered a staggering blow; but Samuel was equal to the emergency. Twenty years later with the Philistines as strong as ever he said to all the house of Israel, "If ye do return unto Jehovah with all your heart, then put away the foreign gods and the Ashtaroth from among you and direct your hearts unto Jehovah and serve him only; and he will deliver you out of the hand of the Philistines" (I Sam. 7:3). This was a true prophetic word and the people heeded it. He gathered the people together at Mizpah that he might pray for them and confess their sins. Even while they were assembled the Philistines came to attack them; but Jehovah heard his prayer and delivered Israel (I Sam. 7:5-14). Unfortunately in Samuel's old age his sons whom he appointed judges dishonored their father as Eli's sons dishonored him. Hence the dissatisfied people asked that they might have a king like the nations around them. At first offended at their request he later yielded. It was he who under the divine guidance chose Saul as king. His address to the people urging that they and their new king should obey Jehovah is in true prophetic style (I Sam. 12:1-17). When Saul proved an unworthy king it was Samuel who under God chose David and anointed him

to be king at Saul's death (I Sam. 16:1-13). Samuel
was the greatest figure in the religious as well as the
political life of Israel from Moses to David. This great
prophet was the instrument in Jehovah's hand not only to
establish the kingdom under its greatest king, but also
to establish its religion more firmly than at any time since
Israel entered the promised land.

There are certain features of prophecy in Samuel's
day which show its primitive character. Apparently a
prophet was sought somewhat as a claivoyant is sought
today. When Saul was seeking his father's asses, his servant said, "Behold now there is in this city a man of God,
and he is a man that is held in honor; all that he saith
cometh surely to pass: now let us go thither; peradvanture
he can tell us concerning our journey whereon we go"
(I Sam. 9:6). Apparently it was customary to pay a
prophet for such a consultation, for Saul was unwilling to
consult Samuel without a present (I Sam. 9:7-8). In this
connection it is said that a prophet was formerly called a
seer (I Sam. 9:9). Prophets in that day seem to have
gone in bands and to have used musical instruments to
induce the ecstatic condition in which they could prophesy,
for Samuel told Saul that he would "meet a band of
prophets coming down from the high place with a psaltery
and a timbrel and a pipe and a harp before them; and they
will be prophesying: and the Spirit of Jehovah will come
mightily upon thee and thou shalt prophesy with them,
and shalt be turned into another man" (I Sam. 10:5-6).
From this the proverb arose, "Is Saul also among the
prophets?" (I Sam. 10:11-12). Years afterward when
Saul had become mentally deranged the record states that

"an evil spirit from God came mightily upon him and he prophesied in the midst of the house" (I Sam. 18:10). On another occasion when David was with Samuel and Saul sent men to take him, "when they saw the company of the prophets prophesying and Samuel standing as head over them, the Spirit of God came upon the messengers of Saul and they also prophesied" (I Sam. 19:20). When Saul heard of it he sent a second group of messengers and later a third, but each of them was overcome by the prophetic ecstasy. Finally Saul went himself "and the Spirit of God came upon him also, and he went on and prophesied, until he came to Naioth in Ramah. And he also stripped off his clothes, and he also prophesied before Samuel, and lay down naked all that day and all that night" (I Sam. 19:23-24).

It is evident from these incidents that in the schools of the prophets of which Samuel was the founder, prophesying was some sort of ecstatic utterance which was poured forth under the influence of emotional excitement. It was akin to madness. The phenomenon may have been similar psyologically to the speaking with tongues and prophesying in the early Christian church (Acts 2:1-21; 19:6; I Cor. 14:1-40; I Thess. 5:20). A susceptible man like Saul was liable to do very startling things under the influence of great emotional excitement, things similar to those which sometimes occur in revival meetings. But on the other hand a sane man was greatly stirred by the Spirit of God and induced to come into closer relation with God. At its best prophecy had much of ecstasy about it; and at its worst this ecstasy led to extravagances. Such were the possibilities for good or ill in the gift of prophecy.

Saul consulted the witch of Endor because Jehovah no longer answered him "by dreams or by Urim or by prophets" (I Sam. 28:6, 15).

(4) THE NATION AND THE INDIVIDUAL.

In spite of the centrifugal effect of the settlement Israel in the promised land, religion during this period remained a national far more than an individual matter. It was natural that a strong sense of national unity should prevail during the conquest. The national life of Israel was so founded in their religion that it is difficult to separate their political from their religious concerns. This comes into prominence in the case of Achan. When he took part of the spoil of Jericho which had been devoted to Jehovah the punishment came on the whole people. The account says: "The children of Israel committed a trespass in the devoted thing; for Achan the son of Carmi, the son of Zabdi, the son of Zerah of the tribe of Judah took of the devoted thing: and the anger of Jehovah was kindled against the children of Israel" (Josh. 7:1). The people were guilty because of the act of one man. The rehearsal of his anceestry and his tribe is to emphasize the thought that he could not act as an individual but only as a member of his family, his tribe, his nation (Josh. 7:16-18). The inquiry by tribes, by families, by households and then man by man had the same purpose. Long afterward Phinehas and the princes who were with him said, "Did not Achan the son of Zerah commit a trespass in the devoted thing and that man perished not alone in his iniquity" (Josh. 22:20). The whole story is typical of the relation of the individual to the nation.

While this strong sense of national unity had its good

side, it had its dangers also. It was calculated to produce a national pride which was hostile to Jehovah. Something of this seems to have been appreciated by Gideon when he prepared to attack the Midianites: "Jehovah said unto Gideon, The people that are with thee are too many for me to give the Midianites into their hand, lest Israel vaunt themselves against me, saying Mine own hand hath saved me" (Judges 7:2). It was on this account that the number was reduced from 32,000 to 10,000 and then to only 300. The three hundred must act for the whole nation, but the whole nation must trust in Jehovah as their Deliverer. Even the exploits of Samson were recounted, not because of his personal prowess but because he delivered Israel from the Philistines (Judges 13:5). His ruling passion even in death was to destroy the Philistines (Judges 16:30).

The religion of the individual as in the time of Moses was merged in the religion of the nation (see p. 136). In this whole period there was no mention of the idea of salvation from sin. The judges saved or delivered Israel from the hostile nations around them (Judges 2:16, 18; 3:9, 31; 8:22; 10:12-14; 12:2-3; 13:5). Redemption is spoken of only in the sense of securing land by purchase (Ruth 4:4-7). Doubtless the individual who offered a sacrifice thought that he was saved thereby from the consequences of his sins; but the idea was never expressed. Those who came to the feast at Shiloh no doubt went away with a sense of forgiven sin; but their main thought was that by participating in the services of the central sanctuary, they renewed their connection with Israel and so were in covenant relations with Jehovah.

In view of the apostasy during the greater part of this period we should not expect to find many traces of the Messianic hope in this age. Yet we may be sure that pious men like Joshua, Caleb and Samuel treasured the promises which Jehovah had given to his people. Otherwise it could not have shone forth so brightly in the time of David. There are also very few references to the covenant of Jehovah with Israel (Josh. 6:8; 7:11, 15; 23:16). The only allusion to the Messianic hope is in the closing words of Hanna's prayer of thanksgiving, "Jehovah will judge the ends of the earth; and he will give strength unto his king and exalt the horn of his anointed" (I Sam. 2:10). Kirkpatrick well says, "Hannah's prophetic prayer was but partially fulfilled in the king soon to be anointed by her son as the deliverer of Israel; it reaches forward to him whom the Jewish kings foreshadowed, the king Messiah, in whom alone the lofty anticipations of the prophetess are to be completely realized" (Commentary on I Samuel in Cambridge Bible).

(5) THE FUTURE LIFE.

There are very few references to the life after death between Moses and David. When Joshua was about to die he said, "Behold this day I am going the way of all the earth" (Josh. 23:14), an expression which contains no suggestion of belief in the future life. Later it is merely said that he died and was buried (Josh. 24:29-32; Judges 2:8-9). The same colorless expression is used concerning Eleazar (Josh. 24:33). However, it is said that "all that generation were gathered unto their fathers" (Judges 2:10) which doubtless conveyed the same idea as in earlier times (See pp. 35, 36, 144). The record states that Gideon died and was buried (Judges 8:32). The same is said about others in this period (Judges 1:7; 9:49, 54; 10:2, etc.).

Saul evidently believed in a life after death, for he asked the witch of Endor to bring up Samuel who was long dead (I Sam. 28:8, 11). She also claimed that she could bring him up (I Sam. 28:11). The expression to come up evidently alludes to the idea that Samuel was in Sheol which was considered to be below the earth. This is clear in the statement of the witch, "I see a god coming up out of the earth" (I Sam. 28:13). The word used is the usual one rendered God in the Old Testament although it is sometimes used of beings who are close to God, like angels (Ps. 8:5; 97:7), or judges who act in God's name (Exod. 22:8-9, 28). Here it means a ghost, who seemed to be supernatural. Probably the witch of Endor like most other witches was an impostor. She could make those who consulted her believe that she could bring up the dead; but she was not really able to do so. Consequently she was alarmed when she saw Samuel coming up. She cried with a loud voice and said to Saul, "Why hast thou deceived me? for thou art Saul" (I Sam. 28:12). Samuel did not come up as the result of her incantations, but he came up because God wished through him to pronounce sentence on Saul.

There are two expressions in the speech of Samuel to Saul which agree with what we have seen elsewhere, about the condition of the dead in Sheol, as they understood it. Samuel said, "Why hast thou disquieted me to bring me up?" (I Sam. 28:15). Apparently his condition in Sheol was one of rest, perhaps of sleep (Gen. 47:30). That

Sheol was regarded as the abode of all the dead appears from Samuel's words, "Jehovah will deliver Israel also with thee into the hand of the Philistines; and tomorrow shalt thou and thy sons be with me" (I Sam. 28:19). Here is no distinction between heaven or hell. The good Samuel and the bad Saul and his sons go after death to the same place.

(6) THE MORALITY OF THE PERIOD.

The morality of the period was low in many respects. Brutality in war was almost universal (Josh. 6:21; 8:19, 24-29; 10:28-43; Judges 7:25; I Sam. 17:54, 57; 27:8-9, 11; 30:17). Some of the incidents are particularly offensive from our point of view. Joshua's treatment of the five kings who hid in the cave of Makkedah is an example. After rolling stones against the mouth of the cave and leaving them there to die (Josh. 10:18), he came back and brought his wretched victims out. He told the warriors to place their feet upon the necks of the kings. Then he said to the warriors, "Fear not nor be dismayed; be strong and of good courage: for thus shall Jehovah do to all your enemies against whom ye fight" (Josh. 10:25). After this speech he killed the five kings and hung them on five trees until the evening (Josh. 10:26). Equally offensive is the statement that Jehovah told Joshua to hock the horses of the enemy (Josh. 11:6, 9). After Joshua's death the people kept up the same brutality. They captured Adonibezek and cut off his thumbs and his great toes. He deserved it for he confessed that he had done the same thing to seventy other kings (Judges 1:7-8). We cannot say, however, that this makes the act any better. The treachery of Jael inviting Sisera into her tent and when he was asleep, driving a tent-pin through his temples is bad enough (Judges 4:18-22). But the way the prophetess Deborah gloried in Jael's treachery is more shocking still.

"Blessed above women shall Jael be,
The wife of Heber the Kenite.
Blessed shall she be above women in the tent.
He asked water and she gave him milk;
She brought him butter in a lordly dish.
She put her hand to the tent-pin,
And her right hand to the workman's hammer;
And with the hammer she smote Sisera, she smote
    through his head;
Yea, she pierced and struck through his temples.
At her feet he bowed, he fell, he lay,
At her feet he bowed, he fell:
Where he bowed, there he fell down dead.

So let all thine enemies perish, O Jehovah:
But let them that love him be as the sun when he goeth
    forth in his might."

(Judges 5:24-27, 31.)

The women and children of Jabesh-gilead were slain because the men did not go to the assembly at Mizpeh (Judges 21:11). Many were slain at Beth-shemesh because a few looked into the ark (I Sam. 6:19). It is said that Jehovah commanded Israel to kill the women and children of Amalek (I Sam. 15:2-3) and condemned Saul because he spared some of them (I Sam. 15:9-23). "Samuel hewed Agag in pieces before Jehovah in Gilgal" (I Sam. 15:33).

Most of these deeds of cruelty should be blamed directly to those who committed them, yet they should be judged according to the degree of knowledge which they had and not according to the vastly higher standards of Christianity or even of the prophetic period. There is no reason to think that they were hypocrites in imagining that Jehovah commanded them to do these things. As Paul thought that he ought to do many things contrary to the name of Jesus of Nazareth (Acts 26:9), breathing threatening and slaughter against the disciples of the Lord (Acts 9:1), so even the best of the Israelites of this time honestly thought that Jehovah told them to do these things and that they were honoring him by doing so. While we condemn their cruelty and frankly confess that they were mistaken in supposing that Jehovah commanded it, we should not fail to commend them for their zeal for the true religion. In so far as they sinned against light they deserve condemnation, but in so far as they sinned through ignorance they may be forgiven, as Paul was forgiven. He said, "Though I was before a blasphemer and a persecutor and injurious: howbeit, I obtained mercy because I did it ignorantly in unbelief" (I Tim. 1:13). In connection with the slaughter of women and children for deeds which they did not commit, it should be remembered that the preservation of their lives would have been as dangerous for the purity of Israel's religion as the sparing of the fighting men. The fact that these cruel deeds were performed sometimes by men like Samuel, who was one of the greatest instruments of divine revelation, should not trouble us. If David who sinned so outrageously was yet the man after God's own heart (I Sam. 13:14) and the sweet psalmist of Israel (II Sam. 23:1), if Peter who denied his Lord with oaths and curses (Mt. 26:69-75) became the rock upon which Christ built his church (Mt. 16:18), we need not be surprised that God showed the wonders of his grace in the choice of sinful and ignorant men as the instruments for revealing himself.

There are many examples of looseness in sexual relations. The spies lodged in the house of Rahab the harlot (Josh. 2:1). Although some have suggested that the word is used here to mean an innkeeper, the arguments for this view are very weak. Jephthah was the son of a harlot (Judges 11:1). Samson went in to a harlot at Gaza (Judges 16:1). He loved Delilah, forgetting his former wife (Judges 16:4, compare 14:20). Even a Levite had a concubine (Judges 19:2). A man of Gibeah was willing to give his daughter to the wicked men of that place in order to save his guest from the Sodomites (Judges 19:24). The Levite surrendered his concubine to their bestial pleasure (Judges 19:25) and when she was dishonored he cut up her body and sent it throughout the borders of the land to arouse the indignation of the Israelites against the men of Gibeah (Judges 19:26-30). The universal indignation against the town of Gibeah and all the tribe of Benjamin was partly moral (Judges 20:1, 8). The prophetess Deborah seems to have regarded virgins as legitimate spoil of war, for she sang,

"Have they not found, have they not divided the spoil?
A damsel, two damsels to every man."

(Judges 5:30.) Four hundred virgins, captives of war, were brought to the camp at Shiloh and given to the men of Benjamin (Judges 21:12, 14, 19-23). David practised polygamy (I Sam. 25:39-44; 27:3; 30:5, 18).

Jehovah is said to have told Samuel to say that he was coming to Bethlehem to sacrifice, when his real purpose was to anoint a king from the sons of Jesse (I Sam. 16:1-5). He no doubt thought sincerely that this suggestion came to him from Jehovah although in reality it came from his own deceitful heart. However, it is characteristic of the Old Testament to ascribe acts to Jehovah which we would refer to men or to natural causes. Secondary causes drop out of view and God is thought of as doing everything. Even Satan was his instrument. Thus while the chronicler says that "Satan stood up against Israel and moved David to number Israel" (I Chron. 21:1), the author of the book of Samuel says that "the anger of Jehovah was kindled against Israel and he moved David against them, saying, Go number Israel and Judah" (II Sam. 24:1). It was God who incited David to number the people, but he did not do the act himself, but through the instrumentality of Satan. So when it is said that Jehovah told Samuel to take a heifer and to say that he was coming to sacrifice (I Sam. 16:2), the meaning is that this idea providentially occurred to him. Similarly, the statement that an evil spirit from Jehovah troubled Saul (I Sam. 16:14-16, 23; 18:10; 19:9) is the Hebrew way of saying that in the providence of God the evil spirit troubled him. Since to the Hebrew, God is the Creator of all things, he must also have created evil. So the prophet boldly says in God's name, "I form the light and create darkness; I make peace and create evil; I am Jehovah that doeth all these things" (Isa. 45:7). Apparently the moral problem which arises in our minds from considering the good God as the creator of evil, did not disturb the Hebrews.

There are certain incidents in the time between Moses and David which indicate high moral standards. One of these was the faithfulness of Israel to the covenant with the Gibeonites. Even though the Gibeonites deceived Israel and the agreement with them was based upon falsehood, "the children of Israel smote them not, because the princes of the congregation had sworn unto them by Jehovah, the God of Israel" (Josh. 9:18). When the Amorites of the hill-country made a league against Gibeon, the Israelites came to their aid (Josh. 10:6-7). The faith and courage of Caleb, even when eighty-five years of age, command our highest praise. He coveted no easy place and no light task. He asked for his inheritance the hill-country of Hebron because the Anakim were there, saying, "It may be that Jehovah will be with me and I shall drive them out, as Jehovah spake" (Josh. 14:12). The same giants who had terrified the people long before (Num. 13:30-33) were to Caleb an opportunity for the exercise of faith and courage. The cooperation of the tribes east of the Jordan with their brethren has been mentioned in the Mosaic period (Josh. 22:1-9). One scarcely knows what points to speak of in the beautiful story of Ruth. The unselfish request of Naomi that Orpah and Ruth return to Moab (Ruth 1:8-9), gave occasion to Ruth's deathless devotion. "Entreat me not to leave thee and to return from following after thee; for whither thou goest, I will go; and where thou lodgest, I will lodge; thy people shall be my people, and thy God my God; where thou diest will I die, and there will I be buried: Jehovah do so to me and more also, if aught but death part thee and me" (Ruth 1:16-17). The willingness of Boaz that Ruth glean in his field (Ruth 2:9), his generous provision for her (Ruth 2:14-16), his courteous suggestion that it was she who showed kindness rather than he (Ruth 3:10), and his willingness to perform the part of kinsman (Ruth 3:13), are expressions of his noble character. The account of Hannah's piety (I Sam. 1: 11-12, 24-28; 2:1-10) was an appropriate introduction to the story of her great son. The faithfulness of Samuel and his readiness to deny himself when the people demanded a king (I Sam. 12) are the marks of his exalted character. There is something sublime in the confident words of David to the boasting giant Goliath, "Thou comest to me with a sword and with a spear and with a javelin: but I come to thee in the name of Jehovah of hosts, the God of the armies of Israel whom thou hast defied" (I Sam. 17: 45). The ideal friendship of David and Jonathan has become proverbial. "The soul of Jonathan was knit with the soul of David and Jonathan loved him as his own soul" (I Sam. 18:1; 20:17). Jonathan's saying, "Jehovah shall be between thee and me, and between my seed and thy seed forever" (I Sam. 20:42), may be taken as the model of friendship. The way that Jonathan encouraged David and "strengthened his hand in God" (I Sam. 23:16) shows that this friendship had its basis in religion. David's magnanimity in sparing the life of Saul his persecutor (I Sam.. 24:1-7; 26:7-12) shows that he at least was not vindictive. His sense of justice in giving an equal share of the spoil of war to those who protected the property at home (I Sam. 30:21-25) shows that he was broadminded. Perhaps the highest peak of all was reached in the saying of Samuel, "Far be it from me that I should sin against Jehovah in ceasing to pray for you" (I Sam. 12:23). This sin of omission was more heinous in his sight than a positive transgression.

CHAPTER IV.

THE RELIGION OF DAVID.

II Samuel, I Kings 1:1-2:11, I Chronicles 11-29,
Psalms 3-9, 11-30, 32, 34-36, 38, 40-41, 51-65,
69-70, 86, 101, 108-110.

While the events recorded in the first book of Samuel
are a necessary introduction to the classic age of David
and Solomon and shed great light on the religion of those
two kings and of Israel in their time, a clearer picture will
be presented if we begin the consideration of the religion
of David with his accession to the throne and that of the
religion of Solomon with his accession. The historical
sources of information for David's reign are found in
the second book of Samuel, the first book of Kings as far
as 2:11 and chapters 11-29 of the first book of Chronicles.
The Davidic Psalms are also an exceedingly valuable
source for the knowledge of David's personal religion and
to some degree for the knowledge of the religion of the
people. It is, however, a very difficult matter to determine
which Psalms were composed by David. While the arguments cannot be presented in detail, a few outstanding
considerations are stated.

In general the great reputation that David had as the
sweet psalmist of Israel (II Sam. 23:1) and the
organizer of the service of song (I Chron. 6:31; 16:7;

25:1; Ezra 3:10; Neh. 12:24, 36, 45-46; Amos. 6:5) make it reasonable to suppose that he was the author of many Psalms. In the Hebrew Bible seventy-three of them are ascribed to him as their author by titles, which, indeed, were not originally parts of the Psalms, but were added before the Septuagint translation was made. This ancient tradition should not be rejected except for adequate cause. If a Psalm in the first part of the Psalter has a Davidic title, strong reasons are required for denying this claim, because these Psalms were probably collected in the time of David or Solomon. On the other hand, a Psalm with a Davidic title in the latter part of the Psalter has the presumption against it, because most of the Psalms of this part were composed after the exile. Many Psalms contain no historical indications of date. In some cases the style, the words used and the grammatical forms are decisive for a late date. The ideas expressed and the liturgical character of a Psalm may favor a certain date. By the application of these principles, only one Psalm ascribed to David by its title, the 139th, could not possibly have been written by him. Next to this is the 103d, which almost certainly was not David's. Psalms 122, 124, 131, 133, 138, 140-145 were probably not his work. This leaves only three Psalms (108-110) which David wrote in the last book of the Psalter. There is no sufficient reason to doubt that Psalm 86 in the third book and Psalm 101 in the fourth book came from him. The only doubtful Psalms ascribed to him in the first and second books are 31, 37, 39 and 68. While it seems probable that he composed them, some things are against it. Hence we have not considered them as sources for the religion of his time. There is no good reason to doubt that the remaining 56 Psalms mentioned at the head of this chapter came from David.

Twelve Psalms are ascribed by their titles to Asaph (Psalms 50, 73-83), who was a prominent musical leader in David's time (I Chron. 15:16-19; 16:4-7). Psalm 50, which is the only Asaphitic Psalm in the second book, may· have been composed by him, although some of its expressions fit a later time better than his. The references to the desolation of the sanctuary in Psalms 74 (verses 3 and 7) and 79 (verse 1) show that they do not date from David's time. None of the other Asaphitic Psalms fits his time and probably they were not his work. The sons of Asaph succeeded him in the service of song (I Chron. 25:1-9), and the title "Sons of Asaph" became the name of a guild or society of temple musicians (II Chron. 14; 29:13) which lasted until after the exile (Ezra 2:41; Neh. 7:44). Possibly the Psalms ascribed to Asaph were composed by members of this guild, but if so this gives no indication of their dates.

Another such musical guild was called the "Sons of Korah" and eleven Psalms are ascribed to them (42, 44-49, 84, 85, 87, 88). Since this guild also probably dated from David's time and lasted several centuries, the title gives no definite indication of date. Psalm 88 has an additional title as the work of Heman, another musical leader of David's time (I Chron. 6:33; 15:17). While he may possibly have written it, it fits the time of the exile far better than that of David. Ethan, still another temple musician in the days of David (I Chron. 6:44; 15:17, 19), is mentioned as the author of Psalm 89. This, how-

ever, must be a mistake, for it speaks of the rejection of
the Davidic dynasty (verses 38-52), and probably dates
from the time of the exile. The Psalms of Asaph, of
the sons of Korah, of Heman and Ethan will be considered as sources for the religion of later periods.

(1) THE IDEA OF GOD.

David, like Moses, was a practical rather than a theo-
retical monotheist. Although he did not deny the existence of other gods, to his inspired thought they were not
to be compared to Jehovah. At first sight some of his
expressions seem to deny the existence of other deities.
Thus he adored God, saying, "Wherefore thou art great,
O Jehovah God; for there is none like thee, neither is
there any God besides thee, according to all that we have
heard with our ears" (II Sam. 7:22; I Chron. 17:20).
In that Psalm which is more surely Davidic than any
other, occurring as it does, not only in the Psalter, but
also in II Samuel, David says, "Who is God, save Jehovah? And who is a rock, save our God?" (II Sam.
22:32; Ps. 18:31). The poetic, rhetorical character of
these exclamations should not be forgotten. They indicate that in David's thought Jehovah was so vastly
greater than all other deities that in comparison with him
they did not deserve to be called gods. That such is the
true understanding of it seems evident from the words,

"There is none like unto thee among the gods, O Lord,
Neither are there any works like unto thy works;
Thou art great and doest wondrous things;
Thou art God alone" (Ps. 86:8, 10).

Here Jehovah seems to be among the gods, but incom-
parably greater than the others. His works are greater

than their works; but to admit that they have any works at all is to admit that they exist. David believed in the existence of other supernatural beings besides Jehovah. He called them gods because he had no other name by which to call them. Yet he felt that they did not deserve this exalted name. He probably did not concede to them any more power than he conceded to the angels who were, in a certain sense, supernatural beings. Hence while we should not call David a monotheist, in the sense that men are monotheists who deny the existence of Jupiter, Juno and other deities except the one living and true God, he was almost as true a monotheist as a Christian of our time who believes that although Satan is not omnipotent and God could crush him at any time, he is vastly more powerful than any man and is as great as the Greeks and Romans thought their lesser deities to be.

David thought of Jehovah as the Maker and Owner of the whole world.

"The earth is Jehovah's and the fulness thereof;
The world and they that dwell therein,
For he hath founded it upon the seas,
And established it upon the floods."

(Ps. 24:1-3). He spoke of the heavens as the work of Jehovah's fingers and the moon and stars as ordained by him (Ps. 8:3). He sang,

"The heavens declare the glory of God,
And the firmament showeth his handiwork."

(Ps. 19:1). He thought of Jehovah as the Judge not merely of Israel, but of all nations, for he said,

"Jehovah sitteth as king forever:
He hath prepared his throne for judgment.

And he will judge the world in righteousness,

He will minister judgment to the peoples in uprightness"
(Ps. 9:7-8). He looked forward to the time when all
nations shall be converted to Jehovah.

"All the ends of the earth shall remember and turn
　　unto Jehovah;

And all the kindreds of the nations shall worship before
　　thee.

For the kingdom is Jehovah's;

And he is the ruler over the nations" ˙
(Ps. 22:27-28).

"O thou that hearest prayer,

Unto thee shall all flesh come   .   .   .

Thou art the confidence of all the ends of the earth,

And of them that are afar off upon the sea"
(Ps. 65:2, 5).

"All nations whom thou hast made shall come and wor-
　　ship before thee, O Lord;

And they shall glorify thy name"
(Ps. 86:9).

Together with David's conception of the universal
dominion of Jehovah, he thought of him as residing in
the sanctuary at Jerusalem. So he sang,

"I cry unto Jehovah with my voice,

And he answereth me out of his holy hill"
(Ps. 3:4).

"Sing praises to Jehovah, who dwelleth in Zion"
(Ps. 9:11). The same conception is found in Ps. 5:7;
11:4; 14:7; 20:2; 28:2 and 65:1, 4. David also spoke
of God as having his throne in heaven and being there
(Ps. 11:4; 14:2; 18:9; 20:6; 53:2; 57:3). Indeed, the

two ideas did not seem contradictory to him, for he brought them together, saying,

"Jehovah is in his holy temple;

Jehovah, his throne is in heaven;

His eyes behold, his eyelids try, the children of men" (Ps. 11:4). While possibly the heavens are thought of in this verse as the temple, in any case it shows that David did not think of God as confined to the sanctuary at Jerusalem. The thunder was poetically designated the voice of Jehovah (Ps. 29:3-9).

Several attributes of God were mentioned by David. His power is referred to (Ps. 24:8; 65:6), which David, like others in Israel, regarded as omnipotence. He spoke of his eternity (Ps. 9:7; 10:16; 29:10), of his justice (II Sam. 22:26-28, 31; Ps. 7:11; 18:25-27, 30), his goodness (I Chron. 16:34; Ps. 25:8; 34:8), his mercy (I Chron. 16:34, 41; Ps. 5:7; 25:10; 32:10; 36:5; 86:15), and his truth (Ps. 19:9; 25:10; 36:5; 40:10-11). As a God of righteousness, he demands righteousness in his worshippers (Ps. 5:4-6; 7:3-5, 8-11; 11:4-7; 15:1-5; 24:3-6). God was thought of as doing everything that is done in the world, even when he does it through an instrument. Thus he is said to have moved David to number the people (II Sam. 24:1) even though Satan did it (I Chron. 21:1). There seems to have been a great reverence for the name of God as the revelation of his character (I Chron. 13:6; Ps. 20:1, 7; 54:1).

The Angel of Jehovah was less prominent in the time of David than in the previous period. There was a pestilence in the land. "And when the angel stretched out his hand toward Jerusalem to destroy it, Jehovah repented

him of the evil and said to the angel that destroyed the
people, It is enough; now stay thy hand. And the angel
of Jehovah was by the threshing-floor of Araunah the
Jebusite. And David spake unto Jehovah when he saw
the angel that smote the people, and said, Lo, I have sinned
and I have done perversely; but these sheep, what have
they done? let Thy hand, I pray thee, be against me and
against my father's house" (II Sam. 24:16-17). The
parallel account amplifies the statement of verse 17 that
David saw the angel. It says, "David lifted up his eyes
and saw the angel of Jehovah standing between earth and
heaven having a drawn sword in his hand stretched out
over Jerusalem. Then David and the elders clothed in
sackcloth fell upon their faces. And David said unto
God, Is it not I that commanded the people to be numbered? even I it is that have sinned and done very
wickedly; but these sheep, what have they done? let thy
hand, I pray thee, O Jehovah my God, be against me, and
against my father's house; but not against thy people,
that they should be plagued" (I Chron. 21:16-17).

At first sight the angel of this incident appears to be
an ordinary angel, a messenger or agent of Jehovah, not
a theophany. God is said to have sent the angel (I Chron.
21:15) and when he had destroyed sufficiently, God commanded him to stop. He was, apparently, subordinate to
God and not God himself. Upon the other hand, he is
called the angel of Jehovah, the usual title of the theophany (Gen. 16:7, 9, 10; 22:11, 15; Exod. 3:2; Num.
22:22-27, 31, 32, 34, 35; Judges 2:1, 4; 6:11, 12, 21, 22;
13:3, 13, 15-18, 20, 21), and the chronicler says that
David saw the Angel of Jehovah standing between earth

and heaven having a drawn sword in his hand stretched out over Jerusalem. The context makes it clear that this was not an appearance of Jehovah which was visible to physical sight. The angel which Jehovah sent was the pestilence from which many people died, from Dan even to Beersheba (II Sam. 24:15; I Chron. 21:14). Therefore he is called a destroying angel and is represented as having a drawn sword in his hand (I Chron. 21:15-16). David saw no physical form, but he perceived that Jerusalem was doomed unless the pestilence was stayed. The prophet Gad also saw no physical form (I Chron. 21:18), but received a revelation in his heart that if David built an altar unto Jehovah in the threshing-floor of Araunah (Called Ornan in I Chronicles) the pestilence would be stayed. The staying of the plague is spoken of literally in II Samuel (24:25), while in I Chronicles the same event is described in figurative fashion: "Jehovah commanded the angel; and he put up his sword again into the sheath thereof" (I Chron. 21:27). Thus the case is parallel to the statement of Isaiah, "the angel of Jehovah went forth and smote in the camp of the Assyrians a hundred and fourscore and five thousand; and when men arose in the morning, behold these were all dead bodies" (Isa. 37:36, compare II Kgs. 19:35). In both cases the destructive agent which God used was not a literal angel with drawn sword, but a pestilence.

There are two references to the angel of Jehovah in Davidic Psalms.

"The angel of Jehovah encampeth round about them
    that fear him
And delivereth them"
(Ps. 34:7).

"Let them (the enemies of Jehovah) be as chaff before
    the wind,
And the angel of Jehovah driving them on.
Let their way be dark and slippery,
And the angel of Jehovah pursuing them"

(Ps. 35:5-6). In both these Psalms the language is
figurative. The angel of Jehovah cannot encamp around
us in any literal sense unless he has an army of other
angels with him. The meaning which is evident from the
context is that God protects his people from harm. In
the other Psalm the angel of Jehovah is represented as
pursuing his enemies as chaff is driven before the wind.

There are a few references to the spirit in the reign of
David. "Then the spirit came upon Amasai, who was
chief of the thirty and he said, Thine are we, David, and
on thy side, thou son of Jesse: peace, peace be unto thee,
and peace be to thy helpers; for thy God helpeth thee"
(I Chron. 12:18). This was a case of inspiration. While
we know that it was the third person of the Trinity who
inspired Amasai, there is no hint of this Christian conception in the story, and the people of that time had no
idea of distinctions in the Godhead. By the spirit is
meant merely the overpowering influence of God himself.
Similarly, David sang in the little poem called his "last
words,"

"The Spirit of Jehovah spake by me,
And his word was upon my tongue"

(II Sam. 23:2). The Spirit of Jehovah here is not the
third person of the Trinity, but Jehovah himself inspiring
David to speak certain words. If the word referred to
were the word of the Spirit of Jehovah, the pronoun

would usually be feminine—not his word but her word—
for the Hebrew word for spirit is feminine, except in a
few cases. While the gender of the pronoun is not decisive, the next verse is,

"The God of Israel said
The Rock of Israel spake to me"
(II Sam. 23:3). Clearly this refers to the same action as
the previous verse. God speaking to David and the Spirit
of Jehovah speaking by (or in) David were one and the
same thing.

An illuminating passage occurs in David's great penitential Psalm.

"Create in me a clean heart, O God;
And renew a right spirit within me.
Cast me not away from thy presence;
And take not thy holy spirit from me.
Restore unto me the joy of thy salvation;
And uphold me with a willing spirit"
(Ps. 51:10-12). In each of these verses the spirit is
spoken of—a right spirit, God's holy spirit, a willing
spirit. There is only one other place in the Old Testament where the words "holy spirit" occur (Isa. 63:10-
11). Since holiness is often mentioned as an attribute
of God, it is not surprising that in these two places it
should be used of the spirit of God. Yet the holy spirit
in the Psalm and in Isaiah is not identical with the Holy
Spirit in the New Testament, even though the work of
the spirit of God in the old dispensation prepared for the
coming of the Holy Spirit. Even during the incarnation
"the Spirit was not yet given; because Jesus was not yet
glorified" (Jno. 7:39). The full manifestation of the

Holy Spirit in the world did not occur until the day of Pentecost (Jno. 14:16-17, 26; 15:26; 16:7, 13; Luke 24: 49; Acts 1:4-5, 8; 2:1-4, 14-21, 33). That day was to the life of the Holy Spirit what the birth of Christ was to the second person of the Trinity. Yet as the theophanies of the Old Testament were temporary foregleams of the incarnation of Christ, so the work of the spirit of Jehovah in the old dispensation foreshadowed and prepared for the coming of the Holy Spirit to abide with us forever. David and the other Old Testament characters had no conception of all this. To them the spirit of Jehovah was Jehovah himself exerting his influence in the world and among men. So David felt that when there was a right spirit within him, when God upheld him with a willing spirit, the spirit of God's holiness was his.

(2) THE CEREMONIES OF RELIGION.

When David came to the throne and for a large part of his reign there was no fully constituted sanctuary. The tabernacle which had been at Shiloh during the time of the judges (Josh. 18:1; Judges 18:31; 21:19) and was still there in the youth of Samuel (I Sam. 1:3, 24; 2:14) lost its glory when the ark was taken from it and captured by the Philistines (I Sam. 4:3-4, 21). During the reign of Saul, the high priest Ahimelech was at Nob (I Sam. 21:1) which was called the city of the priests (I Sam. 22:19). The tabernacle must have been there, because it was there that Ahimelech gave David and his men the showbread to eat (I Sam. 21:2-6; Mk. 2:26). In the reign of David the tabernacle and the altar of burnt-offering were in the high place at Gibeon (I Chron. 21:29); but how and when they were moved there we do not know. At any rate it was an imperfect sanctuary because the ark of the covenant, the symbol of Jehovah's presence, was not in it. Meanwhile the ark remained at Kirjath-jearim (I Chron. 13:5) which, however, was not a place of pilgrimage or public worship (I Chron. 13:3).

Toward the end of David's reign, after he had captured Jerusalem and made it his capital, and after he had subdued the surrounding nations, he brought up the ark from Kirjath-jearim to the tent which he pitched for it on Mount Zion (II Sam. 6:1-19; I Chron. 13:1-14; 15:25-16:1). This was an occasion of great rejoicing because it meant the reconstituting of the worship of Jehovah which had been lost when the ark was taken from the tabernacle at Shiloh nearly a century before. The record says that David set the ark in the tent that he had pitched for it (II Sam. 6:17; I Chron. 15:1; 16:1). In each case it is called a tent and not a tabernacle. The tabernacle and the altar of burnt-offering were still in the high place at Gibeon (I Chron. 21:29). There is no description of the tent which David pitched for the ark on Mount Zion. We do not know whether it had a holy of holies and a holy place as the tabernacle had. The ark was in the midst of the tent. When Zadok and the priests started to carry the ark from Jerusalem when David left the city during the rebellion of Absalom, at the king's command they took it back (II Sam. 15:24-29).

Although the presence of the ark in the tent of Jerusalem gave it preeminence, the tabernacle at Gibeon was not abandoned. The priests and Levites who were with David carrying the ark to Jerusalem (I Chron. 15:11-15) "offered burnt-offerings and peace-offerings before God" there (I Chron. 16:1). Nevertheless Zadok and the other priests continued to live "before the tabernacle of Jehovah in the high place that was at Gibeon" and they offered burnt-offerings there continually, morning and evening (I Chron. 16:39-40). This divided worship continued throughout David's reign. At the beginning of Solomon's reign he left Jerusalem and "went to Gibeon to sacrifice there, for that was the great high place" (I Kgs. 3:4). The chronicler mentions the two sanctuaries together in Solomon's time. "Solomon, and all the assembly with him, went to the high place that was at Gibeon; for there was the tent of meeting of God, which Moses the servant of Jehovah had made in the wilderness. But the ark of God had David brought up from Kirjath-jearim to the place that David had prepared for it; for he had pitched a tent for it at Jerusalem. Moreover, the brazen altar that Bezalel the son of Uri the son of Hur, had made, was there before the tabernacle of Jehovah; and Solomon and the assembly sought unto it" (II Chron. 1:3-5). This incident shows clearly that Jerusalem had not yet become the place of national worship.

David was not satisfied with this condition of things. He said to Nathan the prophet, "See now, I dwell in a house of cedar, but the ark of God dwelleth within curtains" (II Sam. 7:2; I Chron. 17:1). It was his desire to build a temple which would be a suitable dwelling for the ark and where the full sacrificial service could be carried on. At first Nathan consented, but later God told him to tell David that Jehovah did not desire him to build him a temple, but that his son should do so (II Sam. 7:5-13; I Chron. 17:3-12). The reason that David could not build the temple was because he was a man of war (I Chron. 22:8). So David did not build the temple; but he gathered a large amount of valuable material which Solomon could use for that purpose (I Chron. 22:14-16). He also at the divine command built an altar to Jehovah in the threshing-floor of Araunah the Jebusite where the temple later stood (II Sam. 24:18-25; I Chron. 21:18-26).

David divided the Levites into those who had the oversight of the house of Jehovah and those who were officers and judges (I Chron. 23:4). Some were doorkeepers and others were musicians (I Chron. 23:5). They were divided into courses by lot (I Chron. 23:6-32; 24:3-31; 25:8-31; 26:1-32). David also introduced music into the worship (II Sam. 6:5; I Chron. 13:8; 15:16-24; 16:4-6) and organized the choirs (I Chron. 25:1-8).

There were two high priests during David's reign, Zadok, the son of Ahitub, and Abiathar the son of Ahimelech. The last two names are reversed in II Sam. 8:17; I Chron. 18:16 and I Chron. 24:6. Zadok was descended from Eleazar, the third son of Aaron, while Abiathar was descended from Ithamar, Aaron's youngest son (I Chron. 24:3). Zadok belonged to the older line, but Abiathar to the line which had been on the highpriestly throne since Eli. Although the two priests are often mentioned together, the name of Zadok always comes first and he seems to have been favored by David (II Sam. 15:24, 35; 17:15; 19:11; 20:25; I Chron. 15:11). In David's old age, Abiathar sided with Adonijah who tried to seize the throne, but Zadok remained loyal to the king (I Kgs. 1:7-8). When Solomon was anointed, Zadok became the sole priest (I Chron. 29:22).

There is only one passage in the literature of David's reign where the sacred times of worship are mentioned. In describing the duties of the Levites the chronicler says that they were "to offer all burnt-offerings unto Jehovah, on the sabbaths, on the new moons and on the set feasts in number according to the ordinance concerning them, continually before Jehovah" (I Chron. 23:31). While it is strange that neither the sabbatical year, the year of jubilee nor any of the feasts is referred to in this time, we are not justified in concluding that they were not observed.

The only allusions to sacrifices in David's reign were in connection with important occasions. When David brought up the ark to Jerusalem he offered burnt-offerings and peace-offerings (II Sam. 6:17-18; 1 Chron. 16:1). When he built the altar on the threshing-floor of Araunah he offered burnt-offerings and peace-offerings (II Sam. 24:25; I Chron. 21:26). When Solomon was anointed "they sacrificed sacrifices unto Jehovah, and offered burnt-offerings unto Jehovah—even a thousand bullocks, a thousand rams and a thousand lambs with their drink-offerings and sacrifices in abundance for all Israel" (I Chron. 29:21). David displayed his knowledge of the ritual of the drink-offering when he exclaimed:

"Their sorrows shall be multiplied that give gifts to
    another god:
Their drink-offerings of blood will I not offer"
                                            (Ps. 16:4).

On another occasion he sang:
"Sacrifice and offering thou hast no delight in;
Mine ears hast thou opened

Burnt-offering and sin-offering hast thou not required.
Then said I, Lo I am come
In the roll of the book it is written of me:
I delight to do thy will, O my God;
Yea thy law is within my heart."

(Ps. 40:6-8.)

When he had committed his great sin he cried out in deep penitence:

"Thou delightest not in sacrifice; else would I give it:
Thou hast no pleasure in burnt-offering.
The sacrifices of God are a broken spirit:
A broken and a contrite heart, O God, thou wilt not
despise." (Ps. 51:16-17.)

When, however, there is genuine penitence in the heart, then God delights in the sacrifices of righteousness, in burnt-offering and whole burnt-offering. Then will they offer bullocks upon God's altar (Ps. 51:19).

In another Psalm, after praying for deliverance from his enemies and uttering imprecations against them, he says:

"I will praise the name of God with a song,
And will magnify him with thanksgiving.
And it will please Jehovah better than an ox,
Or a bullock that hath horns and hoofs."

(Ps. 69:30-31.)

These expressions show a fine appreciation of the proper relation between the ceremonies of religion and the religion of the heart. They show that through bitter experience David had learned the truth of Samuel's words, "Behold, to obey is better than sacrifice and to hearken than the fat of rams" (I Sam. 15:22). They also anticipate the noble teaching of the prophets (Isa. 1:11-13; Jer. 7:21-23; Hos. 6:6; Amos 5:22; Mic. 6:6-8).

David was the first to mention the custom of prayer toward the sanctuary at Jerusalem. He sang:

"In thy fear will I worship toward thy holy temple."
(Ps. 5:7.)

"Hear the voice of my supplications, when I cry unto thee,
When I lift up my hand toward thy holy oracle."
(Ps. 28:2.)

In Solomon's prayer at the dedication of the temple he referred repeatedly to prayer being offered toward it (I Kgs. 8:35, 38, 42, 44, 48). When Jonah prayed he looked toward the temple (Jon. 2:4). Daniel in Babylon prayed three times a day with his windows open toward Jerusalem (Dan. 6:10). Mohammed took this custom of praying toward Jerusalem from the Jews, but later he made the old heathen shrine at Mecca the direction of prayer. In every mosque there is a kibla (facing point) to indicate the direction of the holy city.

When Joab slew Abner, David declared that he and his kingdom were innocent of Abner's blood. "Let it fall," said he, "upon the head of Joab, and upon all his father's house; and let there not fail from the house of Joab one that hath an issue or that is a leper or that leaneth on a staff or that falleth by the sword or that lacketh bread" (II Sam. 15:29). The horror of this malediction was increased by the fact that anyone who had an issue or was a leper was ceremonially unclean and excluded from the sanctuary (Lev. 13:45-46; 15:1-18). There is an incidental allusion to the law of ceremonial uncleanness in the story of David's sin. The record says that David lay with Bathsheba "for she was purified from her uncleanness" (II Sam. 11:4). The reference is to the law that a woman was ceremonially unclean during the time of her menstrual issue and if any man lay with her at that time, her impurity would be upon him (Lev. 15:19-24).

Although it is not said that circumcision was practiced by the Israelites in David's time, the indirect evidence of it is very strong. The Philistines are referred to with contempt as the uncircumcised (I Sam. 14:6; 17:26, 36; 31:4; II Sam. 1:20; I Chron. 10:4). This clearly implies that the Israelites, like the Edomites, Moabites and Ammonites were circumcised. David secured Michal, the daughter of Saul, as his wife by bringing the king a hundred foreskins of the Philistines (I Sam. 18:24, 27; II Sam. 3:14).

The only reference to a vow in the narrative of David's reign is to that of Abalom. He said to David his father, "I pray thee let me go and pay my vow which I have vowed unto Jehovah in Hebron. For thy servant vowed a vow while I abode at Geshur in Syria, saying, If Jehovah shall indeed bring me again to Jerusalem, then I will serve Jehovah" (II Sam. 15:7-8). The suggestion that Absalom would pay his vow to Jehovah in Hebron was a plausible one, since he was born there (II Sam. 3:3). A vow was regarded as such a solemn thing (Num. 30:2; Deut. 23:21-23) that David did not refuse Absalom's request even though he may have suspected that it was only an excuse to make trouble for the king. There are several references to vows in Davidic Psalms (Ps. 22:25; 56:12; 61:5, 8; 65:1). The most typical instance is that in the sixty-first Psalm:

"Thou, O God, hast heard my vows:

Thou hast given me the heritage of those that fear thy name.

Thou wilt prolong the king's life;

His years shall be as many generations.

So will I sing praise unto thy name forever,

That I may daily perform my vows."

(Ps. 61:5-6, 8.)

David was evidently in danger of death. He made a vow that if God would prolong his life he would make a daily payment or offer a daily sacrifice of thanksgiving.

(3) PROPHECY.

In David's time the prophet was an officer of the royal court whom the king consulted about religious matters. So he consulted Nathan concerning the building of the temple (II Sam. 7:2; I Chron. 17:1). Gad, who was called David's seer (II Sam. 24:11; I Chron. 21:9), told the king the punishment which would come to him for numbering the people. The prophets of David's time were evidently accustomed to use musical instruments, for the leaders of the sacred music are said to have prophesied with harps, with psalteries and with cymbals (I Chron. 25:1). Heman, one of those leaders, was called "the king's seer in the words of God, to lift up the horn" (I Chron. 25:5). This probably means that he played musical instruments as the seers or prophets did. It seems to have been a part of the prophet's duty to write a history of the reign. So the chronicler says, "The acts of David the king, first and last, behold they are written in the history of Samuel the seer, and in the history of Nathan the prophet and in the history of Gad the seer" (I Chron. 29:29). This is the first mention of a prophet's writing a book. It was not, however, a book of prophetic discourses, but a history written from the prophetic standpoint.

(4) PERSONAL RELIGION.

The most remarkable phenomenon of David's religion is its large personal element. Although this element may be discovered in the deeds and words of Moses and of Samuel, the mass of the people merged their religion in the religion of the nation. Direct relation between the individual and Jehovah was almost unknown (see pp. 65-66). Although David, like other Israelites, felt himself a child of the covenant between Jehovah and Israel, it is surprising how seldom his Psalms speak of the nation or identify him with them. Usually he speaks in ths first person singular, only rarely in the first person plural (Ps. 60:1-3, 10-12; 65:4-5; 108:6). There are only a few references to the nation in surely Davidic Psalms (Ps. 3:8; 7:7-8; 9:11; 14:7; 18:43-45; 25:22; 28:9; 29:11; 51:18; 53:6; 59:13; 69:35; 108:8). Often he speaks of his enemies, pleads for deliverance from them and even calls down maledictions upon them. Since he was king they were also the enemies of the nation. Yet these Psalms do not often reflect a national consciousness. Some Psalms are impersonal, such as Psalms 8, 15, 19, 24, 29, 65, and 110, while others are partly personal and partly impersonal, such as Psalms 7, 11, 12,

18, 22, 34, 35, 36, 41, and 69. Yet by far the largest element in David's Psalms is personal. He prays for deliverance from trouble; he prays for victory over his enemies; he confesses his own sins; he thanks God for caring for him; he adores God for his greatness and his goodness. Under all circumstances he feels himself in the presence of God.

It is this personal element in the Psalms and particularly in David's Psalms which has given them their timelessness. The cry of the distressed soul, the confession of the sinner, the outpouring of thankfulness to God were not different in David's time from what they are today. His emotions as expressed in the Psalter are elemental and universally human. Space will suffice to mention only a few of the greatest examples.

Nowhere else did David express more simply and beautifully his genuine faith that Jehovah cared for him and would care for him in all future experiences than in the twenty-third Psalm.

"Jehovah is my shepherd; I shall not want.

He maketh me to lie down in green pastures;

He leadeth me beside still waters.

He restoreth my soul;

He guideth me in the paths of righteousness for his name's sake.

Yea though I walk through the valley of the shadow of death,

I will fear no evil; for thou art with me;

Thy rod and thy staff, they comfort me.

Thou preparest a table before me in the presence of mine enemies;

Thou anointest my head with oil;
My cup runneth over.
Surely goodness and lovingkindness shall follow me
all the days of my life;
And I shall dwell in the house of Jehovah forever."
These are not the words of a theorist in religion. They
are the sincere outpouring of the soul of a man who lived
in fellowship with God. They present the religion of
experience. God was very real to David, not a figment
of the imagination, not like a character in a book, but a
living person who was always present and near. As real
as David was to the sheep of his father Jesse, so real was
God to David. David did not draw his figure for Jehovah's relation to him from the symbolism of the tabernacle or the Mosaic ritual, but from the secular occupation of his daily life. God was to him not the God of
the sabbath and the feasts, not the God of the sanctuary
merely, but the God of every day, the God of the hills
and valleys about Bethlehem. God was to him not the
God of Israel only, whose guidance had brought them
through the wilderness to the land of promise, but his
own personal God who cared for him as tenderly as if
he had no one else to care for. David's heart thrilled
when he thought, "What I did for the sheep when I was
a lad, Jehovah does for me every day." This is no cold,
formal, ceremonial religion in which duty has the chief
place, correct but lifeless. It is rather the religion of
passionate love, the love of God for David, the love of
David for God. Its faith is not argumentative but like the
simple, unreasoning, almost stupid, faith of the sheep in
the shepherd. We cannot understand the religion of

Israel unless we appreciate the fact that there was a man with a faith like that which he had not gained by philosophical speculation and which he did not formulate in the abstract propositions of a creed, but which was to him as real and vital as his daily occupation. Nor was David alone in this faith. Perhaps the majority of the people, then as now, were too unspiritual, too much engaged with their own little lives, to see that God was in their lives; but we may be sure that many a Levite's heart was stirred as he sang this Psalm in the temple, and that many a humble believer was in conscious daily communion with Jehovah as truly as the shepherd king.

It is astounding that the man who wrote the twenty-third Psalm was guilty of the bestial sin and the cowardly, treacherous sin which he confesses in the fifty-first Psalm. Yet it is a passionate nature like his which displays such glaring inconsistencies. He was passionate in his love for God as he was passionate in his relation to Bathsheba, and he did not restrain either passion. Like Peter, who said, "If all shall be offended in thee, I will never be offended" (Mt. 26:33), and yet within a few hours denied his Lord with oaths and curses (Mt. 26:74), David was great in his sin as he was great in his religion. And, David made no attempt to conceal his sin when his conscience was awakened by the searching words of Nathan, "Thou art the man" (II Sam. 12:7). The same blood-red sincerity which found expression in the twenty-third Psalm speaks in the fifty-first.

"Have mercy upon me, O God, according to thy loving-kindness:

According to the multitude of thy tender mercies blot
out my transgressions.
Wash me thoroughly from mine iniquity,
And cleanse me from my sin.
For I know my transgressions;
And my sin is ever before me.
Against thee, thee only have I sinned,
And done that which is evil in thy sight;
That thou mayest be justified when thou speakest,
And be clear when thou judgest.
Behold I was brought forth in iniquity;
And in sin did my mother conceive me.
Behold, thou desirest truth in the inward parts;
And in the hidden part thou wilt make me to know
wisdom.
Purify me with hyssop, and I shall be clean:
Wash me and I shall be whiter than snow."

This is no formal confession of sin. No liturgical formula
could ever express it. It is the cry of a sin-stricken conscience which sees the facts as they really are. The holy
God and his own black sin were so real, so vivid to him
that his heart was in agony. The whole world was forgotten as his wicked soul was exposed to the light of
God's face. He cried out to Jehovah with no plea of
extenuating circumstances, no mathematical calculation of
his guilt. He cast himself helpless on the mercy and
lovingkindness of God. David was great in his repentance as well as in his sin. It is a tremendous evidence of
the virility of Israel's religion that there was a man who
could feel sin so deeply and repent so wholeheartedly as
David did. Dreadful as was the bad example of the king

in his awful sin, the example of his complete repentance must have stirred many another sinner to offer to God the sacrifice of a broken spirit, the broken and contrite heart which God does not despise (Ps. 51:17). It was out of the fulness of his own experience that David sang:

"Blessed is he whose transgression is forgiven,
Whose sin is covered.
Blessed is the man unto whom Jehovah imputeth not iniquity,
And in whose spirit there is no guile.

I acknowledge my sin unto thee,
And mine iniquity did I not hide.
I said I will confess my transgressions unto Jehovah:
And thou forgavest the iniquity of my sin."

(Ps. 32:1-2, 5).

It was in the same practical and genuine way that David met the many troubles of his life. Each one of them was the opportunity to pour out his troubled soul toward God. In an agony which foreshadowed the supreme agony of the ages he cried out:

"My God, my God, why hast thou forsaken me?
Why art thou so far from helping me and from the words of my groaning?
O my God, I cry in the daytime, but thou answerest not:
And in the night season, and am not silent."

(Ps. 22:1-2.)

It would not have been such an agony for him to be forsaken of God, if he had not known the consciousness of his presence.

On another occasion he prayed:

"Save me, O God, for the waters are come in unto my
  soul.
I sink in deep mire, where there is no standing;
I am come into deep waters, where the floods overflow
  me.
I am weary with my crying; my throat is dried:
Mine eyes fail while I wait for my God."
                                            (Ps. 69:1-3.)

Knowing the bitter dregs of sorrow, David also knew
what it meant to have his prayer for deliverance answered.
And when the answer came he was as genuine in his
thanksgiving as he had been in his cry for help. He says:
"I waited patiently for Jehovah;

And he inclined unto me and heard my cry.
He brought me up also out of a horrible pit, out of
  the miry clay:
And he set my feet upon a rock and established my
  goings.
And he hath put a new song in my mouth, even praise
  unto our God:
Many shall see it and fear,
And shall trust in Jehovah."   (Ps. 40:1-3.)

We can hear the echo of his own experience in his words:
"Many are the afflictions of the righteous;
But Jehovah delivereth him out of them all."
                                            (Ps. 34:19.)

Nor was it only that God delivered him out of his
afflictions. He knew what it was to have the uplifting
sense of God's presence even while the trouble was with
him, for he sang:

"In the day of trouble he will keep me secretly in his
 pavilion:
In the covert of his tabernacle will he hide me;
He will lift me up upon a rock."   (Ps. 27:5.)
What wonder that he sang:
"I will bless Jehovah at all times:
His praise shall continually be in my mouth.
My soul shall make her boast in Jehovah:
The meek shall hear thereof, and be glad."

(Ps. 34:1-2.)

In all these experiences David was not alone.   Many
others in his time, as in every time, have cried out of the
depths to God and have received his answer of peace.

One other quality of David's personal religion should
be mentioned, its spirituality.   It should not be compared
with the spirituality of the apostle John or of Paul.   Yet
considering the imperfect knowledge of God, which he
had, it is remarkable.   When David sang:

Surely goodness and lovingkindness shall follow me
 all the days of my life,
And I shall dwell in the house of Jehovah forever,"

(Ps. 23:6.)

he did not mean that he wanted to live all his days in the
tent at Jerusalem where the ark was or in the tabernacle
at Gibeon.   His desire was that he should be so conscious
of God's presence that the whole world would be God's
house to him and all he did would be as holy as the services of the sanctuary.   This is evident from his other
words:

"One thing have I asked of Jehovah that will I seek
 after:

That I may dwell in the house of Jehovah all the days
    of my life,
To behold the beauty of Jehovah,
And to inquire in his temple."   (Ps. 27:4.)

This was as noble an ambition as a man could have who
had not received the gift of the Holy Spirit.

(5) SIN AND FORGIVENESS.

As we have seen in David's personal religion, he made
a great advance in the conception of sin. Apparently he
regarded it as universal among men, for he said:

"Jehovah looked down from heaven upon the children
    of men,
To see if there were any that did understand,
That did seek after God.
They are all gone aside; they are together become filthy;
There is none that doeth good, no not one."
                (Ps. 14:2-3, compare 53:2-3.)

While sin in the Old Testament is mostly a matter of
conduct, David realized that it had its origin in a sinful
nature and that a mere change of conduct is not a sufficient remedy. This is what he meant when he said:

"Behold I was brought forth in iniquity;
And in sin did my mother conceive me.
Behold thou desirest truth in the inward parts;
And in the hidden part thou wilt make me to know
    wisdom."   (Ps. 51:5-6.)

He did not ask merely that his conduct be changed, but he
prayed:

"Create in me a clean heart, O God;
And renew a right spirit within me."   (Ps. 51:10.)

The real significance of sin according to David lay in the

fact that it was committed against God no matter who
the human victims were. After his sin against Bathsheba
he said to God:

"Against thee, thee only, have I sinned,
And done that which is evil in thy sight."

(Ps. 51:4.)

He realized the corrupting nature of sin, for he said:

"Innumerable evils have compassed me about;
Mine iniquities have overtaken me, so that I am not
    able to look up;
They are more than the hairs of mine head;
And my heart hath failed me."   (Ps. 40:12.)

David knew that only God can forgive sin and renew
the life. Therefore he prayed to him repeatedly for forgiveness (II Sam. 24:10; I Chron. 21:8; Ps. 25:7, 11,
18; 32:3-5; 51:1-2, 9). To his view the greatness of
sin was no reason that God would not forgive it. On the
contrary, he used this as an argument, saying:

"For thy name's sake, O Jehovah,
Pardon mine iniquity, for it is great."   (Ps. 25:11.)

He had a keen sense of individual responsibility for sin,
that no one should be punished except the guilty party.
When the pestilence broke out on account of his sin in
numbering the people, and many people and cattle died,
David said to Jehovah, "Lo I have sinned, and I have
done perversely; but these sheep, what have they done?
Let thy hand, I pray thee, be against me and against my
fathers' house" (II Sam. 24:17; I Chron. 21:17). He
realized that unless the sinner acknowledged his sin he
could not be forgiven (Ps. 32:5; 38:18; 51:3). He
seemed to appreciate the distinction between the sinful

condition and the sinful standing before God when he said:

"Blessed is the man unto whom Jehovah imputeth not iniquity

And in whose spirit there is no guile." (Ps. 32:2.)

He desired not merely that God would forgive him, but that his sinful nature might be changed (Ps. 51:9-10). He knew that no animal sacrifice, however great, was adequate to atone for sin (Ps. 40:6-8; 51:16-17; 69:30-31). God demands nothing from the sinner but genuine penitence, heartfelt thanksgiving and obedience to his will.

(6) THE MESSIANIC HOPE.

In the strict sense of the word, the Messianic hope dates from David, for the word Messiah which means "anointed," referred to the king of the David dynasty. Although the priest was called by this name in Leviticus (4:3, 5, 16; 6:22), it became the special title of the king from the time of Saul and onward (I Sam. 2:10, 35; 16:6; 24:6, 10; 26:9, 11, 16, 23, etc.; Ps. 2:2; 18:50; 20:6; 28:8; 84:9; 89:38, 51; 132:10, 17; Lam. 4:20; Hab. 3:13). Although the king on the throne at any time was called the Anointed, the Messiah, with the fall of the kingdom of Judah and the fall of the Davidic dynasty, it came to be the definite title of the Ideal King of David's line whose coming was told to him.

While this hope witnessed a great advance in David's time, it did not begin then. Its antecedents are found in the promise that the seed of the woman should bruise the serpent's head (Gen. 3:15), that in the seed of Abraham all the families of the earth should be blessed (Gen.

12:1-3), that the sceptre should not depart from Judah till he come whose it is (Gen. 49:10), and that a star should rise out of Jacob (Num. 24:17-19). Especially the last two of these predictions connect the hope with a coming king. There was, however, until David's time, a certain vagueness in the expectation. This was mostly cleared away by the predictions of his time.

The basal passage is connected with Jehovah's refusal to allow David to build a temple. At first the prophet Nathan gave his consent (II Sam. 7:3; I Chron. 17:2), but that night the word of Jehovah came to him that he was to tell the king that he should not build the temple (II Sam. 7:5-7; I Chron. 17:4-6). After promising success to David, he added these significant words, "When thy days are fulfilled and thou shalt sleep with thy fathers, I will set up thy seed after thee, that shall proceed out of thy bowels, and I will establish his kingdom. He shall build a house for my name and I will establish the throne of his kingdom forever. I will be his father and he shall be my son; if he commit iniquity, I will chasten him with the rod of men and with the stripes of the children of men; but my lovingkindness shall not depart from him as I took it away from Saul, whom I put away before thee. And thy house and thy kingdom shall be made sure forever before thee; thy throne shall be established forever. According to all these words and according to all this vision, so did Nathan speak unto David" (II Sam. 7:12-17; I Chron. 17: 11-15).

While this promise refers primarily to Solomon, it is evident that it looks far beyond him. The seed of David, like the seed of the woman (Gen. 3:15), and the seed of

Abraham (Gen. 17:7-8) was an inclusive term for all his descendants in successive generations. That is specially clear from the promise to establish his kingdom and his throne forever (II Sam. 7:13, 16; I Chron. 17:12, 14). David understood it in this sense, for in his prayer of thanksgiving he said, "Who am I and what is my house that thou hast brought me thus far? And this was yet a small thing in thine eyes, O Lord Jehovah; but thou hast spoken also of thy servant's house for a great while to come; and this too after the manner of men, O Lord Jehovah! . . . And now, O Lord Jehovah, thou art God and thy words are truth, and thou hast promised this good thing unto thy servant: now therefore let it please thee to bless the house of thy servant, that it may continue forever before thee; for thou, O Lord Jehovah, hast spoken it; and with thy blessing let the house of thy servant be blessed forever" (II Sam 7:18-19, 28-29; I Chron. 17:16-17, 26-27.

This promise of the eternal establishment of his dynasty remained the most precious possession of David. He realized that his family fell far short of being worthy of it. Hence there arose in his heart the conviction that if this promise was to be fulfilled there must come some day an Ideal King in his line. This thought is reflected in the beautiful poem called the last words of David.

"The God of Israel said,
The Rock of Israel said to me:
One that ruleth over men righteously,
That ruleth in the fear of God,

He shall be as the light of the morning when the sun
  riseth,
A morning without clouds,
When the tender grass springeth out of the earth,
Through clear shining after rain.
Verily my house is not so with God;
Yet he hath made with me an everlasting covenant,
Ordered in all things and sure:
For it is all my salvation and all my desire,
Although he maketh it not to grow."

(II Sam. 23:3-5.)

This Ideal King of David's line became the great hope of
the royal house and of Israel, the Messianic hope in the
strict sense. David referred to it in his farewell charge to
Solomon (I Kgs. 2:4). It lies at the basis of his typically
Messianic Psalms (Ps. 22, 40, 69). It found expression
in the 110th Psalm (verses 1-2, 5-7). It was preserved
in the memory of Solomon, who described the character
and work of the Ideal King (Ps. 72). It was expressed
repeatedly by the prophets (Isa. 9:6-7; 11:1-5; Jer. 23:5-
6; 33:17, 21; Amos 9:11; Mic. 5:2-6). The Ideal King
was spoken of as a branch on the Davidic family tree
(Isa. 4:2), and Branch came to be a proper name of the
Messiah (Jer. 23:5; 33:15; Zech. 3:8; 6:12). So closely
was the Messiah identified with David that sometimes he
was called David (Jer. 30:9; Ezek. 34:23-24; 37:24-25;
Hos. 3:5). The promise was called the "sure mercies of
David" and the future David is called "a witness to the
peoples, a leader and commander to the peoples" (Isa.
55:3-4). The term "Son of David" came to be a title
of the Messiah as is seen repeatedly in the New Testa-

ment (Mt. 9:27; 12:23; 15:22; 20:30-31; 21:9, 15; 22:41-45, etc.) On this account Matthew called his gospel for the Jews "the book of the generations of Jesus Christ, the son of David, the son of Abraham" and opened it with the genealogy of Christ through David (Mt. 1:1-16). The Revelation also refers to Christ as the Root of David (Rev. 5:5) and the root and offspring of David (Rev. 22:16).

This brief review of the passages which connect the Messiah with David shows how the promise that God would establish his throne forever became the chief source of the Messianic idea and of the idea of the kingdom of God. It is significant that it was renewed most emphatically by Jeremiah at the very time when in the literal sense the dynasty of David was about to be overthrown (Jer. 23:5-6; 33:14-22). This most spiritual of the prophets seems to have had some slight conception that the Messiah, the Son of David would not be a political, but a spiritual king. Yet his ideas on this subject fell far short of the New Testament idea of a spiritual King and a spiritual kingdom. If even the apostles, after hearing the parables of Our Lord concerning the kingdom, still fancied that he was a political king, we need not expect to find so highly spiritual an idea in the Old Testament. "Except one be born anew, he cannot see the kingdom of God" (Jno. 3:3). The things of the Spirit of God are "spiritually judged" (I Cor. 2:14).

An entirely new and very important element in the messianic expectation emerges in the time of David. It is the suffering of the Messiah at the hands of his persecutors. This idea is not as yet clearly predicated of the

coming King and probably David himself had a very faint
conception of it. Yet he, the type of Christ, as he passed
through sufferings at the hand of Saul and at the hand
of Absalom and other enemies, was guided by the Spirit
of God to use language which transcended his own experience and found its highest fulfilment in the sufferings
and death of Jesus Christ. The greatest of these passages is the twenty-second Psalm which is second only
to the fifty-third chapter of Isaiah as a clear prediction of
the suffering Saviour. In one respect it is superior even
to that wonderful prophecy, viz., that it lets us in to the
thoughts of the Sufferer in the time of his deepest anguish.
It was the more vivid because it was not an ideal picture
of a Sufferer in the future, but a literal picture of the
mental and physical anguish of David. The typical interpretation does not detract from its significance, but
adds to it. While there is a Messianic element throughout
the Psalm, the most important verses are as follows:

"My God, my God, why hast thou forsaken me?
Why art thou so far from helping me, and from the
    words of my groaning?
O my God, I cry in the daytime, but thou answerest
    not;
And in the night season and am not silent.
But thou art holy,
O thou that inhabitest the praises of Israel.
Our fathers trusted in thee;
They trusted and thou didst deliver them.
They cried unto thee and were delivered:
They trusted in thee and were not put to shame.
But I am a worm and no man;

A reproach of men and despised of the people.
All they that see me laugh me to scorn:
They shoot out the lip, they shake the head, saying,
Commit thyself unto Jehovah; let him deliver him:
Let him rescue him, seeing he delighteth in him.

I am poured out like water,
And all my bones are out of joint:
My heart is like wax;
It is melted within me.
My strength is dried up like a potsherd;
And my tongue cleaveth to my jaws,
And thou hast brought me into the dust of death.
For dogs have compassed me:
A company of evil-doers have inclosed me;
They pierced my hands and my feet.
I may count all my bones.
They look and stare upon me;
They part my garments among them,
And upon my vesture do they cast lots."

(Ps. 22:1-8, 14-18.)

Our Lord took the opening words of this Psalm as the expression of his feeling when he hung upon the cross because in their essence they were his (Mt. 27:46; Mk. 15:34). It was his Spirit who inspired them and in his sufferings, as in his triumph, he was the Son of David. While his quotation ended with the opening words, the following words reflect his mental anguish as he suffered for our sins. He was made sin on our behalf (I Cor. 5:21) and so he felt himself forsaken by the holy God (verse 3). By taking our sinful place he had lost his claim on God to answer his prayer. So intense was his agony that he was not like a man. "His visage was so marred more than any man, and his form more than the sons of men" (Isa. 52:14). He was a worm despised by all who saw him (verse 6). "They that passed by railed on him, wagging their heads and saying—He trusted in God; let him deliver him now, if he desireth him" (Mt. 27:39, 43). In his emaciation he seemed like water poured out and his bones seemed out of joint (verse 14). By his intense thirst, due to loss of blood, his strength was dried up, his tongue clave to his jaws and he was at the point of death (verse 15). His persecutors pierced his hands and his feet (verse 16). His skin was drawn so tight over his bones that he could count them and they forced themselves upon his attention (verse 17). His persecutors even parted his garments among them and cast lots for them (verse 18, compare Mt. 27:35; Jno. 19:23-24). Surely the cross cast its shadow over David when he wrote these words. Kirkpatrick was justified in saying, "These sufferings were so ordered by the Providence of God as to be typical of the sufferings of Christ; the record of them was so shaped by the Spirit of God, as to foreshadow, even in detail, many of the circumstances of the crucifixion" (Cambridge Bible on the Psalms).

In a general way the sixty-ninth Psalm presents a similar picture of the typical sufferings of David. It is, however, on a lower plane, since the Psalmist found it necessary to confess his sins (verse 5), and since he gave himself over to imprecating his enemies (verses 22-28). Like Christ, he knew that his enemies hated him without a cause (verse 4, compare Jno. 15:25). Like

Christ, he was mocked by his enemies (verses 11-12, compare Mt. 27:38-44). In a very literal sense, reproach broke Christ's heart (verse 20), for the immediate cause of his death was not the crucifixion, but the bursting of his heart due to his extreme mental anguish in bearing the sin of man (See Stroud's Physical Cause of the Death of Christ). They gave David sour wine to drink as they did the crucified Saviour (verse 21, compare Jno. 19:28-30). Besides these remarkable foreshadowings of the Man of Sorrows, David epitomized his own life and unknowingly epitomized the life of his Greater Son when he said, "The zeal of thy house hath eaten me up" (Ps. 69:9). It was his consuming passion to build a house for God where he could be worshipped in purity. This also was the consuming passion of Christ's life. All who opposed him became thereby the enemies of God. Hence this word of David which expresses the moving power of his imprecations against the enemies of God, was appropriately applied to Our Lord when in his righteous indignation "he made a scourge of cords and cast all out of the temple, both the sheep and the oxen; and he poured out the changers' money and overthrew their tables; and to them that sold the doves he said, Take these things hence, make not my Father's house a house of merchandise" (Jno. 2:15-16). Luke also was right in applying the words which David spoke concerning his enemies to Judas Iscariot who made himself the enemy of Christ (verse 25, compare Acts 1:20).

Second in importance only to the two Psalms just discussed is the brief Davidic poem which we call the one hundred tenth Psalm. The probable reason that it was not put in the Psalter of David's time is because it is a prophecy rather than a Psalm. The word rendered "saith" in the first verse is the common prophetic word. Yet this Psalm is Messianic throughout.

"Jehovah saith unto my Lord, Sit thou at my right hand,
Until I make thine enemies thy footstool.
Jehovah will send forth the rod of thy strength out of Zion:
Rule thou in the midst of thine enemies.
Thy people offer themselves willingly
In the day of thy power, in holy array:
Out of the womb of the morning
Thou hast the dew of thy youth.
Jehovah hath sworn and will not repent:
Thou art a priest forever
After the order of Melchizedek.
The Lord at thy right hand
Will strike through kings in the day of his wrath.
He will judge among the nations
He will fill the places with dead bodies;
He will strike through the head in many countries.
He will drink of the brook in the way;
Therefore will he lift up the head."

(Ps. 110:1-7.)

While the imagery of this Psalm, especially near its close, was drawn from the wars of David, it is not typical in the usual sense. David speaks of the Messiah not as his son, but as his Lord and he quotes the words of Jehovah to the Messiah, words which find their fulfilment in the sitting of Christ at the right hand of God, from which place of power he waits expectantly until all his enemies are subdued (Mt. 22:41-45; Mk. 12:35-37; Luke 20:41-44; Acts 2:32-36; Heb. 1:3). The Psalm also introduces the entirely new idea of the union of the priestly and kingly offices in the Messiah. As Melchizedek was both king and priest, so will Christ be (verse 4, compare Heb. 5:6, 10; 6:20; 7:1-17). Therefore the war in which he leads his followers is a holy war. The soldiers are clad in holy array (verse 3). Jehovah fights on their side (verse 5). Victory is sure.

It is only in a general way that the eighth Psalm should be regarded as Messianic. In it David refers to mankind, saying:

"When I consider thy heavens, the work of thy fingers,
The moon and the stars which thou hast ordained;
What is man that thou art mindful of him?
And the son of man, that thou visitest him?
For thou hast made him but little lower than God,
And crownest him with glory and honor.
Thou makest him to have dominion over the works of
thy hands;
Thou hast put all things under his feet."

(Ps. 8:3-6.)

While the son of man here is a designation of the race and not a reference to the Messiah, these words were appropriately applied to Christ by the author of the Epistle to the Hebrews, because Christ was the head of the human race. In becoming incarnate he took a position but a little lower than such divine beings as the angels. As the head of humanity, God will give him dominion over all things (Heb. 2:5-9). The Messianic title "Son of

Man," which Our Lord took for himself, is not derived
from this Psalm but from Dan. 7:13-14 (Jno. 12:34).

The Messianic element in the sixteenth Psalm is quite
different.   Praying to God for deliverance from trouble,
David receives the assurance that he will not die.   He
says:

"Thou wilt not leave my soul to Sheol;
Neither wilt thou suffer thy holy one to see corruption."
(Ps. 16:10.)

The same loving care which kept David for the time from
going to Sheol brought Christ back from Sheol after he
had gone there.   Here, as always, the antitype is greater
than the type, the fulfilment greater than the prediction.
Yet in view of David's typical relation to the Messiah,
Peter was justified in referring these words as well as
the verses before and after to Christ (Acts 2:24-31).

There is a typically Messianic element in the fortieth
Psalm.   Thanking God for his deliverance, David feels
that he must express his gratitude not by sacrifice and
offering, but by obedience.

"Sacrifice and offering thou hast no delight in;
Mine ears hast thou opened:
Burnt-offering and sin-offering hast thou not required.
Then said I, Lo, I am come;
In the roll of the book it is written of me:
I delight to do thy will, O my God;
Yea thy law is within my heart."   (Ps. 40:6-8.)

The words in which David expressed his devotion to God
are appropriately applied to the supreme consecration of
the Son of God when he left his father's throne and took
upon him our human nature to do God's will (Heb. 10:5-

10). The principal obstacle to the doing of God's will on David's part was that his ears were dull to hear and his will was dull to do it. Therefore God opened his ears to hear his voice and obey. Christ had no such need. He needed only a human body which he could use as the instrument of the divine will. When this was supplied, immediately he said, "Lo I am come to do thy will, O God." Thus the Hebrew ("Mine ears hast thou opened") was appropriate to David, while the Greek paraphrase in the Septuagint ("A body didst thou prepare for me") was appropriate to Christ. While the two versions are superficially quite different the essential idea is the same in both.

(7) THE FUTURE LIFE.

The literature of David's time shows a considerable advance beyond the earlier conception of the future life. When David was about to die he said, "I am going the way of all the earth" (I Kgs. 2:2), using the same expression which Joshua had used (Josh. 23:14). The old expression to sleep with one's fathers also occurs (II Sam. 7:12; I Kgs. 1:21; 2:10) and David prays, "Lighten mine eyes lest I sleep the sleep of death" (Ps. 13:3). Death is described as going to be with one's fathers (I Chron. 17:11). Sheol was dreaded as in earlier times. When in danger of death, David said, "the cords of Sheol were round about me" (II Sam. 22:6; Ps. 18:5) as though they were dragging him to Sheol. He counted it a great blessing that God had saved him from going to Sheol. "O Jehovah, thou hast brought up my soul from Sheol. Thou hast kept me alive that I should not go down to the pit" (Ps. 30:3). Here, as elsewhere, the pit is another name for Sheol. David thanked God, saying, "Thou hast delivered my soul from the lowest Sheol" (Ps. 86:13). Here, as in Moses' farewell song, the expression, "the lowest Sheol" (Deut. 32:22), does not imply that Sheol was divided into different parts. It means merely that it was in the lowest parts of the earth (Ps. 63:9). Looking into the face of death, David exclaimed, "Thou wilt not leave my soul to Sheol; neither wilt thou suffer thy holy one to see corruption" (Ps. 16:10). He had faith that God would not abandon him to the power of Sheol. Although to him this meant that he should not die it looked forward to a salvation from death for Christ through his resurrection (Acts 2:24-32). A possible hint of such a resurrection is also found in David's words, "As for me I shall behold thy face in righteousness; I shall be satisfied, when I awake, with beholding thy form" (Ps. 17:15). This awaking from the sleep of death and beholding the face and form of God was also the faith of Job (19:25-27).

While the righteous are to be saved from going to Sheol as long as possible and even when they go there, there is hope of their coming back, Sheol was thought of as the appropriate place for the wicked. "The wicked shall be turned back into Sheol, even all the nations that forget God" (Ps. 9:17). David prayed against his enemies, "Let death come suddenly upon them. Let them go down alive into Sheol; for wickedness is in their dwelling, in the midst of them" (Ps. 55:15). He charged Solomon concerning Joab, "Let not his hoar head go down to Sheol in peace" (I Kgs. 2:6), and concerning Shimei, "Thou shalt bring his hoar head down to Sheol with blood" (I Kgs. 2:9). These complementary ideas (1) that God would save the righteous from Sheol and (2) that he would bring the wicked to Sheol, while not indicating any distinction between the condition of the righteous and the wicked after death, nevertheless prepared for this doctrine.

The sweet psalmist of Israel had no conception of a blessed communion with God in the future life. He sang, "In death there is no remembrance of thee: in Sheol who shall give thee thanks?" (Ps. 6:5). He pleaded with God, "What profit is there in my blood, when I go down to the pit? Shall the dust praise thee? Shall it declare thy truth?" (Ps. 30:9). This is like the statement of Hezekiah after God saved his life (Isa 38:18-19) and those of later psalmists (Ps. 88:10-12; 115:17). Much as David dreaded Sheol and often as he prayed that his going there might be postponed, he knew that the day of his going must come. After the death of his child he said, "Can I bring him back again? I shall go to him, but he will not return to me" (II Sam. 12:23). Here is no resurrection faith. Beyond death is that bourne from which no traveller returns. Religion even to David was a matter of this life rather than the life to come.

(8) REVELATION AND INSPIRATION.

When David was fleeing from Jerusalem on account of Absalom's rebellion, Shimei cursed him. Abishai, one of David's followers, offered to slay Shimei but David answered, "Because he curseth and because Jehovah hath said unto him, curse David; who shall say, Wherefore hast thou done so? And David said to Abishai, and to all his servants, Behold my son who came forth from my bowels, seeketh my life; how much more may this

Benjamite now do it? let him alone and let him curse;
for Jehovah hath bidden him" (II Sam. 16:10-12).
Looked at superficially it would seem that Jehovah inspired Shimei to curse David, actually tempted him to do
wrong. This seems a contradiction to the statement that
God does not tempt men to do evil (Jas. 1:13). If the
inspiration of David was nothing more than this, it gives
us no guarantee of a genuine divine revelation in his
words. Here, however, as elsewhere in the Old Testament, Jehovah is represented as doing that which he only
permits. Thus Jehovah moved David to number the people
(II Sam. 24:1) by permitting Satan to tempt him (I
Chron. 21:1). He permitted Joseph's brethren to sell
him into Egypt and overruled their wickedness for the
deliverance of Egypt from famine (Gen. 45:5; 50:20).
He allowed Judas to betray Christ and the Roman soldiers
to crucify him, turning the results of their sin into the
means of saving mankind (Acts 2:23). So God makes
the wrath of man to praise him (Ps. 76:10). So he
used Shimei to chastise David. This was a very different
thing from the direct influence of God upon David and
other inspired men by which the Almighty used them as
the instruments of revelation. The cursing of Shimei
was providential. So God used the bad advice of Hushai
as a means to bring about the destruction of Absalom
(II Sam. 17:14).

David gave to Solomon the plan of the temple which
"he had by the Spirit" (I Chron. 28:12). It is clear that
this does not refer to any external revelation to David.
Jehovah worked upon the mind of David so that he was
convinced that the plan of the temple which he gave to

Solomon was Jehovah's plan. Therefore the chronicler wrote, "All this, said David have I been made to understand in writing from the hand of Jehovah, even all the works of this pattern" (I Chron. 28:19). David knew that the thoughts of his mind were not of his own making but came from God. Therefore he sang, "The Spirit of Jehovah spake by me, and his word was upon my tongue" (II Sam. 23:2).

(9) SATAN.

The first mention of Satan by name occurs in the time of David. The chronicler says, "Satan stood up against Israel and moved David to number Israel" (I Chron. 21:1). David prayed against his enemy (or possibly David quotes the words of his enemy against him), "Let Satan stand at his right hand" (Ps. 109:6). The Revised Version renders this word "an adversary" in the latter passage and possibly it should be a common noun in the former verse. It occurs as a common noun several times (Num. 22:22, 32; I Sam. 29:4; II Sam. 29:22; I Kgs. 11:14, 23, 25). In both the passages quoted it is used without the definite article, while in Job (1:6-9, 12; 2:1-4, 6-7) and Zechariah (3:1-2) it has the article. Satan is preeminently the adversary of men. Although the name does not occur until David's time, it was he who tempted Eve (Gen. 3:1-4, see p. 21). He is not represented as omnipotent. Yet he has power to suggest evil thoughts to men. He has, however, only that power which Jehovah permits him to exercise, for the prophetic writer dropping out the secondary cause says that Jehovah moved David to number Israel (II Sam. 24:1). The conception of Satan is a judicial one. According to the custom of the court, he stood up to act as an adversary against Israel (I Chron. 21:1). David wished Satan to stand at the right hand of his enemy (Ps. 109:6) which was the position of the accuser in court (Zech. 3:1). While the conception of Satan in David's time was not developed into that of the Prince of all the forces of wickedness in the world, he seems to have thought of him as the tempter, accuser and adversary of the people of God.

(10) THE MORALITY OF DAVID AND HIS TIME.

The character of David should be judged by the moral standards which he possessed. He slew the Amalekite who confessed that he had killed Saul (II Sam. 1:14-16) and the men who killed Ish-bosheth, Saul's son, David's men brutally cutting off their hands and their feet (II Sam. 4:5-12). He hocked the horses of his enemies (II Sam. 8:4; I Chron. 18:4). He cut the Ammonites with saws, harrows, and axes (I Chron. 20:3).

On the other hand, David showed his magnanimity by mourning for Saul who had persecuted him so cruelly (II Sam. 1:11-12). This magnanimity is heightened by the fact that David coupled his mourning for Saul his persecutor with that for Jonathan his best friend. The dirge he sang for them is the most beautiful in scripture (II Sam. 1:19-27). He blessed the men of Jabesh-gilead who buried Saul (II Sam. 2:4-7). He lamented for Abner who had been his enemy (II Sam. 3:33-34) and "said unto his servants, Know ye not that there is a prince and a great man fallen this day in Israel?" (II Sam. 3:38). He condemned Joab for executing vengeance on Abner (II Sam. 3:28-30). He inquired whether there were any survivors of the house of Saul that he might show kind-

ness to them for Jonathan's sake (II Sam. 9:1); and
when he heard of Mephibosheth, Jonathan's son who
was lame, he gave him back all the property of Saul and
had him eat continually at the king's table (II Sam. 9).
He showed a friendly attitude toward the king of Ammon,
an attitude which was so much above the custom of the
time that the Ammonites thought he had some ulterior
purpose (II Sam. 10:1-5; I Chron. 19:1-5). He loved
his son Absalom in spite of his evil deeds and his rebellion
(II Sam. 13:39; 14:1). Even though he had to defend
his government against Absalom he told the generals,
"Deal gently for my sake with the young man, even with
Absalom" (II Sam. 18:5, compare verse 12). When news
came from the war, his first concern was not for his kingdom but for his wayward son; and when he knew that
Absalom was dead, he cried out in agony, "O my son,
Absalom, my son, my son Absalom! would I had died for
thee, O Absalom, my son, my son!" (II Sam. 18:33).
No other verse of the Old Testament opens up the heart
of God toward sinful men like this. David forgave Shimei who had cursed him (II Sam. 19:16-23). Yet he
charged Solomon to kill him after his death (I Kgs. 2:9).

Some of the imprecations of David's Psalms are against
the enemies of God.

"There is no faithfulness in their mouth;
Their inward part is very wickedness;
Their throat is an open sepulchre;
They flatter with their tongue.
Hold them guilty, O God;
Let them fall by their own counsels;

Thrust them out in the multitude of their transgressions;
For they have rebelled against thee."

(Ps. 5:9-10.)

"The nations are sunk down in the pit that they made:
In the net which they hid is their own foot taken.
Jehovah hath made himself known, he hath executed
    judgment:
The wicked is snared in the work of his own hands.
The wicked shall be turned back into Sheol,
Even all the nations that forget God."

(Ps. 9:15-17.)

"Give them·according to their work, and according to
    the wickedness of their doings:
Give them after the operation of their hands;
Render to them their desert.
Because they regard not the works of Jehovah,
Nor the operation of his hands,
He will break them down and not build them up."

(Ps. 28:4-5.)

Sometimes, however, David's imprecations were personal
and vindictive.

"Strive thou, O Jehovah, with them that strive with me:
Fight thou against them that fight against me.
Take hold of shield and buckler,
And stand up for my help.
Draw out also the spear and stop the way against them
    that pursue me:
Say unto my soul, I am thy salvation.
Let them be put to shame and brought to dishonor
    that seek after my soul:

Let them be turned back and confounded that devise
   my hurt.
Let them be as chaff before the wind,
And the angel of Jehovah driving them on.
Let their way be dark and slippery,
And the angel of Jehovah pursuing them.
For without cause have they hid for me their net in
   a pit;
Without cause have they digged a pit for my soul.
Let destruction come upon him unawares;
And let his net that he hath hid catch himself:
With destruction let him fall therein.
And my soul shall be joyful in Jehovah:
It shall rejoice in his salvation."

(Ps. 35:1-9.)

The great provocation that David had is evident in some
of the Psalms.

"It was not an enemy that reproached me;
Then I could have borne it:
Neither was it he that hated me that did magnify him-
   self against me;
Then I would have hid myself from him:
But it was thou, a man mine equal,
My companion and my familiar friend.
We took sweet counsel together;
We walked in the house of God with the throng.
Let death come suddenly upon them,
Let them go down alive in Sheol;
For wickedness is in their dwelling in the midst of
   them.

As for me I will call upon God;
And Jehovah will save me."

(Ps. 55:12-16.)

"The righteous shall rejoice when he seeth the ven-
geance:
He shall wash his feet in the blood of the wicked;
So that men shall say, Verily there is a reward for
the righteous:
Verily there is a God that judgeth in the earth."

(Ps. 58:10-11.)

While this is far from the spirit of Christ who commanded us to love our enemies, we need not be severe in
our condemnation of David. He lived in a crude world
which knew no law but that of retaliation toward one's
enemies. He knew very little of the love of God for
sinners and almost nothing at all of the rewards and punishment of the future life. Hence his desire for the
punishment of his enemies was for the most part in this
life.

David's record in sexual relations was far from good.
He took other wives besides the two he had before ascend-
ing the throne (II Sam. 3:2-5). He also had concubines
(II Sam. 5:13; I Chron. 14:3). His great sin against
Bathsheba and Uriah is told without excuse and it cannot
be defended (II Sam. 11). "The thing that David had
done displeased Jehovah" (II Sam. 11:27) and Nathan
condemned him unsparingly (II Sam. 12:1-14). His
statement to David, "thou hast given great occasion to the
enemies of Jehovah to blaspheme" (II Sam. 12:14) shows
that Nathan had a lofty idea of the duty of the king to
set a worthy example to his people. David repented sin-

cerely for these sins and freely confessed his guilt (Ps. 51).

The slaying of Uzzah for touching the ark when the oxen stumbled seems unnecessarily severe (II Sam. 6:6-8; I Chron. 13:9-11), but was doubtless calculated to teach Israel the sanctity of the ark. It seems unjust to us that Jehovah punished David for numbering the people (II Sam. 24:10-14), although he had moved him to do it (II Sam. 24:1). This is explained, however, by the statement of the chronicler that God was not the direct cause of David's act. He merely allowed Satan to tempt him (I Chron. 21:1).

The fact that the sanctuary at Jerusalem was supported in part by spoil taken in war (I Chron. 26:27) shows the low moral and religious standards of the time. The wickedness in David's family is another such indication. Amnon, one of David's sons, treacherously forced his half-sister Tamar (II Sam. 13:1-19). In vengeance Absalom caused Amnon's death (II Sam. 13:20-29). Joab, David's general, started to kiss Amasa and then killed him (II Sam. 20:9-10).

The followers of David seem to have been devoted to him. When there was war, they said, "Thou shalt go no more out with us to battle, that thou quench not the lamp of Israel" (II Sam. 21:17). The noblest example of such devotion was Ittai the Gittite, who stayed loyally by him during the rebellion of Absalom, saying, "As Jehovah liveth, and as my lord the king liveth, surely in what place my lord the king shall be, whether for death or for life, even there also will thy servant be" (II Sam. 15:21).

CHAPTER V.

THE RELIGION OF SOLOMON.

I Kings 2:12-11:43, II Chronicles 1-9, Psalms 72 and
127, Proverbs 1-29, Song of Solomon.

The special sources for our knowledge of the religion
of Solomon and Israel in his time are those indicated
above. Yet even if these sources contain no indication as
to the continuance of some ceremony of earlier times or
some earlier religious idea, it is to be presumed that this
ceremony was observed in Solomon's time and this religious idea was held unless there is some indication
against it. This is particularly true if the ceremony or
the idea in question is mentioned after Solomon's time
as well as before it. It is unreasonable to expect a full
account of the religion, both in its external and its spiritual
aspects, in each period. We mention only those things
which are new in this period or which mark a change
from the religion of earlier times. To get a complete
picture of the religion of Solomon it is not sufficient to
study the literature of his time. One should familiarize
himself with the religion of Israel in earlier times, particularly the time of David. There is every reason to
believe that the religion of Solomon's day differed very
little from that of his father. The chief changes came
in connection with (1) the building of the temple and
(2) the beginning of a new class of writing which is
commonly called the Wisdom Literature.

Solomon was the founder of this kind of literature
and the book of Proverbs is its oldest example. The
book of Job is a problem book and has important points

of resemblance to Proverbs (compare, for example, Job 28 with Proverbs 8). While there are features in the book of Job which seem to indicate the time of Solomon or soon after, the date of the book is so uncertain that it is safer to regard it as a source for the religion of a later time. The only other example of the Wisdom Literature in the canonical writings of the Old Testament is the book of Ecclesiastes. Linguistic considerations show conclusively that Solomon could not have written it, and indeed when properly understood the book does not claim to have been written by him. The author of a much later time used the great name of Solomon as a literary device. The case of the book of Proverbs—or at least the greater part of it—is quite different. Although the book contains evidence of editing in the time of Hezekiah (Prov. 25:1), the proverbs themselves are presented as the work of Solomon (Prov. 1:1; 10:1, compare I Kgs. 4:32) and there is no sufficient reason for denying this claim. Chapter 30, by its heading, is ascribed to Agur and chapter 31 to King Lemuel. Although neither of these men is known elsewhere, the position of the chapters after the proverbs which "the men of Hezekiah copied out" (Prov. 25:1) makes it probable that they were at least as late as Hezekiah. Internal indications favor a date later still. Concerning Psalms 72 and 127 and the Song of Solomon, it is sufficient to state that they claim to be the work of Solomon and that this claim is not contradicted by a study of their contents.

(1) THE IDEA OF GOD.

It might be expected that the building of Solomon's

temple and the establishment of the ritual in greater splendor than ever before would have lowered the conception of the spirituality of Jehovah. The magnificence of the ritual may have helped some worshippers, as it did Isaiah, some two and a half centuries later, to get a vision of the Lord high and lifted up with his train filling the temple (Isa. 6:1). To most of them it probably had the opposite effect. Some remembered the simple tabernacle at Gibeon (II Chron. 1:3-6) with its ancient associations from the time of Moses, a tabernacle so simple that it left room for the greatness of God. This new and splendid temple, on the other hand, absorbed the attention to the exclusion of God. That Solomon at least did not yield to this tendency is evident from his prayer at the dedication of the sanctuary, a prayer which marks a distinct advance in the idea of God and prepares for the noble conceptions of his spirituality in the writings of the prophets and of the New Testament. This is seen in three particulars:

(a) The Uniqueness of Jehovah. As in David's time, Jehovah is regarded as vastly superior to all other deities, although the existence of those deities is not denied. Thus Solomon prays: "O Jehovah, the God of Israel, there is no god like thee in heaven above or on earth beneath who keepest covenant and lovingkindness with thy servants that walk before thee with all their heart" (I Kgs. 8:23; compare also I Kgs. 8:60; II Chron. 2:5-6; 6:14).

(b) The Transcendence of Jehovah. Solomon realized the insufficiency of the temple and indeed of any building or place to contain Jehovah, for he said: "Will God in very deed dwell on the earth? Behold heaven and the heaven of heavens cannot contain thee; how much less this house that I have builded" (I Kgs. 8:27; II Chron. 2:5-6; 6:18). Although the temple was the place of Jehovah's name, the king did not think of God as dwelling in the temple. He prayed "that thine eyes may be open toward this house night and day" (I Kgs. 8:29; II Chron. 6:20). Although prayer was to be made in the temple and toward the temple, Jehovah would hear and answer in heaven His dwelling place (I Kings 8:22, 29, 30, 32, 34, 36, 39, 43, 45, 49, 54; II Chron. 6:21, 23 25, 30, 33, 35, 39).

(c) The Universality of Jehovah. This appears from the fact that Solomon expected foreigners to worship Jehovah at Jerusalem. He prayed, "Moreover concerning the foreigner, that is not of thy people Israel, when he shall come out of a far country for thy name's sake (for they shall hear of thy great name, and of thy mighty hand, and of thine outstretched arm) ; when he shall come and pray toward this house; hear thou in heaven thy dwelling-place and do according to all that the foreigner calleth to thee for; that all the peoples of the earth may know thy name, to fear thee as doth thy people Israel and that they may know that this house which I have built is called by thy name" (I Kgs. 8:41-43; II Chron. 6:32-33). Jehovah was to be the God of all men.

Besides this great prayer there are other indications of the loftiness of Solomon's conception of the deity. He says :

"Jehovah by wisdom founded the earth ;

By understanding he established the heavens,

By his knowledge the depths were broken up,
And the skies drop down the dew."

(Prov. 3:19-20.)

Jehovah not only fashioned the world into its present
form, but he brought into being the raw material, the
clods from which it was made, for Wisdom personified
says that he existed

"While as yet he had not made the earth, nor the fields,
Nor the beginning of the dust of the world."

(Prov. 8:26.)

Jehovah's control of everything is boldly affirmed.

"Jehovah hath made everything for its own end,
Yea, even the wicked for the day of evil."

(Prov. 16:4.)

Without him all human effort is vain.

"Except Jehovah build the house,
They labor in vain that build it:
Except Jehovah keep the city,
The watchman waketh but in vain."

(Ps. 127:1.)

He is the All-seeing One.

"The eyes of Jehovah are in every place,
Keeping watch upon the evil and the good."

(Prov. 15:3.)

"Sheol and Abaddon are before Jehovah;
How much more then the hearts of the children of
men!"   (Prov. 15:11.)

Jehovah is the arbiter in all human matters.

"The lot is cast into the lap;
But the whole disposing thereof is of Jehovah."

(Prov. 16:33.)

"The refining pot is for silver, and the furnace for gold;
But Jehovah trieth the hearts."   (Prov. 17:3.)
"Every way of a man is right in his own eyes;
But Jehovah weigheth the hearts."   (Prov. 21:2.)
"If thou sayest, Behold we knew not this;
Doth not he that weigheth the hearts consider it?
And he that keepeth thy soul, doth not he know it?
And shall not he render to every one according to his
work?"   (Prov. 24:12.)
That which happened was regarded as being from Je-
hovah. Thus Adonijah said to Bathsheba, "Thou knowest
that the kingdom was mine and that all Israel set their
faces on me, that I should reign: howbeit the kingdom
is turned about, and is become my brother's; for it was
his from Jehovah" (I Kgs. 2:15).

In the song of Solomon beneath the passionate love of
himself and Shulamite, the king depicts love in its noblest
form between God and the devout soul. "It cannot be
doubted," says Andrew Harper in his Commentary on
the Song, "that there are in the literatures of the East
tales of love between man and woman, dealing with real
persons or at least with persons believed to be real, which
nevertheless are intended to teach how the soul ought to
love God." Dr. Harper gives examples of such tales
from Persian and other literatures. As in them the mystical sense is not stated distinctly, but is to be inferred.
Possibly there is a hint of it in the statement that love is
"a very flame of Jehovah" (Song 8:6). Thus in this
marriage song may be seen an evidence of that true religion which transcends all ceremonies and consists in
the communion of the soul with God.

(2) THE CEREMONIES OF RELIGION.

In the beginning of Solomon's reign the worship of Jehovah was carried on in many places. "The people sacrificed in the high places, because there was no house built for the name of Jehovah until those days. And Solomon loved Jehovah, walking in the statutes of David his father: only he sacrificed and burnt incense in the high places" (I Kgs. 3:2-3). The greatest of the high places was at Gibeon where the tabernacle was (I Kgs. 3:4-5; II Chron. 1:3). At the same time the ark which had come down from the time of Moses was in the tent which David pitched for it at Jerusalem and the altar from the same time was in front of it (I Kgs. 3:15; I Chron. 1:4-5). Worship was carried on at both places.

Carrying out the wishes of David, Solomon built a magnificent temple on Mount Zion on the threshing floor of Araunah the Jebusite (I Kgs. 6; II Chron. 3). For this purpose David had gathered a large amount of material (I Chron. 22:2-5; 28:11-29:9). Solomon enlisted a large force of workmen in Israel (I Kgs. 5:13-17). Hiram, king of Tyre, also gathered material and furnished workmen for him (I Kgs. 5:1-12, 18). He began the building in the fourth year of his reign (I Kgs. 6:1) and finished it in the eleventh year (I Kgs. 6:38).

In general the plan of the temple was the same as that of the tabernacle (see pp. 76-80), but the materials of which it was made were different and the building was larger and much more handsome. The outer walls were of stone while the interior and the roof were of wood. The holy of holies was a perfect cube, as in the tabernacle, to symbolize the perfection of Jehovah who dwelt there.

It was, however, twenty cubits in each dimension, while that in the tabernacle had been ten cubits (I Kgs. 6:16, 20). It was overlaid with pure gold. The ark of the covenant was placed there (I Kgs. 8:6); but there were new and much larger cherubim over it (I Kgs. 6:23-28; 8:7; II Chron. 3:10-13). The partition between the holy place and the holy of holies was not a curtain as in the tabernacle, but was made of cedar wood with doors of olive wood (I Kgs. 6:16, 31-32).

The holy place was forty cubits long by twenty wide and thirty high (I Kgs. 6:17; II Chron. 3:3, 8). The holy place of the tabernacle had been only ten by twenty cubits. The altar of incense, as in the tabernacle, stood in the holy place just before the partition which separated it from the holy of holies. It was made of cedar covered with gold (I Kgs. 6:20, 22), while the one in the tabernacle had been made of acacia wood. While the tabernacle had only one candlestick which stood on the south side of the holy place, the temple had ten candlesticks, five of them standing on one side of the holy place and five on the other side (I Kgs. 7:49; II Chron. 4:7). There were also ten tables for showbread, five of which stood on one side of the holy place and five on the other (II Chron. 4:8, 19). Apparently, however, only one of these tables was used at a time (II Chron. 13:11).

There was a three-story building against the two sides and the back of the temple which was used for storage and for officials (I Kgs. 6:5-10). A handsome portico was in front of the temple and two brazen pillars called Boaz ("In him is strength") and Jachin ("He doth establish") stood by it (I Kgs. 7:15-22; II Chron. 3:15,

17). The temple had two courts, the court of the priests and the great court (II Chron. 4:9, compare II Kgs. 23:12; Jer. 36:10). These courts were separated by a wall of stone and cedar (I Kgs. 6:36; 7:12). The brazen altar stood in the court of the priests (I Kgs. 8:64; II Kgs. 16:14; II Chron. 15:8). It was much larger than that in the court of the tabernacle, being twenty cubits each way and ten cubits high (II Chron. 4:1). A round molten sea, ten cubits in diameter, also stood in the priest's court (I Kgs. 7:23-37) and was used for the priests to wash in. Besides this there were ten brazen lavers, five of them on one side of the court and five on the other side (I Kgs. 7:38-39). They were used for washing the things which belonged to the burnt-offering (II Chron. 4:6). The great court was for the children of Israel (I Kgs. 8:14; II Chron. 7:3). It was paved (II Chron. 7:3) and surrounded by a wall (II Chron. 4:9).

The ceremony of dedicating the temple was very impressive. "Solomon assembled the elders of Israel and all the heads of the tribes, the princes of the fathers' houses of the children of Israel unto King Solomon in Jerusalem to bring up the ark of the covenant of Jehovah out of the city of David which is Zion" (I Kgs. 8:1). The priests carried the ark and the holy vessels (I Kgs. 8:4). After sacrifices had been offered and the ark and the other things put in their proper places, the priests came out of the temple. "The cloud filled the house of Jehovah so that the priests could not stand to minister by reason of the cloud; for the glory of Jehovah filled the house of Jehovah" (I Kgs. 8:10-11; II Chron. 5:13-14). Not only did worshippers pray to Jehovah in the

temple, but in distant places they prayed toward it (I Kgs.
8:30, 35, 38, 42, 44, 48; II Chron. 6:20, 21, 29, 32, 34,
38, compare p. 220). The horns of the brazen altar, as
in David's day, furnished a place of asylum. At first
Benaiah would not slay Joab who fled there, but he did
so when Solomon commanded him (I Kgs. 2:28-35).

The temple was often called a house or the house of
Jehovah (I Kgs. 5:2, 3, 5, 17, 18; 6:1-10, etc.). Like
the tabernacle it was thought of as his dwelling. On
account of its splendor the same word which is sometimes used of the royal palace (I Kgs. 21:1; II Kgs.
20:18; II Chron. 36:7; Ps. 45:15, etc.) was given also
to the temple (I Kgs. 6:3, 5, 17, 33; 7:21, 50, etc.). Now
at last Jehovah dwelt in a house which in splendor and
beauty was as worthy of him as the wealth of Solomon
and the skill of his workmen could make it.

Solomon made a change in the highpriestly succession.
He "thrust out Abiathar from being priest unto Jehovah, that he might fulfil the word of Jehovah, which
he spake concerning the house of Eli in Shiloh" (I Kgs.
2:27). This brought to an end the succession from Ithamar, the youngest son of Aaron, which had been on the
highpriestly throne since the time of Eli. Solomon made
Zadok, who was descended from Eleazar, Aaron's third
son, high priest in Abiathar's stead (I Kgs. 2:35). Thus
the older line was restored. Solomon followed the arrangement of the duties of the priests and Levites which
had been established by David. "He appointed according
to the ordinance of David his father, the courses of the
priests to their service, and the Levites to their offices, to
praise and to minister before the priests, as the duty of

every day required; the doorkeepers also by their courses at every gate: for so had David the man of God commanded" (II Chron. 8:14).

The holy times of the year and the required sacrifices seem to have been observed after the temple was built. In sending to Hiram, king of Tyre, to ask his aid in the construction of the temple, Solomon said, "Behold I am about to build a house for the name of Jehovah my God, to dedicate it to him and to burn before him sweet spices, and for the continual showbread, and for the burnt-offerings morning and evening, on the sabbaths and on the new moons and on the set feasts of Jehovah our God. This is an ordinance forever to Israel" (II Chron. 2:4). On another occasion it is said, "Then Solomon offered burnt-offerings unto Jehovah on the altar of Jehovah which he had built before the porch, even as the duty of every day required, offering according to the commandment of Moses, on the sabbaths and on the new moons, and on the set feasts, three times in the year, even in the feast of unleavened bread and in the feast of weeks and in the feast of tabernacles" (II Chron. 8:12-13). The great feast at the dedication of the temple was in the seventh month (I Kgs. 8:2; II Chron. 5:3) and may have been connected with the glad feast of tabernacles or ingathering (see pp. 101-103). The sacrifices on that occasion were specially significant. "Solomon offered for the sacrifice of peace-offerings, which he offered unto Jehovah, two and twenty thousand oxen and a hundred and twenty thousand sheep. So the king and all the children of Israel dedicated the house of Jehovah. The same day did the king hallow the middle of the court that was before the house of Jehovah: for there he offered the burnt-offering and the meal-offering and the fat of the peace-offerings, because the brazen altar that was before Jehovah was too little to receive the burnt-offering and the meal-offering and the fat of the peace-offerings. So Solomon held the feast at that time and all Israel with him, a great assembly from the entrance of Hamath unto the brook of Egypt, before Jehovah our God, seven days and seven days, even fourteen days" (I Kgs. 8:63-65; II Chron. 7:5, 7-8).

The ceremonies of religion in Solomon's time were by no means always unspiritual. The ethical element is prominent in the prayer of the king when he dedicated the temple. He recognized the fact of sin and the necessity of punishment. "If a man sin against his neighbor and an oath be laid upon him to cause him to swear, and he come and swear before thine altar in this house; then hear thou in heaven and do and judge thy servants, condemning the wicked, to bring his way upon his own head, and justifying the righteous, to give him according to his righteousness" (I Kgs. 8:31-32). He said, "Thou, even thou only knowest the hearts of all the children of men" (I Kgs. 8:39). He recognized that all men are sinners (I Kgs. 8:46). In the book of Proverbs there are indications of the same ethical quality in Solomon's religion. He said:

"The sacrifice of the wicked is an abomination to Jehovah;
But the prayer of the upright is his delight."
(Prov. 15:8.)

"Jehovah is far from the wicked;
But he heareth the prayer of the righteous."
                                        (Prov. 15:29.)
"To do righteousness and justice
Is more acceptable to Jehovah than sacrifice."
                                        (Prov. 21:3.)
"The sacrifice of the wicked is an abomination;
How much more when he bringeth it with a wicked
    mind."   (Prov. 21:27.)
"He that turneth away his ear from hearing the law,
Even his prayer is an abomination."   (Prov. 28:9.)
Such proverbs were necessary in a time when even a
harlot gave sacrifices of peace-offerings and paid vows
(Prov. 7:14).

It is a blot on Solomon's record that although he was
so zealous in establishing the worship of Jehovah he
yielded to idolatry. "It came to pass when Solomon was
old that his wives turned away his heart after other gods:
and his heart was not perfect with Jehovah his God, as
was the heart of David his father. For Solomon went
after Ashtoreth, the goddess of the Sidonians, and after
Milcom, the abomination of the Ammonites . . . Then
did Solomon build a high place for Chemosh, the abomination of Moab in the mount that is before Jerusalem,
and for Molech, the abomination of the children of Ammon. And so did he for all his foreign wives, who burnt
incense and sacrificed unto other gods" (I Kgs. 11:4-5,
7-8). The nature of this idolatrous worship has been
described elsewhere (pp. 184-185). Not Solomon alone
but many of the people worshipped these foreign gods
(I Kgs. 11:33).

(3) PROPHECY.

The condition of prophecy seems to have been the same in the reign of Solomon as in that of David. The most important prophet mentioned in Solomon's reign was Ahijah the Shilonite. When Jeroboam the son of Nebat was plotting against the king, the prophet went to him clad in a new garment. He rent the garment in twelve pieces and said to Jeroboam, "Take thee ten pieces; for thus saith Jehovah the God of Israel, Behold I will rend the kingdom out of the hand of Solomon and will give ten tribes to thee . . . because that they have forsaken me and have worshipped Ashtoreth the goddess of the Sidonians; Chemosh ,the god of Moab, and Milcom, the god of the children of Ammon. . . . I will take the kingdom out of his son's hand and will give it unto thee, even ten tribes. And unto his son will I give one tribe that David my servant may have a lamp alway before me in Jerusalem, the city which I have chosen to put my name there. And I will take thee and thou shalt reign according to all that thy soul desireth and shalt be king over Israel. And it shall be, if thou wilt hearken unto all that I command thee and wilt walk in my ways and do that which is right in mine eyes, to keep my statutes and my commandments, as David my servant did; that I will be with thee and will build thee a sure house, as I built for David and will give Israel unto thee. And I will for this afflict the seed of David but not forever" (I Kgs. 11:31, 33, 35-39).

This remarkable prophecy is according to the best prophetic principles. The symbolic action which accompanied it has many parallels among the writing prophets of later times. The prediction is grounded in a profound insight into the true principles of the divine government of Israel. Ahijah recognized that while Jehovah was absolutely true to his covenant with David (II Sam. 7:12-17), the time and the manner of the fulfilment were conditioned upon the conduct of David's successors on the royal throne. Jehovah would not reject the line of David as he rejected Saul, but if they sinned he would chastise them. Jeroboam and the kingdom of Israel were Jehovah's instruments for this chastisement. This gave a certain legitimacy to Jeroboam and the Northern Kingdom. They were to be in a lower sense successors of David and if they were faithful they would receive the divine favor. Nevertheless, no matter what happened, the exclusive royal power must some day come back to David's line. God will not afflict the seed of David forever. Here is inspired foresight which is based upon inspired insight.

As in David's reign the prophet was attached to the royal court and one of his chief duties was to write the history of the reign, not merely for the sake of record, but in order to preserve permanently the religious and moral interpretation of the events. So it is said at the end of the chronicler's account of Solomon's reign, "Now the rest of the acts of Solomon, first and last, are they not written in the history of Nathan the prophet, and in the prophecy of Ahijah the Shilonite and in the visions of Iddo the seer concerning Jeroboam the son of Nebat?" (II Chron. 9:29). In the similar statement at the end of David's reign, Samuel the seer, Nathan the prophet and Gad the seer are mentioned (I Chron. 29:29). While

Samuel and probably Gad died before Solomon came to the throne, Nathan remained an officer of the royal court even though the king changed. Furthermore, there was a certain official recognition of Ahijah the Shilonite and Iddo the seer, even though the prophecy of the former and probably that of the latter was not favorable to Solomon. Iddo was one of the official historians of the next two reigns (II Chron. 12:15; 13:22).

(4) THE MESSIANIC HOPE.

Solomon referred to the Messianic hope in his prayer at the dedication of the temple. "Now therefore O Jehovah the God of Israel, keep with thy servant David my father that which thou hast promised him, saying, There shall not fail thee a man in my sight to sit on the throne of Israel, if only thy children take heed to their way, to walk before me as thou hast walked before me" (I Kgs. 8:25; II Chron. 6:16). A little later Jehovah renewed this promise to Solomon (I Kgs. 9:4-5; II Chron. 7:17-18).

Psalm 72 is Solomon's prayer for himself and his successors in the Davidic line. Throughout it recognizes the Messianic hope which was connected with that dynasty, particularly in the form which David gave it in his "last words" (II Sam. 23:1-7). The greatest necessity of the Messianic King as Solomon viewed it was righteousness. As he prayed for this for himself and for his son his vision was strengthened by inspiration and prayer passed over into prediction of the Ideal King.

"Give the king thy judgments, O God,
And thy righteousness unto the king's son.
He will judge thy people with righteousness

And thy poor with justice.
The mountains shall bring peace to the people,
And the hills in righteousness.

*   *   *   *   *   *   *

He will come down like rain upon the mown grass,
As showers that water the earth.

*   *   *   *   *   *   *

He shall have dominion also from sea to sea,
And from the River unto the ends of the earth.

*   *   *   *   *   *   *

There shall be abundance of grain in the earth upon the
top of the mountains,
The fruit thereof shall shake like Lebanon
And they of the city shall flourish like grass of the
earth.
His name shall endure forever;
His name shall be continued as long as the sun;
And men shall be blessed in him;
All nations shall call him happy."

(Ps. 72:1-3, 6, 8, 16-17).

Here are several important elements of Messianic prediction; (1) justice especially for the poor, (2) peace, (3)
fertility, (4) universal dominion and (5) eternal reign.

In the crowning passage of the book of Proverbs wisdom is personified and represented as being with God before all creation, the master-workman through whom he
made all things. Thus Wisdom says,

"Jehovah possessed me in the beginning of his way,
Before his works of old.
I was set up from everlasting, from the beginning,
Before the earth was — — —

Then I was by him, as a master workman;
And I was daily his delight,
Rejoicing always before him,
Rejoicing in his habitable earth;
And my delight was with the sons of men."

(Prov. 8:22-23, 30-31).

While this extraordinary passage is not strictly Messianic since it does not refer to the Son of David, and while Solomon could not see in it a distinction of persons in the godhead, it foreshadowed the relation between the Father and Son and prepared the way for the New Testament doctrine of the Logos (Jno. 1:1-5). Therefore it should be mentioned in connection with the history of the Messianic hope.

(5) THE FUTURE LIFE.

There are only a few new elements in the conception of the future life in Solomon's time. When Solomon died he is said to have slept with his fathers (I Kgs. 11:43; II Chron. 9:31). Sheol and the pit are represented as swallowing those who die, for murderers say, of their victims,

"Let us swallow them up alive as Sheol,
And whole as those that go down into the pit"

(Prov. 1:12).

A new name for Sheol is Abaddon which means destruction or ruin

"Sheol and Abaddon are never satisfied"

(Prov. 27:20).

Sheol is represented as in David's time as the appropriate place for the wicked, a place from which the righteous shall be delivered, at least for a time. Thus Solomon says concerning an impure woman,

"Her feet go down to death,
Her steps take hold on Sheol"

(Prov. 5:5)

"Her house is in the way to Sheol,
Going down to the chambers of death"

(Prov. 7:27).

Indeed the wise man says of the man who goes in to her,
"He knoweth not that the dead are there;
That her guests are in the depths of Sheol"

(Prov. 9:18).

He also says,
"The man that wandereth out of the way of under-
standing
Shall rest in the assembly of the dead"

(Prov. 21:16).

The word for "dead" in the last two verses is "rephaim" which is a special designation of the inhabitants of the lower world (Ps. 88:10; Prov. 2:18; Isa. 14:9; 26:19) and may be rendered "shades" or "ghosts."

If Sheol is the appropriate place for the wicked, on the other hand Solomon says,

"To the wise the way of life goeth upward,
That he may depart from Sheol beneath"

(Prov. 15:24).

By chastisement a child may be kept from going to Sheol.
"Withhold not correction from the child;
For if thou beat him with the rod, he will not die.
Thou shalt beat him with the rod,

And shalt deliver his soul from Sheol"

(Prov. 23:13-14).

Sheol was a dark and mysterious place to men, for as proof of God's all-seeing vision Solomon said,

"Sheol and Abaddon are before Jehovah;
How much more then the hearts of the children of
men"

(Prov. 15:11).

Death and Sheol were considered as irresistible for
"Love is strong as death
Jealousy is cruel as Sheol" (Song 8:6).

(6) THE MORALITY OF SOLOMON AND HIS TIME.

It is not surprising that the greatest moral defect in the life of Solomon was in his sexual relations, for he was the child of David and Bathsheba. He had seven hundred wives, princesses and three hundred concubines. "His wives turned away his heart" (I Kgs. 11:3). The frequent warnings of the Proverbs against the strange woman and sexual impurity (2:16-19; 5:3-20, 24-33; 7:5-27; 9:13-18; 23:27-28) show that these evils were common in Solomon's time and that he had a keen realization of the ruin which comes from them.

He also warned against the evils of strong drink which was doubtless common in his day.

"Wine is a mocker, strong drink a brawler;
And whosoever erreth thereby is not wise"

(Prov. 20:1).

"Be not among winebibbers,
Among gluttonous eaters of flesh;

For the drunkard and the glutton shall come to poverty;
And drowsiness will clothe a man with rags"

(Prov. 23:20-21).

"Who hath woe? who hath sorrow? who hath contentions?

Who hath complaining? who hath wounds without
cause?

Who hath redness of eyes?

They that tarry long at the wine,

They that go to seek out mixed wine.

Look not thou upon the wine when it is red,

When it sparkleth in the cup,

When it goeth down smoothly.

At the last it biteth like a serpent,

And stingeth like an adder"

(Prov. 23:29-32).

Solomon displayed the cruelty which is characteristic
of oriental monarchs. He put his half-brother Adonijah
to death because he thought that his request for Abishag
as his wife meant an intrigue to obtain the throne (I
Kgs. 2:22-25). He caused the death of Joab even at the
horns of the altar whither he had fled for safety (I Kgs.
2:28-35). He had Shimei slain because he broke the
oath not to leave Jerusalem (I Kgs. 2:36-46).

Solomon's respect for his mother presents a beautiful
picture (I Kgs. 2:19-20). His choice of a wise and
understanding heart rather than long life or riches or
victory over his enemies was itself a mark of wisdom
(I Kgs. 3:5-15; II Chron. 1:7-12). An example of his
practical shrewdness is found in the story of the two
women who claimed the same child (I Kgs. 3:16-28).

Although the taxation must have been very heavy to carry on all his building operations (I Kgs. 12:4; II Chron. 10:4), his reign was distinguished for justice toward rich and poor alike.

The book of Proverbs is full of the exaltation of righteousness. It is presented as the only way to true success. Although many of the maxims deal with matters of expediency, they never descend to selfish trickiness. The wisdom and the folly of the book are not worldly, but religious. The religious basis of morality appears in many passages.

"The fear of Jehovah is the beginning of knowledge"
(Prov. 1:7).

"My son if thou wilt receive my words,
And lay up my commandments with thee;
So as to incline thine ear unto wisdom,
And apply thy heart to understanding;
Yea if thou cry after discernment
And lift up thy voice for understanding,
If thou seek her as silver,
And search for her as for hid treasures,
Then shalt thou understand the fear of Jehovah,
And find the knowledge of God"
(Prov. 2:1-5).

"Trust in Jehovah with all thy heart,
And lean not upon thine own understanding:
In all thy ways acknowledge him,
And he will direct thy paths"   (Prov. 3:5-6).

"A false balance is an abomination to Jehovah,
But a just weight is his delight"   (Prov. 11:1).

"He that oppresseth the poor reproacheth his Maker;
But he that hath mercy on the needy honoreth him"
(Prov. 14:31).

"The eyes of Jehovah are in every place,
Keeping watch upon the evil and the good"
(Prov. 15:3).

"All the ways of a man are clean in his own eyes;
But Jehovah weigheth the spirits"   (Prov. 16:2).

"He that hath pity upon the poor lendeth unto Jehovah,
And his good deed will he pay him again"
(Prov. 19:17).

"The rich and the poor meet together:
Jehovah is the maker of them all"   (Prov. 22:2).

These are but a few of the gems of truth in this book
which show how the morality which Solomon taught was
grounded in the fear of Jehovah.

Although the representations of the Song of Solomon
seem too sensuous according to Christian standards, they
were not regarded as indelicate or immoral according to
the customs of that day.

CHAPTER VI.

The Religion from Solomon to Amos.

I Kings 12-22; II Kings 1:1-14:22; II Chron. 10-25.

The period covered in this chapter begins with the accession of Rehoboam as king of Judah and continues as far as the accession of Uzziah. It follows the northern kingdom of Israel from its founding by Jeroboam the son of Nebat to the beginning of the reign of Jeroboam the son of Joash. The only Biblical sources for the religion of this time are the chapters of the books of Kings and Chronicles mentioned above. While it is quite possible that some of the anonymous Psalms were composed in this time, it is so uncertain that it is safer to consider them later. The same may be said concerning the book of Job.

During this period of nearly two centuries the religion of Jehovah was in mortal combat with the older religions of Palestine and the neighboring lands. The most powerful of these was the worship of the Baalim which was essentially that of the reproductive power of nature both in the vegetable and animal kingdoms. This worship took different forms in different places according to their physical features. Thus there were many Baalim (see pp. 181-184). Although the northern kingdom of Israel was much more influenced by the religion of the Baalim than the kingdom of Judah, that influence was often felt in the southern kingdom. Sometimes as in the reign of Ahab, the worship of Jehovah existed side by side with the worship of the Baalim, tending toward an amalgamation of the two. At other times the people gave themselves over almost exclusively to the Baal worship. There were several periods of reform when under the leadership of the king or the priest the people returned to the pure worship of Jehovah with more or less thoroughness. The most important such period in the kingdom of Israel was that of Jehu whose burning zeal for Jehovah against the Baalim showed itself in slaying the sons of Ahab and many worshippers of Baal (II Kgs. 10:18-25). "They brought forth the pillars that were in the house of Baal and burned them. And they broke down the pillar of Baal and broke down the house of Baal, and made it a draught-house unto this day. Thus Jehu destroyed Baal out of Israel" (II Kgs. 10:26-28). In the kingdom of Judah the reign of Asa was a period of reform. "He took away the foreign altars and the high places and brake down the pillars and hewed down the Asherim and commanded Judah to seek Jehovah, the God of their fathers, and to do the law and the commandment. Also he took away out of all the cities of Judah the high places and the sun-images; and the kingdom was quiet before him" (II Chron. 14:3-5). To some degree the people must have gone back to their evil ways in the reign of his son Jehoshaphat for it was necessary for him to take away the high places and the Asherim again (II Chron. 17:6). Indeed it was very difficult to make this a lasting reform, for later in Jehoshaphat's reign the chronicler says "the high places were not taken away; neither as yet had the people set their hearts unto the God of their fathers" (II Chron. 20:33).

The marriage of Jehoram, the son of Jehoshaphat, to Athaliah, the able but wicked daughter of Ahab and Jezebel, had a very damaging influence upon the religion of Judah (II Kgs. 8:18; II Chron. 21;6, 11). Jehoiada the high priest saved the day. He caused the death of Athaliah and he "made a covenant between Jehovah and the king and the people, that they should be Jehovah's people; between the king also and the people. And all the people of the land went to the house of Baal and brake it down; his altars and his images brake they in pieces thoroughly, and slew Mattan the priest of Baal, before the altars. And the priest appointed officers over the house of Jehovah" (II Kgs. 11:17-18; II Chron. 23: 16-18).

The immediate effect of the establishment of the separate kingdom of Israel by Jeroboam, the son of Nebat, was the separation of the worship of that kingdom from the legitimate worship at Jerusalem. Jeroboam fearing the effect of his people going to Jerusalem to worship, made two calves of gold which he set up at Bethel and Dan and said, "Behold thy gods, O Israel, which brought thee up out of the land of Egypt" (I Kgs. 12:28). These calves were meant to represent Jehovah. The words which Jeroboam spoke concerning them are almost identical with those which Aaron had spoken concerning the golden calf which he made in the wilderness. "These are thy gods, O Israel, which brought thee up out of the land of Egypt" (Exod. 32:8). The worship of them was a violation of the second rather than the first commandment. Jeroboam established high places and appointed priests who were not of the tribe of Levi. The Levitical priests fled to Judah (I Kgs. 13:33-34; II Chron. 11:13-15). He also established a feast at Bethel in the eighth month to take the place of the feast of tabernacles at Jerusalem (I Kgs. 12:32-33). In spite of these defections from the worship of Jehovah, there were always many people who remained true to Him, who did not bow the knee to Baal nor kiss him (I Kgs. 19:18).

(1)   THE IDEA OF GOD.

The period from the defection of the ten tribes to the writing prophets witnessed no forward movement in the conception of God. At its best it merely handed on that which came from earlier times. No great statements of the spirituality of God like those of Moses, David or Solomon come from this time, unless possibly some of the Psalms belong here. Jehovah is thought of as the doer of all things. The separation of the northern kingdom was brought about by Him (I Kgs. 12:15; II Chron. 10:15). It was He who made Jeroboam king (I Kgs. 14:7-8; II Chron. 11:4), who made Baasha king (I Kgs. 16:2). It was of God to destroy Amaziah (II Chron. 25:20). The gentile nations were also under His control, for He gave victory to Syria through Naaman (II Kgs. 5:1). Jehoshaphat prayed: "O Jehovah, the God of our fathers, art not thou God in heaven? and art not thou ruler over all the kingdoms of the nations? and in thy hand is power and might so that none is able to withstand thee" (II Chron. 20:6).

In the kingdom of Israel the worship of Jehovah in the form of a golden calf at Bethel and another at Dan (I Kgs. 12:28-33), must have lowered the spiritual ideas of the divine nature. Undoubtedly the great mass of the people thought of Jehovah as the god only of Israel, greater than other gods, yet only one of them. The servants of Benhadad thought that Jehovah was a god of the hills and that if they could meet Israel in the plain they could conquer them (I Kgs. 20:23). To meet this narrow conception of deity a man of God told Ahab that Jehovah would give Israel the victory anywhere (I Kgs. 20:28). Naaman asked for two mules' burden of earth that he might take it to Syria and on it as a piece of the territory of Israel worship Israel's God (II Kgs. 5:17). On the other hand Abijah said that the idols of Jeroboam were no gods (II Chron. 13:9). Yet even this statement should not be understood as a denial of their existence. It meant only that in comparison with Jehovah they did not deserve to be called gods.

The Angel of Jehovah who appeared to Elijah (I Kgs. 19:5-7; II Kgs. 1:3, 15) was a theophany like those of earlier times. (See pp. 26-27, 56, 161-164, 209-212.)

(2) THE CEREMONIES OF RELIGION.

The principal worship of the kingdom of Judah was carried on in the temple at Jerusalem throughout this period. However, there were rival places of worship during many reigns. Thus there were high places, pillars and Asherim in the reign of Rehoboam (I Kgs. 14:23). Asa "removed all the idols that his fathers had made" (I Kgs. 15:12-13) but he did not take away the high places (verse 14). He suppressed the worship of other gods, but he did not suppress the worship of Jehovah in high places. (But compare II Chron. 14:3, 5). These high places continued in the reign of Jehoshaphat (I Kgs. 22:43; II Chron. 20:33; but compare II Chron. 17:6).

Jehoram made high places in Judah (II Chron. 21:11). The sons of Athaliah, the daughter of Ahab, broke up the house of Jehovah at Jerusalem and bestowed its dedicated things upon the Baalim (II Chron 24:7). When she was slain and Jehovah made king "Jehoiada made a covenant between Jehovah and the king and the people that they should be Jehovah's people" (II Kgs. 11:17; II Chron. 23:16). The people broke down the house of Baal at Jerusalem, broke the images of Baal and slew Mattan, the priest of Baal (II Kgs. 11:18; II Chron. 23:17). This reform lasted until the death of Jehoiada. Then the princes of Judah forsook the house of Jehovah and served Asherim and idols (II Chron. 24:17-19). Amaziah worshipped the gods of Edom whom he conquered (II Chron. 25:14-15).

The religious record of the northern kingdom is distinctly worse than that of the southern. Throughout all the reigns the golden calves which Jeroboam set up at Bethel and Dan for the worship of Jehovah continued to be a constant cause of idolatry. The high places of Israel like those of Judah were for the worship of Jehovah. Israel made Asherim (I Kgs. 14:15). When Ahab married Jezebel, the daughter of Ethbaal, king of the Sidonians, a great impulse was given to the worship of Baal in Israel (I Kgs. 16:31-33; 21:26). There were four hundred and fifty prophets of Baal and four hundred prophets of the Asherah (I Kgs. 18:19). Nevertheless the worship of Jehovah was not abandoned even in Ahab's reign. Obadiah who was over Ahab's household feared Jehovah greatly (I Kgs. 18:3, 12) and even then there were at least a hundred prophets of Jehovah (I Kgs. 18:

4, 13). The spectacular contest between Elijah and the prophets of Baal had only a temporary effect in turning Israel to Jehovah (I Kgs. 19:10). Ahaziah of Israel worshipped Baal (I Kgs. 22:53) and inquired of Baal-zebub, the god of Ekron (II Kgs. 1:2). Jehoram was somewhat better, for "he put away the pillar of Baal that his father had made" (II Kgs. 3:2). Jehu made a thorough-going destruction of the pillars of Baal and his temple (II Kgs. 10:26-28), but he retained the golden calves of Bethel and Dan (verse 29). Jehoahaz, Jehu's son, undid the reforms of his father and was delivered into the hands of Hazael, king of Syria. When Jehoahaz repented and prayed, Jehovah hearkened to him (II Kgs. 13:1-4).

The establishment of the kingdom of Israel had a marked effect upon the priesthood. Doubtless Jeroboam thought that if he retained the Levitical priesthood who had hitherto regarded the temple at Jerusalem as their principal sanctuary, it would be difficult to keep his people loyal. So he "made priests from among all the people, that were not of the sons of Levi" (I Kgs. 12:31). "Whosoever would, he consecrated him, that there might be priests of the high places" (I Kgs. 13:33). Having dispossessed the Levitical priesthood he drove them out of his land. Hence "the priests and the Levites that were in all Israel resorted to him (Rehoboam) out of all their border. For the Levites left their suburbs and their possession, and came to Judah and Jerusalem; for Jeroboam and his sons cast them off, that they should not execute the priests' office unto Jehovah; and he appointed him priests for the high places and for the he-goats and

for the calves which he had made" (II Chron. 11:13-15,
compare 13:9). While this meant a great lowering of
the quality of the priesthood in the kingdom of Israel,
it also meant a large increase in the number of the priests
in the kingdom of Judah. There were more priests and
Levites in the southern kingdom than were needed at the
temple in Jerusalem or could be supported by it. This
fact doubtless had an important part in the establishment
and maintenance of the high places. The whole country
was full of priests.

It is altogether probable that the priesthood of the
kingdom of Judah remained true to Jehovah. They may
not have had a very spiritual conception of his nature.
They were so much concerned with the externals of his
worship that its inner spirit was often unknown to them.
Nevertheless they were zealous for him. This shows itself most prominently in the case of the high priest
Jehoiada. He resisted with all his power the efforts of
Athaliah to make Baal worship the religion of Judah.
His zeal was successful (II Kgs. 11:9-20; II Chron. 23:
8-21). The fact that in the next period the great prophets
found the priests as their greatest foes makes it probable
that even in this time they were the foes of progress in
religion. Yet they were undoubtedly a strong conservative force for the keeping of the religious conceptions
which had come down from the fathers. The line of
Zadok who was descended from Eleazar, the third son of
Aaron, held the highpriestly office throughout all this
period.

There are only two allusions to the sabbath in the history of this time. When the child of the Shunammite

woman died and she proposed to her husband that she should go to Elisha, he answered, "Wherefore wilt thou go to him to-day? It is neither new moon nor sabbath" (II Kgs. 4:23). This implies that it was customary to make pilgrimages to consult the prophet on the new moon or on the sabbath. Evidently as in earlier and later times these were regarded as holy days. The other reference is in the story of Jehoiada's plot for the murder of Athaliah. It refers to the fact that the arrangement of the guard at the temple and at the royal palace was different on the sabbath day from that on other days (II Kgs. 11:5, 7, 9; II Chron. 23:4, 8). This seems to imply that there were religious observances on the sabbath day which required a larger guard at the temple than on other days. The only reference to a feast is as follows, "Jeroboam ordained a feast in the eighth month, on the fifteenth day of the month, like unto the feast, that is in Judah" (I Kgs. 12:32). Probably the feast in Judah to which the author refers was the feast of tabernacles or ingathering which was celebrated for seven days beginning on the fifteenth day of the seventh month, just one month before the feast which Jeroboam established (see pp. 101-103). As the most joyful feast of the year it would be hardest for the people of the ten tribes to give up when they were separated from the kingdom of Judah. Therefore Jeroboam established it at Bethel; but in order to distinguish it from the feast in Judah he placed it one month later than the appointed time. The establishment, however, shows that in Jeroboam's time the feast of tabernacles was celebrated in Judah. And if it was celebrated in his time there is no reason to doubt that it continued to be celebrated throughout the following centuries.

While we cannot affirm that the full sacrificial system of the Mosaic law was observed during this period, there are clear indications that sacrifices of various kinds were common. "Jeroboam said in his heart, Now will the kingdom return to the house of David if this people go up to offer sacrifices in the house of Jehovah in Jerusalem" (I Kgs. 12:26-27). This implies that it had been customary to go to Jerusalem to sacrifice. Near the end of the period under review, in the account of the collection for the repair of the temple in the days of Joash, the record says, "the money for the trespass-offerings and the money for the sin-offerings was not brought into the house of Jehovah: it was the priests'" (II Kgs. 12:16). Trespass-offerings and sin-offerings were evidently very common. Similarly one of the reforms of Jehoiada was to appoint "the officers of the house of Jehovah under the hand of the priests the Levites, whom David had distributed in the house of Jehovah, to offer the burnt-offerings of Jehovah, as it is written in the law of Moses" (II Chron. 23:18). "They offered burnt-offerings in the house of Jehovah continually all the days of Jehoiada" (II Chron. 24:14). There are also incidental references to the time of the morning oblation (II Kgs. 3:20) and the time of the evening oblation (I Kgs. 18:29) which imply that these oblations were familiar.

The only reference in the records of this time to the idea of ceremonial uncleanness is in the account of Jehoiada's reforms. "He set the porters at the gates of the house of Jehovah, that none that was unclean in anything should enter in" (II Chron. 23:19). Since one of the main provisions of the law concerning ceremonial uncleanness was that the unclean person could not enter the sanctuary (pp. 113, 115, 116), this statement of the chronicler implies that this law was in force. The law of Israel concerning the leper (p. 114) did not apply to Naaman the Syrian who came to Elisha to be cured. Yet the command of Elisha, "Go and wash in the Jordan seven times and thy flesh shall come again to thee and thou shalt be clean" (II Kgs. 5:10) shows that the prophet recognized that as a leper Naaman was unclean. Although circumcision is not mentioned in this period, it is safe to conclude that it was practised. Similarly the silence of the history concerning tithes, vows and Nazirites does not justify us in concluding that the laws concerning them did not exist.

While doubtless very few of the worshippers penetrated to the spiritual meaning of the ceremonies of religion, there is one set of expressions which seems to show that some of them did. The kings were judged by the official historians according to their attitude of heart toward Jehovah and not according to their correctness in observance of the ceremonial. So, for example, it was written of Abijam that "his heart was not perfect with Jehovah his God as the heart of David his father" (I Kgs. 15:3), and on the other hand, "the heart of Asa was perfect with Jehovah all his days" (I Kgs. 15:14; II Chron. 15:17).

(3) PROPHECY.

Prophets are more prominent in this period than ever before, both in Judah and Israel. Shemaiah the man of God was an adviser of Rehoboam (I Kgs. 12:22-24; II

Chron. 12:5, 7). A man of God from Judah prophesied against the altar at Bethel by the word of Jehovah (I Kgs. 13:1-2). An old prophet in Bethel approved of him (I Kgs. 13:11-32). Ahijah the prophet of Shiloh received a revelation concerning Jeroboam's wife and foretold the fall of his house (I Kgs. 14:1-16). An unnamed prophet spoke the word of Jehovah to Ahab (I Kgs. 20:13-14, 22). Micaiah was a prophet of Jehovah (I Kgs. 22:8). The sons of the prophets at Bethel, Jericho and elsewhere (II Kgs. 2:3, 5, 15; 4:1, 38; 5:22; 6:1; 9:1) were guilds or schools of professional prophets. Iddo is called a seer (II Chron. 12:15) and a prophet (II Chron. 13:22); Oded is called a prophet (II Chron. 15:8) and Hanani a seer (II Chron. 16:7).

Greatest of them all was Elijah who was the founder of prophecy in the narrower sense. Although like Nathan and Gad he was adviser to the king, he far exceeded them in moral courage. His fiery zeal for righteousness and for the extermination of the Baal worship became the model for all later prophets. The writing prophets cannot be understood without him. If Moses was the great lawgiver, Elijah was the great prophet (Mt. 17:3, etc.). He was guided by the word of Jehovah (I Kgs. 17:2, 5, 8, 14, 16, 24; 18:1). He went to Horeb, the mount of God, because in the emergency of his life when his victory over Baal was seen to be temporary, he needed a revelation such as Moses had received there (I Kgs. 19:8-18). His recognition of Jehovah's presence in the still small voice rather than in the wind, the earthquake or the fire (I Kgs. 19:11-13) shows his appreciation of the spirituality of Jehovah and of his religion. Elisha lacked the moral vigor of his great master. He was a wonder worker rather than a religious reformer.

(4) THE MESSIANIC HOPE.

There is no advance in the Messianic hope in this period. Indeed there are very few allusions to it. Since from the time of David and onward this hope was indissolubly connected with the Davidic dynasty, the fortunes of that dynasty were closely related to the preservation of the hope. Accordingly the loss of prestige which the family of David suffered when Jeroboam led a successful revolt against them and took away ten tribes, leaving to them only one, meant corresponding loss of prestige for the Messianic idea. It was the tribe of Judah which remained true to David's line, the tribe in which the Messiah was to come (Gen. 49:10). It was therefore in the kingdom of Judah only that the Messianic hope existed. In spite of the wickedness of Jehoram the son of Jehoshaphat, Jehovah did not reject Judah or the Davidic line "for David his servant's sake, as he promised him to give unto him a lamp for his children alway" (II Kgs. 8:19; II Chron. 21:7). The promise referred to is that to David that his descendants should sit forever on his throne (II Sam. 7:12-17). Another allusion to this promise in which the Messianic hope is hidden was given when the high-priest Jehoiada made the boy Joash king. He said to the people, "Behold the king's son shall reign, as Jehovah hath spoken concerning the sons of David" (II Chron. 23:3). Although the hope is not mentioned in connection with the other kings of this period, it was no doubt cherished by those who hid God's word in their hearts.

(5) REVELATION AND INSPIRATION.

The common designation for a divine revelation was "the word of God" or "the word of Jehovah." When, for example, "the word of God came unto Shemaiah" he introduced his words by the familiar formula, "Thus saith Jehovah" (I Kgs. 12:22-24). A man of God prophesied against the altar at Bethel by the word of Jehovah (I Kgs. 13:1-2). Another prophet lyingly told him that an angel had spoken to him by the word of Jehovah. When the former prophet heeded this apparently divine revelation, the latter foretold his death for his disobedience (I Kgs. 13:11-25). Similarly, Jehovah is said to have put a lying spirit into the mouths of his prophets that he might destroy Ahab at Ramoth-gilead (I Kgs. 22:19-23; II Chron. 18:20-22). Such statements can be understood only when we recognize that the word of Jehovah does not constitute the ipsissima verba of God, but the revelation of God as it came through the obscuring medium of sinful and fallible men.

There are no inspired books from this period except the brief records of Kings and Chronicles. In these records, however, there are several short revelations. Elijah was guided by the word of Jehovah (I Kgs. 17:2, 5, 8, 14, 16, 24; 18:1; 19:9). He recognized Jehovah's revelation in the still small voice (I Kgs. 19:11-13). The statements that "the Spirit of God came upon Azariah" (II Chron. 15:1) and "upon Zechariah" (II Chron. 24:20) and that "the Spirit of Jehovah came upon Jehaziel" (II Chron. 20:14), do not indicate a belief in the Spirit of God as a distinct person of the Trinity, but refer to the energy of God working through men.

(6) The Future Life.

The doctrine of the life after death received no important addition in this period. The old phrase, to sleep with one's fathers, occurs many times (I Kgs. 14:20, 31; 15:8, 24; 16:6, 28; 22:50; II Kgs. 8:24; 10:35; 13:9, 13; 14:16, 22; II Chron. 12:16; 14:1; 16:13; 21:1). This expression, however, is not used except in one instance (II Kgs. 14:19, 22) when a man died a violent death (I Kgs. 15:28; 16:10, 18; 22:35, 37; II Kgs. 9:24, 33; 11:16; 12:20; II Chron. 24:25), possibly because such a death was inconsistent with the peacefulness of sleep.

The story of the ascension of Elijah indicates a belief in the future life. It is said that Jehovah took him up by a whirlwind into heaven (II Kgs. 2:1, 11), that he would take him away (II Kgs. 2:3, 5), and that he was taken from Elisha (II Kgs. 2:9-10). The sons of the prophets believed that he was still alive, for they sought him but did not find him (II Kgs. 2:15-18). They believed that he was among the dead although he did not die. The story of Elisha's raising the Shunammite's son from the dead (II Kgs. 4:32-37), and the story of the dead body coming to life when it touched the bones of Elisha (II Kgs. 13:20-21) also betray the common belief that death does not end human life. It is somewhat strange that Sheol is not mentioned in the records of this period; but there is no reason to doubt that the conception was the same as in the time of David and Solomon.

(7) Satan.

Satan is not mentioned by name in the literary sources which have come down to us from this time. There is,

however, a narrative which sheds considerable light upon
the idea of Satan. It is in the prophecy of Micaiah to
Ahab. He said, "I saw Jehovah sitting on his throne and
all the host of heaven standing by him on his right hand
and on his left. And Jehovah said, Who shall entice Ahab,
that he may go up and fall at Ramoth-gilead? And one
said on this manner; and another said on that manner.
And there came forth a spirit (Hebrew, the spirit) and
stood before Jehovah, and said, I will entice him. And
Jehovah said unto him, Wherewith? And he said, I will
go forth and will be a lying spirit in the mouth of all his
prophets. And he said, Thou shalt entice him, and shalt
prevail also; go forth and do so. Now therefore Jehovah
hath put a lying spirit in the mouth of all these thy
prophets; and Jehovah hath spoken evil concerning thee"
(I Kgs. 22:19-23; II Chron. 18:18-22).

The picture presented in this passage is similar to that
in the prologue to the book of Job. Here the host of
heaven is represented as gathered before Jehovah. There
the sons of God present themselves before him (Job 1:6;
2:1). The host of heaven and the sons of God are but
different names for the angels. Here Jehovah asks the
assembled host, "Who shall entice Ahab, that he may go
up and fall at Ramoth-gilead?" One suggests one way
and another another way of accomplishing this result.
At last one spirit more subtle than the rest proposes to
be a lying spirit in the mouth of Ahab's prophets in order
by smooth words to lure him to destruction. Jehovah permits him to carry out this plan and he does so with the
expected result. In the prologue of Job, Jehovah draws
the attention of Satan to the righteousness of Job and

permits Satan to tempt Job, at first confining his power
to Job's family and property (Job. 1:12-19), but later
giving his body also into Satan's control, provided only
he spares his life (Job. 2:4-8). The parallel is so exact
that we cannot doubt that the spirit who stood before
Jehovah and proposed to be a lying spirit in the mouth
of Ahab's prophets was none other than Satan himself.
He was the adversary and tempter of man. He had
great power but only that power which God permitted
him to have and to exercise. He enticed Ahab to go up
to Ramoth-gilead to his destruction, but only because
Ahab was willing to be enticed. Ahab adjured Micaiah
to tell the truth. Yet he insisted that the truth must be
something to his advantage (I Kgs. 22:13-18; II Chron.
18:12-17). Satan tempted Ahab and Ahab yielded. Satan
tempted Job but Job maintained his integrity. In both
cases God used Satan to accomplish his purpose. He
used Satan to tempt Ahab as he had used him to tempt
David (II Sam. 24:1, compare I Chron. 21:1).

(8) THE MORALITY OF THE PERIOD.

The same brutalities were apparently practised in war
as in earlier times. In this respect, however, Judah and
Israel were better than the other nations. The servants
of Benhadad, king of Syria, said to him, "We have heard
that the kings of the house of Israel are merciful kings"
(I Kgs. 20:31). Nevertheless deeds of violence were
common. At the command of Jehu seventy sons of Ahab
were slain and their heads sent to Jezreel (II Kgs. 10:7-
11). He also murdered the brethren of Ahaziah, king
of Judah (II Kgs. 10:13-14; II Chron. 22:7-9). He
gathered together the prophets and priests of Baal to

a great assembly pretending that he had a sacrifice to offer to Baal. Then he slew them (II Kgs. 10:18-28). Athaliah and her followers were slain by the priest Jehoiada, although he would not do it in the house of Jehovah (II Kgs. 11:15-16, 20; II Chron. 23:14-15). Mattan the priest of Baal was slain before the altars (II Kgs. 11:18; II Chron. 23:17). Amaziah slew the murderers of his father Joash, but did not slay their children because he remembered the words of Jehovah to Moses that the children should not be put to death for the fathers (II Kgs. 14:5-6; II Chron. 25:3-4). He slew ten thousand Edomites (II Kgs. 14:7; II Chron. 25:11) and as many more were thrown down from a rock (II Chron. 25:12). Jehoram slew his brothers (II Chron. 21:4). Joash (II Chron. 24:25) and Amaziah (II Chron. 25:27) were assassinated.

Although these facts show the low moral standards of the time, they present no moral difficulty in connection with the revelation. The case is different when it is stated that Jehovah commanded Jehu to smite the house of Ahab to avenge the blood of his prophets (II Kgs. 9:6-10), that Jehovah commended him for carrying out this brutal command (II Kgs. 10:30), and that he had anointed him king for this purpose (II Chron. 22:7). While Jehu's zeal for righteousness and for the purity of religion was from Jehovah, the brutal way that that zeal showed itself was from his own sinful heart. However, the house of Ahab deserved their punishment and in a more orderly condition of society they would have received it at the hands of the regular officers of the law. Elijah was not wrong in supposing that he was carrying out God's will when he slew the prophets of Baal (I Kgs. 18:40).

There were sodomites in Judah in the reign of Rehoboam, but they were regarded as abominations (I Kgs. 14:24). Asa put them away (I Kgs. 15:12). Rehoboam and his sons (II Chron. 11:21, 23), Abijah (II Chron. 13:21), Jehoram (II Chron. 21:17), and even the zealous priest Jehoiada (II Chron. 24:3) practiced polygamy. Elah, king of Israel drank himself drunk (I Kgs. 16:9), as did Benhadad of Syria and thirty-two other kings (I Kgs. 20:16). Such examples of wickedness in high places must have resulted in the condition to which David refers, that "the wicked walk on every side when vileness is exalted among the sons of men" (Ps. 12:8). In spite, however, of such wickedness, there were certainly many both in Judah and Israel who lived moral lives according to the standards of the times. It is refreshing after reading of the sins of Rehoboam to come upon the statement that "in Judah there were good things found" (II Chron. 12:12).

CHAPTER VII.

THE RELIGION OF THE EIGHTH CENTURY.

II Kings 14:23-21:26; II Chron. 26-33; Amos; Hosea; Isaiah; Micah; Psalms 2, 42-50, 66-68, 75-76, 78, 80, 84; Job.

The most important feature of this period was the rise of prophecy in its four great representatives, Amos, Hosea, Isaiah and Micah. They. are called eighth-century prophets although Isaiah and Micah probably continued to prophesy well on into the seventh century. Hence the period covered by these prophets was approximately from 750 to 680 B. C. It is most convenient to include among the sources for the religion of this time the historical records of the northern kingdom from the accession of Jeroboam, the son of Joash, to the fall of Samaria (790-722 B. C.) and the historical records of the kingdom of Judah from the accession of Uzziah to the death of Amon, the son of Manasseh (775-640 B. C.). Although the books of Hosea and Isaiah are dated in the days of Uzziah, Jotham, Ahaz and Hezekiah (Hos. 1:1; Isa. 1:1) and the book of Micah in the last three of these reigns (Mic. 1:1), it is reasonably supposed that the later chapters of Isaiah (40-66) and possibly parts of the last two chapters of Micah were given by those prophets during the wicked reign of Manasseh (698-642 B. C.)

The inclusion of the Psalms mentioned above and of the book of Job in this period is somewhat a matter of conjecture. Space will not permit a full statement of the reasons for this assignment. Suffice it to say that Psalms 46, 48, 66 and 76 fit remarkably well in the time of Sennacherib's invasion (701 B. C.). The date of the other Psalms is more uncertain. While the date of the book of Job cannot be fixed with certainty, there is no more probable theory than that it was contemporaneous with the so-called Deutero-Isaiah (chapters 40-55) which was spoken and then written for the comfort of the faithful remnant in Israel who saw the exile impending as well as for those who later experienced it. The book receives a new meaning if its purpose was to show from the example of an individual righteous sufferer and his restoration how the small but faithful remnant of God's people should suffer in the exile and then be restored. Possibly this purpose is reflected in the expression that "Jehovah turned the captivity of Job" (Job 42:10).

It is somewhat difficult to determine the best way to present the religion of this period as found in the sources mentioned above. If the dates of these sources were equally sure, all of them might be grouped together as was done in earlier chapters and the religion be presented under the various subjects dealt with. Since, however, this is not the case, it is better to deal separately with the historical sections, the four books of prophecy, the eighteen Psalms and the book of Job. The religion as presented in the historical sections and the four prophetic books certainly belongs to this period. Those religious features of the Psalms mentioned above and of the book of Job which are not found also in the historical sections and the prophetic books, are not so surely features of this period. Since, however, we have been influenced in dating these Psalms and the book of Job by their points of resemblance to the eighth-century history and prophets, it will be found that the points of variation are not great, and the religion of the period is nearly the same whether these sources of uncertain date be included or not. Another advantage of treating the sources separately is that by this means the student can gain a clear view of the special contribution of each one of the sources to the religon of this time.

Our first question, then is, What religious ideas were prominent in this period as the history presents them in Kings and Chronicles? So far as the northern kingdom is concerned we are unable to answer this question from the historical records. Were it not for the books of Amos and Hosea our knowledge of the religion of Israel in this time would be meager indeed. *Jeroboam the son of Joash* reigned forty-one years. It was a time of great political prosperity. The king "restored the border of Israel from the entrance of Hamath unto the sea of the Arabah according to the word of Jehovah, the God of Israel, which he spake by his servant Jonah the son of Amittai, the prophet who was of Gath-hepher" (II Kings 14:25). This was a special mark of Jehovah's favor and evidenced his determination not to blot out the name of Israel from under heaven (verses 26-27). Clearly there must have been a faithful remnant in Israel as there was in Judah who were true to the worship of Jehovah as they knew it. Nevertheless religious conditions were far from good.

The statement that the king "departed not from all the sins of Jeroboam the son of Nebat wherewith he made Israel to sin" (II Kings 14:24) does not necessarily indicate a condition worse than that of other periods, for similar statements are found concerning other kings of Israel (I Kings 15:34; 16:26, 31; 22:52; II Kings 3:3; 10:29, 31; 13:2, 6, 11; 15:9, 18, 24, 28; 17:21-22). Yet with such a king upon the throne it is not surprising that the books of Amos and Hosea represent sins of luxury and oppression as rampant among the wealthy classes of society.

After the death of Jeroboam there was almost continuous confusion in the northern kingdom. *Zechariah the son of Jeroboam* was assassinated by *Shallum* who was slain after a reign of one month by *Menahem*. Menahem retained his throne for ten years only by paying a large tribute to Pul (Tiglath-pileser). He was followed by his son *Pekahiah* who was soon slain by his captain *Pekah*. In Pekah's brief reign Tiglath-pileser invaded the land and carried away many captives. *Hoshea* slew Pekah and seized the throne. Finally when Hoshea rebelled against Assyria, Shalmaneser besieged Samaria. The city fell to his successor Sargon and the tribes of the northern kingdom were carried into exile. All of these kings of Israel continued the wickedness and idolatry of Jeroboam's reign (II Kings 15:9, 18, 24, 28; 17:2). The latter part of Hosea's book (chapters 4-14) reflects the troubled conditions of these times. There are also points of contact with some of the prophecies of Isaiah. Doubtless the same evil conditions, both moral and religious, obtained which characterized the reign of Jeroboam.

The period under review covers the reigns of six kings of Judah: Uzziah, Jotham, Ahaz, Hezekiah, Manasseh and Amon. *Uzziah* (called Azariah in II Kings 14:21; 15:1-8, 17-27; I Chron. 3:12) seems to have come to the throne before the death of his father Amaziah (II Kings 14:17-22). His reign lasted fifty-two years and like that of Jeroboam the son of Joash of the northern kingdom with whom he was in part contemporary, it was a time of great prosperity. Early in his reign he delivered Judah from bondage to Israel. He was successful in war against the Philistines and Arabians and the Chronicler says: "His name spread abroad even to the entrance of Egypt; for he waxed exceeding strong . . . his name spread far abroad; for he was marvellously helped till he was strong" (II Chron. 26:8, 15). He reorganized the army and improved the conditions of agriculture. The verdict of the historians on the morals and religion of his reign is in general favorable. The prophetic historian states: "He did that which was right in the eyes of Jehovah, according to all that his father Amaziah had done. Howbeit the high places were not taken away; the people still burnt incense in the high places" (II Kings 15:3-4). The Chronicler's statement is more definite: "He set himself to seek God in the days of Zechariah, who had understanding in the vision of God; and as long as he sought Jehovah, God made him to prosper" (II Chron. 26:5). Alas, in his prosperity and pride he dishonored Jehovah. "When he was strong, his heart was lifted up so that he did corruptly and he trespassed against Jehovah his God, for he went into the temple of Jehovah to burn incense upon the altar of incense" (II Chron.

26:16). For this sin he was smitten with leprosy and was compelled to live in a separate house until his death. During this period his son Jotham reigned in his stead. The great earthquake in his reign from which Amos dates his prophecy (Amos 1:1) was long remembered (Zech. 14:5) and was represented by Josephus as a divine judgment for his sin. It was in the year of Uzziah's death that Isaiah had the vision by which he was ordained to the prophetic office (Isa. 6:1). Amos and Hosea also prophesied during his reign (Amos 1:1; Hos. 1:1) but their ministry related for the most part to the northern kingdom.

The greater part of the reign of *Jotham* was apparently before the death of Uzziah his father. His policy was like that of his father. He conquered the Ammonites and carried on extensive building operations. Morally and religiously his reign was almost exactly like that of his father. On the whole he did that which was right in the eyes of Jehovah; but the high places were not taken away (II Kings 15:34-35). In particular he was not guilty of the sin of his father in entering into the temple of Jehovah (II Chron. 27:2). He "became mighty because he ordered his ways before Jehovah his god" (II Chron. 27:6). The statement that "the people did yet corruptly" (II Chron. 27:2) probably refers to the worship at the high places (compare II Kings 15:34-35).

The record of the reign of *Ahaz* is very different from that of his father Jotham and his grandfather Uzziah. Indeed no king of the Davidic line before him equalled him in idolatry and no king after him exceeded him except Manasseh. "He did not that which was right in the eyes of Jehovah his God like David his father. But he walked in the way of the kings of Israel, yea and made his son to pass through the fire, according to the abominations of the nations whom Jehovah cast out from before the children of Israel. And he sacrificed and burnt incense in the high places and on the hills and under every green tree" (II Kings 16:2-4). The expression "he caused his son to pass through the fire" refers to human sacrifice. It was a part of the worship of Molech the god of the Ammonites (Lev. 18:21; II Kings 23:10) and was practised also by the king of Moab (II Kings 3:27). Ahaz was the first king to introduce this abominable rite into Judah; but it was practised in the northern kingdom (II Kings 17:17) and later by Manasseh (II Kings 21:6). Micah and Jeremiah referred to it (Mic. 6:7; Jer. 7:31; 19:5). Offering sacrifice and burning incense under green trees were part of the worship of Baal. The Chronicler says that Ahaz made molten images for the Baalim and burnt incense in the valley of the son of Hinnom (II Chron. 28:2-3). On account of his sin, in which doubtless the people joined, God delivered Judah to Rezin king of Syria and Pekah of Israel, who carried away many captives. Ahaz appealed for help to Tiglath-pileser and gave him the silver and gold from the temple. When Tiglath-pileser came to Damascus Ahaz went thither to pay him homage. He saw there an altar which impressed him and at his command Urijah the priest built one like it beside the brazen altar in the court of the temple at Jerusalem. When he returned Ahaz commanded the priest to offer sacrifices on this heathen altar, retaining the brazen altar for the king to "inquire by" (II Kings 16:15). This has been thought to refer to divination by the inspection of the entrails of sacrificed victims, which was practised in Babylonia (Ezek. 21:21). The Chronicler says that Ahaz "sacrificed unto the gods of Damascus which smote him; and he said, Because the gods of the kings of Syria helped them, therefore will I sacrifice to them that they may help me. But they were the ruin of him and of all Israel. And Ahaz gathered together the vessels of the house of God and cut in pieces the vessels of the house of God and shut up the doors of the house of Jehovah; and he made him altars in every corner of Jerusalem. And in every city of Judah he made high places to offer incense unto other gods and provoked to anger Jehovah, the God of his fathers" (II Chron. 28:23-25). While there were certainly some of the people who still worshipped Jehovah, the king and most of his people were idolaters. It is not surprising that such a king was impervious to the message of Isaiah and unwilling to believe the words of Jehovah (Isa. 7:1-17). He would not believe. Therefore he was not established (Isa. 7:9).

There is one incident which relieves somewhat the dark picture of this time (II Chron. 28:8-15). When the army of Israel carried away captives from Judah, a prophet named Oded urged them to send them back lest the wrath of Jehovah be on them. Others stood by the prophet. The captives were sent back to Jericho, clothed and with food and drink for the journey. This beautiful story receives added value from the fact that Oded recognized the captives of Judah not as enemies of Israel but as brethren (II Chron. 28:8, 11). He recognized also that while the defeat of Judah was the divine judgment for their sins, Israel was also guilty. It was their awakened conscience concerning their own sin which made them charitable and forgiving toward their brethren of Judah. This sense of the ethical character of the relations between nations is the fundamental teaching of Amos.

The reign of *Hezekiah* stands out preeminently among all those of the divided kingdom. No other king after David was so loyal to Jehovah. There can be no doubt that this was chiefly through the influence of the great prophet Isaiah, an influence which must have been exerted even before Hezekiah came to the throne. The prophetic historian summarizes his reign as follows: "He did that which was right in the eyes of Jehovah, according to all that David his father had done. He removed the high places and brake the pillars and cut down the Asherah; and he brake in pieces the brazen serpent that Moses had made; for unto those days the children of Israel did burn incense to it; and he called it Nehushtan. He trusted in Jehovah the God of Israel; so that after him was none like him among all the kings of Judah, nor among them that were before him. For he clave to Jehovah; he departed not from following him, but kept his commandments which Jehovah commanded Moses. And Jehovah was with him; whithersoever he went forth he prospered" (II Kings 18:3-7). The Chronicler tells that in the first year of his reign, in the first month he opened the doors of the house of Jehovah and repaired them and caused the Levites to sanctify themselves and the house (II Chron. 29:3-17). When the Levites reported that they had finished cleansing the house Hezekiah with the princes offered sacrifices of thanksgiving (II Chron. 29:18-36).

He invited all Israel and Judah to keep the passover (II Chron. 30:1-9). Although many in Ephraim and Manasseh mocked the messengers, others accepted the invitation (verses 10-12). The feast was kept in Jerusalem with great joy, "for since the time of Solomon the son of David king of Israel there was not the like in Jerusalem" (II Chron. 30:26). The idols in Judah, Benjamin, Ephraim and Manasseh were destroyed (II Chron. 31:1). Hezekiah also appointed the courses of priests and Levites and re-established the ordinances of the temple (II Chron. 31:2-19). "Thus did Hezekiah throughout all Judah; and he wrought that which was good and right and faithful before Jehovah his God. And in every work that he began in the service of the house of God and in the law and in the commandments, to seek his God, he did it with all his heart and prospered" (II Chron. 31:20-21).

The siege of Samaria by Shalmaneser began in the fourth year of Hezekiah's reign and the fall of the city and the kingdom of Israel occurred in his sixth year (II Kings 18:9-12). Eight years later the king of Assyria invaded Judah. Hezekiah submitted to him paying a large tribute and giving to him all the silver in the temple and in his own house (II Kings 18:13-15). Later in 701 B. C. Sennacherib invaded Judah again. He took a large amount of booty and besieged Jerusalem. Rabshakeh the Assyrian officer tried to stir up rebellion among the people and sent an insulting message to Hezekiah (II Kings 18:17-37). In his distress Hezekiah appealed to Isaiah who told him not to be afraid (II Kings 19:1-7). Sennacherib sent a threatening letter to Hezekiah and the king took the letter into the temple and spread it before Jehovah (II Kings

19:14). In answer to his prayer Jerusalem was delivered. Pestilence broke out in the Assyrian camp and killed 185,-000 men compelling the remnant of the army to return to Nineveh (II Kings 19:15-37). This divine deliverance has an important place in the prophecies of Isaiah. The narrative is rather difficult to disentangle because the two Assyrian invasions are not distinguished. Nevertheless the deliverance was one of the greatest in the history of Judah and it had a great influence in stimulating faith in God (Cp. Psalms 46, 48, 66, 76).

It was probably soon after the first Assyrian invasion that Hezekiah suffered a serious illness. In answer to his prayers his life was spared for fifteen years in token of which the shadow went back on the dial ten steps (II Kings 20:1-11). After this messengers came from the crafty king of Babylon, Merodach-baladan (called Berodach-baladan in II Kings 20:12), ostensibly to congratulate Hezekiah on his recovery but in reality to secure his cooperation in a conspiracy against Assyria. The king foolishly showed them all his treasures. Then Isaiah told Hezekiah that the time would come when all these treasures would be carried away to Babylon (II Kings 20:12-19).

Hezekiah was succeeded by his son *Manasseh* who undid the religious reformation of his father. "He did that which was evil in the sight of Jehovah, after the abominations of the nations whom Jehovah cast out before the children of Israel. For he built again the high places which Hezekiah his father had destroyed; and he reared up altars for Baal and made an Asherah, as did Ahab king of Israel and worshipped all the host of heaven and served them. And he built altars in the house of Jehovah whereof Jehovah said, In Jerusalem will I put my name. And he built altars for all the host of heaven in the two courts of the house of Jehovah. And he made his son to pass through the fire and practised augury and used enchantments and dealt with them that had familiar spirits and with wizards: he wrought much evil in the sight of Jehovah to provoke him to anger" (II Kings 21:2-6). He also put the graven image of the Asherah in the temple. The way that this wicked king led his people astray is described by the historian in the words, "Manasseh seduced them to do that which is evil more than did the nations whom Jehovah destroyed before the children of Israel" (II Kings 21:9). The Chronicler's description of his idolatry is almost identical with that in the second book of Kings. While many of these idolatrous practices, such as the worship in high places, the Asherah and the human sacrifice were characteristic of the Baalism of earlier times, the worship of the heavenly bodies was due to the influence of Assyria. The prophets warned Manasseh and the people of a terrible doom for Jerusalem because of their sin, but they heeded not. "Moreover Manasseh shed innocent blood very much till he had filled Jerusalem from one end to another" (II Kings 21:16). The Chronicler records that Manasseh was taken in chains and carried to Babylon and "when he was in distress he besought Jehovah his God and humbled himself greatly before the God of his fathers" who restored him to his kingdom in Jerusalem (II Chron. 33:11-13). There he took away the foreign gods and restored the worship of Jehovah (II Chron. 33:15-16). "Nevertheless the people sacrificed ing...

still in the high places, but only unto Jehovah their God" (II Chron. 33:17). It was probably during the terrible days of the early part of Manasseh's reign that Isaiah gave the prophecies in the last part of his book (chapters 40-66) and that the book of Job was written. They would be of inestimable comfort to the righteous few who remained in Judah.

The record of the brief reign of *Amon* was like that of his father except that he never repented. "He did that which was evil in the sight of Jehovah, as did Manasseh his father. And he walked in all the way that his father walked in, and served the idols that his father served and worshipped them: and he forsook Jehovah the God of his fathers and walked not in the way of Jehovah" (II Kings 21:20-22). The Chronicler adds: "He humbled not himself before Jehovah, as Manasseh his father had humbled himself; but this same Amon trespassed more and more" (II Chron. 33:23). After two years he was assassinated by his servants in his own house. The people punished the conspirators and made his son Josiah king when only eight years old.

CHAPTER VIII.

Amos.

Amos was probably the first of the writing prophets. His book is dated "in the days of Uzziah king of Judah (775-735 B. C.), and in the days of Jeroboam the son of Joash king of Israel (790-749 B. C.) two years before the earthquake" (Amos 1:1). The exact date of this earthquake is unknown; but it was remembered in Zechariah's time more than two centuries later and dated in the reign of Uzziah (Zech. 14:5). Possibly it occurred soon after the death of Jeroboam. Its mention by Amos seems to imply that he regarded it as part of the judgment on Israel which he announced.

Although Amos came from Tekoa in Judah six miles south of Jerusalem, his principal prophecies were uttered at Bethel in the kingdom of Israel where Jeroboam had a palace and a royal sanctuary (Amos 7:13). Early in the reign of Jeroboam the prophet Jonah had foretold that the borders of the northern kingdom should be restored "from the entrance of Hamath unto the sea of the Arabah," i. e., the Dead Sea (II Kings 14:25). This gave Israel greater political power than at any other period of its history. It was also a time of great wealth and luxury; but morals and religion were at a low stage. The prophecies of Amos give no evidence that his ministry in

311

Israel continued into the troublous period which began soon after Jeroboam's death and continued until the fall of Samaria in 722 B. C. Hosea, his contemporary, on the other hand, reflects those conditions in the greater part of his book (chapters 4-14). Probably Amos continued his ministry in Judah after his return from Bethel (Amos 6:1), yet even here he did not live to see the death of Uzziah in 735 B. C. Thus while it is somewhat uncertain whether Amos or Hosea began to prophesy first, it is certain that Hosea's ministry continued longer. The times when these two great prophets of the northern kingdom began their work cannot have been far apart.

The name of the father of Amos is not given and it may be inferred that he was not a member of an influential family. He was "a herdsman and a dresser of sycomore trees" (Amos 7:14). Yet it is should not be thought that he was an ignorant rustic. He had observed nature to good purpose (Amos 3:3-8; 4:13; 9:5-6). Possibly he had gone to Egypt or Damascus to sell hides or wool. He certainly had considerable knowledge of history and the political conditions of his time (Amos 1-2; 9:7). He was less tender in dealing with Israel than Hosea was and this may have been partly due to the fact that he was not prophesying to his own people. Nevertheless he did not regard the northern kingdom as a foreign nation but as an apostate part of the people of God. Although his messages concerned chiefly this apostate part, in a larger sense they were a warning to all the twelve tribes. Thus he said: "Hear this word that Jehovah hath spoken against you, O children of Israel, against the whole family which I have brought up out of the land of Egypt" (Amos 3:1).

Even in his sermon delivered at Bethel he included a woe against Judah (Amos 2:4-5). Addressing both parts of the chosen people he said: "Woe to them that are at ease in Zion and to them that are secure in the mountain of Samaria, the notable men of the chief of the nations, to whom the house of Israel come" (Amos 6:1). He recognized Jerusalem as the rightful religious center of the whole land of Palestine, north as well as south, for he began his sermon at Bethel, saying: "Jehovah will roar from Zion, and utter his voice from Jerusalem; and the pastures of the shepherds shall mourn and the top of Carmel (in the northern kingdom) shall wither" (Amos 1:2).

(1) CONCEPTION OF GOD.

The religion of Amos and of the other prophets of the eighth century has well been described as ethical monotheism. This should not be understood, however, as a denial that the beginnings of monotheism were found long before this time or that earlier Israel conceived of Jehovah as a moral being. The moral law of the Pentateuch, particularly the Ten Commandments, contained the germ of ethical monotheism, for it was promulgated as the law of God (Exod. 20:1-2); but it was addressed only to Israel. Samuel's epoch-making words emphasized the same idea. "Hath Jehovah as great delight in burnt-offerings and sacrifices as in obeying the voice of Jehovah? Behold to obey is better than sacrifice and to hearken than the fat of rams" (I Sam. 15:22); but Samuel's words were spoken to Saul. David's similar words (Ps. 40:6-8; 51:16-17) show that he conceived of God as moral. But

Amos was the first Israelite to apply the moral law of God to Gentile nations as well as to Israel. He condemned Damascus because they "threshed Gilead with threshing instruments of iron" (Amos 1:3), Gaza, because they "carried away captive the whole people, to deliver them up to Edom" (Amos 1:6), Tyre, because they "delivered up the whole people to Edom and remembered not the brotherly covenant" (Amos 1:9), Edom because "he did pursue his brother with the sword and did cast off all pity, and his anger did tear perpetually and he kept his wrath forever" (Amos 1:11), Ammon because they "have ripped up the women with child of Gilead that they may enlarge their border" (Amos 1:13) and Moab because "he burned the bones of the king of Edom into lime" (Amos 2:1). While most of these grounds of condemnation had to do with the relation of the nation concerned to Israel, at least one of them had no connection with Israel. Many narrow-minded Israelites rejoiced when the Moabites burned the bones of the king of Edom into lime. They would have done it themselves if they had had the opportunity. But Amos condemned Moab in the name of Jehovah for this act of brutal sacrilege. In the light of this instance we should not think that the condemnation of the other nations was because their cruelty was visited on Israel. Amos referred to cases he knew about. If Damascus had threshed some other land than Gilead with threshing instruments of iron, if Gaza or Tyre had taken captive other people than Israel and sold them into slavery, if Edom had been unbrotherly to some other people than Israel or Ammon had ripped up the women with child in some other neighboring land than

Gilead, they would have received the same condemnation.
The ground of censure in each case is one of essential
morality. The surrounding nations are not condemned
because they did not accept Jehovah as their god but because they disobeyed the law of their own consciences,
they did not follow the light which they had. In disobeying their consciences Amos conceived that they were disobeying Jehovah; in refusing the light they had they were
refusing Jehovah (compare Rom. 2:12-16). Therefore
Jehovah would punish them.

Neither Judah nor Israel was immune from the same
relentless moral law of Jehovah. Indeed they were worthy
of greater condemnation for their sins because of the
special revelations Jehovah gave them. They sinned
against light. Judah's indictment was: "They have rejected the law of Jehovah and have not kept his statutes
and their lies have caused them to err after which their
fathers did walk" (Amos 2:4). All through the book
the charges against Israel and Judah relate to morals.
"For three transgressions of Israel, yea for four, I will
not turn away the punishment thereof because they have
sold the righteous for silver and the needy for a pair
of shoes; they that pant after the dust of the earth on
the head of the poor and turn aside the way of the meek:
and a man and his father go unto the same maiden, to
profane my holy name, and they lay themselves down
beside every altar upon clothes taken in pledge; and in
the house of their God they drink the wine of such as
have been fined" (Amos 2:6-8). To the rich women of
Israel the voice of Amos thundered: "Hear this word,
ye kine of Bashan, that are in the mountain of Samaria,

that oppress the poor, that crush the needy that say unto their lords, Bring and let us drink" (Amos 4:1). On another occasion he described the sinners of Israel as follows: "They hate him that reproveth in the gate and they abhor him that speaketh uprightly. Forasmuch therefore as ye trample upon the poor and take exactions from him of wheat: ye have built houses of hewn stone, but ye shall not dwell in them; ye have planted pleasant vineyards but ye shall not drink the wine thereof. For I know how manifold are your transgressions, and how mighty are your sins; ye that afflict the just, that take a bribe and that turn aside the needy in the gate" (Amos 5:10-12). "Ye have turned justice into gall and the fruit of righteousness into wormwood" (Amos 6:12). "Hear this, O ye that would swallow up the needy and cause the poor of the land to fail, saying, When will the new moon be gone, that we may sell grain? and the sabbath that we may set forth wheat, making the ephah small and the shekel great and dealing falsely with balances of deceit; that we may buy the poor for silver and the needy for a pair of shoes and sell the refuse of the wheat?" (Amos 8:4-6). The high-water mark of the book is reached in Amos 3:2 where Jehovah proclaims to Israel: "You only have I known of all the families of the earth: therefore I will visit upon you all your iniquities." It is the principle so often found in the New Testament, that the just punishments of God are proportioned to knowledge and opportunity (Luke 12:47-48; John 3:19; 9:41; 15:22, 24; Rom. 2:12-16; Jas. 4:17; II Pet. 2:21).

Amos revealed his conception of Jehovah not by a theological description of the divine nature and attributes

but by the thunders of the moral law. The God that
demands righteousness of his people that says: "Let
justice roll down as waters and righteousness as a mighty
stream" (Amos 5:24), must himself be righteous. Israel
had been condemned for their sins before, but the divine
moral law had never before been applied to Gentile nations. If the divine moral law is applicable outside of
Israel, if as far as Amos can see it is universal, then
there is but one God, Jehovah. It is not surprising that
the first prophet who applied the moral law to the Gentiles was the first complete monotheist. His universalism
is so amazing that he seems in one passage to deny the
preëminence of Israel. "Are ye not as the children of
the Ethiopians unto me, O children of Israel? saith
Jehovah. Have not I brought up Israel out of the land
of Egypt and the Philistines from Caphtor and the
Syrians from Kir?" (Amos 9:7). It would, however,
be a serious error to conclude that Amos gave Israel no
preëminence over the Philistines, and Syrians. He was
seeking to humble Israel from the proud thought that
Jehovah cared only for them. Elsewhere he clearly
recognized that they were the chosen people (Amos
3:2; 9:8-15).

Although the greatest emphasis of Amos was on the
righteousness of God, other aspects of the divine nature
were not ignored. Whatever happens God is the cause
of it "Shall evil befall a city, and Jehovah hath not done
it?" (Amos 3:6 cp. Isa. 45:7). Jehovah is the Creator
and he knows the inner thoughts of men. "He that
formeth the mountains, and createth the wind and declareth unto man what is his thought; that maketh the

morning darkness and treadeth upon the high places of the earth, Jehovah, the God of hosts is his name" (Amos 4:13). "Seek him that maketh the Pleiades and Orion and turneth the shadow of death into the morning and maketh the day dark with night; that calleth for the waters of the sea and poureth them out upon the face of the earth" (Amos 5:8). "The Lord Jehovah of hosts is he that toucheth the land and it melteth and all that dwell therein shall mourn; and it shall rise up wholly like the River and shall sink again like the River of Egypt; it is he that buildeth his chambers in the heavens and hath founded his vault upon the earth; he that calleth for the waters of the sea and poureth them out upon the face of the earth; Jehovah is his name" (Amos 9:5-6). The monotheism of the prophet is evident also from his referring to an idol or a false god as non-existent "a thing of nought" (Amos 6:13). The place of idolatrous worship in the territory of Damascus is called Aven (Amos 1:5) which means wickedness. The reference is probably to Baalbek where the sun was worshipped as at On in Egypt and some suppose that it was called On. If so, Aven may have been a play on that name.

(2) THE CEREMONIES OF RELIGION.

Several places of worship are mentioned, not only Bethel and Dan, where Jeroboam I had set up the golden calves as images of Jehovah nearly two centuries before (I Kings 12:28-30) but also Gilgal and Beersheba (Amos 4:4-5; 5:5; 8:14). Bethel in particular is called "the king's sanctuary" (Amos 7:13). It held a place in the religion of the northern kingdom similar to that which

Jerusalem held in Judah. We cannot suppose that Amos
approved of these rival sanctuaries to the temple at Jerusalem. Yet he was concerned with something even more
fundamental than the true place of worship, the fact
that the worship was not sincere but was accompanied
by many forms of unrepented sin. It was on this account that Jehovah would punish these sanctuaries. "In
the day that I shall visit the transgressions of Israel upon
him, I will also visit the altars of Bethel; and the horns
of the altar shall be cut off and fall to the ground" (Amos
3:14). Sarcastically he told them to go on in their wicked
way until they were destroyed. "Come to Bethel and
transgress, to Gilgal, and multiply transgression; and
bring your sacrifices every morning and your tithes every
three days; and offer a sacrifice of thanksgiving of that
which is leavened, and proclaim freewill-offerings and
publish them: for this pleaseth you, O ye children of
Israel, saith the Lord Jehovah" (Amos 4:4-5). Amos
saw a vision of the destruction of the sanctuary at
Bethel (Amos 9:1). He proclaimed, "Thus saith
Jehovah unto the house of Israel, Seek ye me and
ye shall live; but seek not Bethel nor enter into Gilgal
and pass not to Beersheba; for Gilgal shall surely go
into captivity and Bethel shall come to nought" (Amos
5:4-5). The moral ground of these judgments comes
out most clearly in the bold words, "I hate, I despise your
feasts and I will take no delight in your solemn assemblies. Yea though ye offer me your burnt-offerings and
meal-offerings, I will not accept them; neither will I regard the peace-offerings of your fat beasts. Take thou
away from me the noise of thy songs; for I will not

hear the melody of thy viols. But let justice roll down as waters and righteousness as a mighty stream" (Amos 5:21-24).

Beersheba is mentioned as a sanctuary nowhere else than in this book and it is specially surprising that the people of the northern kingdom should have gone there to worship, for the usual road led through the territory of Judah. Possibly they reached it by the coastal plain or by a route east of the Jordan. It was probably no more than one of the high places of which there were many in the land, both north and south. Thus the prophet foretells: "The high places of Isaac shall be desolate and the sanctuaries of Israel shall be laid waste" (Amos 7:9).

There were professional prophets in the land, for Amaziah charged Amos with being one of them, men who prophesied for pay. He said: "O thou seer, go flee thou away into the land of Judah and there eat bread and prophesy there" (Amos 7:12). Amos denied that he was a professional prophet, a member of one of the prophetic guilds called "sons of the prophets" (II Kings 2:3, 5, 15; 4:1, 38; 5:22; 6:1; 9:1). He said: "I was no prophet neither was I a prophet's son; but I was a herdsman and a dresser of sycomore trees and Jehovah took me from following the flock and Jehovah said unto me, Go prophesy unto my people Israel" (Amos 7:14-15). Although these prophetic guilds had their origin in Samuel's day in a desire for mutual edification (see pp. 189-191) and in Elijah's time they had not lost their primary purpose (see pp. 289-290), they had probably lowered the prophetic office by the time of Amos to a profession with its official garb and its cant phrases. Such false prophets were among the greatest foes of the true prophets whom Jehovah had called (Isa. 9:15; 28:7; Jer. 2:8; 5:31; 6:13; 8:10; 14:13-18; 23:11, 13-17, 21, 25-28, etc. Ezek. 13:3-4; Mic. 3:5, 6, 11; Zeph. 3:4).

(3) THE DAY OF JEHOVAH.

This familiar expression occurs in the book of Amos for the first time. Yet it occurs in a way which implies that it was already common among the people. They employed it to mean a day in the near future when Jehovah would give Israel victory over all their enemies. Since Jehovah was their God and they were his people, they thought that this victory would come, whether they were righteous or sinful. Amos took this expression and transformed it to mean the day when Jehovah will punish the wicked even in Israel. "Woe unto you that desire the day of Jehovah! Wherefore would ye have the day of Jehovah? It is darkness and not light. As if a man did flee from a lion and a bear met him; or went into the house and leaned his hand on the wall and a serpent bit him. Shall not the day of Jehovah be darkness and not light? even very dark and no brightness in it?" (Amos 5:18-20). This conception of the day of Jehovah as the day of judgment became a common one with the prophets (Isa. 2:12; 13:6, 9; 34:8; Ezek. 13:5; 30:3; Joel 1:15; 2:1-2, 11, 31; 3:14; Zeph. 1:7, 14; Zech. 14:1) and prepared the way for the New Testament doctrine of the final judgment.

(4) THE MESSIANIC HOPE.

Like the other prophets Amos lighted up his terrible words of doom for the wicked majority of the people of God with blessed words of hope for the righteous minority. He had a duty to the whole people, to the wicked to warn them of the wrath of Jehovah for their sins, and to the righteous to encourage them not to lose their faith in the purposes of Jehovah concerning his people. The righteous must have thought: If Israel goes into exile for their sins, will the promises of Jehovah fail? Can God's purpose be thwarted forever by the sin of man? It is in answer to such vital questions that Amos and the other pre-exilic prophets gave their glorious Messianic promises.

Although Amos did not mention Assyria by name he clearly referred to that power when he said: "Behold I will raise up against you a nation, O house of Israel, saith Jehovah, the God of hosts; and they shall afflict you from the entrance of Hamath unto the brook of the Arabah" (Amos 6:14), the full extent of the territory of the northern kingdom as foretold by Jonah (II Kings 14:25). His predictions of the captivity of the kingdom of the ten tribes are unequivocal. "Gilgal shall surely go into captivity" (Amos 5:5). "I will cause you to go into captivity beyond Damascus, saith Jehovah, whose name is the God of hosts" (Amos 5:27). "Therefore shall they now go captive with the first that go captive and the revelry of them that stretched themselves shall pass away" (Amos 6:7). To Amaziah he said: "Thou thyself shalt die in a land that is unclean and Israel shall surely be led away captive out of his land" (Amos 7:17). So far there is no hope; but in the ninth chapter hope comes in clearly "Behold the eyes of the Lord Jehovah are upon the sinful kingdom and I will

destroy it from off the face of the earth; save that I will
not utterly destroy the house of Jacob, saith Jehovah. For
lo I will command and I will sift the house of Israel
among all the nations, like as grain is sifted in a sieve,
yet shall not the least kernel fall upon the earth. All the
sinners of my people shall die by the sword, who say,
The evil shall not overtake nor meet us" (Amos 9:8-10).
This prediction relates not merely to the northern kingdom but to the whole family of Israel (cp. Amos 3:1).

The Messianic prediction of Amos is closely related to
the promise of perpetual dominion to the dynasty of David
(II Sam. 7:12-16; I Chron. 17:11-14) as well as to the
promises concerning the future of Israel. He foresaw
that the house of David would become like one of the
humble booths in which Israel lived in the wilderness, for
such is the meaning of the word rendered "tabernacle" in
Amos 9:11. He did not foretell definitely a personal
Messiah. Yet this is implied by the restoration of the
Davidic dynasty as in the glorious days of David and
Solomon. Great fertility shall characterize this future
time. Not only will Jehovah bring his people back from
captivity but he will establish them forever in their land.
"In that day will I raise up the tabernacle of David that
is fallen, and close up the breaches thereof; and I will
raise up its ruins, and I will build it as in the days of old;
that they may possess the remnant of Edom and all the
nations that are called by my name, saith Jehovah that
doeth this. Behold the days come, saith Jehovah, that the
plowman shall overtake the reaper and the treader of
grapes him that soweth seed; and the mountains shall drop
sweet wine and all the hills shall melt. And I will bring

back the captivity of my people Israel and they shall build
the waste cities and inhabit them; and they shall plant
vineyards and drink the wine thereof; they shall also make
gardens and eat the fruit of them.   And I will plant them
upon their land and they shall no more be plucked up out
of their land which I have given them, saith Jehovah thy
God" (Amos 9:11-15).   While the return from exile in
Babylon was a partial fulfillment of these words, it did
not exhaust them, for Israel certainly was plucked up out
of its land and scattered among the nations again when
Jerusalem fell in 70 A. D.   So they continue till our own
time.   The complete fulfilment of the prediction of Amos
is still future, in the time to which Isaiah refers when "the
Lord will set his hand again the second time to recover
the remnant of his people that shall remain from Assyria
and from Egypt and from Pathros and from Cush and
from Elam and from Shinar and from Hamath and from
the islands of the sea" (Isa. 11:11).

(5)   REVELATION AND INSPIRATION.

While the book of Amos sheds little light on the method
of revelation and inspiration, their effect upon the prophet
comes out clearly.   By several illustrations drawn from
his own experience he argues that every effect must have
its adequate cause and that every cause produces its necessary effect.   If two persons are seen walking together in
the wilderness, it cannot be by accident.   They must have
made an appointment (Amos 3:3).   If a lion roars, he
must have taken the prey (Amos 3:4).   If a bird falls
when on the earth, it must have been caught in a trap
(Amos 3:5).   If a trumpet is blown in the city, the people

are alarmed at the warning of an approaching enemy (Amos 3:6). These illustrations lead up to the remarkable statements: "Surely the Lord Jehovah will do nothing except he reveal his secret unto his servants the prophets. The lion hath roared: who will not fear? The Lord Jehovah hath spoken: who can but prophesy?" (Amos 3:7-8). These words assert the fact of divine revelation in no uncertain terms. But more remarkable than the fact of revelation is its effect upon its recipient. He felt the compulsion of the divine inspiration within him, that he could no more help prophesying than a lion could help roaring when it had taken the prey. As R. F. Horton well says (The New Century Bible in loc), "He lays bare his bosom and allows men to see the unalterable certainty, sure as cause and effect, that it is God in his soul, God speaking and acting within him that produces the utterance." It was the same inner compulsion which made Jeremiah declare: "If I say I will not make mention of him nor speak any more in his name, then there is in my heart as it were a burning fire shut up in my bones and I am weary with forbearing and I cannot contain" (Jer. 20:9), which made Peter and John say: "We cannot but speak the things which we saw and heard" (Acts 4:20) and which led Paul to exclaim: "Necessity is laid upon me; for woe is unto me if I preach not the gospel" (I. Cor. 9:16).

The most terrible woe in this book is given in these words: "Behold the days come saith Jehovah, that I will send a famine in the land, not a famine of bread nor a thirst for water, but of hearing the words of Jehovah. And they shall wander from sea to sea, and from the north even to the east; they shall run to and fro to seek the word of Jehovah and shall not find it" (Amos 8:11-12). Israel will be in the same sad case as forsaken Saul who sought Jehovah but received no answer "neither by dreams nor by Urim, nor by prophets" (I Sam. 28:6).

(6)   THE FUTURE LIFE.

There is only one allusion to the life after death in this book and that is incidental. When the prophet speaking in God's name foretells the doom of his rebellious people, he says that none can escape him, "Though they dig into Sheol, thence shall my hand take them; and though they climb up to heaven, thence will I bring them down" (Amos 9:2). Amos, like all other Old Testament writers, thought of Sheol as being under the earth, the underworld (Job 11:8; Isa. 14:9, 11). There is no reason to think that his ideas concerning the future life differed from those of earlier periods. His interest was in this life and not in the life to come.

(7)   MORALITY OF THE TIME.

The first two chapters reveal the special sins for which the small nations near Israel were condemned: cruelty in war (Amos 1:3), the slave trade (Amos 1:6, 9), brutality to women with child (Amos 1:13) and sacrilege toward the body of a hostile king (Amos 2:1). Israel was guilty of social sins as well as sins of appetite. The oppression of the poor by the rich is mentioned more often than any other offence (Amos 2:6-8; 4:1; 5:11; 8:4, 6). Associated with this were bribery and corruption in their courts (Amos 5:10, 12; 6:12). Licentiousness (Amos 2:7), drunkenness (Amos 4:1; 6:6) and probably gluttony (Amos 6:4) are also mentioned. Apparently there was a feeling of suspicion so that men did not regard it as safe to speak their minds concerning the powers that be. "Therefore he that is prudent shall keep silence in such a time; for it is an evil time" (Amos 5:13, cp. Eccl. 10:20).

The most serious aspect of the sins of Israel was that they were committed against light and love. Jehovah, speaking through Amos, reminded them of his gracious dealings in the past and especially his revelations to them. "Yet destroyed I the Amorite before them whose height was like the height of the cedars and he was strong as the oaks; yet I destroyed his fruit from above and his roots from beneath. Also I brought you up out of the land of Egypt and led you forty years in the wilderness, to possess the land of the Amorite. And I raised up of your sons for prophets, and of your young men for Nazirites. Is it not even thus, O ye children of Israel? saith Jehovah. But ye gave the Nazirites wine to drink and commanded the prophets saying, Prophesy not" (Amos 2:9-12).

CHAPTER IX.

Hosea.

The book is dated "in the days of Uzziah, Jotham, Ahaz and Hezekiah, kings of Judah and in the days of Jeroboam the son of Joash, king of Israel" (Hos. 1:1). There are two surprising things about this date, (1) that the prophet mentions Jotham, Ahaz and Hezekiah, although Uzziah (775-735 B. C.) survived Jeroboam (790-749 B. C.) by fourteen years; (2) that he does not mention the kings of Israel after Jeroboam. The probable explanation is that although Hosea was a native of the northern kingdom, he looked upon it as an apostate kingdom which had separated itself from the legitimate dynasty of David. Therefore he dated his book first in the reigns of the kings of Judah rather than in the reign of his own king. He did not mention the kings of Israel after Jeroboam because it was a time of great confusion, when four times the throne was obtained by regicide. Such events emphasized the illegitimacy of the kings. That such was Hosea's attitude toward the kings of Israel is evident in the later part of his book. He says in God's name: "They have set up kings, but not by me; they have made princes, and I knew it not" (Hos. 8:4). It may be also to the kings of Israel that Hos. 13:10-11 refers, although the language suggests a reference to the people's asking for a king in Samuel's time (cp. I Sam. 8:4-22). "Where now is thy king that he may save thee in all thy cities? and thy judges of whom thou saidst, Give me a king and princes? I have given thee a king in mine anger and have taken him away in my wrath." The same attitude toward the king of Israel is reflected in the statement: "As for Samaria, her king is cut off as foam upon the water" (Hos. 10:7).

The prophetic ministry of Hosea began near the end of the reign of Jeroboam when Israel was politically more prosperous than at any other period of her history (cp. II Kings 14:25) and when wealth and luxury prevailed. Morality, however, was at a low ebb. It was about the same time that Amos began his ministry in Israel. The first three chapters of Hosea are the only ones which probably belong in the reign of Jeroboam. The later chapters (4-14) give many evidences of the troubled conditions which followed the death of that powerful king. Thus Hosea's ministry continued long after the return of Amos to Judah but not until the Syro-Ephraimite war against Judah in 734 B. C.

Hosea gave his prophecies to the northern kingdom but like Amos he had the whole people of God in view. He foresaw the time when Judah and Israel should be reunited under one king, for he said: "The children of Judah and the children of Israel shall be gathered together and they shall appoint themselves one head, and shall go up from the land" (Hos. 1:11). He did not ignore the sins of Judah nor the punishment which would result from them but frequently he mentioned the two parts of the people of God together as under the divine condemnation. "Though thou, Israel, play the harlot, yet let not Judah

offend; and come not ye unto Gilgal, neither go ye up to
Beth-aven, nor swear, As Jehovah liveth" (Hos. 4:15).
"The pride of Israel doth testify to his face: therefore
Israel and Ephraim shall stumble in their iniquity; Judah
also shall stumble with them. . . . The princes of Judah
are like them that remove the landmark: I will pour out
my wrath upon them like water. Ephraim is oppressed,
he is crushed in judgment; because he was content to
walk after man's command. Therefore am I unto
Ephraim as a moth and to the house of Judah as rotten-
ness. When Ephraim saw his sickness and Judah saw his
wound, then went Ephraim to Assyria and sent to King
Jareb: but he is not able to heal you, neither will he cure
you of your wound. For I will be unto Ephraim as a
lion and as a young lion to the house of Judah: I, even I,
will tear and go away; I will carry off and there shall be
none to deliver" (Hos. 5:5, 10-14). "O Ephraim, what
shall I do unto thee? O Judah, what shall I do unto
thee? for your goodness is as a morning cloud, and as the
dew that goeth early away" (Hos. 6:4). "Israel hath
forgotten his Maker, and builded palaces; and Judah hath
multiplied fortified cities: but I will send a fire upon his
cities and it shall devour the castles thereof" (Hos. 8:14).
"Ephraim feedeth on wind, and followeth after the east
wind: he continually multiplieth lies and desolation; and
they make a covenant with Assyria and oil is carried into
Egypt. Jehovah hath also a controversy with Judah and
will punish Jacob according to his ways; according to his
doings will he recompense him" (Hos. 12:1-2). Even
though this great prophet of the northern kingdom placed
Israel and Judah under equal condemnation for their sins

as Amos had done before him, he saw clearly a distinction between them. Speaking in Jehovah's name he said: "I will no more have mercy upon the house of Israel, that I should in any wise pardon them. But I will have mercy upon the house of Judah and will save them by Jehovah their God and will not save them by bow, nor by sword, nor by battle, by horses, nor by horsemen" (Hos. 1:6-7). Israel had sinned away its day of grace; but there was still hope for Judah in repentance and in the lovingkindness of Jehovah. His promises to His people could not be thwarted by their sins.

The most significant fact about the message of Hosea is that it came directly out of his own experience as interpreted to him by the Spirit of God. On this account he has been called the Jeremiah of the northern kingdom, for Jeremiah's message also was related closely to his tragic experiences. Since, however, Jeremiah was more than a century later and was influenced greatly by Hosea, it would be more accurate to call him the Hosea of the seventh century. The experience of Hosea from which his message was derived consisted in the unfaithfulness of his wife Gomer. Some interpreters have regarded this story as unhistorical, a mere allegory of the unfaithfulness of Israel to Jehovah. Their chief argument is, that God would not command the prophet to take a harlot for his wife. Not only is such a thought an aspersion upon the holiness of God and morally repulsive but such a marriage would have reduced greatly if it did not completely destroy Hosea's influence with his people. It is pointed out that priests were expressly prohibited to marry harlots (Lev. 21:7) and that a prophet must be equally pure.

This view, however, is based upon a misinterpretation of Hos. 1:2. God did not command Hosea to marry a harlot. The expression a wife or woman of whoredom (Hos. 1:2) does not necessarily mean a woman who had already committed acts of impurity. If Hosea had meant such a woman he would have used the common word for a harlot. The expression "a woman of whoredom" resembles the expressions "a woman of grace" (A. R. V. "a gracious woman." Prov. 11:16), "a woman of contentions" (A. R. V. "a contentious woman." Prov. 21:9) and "a woman of worthiness" (A. R. V. "a worthy woman." Prov. 31:10). Each of these expressions refers to inherent character and tendency, not to conduct. Gomer, the wife of Hosea, had an impure character and tendency even before he married her; but there is no hint of this character showing itself in conduct until some years after marriage. Most decisive in favor of this interpretation is the fact that if Gomer had been guilty of acts of impurity before marriage, she would not have been a true representative of Israel. Both Hosea and Jeremiah refer to Israel's faithfulness to Jehovah at the beginning of their history (Hos. 2:15; 6:4; 9:10; 11:1; Jer. 2:2-3). The spirit of whoredom was in Israel as in Gomer (Hos. 4:12; 5:4) but it did not show itself immediately.

Furthermore there is no reason to think that Hosea knew of this tendency to impurity in Gomer before he married her. He did not make this tragic discovery until after the birth of Gomer's second child, Lo-ruhamah. The birth of Jezreel, the first child, is described in the words "she conceived and bare him a son" (Hos. 1:3). Such an expression is frequent in the Old Testament and the man to whom the mother bore the child is always the father of the child (Gen. 6:4; 16:1; 21:3, 7, 9; 22:23; 24:24, etc.). Jezreel was the son of Hosea and Gomer. The name was symbolical of the fact that God would avenge the blood of Jezreel upon the house of Jehu and cause the kingdom of the house of Israel to cease (Hos. 1:4). There is no suggestion in this symbolism of the illegitimacy of the child. But how different is the record concerning the second and the third child. In neither case is it said that Gomer bore the child to Hosea and in both cases the name of the child is suggestive of illegitimacy. The second child was named Lo-ruhamah, the "unpitied one" because Jehovah would have no mercy upon the house of Israel (Hos. 1:6). The third child was named Lo-ammi, "not my people," for Jehovah said to Israel: "Ye are not my people and I will not be your God" (Hos. 1:9). Later these names were changed to Ammi and Ruhamah to foreshadow the fact that God would have pity on Israel and not cast them off in spite of their unfaithfulness (Hos. 1:10; 2:1). Hosea did not cast off these children though he knew that they were not his. He kept them as if they had been his own.

If Hosea did not know of the impurity of Gomer until years after his marriage, how are we to understand the statement of Hos. 1:2, "When Jehovah spake at the first by (margin, with) Hosea, Jehovah said unto Hosea, Go, take unto thee a wife of whoredom and children of whoredom; for the land doth commit great whoredom, departing from Jehovah"? George Adam Smith following W. Robertson Smith states the case well: "When, some years after his marriage, Hosea at last began to be

aware of the character of her whom he had taken to his
home, and while he still brooded upon it, God revealed
to him why He who knoweth all things from the beginning had suffered His servant to marry such a woman;
and Hosea, by a very natural anticipation, in which he is
imitated by other prophets, pushed back his own knowledge of God's purpose to the date when that purpose began actually to be fulfilled, the day of his betrothal. This,
though he was all unconscious of its fatal future, had been
to Hosea the beginning of the word of the Lord. On
that uncertain voyage he had sailed with sealed orders"
(Expositor's Bible. The Minor Prophets. Vol. I, pp.
238-239). A parallel case is the story of Jeremiah's purchase of a field in Anathoth (Jer. 32:6-44). Jeremiah
states that Jehovah told him to buy the field (vs. 6 and
25) although he did not realize at first that it was the
word of Jehovah (vs. 8). Similarly when Hosea looked
back upon his marriage in the light of its tragic results,
he realized that the whole experience from the very beginning had been providential, a word of Jehovah to his
heart. God had led him through this terrific experience in
order that he might reveal to Israel His forgiving love.

That the story of Hosea's marriage to Gomer was an
actual happening and not a mere allegory is evidenced by
the following other considerations: (1) In an allegory
the names are all symbolical. Here, however, while the
names of the children are symbolical, those of Gomer
and her father Diblaim are not so. The fact that the children were given symbolical names no more argues that
the story is an allegory, than the symbolical names of
Isaiah's children (Isa. 7:3; 8:1-4) argue that they did

not exist in real life. (2) Such a story would reflect upon the character of Hosea, if it were not true, and interfere with his usefulness. If he was unmarried it would arouse suspicion of his own impurity; and if he was married to a faithful wife, it would raise suspicion against her. Since the story was true and the facts were well known, it raised no suspicion against him but furnished him with the most powerful and vivid preaching imaginable. He drew his lessons from his own experience. (3) The intense emotion with which Hosea's prophecies were given argues strongly for the reality of his experience. This intense emotion shows itself throughout the book. Hos. 6:4 and 11:1, 3, 4, 8, 9 are notable examples. While we cannot say that Hosea could not have had such intense emotion toward Israel if he had not had the tragic experience of Gomer's unfaithfulness, his emotion is far more natural as the product of his own experience. Hosea came to know God and God's love for Israel through his own love for his unfaithful wife and her children. "He that loveth not knoweth not God; for God is love" (I Jno. 4:8).

(1) The Conception of God.

Since Hosea gained his deep knowledge of God by his own tragic experience, he came to realize that true knowledge of God can be gained in no other way. It is in this experimental sense that we should understand his frequent references to the knowledge of God. The fundamental error of Israel was that they did not know Jehovah. "Hear the word of Jehovah, ye children of Israel; for Jehovah hath a controversy with the inhabitants of the land, because there is no truth nor goodness nor knowledge of

God in the land" (Hos. 4:1). "My people are destroyed
for lack of knowledge: because thou hast rejected knowledge, I will also reject thee" (Hos. 4:6). "Their doings
will not suffer them to turn unto their God; for the spirit
of whoredom is within them and they know not Jehovah"
(Hos. 5:4). "Ephraim is like a silly dove without understanding" (Hos. 7:11). As Gomer did not know Hosea
because she deserted him, her true husband, and went after
her lovers, so Israel did not and could not know Jehovah
because they deserted him and served Baalim (Hos. 2:8,
13; 11:2; 13:1). God's supreme desire for Israel was
that they should have this personal and experimental
knowledge of him. He said: "I desire goodness and not
sacrifice; and the knowledge of God more than burnt
offerings" (Hos. 6:6). "Yet I am Jehovah thy God from
the land of Egypt; and thou shalt know no God but me,
and besides me there is no saviour. I did know thee in
the wilderness, in the land of great drought" (Hos.
13:4-5). Hosea had an imperishable hope that Isreal
would come back to Jehovah and would come to know
him, just as he hoped persistently that Gomer would come
back to her true marital relations with him. In God's
name he foretold: "I will even betroth thee unto me in
faithfulness; and thou shalt know Jehovah" (Hos. 2:20).
The prophet looked forward confidently to the time when
Israel should say: "Let us know, let us follow on to
know Jehovah; his going forth is sure as the morning;
and he will come unto us as the rain, as the latter rain
that watereth the earth" (Hos. 6:3). While this experimental sense of the knowledge of God is very common in
the Old Testament, especially in the expression to know

the name of Jehovah (I Kings 8:43; Ps. 9:10; 91:14; Isa. 52:6; 64:2; Jer. 16:21; Ezek. 39:6-7), it received new depth and force from the experience and teaching of Hosea. It is frequent in the prophecy of Jeremiah, who owed so much to Hosea and who like Hosea derived his prophetic message from experience (Jer. 2:8; 4:22; 9:3, 6, 24; 10:25; 22:16; 24:7; 31:34).

If we inquire what is the content of this experimental knowledge of Jehovah which Hosea gained and which he poured forth so passionately before the people, the book gives answer. It was the love of God for Israel. The prophet learned this great lesson from his own love for Gomer. Loving as God loves he came to know what the love of God really is. Hosea did not love Gomer because she was lovable nor did Jehovah love Isreal because she was lovable. Hosea loved Gomer in spite of her unfaithfulness and Jehovah loved Israel in spite of her sin. Hosea came to appreciate something of the struggle in the heart of God between his righteousness and his love from the same struggle in his own feelings toward his wayward wife. Yet just as love was more powerful than righteousness in Hosea, so was it in Jehovah. He does not speak often of the love of God. Yet it breathes and pulsates in many of his most passionate words. "Jehovah said unto me, Go again, love a woman beloved of her friend and an adultress, even as Jehovah loveth the children of Israel, though they turn unto other gods and love cakes of raisins" (Hos. 3:1). "When Israel was a child, then I loved him and called my son out of Egypt . . . I drew them with cords of a man with bands of love" (Hos. 11:1, 4). "I will heal their backsliding, I will love

them freely; for mine anger is turned away from him"
(Hos. 14:4). These are the only references to the love
of God. Yet how clearly do we feel the infinite love of
God in such words as these. "O Ephraim, what shall I
do unto thee? O Judah, what shall I do unto thee? for
your goodness is as a morning cloud, and as the dew that
goeth early away" (Hos. 6:4). "I taught Ephraim to
walk; I took them on my arms; but they knew not that I
healed them" (Hos. 11:3). Jehovah's inextinguishable
and unconquerable love for Israel, a love which would
ultimately win Isreal to repentance, is the great contribution of Hosea to the history of revelation. It is the beginning of the revelation of the love of God whose greatest
manifestation was the incarnation and the atoning sacrifice
of Jesus Christ. In this sense Hosea was a thoroughly
evangelical prophet.

When we compare the message of Hosea with that of
Amos, the wisdom of revelation becomes evident. The
first necessity for Israel was a realization of the divine
righteousness. If the love of God had been revealed before his righteousness, that love would have appeared as
weak and sentimental; but when God's love is seen against
the background of his righteousness, his impartial justice,
it appears as a love that costs, a love that suffers, a love
that redeems for a price. Hosea did not forgive Gomer because her unfaithfulness seemed to him a trivial thing easily
forgotten and easily forgiven. Jehovah did not forgive
Israel because her sin seemed small to him. He forgave her
in spite of his righteousness and his inexorable demand of
righteousness in his people. His love for Israel made
him suffer when Israel sinned. In spite of the fact that

they deserved their sufferings, that their sufferings were the divine punishment for their sins, "his soul was grieved for the misery of Israel" (Judges 10:16), "in all their affliction he was afflicted . . . in his love and in his pity, he redeemed them" (Isa. 63:9). Thus the message of the righteousness of God in Amos was the necessary preparation for the message of his love in Hosea. In Hosea we see the same conflict between justice and love which called forth David's bitter cry over his wayward and rebellious son: "O my son Absalom, my son, my son, Absalom! would I had died for thee, O Absalom, my son, my son!" (II Sam. 18:33). David's suffering love, however, was helpless. It did not succeed in redeeming Absalom. How different was Hosea's love. At last it won Gomer back. How infinitely different was Jehovah's love. God's love for Israel made him suffer but he was not helpless. God's love made him do what David longed to do but could not. He died for his rebellious children and so redeemed them. While the fullness of this truth remained for the revelation of the New Testament, the experience and teaching of Hosea were among the most important preparations for the cross of Christ. Here as there, "mercy and truth are met together; righteousness and peace have kissed each other" (Ps. 85:10).

There is a marked contrast between Hosea and Amos in respect to breadth. Amos applied the demands of the divine righteousness to the other nations as well as to Judah and Israel (chapters 1 and 2). He represented Jehovah as bringing the Philistines from Caphtor and the Syrians from Kir as truly as he brought Israel up from Egypt (Amos 9:7). There is no such breadth in the teaching of Hosea. He has nothing to say about the Gentile nations. The love of God which he revealed was not a love for all mankind but only for Israel. This was the inevitable result of the sad experience from which Hosea's revelation sprang. The relation of Israel to Jehovah was like that of Gomer to Hosea. It was based upon the covenant which Jehovah had graciously made with the nation. He had fulfilled his part of the covenant but Israel had failed in their part. "They like Adam have transgressed the covenant: there have they dealt treacherously against me" (Hos. 6:7). "They have transgressed my covenant, and trespassed against my law" (Hosea 8:1). This covenant-relation is described under the figures of marriage and of fatherhood. Israel was an unfaithful wife and an undutiful son. It was faithlessness to Jehovah, when they worshipped Baalim, when they sought to make covenants with Assyria or Egypt (Hosea 7:11, 13; 8:9) and when they were guilty of immorality. Yet in spite of all their unfaithfulness Jehovah loved them and his love at last would conquer. Kirkpatrick has well said of Hosea: "He gains in depth what he loses in breadth. If the teaching of Amos is wider, that of Hosea is more profound. Not that the one is to be regarded as the rival of the other: each has his proper place in the economy of revelation. But we cannot fail to note that Hosea goes deeper and deals not with action only but with the springs and motives of action. The love of God for his people is a thought which does not appear in Amos. It is prominent in Hosea (3:1; 11:1, 4; 14:4). The term lovingkindness (Heb. hesed) is not found in Amos. It is a characteristic word in Hosea, who uses it to express the natural attitude of Jehovah to his people, and man's natural attitude to his fellow-man, as the reflection of that love (2:19; 4:1; 6:4, 6; 10:12; 12:6)" (Doctrine of the Prophets p. 138).

Although Hosea does not speak of Jehovah's dominion over all nations, there is no reason to doubt that like Amos he was an ethical monotheist. He had a spiritual conception of Jehovah which could not tolerate the representation of him by the calves at Bethel and Dan. "The workman made it, and it is no God; yea, the calf of Samaria shall be broken in pieces" (Hosea 8:6). "Neither will we say any more to the work of our hands, Ye are our gods" (Hosea 14:3). He considered Jehovah the only true God for Israel. "I am Jehovah thy God from the land of Egypt; and thou shalt know no god but me and besides me there is no saviour." (Hosea 13:4). Although from the nature of the theme with which his book deals, it gives no light on his belief concerning the gods of other nations, it is altogether probable that, like his contemporaries Amos, Isaiah and Micah, he would have denied their existence. It would be too much to expect of Hosea that he should proclaim the love of God for all mankind. Such a proclamation in his time could not have been as deep as was his message. The revelation of the love of God for man must begin with one nation. Yet by his emphasis on the love of God for Israel he helped to prepare the way for the greater teaching. "God so loved the world, that he gave his only begotten Son, that whosoever believeth on him should not perish, but have eternal life" (John 3:16).

(2) THE CEREMONIES OF RELIGION.

The book of Hosea presents the same conditions as to the externals of religion as the book of Amos. Bethel, the chief sanctuary of the northern kingdom, is called Beth-aven ("house of iniquity") because of its idolatrous worship (Hos. 4:15; 5:8; 10:5) and once this is shortened to Aven ("iniquity," Hos. 10:8; compare Amos 1:5). Gilgal is referred to as another place of worship (Hos. 4:15; 9:15; 12:11; compare Amos 4:4; 5:5). Hosea condemns the high places of Aven (Hos. 10:8) as Amos had condemned the high places of Isaac (Amos 7:9). Idolatry is mentioned repeatedly. "My people ask counsel at their stock and their staff declareth unto them; for the spirit of whoredom hath caused them to err, and they have played the harlot, departing from under their God. They sacrifice upon the tops of the mountains, and burn incense upon the hills, under oaks and poplars and terebinths, because the shadow thereof is good" (Hos. 4:12-13). "He hath cast off thy calf, O Samaria; mine anger is kindled against them. . . . For from Israel is even this; the workman made it, and it is no God; yea, the calf of Samaria shall be broken in pieces" (Hos. 8:5-6). "And now they sin more and more, and have made them molten images of their silver, even idols according to their own understanding, all of them the work of the craftsmen; they say of them, Let the men that sacrifice kiss the calves" (Hos. 13:2 compare 2:8). In particular the worship of the Baalim was carried on. Israel vainly imagined that their plentiful crops, their silver and their gold, were the gifts of Baal when in reality it was Jehovah who gave them.

"She did not know that I gave her the grain and the new wine, and the oil, and multiplied unto her silver and gold, which they used for Baal" (Margin "made into the image of Baal" Hos. 2:8). "I will visit upon her the days of the Baalim, unto which she burned incense, when she decked herself with her ear-rings, and her jewels, and went after her lovers, and forgat me, saith Jehovah" (Hos. 2:13). "I will take away the names of the Baalim out of her mouth, and they shall no more be mentioned by their name" (Hos. 2:17). "They sacrificed unto the Baalim and burned incense to graven images" (Hos. 11:2). "When he offended in Baal, he died." (Hos. 13:1). Israel loved cakes of raisins (Hos. 3:1) which were eaten in the drunken feasts of the Baal-worship. These feasts as well as her new moons, sabbaths and solemn assemblies were celebrated to the Baalim (Hos. 2:11-13). In fact, the religion of Israel was highly developed on the ceremonial side but utterly lacking on the moral and spiritual side. It may be to this that the strange expression, "Ephraim is a cake not turned" (Hos. 7:8) refers. "Because Ephraim hath multiplied altars for sinning, altars have been unto him for sinning" (Hos. 8:11). "Ephraim is joined to idols; let him alone" (Hos. 4:17).

The attitude of Hosea toward all this idolatrous worship was like that of Amos with this important exception. Amos condemned it because it was empty formalism unaccompanied by righteousness (Amos 4:4-5; 5:4-5, 21-24). Hosea condemned it because, although nominally rendered to Jehovah, it was in reality the worship of the Baalim. Viewed in this light it was unfaithfulness to Jehovah,

treachery against him (Hos. 1:2; 4:12; 9:1). Nevertheless Hosea like Amos recognized the vanity of a merely
ceremonial approach to God.   Sacrifices are insufficient.
"They shall go with their flocks and with their herds to
seek Jehovah; but they shall not find him: he hath withdrawn himself from them" (Hos. 5:6).   "I desire goodness, and not sacrifice; and the knowledge of God more
than burnt-offerings" (Hos. 6:6).   The exhortation of the
prophet shows the true way for a sinful man to approach
God, "Take with you words, and return unto Jehovah;
say unto him, Take away all iniquity, and accept that which
is good: so will we render as bullocks the offering of our
lips" (Hos. 14:2).   The offering which God desired and
would accept was not an animal sacrifice but a broken
spirit, a broken and a contrite heart (Ps. 51:17) which
poured forth its confession of sin in humble penitence.
As the prodigal came back to his father with no offering
but the words of confession, "I have sinned against heaven
and in thy sight: I am no more worthy to be called thy
son" (Luke 15:18-21), words which he had carried in his
bosom from the far country, so must Israel take with them
words and return unto Jehovah.   We should not think that
Hosea condemned sacrifices as such.   They were offensive
to God only when they were not the genuine expression
of penitence.   If Israel rendered to Jehovah as bullocks
the offering of their lips, we may be sure that he would
accept their burnt-offerings.

Israel was led astray by false priests, priests who were
murderers and adulterers.   "As troops of robbers wait for
a man, so the company of priests murder in the way
toward Shechem; yea, they have committed lewdness"

(Hos. 6:9). With such an example before them it is no wonder that the people gave themselves over to immorality. "It shall be, like people, like priest" (Hos. 4:9). Hosea condemned these priests unsparingly, "Hear this, O ye priests, and hearken, O house of Israel, and give ear, O house of the king; for unto you pertaineth the judgment; for ye have a snare at Mizpah and a net spread upon Tabor" (Hos. 5:1). There were also false prophets as we have seen from Amos (7:12-14), of whom Hosea said that they should stumble with the people in the night (Hos. 4:5). They were blind leaders of the blind (Matt. 15:14).

(3) THE FUTURE LIFE.

The book of Hosea contains the germ of an important new revelation concerning the life to come. Here for the first time appears the idea of the resurrection from the dead. We have seen that possibly this idea may be hidden in two Davidic Psalms (Ps. 16:10; 17:15; p. 246); but this is doubtful. The miracle of Elisha's raising the son of the Shunammite from the dead (II Kings 4:32-37) and that of the dead man who revived and stood upon his feet when his body touched the bones of Elisha (II Kings 13:20-21) should also be mentioned (p. 293). In Hosea, however, the idea is much clearer. It is found in two important passages: "Come, and let us return unto Jehovah; for he hath torn and he will heal us; he hath smitten and he will bind us up. After two days will he revive us; on the third day, he will raise us up, and we shall live before him. And let us know, let us follow on to know Jehovah: his going forth is sure as the morning;

and he will come unto us as the rain as the latter rain that watereth the earth" (Hos. 6:1-3). "I will ransom them from the power of Sheol; I will redeem them from death; O death, where are they plagues? O Sheol, where is thy destruction? Repentance shall be hid from mine eyes" (Hos. 13:14). These passages plainly refer to the resurrection of the nation from the exile. Hosea said that when Ephraim "offended in Baal, he died" (Hos. 13:1). This death of the nation was a moral death, a death which was the wages of sin (Rom. 6:23); but it was not eternal death. They had separated themselves morally and religiously from Jehovah and it was appropriate that they should be separated from him geographically. Therefore he cast them out of his land and sent them into exile. But when they repented of their sin and returned to their God, it was appropriate that they should be restored to his land. This was the national resurrection to which Hosea referred. The same idea is developed by Isaiah (26:19) and Ezekiel (37:1-14) and underlies the symbolic experience of Jonah (1:17; compare Matt. 12:40).

It may be that Hosea had no meaning in his words more than the restoration of Israel from exile. But in the light of the New Testament we are justified in concluding that the Holy Spirit guided the prophet to use language in Hos. 6:2 which foreshadowed the resurrection of Christ and in Hos. 13:14 which foreshadowed the resurrection of all true believers from the dead. Hos. 6:2 is not quoted in the New Testament in reference to Christ. Yet our Lord said: "Thus it is written that the Christ should suffer and rise again from the dead the third day" (Luke 24:46), and Paul wrote "that he hath been raised on the third day according to the Scriptures" (I Cor. 15:4). If we search the Scriptures to learn where it was written that Christ should rise from the dead on the third day, we find it in Hos. 6:2 and Jonah 1:17; 2:10. The former passage literally and the latter passages symbolically refer to the resurrection of Israel from the death of the exile. But in both passages the restoration of Israel from the exile foreshadows the resurrection of Christ. This is most clearly seen in the words of Christ, "as Jonah was three days and three nights in the belly of the whale; so shall the Son of Man be three days and three nights in the heart of the earth" (Matt. 12:40).

Paul quotes Hos. 13:14 in reference to the resurrection of those who believe in Christ (I Cor. 15:55). This is not an arbitrary use of a passage whose original meaning related to the restoration of Israel from the exile. Just as the cause of Israel's exile was their sin, so "the sting of death is sin" (I Cor. 15:56) and the restoration from the exile foreshadowed the resurrection of Christ and of all who believe in him. Well did Paul take Hosea's triumphant words to express his triumph over death. The spiritual Israel of the New Testament through Christ gains the victory over the last enemy to be abolished, which is death (I Cor. 15:26). Although Hosea spoke of a resurrection from the exile, it is not likely that he would have used this figure unless he had believed in a resurrection from the dead. Hence his words represent an important stage in the development of the Old Testament doctrine of the future life, a development which found its climax in the prediction of Dan. 12:2, "Many of them that sleep in the dust of the earth shall awake, some to everlasting life, and some to shame and everlasting contempt" (compare John 5:28-29).

(4) THE MESSIANIC HOPE.

Like the other preëxilic prophets, Hosea foresaw the coming of the Messiah in connection with the restoration of Israel from the exile. To him the reëstablishment of Jehovah's people in their land under the Davidic dynasty and the coming of the ideal king of that dynasty were one. He could not see that several centuries would elapse from the restoration of Israel to the coming of Christ. In spite of Judah's sin Jehovah promised: "I will have mercy upon the house of Judah, and will save them by Jehovah their God, and will not save them by bow, nor by sword, nor by battle, by horses, nor by horsemen" (Hos. 1:7). With recollection of God's promise to Abraham (Gen. 22:17) and to David (II Sam. 7:12-16) the prophet foretold: "The number of the children of Israel shall be as the sand of the sea, which cannot be measured nor numbered; and it shall come to pass that, in the place where it was said unto them, Ye are not my people, it shall be said unto them, Ye are the sons of the living God. And the children of Judah and the children of Israel shall be gathered together, and they shall appoint themselves one head and shall go up from the land (Hos. 1:10-11). This prediction of the reuniting of Judah and Israel under one Davidic king is found also in Jeremiah (23:5-6; 50:4-5) and is enlarged upon by Ezekiel (37:15-28). Hosea does not say here who the king of the united people shall be. He is designated merely as "one head" whom Israel shall appoint themselves. In this respect this prophecy resembles that of Jeremiah, "Their prince shall be of themselves, and their ruler shall proceed from the midst of them" (Jer. 30:21). There can, however, be no doubt that Hosea, like Jeremiah, foresaw the Davidic Messianic king as the future head of the chosen people, for he prophesied: "The children of Israel shall abide many days without king, and without prince, and without sacrifice and without pillar, and without ephod, or teraphim; afterward shall the children of Israel return, and seek Jehovah their God, and David their king, and shall come with fear unto Jehovah and to his goodness in the latter days" (Hos. 3:4-5). Here, as in Jer. 30:9; Ezek. 34:23-24; 37:24, the Messiah is called not the son of David but David. He was a second David, as his forerunner, John the Baptist, was a second Elijah (Mal. 4:5; Matt. 11:14; 17:10-13; Mark 9:11-13; Luke 1:17).

The restoration of Israel from the exile, as we have seen, takes the form of a national resurrection. "After two days will he revive us: on the third day he will raise us up, and we shall live before him" (Hos. 6:2; compare 13:14). To Hosea this doubtless meant nothing more than the resurrection of the nation; but by virtue of the typical relation of Israel to Christ we can see that his resurrection on the third day was here foreshadowed. Such a conclusion is justified by the statements of our Lord and of Paul that the resurrection on the third day was "written," i. e:, recorded in Scripture (Luke 24:46), and "according to the Scriptures" (I Cor. 15:4). Hosea 6:2 and Jonah 1:17 are probably the Scriptures referred to (Matt. 12:40). This typical relation of the chosen people to Christ found its highest expression in Isaiah's noble passages concerning the Servant of Jehovah (Isa. 42:1-7; 49:1-7; 50:4-9; 52:13-53:12). Although Hosea like Isaiah wrote of Israel, a greater than Israel is here. The inner meaning, the divine purpose in the call of Israel looked forward to the Messiah. Hosea's deeply spiritual conception of Israel's relation to Jehovah, a conception which grew out of his own experience with Gomer, led him under divine guidance to speak better than he knew. What he meant to say of Israel coming back from exile, the inspiring Spirit said concerning Jesus Christ coming back from the grave.

Another example of a typically Messianic passage is found in Jehovah's word: "When Israel was a child, then I loved him, and called my son out of Egypt" (Hos. 11:1). The designation of Israel as God's son is derived from the words which Jehovah commanded Moses to say to Pharaoh, "Israel is my son, my first-born" (Exod. 4:22). If the whole nation was God's son, this was pre-eminently true of the theocratic king of the nation. Hence the Psalmist represents Jehovah as saying to the king, "Thou are my son. This day have I begotten thee" (Ps. 2:7). Therefore Matthew was entirely justified in applying words which Hosea wrote of Israel to Christ. The child Jesus was in Egypt until the death of Herod "that it might be fulfilled which was spoken by the Lord through the prophet saying, Out of Egypt did I call my son" (Matt. 2:15). The typical elements of Messianic prediction were not usually in such externals. Yet the fulfillment extends here even to the country where Christ lived. The Messiah like Israel was called out of Egypt.

(5) THE MORALITY OF THE TIME.

The moral condition of Israel as reflected in the book of Hosea is the same as that which we have found in Amos. Many of the same sins are mentioned. "There is nought but swearing and breaking faith, and killing, and stealing, and committing adultery; they break out, and blood toucheth blood" (Hos. 4:2). "Whoredom and wine and new wine take away the understanding" (Hos. 4:11). "I will not punish your daughters when they play the harlot, nor your brides when they commit adultery; for the men themselves go apart with harlots, and they sacrifice with the prostitutes" (Hos. 4:14). "They commit falsehood, and the thief entereth in, and the troop of robbers ravageth without (Hos. 7:1). "They are all adulterers; they are as an oven heated by the baker; he ceaseth to stir the fire, from the kneading of the dough, until it be leavened" (Hos. 7:4). "He is a trafficker, the balances of deceit are in his hand: he loveth to oppress" (Hos. 12:7). Even the priests were robbers and adulterers. "As troops of robbers wait for a man, so the company of priests murder in the way toward Shechem; yea, they have committed lewdness" (Hos. 6:9). The king and the princes also rejoiced in the wickedness of the people. "They make the king glad with their wickedness, and the princes with their lies" (Hos. 7:3). It was true of such a time that "the wicked walk on every side, when vileness is exalted among the sons of men" (Ps. 12:8). Oppression of the poor by the rich and bribery and corruption in the courts, which are so prominent in Amos (2:6-8; 4:1; 5:10-12; 6:12; 8:4, 6) are not mentioned by Hosea except in the single reference to oppression (Hos. 12:7).

Yet the approval of wickedness by the king and the princes (Hos. 7:3) makes such offences natural. The crowning sin of Israel from which all others sprang was unfaithfulness to Jehovah, separation from him. "Woe unto them! for they have wandered from me; destruction unto them! for they have trespassed against me: though I would redeem them, yet they have spoken lies against me" (Hos. 7:13). As Gomer was unfaithful to her husband Hosea, so "the land doth commit great whoredom, departing from Jehovah" (Hos. 1:2).

CHAPTER X.

Isaiah.

Isaiah may confidently be called the greatest of the eighth-century prophets. He combined the broad universality of Amos and his passionate demand for righteousness with the deep intensity of Hosea. His book is dated in the reigns of Uzziah, Jotham, Ahaz and Hezekiah, kings of Judah (Isa. 1:1). There are, however, no prophecies in his book which give evidence of dating from the reign of Uzziah. The inclusion of that king's name in the date is probably due to the fact that the call of Isaiah to his prophetic office occurred "in the year that King Uzziah died (Isa. 6:1). This was 735 B. C. Chapters 40-66 are not dated and are separated from chapters 1-35 by a historical section (chapters 36-39). Furthermore, while Isaiah is mentioned by name sixteen times in the earlier chapters (Isa. 1:1; 2:1; 7:3; 13:1; 20:2, 3; 37:2, 5, 6, 21; 38:1, 4, 21; 39:3, 5, 8) he is neither mentioned by name nor referred to in the last twenty-seven chapters of the book. Of these last chapters the section including chapters 40-55 was plainly spoken or written from the standpoint of the exile. Nowhere in these sixteen chapters is the exile foretold, but it is constantly looked upon as already begun and indeed far advanced. The restoration from the exile is foretold and Cyrus is mentioned by name as Jehovah's agent for its accomplishment

(Isa. 44:28; 45:1). These facts, together with differences of style, vocabulary and theological emphasis from the dated writings of Isaiah, have led many scholars to conclude that chapters 40-55 were not the work of Isaiah but were composed by an unknown and supremely great prophet whom they call for convenience Deutero-Isaiah. They are dated about 540 B. C., after the conquests of Cyrus had begun but before he had taken Babylon.

This is not the place to discuss in full the arguments either for or against this critical opinion. It must suffice to state that those who deny that chapters 40-55 could have been written by Isaiah or in his time have failed to appreciate the attitude of the prophet to the great events of his own day. Like Amos, Hosea and the other prophets he regarded himself as a prophet to all the twelve tribes. The exile of any of those tribes was a clear indication that, if the other tribes did not repent of their sins, they would suffer a like fate. The events of Isaiah's day made it easy for him to look upon the exile as in the will of God, already begun, no more to be foretold but to be taken for granted, presupposed. Near the beginning of his ministry, about 734 B. C., Tiglath-pileser "took Ijon, and Abel-beth-maacah and Janoah and Kedesh and Hazor and Gilead and Galilee, all the land of Naphtali; and he carried them captive to Assyria" (II Kings 15:29). Isaiah refers to this desolate territory (Isa. 9:1). He named his second son Maher-shalal-hash-baz ("Hasten-spoil-hurry-booty") so that the boy might be a visible prophecy of the sure fall of the northern kingdom (Isa. 8:1-4). He witnessed the fall of Samaria in 722 B. C. and the captivity of Israel to Assyria (II Kings 17:1-6).

Years afterwards he witnessed the invasion of Judah by Sennacherib (701 B. C.) when it seemed absolutely sure that Jerusalem would fall and the city was saved as if by a miracle (Isa. 36-37). He went to Hezekiah when the king had foolishly shown his treasures to the messengers of Merodach-baladan the crafty king of Babylon and proclaimed in God's name: "Behold the days are coming, when all that is in thy house, and that which thy fathers have laid up in store until this day shall be carried to Babylon; nothing shall be left, saith Jehovah. And of thy sons that shall issue from thee, whom thou shalt beget shall they take away; and they shall be eunuchs in the palace of the king of Babylon" (Isa. 39:6-7). With such a background the standpoint of chapters 40-55 in the exile may be adequately explained as an ideal standpoint of Isaiah himself rather than a real standpoint after the exile had almost run its course. Isaiah did not need to repeat his predictions of the exile. He looked upon it as divinely speaking already present. Such an ideal standpoint in the future is found in such passages as II Chron. 20:37; Isa. 5:13-17; 9:2-7; 10:28-31; 53:4-10; Mic. 1:16; 2:13.

The maintenance of this ideal standpoint in the exile is even more naturally explained on the reasonable assumption that Isaiah gave the prophecies of chapters 40-55 after the beginning of the wicked reign of Manasseh. According to Jewish tradition Isaiah was martyred in that reign. No other reign in Judah witnessed so much wickedness, idolatry and oppression (II Kings 21:1-9, 16). The prophets of Manasseh's time foretold the fall and captivity of Judah because of this wickedness (II Kings 21:10-15) and from that time onward they considered the captivity of Judah as caused especially by the sins of Manasseh's reign (II Kings 23:26-27; 24:3-4; Jer. 15:4). If chapters 40-55 of Isaiah's book were composed then, their standpoint in the exile is entirely explicable. They have been called "The Exile's Book of Consolation"; but the righteous minority who did not share in the sins of Manasseh's time which made the exile sure, needed just such comfort as these chapters contain. As a true prophet of Jehovah, Isaiah did not neglect his duty to comfort the righteous any more than he neglected his duty to proclaim doom for the wicked. The righteous of Manasseh's time might well cry out in agony: Must we suffer for sins we did not commit? If the nation goes into exile, will the promise of God for its glorious future fail? These chapters answer these questions gloriously. We may well believe that they were meant for the comfort not only of the righteous who suffered in the exile but also of the righteous who saw the exile coming. It may be added that this theory of the date of these chapters would also account for their difference in style, vocabulary and theological emphasis. The difference in subject and the old age of the prophet offer sufficient explanation for these phenomena.

The indications of date in chapters 56-66 are quite different from those of chapters 40-55, although the former chapters are not nearly so homogeneous in their temporal standpoint. The temple seems to be standing (Isa. 56:5, 7; 60:7; 61:3; 66:6) and the walls of Jerusalem are to be rebuilt (Isa. 60:10; 61:4). The geographical indications of Isaiah 57:5-7 are those of Palestine rather than Babylonia and the reference to injustice in the courts

(Isa. 59:4-9, 14) fits conditions in Palestine better than
those in Babylonia. Hence many critics designate chapters 56-66 for convenience as Trito-Isaiah and assign it
to a post-exilic date in Jerusalem, mostly the time of Ezra
and Nehemiah. It should be noted, however, that the indications referred to agree with a date in Isaiah's time as
well as with a post-exilic date, while other indications
point clearly away from the later date to the time of our
prophet. The most important emphases of the time of
Ezra and Nehemiah related to the law and to mixed mar-
riages. Yet neither one of these matters is mentioned in
Isaiah 56-66. On the other hand the polemic against
heathen rites (Isa. 57:3-10; 65:3-7) would have been
quite unnecessary in the time of Ezra and Nehemiah. The
exile had cured Israel of this sin. But such a polemic was
very much needed in Manasseh's day (II Kings 21:2-9;
II Chron. 33:2-9). For these and other reasons the
author regards these chapters as the genuine work of
Isaiah. The same arguments also apply to those parts of
Isaiah 1-39 which many modern critics regard as exilic
or post-exilic. We cannot tell how long Isaiah continued
to prophesy in the reign of Manasseh. If he was twenty
years old in the year that Uzziah died (735 B. C.), he
would have been fifty-seven years of age when Manasseh
came to the throne (698 B. C.). The latter king was only
twelve at his accession (II Kings 21:1; II Chron. 33:1).
It is scarcely probable that a boy of that age would have
reversed immediately his father's policy and instituted a
program of idolatry and oppression, at least if this depended on his own initiative. He may, however, even in
his youth have yielded to the powerful influence of those

who were dissatisfied with Hezekiah's suppression of the high places and of idolatry. Isaiah must have continued his ministry until the idolatrous policy was well established and, if the tradition of his martyrdom is true, he was doubtless one of the prophets who condemned it (II Kings 21:10-15). The only definite indication of the duration of his ministry is in the fact that he records the death of Sennacherib and the accession of Esar-haddon which occurred in 681 B. C. in the eighteenth year of Manasseh's reign (Isa. 37:37-38). At that time Isaiah must have been about seventy-five years of age. Thus we may date his ministry from 735 till about 680 B. C.

In contrast with Amos and Hosea the ministry of Isaiah was entirely in the southern kingdom and related for the most part to that kingdom. Several times, however, he referred to the northern kingdom before its fall and he clearly foretold that catastrophe (Isa. 7:8; 8:4; 9:8-12; 17:3; 28:1-4). He showed no favoritism for the kingdom of Judah, but pronounced judgment on "both the houses of Israel" for their sin (Isa. 8:14). He also uttered prophecies concerning Syria, Moab, Egypt, Tyre, Assyria and Babylon. The most remarkable example of his breadth of vision is in the memorable words: "In that day shall Israel be the third with Egypt and with Assyria, a blessing in the midst of the earth; for that Jehovah of hosts hath blessed them, saying, Blessed be Egypt my people, and Assyria the work of my hands, and Israel mine inheritance" (Isa. 19:24-25). This placing of Egypt and Assyria beside Israel reminds us of the challenge of Amos: "Are ye not as the children of the Ethiopians unto me, O children of Israel? said Jehovah. Have not I

brought up Israel out of the land of Egypt, and the
Philistines from Caphtor, and the Syrians from Kir?"
(Amos 9:7). But Isaiah's prediction surpasses the words
of Amos since, while not denying the preeminent role of
Israel as the chosen people of God, it gives to Egypt the
title "my people," usually reserved for Israel, and calls
Assyria "the work of my hands."

Isaiah lived in the capital Jerusalem while his contemporary prophet Micah was like Amos a countryman. His
father's name, Amoz, is given in the title of his book implying that the prophet belonged to an influential family.
He had free access to the kings of Judah. Probably the
greater part of Jotham's reign was during the illness of
his father Uzziah. He survived his father by only a year
or two. It is not certain whether any of Isaiah's prohecies
date from Jotham's reign; but it may safely be inferred
that Isaiah was hostile to Jotham in his failure to remove
the high places (II Kings 15:35). Ahaz also gave little
heed to the warnings of Isaiah (Isa. 7). But the influence
of Isaiah with Hezekiah was very great. The religious
reforms of that good king were doubtless encourged by the
prophet and through his influence the king learned to trust
in God rather than in Egypt. As we have seen Isaiah
certainly did his best to resist the wickedness of Manasseh and he may have forfeited his life for his faithfulness
to his prophetic duty.

(1) CONCEPTION OF GOD.

The extraordinary fullness of the teachings of Isaiah is
due in part to the way in which he assimilated the religious
ideas of earlier periods and brought them into harmonious

relation. This is particularly true of his relation to the conception of God in the writings of Amos and Hosea. The God of Isaiah is inexorable in the demands of his righteousness, like the God of Amos; but he is also a loving God who yearns over his wayward people and pleads with them to repent and be forgiven, like the God of Hosea. This blending of the justice and forgiving love of God is evident in the summary of Isaiah's teaching in the first chapter of his book. The righteous indignation of Jehovah against the sins of Israel, their hollow ceremonialism, is nowhere expressed more vigorously than in verses 10-17. Yet the sorrowing love of the divine heart in verses 2-9 and his forgiving love in verse 18 are like the love of God which Hosea came to know from his unrequited love for Gomer.

Isaiah blends these apparently conflicting ideas in the conception of the holiness of God, which is not so much a divine attribute as the harmonious blending of all the divine attributes, what we may call the godliness of God, the essence of the divine nature. The Hebrew word for holiness means primarily apartness, separation. The holiness of God is thus that which separates him, differentiates him from every other person and all other things. Other persons and things can become holy only by contact with him. The sabbath was holy because he rested on that day (Gen. 2:3). Jerusalem was holy because it was the city of God (Ps. 48:1). The temple was holy and its innermost chamber the holy of holies because God manifested himself there.

The idea of the holiness of God was not new with Isaiah. A large part of the symbolism of the Mosaic tabernacle and ritual was intended to impress this idea upon Israel. In the song of Moses at the crossing of the Red Sea, he exclaimed: "Who is like unto thee, O Jehovah, among the gods? Who is like thee, glorious in holiness, fearful in praises, doing wonders?" (Ex. 15:11). In the Mosaic law God commanded his people: "Sanctify yourselves therefore, and be ye holy; for I am Jehovah your God—Ye shall be holy unto me: for I Jehovah am holy and have set you apart from the peoples, that ye should be mine" (Lev. 20:7, 26). "Joshua said unto the people, Ye cannot serve Jehovah, for he is a holy God; he is a jealous God; he will not forgive your transgression nor your sins." (Josh. 24:19). Hannah sang: "There is none holy as Jehovah; for there is none besides thee, neither is there any rock like our God" (I Sam. 2:2). David exclaimed: "Thou art holy, O thou that inhabitest the praises of Israel" (Ps. 22:3). And God spoke through Hosea saying: "I am God and not man; the Holy One in the midst of thee." (Hos. 11:9). Although this idea was not new, it made a deeper impression on Isaiah than on any earlier writer and he gave it greater prominence than ever before.

This central thought of the divine holiness was burned into the prophet's soul by the awful vision by which he was ordained. The record of this experience is so important for the understanding of his religion that we record it in his own words: "In the year that King Uzziah died I saw the Lord sitting upon a throne, high and lifted up; and his train filled the temple. Above him, stood the seraphim; each one had six wings; with twain he covered his face, and with twain he covered his feet; and with twain he did fly. And one cried unto another and said, Holy, holy, holy is Jehovah of hosts: the whole earth is full of his glory. And the foundations of the thresholds shook at the voice of him that cried, and the house was filled with smoke. Then said I, Woe is me! for I am undone; because I am a man of unclean lips, and I dwell in the midst of a people of unclean lips; for mine eyes have seen the King, Jehovah of hosts. Then flew one of the seraphim unto me, having a live coal in his hand, which he had taken with the tongs from off the altar; and he touched my mouth with it and said, Lo this hath touched thy lips; and thine iniquity is taken away, and thy son forgiven. And I heard the voice of the Lord, saying, Whom shall I send and who will go for us? Then I said, Here am I; send me." (Isa. 6:1-8). Isaiah never forgot this majestic vision of the holy God. The idea runs all through his book. The impressive title "the Holy One of Israel" occurs 25 times in his prophecies (Isa. 1:4; 5: 19, 24; 10:20; 12:6; 17:7; 29:19; 30:11, 12, 15; 31:1; 37:23; 41:14, 16, 20; 43:3, 14; 45:11; 47:4; 48:17; 49:7; 54:5; 55:5; 60:9, 14) besides five other places where the form varies slightly (Isa. 5:16; 29:23; 40:25; 43:15; 49:7). This title occurs three times in the Psalms (71:22; 78:41; 89:18). The 78th Psalm probably dates from Isaiah's time while the others are later. Jeremiah used it twice (Jer. 50:29; 51:5) and Ezekiel calls Jehovah "the Holy One in Israel" (Ezek. 39:7). Thus Isaiah seems to have originated this name of God, although possibly he derived it from Hosea (Hos. 11:9).

Next to Jehovah's holiness and indeed inseparable from it is Isaiah's emphasis upon the majesty of God. Three times in one chapter he speaks of "the terror of Jehovah" and "the glory of his majesty" (Isa. 2:10, 19, 21) and twice elsewhere of "the majesty of Jehovah" (Isa. 24:14; 26:10). The divine majesty is equally prominent with his holiness in the account of his prophetic ordination already quoted (Isa. 6:1-8).

The ethical monotheism of Isaiah is as clear as that of Amos. As the creator of the heavens and the earth Jehovah summons them to listen to his charge against his rebellious people (Isa. 1:2). Twice the prophet says: "Jehovah alone shall be exalted in that day" (Isa. 2:11, 17). God is the judge of all nations and he will punish them for their wickedness. He says: "I will punish the world for their evil and the wicked for their iniquity" (Isa. 13:11). He controls all nations, for the prophet says: "This is the purpose that is purposed upon the whole earth; and this is the hand that is stretched out upon all nations. For Jehovah of hosts hath purposed, and who shall annul it? and his hand is stretched out and who shall turn it back?" (Isa. 14:26-27). "The nations shall rush like the rushing of many waters; but he shall rebuke them and they shall flee far off and shall be chased as the chaff of the mountains before the wind and like the whirling dust before the storm" (Isa. 17:13). Hezekiah regarded Jehovah as the God of all nations, for he prayed: "O Jehovah of hosts, the God of Israel, that sittest above the cherubim, thou art the God, even thou alone, of all the kingdoms of the earth; thou hast made heaven and earth" (Isa. 37:16). He denied the existence of other gods saying: "They were no gods but the work of men's hands, wood and stone" (Isa. 37:19).

The same monotheism appears clearly in chapters 40-66. "Who hath measured the waters in the hollow of his hand and meted out heaven with the span, and comprehended the dust of the earth in a measure, and weighed the mountains in scales and the hills in a balance? Who hath directed the Spirit of Jehovah or being his counsellor hath taught him? With whom took he counsel and who instructed him, and taught him in the path of justice, and taught him knowledge and showed to him the way of understanding? Behold the nations are as a drop of a bucket, and are accounted as the small dust of the balance: behold he taketh up the isles as a very little thing—All the nations are as nothing before him; they are accounted by him as less than nothing and vanity" (Isa. 40:12-15, 17). The prophet shows the foolishness of representing such a God or any God by an idol which man can make (Isa. 40:18-20; 44:9-20; 45:20; 46:6-7). He points men to the sky for a true picture of the greatness of God "To whom then will ye liken me that I should be equal to him? saith the Holy One: Lift up your eyes on high and see who hath created these, that bringeth out their host by number; he calleth them all by name by the greatness of his might, and for that he is strong in power, not one is lacking" (Isa. 40:25-26). Again and again Jehovah is represented as the only true God. "Before me there was no God formed, neither shall there be after me. I, even I, am Jehovah and besides me there is no saviour" (Isa. 43:10-11). "I am the first and I am the last; and besides me there is no God." (Isa. 44:6). "Is there a God besides me? yea there is no Rock: I know not any" (Isa. 44:8). "I am Jehovah and there

is none else; besides me there is no God" (Isa. 45:5).
"There is no God else besides me, a just God and a
Saviour; there is none besides me" (Isa. 45:21). "I
am God and there is none else; I am God, and there is
none like me" (Isa. 46:9).

It is not surprising that the prophet who had such a
lofty conception of the infinite God should look forward
to the time when the religion of Jehovah should become
the religion of all mankind. He boldly proclaimed: "It
shall come to pass in the latter days that the mountain of
Jehovah's house shall be established on the top of the
mountains and shall be exalted above the hills; and all
nations shall flow unto it. And many peoples shall go
and say, Come ye and let us go up to the mountain of
Jehovah, to the house of the God of Jacob; and he will
teach us of his ways, and we will walk in his paths:
for out of Zion shall go forth the law, and the word of
Jehovah from Jerusalem" (Isa. 2:2-3). "In this mountain will Jehovah of hosts make unto all peoples a feast
of fat things, a feast of wines on the lees, of fat things
full of marrow, of wines on the lees well refined. And
he will destroy in this mountain the face of the covering
that covereth all peoples, and the veil that is spread over
all nations" (Isa. 25:6-7). The Servant of Jehovah has
a revelation from God for all nations (Isa. 42:1, 4, 6;
49:1, 6). Jehovah cries out: "Look unto me and be ye
saved all the ends of the earth; for I am God and there
is none else. By myself have I sworn the word is gone
forth from my mouth in righteousness, and shall not return, that unto me every knee shall bow, every tongue shall
swear" (Isa. 45:22-23). "My house shall be called a

house of prayer for all peoples" (Isa. 56:7). "It shall come to pass that from one new moon to another, and from one sabbath to another, shall all flesh come to worship before me, saith Jehovah" (Isa. 66:23).

Isaiah speaks often of the forgiving love of God. With great tenderness he proclaims to Israel: "Come now, and let us reason together, saith Jehovah: though your sins be as scarlet, they shall be as white as snow: though they be red like crimson, they shall be as wool" (Isa. 1:18). After his recovery from sickness Hezekiah thanked God saying: "Thou hast cast all my sins behind thy back" (Isa. 38:17). Jerusalem is represented as having atoned for her own sins by the sufferings of the exile. "Speak ye comfortably to Jerusalem; and cry unto her that her warfare is accomplished, that her iniquity is pardoned, that she hath received of Jehovah's hand double for all her sins" (Isa. 40:2). Elsewhere, however, the prophet speaking in God's name proclaims: "I, even I, am he that blotteth out thy transgressions for mine own sake; and I will not remember thy sins" (Isa. 43:25). "I have blotted out, as a thick cloud, thy transgressions, and, as a cloud, thy sins: return unto me: for I have redeemed thee" (Isa. 44:22). The Servant of Jehovah is represented as suffering and dying for the sins of God's people "Surely he hath borne our griefs and carried our sorrows; yet we did esteem him stricken, smitten of God and afflicted. But he was wounded for our transgressions, he was bruised for our iniquities; the chastisement of our peace was upon him; and with his stripes we are healed. All we, like sheep, have gone astray; we have turned every one to his own way; and Jehovah hath laid on him the iniquity of us all" (Isa. 53:4-6). In the proclamation of the good news of salvation in chapter 55, a proclamation which is based upon the atoning sacrifice of the Servant of Jehovah described in chapter 53, the prophet cries out: "Seek ye Jehovah while he may be found; call ye upon him while he is near: let the wicked forsake his way, and the unrighteous man his thoughts; and let him return unto Jehovah and he will have mercy upon him; and to our God, for he will abundantly pardon" (Isa. 55:6-7).

This book lays the same stress on the experimental knowledge of God which is so marked a feature of Hosea (Hos. 2:20; 4:1, 6; 5:4; 6:3, 6; 7:11; 13:4-5). The lack of such knowledge was the reason for Israel's rebellion against their God. Out of the sadness of his paternal heart God exclaimed: "The ox knoweth his owner and the ass his master's crib; but Israel doth not know, my people doth not consider" (Isa. 1:3). Like Hosea (4:6) Isaiah considered that it was also this lack of knowledge which was the cause of the destruction and captivity of the chosen nation. "Therefore my people are gone into captivity for lack of knowledge; and their honorable men are famished and their multitude are parched with thirst. Therefore Sheol hath enlarged its desire, and opened its mouth without measure; and their glory and their multitude and their pomp, and he that rejoiceth among them, descend into it." (Isa. 5:13-14). "Go and tell this people, Hear ye indeed, but understand not; and see ye indeed, but perceive not. Make the heart of this people fat, and make their ears heavy, and shut their eyes; lest they see with their eyes, and hear with their ears, and understand with their heart and turn again and be healed. Then said I, Lord, how long? And he answered, Until cities be waste without inhabitant, and houses without man, and the land become utterly waste, and Jehovah have removed men far away and the forsaken places be many in the midst of the land" (Isa. 6:9-12). "It is a people of no understanding; therefore he that made them will not have compassion upon them, and he that formed them will show them no favor." (Isa. 27:11). Isaiah foretold the time when Egypt shall have a saving knowledge of Jehovah. "Jehovah shall be known [Margin, 'make himself known'] to Egypt, and the Egyptians shall know Jehovah in that day; yea, they shall worship with sacrifice and oblation, and shall vow a vow unto Jehovah, and shall perform it" (Isa. 19:21). It is because of his conception of experimental knowledge that the prophet uses so many synonyms for the word (Isa. 40:21, 28; 41:20). The reason that men make idols is lack of knowledge (Isa. 44:18-19). God said to Cyrus: "I have surnamed thee, though thou hast not known me— I will gird thee, though thou hast not known me" (Isa. 45:4-5). And of his people he said: "Therefore my people shall know my name: therefore they shall know in that day that I am he that doth speak; behold it is I" (Isa. 52:6). In all these passages knowledge is not merely intellectual but moral and religious. It includes the idea of communion with God, a personal relation to him.

It is characteristic of Isaiah that he not only believed that God ruled all nations but that he used nations and individuals, often without their knowledge, as his instruments for the accomplishment of the divine purpose.

God exclaimed: "Ho Assyrian, the rod of mine anger, the staff in whose hand is mine indignation!" (Isa. 10:5), and in the same connection he asked: "Shall the axe boast itself against him that heweth therewith? Shall the saw magnify itself against him that wieldeth it? as if a rod should wield them that lift it up, or as if a staff should lift up him that is not wood" (Isa. 10:15). God is represented as teaching the farmer how to perform his agricultural work (Isa. 28:26, 29). God permits Sennacherib to invade Judah but, when he has performed the divine purpose, he puts his hook in his nose, his bridle in his mouth, to bring him back to Nineveh (Isa. 37:26-29). He raises up Cyrus (Isa. 41:2, 25; 45:13), and says of him: "He is my shepherd and shall perform all my pleasure, even saying of Jerusalem, She shall be built; and of the temple, Thy foundations shall be laid" (Isa. 44:28). It is in this connection that the remarkable words occur: "I form the light and create darkness; I make peace and create evil; I am Jehovah that doeth all these things" (Isa. 45:7). Here God is thought of as the doer of everything which is done in his world. The human instrument, the secondary causes, drop out of sight and God appears as the great Primal Cause of all events and actions. There is no distinction between that which God causes directly and that which he merely permits. He even creates evil. The same point of view may be found when God is said to have hardened Pharaoh's heart (Ex. 4:21; 7:3; 9:12; 10:1, 20, 27; 11:10; 14:4, 8), although elsewhere Pharaoah is said to have hardened his own heart (Ex. 8:15, 32; 9:34). It occurs again in the record of the evil spirit from God which came upon Saul (I. Sam. 16:14-16; 18:10; 19:9), in the statement that God moved David to number Israel and then punished him for doing so (II Sam. 24), when in reality the temptation came from Satan (I Chron. 21:1), and in the reference to the lying spirit which God put in the mouths of the prophets to entice Ahab to ruin (I Kings 22:19-23; II Chron. 18:18-22). So intense was Israel's belief in the omnipotent sovereignty of God that they could not conceive how anything could transpire which he could not prevent. Since he either did or permitted everything, they represented him as the one who did everything. Nowhere else is this idea expressed so clearly as in the words which Isaiah spoke in God's name.

The angel of Jehovah is mentioned as going forth and smiting 185,000 in the army of Sennacherib (Isa. 37:36). This messenger should not be identified with the theophanies of earlier history (see pp. 26, 56-57, 162-164). No human form is mentioned nor are any words or acts of the angel referred to except his causing the death of the Assyrian soldiers. Apparently it is the scriptural way of saying that God sent a pestilence which killed a large part of the invading army. A similar record is that of the angel who brought a pestilence on Jerusalem in David's time (II Sam. 24:15-17; I Chron. 21:14-17; see pp. 209-211). The expression "the angel of his presence" in Isa. 63:9 refers to the angel who guided the children of Israel from Egypt to Palestine. This also was not an appearance of God in human form but a reference to the fact that God manifested himself in the pillar of cloud and fire to guide his people through the wilderness. God said: "My presence shall go with thee, and I will give thee rest" (Ex. 33:14), and Moses looking back to the exodus declared to Israel that God brought them out with his presence (Deut. 4:37; see pp. 56-57). Seraphim are mentioned in the account of Isaiah's vision at his ordination (Isa. 6:2-3, 6-7) and nowhere else. They are moral beings who guard the throne of God and render praise to him. One of them carried the coal from the altar to cleanse Isaiah's lips. These functions make it probable that they were beings of the angelic order.

One of the two places in the Old Testament where the words "holy spirit" occur is in the book of Isaiah. The other is in David's penitential Psalm (Ps. 51:11). It is quite clear that in neither place is there any reference to the third person of the Trinity. The "holy spirit" in the Old Testament is God himself exerting his influence upon men (see pp. 213-214). Nevertheless it must be admitted that nowhere else in the Old Testament does the spirit of God come so near to personal representation as in Isaiah 63:10-11 "They rebelled and grieved his holy Spirit: therefore he was turned to be their enemy, and himself fought against them. Then he remembered the days of old, Moses and his people, saying, Where is he that brought them up out of the sea with the shepherds of his flock? Where is he that put his holy Spirit in the midst of them?" The use of the expression to grieve the holy Spirit is specially significant. Skinner well says: "The use of this verb marks the highest degree of personification of the spirit attained in the O.T." (Cambridge Bible on Isa. 63:10). Although the New Testament doctrine of the third person of the Trinity should not be read into this passage, it helped to prepare for the fuller doctrine and Paul probably referred to it when he wrote: "Grieve not the Holy Spirit of God, in whom ye were sealed unto the day of redemption" (Eph. 4:30, compare Acts 7:51).

One of the most profound conceptions of the divine nature is found in the statement of Isa. 63:9, "In all their affliction he was afflicted, and the angel of his presence saved them; in his love and in his pity he redeemed them; and he bare them and carried them all the days of old." Nowhere else in the Old Testament is the fact so clearly stated that God suffers with, sympathizes with his wayward children even though their afflictions were the just punishment for their sin. Once it was said that when Israel put away their foreign gods and served Jehovah, "his soul was grieved for the misery of Israel" (Judges 10:16). The suffering love of Hosea for his unfaithful wife reflects the suffering love of Jehovah for apostate Israel. The breaking heart of David over rebellious Absalom (II Sam. 18:33), also reflects the heart of God toward sinners. In all these passages we can see why God incarnate suffered and died for sinful men.

(2) THE CEREMONIES OF RELIGION.

Like the other eighth-century prophets Isaiah abhorred the ceremonies of religion when they were unaccompanied by righteousness and penitence. This is clearly expressed in the first chapter. "What unto me is the multitude of your sacrifices? saith Jehovah: I have had enough of the burnt-offerings of rams, and the fat of fed beasts;

and I delight not in the blood of bullocks or of lambs, or of he-goats. When ye come to appear before me, who hath required this at your hand, to trample my courts? Bring no more vain oblations; incense is an abomination unto me; new moon and sabbath, the calling of assemblies—I cannot away with iniquity and the solemn meeting. Your new moons and your appointed feasts my soul hateth; they are a trouble unto me. I am weary of bearing them. And when ye spread forth your hands, I will hide mine eyes from you; yea, when ye make many prayers, I will not hear: your hands are full of blood. Wash you, make you clean; put away the evil of your doings from before mine eyes; cease to do evil; learn to do well; seek justice, relieve the oppressed, judge the fatherless, plead for the widow" (Isa. 1:11-17). The same attitude toward ceremonialism comes out here and there in the later chapters. Thus he predicted: "In that day shall men look unto their Maker, and their eyes shall have respect to the Holy One of Israel. And they shall not look to the altars, the work of their hands; neither shall they have respect to that which their fingers have made, either the Asherim, or the sun-images" (Isa. 17:7-8, cp. 27:9). God exclaimed: "Forasmuch as this people draw nigh unto me and with their mouth and with their lips do honor me, but have removed their heart far from me and their fear of me is a commandment of men which hath been taught them (Margin, "learned by rote"), therefore, behold I will proceed to do a marvelous work among this people, even a marvelous work and a wonder; and the wisdom of their wise men shall perish, and the understanding of their prudent men shall be hid"

(Isa. 29:13-14). In the splendid passage, which portrays the greatness of God the insufficiency of sacrifice is recognized, for the prophet declares: "Lebanon is not sufficient to burn, nor the beasts thereof sufficient for a burnt-offering" (Isa. 40:16). All the forests of Lebanon would not furnish sufficient wood nor all its beasts sufficient animals for a suitable sacrifice to such an infinite God. Hypocritical fasts are condemned. "Is such the fast that I have chosen, the day for a man to afflict his soul? Is it to bow down his head as a rush, and to spread sackcloth and ashes under him? Wilt thou call this a fast, and an acceptable day to Jehovah? Is not this the fast that I have chosen: to loose the bonds of wickedness, to undo the bands of the yoke, and to let the oppressed go free, and that ye break every yoke? Is it not to deal thy bread to the hungry, and that thou bring the poor that are cast out to thy house? when thou seest the naked, that thou cover him; and that thou hide not thyself from thine own flesh?" (Isa. 58:5-7). The prophet's abhorrence for false ceremonies is strikingly depicted by the bold declaration: "He that killeth an ox is as he that slayeth a man; he that sacrificeth a lamb, as he that breaketh a dog's neck; he that offereth an oblation, as he that offereth swine's blood; he that burneth frankincense, as he that blesseth an idol" (Isa. 66:3).

Many critics think that the prophet who spoke these words could scarcely have spoken such words in praise of the sabbath as we find in chapters 56 and 58. "Blessed is the man that doeth this, and the son of man that holdeth it fast; that keepeth the sabbath from profaning it, and keepeth his hand from doing any evil" (Isa. 56:2).

"If thou turn away thy foot from the sabbath, from doing thy pleasure on my holy day; and call the sabbath a delight, and the holy of Jehovah honorable; and shalt honor it, not doing thine own ways, nor finding thine own pleasure, nor speaking thine own words; then shalt thou delight thyself in Jehovah; and I will make thee to ride upon the high places of the earth; and I will feed thee with the heritage of Jacob, thy father: for the mouth of Jehovah hath spoken it" (Isa. 58:13-14). The critics who deny these words to Isaiah fail to appreciate that for which he was pleading. He was no narrow sabbatarian demanding the cessation of work on the holy day and performance of a fixed ritual; but he recognized that the secularizing of the sabbath meant the downfall of spiritual religion. Amos had spoken against those in the northern kingdom who said: "When will the new moon be gone that we may sell grain? and the sabbath that we may set forth wheat?" (Amos 8:5). If such was the feeling toward the sabbath in the northern kingdom, the same attitude may have prevailed in Judah particularly in the wicked reign of Manasseh. Isaiah plead for a glad, spiritual observance of the day which would make it a means of spiritual development for those who observed it.

There are several references in this book which show that idolatry and various heathen and superstitious rites, forbidden by the Jewish law, were practised in Judah in Isaiah's time. The references in the early part of his book probably relate to conditions in the reign of Ahaz (II Kings 16; II Chron. 28) while those in the last twenty-seven chapters reflect conditions in Manasseh's

reign (II Kings 21:1-9; II Chron. 33:1-9). The oaks
and the gardens mentioned in Isa. 1:29 were the places
where the impure worship of Baal was carried on. Idolatrous worship was imported from foreign countries for
the prophet says: "They are filled with customs from
the east, and are soothsayers like the Philistines, and
they strike hands with the children of foreigners—Their
land also is full of idols; they worship the work of their
own hands, that which their own fingers have made" (Isa.
2:6, 8). Other references to idolatry are found in Isa.
2:20; 10:10-11; 31:7; 40:19-20; 41:7, 29; 42:17; 44:9-
20. Necromancy was practised, for the prophet exhorted
the people: "When they shall say unto you, Seek unto
them that have familiar spirits and unto the wizards that
chirp and that mutter; should not a people seek unto
their God? on behalf of the living should they seek unto
the dead?" (Isa. 8:19; cp. Isa. 28:15, 18). Reference
is made to Topheth, the hill in the valley of the son of
Hinnom, where human sacrifices were offered (II Kings
23:10; Jer. 7:31; 19:6, 13). Ahaz practised this out-
rageous rite (II Kings 16:3; II Chron. 28:3). Therefore Isaiah boldly declared, "A Topheth is prepared of
old; yea, for the king it is made ready; he hath made it
deep and large; the pile thereof is fire and much wood;
the breath of Jehovah, like a stream of brimstone, doth
kindle it." (Isa. 30:33). This was part of the worship
of Molech, the god of the Ammonites. The impure worship of Baal was common in Manasseh's reign, for Isaiah
addressed such worshippers: "Ye that inflame yourselves
among the oaks, under every green tree; that slay the
children in the valleys; under the clefts of the rocks.

Among the smooth stones of the valley is thy portion;
they, they are thy lot; even to them hast thou poured a
drink-offering, thou hast offered an oblation. Shall I
be appeased for these things?" (Isa. 57:5-6). Isaiah
57:8 seems to refer to some heathen emblem which was
set up behind the doors of their houses. The "sacrificing in gardens" (Isa. 65:3) was part of the Baal worship. Some suppose that the "burning incense upon
bricks" in the same verse had to do with the heathen
practice of offering sacrifice on the roofs of the houses
(II Kings 23:12; Jer. 19:13; Zeph. 1:5). Sitting among
the graves (Isa. 65:4) evidently belonged to ancestor
worship. Burning incense upon the mountains (Isa.
65:7) refers to the forbidden worship at the high places.
Two false deities calls Gad (Fortune) and Meni (Destiny) were worshiped by spreading a table before them
with meat and drink for the gods to devour (Isa. 65:11).
Isa. 66:17 probably refers to the heathen method of worship which was carried on under the leadership of one
man standing in the midst of the group. (Ezek. 8:11).

There were false prophets in Isaiah's time, who taught
lies (Isa. 9:15). He said: "The priest and the prophet
reel with strong drink, they are swallowed up of wine,
they stagger with strong drink; they err in vision, they
stumble in judgment" (Isa. 28:7). These false prophets
were men who yielded to the popular demand to hear
smooth rather than right things. The rebellious people
said to the seers, "See not; and to the prophets, Prophesy
not unto us right things, speak unto us smooth things,
prophesy deceits" (Isa. 30:10).

(3) THE FAITHFUL REMNANT.

The doctrine of the faithful remnant in Israel, the godly kernel of the nation who preserved it from destruction and who would survive the chastisement of the exile and reestablish the political and religious life of the nation, was one of the most important parts of Isaiah's teaching. The idea did not originate with him. Amos had already used it when he spoke of "the remnant of Joseph" (Amos 5:15), those of the northern kingdom who should survive the impending invasion. The idea is found in his vivid prophecy: "As the shepherd rescueth out of the mouth of the lion, two legs, or a piece of an ear, so shall the children of Israel be rescued that sit in Samaria in the corner of a couch, and on the silken cushions of a bed" (Amos 3:12). It is implied in his prediction: "Behold the eyes of the Lord Jehovah are upon the sinful kingdom, and I will destroy it from off the face of the earth; save that I will not utterly destroy the house of Jacob, saith Jehovah. For, lo, I will command and I will sift the house of Israel among all the nations, like as grain is sifted in a sieve, yet shall not the least kernel fall upon the earth" (Amos 9:8-9). Micah, also, the contemporary of Isaiah used the expression repeatedly (Mic. 2:12; 4:7; 5:3, 7-8; 7:18). Possibly some of these utterances were before Isaiah's first use of the term. Yet neither Amos nor Micah developed the idea so fully as Isaiah did or made it so central to his message.

The importance of this doctrine for Isaiah is seen in the fact that he embodied it in the name of his oldest son Shear-jashub which means a "remnant shall return." Both of the prophet's sons were given symbolic names so that, as he expressed it, they should be "for signs and for wonders in Israel from Jehovah of hosts" (Isa. 8:18). By their names they were set apart to be living prophecies of important parts of their father's teaching. The oldest son was a prophecy of the fact that Israel would not die out completely as a nation in the exile; for a remnant shall return to God in penitence and having returned to God, they will return from exile to Palestine. The probable reason that Isaiah took Shear-jashub with him when he went to meet Ahaz (Isa. 7:3) was to encourage the king to believe that the confederacy of Ephraim and Syria against him would not succeed.

The first use of the word "remnant" in the book, although probably not the first historically, is illuminating. "Except Jehovah of hosts had left unto us a very small remnant, we should have been as Sodom, we should have been like unto Gomorrah." (Isa. 1:9). The comparison of Israel to Sodom and Gomorrah refers to the fact that in answer to Abraham's prayer God promised to spare Sodom if there were fifty righteous in the city and that Abraham's importunity persisted until God promised to spare it for ten righteous. (Gen. 18:22-33). These ten, if they had been in Sodom, would have been the faithful remnant which would have saved the city. Sodom and Gomorrah perished for lack of a faithful remnant. Israel also would have perished if there had not been a very small faithful remnant in it.

In the passage just quoted and sometimes elsewhere the remnant does not refer to the exiles but to those of that time and earlier whose faithfulness to Jehovah, restrained the divine hand from destroying the nation for its sins. The reference in Isa. 4:2-5 is of this sort "In that day shall the branch of Jehovah be beautiful and glorious, and the fruit of the land shall be excellent and comely for them that are escaped of Israel. And it shall come to pass that he that is left in Zion and he that remaineth in Jerusalem, shall be called holy, even every cne that is written among the living in Jerusalem" (Isa. 4:2-3). This glorious privilege of the remnant cannot be obtained until "the Lord shall have washed away the filth of the daughters of Zion, and shall have purged the blood of Jerusalem from the midst thereof by the spirit of justice and by the spirit of burning" (Isa. 4:4). The city must be purged from its sin. This purging meant the death of the wicked and the suffering of the righteous. But the righteous would survive. An illustration of this occurred at the time of Sennacherib's invasion when Hezekiah sent messengers to Isaiah saying, "Lift up thy prayer for the remnant that is left" (Isa. 37:4).

The case seems different in Isa. 37:31-32 "The remnant that is escaped of the house of Judah shall again take root downward and bear fruit upward. For out of Jerusalem shall go forth a remnant, and out of mount Zion they that shall escape; the zeal of Jehovah of hosts will perform this." Here the remnant seems to consist of those who flee from the city when it is captured by the enemy. Different still is the representation of Isa. 11:11-12, 16 where the exiles whom Jehovah will bring back from foreign countries are called the remnant. "It shall come to pass in that day, that the Lord will set his hand again the second time to recover the remnant of his people that shall remain from Assyria and from Egypt, and from

Pathros, and from Cush, and from Elam, and from Shinar, and from Hamath, and from the islands of the sea. And he will set up an ensign for the nations, and will assemble the outcasts of Israel, and gather together the dispersed of Judah from the four corners of the earth —And there shall be a highway for the remnant of his people that shall remain from Assyria; like as there was for Israel, in the day that he came up out of the land of Egypt."

The remnant means then those who escape and survive any catastrophe of Israel whether by remaining after the invaders have withdrawn, or by fleeing when the city is captured or by living in exile until they can return to Palestine. Indeed it is the survivors of any catastrophe which came on Israel for their sin. · This comes out clearly in the prediction: "It shall come to pass in that day, that the remnant of Israel, and they that are escaped of the house of Jacob, shall no more again lean upon him that smote them, but shall lean upon Jehovah, the Holy One of Israel, in truth. A remnant shall return, even the remnant of Jacob, unto the mighty God. For, though thy people, Israel, be as the sand of the sea, only a remnant of them shall return; a destruction is determined, overflowing with righteousness." (Isa. 10:20-22). More hopeful is the promise: "In that day will Jehovah of hosts become a crown of glory, and a diadem of beauty, unto the residue of his people; and a spirit of justice to him that sitteth in judgment, and strength to them that turn back the battle at the gate" (Isa. 28:5-6). Thus the doctrine of the remnant meant nothing but doom for the wicked but for the righteous it was a glorious hope.

There is another passage in this book where a similar idea is expressed. In foretelling the devastation of an approaching invasion the prophet says: "If there be yet a tenth in it, it also shall in turn be eaten up: as a terebinth, and as an oak whose stock remaineth, when they are felled; so the holy seed is the stock thereof" (Isa. 6:13). The reference is to the fact that if a terebinth or an oak is cut down, it does not die but a new shoot may spring up from its stump (Job. 14:7-9). So when the nation Israel is depopulated, it does not die, for the holy seed, is the stump from which a new and better national life shall spring. To keep this holy seed from corruption was the purpose of all the divine providence toward Israel (Ezra 9:2).

The remnant is mentioned only once in Isaiah 40-66 (46:3). Another similar but even greater idea takes its place, that of Israel as the servant of Jehovah. Unlike the remnant, the servant of Jehovah sometimes is used of the whole nation (Isa. 41:8-9; 44:1-2, 21; 45:4; 48:20; 49:3). Elsewhere, however, he is distinguished from Israel as a whole in a way which suggests that the servant is the godly part of the nation, an idea similar to that of the remnant (Isa. 42:6-7; 49:5-6; 53:8). This doctrine of the remnant to which Isaiah gave such prominence is mentioned often by later writers (Ezra 9:8; Jer. 6:9; 23:3; 31:7; Ezek. 5:10; 6:8; 9:8; 11:13; 14:22; Joel 2:32; Obad. 17; Zeph. 2:7, 9; 3:13; Hag. 1:12, 14; Zech. 8:6, 12; 14:2).

(4) THE MESSIANIC HOPE.

The Messianic element in the book of Isaiah is larger than that of any other book of the Old Testament. The only other book which compares with it in this respect is the Psalms; but while the different parts of the Psalter date from different periods, we have in Isaiah a large mass of Messianic literature which was produced in the lifetime of the prophet whose ministry covered only about fifty years.

The definiteness and fullness of the Messianic picture in Isaiah is also unequalled elsewhere. In some of the passages there is no reference to the Messiah himself by this or any other name. They refer only to his times or his work (Isa. 2:2-4; 25:6-8; 32:1-8, 15-20; 35:1-10). Indeed it is surprising that the only time the title Messiah occurs in this book, it is given to Cyrus (Isa. 45:1, "anointed"). The coming deliverer is often mentioned, however, by other names of great fullness and richness (Isa. 4:2; 7:14; 9:6-7; 11:1, 10; 28:16). The Servant of Jehovah, the greatest character of chapters 40-55, points typically to Christ (Isa. 42:1-7; 49:1-7; 50:4-9; 52:13-53:12) and in chapter 53 the foreshadowing is so vivid and the picture so accurate, both in general outline and details, that Franz Delitzsch was justified in saying: "Every word here is written, as it were, under the cross of Golgotha." The Messiah also speaks of himself in Isa. 61:1-3 and is foreshadowed by the hero from Edom in Isa. 63:1-6.

Nowhere else in the Old Testament is it so difficult to set bounds to the Messianic element. Besides the passages already mentioned there are many others in which Messianic elements occur with more or less definiteness. The

ideas expressed are those which occur in Messianic connections elsewhere. In reading them we feel that we are
in a Messianic atmosphere. This is true whenever the
prophet looks beyond the exile and sees the reëstablishment
of the nation, its righteousness and prosperity. Whenever
he looks beyond the blackness of the nation's immediate
future, the curtain seems to be lifted, if only a little, and
the distant glory of the Messianic times shines through.
Thus in each of the six woes which comprise chapters
28-35 there is something which approaches a Messianic
prediction if it does not quite reach it. The woe against
the drunken nobles (Isa. 28) is relieved by the Messianic promise of verses 14-17; that against Jerusalem
(Isa. 29) by the promise of fertility, prosperity and
righteousness in verses 17-21; the first woe against
the Egyptian party (Isa. 30) by the similar pictures in
verses 18-26; the second woe against this party (Isa. 31-
32) by the description of the society of the Messianic
kingdom (Isa. 32:1-8) and the prosperity, peace and
righteousness of that kingdom (Isa. 32:15-20) ; the woe
against Assyria (Isa. 33) by the vision of the king in his
beauty, his far-reaching land and its prosperity in verses
17-24; and finally the woe against the nations which oppressed Israel (Isa. 34) by the glad promises of fertility
and prosperity for the returning exiles in chapter 35. Messianic elements appear again and again in chapters 54-66,
especially in the glorious words of encouragement (Isa.
54; 59:20; 62; 65:17-25; 66:7-13, 22-24). A special feature of the last chapters of Isaiah is the picture of Jerusalem as it would be after the exile. Sometimes there are
ideal elements in the picture which transcend the local

and political (Isa. 52:1-3; 62:1-12; 65:18-25; 66:10-13, 20) and prepare the way for the New Testament conception of the New Jerusalem, the capital of the kingdom of God (Rev. 3:12; 21:1-27). This is especially true of the beautiful description of the sun rising over the city and the wealth which flows into it both from land and sea (Isa. 60). Its ideal character is revealed in the fact that the city has no need of sun or moon since Jehovah is its everlasting light (verse 19). All these passages contributed their part to the conception of Messianic times.

The Messianic element in this book is so large that only the main ideas of each passage can be mentioned. The first two passages occur the one at the beginning and the other at the end of chapters 2-4, which probably once constituted a little book which was later merged in the larger book of the prophet. George Adam Smith has pointed out that in Isa. 2:2-4 we have a vision of the ideal Jerusalem of the future, in 2:5-4:1 a picture of the actual city as it was in the prophet's time with all its wickedness, and in 4:2-6 "a vision of Jerusalem as she shall be after God has taken her in hand" (The Book of Isaiah, Vol. I, pp. 23-24). In the first picture (2:2-4) nothing is said of the sin of the city or its being punished for it; but on the other hand the glorious fulfillment of the predictions of Isa. 4:2-6 shall not be accomplished until Jehovah has purged the city from her sins (4:4). Although both passages deal with the Jerusalem of the future, in 2:2-4 the prominent thing is the city, while in 4:2-6 it is Jehovah.

The first Messianic passage is Isa. 2:2-4. "And it shall come to pass in the latter days, that the mountain of Jehovah's house shall be established on the top of the mountains, and shall be exalted above the hills; and all nations shall flow unto it. And many peoples shall go and say, Come ye and let us go up to the mountain of Jehovah, to the house of the God of Jacob; and he will teach us of his ways, and we will walk in his paths: for out of Zion shall go forth the law, and the word of Jehovah from Jerusalem. And he will judge between (Margin, "among") the nations, and will decide concerning many peoples, and they shall beat their swords into plowshares and their spears into pruning-hooks; nation shall not lift up sword against nation, neither shall they learn war any more."

This passage occurs with very slight differences in Mic. 4:1-3. There have been four divergent theories to account for this fact: (1) that Isaiah was the author of the passage and Micah quoted it from him; (2) that Micah was the author and Isaiah quoted from him; (3) that both Isaiah and Micah quoted from an earlier prophet, possibly from Joel (Joel 3:10, compare Isa. 2:4; Mic. 4:3); and (4) that the passage dates from post-exilic times and was a later insertion in the books of Isaiah and Micah. While certainty cannot be attained in such a matter, the most probable theory is that Micah was the author and Isaiah quoted it. This seems likely from the fact that the passage is fuller in Micah adding an additional feature (Mic. 4:4) and fits the context better, while in Isaiah it is introduced as though extracted from another source. Even if, however, Isaiah was not the author of this prediction, he gave it the place of honor as the first Messianic passage in his book. It is therefore properly included among his Messianic predictions. The theory that Isaiah and Micah derived it from Joel had little in its favor, even when Joel was considered as the earlier of the three prophets. It is now entirely excluded by the probable date of Joel after the exile.

Skinner has distinguished four main features in this prediction: (1) the preeminence of Zion among the mountains of the world; (2) the extension of the true religion will be accomplished not by conquest but by the moral influence of Israel's theocratic institutions; (3) the nations are not to be absorbed in Israel or ruled by Israel but by Jehovah; and (4) war will end through the just arbitration of Jehovah in international disputes. The only trace of the Old Testament standpoint is the representation of Zion as the centre of Jehovah's reign upon earth. While many Old Testament saints may have understood verse 2 literally of a great physical change by which Zion would become the highest mountain in the world, the New Testament makes it clear that it is figurative of the preeminence of the religion of Zion over all other religions. There is a hint of its figurative character in the fact that all nations are to flow as a river to Mount Zion, the exact opposite of the law of nature. The missionary activity foretold in verse 3 has its fulfilment in the spread of Christianity which shall never cease until all nations gladly submit themselves to the teaching of Jehovah. The idea of the law as proceeding not from Mount Sinai, as in the Old Testament dispensation, but from Mount Zion, where the temple stood and its sacrifices were offered, is suggestive of our Lord's teaching of the new law of love (Jno. 13:34). The word of Jehovah which goes forth from Jerusalem is the glad news of forgiveness through the blood of Christ. Although Isaiah could not appreciate this, it is hidden in his inspired words. The idea of the cessation of war and a reign of peace was prominent in Isaiah's time (Isa. 9:5-7; 11:6-9; Hos. 2:18; Ps. 46:9). According to this passage this glorious day can be ushered in only when all nations submit themselves to the reign of Jehovah, the law of love which proceeds from Zion.

The second Messianic passage is found in Isa. 4:2-6. "In that day shall the branch of Jehovah be beautiful and glorious, and the fruit of the land shall be excellent and comely for them that are escaped of Israel. And it shall come to pass that he that is left in Zion, and he that remaineth in Jerusalem, shall be called holy even every one that is written among the living in Jerusalem; when the Lord shall have washed away the filth of the daughters of Zion, and shall have purged the blood of Jerusalem from the midst thereof, by the spirit of justice and by the spirit of burning. And Jehovah will create over the whole habitation (Margin, "every dwelling-place") of mount Zion, and over her assemblies, a cloud and smoke by day, and the shining of a flaming fire by night; for over all the glory shall be spread a covering. And there shall be a pavilion for a shade in the daytime from the heat, and for a refuge and for a covert from storm and from rain."

While this passage like Isa. 2:2-4 deals with the future Jerusalem, it contains several new features. The first of these is the Messiah himself who is introduced under the name "the branch of Jehovah." This exact expression occurs nowhere else in the Old Testament. The Hebrew word for "branch," however, came later to be a name for the Messiah (Jer. 23:5; 33:15; Zech. 3:8; 6:12) and it should probably be understood in that sense here. This word is not used elsewhere in Isaiah in a Messianic sense but the same conception of the Messiah occurs in Isa. 11:1, 10 and possibly in Isa. 53:2. The idea is that of a new shoot or scion on the Davidic family tree, which has been cut down with only a stump remaining. Like the rest of this passage it relates to the time after the fall of the Davidic dynasty and indeed after the exile. This new king is to be beautiful and glorious to the faithful remnant in Jerusalem. The second new idea is that of the holiness of the remnant, a holiness which is brought about by the purging process through which Jehovah will remove all wickedness from his people. The third idea is that of the protection which Jehovah will give to every dwelling-place in his purified city. As the pillar of cloud and fire protected Israel from their enemies and guided them through the wilderness (Ex. 13:21-22; 14:19-20; Num. 9:15-23; Zech. 2:5), so should every dwelling-place and assembly of the holy city have the protection and blessing of their God. This protection is compared to the booths which sheltered the wandering Israelites from the burning heat of the sun as well as from storm and rain.

The next three Messianic passages have been called Isaiah's Messianic trilogy. In the first the birth of the Messiah is foretold (Isa. 7:14-17); in the second he is represented as already born and his character is portrayed in a series of remarkable names (Isa. 9:6-7); and in the third his spiritual endowment is described as well as the nature of his work (Isa. 11:1-5).

The first of the three was spoken to the royal family when Ahaz had faithlessly refused to ask a sign from Jehovah. "Therefore the Lord himself will give you a sign: behold, a virgin shall conceive, and bear a son, and shall call his name Immanuel. Butter and honey shall he eat, when he knoweth (Margin "that he may know" or "till he know") to refuse the evil, and choose the good. For before the child shall know to refuse the evil and choose the good, the land whose two kings thou abhorrest shall be forsaken. Jehovah will ·bring upon thee and upon thy people, and upon thy father's house, days that have not come from the day that Ephraim departed from Judah—even the king of Assyria" (Isa. 7:14-17).

The traditional interpretation has regarded verse 14 as a prediction of the virgin birth of Christ, especially since it is quoted as fulfilled in that event (Matt. 1:22-23). A careful study of the passage, however, shows that this interpretation is impossible. The word for "virgin" used here is not the common one which with its derivative "virginity" occurs sixty times in the Old Testament and which by its usage necessarily means a virgin (Gen. 24:16; Deut. 22:14-15, 17, 20; Judges 11:37-38) but a far less common word found only seven times in the Old Testament, never shown by the context to connote virginity (Gen. 24:43; Ex. 2:8; Ps. 68:25; Prov. 30:19; Song. 1:3; 6:8; Isa. 7:14). Sometimes the idea of virginity is opposed by the context (Prov. 30:19; Song. 6:8). This less common word is used in the Targum for Judges 19:5 of an unfaithful concubine and in the dialect of Palmyra it was the word for a harlot. It seems to mean a young woman of marriageable age, whether married or not. It

is utterly incredible that, if Isaiah had meant to predict
the virgin birth of Christ, he would have passed by the
common word which necessarily conveyed this idea and
which he used elsewhere five times (Isa. 23:4, 12; 37:22;
47:1; 62:5) and chosen a word which does not necessarily have this meaning and which he never used
elsewhere.

It should be noticed further that even if Isaiah had
used in verse 14 the word connoting virginity, such an
extraordinary idea as the birth of a child without a human
father, an idea absolutely unknown in the Old Testament,
would not be suggested by it. Additional words would
be needed to present such an idea. It is because such
additional and unambiguous words are found in the account of Jesus' birth (Matt. 1:18-20, 25; Luke 1:34-35),
and not because Mary is called a virgin, that we believe
in the virgin birth of Christ. Such additional words
being absent from Isa. 7:14 and the word used not con-
veying this idea, we conclude that the virgin birth of
Christ is not foretold here. Isaiah foretold the birth of
Christ but not that it would be without a human father.
Matthew was correct in regarding Isa. 7:14 as a prediction of the birth of Christ but his words in Matt. 1:22-23
should not be understood as meaning that Isaiah foretold
the manner of his birth. Here as often the fulfillment
exceeded the prediction.

Since the promised sign did not consist in the birth
of Immanuel without a human father, our thought turns
to the child and we find the sign in him, his name and
what is said about him. The child rather than the mother
is the important figure of this passage. This is evidenced

by the fact that while the mother is referred to only once later (Mic. 5:3), Isaiah goes on to speak of the child in verses 15 and 16 as well as in Isa. 8:8, 10; 9:6-7 and 11:1-5, 10.

The name Immanuel means "God is with us." It is a sentence name similar to Daniel ("God is my judge") and Joel ("Jehovah is God"). It does not necessitate the idea of the deity of the child but it does imply that the child would be a strong proof of the presence of God with his people. His birth is represented as imminent. The mother is already pregnant and about to bring forth her son. Events in the near future are to occur before the boy reaches years of discretion (verse 16). The whole impression is that Isaiah expected the birth of the child to occur soon. Yet we cannot find any nearby fulfillment which is altogether satisfactory. The best identification is with Hezekiah. He was a good king of the Davidic line and so might be a type of Christ. He was the owner of the land as Immanuel was (Isa. 8:8). Although Isa. 7:14-17, does not speak of Immanuel as a king or of the royal family, the child of Isa. 9:6-7 and 11:1-5, 10 is a king and probably he is the same child as Immanuel. Yet there seems to be an insuperable obstacle to the identification of Immanuel with Hezekiah in the facts that Ahaz reigned sixteen years and was followed immediately by Hezekiah who was twenty-five at his accession (II Kings 16:2; 18:2; II Chron. 28:1; 29:1). Hence Hezekiah was born nine years before his father came to the throne and even longer before the prediction of Immanuel. There are, however, good reasons for thinking that some mistake

has come in these numbers, perhaps an **error** in trans-
mitting the text. According to II Kings 16:2 and II
Chron. 28:1 Ahaz was only thirty-six when he died while
according to II Kings 18:2 and II Chron 29:1 Hezekiah
was twenty-five when he came to the throne. If this was
so, Ahaz was only eleven years old when his son Hezekiah was born, which is exceedingly improbable. The
whole matter would be explained if Hezekiah was fifteen instead of twenty-five when he came to the throne.
Then Ahaz was twenty-one instead of eleven when his
son Hezekiah was born. Then Hezekiah could be identified with Immanuel, for he was born a year or more
after his father's accession and so after the prediction of
Immanuel's birth. On the whole this seems to us the
most likely explanation. The prediction would then have
its nearby fulfilment in the birth of Hezekiah and Hezekiah would be a type of Christ.

Some commentators identify Immanuel with the second son of Isaiah, Maher-shalal-hash-baz, whose birth is
told in the next chapter (Isa. 8:1-4). The arguments
for this identification are (1) that the birth of Isaiah's
second son is told soon after the prediction of Immanuel
and probably occurred soon after that prediction, and (2)
that which is said about Isaiah's second son (Isa. 8:4) resembles that which is said about Immanuel (Isa. 7:16).
The two names, however, could scarcely have referred
to the same child. While Immanuel, meaning "God is
with us," is in itself a name of blessing, Maher-shalal-
hash-baz, meaning "hasten-spoil, hurry-booty" is a name
of doom. It is true that after the prediction of Immanuel to the whole royal family, Isaiah took him also

as a sign of doom for faithless Ahaz and his people (Isa. 7:17). Immanuel who would be a great blessing to those who accepted him would bring condemnation and punishment upon those who rejected him. Maher-shalal-hash-baz, on the other hand foreshadowed nothing but doom. Furthermore the son of Isaiah was not the owner of the land as Immanuel was (Isa. 8:8). He was not of the royal line and so could not be the child mentioned in Isa. 9:6-7 and 11:1-5, 10. Further still it would be quite unnatural for Isaiah to refer to his own wife as a virgin (Isa. 7:14). Elsewhere he calls' her the prophetess (Isa. 8:3).

Still other commentators think that Immanuel would be a name applied to any child soon to be born, or some child of a woman pointed out in the crowd before the prophet, or perhaps the next generation. Such an ordinary event, however, could not be taken as a sign. Furthermore such a child would not like Immanuel be the owner of the land (Isa. 8:8) or meet the description in Isa. 9:6-7 and 11:1-5, 10.

If no nearby fulfilment for the prediction of Immanuel can be found, we are forced to regard it as a direct prediction of Christ. The serious objection to this view is that the language of Isa. 7:16 seems to require a nearby fulfilment. It is also asked: "How could the birth of Christ, which did not occur until several centuries later, be a sign to Ahaz or the people of his time?" To this it may be fairly replied that according to the prophetic viewpoint when God gave a prediction, its fulfilment was regarded as so absolutely sure that it was as good as done. The promise of Christ's birth would be a sign to the people of the time of Ahaz long before Christ was born. A close parallel is the sign given to Moses at Mount Sinai before he went back to Egypt to deliver Israel. God said to him: "This shall be the token unto thee, that I have sent thee: when thou hast brought forth the people out of Egypt, ye shall serve God upon this mountain" (Ex. 3:12). How futile it seems to us to give Moses a sign which would not be realized until after the deliverance for which the sign was needed. He needed a sign to authenticate his message from God to Israel and to encourage the people to believe and follow him. Yet Moses did not regard this sign as futile. He had God's promise, and that to him was as good as its fulfilment. So the promise of Immanuel's birth could be a sign to the royal family of Ahaz and his people even if Immanuel was not born until centuries later. In any case whether Immanuel is typically prophetic of Christ through Hezekiah or directly prophetic of him, it points to the Messiah and is properly taken in this sense in Mt. 1:22-23. Matthew understood that the prediction did not mean that Immanuel would be his usual name for in close connection with his quotation he refers to the child's name as Jesus (Matt. 1:21). The expression to call a person by a name means that the person shall have the character suggested by the name (Isa. 9:6). Jesus Christ is the supreme proof to us that "God is with us" (II Cor. 1:19-20).

According to Isa. 7:15-16 Immanuel was to grow up at a time when agriculture was impossible because the land was laid desolate by the Assyrian invasion. Hence the child would eat butter (Margin "curds") and wild honey (Isa. 7:22). Eating such food has no magical power to make the eater refuse the evil and choose the good; but the experience of hardship may have moral value. Elsewhere we learn from prophecy that the Messiah would grow up amid hardship and privation (Isa. 52:14; 53:2-3) and the writer to the Hebrews says that he "learned obedience by the things which he suffered" (Heb. 5:8).

The second passage of Isaiah's Messianic trilogy is Isa 9:2-7. "The people that walked in darkness have seen a great light: they that dwelt in the land of the shadow of death, upon them hath the light shined. Thou hast multiplied the nation, thou hast increased their joy: they joy before thee according to the joy in harvest, as men rejoice when they divide the spoil. For the yoke of his burden, and the staff of his shoulder the rod of his oppressor thou hast broken as in the day of Midian. For all the armor of the armed man in the tumult, and the garments rolled in blood, shall be for burning, for fuel of fire. For unto us à child is born, unto us a son is given; and the government shall be upon his shoulder: and his name shall be called Wonderful, Counsellor, Mighty God, Everlasting Father, Prince of Peace. Of the increase of his government and of peace there shall be no end, upon the throne of David, and upon his kingdom to establish it and to uphold it with justice and with righteousness from henceforth even for ever. The zeal of Jehovah of hosts will perform this."

This passage presents a contrast to the other two of these three passages in the fact that while they introduce the Messiah immediately and develop the ideas from him (Isa. 7:14-17; 11:1-16), the figure of the Messiah does not appear until near the end of this passage. Nevertheless the way the passage is bound together as well as the Messianic character of the ideas shows that the Messiah is its central figure. He is introduced as the explanation of the joy, prosperity and peace which characterizes the early verses. The whole prediction has its guarantee in the words, "the zeal of Jehovah of hosts will perform this" (Isa. 9:7; cp. 37:32).

The occasion of the prophecy was the invasion of Galilee by Tiglath-pileser (Isa. 9:1; cp. II Kings 15:29). The inhabitants of this region are "the people that walked in darkness" (verse 2). The light which they see is the relief from misery and bondage which followed the restoration from the exile, but this looked forward to the light of the Messiah. Hence Matthew was right in finding a fulfillment in the dwelling of Christ "in Capernaum, which is by the sea, in the borders of Zebulun and Naphtali" (Matt. 4:12-16). The increase of the population was regarded as a proof of the divine presence and blessing (Ex. 1:12; Isa. 26:15; 49:19; 54:2-3; Hos. 1:10; Acts 7:17). The explanation of their joy is given in the sudden deliverance of the people from oppression as in the sudden and almost miraculous victory of Gideon over the Midianites (Judges 7:19-23; Ps. 83:9; Isa. 10:26). A further explanation is given in the peace which follows symbolized by the destruction of the garments worn in battle. The marginal reading ("every boot of the booted warrior") is preferable. Predictions of peace are characteristic of Isaiah's time (Ps. 46:9; Isa. 2:4; Hos. 2:18). The final explanation of this peace is found in the birth of the Messianic child. This child is viewed as not only born to Israel but as a gift of God to his people (John 3:16). Here as in the case of Immanuel (Isa. 7:14) the names given are not the common designations of the child but were intended as descriptions of his character.

There are eight names in all. The last four, however, should clearly be taken as consisting of two pairs, "Everlasting Father [literally "Father of Eternity"], Prince of Peace." Hence the first four should be regarded as two pairs, literally "Wonder of a Counsellor, God of a Hero." As the ideal king of the Davidic line the Messiah will be wonderful in counsel.

The expression "Mighty God," literally "God of a Hero," has been regarded by many commentators as a hyperbole. It is compared to the divine titles given to the king in ancient Egypt and to the Roman Emperor. Attention is drawn to the fact that this name for God is sometimes used of angels (Ps. 29:1; 89:6). But on the other hand it is never used in the book of Isaiah of any other than God, either the true God (Isa. 5:16; 12:2; 31:3; 40:18; 42:5; 43:12; 45:22) or false deities (Isa. 44:15, 17; 45:20; 46:6). The Israelites made a clear distinction between God and man. While men are sometimes compared to God (Gen. 33:10; Ex. 4:16; 7:1; I Sam. 29:9; II Sam. 14:17; 19:27; Zech. 12:8), they are never called God. Furthermore the exact words rendered Mighty God here occur in the next chapter in reference to the true God (Isa. 10:21). Hence we must conclude that in this title Isaiah predicates deity of the Messiah. This conception is rare in the Old Testament. It is implied, however, in the fact that the Angel of Jehovah was

God in human form. Such passages as Job 19:25-27; Ps. 45:6; Prov. 8:22-31 also imply it. The way that the title "Son of God" is used in the Gospels with the Messianic titles would lead us to suppose that in the time of our Lord the Jews believed in the deity of the Messiah (Matt. 16:16; 26:63; John 1:49; 11:27; 20:31). Such a belief finds strong support here.

The last of the three passages of Isaiah's Messianic trilogy is *chapter* 11. "And there shall come forth a shoot out of the stock of Jesse, and a branch out of his roots shall bear fruit: and the Spirit of Jehovah shall rest upon him, the spirit of wisdom and understanding, the spirit of counsel and might, the spirit of knowledge and of the fear of Jehovah; and his delight shall be (Margin, 'he shall be of quick understanding') in the fear of Jehovah; and he shall not judge after the sight of his eyes, neither decide after the hearing of his ears; but with righteousness shall he judge the poor, and decide with equity for the meek of the earth; and he shall smite the earth with the rod of his mouth, and with the breath of his lips shall he slay the wicked. And righteousness shall be the girdle of his waist, and faithfulness the girdle of his loins."

"And the wolf shall dwell with the lamb, and the leopard shall lie down with the kid; and the calf and the young lion and the fatling together; and a little child shall lead them. And the cow and the bear shall feed; their young ones shall lie down together; and the lion shall eat straw like the ox. And the sucking child shall play on the hole of the asp, and the weaned child shall put his hand on the adder's den. They shall not hurt nor destroy in all my

holy mountain! for the earth shall be full of the knowledge
of Jehovah, as the waters cover the sea."

"And it shall come to pass in that day, that the root of
Jesse, that standeth for an ensign of the people unto him
shall the nations seek; and his resting place shall be
glorious."

"And it shall come to pass in that day, that the Lord
will set his hand again the second time to recover the
remnant of his people, that shall remain from Assyria,
and from Egypt, and from Pathros, and from Cush, and
from Elam, and from Shinar, and from Hamath, and
from the islands of the sea. And he will set up an ensign
for the nations and will assemble the outcasts of Israel,
and gather together the dispersed of Judah from the four
corners of the earth. The envy also of Ephraim shall
depart, and they that vex Judah shall be cut off: Ephraim
shall not envy Judah and Judah shall not vex Ephraim.
And they shall fly down upon the shoulder of the Philistines on the west; together shall they despoil the children
of the east: they shall put forth their hand upon Edom
and Moab; and the children of Ammon shall obey them.
And Jehovah will utterly destroy the tongue of the
Egyptian sea; and with his scorching wind will he wave
his hand over the River, and will smite it into seven
streams, and cause men to march over dryshod. And
there shall be a highway for the remnant of his people,
that shall remain, from Assyria; like as there was for
Israel in the day that he came up out of the land of
Egypt."

This Messianic passage contains three distinct parts.
In the first paragraph (verses 1-5) the Messiah appears

and his endowment and work are described. The second paragraph (verses 6-9) describes the idyllic peace which shall prevail in the animal world in Messianic times. In verse 10 the prophet reverts to the prediction of the Messiah in the first paragraph, showing that he is the central figure of the entire passage. Finally in the last paragraph (verses 11-16) there is a prediction of the restoration of Israel to their land, the reuniting of Judah and Ephraim and the subjugation of Philistia, Edom, Moab and Ammon.

The child of the Davidic line whose birth is foretold in verse 1 is the same as Immanuel (Isa. 7:14) and the prince with the great names (Isa. 9:6-7). He is called "a shoot out of the stock of Jesse" as though to indicate that he would be a second David. Although the word rendered "branch" is not the same as that so rendered in Isa. 4:2; Jer. 23:5; 33:15; Zech. 3:8; 6:12, the idea is similar. The royal line will be like a tree cut down, only the stump or stock remaining in the earth. Yet from this stump a new shoot will come forth, a branch out of his roots shall bear fruit. The Targum gives a Messianic interpretation by the paraphrase: "A king shall come forth from the sons of Jesse and Messiah shall be consecrated from his son's sons." The same idea recurs in verse 10 which Paul quoted as fulfilled in Jesus Christ (Rom. 15:12).

The second verse foretells the spiritual endowment of the Messiah. The seven spirits mentioned here may have suggested John's reference to the seven Spirits that are before God's throne (Rev. 1:4). They are not, however, seven distinct and unrelated spirits, but are well compared with the golden candlestick or lamp-stand (Exod. 25:31-40) which had one central shaft from which sprang three pairs of shafts, seven in all, with a lamp at the top of each (pp. 77-78). So here, the Spirit of Jehovah may be compared to the central shaft. It is the total endowment of the Messiah; but from it spring three complementary pairs of spirits, which Skinner calls his intellectual, practical and religious endowment. Thus wisdom, which in the Old Testament means the ability to adapt means to ends (Ex. 31:2-4; I Kings 3:9-12, 16-28) is balanced by discernment, the ability to distinguish good from bad, true from false; counsel, in which Solomon was supreme, is balanced by might, the ability to carry counsel into action, in which David was supreme; and the knowledge of Jehovah, which means communion with Him, is balanced by the fear of Jehovah, the Old Testament name for the true religion (Ps. 111:10; Prov. 1:7; 9:10). In Isa. 61:1-3 the prophet describes the work which the Messiah will do as the result of this spiritual endowment. In I Cor. 12:4-11 Paul shows how all spiritual gifts which men display are but different manifestations of the same spirit.

The marginal reading of verse 3 is truer to the original. The word rendered "delight" in the text means literally "smelling" and is used whether the smell is pleasant or not (Gen. 27:27; Deut. 4:28; Job 39:25; Ps. 115:6). The idea of delight is found only when the sweetness of the odor is mentioned (Lev. 26:31). The Messiah is represented here as testing by smelling. The criterion by which he tests men and institutions is not external appearance or hearsay but the fear of Jehovah which is in the heart (I Sam. 16:7; I Chron. 28:9). This is rather imperfectly expressed in the marginal rendering, "he shall be of quick understanding in the fear of Jehovah."

Giving justice to the poor and punishing their wicked oppressors (verse 4) was the exact opposite of the conditions in Isaiah's time, especially in the reign of Ahaz (Isa. 1:23; 10:1-2). In this respect the justice of Solomon became the type of the justice of the Messiah (Ps. 72:2, 4, 12-14). The two parts of the Messianic work stand out here in bold relief. To the poor and defenceless he brings even-handed justice. The same justice brings punishment to the wicked. He came "to proclaim the year of Jehovah's favor, and the day of vengeance of our God" (Isa. 61:2).

The second paragraph of this chapter (verses 6-9) has no parallel in the Old Testament in its representation of a state of perfect peace and harmony in the animal world. Skinner states the case well: "The description is not to be interpreted allegorically; as if the wild beasts were merely symbols for cruel and rapacious men. Neither, perhaps, is it to be taken quite literally. It is rather a poetic presentation of the truth that the regeneration of society is to be accompanied by a restoration of the harmony of creation (cp. Rom. 8:19-22)." The key to the understanding of the passage is found in verse 9. There will be no hurtful and destructive forces in Messianic times. The universal spread of the knowledge of Jehovah will have its beneficent effects even in the animal world. As the ground and all that comes out of it were cursed because of man's sin (Gen. 3:17-19) so the redemption of man from sin will include the undoing of the curse upon the ground and upon the animal creation. "The earnest expectation of the creation waiteth for the revealing of the sons of God. For the creation was subjected to vanity, not of its own will but by reason of him who subjected it, in hope that the creation itself also shall be delivered from the bondage of corruption into the liberty of the glory of the children of God. For we know that the whole creation groaneth and travaileth in pain together until now" (Rom. 8:19-22). The way that nature shares in the fate of man and is affected by his sin and by his righteousness comes out in such passages as Gen. 6:7; Deut. 28:1-6, 11-12, 15-19; Ps. 91:13; Ezek. 34:25; Hos. 2:18; Jonah 4:11; Mark 16:18; Luke 10:19. As Isaac Watts sang, Christ "comes to make his blessings flow, far as the course is found." In the interpretation of Isaiah's prophecy, however, its poetic nature should be remembered especially in the interpretation of details. A literal change of the nature of the lion by which it shall become herbivorous is not to be expected. George Adam Smith has well pointed out that much of the fierceness of the wild animals toward man is due to human contact. He quotes Charles Darwin as saying: "It deserves notice that at an extremely ancient period when man first entered any country the animals living there would have no instinctive or inherited fear of him and would consequently have been tamed far more easily than at present" (The Book of Isaiah, Vol. I, p. 195). When man has attained an ideal conception of his true relation to the animal world, the perfect harmony foretold by Isaiah will be realized. This interesting passage probably suggested the representation in the third book of the Sibylline Oracles, lines

936-944. Possibly Virgil derived certain features of his fourth eclogue from the latter book.

Verse 10 designates the Messiah as "the root of Jesse" (cp. Rev. 5:5; 22:16) and predicts that he shall be the ensign or rallying point for all peoples (Isa. 5:26; 11:12; 18:3; 49:22). The word to "seek" used here is used especially of consulting an oracle (Isa. 8:19; 19:3). Thus the prediction implies that all nations shall seek the Messiah to subject their lives to him. Then will the Messiah have realized the fulfillment of his purpose, even as the ark moved forward in the wilderness "to seek out a resting-place" for Israel (Num. 10:33) but never rested permanently until it reached the land of promise (Deut. 12:9; Ps. 132:8, 14). Then indeed will his resting-place be glorious.

The last paragraph foretells a restoration of Israel to their land not only from Assyria and Shinar but from several other countries and indeed from the four corners of the earth. The language is significant. "The Lord will set his hand again the second time to recover the remnant of his people, that shall remain from Assyria and from Egypt, and from Pathros, and from Cush, and from Elam, and from Shinar, and from Hamath, and from the islands of the sea." If this is to be the second time, what was the first? Many commentators think that it was the deliverance from the bondage of Egypt, since the highway for returning Israel from Assyria is compared to that from Egypt in verse 16. If the deliverance from Egypt was the first time, this prediction looks forward only to the return from Babylon as the second time. But this interpretation is unsatisfactory. (1) The deliverance from Egypt could scarcely be described as recovering the remnant of God's people. Israel in Egypt was not a remnant but on the contrary the people were greatly increased before the exodus (Ex. 1:7, 9, 12). (2) The dispersion from which the second restoration is to come is much more extensive than that at the time when they returned from Babylon. It is true that there were Jews at that time in Egypt and possibly in some of the other countries. A few of them may have returned to Palestine after the exile but this movement could scarcely be described as from the four corners of the earth. (3) The Messianic connection favors the belief that the second restoration is still future. (4) The reconciliation of Judah and Ephraim is still future (verse 13). Hence the restoration of which it is a feature must be also future. (5) The fact that the Jews are now much more widely scattered than they were at the time of the exile and yet for the most part they remain distinct from the nations with whom they dwell, suggests that God is keeping them distinct because he intends again the second time to restore them to their land. (6) The land was given them as a perpetual possession (Gen. 17:8; 48:4). If they persisted in disobeying God, they would be cast out of it (Deut. 29:28); but if they repented and returned to Jehovah they would be restored (Deut. 30:1-5). They were sent into exile in Assyria and Babylon because of their sin and they were restored to Palestine when they repented. Again they have been scattered over all the face of the earth because of their sin in rejecting the Messiah (Matt. 23:37-38; Luke 13:34-35). But the time is coming when they shall look unto him whom they have pierced and mourn for him in deep repentance (Zech. 12:10-14; Rev. 1:7). Jesus looking to the future said to Jerusalem, "Ye shall not see me henceforth till ye shall say, Blessed is he that cometh in the name of the Lord" (Matt. 23:39; Luke 13:35). Jerusalem is not to be trodden down of the Gentiles forever but only "until the times of the Gentiles be fulfilled" (Luke 21:24; cp. Rev. 11:2). To the present writer it seems that all these facts point to a future restoration of the Jews to their land when they repent of their sin in rejecting their Messiah, as they were restored when they repented in Babylon. If so, the first time that God put forth his hand to recover the remnant of his people was in the days of Cyrus, Zerubbabel, Ezra and Nehemiah; and the second time is still future. Some commentators find a fulfillment of Isaiah's prediction in the conversion of the Jews to Christianity. This is indeed foretold (Rom. 11:25-26). But the language of Isaiah does not admit of such a figurative interpretation and the prophecies concerning Jerusalem (Matt. 23:37-39; Luke 13:34-35; 21:24; Rev. 11:2) seem to require a literal fulfillment.

The idea of a future reconciliation of Judah and Ephraim is prominent in prophecy (Hos. 1:11; Isa. 11:13; Jer. 23:5-6; 50:4-5; Ezek. 37:16-22). In Ezra's time twelve animals were offered as a sacrifice for all Israel (Ezra 6:17; 8:35). Jesus chose his twelve apostles according to the number of the tribes and he foretold that they should sit upon twelve thrones judging the twelve tribes of Israel (Matt. 19:28; Luke 22:30). Paul spoke of the twelve tribes as existing in his day (Acts 26:7) and James addressed his epistle "to the twelve tribes which are of the Dispersion" (James 1:1). John also in vision saw twelve thousand sealed out of each one of the twelve tribes (Rev. 7:4-8). Where the lost ten tribes are we do not know. None of the many theories of their whereabouts is convincing. But the predictions of their reconciliation with Judah and restoration to their land stand as a promise of God which cannot fail.

One of the most remarkable Messianic passages in Isaiah, both in its universalism and its divine graciousness, is found in Isa. 25:6-8. "And in this mountain will Jehovah of hosts make unto all peoples a feast of fat things, a feast of wines on the lees, of fat things full of marrow, of wines on the lees well refined. And he will destroy in this mountain the face of the covering that covereth all peoples, and the veil that is spread over all nations. He hath swallowed up death for ever; and the Lord Jehovah will wipe away tears from off all faces; and the reproach of his people will he take away from off all the earth; for Jehovah hath spoken it."

The picture is that of the coronation feast of Jehovah on Mount Zion as king of all nations (I Sam. 11:15; I Kings 1:9, 25). It is not, however, a feast which the people give in honor of their king but one which he gives to his people. He is the host and he invites all nations to his coronation feast since they are properly all his people. All the blessings of the feast and the other blessings mentioned are his gracious gifts. In figurative language they signify the admission of all nations to communion with him. Since the feast is spread on Mount Zion, the temple mount, the place of sacrifice, the suggestion is that the deepest spiritual needs of all men would be satisfied there by the atoning sacrifice of Calvary. The figure of a feast to represent spiritual blessings is found in Ps. 36:8; 63:5; and Isa. 55:1-2, as well as in the New Testament in Matt. 22:1-14; Luke 14:15-24 and Rev. 19:9. The provision is rich in quality and abundant in quantity.

The face of the covering that covereth all nations does not refer to spiritual blindness as in II Cor. 3:14-18 but to the custom of covering the face with a veil in times of sorrow and bereavement (II Sam. 15:30; 19:4; Esther 6:12; Jer. 14:3, 4). Jehovah will not only remove this veil of sorrow from all nations but will destroy it so that it can never cover their faces again. In order to accomplish this he swallows up death forever. Paul refers to this as to be fulfilled "when this corruptible shall have put on incorruption, and this mortal shall have put on immortality" (I Cor. 15:54). Following a slightly different Aramaic form he renders: "Death is swallowed up in victory." When Jehovah removes the veil from the faces of sorrowing men, he sees their tears and with infinite tenderness he wipes them away (Rev. 7:17; 21:4). Not forgetful of his chosen people Israel he promises to take away the reproach which has been so large a part of their anguish through all the ages (Deut. 28:37; Ps. 44:14-16; 79:10; Joel 2:17). All this is guaranteed by Jehovah's unfailing word.

Another passage with ultimately Messianic content is *Isa.* 28:14-18. "Wherefore hear the word of Jehovah, ye scoffers, that rule this people that is in Jerusalem: Because ye have said, We have made a covenant with death, and with Sheol are we at agreement; when the overflowing scourge shall pass through, it shall not come unto us; for we have made lies our refuge, and under falsehood have we hid ourselves: therefore thus saith the Lord Jehovah, Behold I lay (Margin "have laid") in Zion for a foundation a stone, a tried stone, a precious corner-stone of sure foundation: he that believeth shall not be in haste. And I will make justice the line, and righteousness the plummet; and the hail shall sweep away the refuge of lies, and the waters shall overflow the hiding-place. And your covenant with death shall be annulled, and your agreement with Sheol shall not stand; when the overflowing scourge shall pass through, then ye shall be trodden down by it."

The historic situation which called forth this prophecy arose during the early years of Sennacherib's reign before he invaded Judah (between 705 and 701 B. C.). During these years Sennacherib was occupied with the rebellion of Merodach-baladan, king of Babylon, who was nominally subject to Assyria but who faithlessly sought independence whenever the king of Assyria turned his back. Shabaka, king of Egypt, took advantage of this situation to incite Judah and the neighboring tributary states to rebel against Assyria. Many of the drunken nobles of Judah welcomed these advances from Egypt; but Isaiah, and through his influence Hezekiah, opposed them and advocated trusting not in Egypt but in Jehovah. It was against these drunken nobles of the Egyptian party that Isaiah spoke this prophecy. He called them scoffers because they had mocked him in words which he quoted from them (Isa. 28:9-10). The covenant with death and the agreement with Sheol to which the prophet referred were the alliance with Egypt which was probably ratified by necromantic rites (Isa. 8:19). The overflowing scourge was the impending Assyrian invasion, which is represented as though the Euphrates or the Tigris were made to overflow Palestine (Ps. 46:3; Isa. 8:7-8). The drunken nobles thought they would be safe when the Assyrian invasion came because of the help of Egypt (Isa. 29:15; 30:1-7, 15-17; 31:1-3; II Kings 18:19-21; Isa. 36:4-6). The covenant with Egypt Isaiah called a refuge of lies. In contrast with this false confidence the prophet speaking in God's name presented the only true foundation for their faith. Their confidence would be swept away but this sure foundation would stand firm.

What is the foundation stone to which Isaiah referred? Skinner says: "It is not Jehovah himself, since it is Jehovah who lays it; it is not the temple nor Mount Zion, nor the Davidic dynasty, for these are at most but visible symbols of a spiritual fact disclosed to the prophet's faith. The foundation stone represents the only element in human history which is indestructible, viz., the purpose of God, and that purpose as historically realized in the relation which he has established between himself and the people of Israel." This statement points in the right direction; but it fails to recognize that the purpose of God in choosing Israel was to reveal himself to all mankind (Gen. 12:3; Ex. 19:5-6; Isa. 42:1, 6; 49:1, 6) and that this would be fulfilled in and through the Messiah. While the stone represents the purpose of God as expressed in his promises, that purpose came to be so completely embodied in Christ that he was the stone. The case of Peter is somewhat similar. After Peter's confession that Jesus was the Messiah, the Son of God, Christ said to him: "Thou art Peter (Greek, Petros), and upon this rock

(Greek, petra) I will build my church" (Matt. 16:18). Christ founded his church on the faith that he was the Messiah, the Son of God. This faith was so embodied in Peter that in a sense he was the rock on which the church was founded. Similarly God's purpose was so embodied in Christ that he was the foundation stone of which Isaiah spoke. Hence Peter was justified in quoting this passage in connection with Ps. 118:22 in reference to Christ (I Peter 2:6-8) and Paul was justified, probably in reference to this passage, in calling Christ the foundation and the chief corner-stone (I Cor. 3:11; Eph. 2:20). The purpose of God had already been expressed in Isaiah's time in the promise of the Messiah. The foundation had been laid in Zion. Those who would not accept this foundation and trust in it would be overthrown. But those who trusted in it would find it indeed "a tried stone, a precious corner-stone of sure foundation" (cp. Isa. 7:9). It is in this sense that this passage points ultimately to Christ.

The society of Messianic times is foretold in *Isa.* 32:1-8. "Behold, a king shall reign in righteousness, and princes shall rule in justice. And a man shall be as a hiding-place from the wind, and a covert from the tempest, as streams of water in a dry place, as the shade of a great rock in a weary land. And the eyes of them that see shall not be dim, and the ears of them that hear shall hearken. And the heart of the rash shall understand knowledge, and the tongue of the stammerers shall be ready to speak plainly. The fool shall be no more called noble, nor the churl said to be bountiful. For the fool will speak folly, and his heart will work iniquity, to practise profaneness, and to utter error against Jehovah, to make empty the soul of the hungry, and to cause the drink of the thirsty to fail. And the instruments of the churl are evil: he deviseth wicked devices to destroy the meek with lying words, even when the needy speaketh right. But the noble deviseth noble things, and in noble things shall he continue."

The society of Messianic times will be ideal from top to bottom. Naturally Isaiah begins with the king, but in doing so he says "a king" rather than "the king" (cp. Ps. 72:1) since the prediction is a general one and not a definite prediction of the Messiah. Of course the king of Messianic times can be none other than the Messiah himself. The righteousness with which he shall reign is mentioned elsewhere in Messianic passages (II Sam. 23:3; Ps. 72:1-4; Isa. 9:7; 11:4-5; Jer. 23:5; 33:15). He is mentioned here, however, merely incidentally. It is natural that with such a righteous king at the head all the lower strata of society should be righteous as Solomon had foretold: "In his days shall the righteous flourish" (Ps. 72:7). Next under the king "princes shall rule in justice." The word for "man" in the second verse is used especially of men of high character or social standing (Ps. 49:2; 62:9) and here stands for one of influence and wealth. Such a man will use his power to protect the weak and his wealth to satisfy the needs of the poor. The intellectual powers will be so strengthened that men will see clearly and hear distinctly. Those who are hasty and precipitate in their speech will learn to be judicious and on the other hand those who hesitate and stammer will speak plainly. Men will be judged by their character rather than by their social position, wealth or power. Accordingly a noble who is a fool will no more be called noble and a rich man who is a churl will not be called bountiful. Men will show what they really are by their deeds. The fool and the churl will show their folly and their churlishness by word and act; while the truly noble will devise noble things and continue to do so.

There are unmistakable Messianic elements in *Isa.* 33: 17-24. "Thine eyes shall see the king (Hebrew, 'a king') in his beauty; they shall behold a land that reacheth afar (Margin, 'a land that is very far off'; Hebrew, 'a land of far distances'). Thy heart shall muse on the terror. Where is he that counted, where is he that weighed the tribute? Where is he that counted the towers? Thou shalt not see the fierce people, a people of a deep speech that thou canst not comprehend, of a strange tongue that thou canst not understand. Look upon Zion the city of our solemnities: thine eyes shall see Jerusalem a quiet habitation, a tent that shall not be removed, the stakes whereof shall never be plucked up, neither shall any of the cords thereof be broken. But there Jehovah will be with us in majesty, a place of broad rivers and streams, wherein shall go no galley with oars, neither shall gallant ship pass thereby. For Jehovah is our judge, Jehovah is our lawgiver, Jehovah is our king; he will save us. Thy tacklings are loosed; they could not strengthen the foot of their mast, they could not spread the sail: then was the prey of a great spoil divided; the lame took the prey. And the inhabitants shall not say, I am sick: the people that dwell therein shall be forgiven their iniquity."

This passage furnishes one of the best illustrations of the fact that as the prophets looked into the future they could not distinguish the near from the far. To them the future seemed as one and they described it as they saw it mingling the near and far in a way which is confusing to us who live after the fulfillment of their words. This prophecy seems to have been spoken when the armies of Sennacherib had laid waste the towns of Judah and besieged the city of Jerusalem. Humanly there seemed no hope of deliverance. Yet Isaiah with sublime faith foretold that the siege would be lifted and the Assyrian army would return to their land (II Kings 19:6-7; Isa. 37:6-7). Here his prophetic eyes are looking toward that blessed deliverance. The siege of the city was a serious blow to the prestige of Hezekiah; but Isaiah says to the people: "Thine eyes shall see a king in his beauty; they shall behold a land that reacheth afar." It is futile to ask whether the king referred to is Hezekiah or the Messiah. If it was Hezekiah, it was that good king arrayed in such splendid garments that he was a type of Christ (Ps. 45:2). The retreat of the Assyrians would restore the lost prestige of the king. The people would look upon him with pride. He would be beautiful in their eyes. This beauty of Hezekiah foreshadowed the beauty of the chiefest among ten thousand and the one altogether lovely (Song 5:10, 16). He is the king in his beauty. His land is to be one of far distances, reaching to the utmost limits promised to Abraham (Gen. 15:18-21; Ex. 23:31; Deut. 1:7-8; Ps. 72:8; Zech. 9:10).

In the next two verses the prophet describes the conditions immediately after the retreat of the Assyrian army. In their new joy the people would meditate on the terror they felt when the hostile soldiers infested the land. They would exclaim: Where have the officers gone who counted

the towers of Jerusalem and collected its tribute? No
more would they hear the Assyrian speech with its deep
gutturals, so harsh and strange to their ears (Isa. 28:11;
Jer. 5:15). But they would see the holy city quiet and
established. The word for river in verse 21 is the one
specially used of the Euphrates (Gen. 15:18; 31:21; Ex.
23:31; Ps. 72:8; Isa. 7:20; Jer. 2:18; Mic. 7:12; Zech.
9:10) and the word for streams is used almost exclusively
of the Nile (Gen. 41:2, 3, 17, 18, etc.). As the capital of
Egypt was on the broad Nile (Nah. 3:8) and Babylon on
the Euphrates, so would the ideal Jerusalem of the future
have its broad river (Ps. 46:4; Isa. 8:6; Ezek. 47:1-5;
Joel 3:18; Zech. 14:8; Rev. 22:1-2) on which no hostile
ship would float. The representation is plainly ideal and
points to the Jerusalem of the last days, especially in its
eternity (verse 20). In verse 23 the prophet addressed
the city in her distressed condition while the Assyrian
army remained. He compared her to a ship whose tacklings are loosed, whose mast had slipped from its base and
whose sails could not be spread. Dropping this figure he
said: "Then was the prey of a great spoil divided; the
lame took the prey." This division of spoil was not made
by the Assyrians but by Israel, who is spoken of as lame
because their ancestor Jacob had limped when the angel
touched the hollow of his thigh (Gen. 32:31). Micah and
Zephaniah used the same figure concerning Israel (Mic.
4:6-7; Zeph. 3:19). Looking forward to the Jerusalem
of Messianic times Isaiah predicts that its inhabitants shall
not be sick. Since sickness was regarded as the punishment for sin (Ps. 103:3; Isa. 1:4-6; Mark 2:5-12) health
would come when their sins were forgiven.

THE SERVANT OF JEHOVAH. The greatest conception
of the book of Isaiah is found in chapters 40-53. It is
that of the Servant of Jehovah. This title occurs twenty
times in these chapters (Isa. 41:8, 9; 42:1, 19; 43:10;
44:1, 2, 21, 26; 45:4; 48:20; 49:3, 5, 6, 7; 50:10; 52:13;
53:11) and never elsewhere in this book. The first time
it occurs the servant is distinctly identified with Israel.
"But thou, Israel, my servant, Jacob whom I have chosen,
the seed of Abraham my friend, thou whom I have taken
hold of from the ends of the earth, and called from the
corners thereof, and said unto thee, Thou art my servant,
I have chosen thee and not cast thee away" (Isa. 41:8-9).
The same is true in several other passages (Isa. 44:1, 2,
21; 45:4; 48:20; 49:3). From this repeated identification
of the servant with Israel one would naturally infer that
the servant refers to Israel wherever the expression occurs.
This inference, however, is impossible; for in other passages the servant is distinguished from Israel. In Isa. 42:6
Jehovah says to the servant: "I will keep thee and give
thee for a covenant of the people, for a light of the
Gentiles." The word for people is that used almost exclusively of Israel. The context also shows that Israel is
meant. But if the servant is to be a covenant of Israel, it
must in some sense be distinct from Israel. This is even
plainer in Isa. 49:5-7 where the servant says: "And now
saith Jehovah that formed me from the womb to be his
servant, to bring Jacob again to him, and that Israel be
gathered unto him . . . yea, he saith, It is too light a
thing that thou shouldst be my servant to raise up the
tribes of Jacob, and to restore the preserved of Israel: I
will also give thee for a light to the Gentiles, that thou

mayest be my salvation unto the end of the earth." Obviously if the servant is to bring Jacob back to God, to gather Israel to God, to raise up the tribes of Jacob and to restore the preserved of Israel, he must be in some sense distinct from Israel.   In chapter 53 the prophet speaking for the nation distinguishes Israel from the servant. "He (the servant) grew up before him (Jehovah) as a tender plant, and as a root out of a dry ground: he hath no form nor comeliness; and when we (Israel) see him (the servant), there is no beauty that we should desire him" (Isa. 53:2). This distinction between Israel and the servant is found in verses 2, 3, 4, 5, 6. It is even clearer in verse 8 where the prophet says: "He (the servant) was cut off out of the land of the living for the transgression of my people (Israel) to whom the stroke was due." If the servant, as represented here, suffers and dies for the sins of Israel, he must be in some sense distinct from Israel.

Furthermore in some of these passages the servant is so definitely represented as a person, an individual, that we naturally conclude that an individual must be meant. He is addressed by the singular pronoun (Isa. 41:8, 9; 42:6; 44:2, 3, 21, 22; 49:3, 6, 7), he speaks of himself with the singular pronoun (Isa. 49:1, 2, 3, 4, 5; 50:4, 5, 6, 7, 8, 9) and he is spoken of by the singular pronoun (Isa. 42:1, 2, 3, 4; 52:13, 14, 15; 53:2, 3, 4, 5, 6, 7, 8, 9, 10, 11, 12). We must remember that the nation, or a part of it, is often personified in the Old Testament and represented as an individual (Ex. 14:25; Num. 20:18-19; Deut. 2:26-29; Josh. 9:7; 17:14; Judges 1:3; 20:23; Ps. 44:4, 6; 129:1-3; Isa. 25:1-4; Jer. 10:19-25; Lam. 1:1-22;

3:1-21, 24, 48-63; Hab. 3:14). Personification of a nation or a part of it is carried much further in the Old Testament than is customary with us. Hence it is argued that in the Servant of Jehovah passages we have a personification of Israel or a part of Israel rather than a person. This view is supported by the fact that some of the ideas found in the passages where the personification is strongest occur elsewhere of Israel. In Isa. 50:6 the servant says: "I gave my back to the smiters, and my cheeks to them that plucked off the hair; I hid not my face from shame and spitting." A similar expression is put into the mouth of Israel in Ps. 129:1-3, "Many a time have they afflicted me from my youth up, let Israel now say . . . The plowers plowed upon my back; they made long their furrows." Since the Psalmist referred to the afflictions of the exile, the natural inference is that Isa. 50:6 has the same meaning. The servant is represented in Isa. 53:4-6, 8, 11 as bearing the sin of Israel. The same conception is found in Lam. 5:7 where the generation of Israel which suffered from the devastation of Jerusalem says: "Our fathers sinned and are not; and we have borne their iniquities." Here again the inference is that the picture of the suffering servant in chapter 53 is the picture of Israel suffering during the exile, not only those who remained in desolate Jerusalem but those in captivity in Babylon. The same idea is found in the proverb by which the generation of the exile protested against their suffering for the sins of their ancestors. "The fathers have eaten sour grapes and the children's teeth are set on edge" (Jer. 31:29; Ezek. 18:2). The fall of Jersalem and the exile of Judah were represented as being especially for the sins of Manasseh's reign (II Kings 21:10-15; 23:26-27; 24:3-4; Jer. 15:4). Isaiah prophesying in that reign might well depict the sufferings of the exile in the picture of the vicarious suffering servant. The servant is represented as dying and rising again in Isa. 53:8-12. Similarly the exile is represented as the death of the nation and the restoration as a resurrection in Ezek. 37:1-14; Hos. 6:2; 13:14 and probably in Isa. 25:8; 26:19. All these indications point toward the conclusion that when the Servant of Jehovah is distinguished from the nation as a whole, it refers to the generation of Israel which suffered in the exile.

This idea is confirmed by a comparison of the conception of the Servant of Jehovah when distinguished from the whole nation with that of the faithful remnant so prominent in the first part of Isaiah's book. The remnant saved Jerusalem in Isaiah's time from complete extermination (Isa. 1:9). The remnant would be purged by the sufferings of the exile but would survive (Isa. 4:2-4; 10:20-22; 11:11-12, 16; 37:31-32). The same was true of the Servant of Jehovah. The remnant was holy, faithful to Jehovah (Isa. 4:3; 10:20). So the Servant of Jehovah is righteous (Isa. 42:1-3), "honorable in the eyes of Jehovah" (Isa. 49:5); he submits to Jehovah's will (Isa. 50:5-6); "he had done no violence, neither was any deceit in his mouth" (Isa. 53:9). The representations are so similar that we are driven to the conclusion that they are the same. The Servant of Jehovah when distinguished from Israel is none other than the faithful remnant of Israel, the righteous few in the time of the

exile who would save the nation from extinction and re-
ëstablish the national life.

Many commentators are satisfied to regard the Servant
of Jehovah as always representing Israel, although it is
sometimes the nation as it actually was and sometimes the
nation as God wished it to be. This interpretation completely excludes the personal, Messianic explanation of the
Servant. It is the usual Jewish interpretation, although
a few of the best Jewish commentators have identified the
Servant in chapter 53 with the Messiah and it is not improbable that in New Testament times the number of Jews
who interpreted the suffering Servant Messianically was
greater than it was after the disputes with the Christians
in the second century which centered about this chapter.

Other commentators while not denying that the Servant
was Israel or sometimes the faithful part of Israel, find
in Isa. 42:1-7; 49:1-7; 50:4-9; 52:13-53:12 predictions
of the Messiah which have been fulfilled in part and are
to be completely fulfilled by Jesus Christ. Peake states
the case well: "We may solve the difficulty if we can
identify Jesus with Israel . . . If then, the qualities
which constituted for the prophet Israel's essential meaning, its place in universal history, were qualities which
existed in a very mixed and imperfect form in the nation,
but were embodied and perfectly realized in an individual,
we may think of that individual as concentrating within
himself the essential Israel. Now we believe that this is
precisely the place Jesus fills in history and that the functions only partially fulfilled by Israel were completely discharged by him. In him the long revelation of God in
Israel attained its climax and goal" (The Problem of Suf-

fering, pp. 65-66). This statement recognizes the true
relation of Israel to the coming Messiah by virtue of
which statements which were originally made concerning
Israel could be applied directly to Christ (Hos. 11:1; cp.
Matt. 2:15). It was not merely the king, the prophet or
the priest in Israel who were the types of Christ by virtue
of their office, but the whole nation was a type of him in
so far as it realized in character and conduct the call of
God to be his Servant. The case is stated somewhat dif-
ferently in Davis' "Dictionary of the Bible": "The view
most widely entertained by modern commentators is that
the Servant of the Lord in these chapters is Israel, the
eye of the prophet being fixed sometimes on the nation
as a whole, sometimes on the godly portion, sometimes on
that perfect representative of Israel, that Israelite indeed,
Christ." Better still is the way which Franz Delitzsch
puts it: "The conception of the Servant of Jehovah is as
it were a pyramid of which the basis is the people of
Israel as a whole, the central part Israel according to the
spirit and the summit the person of the mediator of salvation who arises out of Israel." The advantage of this
figure is that it unifies the whole conception. It is not
that sometimes the prophet speaks of one thing and sometimes of another thing unrelated to it. It is rather that
he always speaks of Israel but as he broods on Israel as
Balaam did, its divine call and future destiny (Num.
24:15-19) he sees the Messiah arising out of Israel and
guided by the Spirit of God he uses language of Israel
which presents the clearest picture of Christ in the Old
Testament. Somewhat similar to Delitzsch's statement is
that of Oehler: "The prophetic view ascends in these

discourses step by step, as it were, from the broad space covered by the foundations of a cathedral up to the dome on which the cross is planted."

The use which the New Testament makes of the Servant of Jehovah passages justifies and confirms the Messianic interpretation. Matthew quotes Isa. 42:1-4 as fulfilled by Christ (Matt. 12:15-21). Paul and Barnabas referred to Isa. 49:6 to justify their turning to the Gentiles (Acts 13:46-47). Although this use cannot be called a directly Messianic interpretation, it refers the passage to Messianic times. The statement of Luke 9:51 that Jesus "stedfastly set his face to go to Jerusalem" while not a quotation is probably a reference to the words of the Servant in Isa. 50:7, "I set my face like a flint." Paul quoted Isa. 52:15 as justification for his preaching the gospel where Christ was not already named (Rom. 15:20-21). This again is not a directly Messianic interpretation but it applies the passage to Messianic times. John quoted Isa. 53:1 as fulfilled in Christ (John 12:37-38). Paul quoted the same verse as fulfilled in the preaching of the gospel (Rom. 10:16). Matthew quoted Isa. 53:4 as fulfilled by Christ (Matt. 8:17) and Peter gave a free paraphrase of Isa. 53:4-6 in reference to Christ (I Peter 2:24-25). Peter also referred Isa. 53:9 to Christ (I Peter 2:22). The Ethiopian eunuch read Isa. 53:7-8 and asked Philip, "Of whom speaketh the prophet this, of himself, or of some other? And Philip opened his mouth, and beginning from this scripture preached unto him Jesus" (Acts 8:32-35). Finally our Lord himself quoted Isa. 53:12 as fulfilled in him (Luke 22:37). Even if Isa. 53 were not quoted in the New Testament in reference to

Jesus, a fair exegesis would require the Messianic interpretation. Since, however, there are such quotations and
references, this interpretation is even surer. The impression produced upon the thoughtful Christian reader
of this chapter is that here we have an inspired picture of
Jesus not only in the broad outlines of his saving work
but in such details as his silence under suffering (Isa.
53:7), his being crucified between two malefactors, and
his being buried in a rich man's tomb (Isa. 53:9). It is
surprising that Isa. 50:6 is not quoted in the New Testament in reference to Christ. Yet the representation of
him is amazingly accurate.

Besides the quotations and references of Servant of
Jehovah passages in the New Testament as relating to
Jesus or fulfilled in him, he was called God's servant four
times with probable allusion to the conception in Isaiah.
Thus Peter said: "The God of Abraham, and of Isaac
and of Jacob hath glorified his Servant Jesus" (Acts
3:13) and again: "Unto you first God, having raised up
his Servant, sent him to bless you, in turning away everyone of you from your iniquities" (Acts 3:26). Peter and
John prayed: "Of a truth in this city against thy holy
Servant, Jesus, whom thou didst anoint, both Herod and
Pontius Pilate, with the Gentiles and the peoples of Israel
were gathered together" (Acts 4:27) ; and they asked God
"that signs and wonders may be done through the name
of thy holy Servant Jesus" (Acts 4:30'). In all four of
these verses the Greek word rendered Servant is the one
by which the Septuagint usually translates the Hebrew
word in Isaiah and elsewhere. Mary used the same word
in the Magnificat when she sang: "He hath given help to

Israel his servant" (Luke 1 :54). God indeed gave help
to his servant Israel by raising up his Servant Jesus, as
well as by his life and death. When Paul wrote that
Christ "emptied himself, taking the form of a servant"
(Phil. 2:7) he used a different Greek word. While this
other word is sometimes used by the Septuagint in rendering the Hebrew, it is doubtful whether Paul in using
it meant to give Jesus the title Servant of Jehovah.

Although our Lord is called God's Servant only five
times in the New Testament (Matt. 12:18; Acts 3:13, 26;
4:27, 30) and one of the five is a quotation from Isaiah
(Matt. 12:18; cp. Isa. 42:1), the conception of his mission
as one of service for God is prominent in his sayings. He
said: "My meat is to do the will of him that sent me,
and to accomplish his work" (John 4:34) ; "I seek not
mine own will, but the will of him that sent me" (John
5:30) ; "I am come down from heaven, not to do mine own
will, but the will of him that sent me" (John 6:38). He
looked forward to his approaching death as service for
God, for he said: "Therefore doth the Father love me,
because I lay down my life, that I may take it again. No
one taketh it away from me, but I lay it down of myself.
I have power to lay it down and I have power to take it
again. This commandment received I from my Father"
(John 10:17-18). In the garden of Gethsemane he
prayed: "My Father, if it be possible, let this cup pass
away from me; nevertheless not as I will, but as thou
wilt" (Matt. 26:39; cp. Matt. 26:42; Mark 14:36; Luke
22:42). At the end of his life he prayed: "I glorified
thee on the earth, having accomplished the work which
thou hast given me to do" (John 17:4). And when he

cried on the cross: "It is finished" (John 19:30) he doubtless referred to the work which God gave him to do. Jesus was preeminently the Servant of Jehovah and the service which he rendered for Jehovah and the way in which he rendered it are accurately portrayed in these predictions of Isaiah. His features are so plainly depicted here that it can be a portrait of no one else.

An interesting and important feature of the Servant of Jehovah passages is that they represent him not as a king but as performing prophetic and priestly functions. Isaiah had foretold the coming of the Messianic king (Isa. 9:6-7; 11:1, 4; 32:1; 33:17) but had said nothing hitherto about the prophetic and priestly work of the Coming One. Moses had foretold such a prophet (Deut. 18:15-19); but of the priestly work of the Messiah, almost nothing is found in the Old Testament outside of Isaiah. Furthermore the prophetic work of the Servant leads up to his priestly work in these passages. The Servant of Jehovah whose call is described in Isa. 42:1-7 carries out that call in Isa. 49:1-7 by preaching as a prophet to the nations. In Isa. 50:4 he still views his work as prophetic, for he says: "The Lord Jehovah hath given me the tongue of them that are taught, that I may know how to sustain with words him that is weary." He is still a preacher in chapter 50 but one whose preaching is rejected and he is persecuted. In chapter 53 this persecution leads on to the death of the Servant and that death is represented as a sacrifice which the Servant offers voluntarily for the sins of men. This is priestly work and it is this priestly work which gives him the exalted position among the great of earth. It is not as a kingly conqueror that he attains the highest place but as a priest who offers himself as his sacrifice. "Therefore will I divide him a portion with the great, and he shall divide the spoil with the strong; because he poured out his soul unto death and was numbered with the transgressors; yet he bare the sin of many, and made intercession for the transgressors" (Isa. 53:12). In fulfillment of these words the cross of Christ has become his crown. Thus Isaiah presents the kingly work of the Messiah in the first part of his book (chapter 1-39) and his prophetic and priestly work in the later part (chapters 40-53). Although Israel is the Servant of Jehovah, and in particular the faithful remnant of Israel, this noble title is specially applicable to such officers of the nation as the prophet and the priest.

It cannot be by accident that the Servant of Jehovah is mentioned only in the singular in chapters 40-53 and only in the plural in chapters 54-66. The climax having been reached in chapter 53 no further development is possible. The Servant of Jehovah having given his life as a sacrifice for sin, having risen from the dead and made intercession for the transgressors, his work is finished. But there is possible a multiplication of the Servant in the person and work of others. In this sense the word occurs eleven times in the plural (Isa. 54:17; 56:6; 63:17; 65:8, 9, 13, 14, 15; 66:14). Isaiah concludes a description in chapter 54 of the glorious future of Israel by the statement: "This is the heritage of the servants of Jehovah, and their righteousness which is of one, saith Jehovah" (Isa. 54:17). The servants of Jehovah get their position and their privileges from the Servant of Jehovah. These servants are not confined to Israel for the prophet speaks of "the foreigners that join themselves to Jehovah, to minister unto him, and to love the name of Jehovah, to be his servants" (Isa. 56:6). In chapter 65 the title "servants of Jehovah" is used of the faithful element in Israel, almost as a synonym of the faithful remnant. Thus Jehovah says to the unfaithful Israelites: "Behold, my servants shall eat, but ye shall be hungry; behold, my servants shall drink, but ye shall be thirsty; behold, my servants shall rejoice, but ye shall be put to shame" (Isa. 65:13). The same contrast is found in Isa. 66:14: "The hand of Jehovah shall be known toward his servants; and he will have indignation against his enemies."

The title servant of God had been given to many before Isaiah's time, such as Abraham (Gen. 26:24), Moses (Num. 12:7, etc.), Joshua (Josh. 24:29) and David (Ps. 89:20). It is used of Moses no less than thirty-eight times. Isaiah's usage must have given it new force. Possibly this usage was in the minds of Paul and James when they took it for their own (Tit. 1:1; Jas. 1:1). Certainly no one can be a true servant of God unless he receives the spirit of God's great Servant, Jesus Christ, and lets that spirit control and empower him.

The passages in which the Servant of Jehovah is most personal and therefore Messianic are Isa. 42:1-7; 49:1-7; 50:4-9 and 52:13-53:12. In the first of these Jehovah introduces his Servant to Israel and the nations: "Behold, my servant, whom I uphold; my chosen in whom my soul delighteth: I have put my Spirit upon him; he will bring forth justice to the Gentiles. He will not cry, nor lift up his voice, nor cause it to be heard in the street. A bruised reed will he not break, and a dimly burning wick will he not quench: he will bring forth justice in truth. He will not fail (Margin, 'burn dimly') nor be discouraged (Margin, 'bruised'), till he have set justice in the earth; and the isles shall wait for his law. Thus saith God Jehovah, he that created the heavens, and stretched them forth; he that spread abroad the earth and that which cometh out of it; he that giveth breath unto the people upon it, and spirit to them that walk therein: I Jehovah have called thee in righteousness, and will hold thy hand, and will keep thee, and give thee for a covenant of the people for a light of the Gentiles; to open the blind eyes to bring out the prisoners from the dungeon, and them that sit in darkness out of the prison house."

The Septuagint renders the first verse "Jacob my servant—Israel my elect" while the Targum reads "Behold, my servant the Messiah." The passage undoubtedly recalls the divine purpose in the call of Abraham and later the call of the nation Israel. In calling Abraham, God said: "In thee shall all the families of the earth be blessed" (Gen. 12:3) and in his last renewal of this promise to Abraham, God said: "In thy seed shall all the nations of the earth be blessed" (Gen. 22:18). This promise was renewed to Isaac (Gen. 26:4) and to Jacob (Gen. 28:14). So when God called Israel at Mount Sinai he did not cast off other nations, for he said: "All the earth is mine" (Ex. 19:5). Israel was to be God's instrument to bring the knowledge of himself to all mankind. They were to be a kingdom of priests (Ex. 19:6) priests for the nations. Israel as a nation fell short of this high calling. Hence that which Isaiah said of Israel was to be fulfilled by that true Israelite, that true Servant of Jehovah, Jesus the Messiah. "He will bring forth justice to the Gentiles." He is God's chosen, in whom his soul delighteth (Matt. 3:17; 17:5). In bringing forth justice to the Gentiles the Servant will show the noble qualities which descended to Israel from Abraham (Gen. 13:7-11) rather than the self-assertiveness which came from Jacob (Gen. 25:27-34; 27:1-29). He will be like the still, small voice rather than the wind, the earthquake or the fire (I Kings 19:11-12). Although his forerunner is "the voice of one crying in the wilderness" (Isa. 40:3; Matt. 3:3) he avoids publicity (Matt. 8:4; 9:30; 12:16; Mark 3:12; 5:43; 7:36; 8:30; 9:9; Luke 8:56; 9:21).

He deals gently with penitent and discouraged souls. He strengthens the weak and fans into a flame the least spark of goodness or noble aspiration. It was in this way that Jesus dealt with the adulteress (John 8:11) and the dying thief (Luke 23:39-43). Contact with him brought out the best in men. Nor was this sympathy a sign of weakness in him. Verse 4 makes this clear by the fact that the word rendered "fail" is from the same stem as that rendered "dimly burning" in verse 3 and the word rendered "be discouraged" is from the same stem as that for "bruised." The Servant is able to strengthen the weak because he is never weak himself; to encourage the downcast because he is never discouraged. The distant isles wait expectantly for his law as Israel waited for the law from Mount Sinai. Jehovah the Creator and sustainer of the world pledges his omni-

potence to sustain the Servant whom he has called until
he shall accomplish his two-fold work, to be a covenant
for Israel and a light for the Gentiles. He will open the
blind eyes of Israel (Isa. 42:18-20) and bring them out
of the prison of captivity (Isa. 42:22; 49:9; Zech.
9:11-12).

The Servant whose call and work have been described
in Isa. 42:1-7 takes up that work in *Isa.* 49:1-7. "Listen
O isles, unto me; and hearken, ye peoples from far: Jehovah hath called me from the womb; from the bowels
of my mother hath he made mention of my name: and
he hath made my mouth like a sharp sword; in the shadow
of his hand hath he hid me: and he hath made me a
polished shaft; in his quiver hath he kept me close; and
he said unto me, thou art my servant; Israel in whom I
will be glorified. But I said, I have labored in vain, I
have spent my strength for naught and vanity; yet surely
the justice due to me is with Jehovah, and my recompense
with my God. And now saith Jehovah that formed me
from the womb to be his servant, to bring Jacob again
to him, and that Israel be gathered unto him; (for I am
honorable in the eyes of Jehovah, and my God is become
my strength); yea, he saith, It is too light a thing that
thou shouldest be my servant to raise up the tribes of
Jacob, and to restore the preserved of Israel: I will also
give thee for a light to the Gentiles, that thou mayest
be my salvation unto the end of the earth. Thus saith
Jehovah, the Redeemer of Israel, and his Holy One, to
him whom man despiseth, to him whom the nation abhorreth, to a servant of rulers: Kings shall see and arise;
princes, and they shall worship; because of Jehovah that

is faithful, even the Holy One of Israel, who, hath chosen thee."

The section of the book which follows the first Servant passage (Isa. 42:1-7) and precedes this contains much which was calculated to encourage Israel to perform its true work. The Servant is mentioned ten times (Isa. 42:19; 43:10; 44:12, 21, 26; 45:4; 48:20). The promise of Cyrus also occurs in this section (Isa. 44:28-45:4). George Adam Smith presents the relation of Cyrus and the Servant to the purpose of God for Israel in a very striking way: "On the ship of Israel's fortunes—as on every ship and on every voyage—the prophet sees two personages. One is the Pilot through the shallows, Cyrus, who is dropped as soon as the shallows are past; and the other is the captain of the ship, who remains always identified with it—the Servant. The Captain does not come to the front till the Pilot has gone; but both alongside the Pilot, and after the Pilot has been dropped, there is every room for his office" (The Book of Isaiah Vol. II p. 288). The part of Cyrus in the restoration of Israel was to permit their return to Palestine. This part was essential but temporary. The Servant's part was to bring Israel back and establish them in their land. This work was permanent. Accordingly Cyrus is mentioned for the last time in Isa. 48:14-15 before the Servant takes up his task in Isa. 49:1-7. The promise that Cyrus would permit the return of the exiles, a new policy in human history, was an immense encouragement to Israel to do the Servant's work which Jehovah had laid upon them.

With such encouragement the Servant begins his prophetic work. He addresses the distant isles (Isa. 49:1) since God had said: "The isles shall wait for his law" (Isa. 42:4). If the distant isles hear his words, much more will those places nearer by. He speaks of himself, telling how God had called him, even from his birth (Isa. 42:6-7), that God had made his mouth like a sharp sword, so that his prophetic preaching should be penetrating and incisive. God held him back, as a soldier keeps his arrow in the quiver until he is ready to shoot it. So God held back his true Servant, Jesus Christ, until "the fulness of the time came" (Gal. 4:4; cp. Mark 1:15).

That Israel is not absent from the conception of the Servant in this passage is evidenced by the mention of Israel as the Servant in verse 3 and by Israel's words of discouragement in verse 4. The true Servant, the inner kernel of the nation, Jesus Christ, cannot speak these words, for he is never discouraged (Isa. 42:4). Jehovah's answer to the Servant's discouragement is to give him a larger work to do. It is not enough that he shall bring Israel back to their land. He must also be a light to the Gentiles (Isa. 49:6; cp. 42:6), God's "salvation unto the end of the earth." This world-wide work which was not performed by Israel as a whole is carried out by Christ and his disciples (Acts 13:47). In verse 7 the Servant is seen as one "whom man despiseth," "whom the nation abhorreth" (cp. Isa. 53:2-3). He is not only the Servant of Jehovah, but "a servant of rulers," referring doubtless to the dominion of the Babylonian kings over Israel. Yet kings shall pay homage to him because of Jehovah's presence with him (cp. Isa. 52:15).

This idea that men despise the Servant and the nation abhors him prepares the way for the picture of his being persecuted in Isa. 50:6 and that of his violent death in Isa. 53:7-9.

That the speaker in Isa. 50:4-9 is none other than the Servant of Jehovah is proven not only by the resemblance of the things said to those said elsewhere of the Servant but also by the reference to the voice of God's servant in Isa. 50:10. The Servant says: "The Lord Jehovah hath given me the tongue of them that are taught (Margin, 'disciples'), that I may know how to sustain with words him that is weary: he wakeneth morning by morning, he wakeneth mine ear to hear as they that are taught (Margin, 'disciples'). The Lord Jehovah hath opened mine ear, and I was not rebellious, neither turned away backward. I gave my back to the smiters, and my cheeks to them that plucked off the hair; I hid not my face from shame and spitting, for the Lord Jehovah will help me; therefore have I not been confounded: therefore have I set my face like a flint, and I know that I shall not be put to shame. He is near that justifieth me; who will contend with me? let us stand up together: who is mine adversary? let him come near to me. Behold, the Lord Jehovah will help me; who is he that shall condemn me? behold, they all shall wax old as a garment; the moth shall eat them up" (Isa. 50:4-9).

Although the Servant is not mentioned between Isa. 49:1-7 and this passage, the intervening words are full of comfort and were intended to encourage the Servant to perform his work even though this meant cruel persecution. Here as in Isa. 49:1-7 he speaks of his prophetic

work. As a true prophet of God, a true disciple he needed
two things: an attentive ear and the power of speech.
Accordingly the Lord Jehovah gave him the tongue and
the ear of the disciple. He must hear God's message and
then deliver it to his hearers without fear or favor. The
Servant learned in particular how to speak the comforting word to the weary. This recalls Jehovah's words at
his call: "A bruised reed will he not break, and a dimly
burning wick will he not quench" (Isa. 42:3). It also
recalls the Servant's most comforting words: "Come
unto me, all ye that labor and are heavy laden, and I
will give you rest. Take my yoke upon you and learn
of me; for I am meek and lowly in heart: and ye shall
find rest unto your souls. For my yoke is easy, and my
burden is light" (Matt. 11:28-30). No one else knows
so well as Jesus how to sustain with words him that is
weary. In him the true Servant of Jehovah speaks.

As a true disciple the Servant does not rebel or turn
away backward if Jehovah commands him to do a hard
or thankless task. He even submits willingly if he is
persecuted because of his faithfulness to Jehovah's message. While the persecution of verse 6 may refer figuratively to the sufferings of Israel in the exile (cp. Ps.
129:1-3) it had its literal fulfilment in the persecution
of Christ (Matt. 26:67; 27:26, 30; Mark 10:34; 14:65;
15:15, 19; Luke 18:32; 22:63; John 18:22; 19:1). He
submitted without complaint to these cruelties and insults as later he uttered no protest when he was led away
to die (Isa. 53:7). He was able to endure his sufferings
patiently because the Lord, Jehovah helped him (Luke
22:43). The word for "confounded" in verse 7 is from

the same stem as that rendered "shame" in verse 6. Although insults were heaped on his innocent head, they awakened no resentment in his pure soul. He was not confounded, put to confusion. Insult and mockery rolled off from him and left him more majestic and royal than any king. Helped by Jehovah he set his face like a flint to go through all the agony knowing that he could never be put to shame.

Luke probably referred to this verse when he said that after the transfiguration where Jesus learned that his death was at hand (Luke 9:31), he "stedfastly set his face to go to Jerusalem" (Luke 9:51). The Greek verb which Luke used in this verse is from the same stem as the adjective which the Septuagint uses in Isa. 50:7. From that time the cross cast its shadow over him (Luke 9:53; 12:50; 13:22; 17:11; 18:31; 19:11, 28). In verses 8-9 the sufferings of the Servant take the form of a legal contest between him and his persecutors. Confident that Jehovah is on his side he challenges his adversaries to the contest. He will survive the ordeal, but they will "wax old as a garment; the moth shall eat them up."

The climax of the presentation of the Servant of Jehovah is reached in *Isa.* 52:13-53:12, the most precious passage to the Christian in the entire Old Testament. "Behold my servant shall deal wisely (Margin, 'prosper'), he shall be exalted and lifted up, and shall be very high. Like as many were astonished at thee (his visage was so marred more than any man, and his form more than the sons of men), so shall he sprinkle (Margin, 'startle') many nations; kings shall shut their mouths at him; for that which had not been told them shall they see; and that which they had not heard shall they understand (Margin, 'consider')."

"Who hath believed our message? and to whom hath the arm of Jehovah been revealed? For he grew up before him as a tender plant, and as root out of a dry ground: he hath no form nor comeliness; and when we see him, there is no beauty that we should desire him (Margin 'that we should look upon him, nor beauty that we should desire him'). He was despised, and rejected of men; a man of sorrows, and acquainted with grief: and as one from whom men hide their face he was despised; and we esteemed him not."

"Surely he hath borne our griefs, and carried our sorrows; yet we did esteem him stricken, smitten of God, and afflicted. But he was wounded for our transgressions, he was bruised for our iniquities; the chastisement of our peace was upon him; and with his stripes we are healed. All we like sheep have gone astray; we have turned every one to his own way; and Jehovah hath laid on him the iniquity of us all."

"He was oppressed, yet when he was afflicted, he opened not his mouth; as a lamb that is led to the slaughter, and as a sheep that before its shearers is dumb, so he opened not his mouth. By oppression and judgment he was taken away; and as for his generation who among them considered that he was cut off out of the land of the living for the transgression of my people to whom the stroke was due? And they made his grave with the wicked, and with a rich man in his death; although (Margin, 'because') he had done no violence, neither was any deceit in his mouth."

"Yet it pleased Jehovah to bruise him; he hath put him to grief: when thou shalt make his soul an offering for sin he shall see his seed, he shall prolong his days, and the pleasure of Jehovah shall prosper in his hand. He shall see of the travail of his soul, and shall be satisfied: by the knowledge of himself (Margin, 'by his knowledge') shall my righteous servant justify many; and he shall bear their iniquities. Therefore will I divide him a portion with the great, and he shall divide the spoil with the strong; because he poured out his soul unto death, and was numbered with the transgressors: yet he bare the sin of many, and made intercession for the transgressors."

The Servant of Jehovah is not mentioned between Isa. 50:4-9 and the beginning of this passage. Yet the whole section is full of encouragement to the Israelites to consider their noble origin, their divine call, and to receive the great salvation which Jehovah was about to offer them through his Servant. The Servant is mentioned by name only at the beginning (Isa. 52:13) and near the end of this passage (Isa. 53:11). Yet he is the subject of it all. George Adam Smith well says: "Most wonderful and mysterious of all is the spectral fashion in which the prophecy presents its Hero. He is named only in the first line and once again: elsewhere he is spoken of as 'he.' We never hear or see himself. But all the more solemnly is he there: a shadow upon countless faces, a grievous memory on the hearts of the speakers. He so haunts all we see and all we hear, that we feel it is not art, but conscience, that speaks of him" (The Book of Isaiah Vol. II p. 356).

Great as is the advance in the conception of the Servant in the last passage (Isa. 50:4-9), here it is vastly greater still. There he is a prophet who suffers persecution. Here this persecution goes to the length of judicial murder and the persecution and death are represented as a vicarious sacrifice for the sins of his people, a sacrifice by which they are justified. The idea of the innocent members of the nation suffering for the sins of their fellow Israelites was a familiar one. When Achan took from the spoil of Jericho it was said: "The children of Israel committed a trespass in the devoted thing" (Josh. 7:1; cp. verses 11, 13, 15, 25). The same idea underlies Deut. 21:1-9 and Judges 20:1-16. Righteous men felt the guilt of the nation as their own. So Daniel in exile would pray: "We have sinned, and have dealt perversely, and have done wickedly, and have rebelled, even turning aside from thy precepts and from thine ordinances" (Dan. 9:5; cp. verses 7-11, 20). Nehemiah also although righteous took the sins of Israel as his own (Neh. 1:6-7). But aside from this chapter there is no instance in the Old Testament of an innocent man atoning for the sins of others by his suffering or death. That was accomplished by the death of an animal. The offerer or the priest acting for him put his hand on the head of the animal as an indication that it was a substitute and atonement for him (Lev. 1:4; 3:2, 8, 13; 4:4, 15, 24, 29, 33; 8:14, 18, 22; 16:21).

There are good reasons for thinking that the fifty-third chapter of Isaiah relates the sufferings and death of the Servant to the sacrificial system of atonement and so prepared for the New Testament conception of that sacrificial system as pointing forward to the perfect sacrifice of Christ (Heb. 10:1-14). This is suggested, not only by the references to substitution and expiation so prominent in the sacrificial system but by the fact that the Servant is compared to a lamb that is led to the slaughter (Isa. 53:7) and that his soul was an offering for sin, literally a trespass-offering (Isa. 53:10), the word so commonly used in Leviticus (Lev. 5:6, 7, 15, 16, 18, 19, etc.). The designation "Lamb of God" by which John the Baptist referred to Christ (John 1:29, 36) was probably a reference to Isa. 53:7, for his statement that this lamb "taketh away the sin of the world" has a close resemblance to the Septuagint rendering of Isa. 53:4. Not only are parts of this chapter quoted in the New Testament as fulfilled in Christ (Matt. 8:17; Luke 22:37; John 12:38; Acts 8:32-35) or referred to him (I Pst. 2:22, 24-25); but there is other evidence that this was the usual interpretation. Paul said: "Christ died for our sins according to the scriptures" (I Cor. 15:3) and in several other passages it is evident that the death of Christ was regarded as foretold in the Old Testament (Matt. 26:24; Luke 24:25-26; Acts 17:2-3; 26:22-23). Yet there is no other passage in the Hebrew scriptures where the death of the Messiah is foretold if not here. The conclusion is inevitable that the apostles and Christ himself regarded the suffering Servant of Isa. 53 as a type of the Messiah.

There are important resemblances between the picture of the Suffering Servant in Isa. 53 and that of the sufferer in the passion Psalms (22, 40, 69). The suffering Psalmist says: "I am a worm, and no man; a reproach of men, and despised of the people" (Ps. 22:6), and it is written of the Suffering Servant: "His visage was so marred more than any man, and his form more than the sons of men—He hath no form nor comeliness that we should look upon him; nor beauty that we should desire him. He was despised, and rejected of men; a man of sorrows and acquainted with grief: and as one from whom men hide their face he was despised; and we esteemed him not" (Isa. 52:14; 53:2-3). The description of the mockery and insult heaped upon the suffering Psalmist goes much further than that in Isa. 53 (Ps. 22:7-8, 13, 18; 40:14-15; 69:4, 7-12, 19-21). The nearest approach to it is in the words of the Servant in Isa. 50:6: "I gave my back to the smiters, and my cheeks to them that plucked off the hair; I hid not my face from shame and spitting." Many of the insults mentioned in the passion Psalms are those which were inflicted on Christ and they are quoted as fulfilled in him (See pp. 237-241).

There is little doubt that the sufferings of the Psalmist particularly as presented in Psalms 22 and 69, influenced Isaiah in the picture of the suffering Servant in Isa. 50:6, 52:14 and 53:2-3. Yet there are two important differences between the suffering Psalmist and the Suffering Servant: (1) The suffering and persecution of the Psalmist is never represented as resulting in his death. On the contrary he thanked God for delivering him from suffering (Ps. 22:21, 24-25; 40:1-3; 69:29-30, 33). (2) The sufferings of the Psalmist are not represented as vicarious or as atoning for the sins of others. It is true that in thanksgiving to God for his deliverance the Psalmist offers a sacrifice in which the meek share (Ps.

22:25-26, 29; 69:30, 32); but this is a thank-offering rather than a sin-offering. Furthermore the sufferings of the Psalmist and the death of the animal are not connected with each other. In both these respects the Suffering Servant of Isa. 53 goes far beyond the suffering Psalmist. He dies and that too not for his own sins but for the sins of his people. His death is the atonement for their sins by virtue of which they are justified (Isa. 53:3, 11').

There is also a resemblance between the sufferings of Job and those of the Servant of Jehovah. The disease from which Job suffered was probably a form of leprosy called elephantiasis, the symptoms of which are indicated in Job 2:7-8, 12; 3:25; 7:3-5, 14-15; 13:28; 16:8; 19:17-20, 26; 30:17-18, 27, 30). The Servant of Jehovah is also represented as suffering from leprosy. This shows itself from the fact that many were astonished (literally, horrified) at his appearance (Isa. 52:14; cp. Lev. 13:45-46; Job 2:12; 19:19; Luke 17:12-13), the disfigurement of his countenance. He was "as one from whom men hide their face" (Isa. 53:3). The word rendered "sorrows" in this verse and verse 4 may be translated literally "pains" (Job 33:19; Jer. 51:8) and the word for "grief" is the common one for "sickness" and usually so translated (Deut. 7:15; 28:59, 61; I Kings 17:17; II Kings 1:2, etc.) The verb rendered "put him to grief" in Isa. 53:10 means literally "made him sick" and is from the same stem as the noun for "sickness" in verses 3-4. Most conclusive of all the verb rendered "stricken" in Isa. 53:4 is the same which is used of God's smiting Uzziah with leprosy (II Kings 15:5) and the word for "stroke" in Isa. 53:8 is the one used many times of the stroke or plague of leprosy (Lev. 13:2, 9, 12, 13, 20, 25, 27, etc.) Certain Jewish Rabbis taking these statements literally expected that the Messiah would be a leper. It may be that the representation in Isa. 53 is derived in this respect from Job. Another resemblance between Job and the Servant of Jehovah is in the fact that both survived their sufferings and the end of the story of each was one of triumph (Job 42:10-17; Isa. 53:10-12).

There are, however, more important differences between them. Like the suffering Psalmist Job's sufferings did not result in his death and his sufferings are not represented as vicarious or atoning. The nearest approach to the vicarious idea is in the significant statement that "Jehovah turned the captivity of Job, when he prayed for his friends" (Job 42:10). The turning-point in the fortunes of Job was when he had learned the lesson of magnanimity toward the friends who had added so much to his suffering. So the Suffering Servant made intercession for the transgressors (Isa. 53:12). Job's prayer for his friends reminds us of our Lord's command, "Pray for them that despitefully use you" (Luke 6:28) and of his prayer for his persecutors when he was crucified, "Father, forgive them; for they know not what they do." (Luke 23:34) which was echoed by the prayer of the martyred Stephen, "Lord, lay not this sin to their charge" (Acts 7:60). It is in the true spirit of vicarious sacrifice. Yet the Servant of Jehovah carried that spirit much further by dying for his enemies as well as for his friends (John 15:13; Rom. 5:7-8).

The fifteen verses of this passage are clearly divided into five sections of three verses each, the first words of each section indicating its subject: (1) The exaltation and humiliation of the Servant, *Isa.* 52:13-15; (2) The message concerning the Servant unheeded, *Isa.* 53:1-3; (3) The cause of the Servant's sufferings, *Isa.* 53:4-6; (4) The submission of the suffering Servant, *Isa.* 53:7-9; (5) The rewards of the suffering Servant, *Isa.* 53:10-12.

This is not the place for detailed exegesis of this supreme passage. Nevertheless a few additional remarks are needed to bring out its full meaning. The Targum of Jonathan gives a Messianic interpretation to the entire passage by the rendering "my servant the Messiah" in Isa. 52:13. The first section (52:13-15) sums up in a way the theme of the fifteen verses by the strange manner in which it combines the exaltation and humiliation of the Servant. The humiliation is more fully described in 53:1-9 and the exaltation appears again in 53:10-12. The first section does not make the relation between the humiliation and the exaltation clear. Yet it seems to imply that which is clearly revealed in 53:10-12 that the Servant was humbled that he might be exalted. The marginal reading "prosper" is better than "deal wisely" (52:13). The Hebrew verb has both meanings. It means to have that success which comes from wise and prudent conduct (Josh. 1:7-8; I Sam. 18:5, 14; II Kings 18:7; Prov. 17:8; Jer. 10:21; 23:5). Here, however, as the context shows the emphasis is on the success. The humiliation and exaltation of the Servant as presented here have points of resemblance to Paul's description in Phil. 2:5-11. The Hebrew word is very imperfectly translated "astonished" (52:14) in the weakened sense which that English word has today. It means to be appalled, awe-struck, horrified (Lev. 26:32; Jer. 2:12; Ezek. 26:16; 27:35; 28:19). Jehovah addresses the Servant in the beginning of the verse and then, as if speaking to bystanders, explains why many were horrified at him. The literal rendering is "disfigurement from man was his visage" which makes no sense in English. Delitzsch brings out the meaning well by his comment. "From man, away from what is human, i.e. such that his appearance and the impression it made were not like those of a man, nor of other children of men in general." A similar idea is found in Ps. 22:6. The rendering "sprinkle" (52:15) is probably incorrect. While the verb has this meaning elsewhere, its object is always the liquid and never that on which it is sprinkled (Ex. 29:21; Lev. 4:6, 17, etc.). The marginal reading "startle," which is derived from an Arabic verb and is not found elsewhere in the Old Testament, is preferable. It refers to the fact that the Servant will surprise many nations. In token of this surprise kings shut their mouths at him, speechless with astonishment (Job 29:9; Ezek. 16:63; Mic. 7:16). The cause of their surprise is that they have witnessed something hitherto unheard-of and unthought-of. What this is appears in the following verses to be that the humiliation of the Servant is the means of his exaltation.

The speaker in 53:1-9 cannot be the Gentile nations just mentioned, as many commentators think, for the expression "my people" (verse 8) would be meaningless in their mouths. It is the prophet who speaks associating with himself the other Israelites of his time. He asks the rhetorical question whether any have believed the message of Israel. That message to the nations was the amazing fact that the Servant is to gain undying glory not by conquest but by humiliation. Israel humbled in the exile will be greater than ever before. Christ crucified will become Christ victorious. This glorious truth had been revealed to no one as Cheyne well says: "The 'Arm' must be made bare in heaven (comp. 34:5), and only a few have eyes to see such supramundane sights, when nothing on earth, seems to suggest them."

The reason that so few believed the message of Israel is given in verse 2. It is because Israel the Servant in his origin and external appearance lacked those things which generally attract men. The Servant emerging from Israel in the exile is an unattractive figure. Christ also, born in a manger, living in despised Nazareth (John 1:46), his followers mostly obscure (John 7:48), was a root out of a dry ground. Christ crucified was a stumbling block to the Jews and foolishness to the Gentiles (I Cor. 1:23). The parallelism of Isa. 53:2 as well as the Hebrew construction favor the marginal translation, "that we should look upon him; nor beauty that we should desire him."

The Servant is represented in verse 3 as acquainted with sickness. The Hebrew word to be "sick" was used not only of disease but of Ahaziah when he was injured by a fall (II Kings 1:2) and of others who were wounded in battle (I Kings 22:34; II Chron. 18:33; 35:23). It might refer figuratively to Israel's sufferings in the exile (cp. Ps. 129:3) and literally to the physical sufferings of Christ. Since, however, the sickness of the Servant is that of leprosy, and not due to an accident or a wound, it is better to take the word figuratively in the sense of grief (Isa. 17:11; Jer. 10:19; Amos 6:6).

Verse 4 introduces a strong contrast between Israel and the Servant. Israel thought that the Servant suffered for his own sins, that he was stricken, smitten of God and afflicted. But in reality he bore the griefs and carried the sorrows of Israel. Isaiah looking forward from Manasseh's wicked reign to the generation of Israel that suffered in the exile declared: "He was wounded for our transgressions, he was bruised for our iniquities; the chastisement of our peace was upon him; and with his stripes we are healed." Yet this vicariousness of Israel's sufferings in exile (Lam. 5:7) was an imperfect vicariousness, for they were by no means free from sin. The complete fulfilment is found only in the perfect vicariousness of the sufferings of Christ the sinless one. The chastisement of our peace means the chastisement by which our peace is secured. "We have peace with God through our Lord Jesus Christ" (Rom. 5:1). Sin is individualistic, scattering (Gen. 11:8). Each sinner goes his own way like a wandering sheep. Redemption is gathering, centralizing. Jehovah gathers all the sins together and focuses them on the innocent head of the Servant.

George Adam Smith has a fine passage on the silence of the Suffering Servant, "Now silence under suffering is a strange thing in the Old Testament—a thing absolutely new. No other Old Testament personage could stay dumb under pain, but immediately broke into one of two voices—voice of guilt or voice of doubt. In the Old

Testament the sufferer is always either confessing his guilt to God, or, when he feels no guilt, challenging God, in argument. David, Hezekiah, Jeremiah, Job, and the nameless martyred and moribund of the Psalms, all strive and are loud under pain. Why was this Servant the unique and solitary instance of silence under suffering? Because he had a secret which they had not. . . . He had no guilt of his own, no doubt of his God. But he was conscious of the end God had in his pain, an end not to be served in any other way, and with all his heart he had given himself to it." (The Book of Isaiah Vol. II pp. 375-376). Christ was silent under suffering because he had no sin of his own to confess and because he was in perfect harmony with the divine plan of redemption by which he suffered and died for the sins of his people (Matt. 26:63; 27:12-14; John 19:9-10; I Pet. 2:23).

"Oppression and judgment" by a common Hebrew idiom means an oppressive judgment. The Servant was put to death by an unjust judgment. His death was a judicial murder. His contemporaries did not realize the true cause of his death, which was the transgression of Israel. Although the words "my people" are usually spoken by God (Isa. 40:1; 43:20; 47:6; 51:4, 16, etc.), the people are occasionally represented as belonging to the king or some other member of the nation (Isa. 7:2, 17; 13:14; 22:4). Here it is the prophet who calls Israel "my people." The expression "they made his grave with the wicked" should not be understood as meaning that Israel made the grave of the Servant with the wicked. It is rather indefinite as though it were said: "His grave was made." The association of the wicked and the rich,

like that of the poor and the righteous, was natural in
Isaiah's time because most of the righteous were poor
and they were oppressed by the rich landowners (Isa.
5:8; Mic. 2:2). The faithful remnant of Israel suffered in the exile, with the wicked. Christ also was crucified between two robbers and was buried in the tomb
of the rich man, Joseph of Arimathea. The rendering
"although he had done no violence, neither was any deceit in his mouth" and the marginal rendering "because
he had done no violence" are equally permissible. The
former would mean that he was humiliated by dying with
the wicked and being buried with them, although he
was innocent, an idea which agrees with the identification of the Servant with the generation of Israel which
suffered in the exile. The marginal rendering "because"
agrees better with the New Testament. It suggests that
Jesus received the honor of being buried in the rich man's
tomb because he was innocent.

The rendering "it pleased Jehovah to bruise him" gives
a wrong impression to the English reader as though Jehovah took delight in the suffering of the Servant. The
meaning is merely that it was Jehovah's will to bruise him,
he had determined to do so (Deut. 25:7-8; Ruth 3:13;
I Kings 9:1, etc.). The prophet mentions three blessed
results which will follow when Jehovah makes the soul of
the Servant an offering for sin: (1) he shall see his seed;
(2) he shall prolong his days; and (3) the pleasure, or
rather the will, purpose of Jehovah shall prosper in his
hand. This clearly implies the resurrection of the Servant.
After he dies and as a result of his death these things shall
follow. It was counted a special honor to live to see one's

descendants of later generations (Gen. 50:23). So the Servant risen from the dead would see many generations of his followers, his spiritual seed, saved by his great sacrifice (Ps. 22:30). He prolongs his days after death. "Christ being raised from the dead dieth no more; death no more hath dominion over him" (Rom. 6:9). The divine purpose in the death of Christ, the purpose of redeeming the world from sin, will go on to glorious fruition in his hand, as Jesus said: "I, if I be lifted up from the earth, will draw all men unto me" (John 12:32).

Jehovah must be the speaker in verse 11, for only he can use the expression "my righteous servant." The Servant shall look with satisfaction upon the blessed results of his pain and labor. The Hebrew word is never used in the sense of the labor of child-birth. The marginal translation "by his knowledge" is much more accurate than that in the text, "by the knowledge of himself." It is by his complete knowledge of God, man, sin and the way of salvation that the Servant is able to justify many. Jehovah is probably the speaker also in verse 12. It is he who gives his Servant the highest place among the great of earth because of his priestly sacrifice. The "therefore" at the beginning of this verse reminds us of the "wherefore" in Phil. 2:9. "Wherefore (because he was obedient unto death, even the death of the cross) also God highly exalted him, and gave unto him the name which is above every name." Others have been great in their lives. Christ's supreme greatness was in his death. Others have been great because they sought their selfish advantage and crushed others. Christ was great because he gave himself to the service of God and the salvation of men. The

spoil of his warfare is the souls of men. His soul is
represented as poured out because it was thought of as
residing in the blood (Gen. 9:4; Lev. 17:11, 14). The
last and crowning work of the Servant is intercession for
the transgressors. This work cannot be done until after
his vicarious and atoning death, since that sacrifice furnishes the supreme argument of his intercession. Even
the sacrifice of Christ would not have been efficacious if
he had not as our great high-priest carried the precious
blood of his sacrifice into the holy of holies "to appear
before the face of God for us" (Heb. 9:24). "He is able
to save to the uttermost them that draw near unto God
through him, seeing he ever liveth to make intercession
for them" (Heb. 7:25).

There are two Messianic passages in this book after the
revelation of the Servant of Jehovah. The first is *Isa.*
61:1-3. "The Spirit of the Lord Jehovah is upon me;
because Jehovah hath anointed me to preach good tidings
unto the meek; he hath sent me to bind up the broken-
hearted, to proclaim liberty to the captives, and the opening of the prison to them that are bound; to proclaim the
year of Jehovah's favor, and the day of vengeance of our
God; to comfort all that mourn; to appoint unto them
that mourn in Zion, to give unto them a garland for ashes,
the oil of joy for mourning, the garment of praise for the
spirit of heaviness; that they may be called trees of righteousness, the planting of Jehovah, that he may be glorified."

Some commentators think that it is the Servant of Jehovah who speaks in these verses as he does in Isa. 49:
1-6 and 50:4-9. There are indeed certain resemblances

between this and the Servant passages which might seem to argue for this conclusion. The speaker here makes a proclamation concerning his work in true prophetic style as the Servant does in Isa. 49:1-6 and 50:4-9. The Spirit of Jehovah is upon him as upon the Servant (Isa. 42:1). The work which the speaker here is anointed to do has points of similarity to that of the Servant. He speaks words of comfort to the broken-hearted (cp. Isa. 42:3; 50:4). He proclaims release to the captives (cp. Isa. 42:7). But on the other hand the speaker of Isa. 61:1-3 merely makes a proclamation. He does not perform a work of deliverance as the Servant does (Isa. 42:7; 49:5-6; 53:4-6, 10-12). His work is exclusively prophetic and not priestly. The proclamation of "the day of vengeance of our God" (Isa. 61:2) is entirely out of harmony with the prophetic work of the Servant. There is no suggestion in Isa. 61:1-3 that the proclamation is to the Gentiles as is the case in Isa. 42:1, 6; 49:1, 6. Finally, if the speaker in Isa. 61:1-3 were the Servant, it would be an anticlimax after the high point of the presentation of the Servant in chapter 53. The Servant is never mentioned in this book after that chapter. For all these reasons the speaker in these verses is not the Servant but the prophet. The points of resemblance to the Servant passages are due to the fact that the prophet was one of Jehovah's servants. He was subordinate to the great Servant of Jehovah and did a part of his work. Yet as a true prophet he was a type of the great prophet, Jesus Christ. He used words of himself which find their complete fulfillment in Christ.

The anointing of a prophet is mentioned elsewhere only in I Kings 19:16, although in Isa. 42:1 Jehovah said that he had put his Spirit upon his Servant to equip him for his prophetic work. Isaiah had foretold that the Spirit of Jehovah would rest upon the Messiah (Isa. 11:2). There, however, the emphasis is upon the Spirit with which he is anointed and that Spirit is described, while here the emphasis is upon the work for which he is anointed. The word for "meek" means poor as well as meek. It was probably to this clause that Christ referred when he mentioned the fact that "the poor have good tidings preached to them" as the crowning proof of his Messiahship (Matt. 11:5). The word for "liberty" is used especially of the release of slaves from bondage in the year of jubilee (Lev. 25:10; Jer. 34:8, 15, 17; Ezek. 46:17). As the heralds with their trumpets on the day of atonement in that year proclaimed liberty from bondage throughout the land, unto all the inhabitants thereof (Lev. 25:8-10), so the prophet proclaimed release from the bondage of the exile and so Christ by his perfect atonement proclaimed release from the bondage of sin.

This year of jubilee is called the year of Jehovah's favor. While the period of Jehovah's favor is a year, that of his vengeance is only a day (Isa. 34:8; 63:4). Jehovah has no pleasure in the death of the wicked but that the wicked turn from his evil way and live (Ezek. 18:32; 33:11). Yet the righteousness of God requires that he shall do this strange work of vengeance (Isa. 28:21). There is a rhetorical play on words in the expression "a garland for ashes." The two Hebrew words differ only in the order of their three letters. The former means the beautiful turban which was worn only on a festal day (Ex. 39:28; Isa. 61:10; Ezek. 24:17, 23) while ashes were put on the head as a sign of mourning (II Sam. 13:19; Esther 4:1). Various attempts have been made to reproduce this paronomasia in other languages. Thus the Vulgate renders "coronam pro cinere," Cheyne suggests the German "schmuck statt schmutz" and Moffatt has "coronals for coronachs." The idea may be given quite freely as "a crown for a cross." Anointing the head with oil was a mark of honor and courtesy (Ps. 23:5; 45:7; Luke 7:46). All this work of the Messiah is done not merely that the recipients of these blessings shall be permanently established, rooted as trees of righteousness, the planting of Jehovah, but that God may be glorified.

Our Lord read the early part of this passage near the beginning of his public ministry in the synagogue at Nazareth (Luke 4:16-19) and when he had closed the book he announced: "To-day hath this scripture been fulfilled in your ears" (Luke 4:21). Thus he applied it directly to himself, an interpretation which is entirely justified. It is significant that he did not read the whole passage. He stopped after announcing the acceptable year of Jehovah and did not proceed to announce the day of vengeance of our God. This is in perfect agreement with his work. He did not come the first time to announce the day of vengeance but the year of jubilee. His message was one of joy and not of doom, release from the power and the penalty of sin. He said: "I came not to judge the world, but to save the world" (John 12:47). But when he shall come the second time in his glory, then he will judge all the nations (Matt. 25:31-32) and to some

he will say: "Depart from me, ye cursed, into the eternal
fire which is prepared for the devil and his angels" (Matt.
25:41). This is also Messianic work. It will be the day
of vengeance of our God.

The last Messianic passage in this book is *Isa.* 63:1-6.
"Who is this that cometh from Edom with dyed garments
from Bozrah? this that is glorious in his apparel, marching in the greatness of his strength? I that speak in
righteousness, mighty to save. Wherefore art thou red
in thine apparel, and thy garments like him that treadeth
in the winevat? I have trodden the winepress alone; and
of the peoples there was no man with me: yea, I trod
them in mine anger, and trampled them in my wrath; and
their lifeblood is sprinkled upon my garments, and I have
stained all my raiment. For the day of vengeance was in
my heart, and the year of my redeemed is come. And I
looked, and there was none to help; and I wondered that
there was none to uphold: therefore mine own arm
brought salvation unto me; and my wrath, it upheld me.
And I trod down the peoples in mine anger, and made
them drunk in my wrath, and I poured out their lifeblood on the earth."

There is no doubt, as many commentators suggest, that
the majestic figure which the prophet sees in his vision
coming up the narrow valley from Edom to Jerusalem is
none other than Jehovah himself. This is made probable
by the fact that the hero from Edom uses language in
verse 5 which closely resembles that which is said of Jehovah in Isa. 59:16. "He saw that there was no man,
and wondered that there was no intercessor: therefore
his own arm brought salvation unto him; and his right-

eousness, it upheld him." In this sense George Adam Smith is right in calling this a drama of divine vengeance. Yet the very idea of Jehovah appearing in human form is suggestive of the incarnation. That which the hero says of himself, while in no sense unnatural if Jehovah is the speaker, is strongly suggestive of the Messiah. In answer to the prophet's question: "Who is this that cometh from Edom?" the hero describes himself in the words: "I that speak in righteousness, mighty to save"; and when the prophet asks him why his garments are red as if he had been treading grapes in the winevat, he replies: "I have trodden the winepress alone; and of the peoples there was no man with me: yea, I trod them in mine anger and trampled in my wrath; and their lifeblood is sprinkled upon my garments, and I have stained all my raiment." The hero is represented as angry against other nations because they would not help in his conflict with Edom. Therefore he turned against the peoples and trod them down as one treads grapes in the winepress. Their blood was sprinkled on him as the juice of the grapes is sprinkled on the one treading the winepress.

Edom is mentioned as a typical foe of Israel, perhaps also because the name resembles the Hebrew word for "blood." The hostility of Israel to Edom began even before the birth of Jacob and Esau from whom the two nations were descended (Gen. 25:21-22). It was fed by Jacob's tricking Esau out of the birthright and the blessing (Gen. 25:27-34; 27:1-45). When the Israelites were on the way to Canaan the king of Edom refused their request to pass through his land (Num. 20:14-21). David conquered the Edomites (II Sam 8:14). Amos condemned Edom because of its unbrotherly conduct toward Israel (Amos 1:11-12). After Isaiah's time Edom showed its bitter enmity by rejoicing in the fall of Jerusalem and cutting off fugitives from the city (Ps. 137:7; Obad. 10-14). It does not appear that Edom ever ruled over Israel. Yet the hero who has returned from conquering Edom says: "The day of vengeance was in my heart, and the year of my redeemed (Margin, 'my year of redemption') is come," using expressions similar to the "year of Jehovah's favor, and the day of vengeance of our God" which was announced by the Messiah (Isa. 61:2). The punishment of Edom is represented as the means of redeeming Israel. This is an ideal picture of the way Jehovah will conquer all his enemies. The surprise of the hero that there were none to help him in his conflict with Edom is a hint of its ideal and typical character.

These considerations show that John did not follow an arbitrary exegesis when he found a fulfillment of this passage in the passion of Jesus Christ. He says that the nations were cast into the winepress of the wrath of God and the winepress was trodden without the city, a clear allusion to Calvary (Rev. 14:19-20). In a later passage he calls Christ "Faithful and True." "He is arrayed in a garment sprinkled with blood: and his name is called The Word of God . . . He treadeth the winepress of the fierceness of the wrath of God, the Almighty. And he hath on his garment and on his thigh a name written, King of Kings, and Lord of Lords" (Rev. 19:13, 15-16). The hero from Edom is the same as the hero from Calvary. It is true that the blood on the hero's garments is not his own blood but that of his enemies. It is therefore a mistake to read into Isaiah's prophecy the doctrine of the atonement. It speaks of a great victory over the enemies of God. But the cross of Christ was just such a victory. In one sense his passion was a combat with the powers of darkness (Luke 22:53). It was in reference to his death that he said: "Now is the judgment of this world: now shall the prince of this world be cast out" (John 12:31); "I will no more speak much with you for the prince of this world cometh: and he hath nothing in me" (John 14:30). "The prince of this world hath been judged" (John 16:11). Beyond the hero which Isaiah saw returning from victory over Edom, we can see the hero Christ returning from his victory over Satan at Calvary. He can describe himself in a meaning Isaiah could not know in the memorable words: "I that speak in righteousness, mighty to save." He, too, is "glorious in his apparel, marching in the greatness of his strength." He, too, has trodden the winepress alone; for "there was no other good enough to pay the price of sin." His own arm brought salvation unto him. Isaiah called him "Mighty God," literally a God of a hero (Isa. 9:6). The spirit of this passage is caught in the words of the hymn:

> "Look, ye saints, the sight is glorious;
> See the Man of Sorrows now;
> From the fight returned victorious,
> Every knee to him shall bow:
> Crown Him! Crown Him!
> Crowns become the Victor's brow."

(5) THE GOSPEL IN ISAIAH.

No other Old Testament book contains such a large
element of the gospel as Isaiah. He was preëminently
the evangelical prophet. While woes against sinners are
not lacking, the joyful proclamation of universal salvation
was his favorite theme. This was to be expected because
there is such a large number of Messianic passages. The
gospel of forgiveness, the gospel of the grace of God is
specially prominent in Isa. 53. The very idea of the
gospel and its related words began with Isaiah. It is
found in the name of that mysterious character of chapters 40-55 who is called in English "one that bringeth good
tidings." It is only one word in Hebrew and might well
be rendered by the old English word, gospeller, or its
equivalent of Latin origin, evangelist.

It is found only in chapters 40-55. "O thou that tellest
good tidings to Zion, get thee up on a high mountain; O
thou that tellest good tidings to Jerusalem, lift up thy
voice with strength; lift it up, be not afraid; say unto the
cities of Judah, Behold your God" (Isa. 40:9). "I am
the first that saith unto Zion, Behold, behold them; and I
will give to Jerusalem one that bringeth good tidings"
(Isa. 41:27). "How beautiful upon the mountains are
the feet of him that bringeth good tidings, that publisheth
peace, that bringeth good tidings of good, that publisheth
salvation, that saith unto Zion, Thy God reigneth" (Isa.
52:7). It is the messenger who runs ahead to tell Jerusalem and the cities of Judah the glad news that the exiles
are coming home. The Septuagint usually renders it by
a participle from the Greek verb which was taken over
into Latin and from Latin into English in which it is

"evangelize." The good news is the evangel and the announcer of it is sometimes called an evangelist. The New Testament derives its usage from the Septuagint. It uses the Greek noun in the sense of "gospel" seventy-six times, the verb meaning to preach the gospel twenty-five times and the noun evangelist three times. Preaching the gospel is proclaiming the good news of salvation from sin through Jesus Christ. It had its prototype in the work of the herald who came running to Jerusalem with the glad news that the exiles were coming back and the city would be rebuilt. The first announcement of the gospel in the New Testament was in the words of the angel to the shepherds: "Behold, I bring you good tidings of great joy which shall be to all the people: for there is born to you this day in the city of David a Saviour, who is Christ the Lord" (Luke 2:10-11). Its spirit like that of every later announcement is like that of the one who brought good tidings to Jerusalem and the cities of Judah.

The gospel is nowhere more prominent in Isaiah than in *chapter* 55 where Jehovah gives the invitation to all men to accept a full and free salvation: "Ho, every one that thirsteth, come ye to the waters, and he that hath no money; come ye, buy, and eat; yea, come, buy wine and milk without money and without price. Wherefore do ye spend money for that which is not bread? and your labor for that which satisfieth not? hearken diligently unto me and eat ye that which is good, and let your soul delight itself in fatness. Incline your ear, and come unto me; hear, and your soul shall live: and I will make an everlasting covenant with you, even the sure mercies of David. Behold, I have given him for a witness to the peoples, a leader and commander to the peoples. Behold, thou shalt call a nation that thou knowest not; and a nation that knew not thee shall run unto thee because of Jehovah thy God, and for the Holy One of Israel; for he hath glorified thee."

"Seek ye Jehovah while he may be found; call ye upon him while he is near: let the wicked forsake his way and the unrighteous man his thoughts; and let him return unto Jehovah, and he will have mercy upon him; and to our God, for he will abundantly pardon. For my thoughts are not your thoughts, neither are your ways my ways, saith Jehovah. For as the heavens are higher than the earth, so are my ways higher than your ways, and my thoughts than your thoughts. For as the rain cometh down and the snow from heaven, and returneth not thither, but watereth the earth, and maketh it bring forth and bud, and giveth seed to the sower and bread to the eater; so shall my word be that goeth forth out of my mouth: it shall not return unto me void, but it shall accomplish that which I please and it shall prosper in the thing whereto I sent it. For ye shall go out with joy, and be led forth with peace: the mountains and the hills shall break forth before you into singing; and all the trees of the field shall clap their hands. Instead of the thorn shall come up the fir-tree; and instead of the brier shall come up the myrtle-tree: and it shall be to Jehovah for a name, for an everlasting sign that shall not be cut off."

This proclamation of the gospel is based upon the saving work of the Servant of Jehovah which is fully described in the fifty-third chapter. It comes at the end of the section of the book which is commonly called Deutero-Isaiah in which the Servant is to bring Israel back from the exile in Babylon to Palestine. Yet only in the last two verses is that return mentioned. Israel must return to Jehovah before they can return to Palestine. They must repent of their sins or even the atonement by the Servant cannot be efficacious for them. Since repentance is an individual and not a national matter the proclamation is addressed to the individuals in the nation. Not even the New Testament contains a more thoroughly evangelical proclamation of the gospel than this. Salvation is not something to be purchased. It is absolutely free, "without money and without price." Yet it is rich and life-giving, as life-giving as water to the thirsty, as nourishing as milk and as joy-giving as wine. Jehovah tries to dissuade his people from spending money and giving labor for that which cannot satisfy the soul. Instead he offers them freely nourishment by which their soul will delight itself in fatness. This comes from accepting Jehovah's invitation. He will make an everlasting covenant with them, even the sure mercies of David. This refers to the covenant with David when God promised to establish his throne forever and that the Messiah should arise in his royal line (II Sam. 7:12-16), a covenant which David said was "ordered in all things and sure" (II Sam. 23:5). The introduction of this covenant with David here shows that the Servant of Jehovah of chapter 53 is none other than the Messiah. If the Israelites accept this covenant they will become a missionary nation. They will call a nation that they knew not; and another nation which knew them not shall run unto them because of Jehovah their God.

In true evangelical style the prophet urges the people to seek Jehovah while he may be found, to call upon him while he is near, implying that, if the invitation is refused too long, it will be too late. In order to seek Jehovah, the wicked must leave his own way and his own thoughts which are so different from Jehovah's ways and thoughts. It is at first discouraging when we learn that God's thoughts and ways are as much higher than man's as the heavens are higher than the earth. If so, how can we ever find God? We cannot scale heaven. But our discouragement is dispelled immediately when we learn that we do not need to scale heaven to find God and to learn his thoughts and ways. He has bridged the gulf between himself and us from the side of heaven. Pursuing the same figure, he says that his word is like the rain and the snow which come down from heaven and do not return thither until they have watered the earth and made it bring forth and bud, giving seed to the sower and bread to the eater. Then the rain and snow are drawn up to heaven again. So God's word makes the heart of man fertile. It brings forth noble virtues which show themselves in noble deeds. As some of the food of earth is eaten and some is kept to be seed for another season, so the soul of man feeds on the word of God and yet has plenty to sow as spiritual seed in other hearts. And as the moisture of earth returns in vapor to heaven, so God's word comes back to him not void but transmuted into the praise and worship of men.

The evangelical character of the book of Isaiah shows itself by its doctrine of forgiveness. The Old Testament has no other gospel, no other good news more glorious than the words of Isa. 1:18 "Come now, and let us reason together, saith Jehovah: though your sins be as scarlet, they shall be as white as snow; though they be red like crimson, they shall be as wool." In describing the Jerusalem of the last days the prophet says: "The people that dwell therein shall be forgiven their iniquity" (Isa. 33:24). To desolate Jerusalem he proclaims that her warfare is accomplished, her iniquity is pardoned (Isa. 40:2). Jehovah cries out to his people: "I, even I, am he that blotteth out thy transgressions for mine own sake; and I will not remember thy sins" (Isa. 43:25). "I have blotted out, as a thick cloud, thy transgressions, and, as a cloud, thy sins: return unto me, for I have redeemed thee" (Isa. 44:22). Similarly Hezekiah exclaimed: "Thou hast cast all my sins behind thy back" (Isa. 38:17). Although forgiveness is not distinctly mentioned in chapter 53, it is implied in the statement that the Servant was wounded for our transgressions, bruised for our iniquities; the chastisement of our peace was upon him; and with his stripes we are healed (Isa. 53:5). In the gospel proclamation we have just examined, Isaiah says that our God will abundantly pardon or, more literally, he will multiply to pardon (Isa. 55:7). This forgiveness, which we know has cost the cruel sufferings and death of the Servant of Jehovah, is the very essence of the gospel.

The evangelical character of this book appears strikingly in its vocabulary. The words which from the New Testament we associate with the gospel are the most prominent words in Isaiah. Thus the words to save and salvation, both of them from the stem from which the name Jesus comes, occur more often in Isaiah than in

any other book either of the Old or the New Testament
with the single exception of the Psalms. The word
Saviour from the same stem is found eight times in Isaiah
and only seven times in all the rest of the Hebrew scriptures. These words are used almost exclusively of the
act of God. It is he who saves. The salvation is his.
He is the Saviour. The salvation is often not primarily
religious, a salvation from sin, but from some earthly
enemy, political or military (Isa. 25:9-10; 35:4; 37:20,
35; 49:25). We have seen this secular use in the word
in the time of Moses (p. 135).

It is often difficult to determine whether there is any
thought of salvation from sin as it occurs in certain connections in the book of Isaiah. For example in Isa.
12:2-3 we read: "Behold, God is my salvation; I will
trust, and will not be afraid: for Jehovah, even Jehovah,
is my strength and song; and he is become my salvation.
Therefore with joy shall ye draw water out of the wells
of salvation." While probably the reference is primarily
to a political or military salvation, the figure of drawing
water out of the wells of salvation, seems to suggest something beyond this. Since political or military salvation
was wrought for Israel only when they repented of their
sins, it might be a type of salvation from sin. This may
be the case in Isa. 43:3; 45:17; 51:6, 8; 59:1-2; 63:1.
There are, however, a few passages in which the spiritual
conception of salvation is certainly present. Such is Isa.
64:5-6 "Behold, thou wast wroth, and we sinned: in them
have we been of long time; and shall we be saved? For
we are all become as one that is unclean and all our
righteousnesses are as a polluted garment." Possibly the

idea is that if they repented they would be saved from Babylon. Yet the emphasis upon their sins seems to suggest that their real foe was not Babylon but the sin which brought them there. If so, the salvation for which they longed would not be from Babylon so much as from sin.

It is impossible to exclude the spiritual idea of salvation from such a passage as Isa. 45:22-23. "Look unto me and be ye saved, all the ends of the earth; for I am God, and there is none else. By myself have I sworn, the word is gone forth from my mouth in righteousness, and shall not return, that unto me every knee shall bow, every tongue shall swear." This salvation of all the ends of the earth cannot refer to the gathering of the scattered exiles of Israel back to Palestine. It cannot be a political salvation. As the context shows it means that all nations shall submit to the beneficent rule of Jehovah. This is salvation from sin and error. The same lofty idea of salvation is found in Isa. 49:6 when Jehovah says to his Servant: "I will also give thee for a light to the Gentiles, that thou mayest be my salvation unto the end of the earth." To a certain extent this prediction was fulfilled by the spiritual influence of the Jews of the dispersion and of the Septuagint version upon the ancient world; but the complete fulfilment comes from Jesus Christ and those who carry the saving knowledge of him to the earth's utmost bound. It is surprising that in no one of the seven verses where Jehovah is called Saviour in Isaiah (43:3, 11; 45:15, 21; 49:26; 60:16; 63:8) is the idea of salvation from sin present. Nevertheless the use of the word helped to prepare for its application to Christ in the New Testament, especially as the Saviour from sin (Acts 5:31; Tit. 2:13-14; 3:5-6; II Pet. 2:20; I John 4:14).

The use of the words to redeem and Redeemer in Isaiah is similar to that of the words to save and Saviour. Jehovah redeems and he is called the Redeemer. He re∙ deems Israel from Babylon (Isa. 48:20). He redeems Jerusalem from foreign bondage (Isa. 52:9). He redeemed his people from the bondage of Egypt (Isa. 63:9). The title Redeemer is used thirteen times by Isaiah, more often than in any other book of the Old Testament. It is used only of Jehovah (Isa. 41:14; 43:14; 44:6, 24; 47:4; 48:17; 49:7, 26; 54:5, 8; 59:20; 60:16; 63:16). Yet in no one of these verses is there any evidence that the redemption is spiritual. The case seems to be different in Isa. 44:22 where Jehovah says: "I have blotted out, as a thick cloud, thy transgressions, and, as a cloud, thy sins: return unto me; for I have redeemed thee." This seems to be redemption from sin. In any case the usage of these terms by Isaiah helped to prepare for their use in the New Testament in the high spiritual sense of Christ's redemption from sin (Rom. 3:24; Gal. 3:13; 4:5; Eph. 1:7; Col. 1:14; Tit. 2:14).

Space forbids a full description of the evangelical element in this book. Suffice it to say that nowhere else is the saving work of Christ so perfectly foreshadowed in the Old Testament as in Isa. 53. The doctrine of the atonement which Paul made the central theme of his preaching (I Cor. 2:2; Gal. 6:14), the very center of the gospel, is set forth clearly in this chapter. The representation of the feast which Jehovah will make in Mount Zion for all nations (Isa. 25:6) is also thoroughly evan-

gelical; and the statement that in all Israel's afflictions
Jehovah was afflicted (Isa. 63:9) prepares for the New
Testament statement that "God so loved the world that
he gave his only begotten Son, that whosoever believeth on
him should not perish, but have eternal life" (John 3:16).
In a general sense the two dispensations may be described
as the Law and the Gospel. Yet there is much gospel in
the Old Testament, especially in the book of Isaiah.

(6) FAITH.

The doctrine of faith is a New Testament doctrine.
Since the Law was the central thing in the old dispensation it was natural that the principal emphasis should be
laid on obedience rather than on faith. The new dispensation, on the other hand, having the Gospel as its central theme, naturally exalts faith to a position of great
importance. In this characterization of the two dispensations, however, as in every generalization of their main
features, the whole story is not told. The element of
gospel is not lacking in the Old Testament nor the element of law in the New. Consequently although faith
in the Old Testament has a position subordinate to obedience, its position is by no means unimportant, particularly as a preparation for its high place in the New Testament.

Isaiah was the great prophet of faith. Nevertheless
it did not begin with him. The beginning of the doctrine
of faith is in the story of Abraham. God had promised
him to multiply his seed as the stars of the heaven and
that in his seed should all the families of the earth be
blessed (Gen. 12:1-3; 13:16; 15:5). Yet Abraham had
no seed and Sarah his wife was barren. Every human

indication pointed to a failure of the divine promise. Yet when God renewed the promise to Abraham, "he believed in Jehovah; and he reckoned it to him for righteousness" (Gen. 15:6; cp. Rom. 4:3; Gal. 3:6; Jas. 2:23). That was faith indeed. Abraham was well called the father of the faithful, not only because he failed in none of his duty to God, but in the original sense of the word, that he was full of faith (Gal. 3:7, 9).

Faith is a prominent feature in the story of the deliverance of Israel from Egypt. When God commanded Moses to go from Midian to deliver the people from the bondage of Egypt, Moses complained that they would not believe that God had appeared to him (Exod. 4:1). God graciously encouraged their faith by a series of signs (Ex. 4:1-9). Convinced by these signs Israel believed (Ex. 4:31). Later when God brought his people safely through the Red Sea and destroyed the pursuers, "Israel saw the great work which Jehovah did upon the Egyptians, and the people feared Jehovah: and they believed in Jehovah, and in his servant Moses" (Ex. 14:31). This was faith but it was on a much lower plane than the faith of Abraham. Abraham believed when all the evidence except God's promise was against it. Israel believed only when proofs were submitted to them. So Thomas would not believe that Jesus had risen from the dead until he saw in his hands the print of the nails, put his finger into the print of the nails and put his hand into his side (John 20:25). His Master graciously gave him this proof but in doing so he said: "Because thou hast seen me thou hast believed: blessed are they that have not seen, and yet have believed" (John 20:29). Abraham had this blessedness of believing without seeing. Israel believed only when they saw. The Psalms of David's time and later are full of expressions of faith in God (Ps. 11:1; 13:5; 16:1; 18:2; 22:4-5, etc.).

With such a background the doctrine of faith makes a distinct advance in Isaiah. This appears first in the incidents which led to the giving of the sign Immanuel (Isa. 7:1-17). Ahaz appears in this story as a man without faith in God. He was terrified by the alliance of Syria and Samaria against him so that his heart and that of his people trembled like the trees before the wind. He was inspecting the water supply to decide whether Jerusalem could hold out in a long siege. He had made up his mind to appeal to Assyria against his enemies. In all respects he was a materialist. While nominally a worshipper of Jehovah he had no real faith in him as against such powerful foes. Isaiah tried to encourage his faith. He took with him Shear-jashub his son, whose name made him a living prophecy that Israel would survive the exile. He said to the king: "Take heed, and be quiet; fear not, neither let thy heart be faint, because of these two tails of smoking firebrands, for the fierce anger of Rezin and Syria, and of the son of Remaliah." He assured him that the confederacy against him would fail and Ephraim be broken in pieces within sixty-five years. He announced to the whole royal family: "If ye will not believe, surely ye shall not be established."

This was sublime faith on the part of Isaiah, for he knew the power of Syria and Samaria as well as Ahaz knew it. He realized the necessity of an adequate water supply for the city as much as the king. He knew that

Assyria was the most powerful nation on earth. But above and beyond all material things he saw Jehovah, the God of the whole earth and he knew that faith in him gives firmness and stability to character. In announcing this principle he made a striking play on words, for the word rendered to be established is but a different form of that rendered to believe. Its primary meaning is to confirm, support. One who believes counts the object of his faith as firm, reliable, trustworthy. This faith returns with blessing into his own soul and he is confirmed, established. Skinner well says: "The words mark an epoch in the history of revelation; never before probably had the distinctively religious principle of faith been so plainly exhibited as the touchstone of character and of destiny" (Commentary on Isa. 7:9). But it was all to no avail. Ahaz refused to trust in Jehovah. He refused to ask the sign which Isaiah invited him to do. So he lost the stability which faith in God alone could give. He sought the aid not of Jehovah but of Assyria. The aid was given but at the ultimate cost of the invasion and downfall of his kingdom (Isa. 7:17).

Isaiah's second great passage on faith is in the glorious words "Thou wilt keep him in perfect peace, whose mind is stayed on thee; because he trusteth in thee" (Isa. 26:3). Literally translated it is: "A steadfast mind (or imagination) thou wilt keep—peace, peace—because on thee has he trusted." The same word for imagination occurs in Gen. 6:5 and 8:21. The word for steadfast is rendered established in Ps. 112:8, a verse similar to this. "His heart is established, he shall not be afraid." In the previous verse the Psalmist expresses the same idea with a different word, "his heart is fixed, trusting in Jehovah" (Ps. 112:7). The idea of Isaiah's words is similar to that of Isa. 7:9. If by faith in God a man allows his imagination to picture before him the resources of the Infinite and Omnipotent One, nothing can possibly disturb his equanimity. He will see the whole mountain full of horses and chariots of fire round about him (II Kings 6:17). This verse goes beyond Isa. 7:9 in showing more clearly the psychological working of faith on the mind and laying greater stress on the peace which results from it.

The next passage on faith, as probably the one just mentioned, was occasioned by the fact that in Hezekiah's reign a powerful party of the nobles favored an alliance with Egypt against Assyria. They had as little faith in Jehovah as Ahaz had and they had even less worldly wisdom, for Rabshakeh was right when he said: "Behold, thou trustest upon the staff of this bruised reed, even upon Egypt, whereon if a man lean, it will go into his hand and pierce it; so is Pharaoh king of Egypt to all that trust on him" (Isa. 36:6). Isaiah opposed this Egyptian alliance. He urged the king and the nobles to trust neither in Egypt nor Assyria but in Jehovah. To confirm their faith in God he spoke God's words: "Behold, I lay in Zion for a foundation a stone, a tried stone, a precious corner-stone of sure foundation: he that believeth shall not be in haste" (Isa. 28:16). Here is the same idea of the firmness and stability which comes from faith in God and his promises, "How firm a foundation ye saints of the Lord, is laid for your faith in his excellent word." It has been suggested that the words "he that believeth shall not be in haste" are thought of as the inscription on the corner-stone. However this may be, they express the idea that the man who believes in the promises of God will not be in haste to protect himself by human alliances. Calmly will he stand his ground, not trembling like Ahaz, not making an alliance with Egypt like the nobles of that time, but with a steadfast imagination and therefore in perfect peace.

From the same period of Isaiah's ministry came another great message of faith, "In returning and rest shall ye be saved; in quietness and in confidence shall be your strength" (Isa. 30:15). In spite of Isaiah's advice, messengers had gone to Egypt (Isa. 30:1-5). The prophet describes their journey through the deserts, the asses and camels carrying rich presents to secure an alliance (Isa. 30:6). In opposition to such faithlessness and folly he announces the true policy for Judah. Politically speaking it is for the messengers to return from Egypt to Palestine and to rest there. Religiously speaking it is for the rulers of Judah to keep quiet and place their confidence in Jehovah. So only will the nation be saved and become strong. Here again is the idea of stability through faith in God, salvation by faith. Although its occasion was political, its profound truth is equally applicable to individual experience. The nobles refused this teaching with the result that Sennacherib invaded Judah, besieged Jerusalem and but for a divine interposition the city would have fallen (Isa. 36-37). Psalm 46 which was probably written after the lifting of the siege seems to reflect Isaiah's word when it says "Be still and know that I am God" (Ps. 46:10). It is in quiet confidence in God that national and individual strength are attained. Isaiah emphasized this truth again when he said: "The work of righteousness shall be peace; and the effect of righteousness, quietness and confidence for ever" (Isa. 32:17).

Rabshakeh the Assyrian officer did his best to undermine the faith of the inhabitants of Jerusalem in Jehovah. He pretended that Jehovah was displeased, because Hezekiah had done away with the worship at the high places (Isa. 36:7; cp. II Kings 18:4-5) and that Jehovah had sent the Assyrian army to punish him for this wrong (Isa. 36:10). He claimed that Israel could get no more help from Jehovah against the Assyrian army than the other nations had gotten from their gods (Isa. 36:18-20). In this emergency Isaiah encouraged the faith of Hezekiah (Isa. 37:5-7). Later when Sennacherib sent a blasphemous letter to Hezekiah defying Jehovah (Isa. 37:9-13), the king in simple faith went up to the temple, spread the letter before Jehovah (Isa. 37:14) and prayed for deliverance from Assyria. This sublime act of faith has been the model of every true believer for his conduct in difficulty since that day.

(7) THE FUTURE LIFE.

The writings of Isaiah mark a great advance beyond the conception of the future life in the writings of earlier inspired men. While there is no reason to think that he had a different idea of Sheol, the abode of the dead, from that which had prevailed before him (pp. 35-36, 143-145, 193-195, 245-247, 273-275, 293) the idea is expressed more fully by Isaiah than by any other writer of the Old Testament. Not only did he predict the exile of Israel because of their sins but he added: "Therefore Sheol hath enlarged its desire, and opened its mouth without measure; and their glory, and their multitude, and their pomp, and he that rejoiceth among them, descend into it" (Isa. 5:14). Sheol is viewed as an insatiable monster which devours all men (Prov. 1:12; 30:15-16). When Isaiah offered Ahaz a sign of the truth of his words he said: "Make it deep to Sheol" (Isa. 7:11) as if to suggest a resurrection from the dead. In the woe against Babylon there is one of the clearest descriptions of the condition of life in Sheol, the weak and shadowy existence of the shades who dwell there. They are represented as disturbed from their sleep by the coming of those from Babylon. "Sheol from beneath is moved for thee to meet thee at thy coming; it stirreth up the dead (Margin, 'shades') for thee, even all the chief ones of the earth; it hath raised up from their thrones all the kings of the nations. All they shall answer and say unto thee, Art thou also become weak (literally 'sick') as we? Art thou become like unto us? Thy pomp is brought down to Sheol, and the noise of thy viols: the worm is spread under thee, and worms cover thee" (Isa. 14:9-11).

Later in this woe we meet the same idea. "Thou shalt be brought down to Sheol, to the uttermost parts of the pit—All the kings of the earth, all of them, sleep in glory, every one in his own house. But thou art cast forth away from thy sepulchre like an abominable branch, clothed with the slain, that are thrust through with the sword, that go down to the stones of the pit; as a dead body trodden under foot" (Isa. 14:15, 18-19). Isaiah charged the drunken nobles of the Egyptian party with having made a covenant with death and an agreement with Sheol to protect them against the Assyrian invasion (Isa. 28:15, 18). The reference is probably to necromantic rites by which they sought to confirm their alliance with Egypt. Such rites are mentioned in Isa. 8:19. "When they shall say unto you, Seek unto them that have familiar spirits and unto the wizards that chirp and that mutter: should not a people seek unto their God? on behalf of the living should they seek unto the dead?" Isaiah said: "The captive exile shall speedily be loosed; and he shall not die and go down into the pit, neither shall his bread fail" (Isa. 51:14). He said to the wicked that he had debased himself even unto Sheol (Isa. 57:9).

In Hezekiah's song of thanksgiving after he recovered from sickness he expressed the idea which was found in Davidic Psalms (6:5; 30:9), that there is no remembrance of God or praise of him in Sheol. It is only in this life that communion with God is possible. Hezekiah sang: "I said, in the noontide of my days I shall go into the gates of Sheol. I am deprived of the residue of my years. I said, I shall not see Jehovah, even Jehovah, in the land of the living. I shall behold man no more with the inhabitants of the world—Sheol cannot praise thee, death cannot celebrate thee: They that go down into the pit cannot hope for thy truth. The living, the living, he shall praise thee, as I do this day: The father to the children shall make known thy truth" (Isa. 38:10-11, 18-19). George Adam Smith has a remarkable chapter on this incident of Hezekiah's illness which he calls "An Old Testament Believer's Sick-bed; or the Dif-

ference Christ has Made." He compares Hezekiah's idea
of the future life with that of Paul who desired "to depart and be with Christ; for it is very far better" (Phil.
1:2, 3); and with that of John who pictured the joy of
the redeemed in heaven (Rev. 7, 21, 22) and he points
out that this difference has been made by the fact of
Christ's resurrection. It is Christ who has "brought life
and immortality to light through the gospel" (II Tim.
1:10). Hezekiah knew nothing of this. Therefore he
had no hope in the future life. (The Book of Isaiah
Vol. I, p. 405).

Isaiah's most important contribution to the doctrine
of the future life does not consist in a fuller description
of Sheol but in two clear predictions of the resurrection.
The first is found in his beautiful description of the
coronation feast of Jehovah which is to usher in the Messianic age (Isa. 25:6-8). In this connection he says that
Jehovah "hath swallowed up death for ever," a statement
which Paul says will be fulfilled when "this mortal shall
have put on immortality" (I Cor. 15:54). The second
passage shows that Isaiah did not believe that the resurrection must wait till the Messianic age, for he foretold:
"Thy dead shall live; my dead bodies shall arise. Awake
and sing, ye that dwell in the dust; for thy dew is as the
dew of herbs, and the earth shall cast forth the dead"
(Isa. 26:19).

The context shows that primarily the resurrection foretold here is the resurrection of Israel from the exile,
an idea which we have already met in Hosea 6:2 and
13:14 and which is fully developed in Ezek. 37:1-14.
Yet as Hos. 6:2 is a typical prediction of the resurrection

of Christ, so Isa. 26:19 is a prediction of the resurrection of the just (Luke 14:14). It is not a general resurrection. As only the faithful remnant in Israel would be restored after the exile, so only the righteous will rise from the dead. Although neither Isa. 25:8 nor 26:19 comes near the New Testament doctrine of the resurrection, they represent the highest point of the Old Testament conception of the future life with the single exception of Dan. 12:2.

On the other hand the germ of the doctrine of Hell as the place of eternal punishment is found in the last verse of this book (Isa. 66:24). Here God foretells that the inhabitants of the New Jerusalem "shall go forth, and look upon the dead bodies of the men that have transgressed against me: for their worm shall not die, neither shall their fire be quenched; and they shall be an abhorring to all flesh." The reference is to a place in the valley of Hinnom south of Jerusalem where Ahaz (II Chron. 28:3) and Manasseh (II Chron. 33:6) offered their children as burnt-offerings to Molech. Josiah defiled it to prevent this abomination (II Kings 23:10) and it became the place for the refuse of the city including the dead bodies of animals (Jer. 7:32). How far this use of the place had extended in Isaiah's time is unknown. To cast human bodies unburied in such a place was the greatest indignity. The worms were constantly devouring them, and so great was the refuse that the fire which consumed it never went out. The idea of Isaiah is the loathsome spectacle of the bodies of the wicked being so consumed. But in the New Testament the expression "where their worm dieth not, and the fire is not quenched"

(Mark 9:48) is used of the perpetual torment of the wicked. Furthermore the Hebrew name for the valley of Hinnom is used in the New Testament in the form Gehenna which is translated as hell in the text but transliterated as Gehenna in the margin (Matt. 5:22, 29, 30; 10:28; 18:9; 23:15, 33; Mark 9:43, 45, 47; Luke 12:5; Jas. 3:6). Since the passage in Isaiah concerns the Jerusalem of the last days this eschatological use is justified. Although the worm that dieth not and the fire that is not quenched are not used by Isaiah to represent punishment, the whole picture foreshadows the casting of the wicked out of the holy city with the utmost indignity.

The Servant of Jehovah is represented as living and working after his death. After Jehovah has made the soul of the Servant a trespass-offering, "he shall see his seed, he shall prolong his days, and the pleasure of Jehovah shall prosper in his hand" (Isa. 53:10). While this prediction had a partial fulfilment in the resurrection of Israel after the exile (Hos. 6:2; 13:14; Isa. 25:8; 26:19; Ezek. 37:1-14), the only complete fulfilment was in the resurrection and continuing work of Jesus Christ.

(8) MORALITY OF THE TIME.

Isaiah spoke of sin as rebellion against God (Isa. 1:2-4) and as an incurable disease (Isa. 1:5-6). In his time the same sins existed in Judah which Amos and Hosea had condemned in the northern kingdom. The rich oppressed the poor, defrauding them of their rights by bribery in the courts. Robbery and murder were common. Defenceless orphans and widows received no justice in the courts. In his terrible arraignment of Judah which forms the introduction to his book he said: "Your hands are full of blood—seek justice, relieve the oppressed, judge the fatherless, plead for the widow" (Isa. 1:15, 17). He lamented over wicked Jerusalem "How is the faithful city become a harlot! she that was full of justice! righteousness lodged in her, but now murderers. Thy princes are rebellious, and companions of thieves; everyone loveth bribes, and followeth after rewards: they judge not the fatherless, neither doth the cause of the widow come unto them" (Isa. 1:21, 23). "Jehovah will enter into judgment with the elders of his people, and the princes thereof: It is ye that have eaten up the vineyard; the spoil of the poor is in your houses: what mean ye that ye crush my people, and grind the face of the poor? saith the Lord, Jehovah of hosts" (Isa. 3:14-15).

Isaiah condemned the land-grabbing of the rich nobles. "Woe unto them that join house to house, that lay field to field, till there be no room, and ye be made to dwell alone in the midst of the land" (Isa. 5:8; cp. Mic. 2:2, 9). He had a special woe for those who obliterated moral distinctions. "Woe unto them that call evil good, and good evil; that put darkness for light, and light for darkness; that put bitter for sweet and sweet for bitter!—that justify the wicked for a bribe and take away the righteousness of the righteous from him" (Isa. 5:20, 23). Another woe was uttered against the unjust judges. "Woe unto them that decree unrighteous decrees, and to the writers that write perverseness: to turn aside the needy from justice, and to rob the poor of my people of their right, that widows may be their spoil, and that they may make the fatherless their prey" (Isa. 10:1-2). The prophet speaks of those "that make a man an offender in his cause, and lay a snare for him that reproveth in the gate, and turn aside the just with a thing of nought" (Isa. 29:21). This probably refers to the practice of making a man out as an offender in a legal case when he is not, of catching by trickery a judge or a private individual who dares to stand for justice in the court and of defrauding the just of their rights by some empty pretext. It is probably to the same practices that Isaiah refers when he says that the churl "deviseth wicked devices to destroy the meek (Margin "poor") with lying words, even when the needy speaketh right" (Isa. 32:7).

Drunkenness must have been very common for it is often condemned. "Woe unto them that rise up early in the morning that they may follow strong drink; that tarry late into the night till wine inflame them! And the harp and the lute, the tabret and the pipe, and wine, are in their feasts" (Isa. 5:11-12). "Woe unto them that are mighty to drink wine, and men of strength to mingle strong drink " (Isa. 5:22). Isaiah had spoken a woe against the drunkards of the northern kingdom. "Woe to the crown of pride of the drunkards of Ephraim, and to the fading flower of his glorious beauty, which is on the head of the fat valley of them that are overcome with wine—the crown of pride of the drunkards of Ephraim shall be trodden under foot" (Isa. 28:1, 3). Years after the fall of Samaria, Isaiah repeated this woe to the drunken nobles of the Egyptian party saying as it should be translated, "And these also reel with wine, and stagger with strong drink; the priest and the prophet reel with strong drink, they are swallowed up of wine, they stagger with strong drink; they err in vision, they stumble in judgment. For all tables are full of vomit and filthiness, so that there is no place clean" (Isa. 28:7-8). These were the drunken nobles who mocked Isaiah (Isa. 28:9-10). Toward the end of his life probably in the reign of Manasseh the prophet referred to those who say: "Come ye, I will fetch wine, and we will fill ourselves with strong drink; and to-morrow shall be as this day, a day great beyond measure" (Isa. 56:12).

We should not conclude that such sins of oppression, murder, and drunkenness were universal in Judah at that time. It was the rich and powerful who were guilty of such things. While not much is known of the life of the common people, the way the poor and the righteous are spoken of as synonyms implies that many of them were not only pious but had high moral character. The faithful remnant, without which the nation would not have survived the exile, were mostly of the poor people. In describing the society of the Messianic kingdom (Isa. 32:1-8) all are to be righteous from the king down to the common people. Men of wealth and influence are to use their power for the protection of the weak. Men shall be judged by their inherent worth and not by the accidents of title or property.

An example of faithfulness and idealism in high office is seen in Eliakim the prefect of the palace for part of Hezekiah's reign. He succeeded to Shebna who had not been faithful (Isa. 22:19-20). Eliakim would be a father to the inhabitants of Jerusalem and to the house of Judah. Jehovah said, "I will fasten him as a nail in a sure place; and he shall be for a throne of glory to his father's house"

(Isa. 22:23). Eliakim was evidently the kind of man of whom Isaiah foretold. "A man shall be as a hiding-place from the wind, and a covert from the tempest, as streams of water in a dry place, as the shade of a great rock in a weary land" (Isa. 32:2).

He was not the only man of high character and high position in Judah, for Isaiah said: "He that walketh righteously, and speaketh uprightly; he that despiseth the gain of oppressions, that shaketh his hands from taking a bribe, that stoppeth his ears from hearing of blood, and shutteth his eyes from looking upon evil: he shall dwell on high; his place of defence shall be the munitions of rocks; his bread shall be given him; his waters shall be sure" (Isa. 33:15-16). This noble picture of a righteous man which resembles Psalm 15 and Psalm 24:3-6, may well have been drawn from life. A lofty conception of righteousness is implied also by the confession of Isa. 64:6, "All our righteousnesses are as a polluted garment." The evangelical prophet felt that even the noblest efforts of Israel to do God's will were so tainted with impure motives, so imperfect in accomplishment, that they were like a polluted garment. Such were natural words for the prophet whose long ministry had been begun and inspired by a vision of God in his holiness (Isa. 6:1-8), a vision which he never forgot.

CHAPTER XI

Micah

The first verse of this prophecy indicates not only its date and scope but also something of its character. "The word of Jehovah that came to Micah the Morashtite in the days of Jotham, Ahaz and Hezekiah, kings of Judah, which he saw concerning Samaria and Jerusalem" (Mic. 1:1). The three kings mentioned are the last three of the four in the headings of the books of Isaiah and Hosea. Thus Micah began his prophetic ministry somewhat later than Hosea and Isaiah. On the other hand while the evidence from the book of Hosea shows that that prophet finished his work before Micah, the evidence from the latter part of Isaiah shows that he continued to prophesy after Micah had ceased. It is possible that parts of chapters six and seven date like Isa. 40-55 from the reign of Manasseh; but this is not so clear as in the latter case.

It is customary to speak of Micah as a prophet of the kingdom of Judah. Not only the heading of his book, however, but several indications in it show that he prophesied concerning the northern as well as the southern kingdom. In fact, the parts of his book relating to the northern kingdom, are proportionately much larger than those of Isaiah. He couples the two together. "For the transgression of Jacob is all this, and for the sins of the house of Israel. What is the transgression of Jacob? is it not Samaria? and what are the high places of Judah? Are

they not Jerusalem? Therefore I will make Samaria as
a heap of the field, and as places for planting vineyards"
(Mic. 1:5-6). Here Jacob seems to be a designation of
the northern kingdom. The natural inference is that the
name is used in the same sense in Mic. 3:1, 8, 9. The
absence of the mention of Judah, however, makes this
uncertain. Micah never calls the northern kingdom
Ephraim, the usual designation in Hosea. It was apparently to Judah that he said: "The statutes of Omri
are kept, and all the works of the house of Ahab and ye
walk in their counsels" (Mic. 6:16). Judah had evidently
gone into the same wickedness which characterized the
darkest period in the history of the northern kingdom
(II Kings 16:3).

Like the other prophets Micah regarded Jerusalem as
the true center of Jehovah's worship and rule. The holy
temple of Jehovah is at Jerusalem (Mic. 1:2). Jerusalem is the gate of Jehovah's people (Mic. 1:9). In
the latter days the law shall go forth from Zion and the
word of Jehovah from Jerusalem (Mic. 4:2). Jehovah
will reign over his people in Mount Zion from henceforth even for ever (Mic. 4:7). It is the mountain of
Jehovah's house in Jerusalem which shall be established
on the top (Margin "at the head") of the mountains
(Mic. 4:1). Although Micah looked upon Jerusalem as
a sink of iniquity (Mic. 1:5) and although he foretold
the coming of the Messiah from Bethlehem (Mic. 5:2),
he did not reject Jerusalem as the rightful seat of
Jehovah's dominion.

Micah was a Morashtite. He probably lived at More-
sheth-gath (Mic. 1:14). The name means "a possession

of Gath" and it was probably a small village near Gath. Like Amos he was a man of the country, a rural prophet. Accordingly he was not so much interested as his great contemporary Isaiah in merely political matters. He does indeed foretell the Assyrian invasion and that the land of Assyria shall be laid waste (Mic. 5:5-6). He describes in graphic style the onward march of the Assyrian army and the desolation it brings (Mic. 1:10-16). Yet his chief interest was not in kings and armies but in the common people. He was their champion and his bitterest woes, like those of Amos, were against those who oppressed them. Accordingly the Messiah whom he foretold would not come from the capital or grow up in the royal palace but he too would be a man of the people, coming from Bethlehem which was little to be among the thousands of Judah (Mic. 5:2). There is no reason to believe as some have thought that Micah went to Jerusalem and gave his prophecies there. We do not know who his hearers were. Probably they were the people of his own neighborhood. At any rate his prophecies were later written down and his book became an influential one in the nation.

This book lacks the universalism of Amos and Isaiah. It has almost nothing to say about other nations. It begins by addressing all nations. "Hear, ye peoples, all of you; hearken, O earth, and all that therein is; and let the Lord Jehovah be witness against you, the Lord from his holy temple" (Mic. 1:2). Yet the book is concerned almost entirely with Judah and Samaria. It also lacks the intense passion and depth of Hosea, for there is no evidence that the message of Micah came out of his own experience. There are a number of points of contact between Micah and Isaiah. The prophecy of Mic. 4:1-3 occurs almost word for word in Isa. 2:2-4. Since in Micah there is an additional verse and since it fits the context better than in Isaiah, it is more probable that Micah was the author, although some commentators think that both prophets took it from an earlier author. The idea of the faithful remnant which is so prominent in Isaiah is found also in Micah (2:12; 4:7; 5:3, 7, 8; 7:18). Neither of these prophets, however, took this idea from the other but both derived it from Amos (3:12; 5:15; 9:8-9). Micah never introduces the Servant of Jehovah who is such an important figure in Isa. 40-55. Possibly those chapters were given after Micah's prophetic work was finished. He never uses Isaiah's great name for Jehovah as the Holy One of Israel. There is an interesting reference to Micah's prophecy that Zion should be plowed as a field and Jerusalem should become heaps (Mic. 3:12) in the book of Jeremiah (Jer. 26:18). When the priests and prophets planned to put Jeremiah to death because he had foretold the fall of Jerusalem, the princes and all the people pled to spare his life and cited the words of Micah against the holy city, words even more severe than Jeremiah's. Yet Micah was not put to death. This is one of the few quotations from one prophet in the writings of another.

(1) CONCEPTION OF GOD.

Micah made no important addition to the conception of God presented by Amos and Hosea, the prophets who preceded him. The most which can be said for him is that he received and handed on the great ideas which they had.   He falls so far short of the noble thoughts about God in the writings of his great contemporary Isaiah that we are tempted to conclude that he was not familiar with them.   Living in the lowlands of Judah at some distance from the capital he may have been ignorant of the writings of the court prophet.   He never speaks of the holiness of God, an idea which is so prominent in Isaiah, only once does he speak of the majesty of God (Mic. 5:4), another of Isaiah's great ideas.   We look in vain in this little book for any such revelation of God's holiness and majesty as is found in the vision by which Isaiah was ordained as a prophet (Isa. 6:1-8) or for any such majestic concepton of God's greatness as is revealed in Isa. 40:12-26.

This is not to say, however, that Micah had a low conception of God.   He doubtless believed in the holiness of God as truly as Isaiah did, but his lips were not touched with the live coal from off the altar (Isa. 6:6-7).   He certainly believed that Jehovah was the God of all nations as Amos did for his first words were, "Hear, ye peoples, all of you; hearken, O earth, and all that therein is: and let the Lord Jehovah be witness against you, the Lord from his holy Temple.   For, behold, Jehovah cometh forth out of his place, and will come down, and tread upon the high places of the earth.   And the mountains shall be melted under him, and the valleys shall be cleft, as wax before the fire, as waters that are poured down a steep place" (Mic. 1:2-4).   This is original in its figures, figures which were appropriate to the region where Micah lived.   Yet after this passage he refers only once again to the other nations. It is when he foretells that many nations shall invite other nations to go with them to Jerusalem to worship Jehovah and that Jehovah will judge among many peoples resulting in the cessation of war (Mic. 4:2-3). Micah was not like Jeremiah a prophet unto the nations (Jer. 1:5). Nevertheless he believed that his God was the God of all nations, "the Lord of the whole earth" (Mic. 4:13).

The only place where it looks at first sight as though our prophet regarded Jehovah as merely a national God is Mic. 4:5, "All the peoples walk every one in the name of his god; and we will walk in the name of Jehovah our God for ever and ever." It is clear, however, from the context that this cannot be the meaning, for this verse occurs at the end of the prediction of the universality of Jehovah's worship. The idea probably is that even if other nations refuse to acknowledge Jehovah for the present and foolishly persist in worshipping each one its own god, Israel will persist in serving Jehovah, confident that some day all nations will bow the knee to him.

Micah's name means: "Who is like Jehovah." This conception of the preeminence of God is reflected in Mic. 7:18-19, "Who is a God like unto thee, that pardoneth iniquity, and passeth over the transgression of the remnant of his heritage? he retaineth not his anger for ever, because he delighteth in lovingkindness. He will again have compassion upon us; he will tread our iniquities under foot, and thou wilt cast all their sins into the depths of the sea." This reminds us of the proclamation of the divine nature in Exod. 34:6-7. The statement that Jehovah delighteth in lovingkindness reflects the influence of

Hosea, the great prophet of the love of God. Indeed the idea of the forgiving love of God has another glorious expression in the words "thou wilt cast all their sins into the depths of the sea" (cp. Ps. 103:12; Isa. 38:17; 43:25; 44:22).

(2)   CEREMONIES OF RELIGION.

This book adds nothing to our knowledge of the external rites of religion as practised in that time. It speaks of Jerusalem as one of the high places of Judah, using the term by which the rival sanctuaries are designated (Mic. 1:5). This seems to disparage the worship at the temple. Yet it cannot be meant in this sense, for God is represented as proceeding from that temple (Mic. 1:2) and in the last days the mountain of Jehovah's house is to be established at the head of the mountains (Mic. 4:1).

Micah refers to the idols used in the Baal worship. "All her graven images shall be beaten to pieces, and all her hires shall be burned with fire, and all her idols will I lay desolate; for of the hire of a harlot hath she gathered them, and unto the hire of a harlot shall they return" (Mic. 1:7). The meaning is that the wealth gained by the prostitution carried on as part of the worship of Baal shall be seized by the Assyrians and returned to their heathen temples. Reference is also made to other heathen rites such as witchcraft and soothsaying, and to such idolatrous things as the pillars and Asherim (Mic. 5:12-14). The prophet foretells that in the good time coming Israel will no more worship the work of its hands (Mic. 5:13).

We hear in this book more than once of the false prophets who led the people astray. Such prophets said what the people in their wickedness wished to hear. Thus Micah said: "If a man walking in a spirit of falsehood (Margin, "in wind and falsehood") do lie, saying, I will prophesy unto thee of wine and of strong drink; he shall even be the prophet of this people" (Mic. 2:11). In another connection he said: "The prophets thereof divine for money; yet they lean upon Jehovah, and say, Is not Jehovah in the midst of us? no evil shall come upon us" (Mic. 3:11). The attitude of these false prophets was that of the people in the time of Amos. They thought that Jehovah would never cast off his people, no matter how great their sins were. They looked forward to a day of Jehovah in which Israel would triumph over all its enemies (Amos 5:18-20).

The prophets who encouraged this false hope were not true patriots. True patriotism required them like Amos, Isaiah and Micah to proclaim relentlessly the punishment of Israel for their sins. Only by turning from their sins could Israel be saved. "Thus saith Jehovah concerning the prophets that make my people to err; that bite with their teeth, and cry, Peace; and whoso putteth not into their mouths, they even prepare war against him. Therefore it shall be night unto you, that ye shall have no vision; and it shall be dark unto you, that ye shall not divine; and the sun shall go down upon the prophets, and the day shall be black over them. And the seers shall be put to shame, and the diviners confounded; yea, they shall all cover their lips; for there is no answer of God" (Mic. 3:5-7). These were like the false prophets

of Ezekiel's day who proclaimed peace when there was
no peace (Ezek. 13:10). They were prophets for gain.
To those who paid them they spoke pleasant words, but
they made a holy war in Jehovah's name against those
who dared refuse them. Such false prophets existed
side by side with the true prophets and were their greatest
foes. They were specially prominent in the time of Jeremiah (Amos 2:11-12; 7:14-16; Hos. 4:5; 9:8; Isa. 9:15-
16; 28:7; Jer. 2:8, 26; 5:12-13, 30-31; 8:10; 14:13-15;
23:11, 13-15, 30-32; 27:14-15; 28:5-9, 15-17; 29:8-9;
32:32; 37:19; Lam. 2:9, 14; 4:13; Ezek. 13:2-4, 9-10,
15-16; 14:9-10; 22:25, 28; Zeph. 3:4, Zech. 13:2-6).

Over against such false prophets Micah says of himself: "But as for me, I am full of power by the Spirit
of Jehovah, and of judgment, and of might, to declare
unto Jacob his transgression and to Israel his sin" (Mic.
3:8). As a true prophet of Jehovah he dared to speak
the unpopular word, to denounce the people for their
sins. His power to do this was not of human making.
It came from the fact that he was full of the Spirit of
Jehovah.

Micah like Amos (5:21-24), Hosea (6:6; 14:2) and
Isaiah (1:11-17) recognized the vanity of all religious
ceremonies when accompanied by unrepented sin. He
saw the superiority of the moral above the ceremonial
law. His statement of the relation between religious ceremony and true religion is the most eloquent in his book.
It concludes with a summary of the requirements of
Jehovah which has been called the greatest passage in
the Old Testament. "Wherewith shall I come before
Jehovah, and bow myself before the high God? Shall I

come before him with burnt-offerings, with calves a year old? Will Jehovah be pleased with thousands of rams, or with ten thousands of rivers of oil? Shall I give my first-born for my transgression, the fruit of my body for the sin of my soul? He hath showed thee, O man, what is good; and what doth Jehovah require of thee, but to do justly, and to love kindness, and to walk humbly with thy God?" (Mic. 6:6-8).

This great passage requires careful interpretation. Its rhetorical questions are very searching and indicate the deep yearning of the prophet's soul. He asks himself the deepest question which man can ask, "Wherewith shall I come before Jehovah?" The verb means to come or be in front, to confront, to meet. It occurs in Ps. 88:13, "In the morning shall my prayer come before thee," literally "confront or meet thee," and in Ps. 95:2, "Let us come before his presence with thanksgiving," literally "confront or meet his face." So here it may be translated literally "With what shall I confront or meet Jehovah?" In his deep sense of sin he felt that in God was his only help and he longed to find him as Job cried out in his suffering: "Oh that I knew where I might find him, that I might come even to his seat!" (Job 23:3).

All his experience taught him that he could not meet God empty-handed. He must bring something with him which will insure his acceptance with God. What shall it be? Since Jehovah is the high God, what shall he bring with him when he bows humbly in his presence? The religion of his time taught Micah that a sinful man should bring a burnt-offering to atone for his sin. Feeling his sin great, no small sacrifice would suffice. So in the passion of his soul he asked himself: "Shall I come before him with burnt-offerings, with calves a year old? Will Jehovah be pleased with thousands of rams, or with ten thousands of rivers of oil?" The law required that the calf and the lamb of the burnt-offering should be a year old and without blemish (Lev. 9:3). The prophet's passionate hyperbole, suggesting an offering of thousands of rams, like the royal sacrifice of Solomon at the dedication of the temple (I Kings 8:63; II Chron. 7:5), is something like Isaiah's hyperbole, "Lebanon is not sufficient to burn, nor the beasts thereof sufficient for a burnt-offering" (Isa. 40:16). Even this is exceeded by the suggestion of ten thousands of rivers of oil. The word for river is used especially of the torrents of water which rushed down the wadies of Palestine in the rainy season (Judges 5:21; Am. 5:24, etc.). Oil was used in small quantities in connection with the meal-offerings (Ex. 29:2, 23, 40; Lev. 2:1-2, 4-7; 6:15, 21; 7:10, 12; Num. 8:8). Even one river was far beyond the requirements of a great sacrifice. Ten thousands of rivers of oil is an amount almost beyond thought. Yet even such a sacrifice would not do in seeking the favor of Jehovah.

Since nothing in the Mosaic ritual could suggest an adequate sacrifice for the sinner seeking Jehovah, Micah turns as if in despair to the idolatrous human sacrifices offered to Molech which were forbidden by the law (Lev. 18:21; 20:2) but were offered by Ahaz (II Kings 16:3) by others of the people (II Kings 17:17) and later by Manasseh (II Kings 21:6; Jer. 7:31; 19:5; Ezek. 16:20; 20:26). He cries out: "Shall I give my first-born for my transgression, the fruit of my body for the sin of my soul?" Such a human sacrifice, even if it were his first-born and most beloved son (Gen. 27:19, 32; 48:14, 18; Ex. 4:22-23, etc.), would not avail. All sacrifices, whether Jewish or heathen, failing him, the prophet hears an inner voice answering his question, "Wherewith shall I come before Jehovah, and bow myself before the high God?" The answer is: "He hath showed thee, O man, what is good; and what doth Jehovah require of thee, but to do justly, and to love kindness, and to walk humbly with thy God?"

Hosea had commanded penitent Israel to bring with them words of penitence instead of animal sacrifices (Hos. 14:2). Micah surpassed him by making religion a matter of the heart, of character, rather than any expression of it in deeds or words. In the conscience God has told man that which is morally good (Deut. 30:15). Jehovah made no more than three requirements of man: (1) to do justly; (2) to love kindness, and (3) to walk humbly with his God. The first of the three was the great teaching of Amos (Amos 5:24) and the second that of Hosea (Hos. 6:4, 6; 10:12; 12:6). They relate to morality, the relation of man to his fellow-men. Yet Amos demanded righteousness from men because God is righteous and Hosea demanded kindness because God is kind and loving. Thus morality is not separated from religion but is grounded in it. It is Jehovah who requires man to deal justly with his fellows. Yet as the justice of God is not all of his perfect nature, so true human nature must go beyond justice and love kindness, even as God loves kindness in his dealings with men. Micah puts the crown on justice and kindness by adding the third requirement, to walk humbly with his God. This is religion pure and simple. The word rendered "humbly" is a verb. It occurs elsewhere only in Prov. 11:2 where the context shows that the participle is correctly translated "lowly." The literal translation of Micah's expression is "to make humble thy walk with God." It requires that all man's conduct, his daily walk and conversation, shall be in secret and humble fellowship with his God.

This is the greatest summary of the law in the Old Testament. It reminds us of Moses' summary, "And now, Israel, what doth Jehovah thy God require of thee, but to fear Jehovah thy God, to walk in all his ways, and to love him, and to serve Jehovah thy God with all thy heart, and with all thy soul, to keep the commandments of Jehovah, and his statutes, which I command thee this day for thy good?" (Deut. 10:12-13; cp. pp. 70-71). It also recalls the summary of the law which our Lord took from Deut. 6:5 and Lev. 19:18, "Thou shalt love the Lord thy God with all thy heart, and with all thy soul, and with all thy mind. This is the great and first commandment. And a second like unto it is this, Thou shalt love thy neighbor as thyself. On these two commandments the whole law hangeth, and the prophets" (Matt. 22:37-40). Micah made humble fellowship with God the crown of the religious life. Jesus reversing the order made the love of God the first duty of man and affirmed that the love of his neighbor is like it in binding power. Micah's summary has its New Testament counterpart in James' definition of religion, "Pure religion and undefiled before our God and Father is this, to visit the fatherless and widows in their affliction, and to keep oneself unspotted from the world" (Jas. 1:27).

(3) THE FAITHFUL REMNANT.

The doctrine of the faithful remnant in Israel, the kernel of the new and better nation of the future, is found in the writings of Micah as well as in those of his great contemporary Isaiah. Neither of these prophets, however, took it from the other. It was found before them in the teaching of Amos (Amos 3:12; 5:15; 9:8-9). While in Micah the doctrine is somewhat undeveloped, Isaiah, whose first-born son Shear-jashub ("A remnant shall return") was a living prophecy of this idea, carried it to much greater lengths (Isa. 1:9; 4:2-3; 6:13; 10:20-22; 11:11-12, 16; 28:5-6; 37:4, 31-32; 46:3).

The first mention of the remnant is in Mic. 2:12. "I will surely assemble, O Jacob, all of thee; I will surely gather the remnant of Israel; I will put them together as the sheep of Bozrah, as a flock in the midst of their pasture." Here as elsewhere in Micah the remnant consists of the faithful who are in exile. It is never used of those who remained in Palestine after the mass of the population was carried into captivity. Isaiah uses the term in Micah's sense sometimes (Isa. 10:20-22; 11:11-12, 16) but sometimes in a different sense (Isa. 1:9; 4:3; 37:4, 31-32). Jehovah promises through Micah that he will gather together the remnant of Israel dispersed in exile, as a shepherd gathers his sheep. This gathering is plainly in order to bring the remnant back to their own pasture in Palestine.

This is expressed more fully in Mic. 4:6-7. "In that day, saith Jehovah, will I assemble that which is lame, and I will gather that which is driven away, and that which I have afflicted; and I will make that which was lame a remnant, and that which was cast off a strong nation: and Jehovah will reign over them in Mount Zion from henceforth even for ever." The word rendered "lame" in these two verses occurs elsewhere only in Gen. 32:31 and Zeph. 3:19. In the former passage it is used of Jacob after the angel wrestled with him. When the angel saw that he did not prevail over him, he touched the hollow of Jacob's thigh so that it was strained. Jacob's name was changed to Israel ("he striveth with God" or "God striveth") because he strove with God and prevailed. Jacob "limped upon his thigh." The more common word meaning "lame" occurs fourteen times in the Old Testament (Lev. 21:18; Deut. 15:21; II Sam. 5:6, 8, etc.).

Since Micah passed by this more common word and used the one which was associated with Jacob, he must have meant to compare the nation in exile with their ancestor as he wrestled with the angel and limped upon his thigh. What this tremendous experience was in Jacob's life, that would the exile be in the life of Israel. Jacob prevailed over God only when his character was changed, when he ceased to strive for success by self-seeking as he had done in getting the birthright and the blessing from his brother Esau and his flocks and herds from his uncle Laban. He tried this method with God but without success. Helpless and limping he surrendered to God and by that act he prevailed. God conquered

Jacob before Jacob could conquer God. Jacob's will yielded to God's will before it prevailed with God. Like Paul accepting his thorn in the flesh, when he was weak he became strong (II Cor. 12:10).

The exile would likewise be the turning-point in the life of the nation. They too had sought success for themselves by selfish and wicked means. Such means would bring them at last not to success but to utter failure, to exile in a foreign land. Yet out of Israel with the hollow of its thigh touched and strained, out of Israel helpless and limping, Jehovah would make the remnant over which he would reign in Mount Zion. The remnant would become a strong nation. Zephaniah a century later borrowed this idea from Micah when speaking in Jehovah's name he said: "I will save that which is lame, and gather that which was driven away; and I will make them a praise and name, whose shame hath been in all the earth" (Zeph. 3:19). Ezekiel uses a similar figure concerning the returning exiles although he does not compare them to limping Jacob nor in this connection speak of them as a remnant (Ezek. 34:16).

The next reference to the remnant is in connection with the prediction of the birth of the Messiah at Bethlehem. "Therefore will he give them up, until the time that she who travaileth hath brought forth; then the residue of his brethren shall return unto the children of Israel" (Mic. 5:3). Jehovah will not give up his people to exile forever but only until the birth of Immanuel. The reference is to Isa. 7:14, "A virgin (Margin, "the maiden") shall conceive, and bear a son, and shall call his name Immanuel." When Immanuel is born, the residue of

Immanuel's brethren in exile will be reunited with the body of the nation in Palestine (Isa. 11:11-16; Ezek. 16:55, 61; Hos. 3:5; Zech. 8:13). If Hezekiah may be identified with the Immanuel foretold in Isa. 7:14, the prediction of Micah would mean merely that the exile would last until after the birth of Hezekiah. But the trouble with this interpretation is that the exile did not begin until after Hezekiah was born. It was while he was on the throne that Samaria fell and the exiles of the northern kingdom were carried away. Possibly Micah's prediction was given soon after Isa. 7:14 which was probably in the first year of the reign of Ahaz. Yet even so the context implies that the prophet was looking forward to an event much later than the birth of Hezekiah, viz., the birth of the Messiah of whom Hezekiah may have been a type.

It is strange that Micah should predict that the exile would last until after the birth of the Messiah. It is an illustration of the fact that in forecasting the future the prophets could not distinguish the order of events. Prediction was not history written in advance. The prophets could not distinguish that which was near from that which was far off. So here Micah saw the birth of the Messiah as part of that great movement which would begin with the restoration of Israel from the exile and the reuniting of the scattered elements of the nation. To his view the birth of the Messiah was the most important part of that movement and it seemed to him that it could not begin until the Messiah was born. In this respect Micah's conception resembles that of the Servant of Jehovah in Isaiah. In the near distance Isaiah saw the generation of Israel suffering in the exile and as a distinct feature of that picture he saw the Messiah suffering and dying for the sins of his people. So to Micah the nation would not be restored and reunited until the Messiah was born.

In the same connection Micah foretells that the scattered remnant shall be a blessing among the peoples where they live. "The remnant of Jacob shall be in the midst of many peoples as dew from Jehovah, as showers upon the grass; that tarry not for man, nor wait for the sons of men. And the remnant of Jacob shall be among the nations, in the midst of many peoples, as a lion among the beasts of the forest, as a young lion among the flocks of sheep; who, if he go through, treadeth down and teareth in pieces, and there is none to deliver" (Mic. 5:7-8). This difficult passage seems to bring together two contrasting ideas, (1) the beneficent influence which comes from Jehovah through the scattered remnant of Israel upon the nations around them and (2) the way that Israel shall overthrow and devour those nations. The beneficent influence is compared to that of the dew (Deut. 32:2; Prov. 19:12; Hos. 14:5) and the showers (II Sam. 23:4; Ps. 65:10; 72:6), which make the grass grow without waiting for human cultivation. On the other hand the remnant will be like a lion not only among other wild animals but among defenceless sheep. They will come to dominate those about them.

Micah's last reference to the remnant is in the verse already quoted: "Who is a God like unto thee, that pardoneth iniquity, and passeth over the transgression of the remnant of his heritage" (Mic. 7:18). Even though

the remnant is faithful, it is not entirely free from sin.
God in his mercy passes over the transgression of the
remnant (Prov. 19:11).

It is significant that at least three of Micah's five references to the remnant (Mic. 4:7; 5:3, 7-8) occur in
Messianic connections. As the idea of the faithful remnant in Isaiah prepared for that of the Servant of Jehovah, so the remnant in Micah is closely associated with
the Messiah and his times.

(4) The Messianic Hope.

Aside from his great summary of man's duty to God
(Mic. 6:8), Micah's most important contribution to the
religion of Israel was in his Messianic predictions. If
they lack the depth and the breadth of the Messianic
prophecies of Isaiah, they excel in definiteness. As in
the case of Isaiah, so here also it is difficult to set bounds
to the Messianic element in the book. This is particularly true in chapter 5 where the Messiah and his times
are foretold in connection with events soon after the
prophet's time.

Certain Jewish writers regarded *Mic.* 2:13 as referring
to the Messiah. "The breaker is gone up before them:
they have broken forth and passed on to the gate, and
are gone out thereat: and their king is passed on before
them, and Jehovah at the head of them." Accordingly
the Jews made "the Breaker-through" one of the titles
of the Messiah. The context of the passage might seem
to favor such an interpretation. In verse 12 Jehovah
promises to gather the scattered remnant of Israel like
sheep. Verse 13 plainly refers to the exiles as break-

ing through the barriers which confined them in prison and going out of the gate of the city of their exile under the leadership of Jehovah. In such a connection a reference to the Messiah would not be unnatural. Such a reference is found in a similar context in Mic. 4:8 and 5:2-5. Isaiah also represents the Servant of Jehovah as called to deliver Israel from the prison of the exile (Isa. 42:7; 49:5-6).

On the other hand, neither the title "Breaker-through" nor any title of similar import, is ever used elsewhere of the Messiah. The breaker who is gone up before the assembled exiles is not the Messiah, for he is not mentioned in the previous verse, but Jehovah himself. Their king who is passed on before them might seem to be the Messiah, who certainly would be their king. The following words, however, ("and Jehovah at the head of them") show that the king who leads them is not the Messiah but Jehovah. Otherwise we should have to picture Israel as returning from exile under the dual leadership of the Messiah and Jehovah, an idea never found in prophecy or fulfillment. Jehovah was the king of Israel (Deut. 33:5; I Sam. 12:12; Isa. 41:21; 43:15; 44:6). Thus Mic. 2:13 is similar to Isa. 52:12, "Ye shall not go out in haste, neither shall ye go by flight: for Jehovah will go before you; and the God of Israel will be your rearward." Such being the meaning, the last words of the verse should be translated "even Jehovah at the head of them."

The first Messianic passage in this book is *Mic.* 4:1-4. "But in the latter days it shall come to pass, that the mountain of Jehovah's house shall be established on the top (Margin, "at the head") of the mountains, and it shall be exalted above the hills; and peoples shall flow unto it. And many nations shall go and say, Come ye, and let us go up to the mountain of Jehovah, and to the house of the God of Jacob, and he will teach us of his ways, and we will walk in his paths. For out of Zion shall go forth the law, and the word of Jehovah from Jerusalem; and he will judge between (Margin, "among") many peoples, and will decide concerning strong nations afar off: and they shall beat their swords into plowshares, and their spears into pruning-hooks; nation shall not lift up sword against nation, neither shall they learn war any more. But they shall sit every man under his vine and under his fig-tree; and none shall make them afraid: for the mouth of Jehovah of hosts hath spoken it."

The first three of these four verses occur with a few slight variations in Isa. 2:2-4 and their general interpretation is given in the chapter on that book. As indicated there, Micah was probably the author of the passage and Isaiah took it from him. This seems likely from the additional verse found here. This verse presents the state of individual and domestic peace which will be possible when the nations not only cease from war but cease to prepare for it. It is pictured in language appropriate to the rural district where Micah lived. Each man sitting in peace under his own vine and fig-tree (I Kings 4:25; Zech. 3:10) had a meaning something like our expression to sit by one's own fireside or on one's own hearth. The words "and none shall make them afraid" were proverbial (Lev. 26:6; Job. 11:19; Isa. 17:2; Jer. 30:10; 46:27; Ezek. 34:28; 39:26; Nah. 2:11; Zeph. 3:13).

This blessed state of peace as well as all that goes before in this passage is guaranteed by the fact that the mouth of Jehovah of hosts hath spoken it (Isa. 1:20; 40:5; 58:14).

Mic. 4:8 is essentially Messianic. "And thou, O tower of the flock, the hill of the daughter of Zion, unto thee shall it come, yea the former dominion shall come, the kingdom of the daughter of Jerusalem." The expression "tower of the flock" occurs nowhere else except Gen. 35:21 where the English translators have incorrectly regarded the word for "flock" as a proper name. The shepherds had built a tower near Bethlehem in which they might be protected from storms and from which they might watch their flocks (II Chron. 26:10). Such towers were also built in vineyards (Isa. 5:2). It was near this tower that Benjamin was born and Rachel died when Jacob was returning with his family from Paddan-aram (Gen. 35:16-21). Micah had doubtless seen it. The word for hill is the same as the proper name Ophel used especially of the southern part of the temple hill at Jerusalem (II Chron. 27:3; 33:14; Neh. 3:26-27).

Here Micah apostrophizes the tower of the flock near Bethlehem and the hill Ophel at Jerusalem, declaring that the former dominion, that is the dominion which the Davidic dynasty had before the loss of the ten tribes, shall come back to it. The Targum paraphrases this verse: "And thou Messiah of Israel, who shalt be hidden on account of the sins of Zion, to thee shall the kingdom come." It is going too far to regard the tower of the flock and the hill Ophel as standing symbolically for the Messiah. Indeed the Messiah is not referred to in this verse. It merely foretells that the kingly power once wielded by David and Solomon shall some day come back to Bethlehem and Jerusalem. Since, however, Micah foretold that the Messiah should be born at Bethlehem (Mic. 5:2), this prediction is essentially Messianic. It is based upon the promise which God gave through Nathan to David that he would establish the dominion of his son forever (II Sam. 7:12-16). Solomon still looking forward sang: "He shall have dominion also from sea to sea, and from the River unto the ends of the earth" (Ps. 72:8; cp. Zech. 9:10). Such will be the kingdom of the daughter of Jerusalem.

The last Messianic passage in this book is Mic. 5:2-6. "But thou, Bethlehem Ephrathah, which art little to be among the thousands of Judah, out of thee shall one come forth unto me that is to be ruler in Israel; whose goings forth are from old, from everlasting. Therefore will he give them up, until the time that she who travaileth hath brought forth: then the residue of his brethren shall return unto the children of Israel. And he shall stand, and shall feed his flock in the strength of Jehovah, in the majesty of the name of Jehovah his God: and they shall abide; for now shall he be great unto the ends of the earth. And this man shall be our peace. When the Assyrian shall come into our land, and when he shall tread in our palaces, then shall we raise against him seven shepherds, and eight principal men. And they shall waste the land of Assyria with the sword, and the land of Nimrod in the entrances thereof: and he shall deliver us from the Assyrian, when he cometh into our land, and when he treadeth within our border."

At first sight it might seem natural that Micah should mention Bethlehem as the birthplace of the Messiah, since David was born there and the Messiah was to be descended from David. Further thought, however, shows that Bethlehem was not the natural place. By Micah's time ten kings of David's line had sat upon the royal throne. Yet only David, as far as we know, was born in Bethlehem. All the others were probably born in the palace at Jerusalem. That was the natural place to expect the birth of the greater Son of David. Yet Micah, the rural prophet, the champion of the common people, had the spiritual insight to see that the Messiah would not come from the capital, would not be born in the royal palace, but would be a man of the common people like himself. George Adam Smith with true imagination wrote: "We may conceive how such a promise would affect the crushed peasants for whom Micah wrote, A Saviour, who was one of themselves, not born up there in the capital, foster-brother of the very nobles who oppressed them, but born among the people, sharer of their toils and of their wrongs—it would bring hope to every broken heart among the disinherited poor of Israel" (Expositor's Bible on The Minor Prophets, Vol. I, p. 414).

The birth of the Messiah at Bethlehem instead of Jerusalem seems to imply that the Davidic dynasty would not be reigning at the time. The dynasty would have gone back to its original place before David became king and the royal capital was established at Jerusalem. The Messiah would be, as Isaiah foretold, "A shoot out of the stock of Jesse" (Isa. 11:1). He would be another David, the founder of the dynasty appearing again on earth (Jer. 30:9; Ezek. 34:23-24; 37:25; Hos. 3:5). In the Messiah the dynasty would return to its ideal, not like the weak and wicked kings of later times but like the first and greatest of them all, the king after God's own heart, the king whom the people loved and to whom they looked back with pride.

Yet strictly speaking this is not a prediction of the place of the Messiah's birth. He will come forth, it is true, from Bethlehem—but the coming forth to which the prophet refers is not his birth but something long before. The noun rendered "goings forth" is from the same stem as the verb to come forth. The one that is to be ruler in Israel shall come forth out of Bethlehem. This coming forth was future to Micah; but it would be the culmination of a process which had begun long before his time. The prophet said of the Messiah that his goings forth were from of old, from everlasting or as the margin translates literally "from ancient days." Both expressions refer to the distant past. That rendered "from of old" is used elsewhere sometimes of the past eternity (Deut. 33:15, 27; Ps. 55:19; 68:33; Prov. 8:22-23, etc.), sometimes of the distant past of human history (Ps. 74:2, 12; 77:5, 11; 78:2; Isa. 23:7; Mic. 7:20, etc.) and sometimes even of the far past of individual experience (Job. 29:2). Here it looks back to David three centuries before Micah. The other expression "from ancient days" is used elsewhere only of the distant past of Israel's history. Isaiah used it of the time of Moses (Isa. 63:11), Amos of the period of the united monarchy (Amos 9:11) and Micah and Malachi of Israel's far past (Mic. 7:14; Mal. 3:4).

This usage argues that here it also looks back to David's time. If so the idea is that the human source of the Messiah is in David. Yet the fact that the former expression is used sometimes of the past eternity and that we have here the cumulative effect of two strong expressions seems to hint that the inspiring Spirit was looking back of all human history to the origin of the Messiah in the bosom of the eternal God himself. Horton states the case well, "The solemn addition 'from everlasting' gives a deeper tone to the prophecy which might come as easily to Micah as to any later prophet; it shows that Messiah will not be only David restored, but One who was in the beginning with God. We are not called on to explain away this solemn and wonderful forecast especially when we have seen it fulfilled in the babe of Bethlehem, who came into the world out of the bosom of the Father. Micah could not understand his own deep saying; but how foolish of us to discredit it when history has made its meaning plain" (New Century Bible). We have here then a reference to the preexistence of the Messiah with God (Prov. 8:22-23; John 1:1-2; 17:5; I John 1:2, etc.).

Although then this verse did not primarily foretell the birth of Christ in Bethlehem it was commonly and correctly interpreted in this sense when Jesus was born (Matt. 2:4-6; John 7:42). The chief priests and scribes of the people took it so. It was a legitimate inference from the verse that the Messiah would be born in the same place which was his human origin in David's time. History as Horton suggests has interpreted prophecy.

Verse 3 has been dealt with elsewhere because of its reference to the faithful remnant. The idea is that because God has promised the Messiah, he will give up his people to exile for their sins until the Messiah comes to deliver them. Then the remnant of the Messiah's brethren in exile shall be reunited with those of the children of Israel who remain in Palestine. The lack of perspective between the near and the far has already been mentioned. The Messiah like David is to shepherd his people (verse 4; cp. II Sam. 5:2; Ezek. 34:23; 37:24; John 10:11, 14). The strength by which he shall rule will not be human strength but the strength of Jehovah who appoints him king, especially as revealed in his majestic name. As a result of his beneficent reign his people Israel shall dwell in security (Mic. 4:4). The greatness of the Messiah, however, will not be confined to Israel but will extend to the ends of the earth (Ps. 2:8; 72:8; Zech. 9:10).

The change of standpoint in verse 5 is surprising. As Horton says: "From the great and mystical forecast, which to us is rich with spiritual significance, he turns to the almost prosaic and strictly national politics of his time. The Messiah whom he has foretold, who actually was to be the Saviour of the world, fades into the light of common day, and is simply the leader who shall deliver Jerusalem from the Assyrian, a mere Hezekiah, or his like" (New Century Bible). It is another illustration of the fact that the prophets did not distinguish the near future from the far. As the promise of Immanuel would be the sign of the approaching Assyrian invasion (Isa. 7:14-17), so the promise of the Great Ruler from

Bethlehem would bring peace to his believing people when that invasion came.

The reference to seven shepherds and eight princes may be compared to Job 5:19; Eccl. 11:2; Amos 1:3. The idea is that when the Assyrian invasion comes, Israel will have enough leaders to raise up against them. There is no occasion on which any Jewish leaders wasted the land of Assyria with the sword. Possibly the seven shepherds and eight princes are not Israelites but the Babylonians and Medes who conquered Nineveh. The deliverance of Israel from the Assyrian had its fulfillment in the turning back of Sennacherib's army (Isa. 14:25; 37:36-37). The representation that the Messiah would work this deliverance is not more surprising than that he would bring the exiles back to their homeland (Mic. 5:3-4; cp. Isa. 42:7; 49:5-6). Here as there it may be that that which is wrought by the type is thought of as the work of the Antitype.

(5) THE MORALITY OF THE TIME.

Not much need be said about the morality of the time as reflected in the book of Micah, since it corresponds almost exactly to that which we have seen in the writings of Amos and Hosea who preceded him and of Isaiah, his contemporary prophet. The rich oppressed the poor defrauding them of their lands and even their clothes, "Woe to them that devise iniquity and work evil upon their beds! When the morning is light, they practice it, because it is in the power of their hand. And they covet fields, and seize them; and houses, and take them away: and they oppress a man and his house, even a man and his heritage—Ye strip the robe from off the garment from them that pass by securely as men averse from war. The women of my people ye cast out from their pleasant houses; from their young children ye take away my glory forever" (Mic. 2:1-2, 8-9; cp. Isa. 5:8). They went further to torture their bodies. "Ye who hate the good, and love the evil; who pluck off their skin from off them, and their flesh from off their bones; who also eat the flesh of my people, and flay their skin from off them, and break their bones, and chop them in pieces, as for the pot, and as flesh within the caldron" (Mic. 3:2-3). The rulers and the nobles "abhor justice, and pervert all equity. They build up Zion with blood, and Jerusalem with iniquity. The heads thereof judge for reward, and the priests thereof teach for hire, and the prophets thereof divine for money" (Mic. 3:9-11). Scant measure, false balances, violence and lying were common "Are there yet treasures of wickedness in the house of the wicked, and a scant measure that is abominable? Shall I be pure with wicked balances, and with a bag of deceitful weights? For the rich men thereof are full of violence, and the inhabitants thereof have spoken lies and their tongue is deceitful in their mouth" (Mic. 6:10-12).

How widespread wickedness was is graphically described. "The godly man is perished out of the earth, and there is none upright among men; they all lie in wait for blood; they hunt every man his brother with a net. Their hands are upon that which is evil to do it diligently; the prince asketh, and the judge is ready for a reward; and the great man, he uttereth the evil desire of his soul: thus they weave it together. The best of them is as a brier; the most upright is worse than a thorn hedge" (Mic. 7:2-4). In such a state of society no one dared trust a neighbor, a friend or even his own wife. "Trust ye not in a neighbor; put ye not confidence in a friend; keep the doors of thy mouth from her that lieth in thy bosom. For the son dishonoreth the father, the daughter riseth up against her mother, the daughter-in-law against her mother-in-law; a man's enemies are the men of his own house" (Mic.. 7:5-6).

It is refreshing to turn from such a picture to Micah's glorious picture of true morality and religion "He hath showed thee, O man, what is good; and what doth Jehovah require of thee, but to do justly and to love kindness, and to walk humbly with thy God?" (Mic. 6:8).

CHAPTER XII.

Psalms 2, 42-50, 66-68, 75-76, 78, 80, 84.

There is no more difficult critical question in the Old Testament than the dating of individual Psalms. The cases in which they contain clear historical allusions which help to fix the date are few. Reference to the king may indicate that the Psalm was written before the fall of the monarchy but may leave us in doubt to what period of the monarchy it belongs. Reference to the temple may show that it was standing; but this criterion alone does not fix the date before or after the exile. Apparent historical allusions may refer to events not recorded in the historical books. The criterion of language may indicate a late or an early date but cannot be more definite. Comparison of the ideas expressed with those of dated writings is a very uncertain test, for it is impossible to tell whether the Psalmist originated the ideas or took them from older writings known or unknown.

The general character or structure of the Psalm—for example, liturgical or alphabetical—has some value. Those Psalms which are most surely Davidic are not liturgical. Yet we do not know how soon after David's time this type of Psalm originated. On the other hand there are three alphabetic Psalms ascribed to David as.

514

their author by their inscriptions (Pss. 9, 25, 34) which other considerations do not justify us in denying to him. The position of a Psalm in the Psalter is of considerable value when other criteria fail or are indecisive. Since in general the most surely early Psalms are in the early part of the Psalter and the most surely late Psalms in the later parts of it, the presumption is in favor of an early date for a Psalm in the early part and in favor of a late date for one near the end. This test may be applied with some confidence also to certain groups of Psalms. For example since Psalms 46 and 48 give rather clear evidence of a certain date, it seems fairly safe to date the other Psalms of this group (Pss. 42-45, 47, 49) in the same time, if there is no evidence to the contrary.

When all these criteria are applied, in many cases we can do no more than conjecture with more or less probability as to the time from which the production came. That being so it is unscientific to reject the ancient tradition contained in the inscriptions except for adequate cause. The fact that these inscriptions of authorship are much more numerous in the early part of the Psalter than near the end, while one-third of the Psalms are anonymous in the Hebrew Bible, argues that they represent real tradition and were not arbitrary surmises. In some cases they are not reliable (see pp. 204-205) ; but in the majority of cases they are more worthy of confidence than the unsupported conjectures of modern critics.

When we apply these general principles to determine which Psalms should be dated in the eighth century, the result is the selection of those mentioned at the head of this chapter. In the cases of Psalms 46, 48, 66, and 76, the evidence is so strong that the date is quite sure. In the other cases it is more uncertain. The only Psalm with a Davidic title in the Hebrew Bible assigned to this period is number 68. There are, however, several Korahitic Psalms (Pss. 42-49, 84) and five Asaphitic Psalms (Pss. 50, 75-76, 78, 80) which we have dated in this time. This dating does not require a rejection of the title. Since the Korahitic and Asaphitic guilds were in existence for several centuries, these titles are almost valueless in determining the date (see p. 205). It should be noticed that all the Psalms which we have assigned to this time are found in the first three books of the Psalter. That fact creates a certain degree of probability in favor of a date at least before the exile. The arguments concerning the time of each Psalm will be considered separately. Since in most cases the date is conjectural, it seems better not to group them together but to present the religious conceptions of each Psalm by themselves.

There is a great antecedent probability that there were Psalms of the eighth century. This is seen from two facts: (1) It was a time of renewed literary activity. There are no writings of the Old Testament which are dated in the period between Solomon and Amos unless it be the prophetic and priestly records of that period found in the books of Kings and Chronicles. It seems strange that the inspired writers have left us nothing from so long a time (931-750 B. C.). It is possible that some of the Psalms which we have placed in the eighth century were handed down from an earlier time, such as the reigns of the good kings Asa (911-871 B. C.)

and Jehoshaphat (871-849). The religious reforms of Asa (II Chron. 15:8-15) give some strength to this hypothesis. But we know too little of that time to judge confidently. When we enter the eighth century, however, we are on sure ground. From this time came the first of the writing prophets, Amos, Hosea, Isaiah and Micah. The heading of Prov. 25:1, "These also are proverbs of Solomon, which the men of Hezekiah king of Judah copied out," is another sign of literary activity in this time. Finally, Hezekiah himself wrote a poem when he recovered from his sickness (Isa. 38:9-20) which might well be called a Psalm. Not only does it contain many points of resemblance to Psalms both early and late but its closing verse shows that it was used in the temple worship. "Therefore we will sing my songs with stringed instruments all the days of our life in the house of Jehovah" (Isa. 38:20).

(2) The reign of Hezekiah was a time of religious reformation greater than any which had preceded it. (II Kings 18:4-6). He cast out the idolatry which his father Ahaz had practised and removed the high places. He repaired the temple and cleansed it (II Chron. 29:3, 15-19). He reestablished the orders of Levites, in particular those connected with the musical part of the service (II Chron. 29:25-30). "Hezekiah the king and the princes commanded the Levites to sing praises unto Jehovah with the words of David, and of Asaph the seer" (II Chron. 29:30). The words of David had come down to that time in the collection of Psalms which had been used in the temple from Solomon's day; but if we are correct in assigning Psalms 50, 75, 76, 78 and 80 to this

reign, they may be the words of Asaph the seer to which the Chronicler referred. At any rate it would be a most natural time to supplement the ancient Psalter with Psalms which had not yet found a place in it or which were composed under the impetus of the religious revival. When the Northern Kingdom fell early in Hezekiah's reign (722 B. C.) the religious literature of that kingdom including the book of Hosea passed to the kingdom of Judah. Possibly there were Psalms among them. All these considerations make the assignment of Psalms to the eighth century and in particular to the reign of Hezekiah reasonable.

PSALM 2.

This Psalm has no inscription in the Hebrew Bible but in some texts of the Septuagint it has an inscription as the work of David. It was probably such a Greek text which caused Peter and John to quote the first two verses as "by the mouth of our father David" (Acts 4:25-26). If David had really been its author, the Hebrew text would certainly contain the inscription as it does in 73 other cases. Its absence justifies us in the conclusion that there was no reliable tradition as to its authorship. The internal indications are indecisive also as to its exact date. The language fits an early time with the possible exception of the word rendered "son" in verse 12. It is the usual word for "son" in Aramaic which occurs elsewhere in the Hebrew parts of the Old Testament only in Prov. 31:2 in a chapter which is evidently later. This would argue for a date for the Psalm not earlier than just before the exile, except on the theory that this one

Aramaic word was substituted for the similar Hebrew word long after the Psalm was written. It is, however, not certain that this is the word for "son." Of the four ancient versions only the Syriac renders it so. It may be a Hebrew word meaning "pure" and if so, it furnishes no argument for a late date. The way the king is mentioned in the Psalm seems to indicate that it was written while the Davidic dynasty was standing. The opposition of surrounding nations to the king is thought by some to refer to the wars of David and by others to the confederacy of Syria and Samaria against Ahaz (Isa. 7:1-9). Others still regard it as an ideal picture of all opposition to the kingdom of God. The early position of the Psalm in the first book of the Psalter is a strong argument for an early date. On the whole there is no more likely time for it than that of Ahaz or Hezekiah. The prominence of the Messianic element in the books of Isaiah and Micah makes it reasonable to date this Messianic Psalm in that time.

This is one of the two Messianic Psalms which we have dated in the eighth century (Psalms 2 and 45). Its Messianic character is universally admitted. Verses 1 and 2 are quoted in reference to Christ in Acts 4:25-28; verse 7 in Acts 13:33; Heb. 1:5 and 5:5; and verse 9 in Rev. 12:5 and 19:15. The word rendered "anointed" in verse 2 is Messiah. It should not be thought, however, that it has the same sense as the Greek word Christ in the New Testament. The Messiah of that time was the anointed king of the Davidic dynasty.

The Psalm is thus typically Messianic, referring to the Davidic king of the time and through him to Christ.

Opposition to that king was a vain thing because he did not reign in his own right but as the earthly representative and vicegerent of Jehovah. His kingdom was the kingdom of God in concrete visible form. Hence opposition to the earthly king was in reality opposition to God. God's attitude toward this opposition is represented, as one of laughter and derision at its extreme futility, and then of anger and vexation. His sufficient reply is given in the words, "Yet I have set my king upon my holy hill of Zion" (Verse 6). It is this king who says "I will tell of the decree" (verse 7). The decree to which he refers is the divine adoption and promise of world-wide dominion which he relates immediately. The king says: "Jehovah said unto me, Thou art my son. This day have I begotten thee. Ask of me, and I will give thee the nations for thine inheritance, and the uttermost parts of the earth for thy possession. Thou shalt break them with a rod of iron. Thou shalt dash them in pieces like a potter's vessel" (verse 7-9). In view of all this the Psalmist exhorts the rebellious nations to act wisely by submitting themselves to the Messianic king.

The statement of Jehovah "Thou art my son" does not refer to Christ as the second person of the Trinity and the words, "This day have I begotten thee," do not refer to the eternal generation of the Son of God. It is the Messianic sonship which is spoken of as the entire context shows. Jehovah had adopted Israel as his son in Moses' day, for he commanded Moses to say to Pharaoh: "Israel is my son, my first-born" (Ex. 4:22). This sonship of the nation was recognized by Moses in his farewell song. "Do ye thus requite Jehovah, O foolish people and unwise? Is not he thy father that hath bought thee? He hath made thee and established thee" (Deut. 32:6). Hosea also recognized it, for he spoke Jehovah's words: "When Israel was a child, then I loved him and called my son out of Egypt" (Hos. 11:1!). If the whole nation Israel was the son of God this was preeminently true of the divinely anointed king, the vicegerent of God (II Sam. 7:14). The day on which the king was begotten as the son of God was the day when he was anointed as king. We are not justified in pressing the figure of begetting as though it indicated the deity of the son, especially as it is found in poetry. It merely means that God adopted the king as his son when he became king. Because of the typical relation of the Davidic king to the coming Messiah, the New Testament writers and speakers correctly referred the words of the Psalm to Jesus Christ.

The Messianic predictions of this Psalm are based upon the promise which God gave through Nathan to David in II Sam. 7:12-17. Yet that promise related to the eternity of the Messianic kingdom while this has to do with its world-wide extent. In particular it appropriates for the king the promise which God had given David concerning his son: "I will be his father, and he shall be my son" (II Sam. 7:14). This Psalm resembles one of David's Messianic Psalms (110) in this respect, that the conquests of the Messiah are represented as acquired by force. He is to break the nations with a rod of iron and to dash them in pieces like a potter's vessel (Ps. 2:9; cp. 110:5-6). Solomon's Messianic Psalm (72), however, corresponding to the peaceful character of his time, represents the

Messiah's reign as peaceful, extending from sea to sea and from the river unto the ends of the earth, not by force but because he delivers the needy when he crieth, the poor, that hath no helper (Ps. 72:8, 12). Yet even in Solomon's Psalm the Messiah saves the children of the needy by breaking in pieces the oppressor (Ps. 72:4). This representation of force, military conquest, is a part of the Psalm's typology. That which was true literally of David and the later royal conquerors in the dispensation of the external pointed to that which was true spiritually of Jesus Christ in the dispensation of the Spirit. Christ has his conquests as well as David, but the sword with which he pierces men is the sword of the Spirit, which is the word of God (Eph. 6:17). Christ as well as David makes conquest of the nations by force, but the force by which he conquers them is the force of his suffering and atoning love, for he said: "I, if I be lifted up from the earth, will draw all men unto myself" (John 12:32). Christ as well as David breaks the nations with a rod of iron and dashes them in pieces like a potter's vessel, so that broken up into their constituent elements they may enter the kingdom of our Lord and of his Christ (Rev. 11:15) It is the part of wisdom to submit to such beneficent rule.

Psalms 42 and 43.

These two Psalms are one in no less than forty-six Hebrew manuscripts although all the ancient versions separate them. Their original unity is seen from the progress of thought and from the occurrence of the same refrain in Ps. 42:5, 11 and 43:5. The situation is the same in both. The five verses of Ps. 43 may have been separated for liturgical purposes.

This is the first Korahite Psalm in the Psalter. It is the first of a series of seven Psalms with the inscription "of the sons of Korah" (Pss. 42-49). Four others occur later (Pss. 84, 85, 87, 88). "The Sons of Korah" was the name of one of the guilds of temple musicians which David established and which lasted for several centuries after his time (I Chron. 6:31-38; 15:6-7; 16:41-42; 25:1, 4-5; II Chron. 20:19; 29:14). Hence the inscription gives no definite clue to the date of these Psalms. Nor does internal evidence give much help. The temple and the altar were standing and the worship there was carried on (Ps. 42:4; 43:3-4). But this by itself does not decide between a time before the temple was destroyed in 586 B. C. and after it was rebuilt in 516 B. C. Psalms 46 and 48 of this group, however, give quite definite evidence of coming from the end of the eighth century. The natural inference is that the other Psalms of this group date from about the same time. While it is quite hazardous to insist on a chronological order, we would naturally expect that the first Psalm of the group would be at least as old as the later ones. On the whole the eighth century seems as likely a time as any for these seven Psalms.

There is nothing new here in the conception of God or in any doctrinal matter. It is a Psalm of individual experience. The author, although a Levite, longs to go up to worship at Jerusalem not from a narrow-minded devotion to mere externals but because he longs for communion with God. This expresses itself in the opening words: "As the hart panteth after the water brooks, so panteth my soul after thee, O God. My soul thirsteth for God, for the living God. When shall I come and appear before God?" (Ps. 42:1-2). It was God for whom he yearned. The only reason he desired to go to the temple in Jerusalem was because he believed he would find God there. In this respect we may compare David's devotion to the sanctuary as expressed in Ps. 27:4 and his spiritual devotion to God in Ps. 63:1. Psalm 84, another Korahitic Psalm which we have dated in the eighth century, resembles Psalms 42-43 at so many points that some have thought they were by the same author.

The most important contribution which this Psalm makes to the history of Israel's religion is on the ceremonial side. It shows the ceremonies of the pilgrimage to Jerusalem at the time of the annual feasts more clearly than any other passage in the Bible. The Psalmist says: "These things I remember, and pour out my soul within me, how I went with the throng, and led them to the house of God, with the voice of joy and praise, a multitude keeping holyday" (Ps. 42:4). The word rendered "keeping holyday" means "making the pilgrimage" and is used especially of the pilgrimages to Jerusalem at the national feasts (Ex. 12:14; 23:14; Lev. 23:39-41; Num. 29:12, etc.). The noun from this stem is the same which the Moslems still use for the pilgrimage to Mecca. For the ancient Israelites, as for the Moslems who derived the idea from them, making the pilgrimage included not only the journey to the holy city but all the appointed ceremonies of the feast.

The pilgrims did not make the journey separately or even by families, but in large companies as the Moslems do from Cairo and Damascus. Hence Joseph and Mary went a day's journey before they knew that the boy Jesus was not in the company and they sought him among their relatives and friends who were in the same large company (Luke 2:44). It is not known how large these companies were. Possibly all the pilgrims from a town and its suburbs went together. The journey would be the occasion of much pleasure and mirth; but when the company approached the sacred city they would form in procession, singing glad songs and probably carrying banners (Isa. 30:29). The so-called "Songs of Ascents" (Pss. 120-134) were probably used for this purpose. The author of Psalm 42 says that he remembered the time when he had the honor of leading this procession. The word rendered "led" here is found elsewhere only in Hezekiah's Psalm of thanksgiving. He said: "I shall go softly (Margin, 'as in solemn procession') all my years beecause of the bitterness of my soul" (Isa. 38:15). As Kirkpatrick says, "it seems to denote the slow and stately march of a solemn procession" (Cambridge Bible on Ps. 42:4). No doubt the Psalmist counted it one of his greatest honors that he had been chosen to lead this procession entering the holy city. It was appropriate that one of the Levitical singers should be selected for this honor, for the Levites had had this place when David brought up the ark to Jerusalem (I Chron. 16:4-6). Psalm 24 was probably composed for this occasion.

Psalm 44.

While Psalm 42-43 is individual, this Psalm is distinctly national. The nation was standing but its armies had suffered defeat and Israel had become a reproach to its neighbors (verses 9-16). The Psalmist said: "Thou hast made us like sheep appointed for food, and hast scattered us among the nations" (verse 11). The latter expression might seem to refer to the exile. Yet the remainder of the Psalm and its position with the other Psalms of this Korahitic group (Psalms 42-49), especially Psalms 46 and 48, do not favor this theory. The statement of verse 11 would be satisfied by the invasion of Gilead and Galilee by Tiglath-pileser in 734 B. C. when he carried many captives to Assyria (II Kings 15:29; cp. Isa. 9:1) or by the time that Gaza "carried away captive the whole people, to deliver them up to Edom" (Amos 1:6) or when Tyre "delivered up the whole people to Edom" (Amos 1:9), events which occurred in the eighth century. The exile is excluded as the time of the Psalm by the fact that the Psalmist declares that the catastrophe of the nation was not on account of their sin. He said: "All this is come upon us; yet have we not forgotten thee, neither have we dealt falsely in thy covenant. Our heart is not turned back, neither have our steps declined from thy way" (verses 17-18). But on the contrary the prophets and other Old Testament writers invariably represented the exile as punishment for sin (II Kings 21:10-15; 23:26-27; 24:1-4; Jer. 15:4, etc.).

There is no other time which fits the situation represented in Psalm 44 so well as that of the invasion of Judah by Sennacherib in the end of the eighth century. The Psalmist spoke of "the voice of him that reproacheth and blasphemeth, by reason of the enemy and the avenger" (verse 16). Similarly when Rabshakeh the officer of Sennacherib, defied Jerusalem, Isaiah sent this message to Hezekiah: "Thus saith Jehovah, Be not afraid of the words that thou hast heard, wherewith the servants of the king of Assyria have blasphemed me" (Isa. 37:6). When Hezekiah spread Sennacherib's defiant letter before Jehovah, he did not confess the sins of Judah but merely prayed for deliverance (Isa. 37:14-20). Isaiah also sent a message to Hezekiah saying that Sennacherib had defied and blasphemed the Holy One of Israel (Isa. 37:23-24). Altogether the attitude of Isaiah and Hezekiah was in perfect agreement with that of the author of this Psalm. There is not a verse in the Psalm which does not fit the circumstances of Hezekiah's reign at the time of Sennacherib's invasion.

This Psalm adds no new element to the religion of Israel. Everything in it is found elsewhere before or in this time. The resemblance to Psalm 60, which was written when David suffered some military reverse is specially striking. There, as here, there is no confession of sin. There, as here, victory is considered as possible only through God (Ps. 44:5; cp. Ps. 60:12). Even the language of Psalm 44 is borrowed from Psalm 60 (Ps. 44:9; cp. Ps. 60:1, 10). There are also resemblances between our Psalm and the great historical Psalm of the Asaphitic guild which we have placed in this time. Like Psalm 78 this Korahitic poet begins with recollections of Israel's early history (Ps. 44:1-3). The startling prayer of Ps. 44:23, "Awake, why sleepest thou, O Lord?" has its closest parallel in Ps. 78:65, "Then the Lord awaked as one out of sleep." Another Asaphitic Psalm of this time with resemblances to this is number 80. The Korahite speaks of Jehovah's planting Israel in the Holy Land and making them spread abroad (Ps. 44:2). So the

Asaphite sang: "Thou broughtest a vine out of Egypt: Thou didst drive out the nations, and plantedst it. Thou preparedst room before it, and it took deep root, and filled the land. The mountains were covered with the shadow of it, and the boughs thereof were like the cedars of God. It sent out its branches unto the sea, and its shoots unto the river" (Ps. 80:8-11). These affinities help to fix Psalms 44, 78 and 80 in the same time.

Psalm 45.

It is not easy to fix upon the date of this beautiful Psalm. It surely celebrates the marriage of a king of the Davidic dynasty with a foreign princess. One naturally thinks of the marriage of Solomon with Pharaoh's daughter (I Kings 3:1; II Chron. 8:11) which greatly increased the prestige of Solomon and influenced his foreign policy. Nearly all the phenomena of the Psalm may be explained on this theory. The splendor of the king is like that of Solomon. The reference to myrrh, aloes and cassia fits his time (Ps. 45:8; cp. I Kings 10:2, 10; Song 4:14, etc.). King's daughters were among his honorable women (Ps. 45:9; cp. Song 6:8). Bringing gold from Ophir was one of his accomplishments (Ps. 45:9; cp. I Kings 9:28). The presence of the daughter of Tyre, probably the daughter of the king of Tyre, at the wedding with a present would be natural, for Solomon was in alliance with Hiram the king of Tyre (Ps. 45:12; cp. I Kings 5:1-12). The objection that the king is represented as warlike while Solomon was a man of peace has considerable force. It is not that he wears his sword (Ps. 45:3), for the king might well wear his military uniform at the wedding; but that the Psalmist says: "Thine arrows are sharp. The peoples fall under thee. They are in the heart of the king's enemies" (Ps. 45:5). The prediction concerning the offspring of the marriage is also against the Solomonic date. "Instead of thy fathers shall be thy children, whom thou shalt make princes in all the earth" (Ps. 45:16). Since only David preceded Solomon in that dynasty, this reference to fathers seems unnatural in his time.

The theory that the Psalm celebrates the marriage of Ahab, king of the northern kingdom, with Jezebel, daughter of Ethbaal king of the Sidonians (I Kings 16:31), has little in its favor. It would account for the presence of the daughter of Tyre (Ps. 45:12) at the wedding. The reference to the ivory palaces (Ps. 45:8) would agree with the fact that Ahab built an ivory house (I Kings 22:39). But although it is not recorded that Solomon had such a palace, it is probable that he used some of the ivory imported in his reign (I Kings 10:22; II Chron. 9:21) to decorate his house. He certainly had a great throne of ivory (I Kings 10:18; II Chron. 9:17). It is incredible that a Psalm celebrating Ahab's marriage with wicked and idolatrous Jezebel should have found its way into the Psalter. It is even more incredible that Ahab could have been regarded as a type of the Messiah, as the king of this Psalm certainly was.

Scarcely less objectionable is the theory that the Psalm celebrates the marriage of Jehoram king of Judah with Athaliah daughter of Ahab (II Kings 8:18, 26). Although Jehoram as a descendant of David might have been a type of the Messiah, the evil results of his marriage with

Athaliah, who was no less wicked than her mother Jezebel, were so great that a Psalm celebrating this marriage would never have come into the Psalter. Equally objectionable is the identification of the king of the Psalm with a foreign monarch such as an unknown Persian king, the Egyptian Ptolemy Philadelphus or the Syrian king Alexander. All such theories are broken against the Messianic character of the Psalm.

There remains the theory that the Psalm was written at a later time in reference to Solomon's marriage with Pharaoh's daughter or in reference to the marriage of some later king of the Davidic dynasty with recollections of Solomon's splendor. In either form this theory explains the resemblances to Solomon and the differences from him. There is no later king to whom it could refer more naturally than Hezekiah. As the best king of Judah after Solomon he could well be taken as a type of the Messiah. He was much more warlike than Solomon. In his time the Psalmist could look back to several generations of Hezekiah's ancestors reigning over Judah (Ps. 45:16). The word rendered "mighty one" in Ps. 45:3 is the same which Isaiah used in one of the Messianic titles, "Mighty God" (Isa. 9:6). The position of this Psalm in a group of Korahitic Psalms (Psalms 42-49) of this time and just before the one with the strongest evidence for this date (Psalm 46) makes this the most probable theory.

The Messianic character of Psalm 45 has been recognized in all ages. The Targum paraphrases verse 2, "Thy beauty, O King Messiah exceeds that of the children of men; a spirit of prophecy is bestowed upon thy lips."

The verb rendered "anointed" in verse 7 is from the same stem as the name Messiah (cp. Ps. 2:2 and 84:9). The Epistle to the Hebrews quotes verses 6 and 7 in reference to Christ (Heb. 1:8-9). If the Messianic interpretation be accepted, the marriage of the king receives a new religious significance as symbolizing the relation between Jehovah and his people or the individual believer. This religious interpretation of the marriage of Solomon and Shulammite was the justification for the inclusion of the Song of Solomon in the canon. The marriage relation between Jehovah and Israel received new meaning from the tragic experiences of Hosea. In the New Testament this spiritual interpretation of the marriage relation is transferred to that between Christ and the church (Eph. 5:22-25; Rev. 19:7-8; 21:2; 22:17).

This typical interpretation of the Psalm gives it a new and glorious meaning. The apostrophe to the king "Thou art fairer than the children of men" (verse 2) looks forward to him who to the believer is "the chiefest among ten thousand" and "altogether lovely" (Song 5:10, 16). The grace which was poured into the lips of the king (verse 2) looked forward to the words of grace which proceeded out of the mouth of Christ (Luke 4:22). If the Davidic king could be addressed as "mighty one" (verse 3), much more could he whom Isaiah called "Mighty God" (Isa. 9:6). If the majesty of the king impressed the Psalmist, much more may we be impressed by the majesty of the King of Kings. If the king could be addressed as God because he reigned in God's stead (verse 6), much more could Christ. If even the Davidic king remembering the promise to David (II Sam. 7:13,

16) regarded his throne as eternal (verse 6), much more is the throne of Christ (Isa. 9:7; Luke 1:33; II Peter 1:11). If God anointed the king of Judah with the oil of gladness above his fellows because he loved righteousness and hated wickedness (verse 7), much more is Christ anointed with joy and filled with joy (John 15:11; Heb. 12:2). The exhortation to the bride to forget her own people and her father's house, "So will the king desire thy beauty, for he is thy lord; and reverence thou him" (verses 10-11), has its final fulfilment in our Lord's words, "He that loveth father or mother more than me is not worthy of me; and he that loveth son or daughter more than me is not worthy of me" (Matt. 10:37). Throughout this Psalm we are forced to confess that a greater than Solomon (Matt. 12:42) or Hezekiah is here. The inspired poet looked far beyond Hezekiah when in God's name he proclaimed: "I will make thy name to be remembered in all generations. Therefore shall the peoples give thee thanks forever and ever" (verse 17).

Psalm 46.

Very few Psalms contain such clear evidences of their occasion and date as this. With a probability which approaches certainty it was composed soon after the army of Sennacherib withdrew from Jerusalem in 701 B. C. The refrain which occurs twice in the Psalm (verses 7 and 11) is closely related to the name Immanuel which Isaiah gave to the Messiah in the reign of Ahaz as a sign of the approaching Assyrian invasion (Isa. 7:14-17; 8:8, 10). Immanuel means "God is with us." The Psalmist uses the same expression except for the last syllable when he exclaims "Jehovah of hosts is with us." Like Isaiah he compares the Assyrian invasion to a flood (Ps. 46:3; cp. Isa. 8:7-8; 17:12) and the sure confidence of Jerusalem to the gentle stream which flowed from the Virgin's spring to the pool of Siloam. Isaiah called it "the waters of Shiloah that go softly" (Isa. 8:6). The Psalmist referred to it as "a river, the streams whereof make glad the city of God, the holy place of the tabernacles of the Most High" (verse 4), because the tunnel for the water went under part of the temple enclosure. In the reign of Ahaz this stream had not been brought within the city. Ahaz went out to inspect it "at the end of the conduit of the upper pool" (Isa. 7:3; cp. II Kings 18:17; Isa. 36:2), when the city was threatened with a siege by Syria and Samaria. It was one of Hezekiah's greatest works that "he made the pool, and the conduit, and brought water into the city" (II Kings 20:20). It was near the southern end of this conduit that the Siloam inscription was discovered in 1880. The fact that the Psalmist represents the stream as making glad the holy place of the tabernacles of the Most High is one of the evidences that he wrote after Hezekiah built the conduit under the temple enclosure. Like Isaiah he contrasts the two streams, the one angry and hostile, the other gentle and gracious, making the contrast more striking by omitting the refrain between verses 3 and 4 where the structure of the Psalm seems to require it.

While Isaiah reproved the people for refusing the gracious stream and told them that because of this refusal the Lord would bring up upon them the overflowing flood (Isa. 8:6-8), the Psalmist refers to the flood of the Assy-

rian invasion only to turn from it to the gracious stream
which suggests the coming peace. Jehovah had indeed
allowed the nations to rage, the kingdoms to be moved
(verse 6). He made desolations in the earth by the Assyrian invasion (verse 8). But in reference to the de-
parture of the Assyrian army, the Psalmist said: "He
maketh wars to cease unto the end of the earth. He
breaketh the bow, and cutteth the spear in sunder. He
burneth the chariot in the fire" (verse 9). This emphasis
on peace is prominent in the writings of Isaiah (Isa.
2:4; 9:5-7) and Micah (Mic. 4:3-4). Clearly this Psalm
was written when the withdrawal of the Assyrian army
from the Holy City was fresh in mind. Isaiah foretold
that the city would not fall and it came about as he said
(Isa. 37:33-38).

The contribution of this Psalm to the religion of Israel
is not apparent on the face of it. Yet like all spiritual
things it cannot be measured. It is the great Psalm of
faith. The words faith, believe, trust, confidence do
not occur in it, as God is not mentioned in the book of
Esther. Yet as God though unmentioned is the central
figure of the story of Esther, so faith in God though
unmentioned is the moving principle of this great Psalm.
It is faith in exercise, not reasoned about but practised.
The Psalmist does not say, "I believe," but he believes.
His contribution to the religion of Israel and indeed to
the religion of all ages by his act of faith cannot be
measured.

We should expect to find faith prominent in the Psalms
of this period because Isaiah was the great prophet of
faith (Isa. 7:9; 26:3; 28:16; 30:15; 32:17). Faith had

an important place in David's Psalms (Ps. 11:1; 13:5; 16:1; 18:2; 22:4-5, etc.). It is also found in other eighth-century Psalms besides the one before us (Ps. 2:12; 44:4-8; 48:3; 49:15; 84:12). But no other Psalm of this or any other period equals or exceeds Psalm 46 in its deep undertone of faith. The Psalmist strikes the keynote in the first verse. Speaking for Israel he declares: "God for us is a refuge and strength." Not only is he a shelter from all foes (Isa. 4:6; 25:4) but the strength by which all foes may be conquered (Ps. 84:5). The last part of the verse may be translated literally "a help in distresses he has let himself be found exceedingly" or somewhat more freely "an exceedingly accessible help in trouble." To those who have faith he is a help which is always accessible, easy to find. He does not refuse help to his people but lets himself be found. Isaiah and the faithful in Jerusalem found this true when the city was threatened by Sennacherib. Having had this experience the Psalmist proclaims: "Therefore will we not fear, though the earth do change, and though the mountains be shaken into the heart of the seas; though the waters thereof roar and be troubled, though the mountains tremble with the swelling thereof." These figures represent violent military and political convulsions. No such violent external changes can shake the faith of the nation or the individual who has found in God an accessible help. Fear is the foe of faith. It cannot exist when faith is present (Ps. 23:4; 27:1). Ahaz and his people trembled with fear because they lacked faith in God (Isa. 7:2). Isaiah was not afraid because he had faith in God (Isaiah 7:4).

The earthly symbol of God's presence in Jerusalem was not a mighty river; but the little trickling stream which flowed to the pool of Siloam. To faithless eyes it seemed as nothing compared with the flood of the Assyrian invasion. It went softly (Isa. 8:6). It was like the "still small voice" (Margin, "sound of gentle stillness") in which Elijah recognized God rather than in the wind, earthquake or fire (I Kings 19:11-13). Yet God manifested Himself in that little stream so that to the Psalmist it seemed a river and to Isaiah's faith it would become a mighty river, as though the Euphrates and the Nile were rolled into one (Isa. 33:21). By that symbol God was in the midst of the city. Therefore the city would not be moved even by a flood vastly greater than the Assyrian invasion. The last part of verse 5 is translated literally "at the turning of the morning." It refers to the morning when the people looked on the camp of the Assyrians. Where there had been a mighty army, "behold, these were all dead bodies" (Isa. 37:36). So will God help his people in every time of trouble.

Verse 6 by its brief staccato movement emphasizes the agitation of nations in commotion. Literally rendered it is, "Nations raged. Kingdoms moved. He gave his voice. Earth melts." The raging of the nations reminds us of Ps. 2:1-3, although a different word is used. In contrast to Jerusalem which shall not be moved because God is in the midst of her, Gentile kingdoms will be moved and when God speaks even the solid earth will melt. It is like Nebuchadnezzar's dream of a human image representing by its parts successive empires, Babylonian, Medo-Persian, Greek and Roman. A stone representing the kingdom of God will break the image in pieces and become a great mountain filling the whole earth (Dan. 2:31-35). The kingdom of God "shall break in pieces and consume all these kingdoms, and it shall stand forever" (Dan. 2:44). The Psalmist does not mention the kingdom of God; but in the light of prophecy and subsequent history we may see in the statement that the earth melts at the voice of God a hint of the melting of the nations into the kingdom of God (Rev. 11:15; cp. Ps. 2:8-9).

In the refrain the Psalmist uses the great title Jehovah of hosts, a favorite title of Isaiah which the prophet uses more than sixty times (Isa. 1:9, 24; 2:12, etc.). If such a God is with his people they need not fear their enemies but can say as Elisha did: "They that are with us are more that they that are with them" (II Kings 6:16). The title "God of Jacob" suggests his providential care for the patriarch (Ps. 20:1; 81:1, 4; 84:8, etc.). It is echoed in the exclamation of the post-exilic Psalmist, "Happy is he that hath the God of Jacob for his help" (Ps. 146:5). The word for refuge in verses 7 and 11 is not the same as that in the first verse. It means a secure height or retreat and occurs again in Ps. 48:3. This meaning comes out well in Isa. 33:16 where it is rendered "place of defence." The prophet says of the righteous man "He shall dwell on high; his place of defence shall be the munitions of rocks." Such a place of defence is the God of Jacob to those who trust Him. A similar idea but a different word occurs in Prov. 18:10 "The name of Jehovah is a strong tower. The righteous runneth into it and is safe (Margin, 'is set on high')."

In verses 8-10 the Psalmist invites the nations to look upon the works of God, how he desolates the earth with war and then brings war to an end, so that they may learn to desist from their vain attempt to oppose his Almighty will. Here God is represented as breaking the bow (verse 9) while in Psalm 76 which dates from the same time he breaks the arrows of the bow (Ps. 76:3). The verb rendered "be still" means to relax, do nothing, be quiet. It is rendered stay in I Sam. 15:16. So long as the nations continue to oppose Jehovah, they cannot know that He is God; but if they will give up the fight, surrender to Him, they will recognize His divine nature and know that he will be exalted among the nations, exalted in the earth.

The impulse to faith which this Psalm has given is well illustrated from the life of Martin Luther. In times of despondency he would say to Melancthon: "Come, Philip, let us sing the 46th Psalm." His great hymn which is based upon verses 1-3 breathes the same undaunted faith and courage in the presence of foes which characterized the Psalmist.

> "A mighty fortress is our God,
>   A bulwark never failing,
> Our Helper He amid the flood,
>   Of mortal ills prevailing:
> For still our ancient foe
> Doth seek to work us woe;
> His craft and power are great,
> And armed with cruel hate,
> On earth is not his equal."

Psalm 47.

This Psalm was evidently written to commemorate a victory over the foes of Israel who are regarded as the foes of God. Although it contains no such clear evidences of its occasion as Psalms 46 and 48, its position between them makes it probable that it came from the same time. In general the representation is the same, although less detailed. Jehovah is called Most High as in Ps. 46:4 as well as in Ps. 50:14; 78:17, 35, 56 which date from this time. He is terrible as in Ps. 66:3, 5; 68:35 which are also of this period. Rabshakeh arrogantly called Sennacherib the great king (Isa. 36:4). This title is rightfully applied to Jehovah in Ps. 47:2 and 48:2. God is represented as going up to heaven after his victory (verse 5) as in Ps. 68:18, a contemporary Psalm. The same Hebrew word which is rendered four times "sing praises" in Ps. 47:6 is found in Ps. 66:2, 4; 68:4, 32; 75:9 in Psalms of this time. The bold expression, "the princes of the peoples are gathered together to be the people of the God of Abraham" (Ps. 47:9), has its closest Old Testament parallel in the prediction of Isaiah that Jehovah will say: "Blessed be Egypt my people, and Assyria the work of my hands, and Israel mine inheritance" (Isa. 19:25). Nowhere else are Gentile nations called God's people. In general this Psalm deals with the effect produced upon other peoples by Jehovah's victory. This is exactly the thing for which Hezekiah prayed when he spread the blasphemous letter of Sennacherib before Jehovah. "Now therefore, O Jehovah, our God, save us from his hand, that all the kingdoms of the earth may know that thou art Jehovah, even thou only" (Isa. 37:20).

While Psalm 46 is the triumphant expression of Israel's faith in God as stimulated by the deliverance of Jerusalem from the menace of the Assyrian army, Psalm 47 presents Jehovah as the King over all the earth. In this sense it may be regarded as an expansion of the exhortation of Ps. 46:10 to the Gentile nations to desist from their vain opposition and surrender to Jehovah, learning thereby that he is God. In this Psalm Jehovah is exalted among the nations, exalted in the earth (Ps. 46:10). Its exalted monotheism, its sense of the universal sway of Jehovah corresponds to that of the eighth-century prophets. All nations are invited to acknowledge Jehovah as their king. In token of their joyful allegiance they are to clap their hands as the people of Jerusalem did when Jehoiada brought out the boy Joash, the heir to the throne, from his long hiding and put the crown upon his head (II Kings 11:12). They are to shout for joy as the people did when Samuel presented Saul to them as their king (I Sam. 10:24; cp. Num. 23:21).

The representation is like that of Isaiah of the coronation feast which Jehovah makes in Jerusalem for all peoples (Isa. 25:6). The God who has subdued Sennacherib, the greatest conqueror of his time, is no mere national deity. He and not Sennacherib is the "great King" (Ps. 47:2; cp. Isa. 36:4). Sennacherib was king only of southwestern Asia, but Jehovah is King over all the earth. While he subdues Gentile peoples to the people of God (verse 3), he chooses for Israel their promised inheritance (verse 4). Having come down from heaven to fight for Israel against the Assyrians, he goes up again when the victory is won with a glad shout and the sound of a trumpet (verse 5).

In verse 6 the Psalmist again addresses the nations, inviting them to praise God, the King of Israel. The verb translated "sing praises" is from the stem in the noun for Psalm which is common in the inscriptions. It denotes instrumental rather than vocal music and may be rendered "make melody." The word rendered "understanding" in verse 7 is Maschil which is found in the inscriptions of thirteen Psalms (32, 42, 44, 45, 78, etc.). From its etymology it means a contemplative Psalm but in what sense we do not know. The marginal reading "in a skilful psalm" is better than the text. God has taken his seat upon his royal throne and begun to reign over the nations (verse 8). The inspired poet sees an assembly of the princes of the Gentiles at Jerusalem to become the people of the God of Abraham (verse 9). This title "the God of Abraham" probably refers to the covenant which God made with the patriarch to multiply his seed and give them the holy land (Gen. 26:24; 28:13). Since in Abraham and his seed all the families of the earth are to be blest (Gen. 12:3; 22:18; 26:4; 28:14), it is appropriate that the princes of the peoples should become the people of the God of Abraham (Ps. 72:11; Isa. 49:7). The term "shields of the earth" which is used synonymously with princes in verse 9 is a symbolic designation for rulers as the proper protection of their people. Thus an exilic Psalmist sang: "Our shield belongeth unto Jehovah; and our king to the Holy One of Israel" (Ps. 89:18). The word is translated "rulers" in the text of Hos. 4:18 but more literally "shields" in the margin. The rulers of the earth belong to God. The Psalm closes with a thought similar to that of Ps. 46:10 although a different Hebrew word is used. Greatly is Jehovah exalted.

Psalm 48.

The indications that this Psalm was written when the Assyrian army withdrew and Jerusalem was saved in 701 B. C. are almost as strong as in the case of the 46th Psalm. This is the situation reflected especially in verses 4-6. "For, lo, the kings assembled themselves. They passed by together. They saw it, then were they amazed. They were dismayed, they hasted away. Trembling took hold of them there, pain, as of a woman in travail." The city was not actually besieged although many smaller places were taken and it looked certain that Jerusalem would fall. Sennacherib sent a messenger to demand its surrender. Hezekiah spread the letter before Jehovah and prayed for deliverance. Isaiah came to him with the assurance from Jehovah. "Therefore thus saith Jehovah concerning the king of Assyria. He shall not come unto this city, nor shoot an arrow there, neither shall he come before it with shield, nor cast up a mound against it. By the way that he came, by the same shall he return, and he shall not come unto this city, saith Jehovah. For I will defend this city to save it, for mine own sake, and for my servant David's sake" (Isa. 37:33-35). A pestilence decimated the Assyrian army. Sennacherib unable to proceed against Egypt, as he had intended, returned to Nineveh. Thus Jerusalem was saved. It is objected that the Psalmist speaks of kings assembling and looking upon Jerusalem while Sennacherib was the only king concerned. It should be remembered, however, that this is the language of poetry. If the plural is pressed, it may be suggested that they were probably petty kings subject to Sennacherib. This suggestion is in line with the statement of the king of Assyria: "Are not my princes all of them kings?" (Isa. 10:8).

A remarkable parallel to Psalm 48 is the prophecy of Isa. 33:18-20 of the time of Sennacherib's invasion. "Thy heart shall muse on the terror: Where is he that counted, where is he that weighed the tribute? where is he that counted the towers? Thou shalt not see the fierce people, a people of a deep speech that thou canst not comprehend, of a strange tongue that thou canst not understand. Look upon Zion, the city of our solemnites: thine eyes shall see Jerusalem a quiet habitation, a tent that shall not be removed, the stakes whereof shall never be plucked up, neither shall any of the cords thereof be broken." This corresponds to Ps. 48:4-6 and gives special significance to verses 12-14. Assyrian officers had counted the towers of Jerusalem to see how strong it was and how large an army would be required to take it. After the city was spared the Psalmist invited his hearers to inspect the city for quite another purpose, "Walk about Zion, and go round about her; number the towers thereof. Mark ye well her bulwarks; consider her palaces, that ye may tell it to the generation following, for this God is our God, forever and ever; he will be our guide even unto death" (Ps. 48:12-14).

There are also several linguistic similarites between this Psalm and other writings of the time of Isaiah which confirm the argument. Verses 1 and 8 call Jerusalem "the city of our God" while in Ps. 46:4 it is called "the city of God." Verse 2 says that Mount Zion is "beautiful in elevation" and in Ps. 50:2 it is called "the perfection of beauty." The word for joy in verse 2 occurs nowhere else in the Psalms; but 10 of its 17 occurrences in the Old Testament are in the book of Isaiah. The expression "sides of the north" occurs elsewhere only in Isa. 14:13; Ezek. 38:6, 15 and 39:2. The word for city in this verse occurs only here in the book of Psalms but 10 of its 28 occurrences are in Isaiah. God is called the great King here and in Ps. 47:2 (cp. Isa. 36:4). God is called a refuge in Ps. 48:3 with the same Hebrew word as in Ps. 46:7. The only other place in the Psalms where the word for trembling in Ps. 48:6 occurs is Ps. 2:11. The title "Jehovah of hosts" in Ps. 48:8 is specially frequent in Isaiah and occurs in the refrain in Ps. 46:7 and 11. In verse 10 the Psalmist says "Thy right hand is full of righteousness" and in Isa. 41:10 Jehovah speaks of the right hand of his righteousness. Surely these parallels together with the other indications make the date of this Psalm reasonably sure.

No other Psalm equals this as an expression of the rejoicing of Israel in Jerusalem. Yet their rejoicing in the holy city is not in its location, its palaces, its towers or its bulwarks for their own sake but in Jehovah whose capital it is. It is the city of our God (verses 1 and 8), the city of the great King (verse 2). The high tower of the city is in reality God Himself (verse 3). It is

He who will establish it forever (verse 8). It is the lovingkindness of God in delivering the city on which Israel meditates (verse 9). It is because of God's judgments that Mount Zion is glad (verse 11). The real reason for walking about Zion, numbering its towers, marking well its bulwarks, considering its palaces and telling the results of the inspection to the next generation is because "this God is our God forever and ever. He will be our guide even unto death" (verses 12-14). This Psalm did not come from the heart of a materialist who rejoiced only in physical things but from the inspired mind of a true worshipper of God who saw Him in the towers and bulwarks of the city as well as in the signal deliverance of the city from its most powerful foe.

It should be noted that the temple does not have a prominent place in Psalm 48 as it does in most of the Zion Psalms. In Psalm 24, which was probably written for use when David brought the ark to Jerusalem, the temple is not mentioned because it was not yet built. Yet if this theory of its origin is correct, it was the religious rather than the political aspect of the city that was prominent. In Psalm 84, whch probably dated from the eighth century, the temple is the chief thing throughout. In Psalm 122, which was probably post-exilic, the house of Jehovah is mentioned in the first verse; but the remainder of the Psalm has a political rather than a religious tone. Another post-exilic Psalm (125) refers to the divine protection of the people of God as like that of the mountains around Jerusalem. In Ps. 5:7 and 138:2 prayer toward the temple is spoken of (cp. I Kings 8:30, 35, 38, 42, 44, 48; Dan. 6:10; Jon. 2:4).

In Psalm 48, on the other hand, as is natural from its occasion, the prominent things are the towers, bulwarks and palaces of the city. Yet the Psalmist says: "We have thought of thy lovingkindness, O God, in the midst of thy temple" (verse 9). It is the temple and God's presence in it which makes Jerusalem the city of our God, the city of the great King. The temple is his palace from which he rules the city. Hence the distinction between sacred and secular, between church and state, so familiar in modern thought, cannot be thought of. The whole city is holy. The high-priest is no more a religious officer than the king. Everything in Jerusalem is related to God and therefore holy. It is in this broad sense that we should understand the exclamation, "Great is Jehovah, and greatly to be praised, in the city of our God, in his holy mountain."

Psalm 49.

This is the last of the series of seven Korahitic Psalms (42-49), numbers 42 and 43 being counted as one. Its date is much more conjectural than that of Psalms 46 and 48. Yet the most likely date was in the latter part of the eighth century. It may be called a problem Psalm dealing with wealth, its vanity and transitoriness. The time of Isaiah was one when such problems were engaging the thought particularly of a class of thinkers called the wise. Isaiah speaks of the wise (Isa. 19:12; 29:14; 44:25). Solomon was the author of the oldest book of wisdom. The book of Job which we have dated in the reign of Manasseh, contemporary with Isa. 40-55, was a problem book dealing with the sufferings of the righteous. Not only is Psalm 49 the same kind of writing as Job but it has certain resemblances to it. Ps. 49:6 speaks of those "that trust in their wealth and boast themselves in the multitude of their riches." Job declares that if he were such a man he would be guilty (Job. 31:24-25). The Psalmist says that the beauty of the wicked shall be for Sheol to consume (49:14) and Job says: "Drought and heat consume the snow waters: So doth Sheol those that have sinned" (Job 24:19). The natural inference is that the Psalm dated from a time not far from that of Job.

There are a few other indications of the same time. There is a certain resemblance between the first verse of the Psalm and the beginning of the prophecy of Micah. The Psalmist says: "Hear this, all ye peoples. Give ear, all ye inhabitants of the world," while Micah says: "Hear, ye peoples, all of you; hearken, O earth, and all that therein is" (Mic. 1:2). Psalm 47, which is from this time is also addressed to all peoples (Ps. 47:1). The Psalmist speaks of the rich and poor together (verse 2). The extremes of wealth and poverty were characteristic of the reigns of Uzziah and Jotham in Judah. Verse 11 seems to refer to the large landed estates of the rich. "Their inward thought is that their houses shall continue forever, and their dwelling-places to all generations. They call their lands after their own names." Such large estates existed in Isaiah's time, for he said: "Woe unto them that join house to house, that lay field to field till there be no room" (Isa. 5:8). Micah also said: "They covet fields, and seize them; and houses, and take them away" (Mic. 2:2). It cannot be claimed that the date of this Psalm is at all sure. Yet all things considered, the eighth century, somewhat earlier than Psalms 46-48, seems the most likely time for it.

The most important element in this Psalm for the history of religion relates to the future life. Speaking of the rich it says: "None of them can by any means redeem his brother, nor give to God a ransom for him—that he should still live alway, that he should not see corruption. For he shall see it. Wise men die. The fool and the brutish alike perish" (Ps. 49:7, 9-10). This idea that all must die was not new. But a few verses later the Psalmist says of the wicked rich: "They are appointed as a flock for Sheol. Death shall be their shepherd, and the upright shall have dominion over them in the morning" (Verse 14). Most commentators think that the morning here referred to is not the morning of the resurrection but the morning of the day here on earth when the righteous shall triumph over the wicked. This interpretation is possible but seems unnatural. It is a morning after the death of the wicked. It is more natural therefore to see in it the faint foreshadowing of the morning of the resurrection when the righteous shall be rewarded and the wicked condemned.

This is made probable from the next verse, "God will redeem my soul from the power of Sheol, for he will receive me" (Ps. 49:15). The redemption from the power of Sheol taken by itself might be preventing him from dying or bringing him back from Sheol after he died. In the former case it would correspond to David's statement, "Thou wilt not leave my soul to Sheol; neither wilt thou suffer thy holy one to see corruption" (Ps.

16:10). The next clause, however, decides for the latter meaning. The verb rendered receive is the common one to take and is used elsewhere of God taking a person out of this world. Here it probably refers to the statement concerning Enoch that "he was not, for God took him" (Gen. 5:24). The same word is used of the passage to the future life in Ps. 73:24 "Thou wilt guide me with thy counsel, and afterward receive me to glory." So when the Psalmist says that God will take him he refers to his death. Hence the redeeming from the power of Sheol cannot be preventing him from dying but must be raising him from the dead. The morning of the previous verse also must agreeably to the context be the resurrection morning. It is not surprising that the resurrection should be spoken of in an eighth-century Psalm since Hosea had foreshadowed it by the resurrection of the nation from the exile (Hos. 6:2; 13:14) and Isaiah foretold it more clearly than any earlier writer (Isa. 25:8; 26:19). The Psalmist in his brief references falls far short of these great passages.

Psalm 50.

This is the first "Psalm of Asaph" according to the inscription and indeed the only one in the second book of the Psalter. From this fact we might expect it to be the oldest Asaphitic Psalm and perhaps written by Asaph himself who was a prominent leader of sacred music in David's time (I Chron. 15:16-19; 16:4-7). Indeed it may be the oldest Asaphitic Psalm, although Psalms 75, 76, 78 and 80 with ascription to Asaph probably date from about the same time. But it can scarcely have been written by Asaph himself. Some of the Psalms with this heading date from a much later time. (Ps. 74:3, 7; 79:1). The sons of Asaph succeeded him in the musical service (I Chron. 25:1-9) and the title "sons of Asaph" became the name of one of the guilds of temple musicians which was in existence in the time of Hezekiah (II Chron. 29:13) as well as after the exile (Ezra. 2:41; Neh. 7:44). It is probable that the name Asaph in the inscriptions of the Psalms did not refer to the man of David's time but to the guild of which he was the founder. If so these headings give no more evidence for the date of the Psalms than do those to the sons of Korah.

The indications of date in Psalm 50 are not very definite. It is very improbable that it came from Asaph himself. The formal ceremonialism which it condemns was not characteristic of his age. The strongest evidences of date come from the resemblance of its idea of sacrifice to that of the eighth-century prophets (Ps. 50:8-14; cp. Am. 5:21-25; Hos. 6:6; 14:2; Isa. 1:11-17; Mic. 6:6-8) and in particular the rather close correspondence between the arrangement of the ideas in the Psalm and in the first chapter of Isaiah. In both the heavens and the earth are summoned to witness Jehovah's controversy with his people (Ps. 50:4; cp. Isa. 1:2). In both sacrifices are condemned because they were accompanied by unrepented sin (Ps. 50:8-14; cp. Isa. 1:11-17). In both condemnation of individual sins follows (Ps. 50:17-21; cp. Isa. 1:16-23). While these resemblances do not necessarily indicate a date contemporaneous with Isaiah, they make such a theory reasonable.

There are also a few other phenomena of the Psalm which look in the same direction. The reference to Zion as "the perfection of beauty" (Ps. 50:2) reminds us of Ps. 48:2, "Beautiful in elevation, the joy of the whole earth is Mount Zion." Looking back to Ps. 50:2 and Ps. 48:2 Jeremiah said: "Is this the city that men called the perfection of beauty, the joy of the whole earth?" (Lam. 2:15). The picture fits Jerusalem in the eighth century before Christ. The rare word rendered "shined forth" in Ps. 50:2 is found also in Psalm 80 (verse 1) which probably dates from that time. The word for folds in Ps. 50:9 occurs again in the Psalter only in Ps. 78:70. The word for wild beasts in verse 11 occurs only three times in the Old Testament, the other two being from the eighth century (Ps. 80:13; Isa. 66:11). In the latter place it is translated abundance. Paying vows to God is enjoined in Ps. 50:14 and Ps. 76:11. All things considered, there is no other time in which Psalm 50 fits so well as the eighth century.

The most important contribution to the history of religion in this majestic Psalm is in its lofty conception of sacrifice. The Psalmist does not condemn sacrifice as such. He recognizes God's saints as those who made a covenant with Him by sacrifice (verse 5). God says through the Psalmist to his people: "I will not reprove thee for thy sacrifices, and thy burnt-offerings are continually before me" (verse 8). But he adds: "I will take no bullock out of thy house, nor he-goats out of thy folds. For every beast of the forest is mine, and the cattle upon a thousand hills. I know all the birds of the mountains; and the wild beasts of the field are mine."

If I were hungry, I would not tell thee, for the world is mine and the fulness thereof. Will I eat the flesh of bulls or drink the blood of goats? Offer unto God the sacrifice of thanksgiving, and pay thy vows unto the Most High. And call upon me in the day of trouble. I will deliver thee, and thou shalt glorify me" (verses 9-15). This great passage is in the true spirit of Samuel's epoch-making words, "Behold to obey is better than sacrifice, and to hearken than the fat of rams" (I Sam. 15:22). David had learned this lesson from Samuel (Ps. 40:6-8; 51:16-7) and it echoes through the writings of the eighth-century prophets (Am. 5:21-25; Hos. 6:6; 14:2; Isa. 1:11-17; Mic. 6:6-8). The idea that in offering sacrifices to God we are but giving back to Him that which is His own is unique. The Psalmist strikes especially at the gross conception that sacrifice satisfies the hunger of God. Therefore it was called the bread of God (Lev. 21:6, 8, 17, 21, etc.).

The reason the sacrifices were not acceptable was that they were not the sincere expression of repentant hearts. The offerers were not sorry for their sins and had no intention of turning away from them. The Psalmist speaking in God's name lays bare their guilt, "When thou sawest a thief, thou consentedst with him, and hast been partaker with adulterers. Thou givest thy mouth to evil, and thy tongue frameth deceit. Thou sittest and speakest against thy brother. Thou slanderest thine own mother's son. These things hast thou done and I kept silence. Thou thoughtest that I was altogether such a one as thyself; but I will reprove thee, and set them in order before thine eyes" (verses 18-21).

There is a very striking expression in the last verse quoted. Literally it is "Thou didst compare the being of I Am to thyself" or "Thou thoughtest that I Am was like thee." There is a clear reference to the name of Himself which God gave to Moses. "God said unto Moses, I Am that I Am; and he said, Thus shalt thou say unto the children of Israel, I Am hath sent me unto you" (Ex. 3:14). Speaking in the first person God called Himself I Am. In the mouth of a man it would be in the third person, He Is, which is the translation of the covenant name Jehovah (see pp. 46-48). The wicked people of the Psalmist's time imagined that Jehovah was but a great man with all a man's evil passions, all a man's selfishness. They had no appreciation of his infinite power and wisdom, no sense of his moral attributes. They thought they could please Him by their sacrifices without giving up their wicked ways. They forgot God (verse 22) and especially his justice which might tear them in pieces for their sins. Yet his last words are not words of doom for the wicked but of encouragement for the righteous. "Whoso offereth the sacrifice of thanksgiving glorifieth me, and to him that ordereth his way aright will I show the salvation of God" (verse 23).

Psalm 66.

The date of this anonymous Psalm is uncertain. Verses 9-12 seem to refer to some great crisis through which God had brought his people safely. "Who holdeth our soul in life, and suffereth not our feet to be moved For thou, O God, hast proved us. Thou hast tried us, as silver is tried. Thou broughtest us into the net. Thou layedst a sore burden upon our loins. Thou didst cause men to ride over our heads. We went through fire and through water; but thou broughtest us out into a wealthy place." This crisis occurred while the temple was standing and the sacrifices offered (Ps. 66:13-15). Hence it cannot refer to the exile. Furthermore the description fits a brief crisis rather than such a long misfortune as the exile. There is no other known experience of the nation which fits the description so well as Sennacherib's invasion which ended so abruptly in 701 B. C. It was a terrible trial for Judah. They felt that God had brought them into a net. With a different figure Sennacherib said that he shut up king Hezekiah like a bird in a cage. They felt that God had caused men to ride over their heads, for the Assyrian army captured many towns in Judah and took a large amount of booty. They felt that they had gone through fire and through water; yet suddenly God brought them out into a wealthy place, when the Assyrian army withdrew. The description corresponds to the situation in Isa. 36-37, especially the account of the deliverance in Isa. 37:33-38. It also corresponds to the references to the deliverance in Ps. 46:8-9; 47:3, 5; 48:4-6; 76:3, 5-6; Isa. 33:18-20.

While in the first part of the Psalm the author uses the first person plural as though speaking for the nation, in verses 13-20 an individual speaks. Some have thought that these verses originally constituted a separate Psalm. But this change from the plural to the singular or vice versa is common in the Psalter (Psalms 44, 60, 71, 74, 118). Possibly it is the nation who speaks in Ps. 66:13-

20 as in Ps. 129:1-3. A more likely suggestion, however,
is that here the Psalmist speaks in the name of Hezekiah.
These verses might well be the expression of Hezekiah's
gratitude for his recovery from sickness, which is told
in connection with the invasion of Sennacherib in II
Kings 20 and in Isa. 38. Ps. 66:16 would be appropriate
in Hezekiah's mouth "Come, and hear, all ye that fear
God, and I will declare what he hath done for my soul."
The soul was the seat of life. God had saved his soul
from death. Verse 18 ("If I regard iniquity in my heart,
the Lord will not hear") agrees admirably with Hezekiah's prayer, "Remember now, O Jehovah, I beseech
thee, how I have walked before thee in truth and with a
perfect heart, and have done that which is good in the
sight" (Isa. 38:3).

   In addition to these more definite signs of the occasion of this Psalm, there are a few linguistic parallels
with writings of this time. The word rendered "make
a joyful noise" in Ps. 66:1 is identical with that rendered
shout in Ps. 47:1. Here all the earth is invited to shout
for joy unto God while there all the peoples. The word
which is rendered "sing forth" in Ps. 66:2 occurs four
times in Ps. 47:6 and once in 47:7 and is translated
"sing praises." In Ps. 66:3, 5 the works of God are
said to be terrible and in Ps. 47:2 God himself is terrible.
In Ps. 66:5 we read "Come and see the works of God"
and in Ps. 46:8 "Come, behold the works of Jehovah."
Ps. 66:10 ("Thou, O God, hast proved us. Thou hast
tried us as silver is tried") has a certain resemblance to
Job 23:10 ("When he hath tried me, I shall come forth
as gold"). The idea that God will not hear the prayer

of the impenitent sinner (Ps. 66:18) is found also in Job 27:8-9 and Isa. 1:15. These parallels with eighth-century writings confirm the impression that the Psalm comes from that time.

There is nothing specially new in this Psalm. Its universalism is like that of Psalm 47. Ps. 66:4 says "All the earth shall worship thee, and shall sing unto thee. They shall sing to thy name." So in Ps. 47:9, "the princes of the peoples are gathered together to be the people of the God of Abraham." In both Psalms this result is represented as coming from the proclamation of the deliverance which God has wrought for Israel. This is in line with Hezekiah's prayer for deliverance from Sennacherib "Now therefore O Jehovah our God, save us from his hand, that all the kingdoms of the earth may know that thou art Jehovah, even thou only" (Isa. 37:20). Salvation here is political rather than religious. Yet it tended to the increase of faith among the people of Judah and the knowledge of it among other peoples gave them a new sense of the greatness, the uniqueness of Jehovah, the God of Israel.

Psalm 67.

This anonymous Psalm contains very little indication of its occasion or date. Its joyful tone is like that of the previous Psalm. Its universalism also and in particular the idea in verses 1 and 2 that if God shows his mercy and blessing to Israel, it will result in the knowledge of God coming to all other nations, are similar to Psalms 47 and 66 (cp. Isa. 37:20). The only historical reference is to an abundant harvest (verse 6) and even that is otherwise unknown. The expression "cause his face to shine upon us" (verse 1) resembles one which occurs three times in Psalm 80, "Cause thy face to shine, and we shall be saved" (Ps. 80:3, 7, 19). In both Psalms it is evidently suggested by the priestly benediction of Num. 6:26. Verses 3 and 5, "Let the peoples praise thee, O God; let all the peoples praise thee," resemble Ps. 66:4, "All the earth shall worship thee, and shall sing unto thee. They shall sing to thy name," although the words are quite different. The words of verse 4, "Thou wilt judge the peoples with equity, and govern (Margin, 'lead') the nations upon earth," convey in different words a similar idea to Ps. 47:8, "God reigneth over the nations. God sitteth upon his holy throne." So scant and doubtful are these marks that the date of this Psalm is very uncertain. We cannot say more than that no other time fits it better than the eighth century and no other quite so well. We would scarcely dare to say even this if it did not stand in the Psalter directly after a Psalm with much clearer marks of its time.

This beautiful little Psalm draws its inspiration from the priestly blessing of Num. 6:24-26. "Jehovah, bless thee, and keep thee. Jehovah make his face to shine upon thee, and be gracious unto thee. Jehovah lift up his countenance upon thee, and give thee peace." The word in Ps. 67:1 rendered "be merciful unto us" is the same which in the blessing is translated "be gracious unto thee." The verb to bless in verses 1, 6 and 7 is the same as that in Numbers. The expression "cause his face to shine upon us" is the same as that in the second part of the threefold blessing. Beginning with a prayer for the divine blessing upon Israel in order that salvation may come to all nations the Psalmist comes at last to assured confidence that his prayer is answered. Therefore he exclaims: "God will bless us, and all the ends of the earth shall fear him" (verse 7). The greatest idea of the Psalm is that at last all nations shall give glad homage to the God of Israel. We have already found this great truth in other Psalms of this period (Ps. 47:9; 66:4). It is also prominent in the writings of Isaiah (Isa. 2:2-4; 25:6-7; 56:7) and Micah (Mic. 4:1-3).

Psalm 68.

This majestic Psalm has an inscription as the work of David. Internal evidence, however, makes it clear that in this case as in a few others (Psalms 31, 37, 39, 103, 122, 124, 131, 133, 138-145) the tradition of Davidic authorship is mistaken. The reference to the temple at Jerusalem (verse 29) argues strongly against Davidic authorship. It is true that the tabernacle at Shiloh received this name (I Sam. 1:9; 3:3) and it might be used in poetry of the sanctuary to which David brought up the ark of the covenant (II Sam. 6:12-19; I Chron. 15:25-16:3). Although it was only a tent (II Sam. 6:17; I Chron. 16:1) it contained the ark, which was the symbol of God's presence, and it received an added glory from the fact that the temple was soon to replace it. It may have been this sanctuary to which David referred as the temple in several Psalms (II Sam. 22:7; Ps. 5:7; 11:4; 18:6; 27:4; 29:9; 65:4). The reference in Ps. 68:29, however, will scarcely admit of this interpretation. It presupposes a stately temple which would impress foreign kings. "Because of thy temple at Jerusalem kings shall bring presents unto thee." Furthermore verses 16-18 seem to refer to the building of Solomon's temple.

Possibly the reference to the temple in Ps. 68:29 might be regarded as poetic hyperbole in the mouth of David if there were no other marks in the Psalm of a date after his time. But this is not the case. Verses 1-2 and 20 fit the time of the retreat of Sennacherib's army better than any known experience of David. It was a deliverance (verse 20) which was not the case with David's victories. Verses 12 and 14 also seem to refer to the retreat of Sennacherib. The reference to the tribes of Benjamin, Judah, Zebulun and Naphtali in verse 27 might seem to favor a time before the loss of the northern tribes under Jeroboam. It may, however, be an ideal picture of the future when all twelve tribes are reunited (Isa. 11:12-13; Jer. 3:18; Ezek. 37:15-23; Hos. 1:11). Although the historical allusions of the Psalm are difficult of interpretation, they are much more difficult on the theory of the Davidic date than on that of some later time.

The linguistic evidence makes the Davidic authorship almost impossible. The word for prosperity in verse 6 is from a stem which occurs elsewhere only in Esther and Ecclesiastes. The stem of the word for "parched land" in the same verse is found once in Isa. 58:11 and later only in Ezekiel and Nehemiah. The verb to scatter in verse 30 occurs again only in Dan. 11:24. The words for high (verses 15-16), look askance (verse 16) and thousands upon thousands, literally thousands of repetition (verse 17) are probably also Aramaic. The earliest date which would satisfy the linguistic evidence is the latter part of the eighth century when Aramaic influence began to make itself felt on the Hebrew language.

Abandoning then the traditional Davidic authorship, there is no other time which satisfies the phenomena of the Psalm so well as the end of the eighth century or the early part of the seventh. Verses 1-3 would be appropriate at the time of Sennacherib's invasion. "Let God arise, let his enemies be scattered: let them also that hate him flee before him. As smoke is driven away, so drive them away. As wax melteth before the fire, so let the wicked perish at the presence of God. But let the righteous be glad; let them exult before God: yea let them rejoice with gladness" (Cp. Ps. 46:6, 9; 47:3, 5; 48:4-7; 66:10-12; Isa. 33:18-20; 37:33-38). The word rendered "cast up a highway" in verse 4 occurs in a similar context in Isa. 57:14 and 62:10. With other resemblances with Isa. 40-66 it is used as an argument for dating the Psalm near the end of the exile. But if, as we have seen, Isaiah wrote these chapters in the reign of Manasseh, a date in that time would account for these expressions. Verses 5-6 would be appropriate to this time when there was so much oppression of the weak. Verses 7-10 look back to God's guidance of his people through the wilderness of Sinai and their establishment in the promised land. Verses 11-14 probably refer to the victory over Sisera under Deborah and Barak (verse 12; cp. Judges 5:19, 30; verse 13; cp. Judges 5:16). Yet this sudden victory would have been more significant to the Psalmist if he had witnessed the sudden withdrawal of Sennacherib's army.

Verse 18 uses a figure like that of Ps. 47:5. The latter Psalm says: "God is gone up with a shout" and the former "Thou hast ascended on high." If the former expression refers to God's return to heaven after his victory over the Assyrians, the latter may well refer to the same occasion. Appropriate also to this time are verses 20-21 "God is unto us a God of deliverances; and unto Jehovah the Lord belongeth escape from death. But God will smite through the head of his enemies, the hairy scalp of such a one as goeth on still in his guiltiness." The enemies of God cannot escape punishment even if they hide in the forests of Bashan or the depths of the sea (Verses 22-23; cp. Am. 9:2-3). Verses 24-27 give an ideal description of a future procession of thanksgiving to the temple to celebrate God's victory over his foes. Verses 28-31 represent the nations as submitting to God. The wild beast of the reeds (verse 30) is Egypt (Ps. 74:14; Isa. 27:1) and the bulls and calves represent other hostile nations. The reference to Egypt was appropriate in the reign of Hezekiah when it was stirring up Judah to rebel against Assyria. The invitation to the kingdoms of the earth to worship God (verses 32-34) is peculiarly appropriate to this time, for we have a similar picture in Ps. 47:1; 66:1, 4, 8 and 67:3-5. The representation of God as terrible in verse 35 is like that in Ps. 47:2; 48:6 and 66:3, 5. Altogether the arguments for placing Psalm 68 in this time are very strong.

Kirkpatrick well describes the tenor of this great poem as follows: "The theme of this magnificent Psalm is the march of God to victory. It traces the establishment of His kingdom in Israel in the past; it looks forward to the defeat of all opposition in the future, until all the kingdoms of the world own the God of Israel as their Lord and pay Him homage." In the broad sense it is a Messianic Psalm, not that it mentions the Messiah or his work but that it describes the progress of the kingdom of God to its final glorious consummation. It is in this sense that Paul's reference of verse 18 to Christ can be justified. The Psalmist addressing God says: "Thou has ascended on high, thou hast led away captives. Thou has received gifts among men." God came down from heaven (Gen. 11:5, 7; 18:21; Ex. 3:8; 19:11, 18, 20) to fight against his people's foes who were also his foes. When his victory was complete he returned to heaven, as a true conqueror taking with him a train of captives and a large amount of tribute which he received among men. The Psalmist referred to God's victory over Sennacherib or some other military victory. But Paul was able to see that the God who came down to fight Israel's battles would some day come down far more definitely to fight the battles of men against their spiritual foes. Yea, Paul believed that God had come down in Jesus Christ to do this very thing; and, when his victory over sin and death was complete, he returned to heaven. Therefore he applied to Christ words which referred originally to a military victory, adapting the words from some current paraphrase to his use. "Wherefore he saith, When he ascended on high, he led captivity captive and gave gifts unto men" (Eph. 4:8). Jesus the conqueror returns to heaven with captives in his train. He also has tribute which he has received among men; but Paul speaks not of the tribute which Jesus received among men but of the gifts which he gave to men after his return to heaven. Paul thought especially of the gift of the Holy Spirit who wrought spiritual grace in the hearts of men (Eph. 4:7) and equipped them for their offices in the church (Eph. 4:11).

The picture of God returning to heaven victorious over his foes is like that of the hero from Edom in Isa. 63:1-6. There, as here, the victorious hero is God himself. Yet just as the apostle John with spiritual insight referred to Christ that which Isaiah spoke of Jehovah (Rev. 14:19-20; 19:11-16), so Paul referred to Christ that which the Psalmist spoke of God. Both New Testament passages (Eph. 4:8 and Rev. 19:11-16) are based upon the idea that at Calvary Christ gained a victory over the powers of darkness (Luke 22:53; John 12:31; 14:30; 16:11). In somewhat the same sense Paul speaks of Christ as having despoiled the principalities and the powers, making a show of them openly, triumphing over them (Col. 2:15).

Another great verse in this Psalm is 31. "Princes shall come out of Egypt. Ethiopia shall haste to stretch out her hands unto God" (Ps. 68:31). The word rendered princes occurs only here in the Old Testament and its exact meaning is unknown. The Septuagint translates it ambassadors, a meaning that fits well. If this is the idea, the verse was specially appropriate in that time. The faithless nobles of Judah had sent an embassy to Egypt to seek their aid against Assyria (Isa. 30:1-7; 31:1). This embassy would fail. In contrast the Psalmist predicts that Egypt shall send ambassadors to Jerusalem, seeking the help of Jehovah. Egypt is selected from among foreign nations because it was the earliest oppressor of Israel.

Ethiopia is mentioned because it was so distant (Isa. 18:1, 7; Zeph. 3:10). Isaiah in the same time with this Psalm gave one of his most significant predictions concerning the conversion of Egypt (Isa. 19:19-25) concluding with the remarkable words: "Blessed be Egypt, my people." Tirhakah, who came out to fight against Sennacherib, was king of Ethiopia (Isa. 37:9) and later became king of Egypt.

Psalm 75.

The inscription calls this a Psalm of Asaph, indicating that it was composed by some member of that guild of temple musicians. It has very few marks of date or occasion. Its general tone of thanksgiving and triumph resembles that of Psalm 76 which has clear indications of coming from the time when the Assyrian army was withdrawn and Jerusalem was saved in 701 B. C. The statement of verse 3 ("The earth and all the inhabitants thereof are dissolved") is like that of Ps. 46:6 ("The earth melted") for the same Hebrew word is rendered melted in one place and dissolved in the other. The word rendered "sing praises" in verse 9 occurs in Ps. 47:6, 7; 66:24; 68:4, 32, all three Psalms dating from this time. The title "God of Jacob" in verse 9 is found also in Ps. 46:7, 11; 76:6 and 84:8. Rabshakeh and his associates are accurately described in verse 4 as arrogant and in verse 5 as speaking with a stiff neck (Isa. 36:4-10, 12-20; 37:10-13, 23). These considerations make it a reasonable hypothesis that the Psalm arose from the same occasion as Psalms 46-48, 66-68 and 76.

Verse 3 expresses the same stedfast faith which characterizes the 46th Psalm. In the midst of all the great political convulsions of his time when the earth and all the inhabitants thereof were dissolved, the Psalmist heard God's voice saying: "I have set up the pillars of it." The verb rendered "set up" means literally to measure, regulate, adjust. Since it is God who has adjusted the pillars of the earth, placing them on a solid foundation and in absolute perpendicular, they cannot be overthrown. The Psalmist realized that help did not come from any point of the compass but from God only. While he mentions the east, west and south (verse 6) he fails to mention the north because that was the direction from which the Assyrians came. God appears in this Psalm as the absolute ruler of the world whose justice will visit destruction upon the wicked and will also exalt the righteous.

Psalm 76.

This Asaphitic Psalm gives clear evidence of its occasion. The Septuagint correctly calls it "a song with reference to the Assyrians." This occasion is almost as clear as in Psalms 46 and 48. Verses 5 and 6 vividly portray the destruction of Sennacherib's army: "The stouthearted are made a spoil: They have slept their sleep, and none of the men of might have found their hands. At thy rebuke, O God of Jacob, both chariot and horse are cast into a dead sleep." This is the poetic description of the event which Isaiah describes as follows: "The angel of Jehovah went forth, and smote in the camp of the Assyrians a hundred and fourscore and five thousand; and when men arose early in the morning, behold,

these were all dead bodies" (Isa. 37:36). Besides this
clear evidence of its occasion the Psalm contains several
points of contact with other writings of that time. The
statement of verse 1, "In Judah is God known," resembles
that of Ps. 48:3, "God hath made himself known in her
palaces for a refuge." This Psalmist says: "There he
brake the arrows of the bow, the shield, and the sword,
and the battle" (verse 3), while the author of the 46th
Psalm says: "He breaketh the bow, and cutteth the spear
in sunder" (Ps. 46:9). The reference to the stouthearted
in verse 5 is similar to Isaiah's reference to the stout heart
of the king of Assyria (Isa. 10:12) although a different
word is used. The idea that God is terrible is found in
verses 7, 11, and 12. The word rendered to be feared in
verse 7 is the same as that for terrible in verse 12. Another word from the same stem is translated to be feared
in verse 11. This idea occurs also in Ps. 47:2; 48:6;
66:3, 5 and 68:35. The title "God of Jacob" is found in
verse 6 as in Ps. 46:7, 11; 75:9 and 84:8. The word for
presents in verse 11 is found elsewhere only in Ps. 68:29
and Isa. 18:7. All these marks make it practically certain
that this Psalm was called forth by the retreat of the
Assyrian army in 701 B. C.

The great contribution of this Psalm to the history of
religion is found in verse 10. "Surely the wrath of man
shall praise thee: the residue of wrath shalt thou gird
upon thee." The first statement is sufficiently clear. It is
a general statement occasioned by the Assyrian invasion.
The wrath of the Assyrians expressed itself in their invasion of Judah. Yet God used this wrath as a means
of bringing praise to himself. Not only did the people

of Judah praise God for his deliverance when the Assyrian army withdrew and Jerusalem was saved, but the Psalms of this time speak of the effect which this deliverance would have upon other nations. Those nations would be converted to the God of Israel and would render glad homage to him (Ps. 46:10; 47:1, 7-9; 66:1, 4, 8; 67:2-7; 68:18, 31-32).

The second part of the verse is more difficult to interpret. The expression "the residue of wrath" occurs nowhere else. It would naturally mean that part of wrath which remains after the expression of anger in deed or word. Some think that the wrath of God is referred to, especially since the word is plural in the last part of the verse but singular in the first part. God's wrath was not all spent in his punishment of the Assyrian army. There remained a residue of his wrath which he girded upon himself as one might put a sword in his girdle for future use. But if this be the meaning, the last part of the verse expresses an idea quite different from the first part. It is much more natural to suppose that the wrath of man is referred to in the last half of the verse as it certainly is in the first half. The meaning is then that the residue of human wrath which remains after man has given way to anger, God girds upon himself as an ornament or as a sword. God turns this residue of wrath to his own use. Instead of being used against God it will be used for God. This interpretation makes the two parts of the verse harmonious. The general idea of the whole verse is that God brings good out of evil, using even the wrath of his enemies for his own glory. So viewed it is one of the most important statements of the Old Testament.

It is a presupposition of this great verse that God is absolutely sovereign, using as his instruments not only his friends but his foes. Isaiah gave greater prominence to this idea than any other writer. So God said: "Ho, Assyrian, the rod of mine anger, the staff in whose hand is mine indignation" (Isa. 10:5). When God had made use of the Assyrian to accomplish his purpose in Judah, he said to Sennacherib: "Because of thy raging against me, and because thine arrogancy is come up into mine ears, therefore will I put my hook in thy nose, and my bridle in thy lips, and I will turn thee back by the way by which thou camest" (Isa. 37:29). God said of Cyrus: "He is my shepherd and shall perform all my pleasure, even saying of Jerusalem, She shall be built, and of the temple, Thy foundation shall be laid" (Isa. 44:28). And to Cyrus he said: "For Jacob my servant's sake and Israel my chosen, I have called thee by thy name: I have surnamed thee, though thou has not known me" (Isa. 45:4). It is in this connection that the astounding statement occurs, "I form the light, and create darkness; I make peace, and create evil; I am Jehovah that doeth all these things" (Isa. 45:7).

The Psalmist goes even beyond Isaiah. God not only creates evil but he uses evil as his instrument for the accomplishment of his own glory. This was the way the inspired men of ancient Israel put it who were God-intoxicated, who knew and cared little about secondary causes. To them God did everything that was done in the world. Whether he did it directly or through instruments they did not care. We say: "God overrules." They said: "God rules." We say: "God permits." They said: "God does." Their supreme desire was to know God's purpose. What was God's purpose in the life of the Pharaoh who oppressed Israel? God told Moses to tell him, "For this cause have I made thee to stand, to show thee my power, and that my name may be declared throughout all the earth" (Ex. 9:16). What was God's purpose in allowing Joseph to be sold into Egypt? Joseph said to his brethren: "As for you, ye meant evil against me; but God meant it for good, to save much people alive" (Gen. 50:20). What was God's purpose in permitting David to commit his awful sin? David confessed it. "Against thee, thee only have I sinned, and done that which was evil in thy sight; that thou mayest be justified when thou speakest, and be clear when thou judgest" (Ps. 51:4). What was God's purpose in allowing the man to be born blind? It was "that the works of God should be made manifest in him" (John 9:3). All this is hidden in the Psalmist's great word: "Surely the wrath of man shall praise thee. The residue of wrath shalt thou gird upon thee."

Psalm 78.

This long Asaphitic Psalm gives almost no clue to its occasion or date. It refers to incidents in the history of Israel from the crossing of the Red Sea to the building of Solomon's temple. Although the allusion to the temple does not indicate whether it was still standing (verse 69), the Psalmist's purpose implies that it was. He was warning Israel from their sins in the past and the way God punished them to turn away from sin lest a like fate come upon them. The Psalm does not read as though such a fate as the fall of Jerusalem and the destruction of the

temple had occurred. Similarly the reference to the choice
of David (verses 70-71) seems to imply that the Davidic
dynasty was still ruling. The didactic use of history which
flourished after the exile (Psalms 105-106) is illustrated
in this Psalm. Since this is found in eighth-century
Psalms (Ps. 44:1-3; 66:5-6; 68:7-18) we have ventured
to place this Psalm in that time. The title "Holy One, of
Israel" which occurs about thirty times in the book of
Isaiah and was probably originated by him, is found in
verse 41. This probably indicates a date not earlier than
Isaiah. Zoan is mentioned twice in the Psalm (verses 12
and 43), three times in Isaiah (19:11, 13; 30:4) and only
twice elsewhere.

There are only a few points of contact with eighth-
century Psalms. Verse 2 says: "I will open my mouth in
a parable. I will utter dark sayings of old." Similarly
Ps. 49:4 has: "I will incline mine ear to a parable. I will
open my dark saying upon the harp." Verse 3 ("Which
we have heard and known and our fathers have told us")
may be compared with Ps. 44:1 ("We have heard with
our ears, O God, our fathers have told us."). Verse 55
refers to the same incident as Ps. 44:2 and Verse 65 uses
the figure of God awaking from sleep to punish the
enemies of Israel, a figure found also in Ps. 44:23. These
are not very strong reasons for assigning the Psalm to
the eighth century; but if it were assigned to some other
time, the reasons would be fewer still.

This review of God's dealings with Israel throughout
their history is valuable because it shows at a single glance
the fundamental elements of God's attitude toward Israel
and of Israel toward God. On God's part it was an atti-

tude of repeated and persistent goodness. He revealed himself in the law from Sinai (verses 5-8). He brought them out of Egypt and led them through the wilderness (verses 12-16). He gave them food and drink (verses 23-29). He cleared a place for them in Palestine (verse 55). He punished their enemies (verse 66). He established the temple in Jerusalem (verses 67-69) and the Davidic dynasty (verse 70-72). This goodness was displayed even after their sin. He forgave their iniquity and remembered that they were but flesh (verses 38-39). The thing that stirred him most to anger was their lack of faith (verses 22 and 32) and their hypocrisy (verses 36-37). He punished them only after repeated sin. On the part of Israel it is a record of repeated sin against God's goodness (verses 17, 32, 40 and 56) of doubt of him (verses 22 and 32). "When he slew them, then they inquired after him, and they returned and sought God earnestly" (verses 34). Yet even this repentance was soon followed by hypocrisy. "They flattered him with their mouth, and lied unto him with their tongues" (verse 36). The entire Psalm is a vivid presentation on the one hand of the goodness, the justice and the forgiving love of God and on the other hand of the depravity of the human heart. It sets forth in this practical way the same conception of God and man which appears in the books of the eighth-century prophets.

Psalm 80.

The date of this Psalm of Asaph is uncertain. Lacking better evidence we may accept the suggestion found in the Septuagint which calls it "a Psalm concerning the Assyrians." The internal evidence confirms this. There is no reference to Judah but only to Joseph, Ephraim, Benjamin and Manasseh (verses 1-2). Hence it has been inferred that the author lived in the northern kingdom. It was evidently a time of great affliction apparently due to a foreign invasion (verses 5-6, 12-13, 16). From the prayer in the refrain, "turn us again" (verses 3, 7, 19) some have supposed that the people were already in exile, but verses 12-16 seem to imply that they were still in their own land. All things considered, no other date fits the Psalm so well as a few years before the fall of Samaria, possibly about 740 B. C. when Menahem was on the throne of the northern kingdom. In his reign Tiglath-pileser invaded the land. Menahem bought him off by the payment of a huge tribute which he raised by levying a tax on all the wealthy people of the land. In addition to the devastation wrought by the Assyrians there was this great drain on the national resources (II Kings 15:17-22).

The conditions reflected in the Psalm correspond to that described or rather presupposed in the historical records. There are also a few literary resemblances to writings of this time which look in the same direction. The name Jehovah God of hosts occurs twice in the Psalm (verses 4 and 19) and God of hosts occurs twice (verses 7 and 14). Jehovah of hosts occurs in Isaiah more than sixty times. It is also found in Ps. 46:7, 11; 48:8 and 84:1, 3, 8, 12. Verses 8-11 speak of Israel as a vine which God brought out of Egypt and planted in Palestine, a conception which resembles Isaiah's beautiful song of the vineyard. (Isa. 5:1-7). Verse 5 uses a figure found in Ps. 42:3 and verse 6 is like Ps. 44:13. The word for wild beasts in verse 13 occurs elsewhere only in Ps. 50:11 and Isa. 66:11, both of which come from this time.

There is a striking use of the word to turn again in this Psalm. In the refrain the Psalmist prays: "Turn us again, O God, and cause thy face to shine and we shall be saved" (verses 3, 7, and 19) while in verse 14 he prays, "Turn again, we beseech thee, O God of hosts. Look down from heaven and behold and visit this vine." The refrain is identical in all three places except that there is progress in the way God is addressed. In verse 3 he is addressed merely as God and in verse 7 as God of hosts, while in verse 19 the covenant name is used "Jehovah God of hosts." In the refrain the Psalmist prays that God would turn Israel again while in verse 14 he prays that God himself would turn again. Some commentators think that the prayer of the refrain is for restoration from exile and others that it is for an improvement of the national fortunes. But the exile is not mentioned. The meaning therefore is not the same as the common one to turn or bring back the captivity (Deut. 30:3; Ps. 85:1; 126:4; Jer. 30:3, 18, etc.), an expression which is sometimes used figuratively of a restoration of good fortune (Job 42:10; Ps. 14:7; 53:6, etc.). It is better to regard the refrain as a prayer that God would turn the hearts of his people in true repentance to himself. So Jeremiah represents Ephraim as praying, "Turn thou me and I shall be turned" (Jer. 31:18) and the same prophet pleads for his people, "Turn thou us unto thee, O Jehovah, and we shall be turned" (Lam. 5:21). Ezekiel also uses the same verb of turning from idols (Ezek. 14:6) and from all transgressions (Ezek. 18:30, 32). On the other hand, Ps. 80:14 is a prayer that God would turn from his anger and look favorably toward his people.

There is thus in this Psalm important teaching concerning repentance and at least a suggestion of the great doctrine of reconciliation. The Psalmist felt that Israel was alienated from God and he knew that the cause of this alienation was not in any unwillingness on God's part to look favorably upon his people but in the sin of Israel. So while he prayed that God turn again to his people (verse 14), his great prayer to which he came back with ever increasing urgency was that God would cause his people to repent and come back to him (verses 3, 7, 19). Only God could stir their hard hearts to repentance. Even this must come from him. That it is repentance and not a mere improvement of fortunes for which he prays appears in verse 18, "So shall we not go back from thee. Quicken thou us, and we will call upon thy name." If God by his gracious influence revives his people to a new life of harmony with him, they will show their gratitude by not going back from him again. To accomplish reconciliation with God the one great need was that "they should repent and turn to God, doing works worthy of repentance" (Acts 26:20). This was a preparation for the teaching of the New Testament in which God is never spoken of as being reconciled to man but man is repeatedly spoken of as being reconciled to God (Rom. 5:10; II Cor. 5:18-20; Eph. 2:16; Col. 1:20-22). God is always ready to come back to man as soon as man comes back to God. "I have no pleasure in the death of him that dieth, saith the Lord Jehovah; wherefore turn yourselves, and live" (Ezek. 18:32). This is like the story of the prodigal son. "He arose, and came to his father. But while he was yet afar off his father saw him, and was moved with compassion, and ran, and fell on his neck, and kissed him" (Luke 15:20). The full doctrine is not found in the Old Testament. This Psalm helped to prepare for it.

Psalm 84.

This is the first of two Psalms of the Sons of Korah. Its resemblances to the first Psalm in the earlier Korahite group (Psalms 42-43) are so marked that some have thought that they were written by the same author. Both express great love for the sanctuary at Jerusalem. Both speak of the tabernacles of God (Ps. 84:1; cp. Ps. 43:3). Both use the title "the living God" which is found nowhere else in the Psalter (Ps. 84:2; cp. Ps. 42:2, 8). Both refer to the altar (Ps. 84:3; cp. Ps. 43:4). Praising God is prominent in both (Ps. 84:4; cp. Ps. 42:5, 11). The expression to appear before God occurs in both (Ps. 84:7; cp. Ps. 42:2). The structure of the two Psalms also is similar. Each of them is divided into three stanzas. Each of the stanzas of Psalms 42-43 ends with a refrain, while the stanzas of Psalm 84 are marked off by Selah. Furthermore the middle stanza of Psalms 42-43 is one verse longer than the others while the stanzas of Psalm 84 are of equal length. These resemblances may not prove that the two Psalms were by the same author but they make it probable that they date from the same time.

This conclusion is strengthened by internal evidence and by points of contact with other eighth-century Psalms. The references show that the temple was standing and the pilgrimages made. The anointed of God mentioned in verse 9 must be the king (cp. Ps. 2:2). Hence the Davidic dynasty was standing. God is spoken of as king (verse 3) as in Ps. 44:4; 47:2, 6, 7. He is called Jehovah of hosts (verses 1, 3 and 12) as in Ps. 46:7, 11; 48:8, Jehovah God of hosts (verse 8) as in Ps. 80:4, 19, and God of Jacob (verse 8) as in Ps. 46:7, 11; 76:6. These facts make it probable that Psalm 84 dates from the eighth century, possibly in the reign of Hezekiah.

This Psalm, like Psalms 42-43, which are closely related to it, makes special reference to the pilgrimages to the temple at Jerusalem at the time of the feasts (Ex. 12:14; 23:14; Lev. 23:39-41). "Blessed is the man whose strength is in thee, in whose heart are the highways to Zion" (verse 5). Literally translated the last part of the verse is "highways in their heart." Although Zion is not mentioned, the thought is that the highways which lead from various parts of the land to the holy city are precious because they lead to the place where God manifests himself to his people and where they worship him.

This love of the highways to Zion shows itself not only in relation to those parts of the road which go through fertile and well-watered places, but also to those which go through dark and sterile valleys. "Passing through the valley of Weeping they make it a place of springs. Yea, the early rain covereth it with blessings" (verse 6). The word rendered Weeping resembles the word with that meaning but it is never used in that sense. It is the name of a kind of balsam-tree which may have been so-called from the fact that it exudes gum somewhat as tears drop from the eyes. Such trees are mentioned in II Sam. 5:23-24 and I Chron. 14:14-15 where the translation in the text is mulberry trees and in the margin balsam-trees. These trees grow in dry valleys. The valley mentioned here derived its name from the trees which grew there. Although it was a dry and possibly a dark place, the early rain transformed it into a place of blessings. It was God who sent this transforming rain. Yet the believing pilgrims did not have to wait for the rain. Their faith transformed the dry valley into a place of springs because it was on the way to the dwelling-place of God to whom a later Psalmist sang, "All my springs are in thee" (Ps. 87:7). In reference to such a dark valley David sang, "Yea, though I walk through the valley of the shadow of death, I will fear no evil, for thou art with me" (Ps. 23:4). Having their hearts set on the blessed end of their journey the pilgrims "go from strength to strength. Everyone of them appeareth before God in Zion" (verse 7).

While then the Psalm expresses an intense love for the temple at Jerusalem and even the roads which lead to it, it is not a superstitious or unspiritual love. The love for God is even more prominent than the love for the sanctuary. While the tabernacles of Jehovah seem lovely to his sight and his soul longs and faints for the courts of Jehovah, the heart and the flesh of the Psalmist sing for joy unto the living God. Those who dwell in God's house are blessed because they praise God again and again. The pilgrimage is blessed because it ends in the presence of God. The Psalmist was not emancipated from the external in religion. Yet he was not slavishly devoted to it. His spirituality may not equal that of David when he cried: "O God, thou art my God; earnestly will I seek thee. My soul thirsteth for thee, my flesh longeth for thee, in a dry and weary land, where no water is" (Ps. 63:1). Yet his love for the pure worship of God helped to prepare for the time when the true worship of God was freed from all limitations of place and time (John 4:20-24).

CHAPTER XIII.

Job.

The date of this great book cannot be fixed with any degree of certainty. The condition of life represented in it is patriarchal. From this fact some have placed it very early, even in the time of Moses. But the patriarchal conditions in the story may be due to the skill of the author. Furthermore patriarchal conditions continued in the land of Uz where the scene of the story is laid for many centuries after Moses' day. The book contains no historical allusions which might help to fix its date. The supposed references to the Mosaic law (Job 22:6, 27; 24:2, 9; 31:9, 11, 26-28) are doubtful, for similar laws may have existed in Uz even before Moses' time. Some have supposed that it came from the time of Solomon because of its resemblance to Proverbs, particularly in chapter 28. But this method of writing is found also in the much later books of Ecclesiastes, Ecclesiasticus, and the Wisdom of Solomon. There is no more likely time for its composition than a century or so before the fall of Jerusalem, perhaps in the reign of Manasseh (698-642 B. C.).

The strongest argument for this date is in a consideration of the purpose of the book. It tells the story of a man who suffered great losses, yet maintained his integrity and therefore was restored to prosperity. Why was it written? The most natural answer is that it was

578

written as an encouragement for other righteous people who maintained their integrity in the midst of great trials. No other people needed such a book so much as the small but faithful remnant in Judah in the time of Manasseh. Because of the terrible wickedness of that reign the prophets foretold the sure punishment of the exile (II Kings 21:10-15; 23:26-27; 24:3-4; Jer. 15:4). The righteous few inevitably asked two questions, (1) Will the righteous suffer in the exile with the wicked: and (2) Will the nation survive the exile? The book of Job answers these questions. To the first it replies: Yes, the righteous must suffer with the wicked. To the second it replies: Yes, the nation, or rather the righteous part of it, will survive the exile. The answer it gives is not abstract but is derived from the old tradition of the man of Uz who suffered many losses and endured much suffering but at last was vindicated and restored to prosperity.

The question discussed in the book of Job was a pressing one in the time of Isaiah and later. It is essentially the subject of Psalm 49 which we have dated in the eighth century. The Psalmist deals with the deceitfulness of riches and expresses his conviction that the upright shall have dominion over the wicked rich in the morning (Ps. 49:14). Job deals rather with the sufferings of the righteous. Yet it is but another side of the same subject. It is also the subject of Isa. 40-55. Isaiah goes far beyond the book of Job. Job after long struggle came to believe that his sufferings were not eternal. He would not perish but be vindicated (Job 19:25-27). Isaiah foretold that the sufferings of the righteous would be vicarious and the means of restoration (Isa. 53). Later the subject of the

sufferings of the righteous gave birth to a new emphasis
on individual responsibility (Jer. 31:29-30; Ezek. 18).

It is striking that the disease from which Job suffered
was the same by which Isaiah figuratively described the
sufferings of the Servant of Jehovah. It seems to have
been the form of leprosy known as elephantiasis. The
symptoms of this dreadful malady are mentioned in Job
2:7, 8, 12; 3:25; 7:3-5, 14-15; 13:28; 16:8; 19:17-20,
26; 30:17, 18, 30. The sore boils which were the first
symptom were part of the penalty which God announced
to Israel through Moses if the people persisted in disobedience (Deut. 28:27, 35). The Servant of Jehovah in
Isa. 40-55 who is repeatedly identified with Israel (Isa.
41:8; 44:1-2, 21; 45:4; 48:20; 49:3) is represented as
a leper. The disfiguring of his appearance (Isa. 52:14;
53:2) was on this account. For this reason he was despised as one from whom men hide their face (Isa. 53:3).
The word rendered stricken in Isa. 53:4 and the word for
stroke in Isa. 53:8 were used specially of the stroke or
plague of leprosy (Lev. 13:3, 9, 20; II Kings 15:5). Job
was despised and men hid their faces from him (Job
19:13-19; 30:10). These parallels suggest that, even
though the story of Job has a historical basis, the purpose
of telling it related to Israel. Job may be called a type of
Israel suffering in the exile. The statement that "Jehovah
turned the captivity of Job" (Job 42:10) may be a hint
of this, for although this expression was sometimes used
with the general sense of improving the fortunes (Ps.
14:7; 53:6), it usually referred to a restoration from exile
(Jer. 29:14; Hos. 6:11; Am. 9:14, etc.).

The absolute monotheism of the book also agrees with the theory that it was produced soon after the writings of the eighth-century prophets. It is an ethical monotheism like theirs. The majesty of God in the speech from the whirlwind (Job 38) is like the majesty of God in Isaiah's vision at his ordination (Isá. 6:1-5). Job called God "the Holy One" (Job 6:10) with possible reference to Isaiah's favorite title "the Holy One of Israel." Although the book does not use the word holiness, so common in Isaiah, the idea is there. Even the heavens are not clean in God's sight (Job 15:15; cp. 25:5). Indeed all the phenomena of the book may be explained if it was produced in the reign of Manasseh about the time of Isa. 40-55.

Certain parts of the book have been regarded as later additions. The one concerning which there is the greatest agreement is the speech of Elihu (chapters 32-37). The arguments for regarding this long speech as a later addition to the book are strong. (1) Elihu is never mentioned elsewhere in the book and his arguments are completely ignored. If Elihu had spoken just before the speech of Jehovah from the whirlwind, we should expect that speech to contain some reference to him approving or disapproving; but Jehovah addresses himself only to Job. In the epilogue Jehovah condemns the three friends (Job 42:7-9) but he has not a word for Elihu. (2) At the end of his last speech Job pleads with God to answer him (Job 31:35-40) and chapter 38 is such an answer. It begins, "Then Jehovah answered Job out of the whirlwind and said" (Job 38:1). It is all plain and consecutive, if the speech of Elihu is omitted but very strange if it is retained. (3) The speech of Elihu contributes nothing to the argument of the book. His explanation of Job's sufferings is practically identical with that of the friends. He speaks of the disciplinary purpose of suffering as Eliphaz had done (Job 33:19-28; cp. 5:17-27). (4) The speech of Elihu gives evidence that its author was familiar with the speech of Jehovah and other later parts of the book (Job 33:14; cp. 40:5; Job 36:27; cp. 38:28; Job 37:8; cp. 38:40; Job 37:10; cp. 38:29). The original author of the book would not have made such a mistake as this. (5) The style of the Elihu speech is different from that of the rest of the book. Elihu has been spoken of as a mediator between Job and God. By the skill of the author there are hints of the gathering storm while he is speaking (Job 37:2-22) but these are not sufficient evidence of originality to outweigh the other strong arguments. It is very probable that the Elihu speeches were introduced by another writer. Since, however, there is no way of judging how much later these speeches were inserted, it is best to include them among the sources for the religion of this time. No harm can come from doing so, since these chapters contain nothing of consequence which is not found elsewhere in the book.

Job 27:13-23 and possibly verses 7-12 are probably not parts of the speech of Job. They probably belong to a lost third speech of Zophar, the heading for which may have dropped out of the text. The reasons for this conclusion are as follows: (1) The absence of a speech of Zophar in the third round arouses the suspicion that it has dropped out. (2) The sentiments expressed in these verses do not agree with what Job says elsewhere, but do agree with the views of the friends. Job 27:10 resembles what Eliphaz says in 22:26-27. Job 27:13-23 has many points of contact with Zophar's speech in chapter 20. Compare especially Job 27:13 with 20:29, Job 27:14 with 20:10, Job 27:16-19 with 20:18-21 and Job 27:23 with 20:8. Some have supposed that Job uses these expressions with reference to the sayings of the friends; but such a theory is quite unnatural.

Some commentators regard chapter 28 as a later addition to the book. It has no separate heading and appears at first sight to belong to Job's speech which began in 27:1 or perhaps to the lost third speech of Zophar, if 27:7-23 is indeed such. If, however, Job is the speaker in chapter 28 it is strange that chapter 29 begins, "And Job again took up his parable and said." Chapter 28 has no reference to the situation of Job at the time. Furthermore its style differs from the rest of the book. These arguments are sufficient to show that Job is not the speaker in this chapter, but not sufficient to exclude it from the book as originally written. This grand chapter should be regarded as an insertion by the author of the book at the end of the third round of speeches. Its difference of style is due in the main to the different subject with which it deals. The rare words are mostly in the description of mining and precious stones. The word rendered "surely" at the beginning of the chapter should be translated as often "for" or "because." If so, the chapter will be seen as the illuminating comment of the author on the discussion in which Job and the three friends had engaged. To the author's mind the supreme need of man for the solution of all problems was wisdom which is the gift of God and not to be attained as precious metals and stones are by human skill and effort. Therefore God says to man: "The fear of the Lord, that is wisdom; and to depart from evil is understanding" (Job 28:28).

(1)	THE CONCEPTION OF GOD.

Like the writings of the eighth-century prophets the book of Job was thoroughly monotheistic. This is true of all parts of the book. In the prologue the sons of God present themselves before God and Satan among them (Job 1:6; 2:1). Satan has no power over Job except that which Jehovah gives him (Job 1:12; 2:6). He can only carry out the permission which God gives him. Job thought of God as the omnipotent Creator and Ruler of the world. "He is wise in heart and mighty in strength. Who hath hardened himself against him and prospered? —Him that removeth the mountains and they know it not, when he overturneth them in his anger; that shaketh the earth out of its place, and the pillars thereof tremble; that commandeth the sun and it riseth not, and sealeth up the stars, that alone stretcheth out the heavens, and treadeth upon the waves of the sea; that maketh the Bear, Orion and the Pleiades and the chambers of the south; that doeth great things past finding out, yea marvellous things without number" (Job. 9:4-10).

"With God is wisdom and might; he hath counsel and understanding. Behold, he breaketh down and it cannot be built again. He shutteth up a man and there can be no opening. Behold, he withholdeth the waters and they dry up. Again he sendeth them out and they overturn the earth. With him is strength and wisdom. The deceived and the deceiver are his. He leadeth counsellors away stripped and judges maketh he fools. He looseth the bond of kings and bindeth their loins with a girdle. He leadeth priests away stripped and overthroweth the mighty. He removeth the speech of the trusty and taketh away the understanding of the elders. He poureth contempt upon princes and looseth the belt of the strong. He uncovereth deep things out of darkness and bringeth out to light the shadow of death. He increaseth the nations and he destroyeth them. He enlargeth the nations and he leadeth them captive" (Job 12:13-23).

While these statements do not affirm that God is omnipotent, they imply it. Job never speaks of any other god as having real existence. The only time he refers to idolatry he rejects it. He says: "If I have beheld the sun (Margin, 'light') when it shined, or the moon walking in brightness, and my heart hath been secretly enticed and my mouth hath kissed my hand, this also were an iniquity to be punished by the judges, for I should have denied the God that is above" (Job 31:26-28). Evidently in Job's opinion Jehovah was not one of many gods, not the god of one nation only, but the only living and true God.

While the three friends opposed Job in certain important matters, they found no fault with his monotheism. Evidently they too were monotheists. They do not, it is true, make any such grand statements of the omnipotence of God as those of Job which we have quoted; but on the other hand they never speak of him as one of many deities or as limited in his power. Eliphaz says that God is one "who doeth great things and unsearchable, marvellous things without number, who giveth rain upon the earth

and sendeth waters upon the fields, so that he setteth up
on high those that are low and those that mourn are
exalted to safety. He frustrateth the devices of the crafty
so that their hands cannot perform their enterprise. He
taketh the wise in their own craftiness and the counsel of
the cunning is carried headlong" (Job 5:9-13). Bildad
says of God: "Dominion and fear are with him. He
maketh peace in his high places. Is there any number of
his armies and upon whom doth not his light arise?" (Job
25:2-3). Zophar has no such statements; but there is no
reason to doubt his monotheism.

The magnificent chapter on wisdom, which is not put
into the mouth of Job, but is the direct work of the author
of the book, represents God as the All-seeing One, the
Creator of the world. Man cannot find the way to wisdom; but "God understandeth the way thereof and he
knoweth the place thereof, for he looketh to the ends of
the earth and seeth under the whole heaven to make a
weight for the wind, yea he meteth out the waters by
measure. When he made a decree for the rain and a way
for the lightning of the thunder, then did he see it and
declare it; he established it, yea and searched it out" (Job
28:23-27).

Elihu criticized the three friends and also Job (Job
32:2-3); but it was not for their monotheism. Toward
the end of his speech he recognized in the thunder the
voice of God. "God thundereth marvellously with his
voice. Great things doeth he which we cannot comprehend. For he saith to the snow, Fall thou on the earth,
likewise to the shower of rain, and to the showers of his
mighty rain. . . . Canst thou with him spread out the

sky, which is strong as a molten mirror? . . . Touching the Almighty we cannot find him out. He is excellent in power; and in justice and plenteous righteousness he will not afflict" (Job 37:5-6, 18, 23). He said that God is "perfect in knowledge" (Job 37:16) and that he "hath upon him terrible majesty" (Job 37:22).

The monotheism of the speech of Jehovah out of the whirlwind is grander than anything else in the book. In a series of questions God challenges Job: "Where wast thou when I laid the foundations of the earth? Declare if thou hast understanding. Who determined the measures thereof if thou knowest? Or who stretched the line upon it? Whereupon were the foundations thereof fastened? Or who laid the corner-stone thereof, when the morning stars sang together and all the sons of God shouted for joy?" (Job. 38:4-7). God speaks of his confining the sea (38:8-11), commanding the morning (38:12), reserving the hail against the day of trouble (38:22-23). He asks Job: "Who hath cleft a channel for the waterflood or a way for the lightning of the thunder? . . . Hath the rain a father or who hath begotten the drops of dew? Out of whose womb came the ice? And the hoary frost of heaven, who hath gendered it?" (Job 38:25, 28-29). The implied answer to these questions is that God has made all these things.

Changing the form of the question God asks Job: "Canst thou bind the cluster of the Pleiades, or loose the bands of Orion? Canst thou lead forth the Mazzaroth in their season? Or canst thou guide the Bear with her train? Knowest thou the ordinances of the heavens? Canst thou establish the dominion thereof in the earth?"

(Job 38:31-33). The implication is that God controls all these heavenly bodies. Then returning to the other form of question God asks: "Who hath put wisdom in the inward parts? Or who hath given understanding to the mind?" (Job 38:36) implying that this too is God's work. Finally in the epilogue it is God who changes the fortunes of Job restoring him to his former prosperity. The entire representation of the book is that God controls all things. He is the only God.

One of the frequent ideas of the book is that God is beyond human comprehension. Thus Job said: "Lo he goeth by me and I see him not. He passeth on also, but I perceive him not" (Job. 9:11). He cried out with passionate longing: "Oh that I knew where I might find him, that I might come even to his seat! . . . Behold, I go forward, but he is not there; and backward, but I cannot perceive him; on the left hand when he doth work, but I cannot behold him; he hideth himself on the right hand, that I cannot see him" (Job 23:3, 8-9). After speaking of the marvellous works of God in the heavens, Job said: "Lo, these are but the outskirts of his ways: and how small a whisper do we hear of him! But the thunder of his power who can understand?" (Job 26:14). Evidently he realized the inadequacy of the revelation of God in nature. God charged Job with speaking on matters too deep for him, darkening counsel by words without knowledge (Job 38:2) and in the end he confessed: "Therefore have I uttered that which I understood not; things too wonderful for me, which I knew not" (Job 42:3).

Eliphaz also recognized the element of mystery in God, "who doeth great things and unsearchable, marvellous things without number" (Job 5:9). One of the finest sayings of Zophar is his challenge, "Canst thou by searching find out God? (Margin, 'Canst thou find out the deep things of God?'). Canst thou find out the Almighty unto perfection?" (Job 11:7). Elihu said: "Behold, God is great and we know him not. The number of his years is unsearchable" (Job 36:26). Almost his last words were: "Touching the Almighty, we cannot find him out" (Job 37:23). We should not conclude from such expressions that Job, his three friends and Elihu were agnostics, that they believed that God was unknowable. In the early stage of revelation in which they and the author of the book lived, there was much of mystery in God and his ways. If even the revelation of Jesus Christ and the New Testament still leaves many mysteries, we should not be surprised that these early men felt their knowledge of God very imperfect. Yet Job's faith expressed itself in his memorable words: "I know that my Redeemer liveth" (Job 19:25); and the author of the book points out the true way to the knowledge of God as the climax of his great chapter on the search for wisdom. "Behold, the fear of the Lord, that is wisdom; and to depart from evil is understanding" (Job 28:28).

In his agony of suffering Job realized anew that God is different from man, for he said: "He is not a man, as I am, that I should answer him, that we should come together in judgment" (Job 9:32). At that stage of the argument Job also felt that there was no Mediator between God and Man, for he added: "There is no umpire betwixt us, that might lay his hand upon us both" (Job 9:33). Later he came to see that he had been mistaken, for he affirmed: "Even now, behold, my witness is in heaven, and he that voucheth for me is on high" (Job 16:19). This witness in heaven, this one that vouched for him on high was not exactly a Mediator between God and man, but was God himself, for the sufferer added immediately: "Mine eye poureth out tears unto God, that he would maintain the right of a man with God, and of a son of man with his neighbor" (Job 16:20-21). Job appealed to God against God, to God the merciful against God the persecutor, to God his witness in heaven, the one that vouched for him on high against the God who seemed his enemy. From this terrible experience there came the conviction that there is a distinction in God which we in the light of the New Testament recognize as the distinction between the persons of the Trinity. The doctrine of the Trinity was far beyond Job; yet this idea of distinctions in the divine nature helped to prepare for it. The place where the distinction in God is clearest is Job 19:25-27. "I know that my Redeemer liveth and at last he will stand up upon the earth: and after my skin, even this body, is destroyed, then without my flesh shall I see God, whom I, even I, shall see on my side and mine eyes shall behold and not as a stranger." The Redeemer is God; but he is not the God who persecutes Job but his witness, the one that vouches for him, the one that maintains his right, his next-of-kin who is on his side. This is one of the most profound conceptions in the Old Testament.

Only once is the holiness of God, Isaiah's great idea mentioned in this book. Job once called God "the Holy

One" (Job 6:10) a title which may have been suggested by the one which Isaiah originated, "the Holy One of Israel." The author would not have put this full title into the mouth of Job since he was not an Israelite. Eliphaz had some idea of the holiness of God although he did not use the word, for he said: "He putteth no trust in his holy ones; yea, the heavens are not clean in his sight" (Job 15:15; cp. 4:17-19). Bildad developed the same idea: "How then can man be just with God, or how can he be clean that is born of a woman? Behold, even the moon hath no brightness and the stars are not pure in his sight" (Job 25:4-5).

The friends speak of the righteousness or justice of God. Thus Eliphaz asks: "Shall mortal man be more just than God? Shall a man be more pure than his Maker?" (Job 4:17). Bildad asks: "Doth God pervert justice, or doth the Almighty pervert righteousness?" (Job 8:3). Elihu also refers repeatedly to the righteousness of God. He said: "Far be it from God that he should do wickedness and from the Almighty that he should commit iniquity. . . . Yea, of a surety God will not do wickedly, neither will the Almighty pervert justice" (Job. 34:10, 12). Later he said: "I will ascribe righteousness to my Maker" (Job 36:3; cp. 37:23).

Job speaks of the wisdom and power of God together three times. "He is wise in heart and mighty in strength" (Job 9:4). "With God is wisdom and might" (Job 12:13). "With him is strength and wisdom" (Job 12:16). Similarly Elihu says: "Behold God is mighty and despiseth not any; he is mighty in strength of understanding" (Job 36:5). "He is excellent in power" (Job 37:23).

(2) CEREMONIES OF RELIGION.

The book of Job sheds very little light on the ceremonies of religion which were practised in the time when it was written. Since the author was describing the primitive conditions of the time of Job he purposely avoided elements of a later day. In the prologue we are told that Job offered burnt-offerings according to the number of his children and said: "It may be that my sons have sinned and renounced God in their hearts" (Job 1:5). He also sent and sanctified them. We are not told wherein this sanctifying consisted. Possibly they washed and changed their garments (Gen. 35:2; Ex. 19:10, 14). Nothing is said of a priest in this connection and it is probable that as in primitive times, Job as the head of the family offered the sacrifice himself (Gen. 8:20; 22:2, 3, 6, 7, 8, 13). It is a mark of Job's piety that he did not wait until his children had surely sinned before he sanctified them and offered burnt-offerings. He did so on the chance that in their feasting they had failed to give that reverence to God which is his due. The rendering "renounced" is misleading. The word means literally to bless. Since it was customary to bless anyone in taking leave of him (Gen. 24:60; 47:10; I Kings 8:66), some suppose that it means here to take leave of God, say good-bye to him. Others think that "bless" is a euphemism for "curse" as it is sometimes in English (I Kings 21:10, 13; Job 1:5, 11; 2:5, 9; Ps. 10:3). In either case it scarcely suggests open blasphemy, but rather forgetfulness of God, neglect of him or unintentional irreverence to him. The inwardness of Job's religion is seen in his fear that his children had forgotten God, neglected him, taken leave of him not by overt act but in the heart.

In the epilogue Jehovah commanded the three friends: "Now therefore take unto you seven bullocks and seven rams and go to my servant Job and offer up for yourselves a burnt-offering" (Job 42:8). These were proper animals for a burnt-offering according to the Mosaic law (Lev. 1:3, 5; 9:2). We should not conclude, however, from this fact either that the Mosaic law was in force in the land of Uz in Job's time or that the author of this book improperly attributed to Job's time the ceremonial law of a later day. The Israelites were not the only ancient people who offered burnt-offerings. Even before the Mosaic law was enacted Jethro the Midianite did so (Ex. 18:12). It is entirely within the range of possibility that it was customary to offer bullocks and rams for burnt-offerings in the countries east and south of Canaan from which the three friends came. These are the only references to offerings of any kind in the book (Job 1:5; 42:8). It never mentions any holy building such as a sanctuary, or temple. It never mentions either an altar or a priest. Evidently the religious ceremonies were very primitive in Job's time, at least in his country, although they were highly developed when the book of Job was written.

Eliphaz told Job that if he would turn from his sin, God would forgive and restore him: "Thou shalt make thy prayer unto him, and he will hear thee; and thou shalt pay thy vows" (Job 22:27). The reference is apparently to the custom of vowing to God that one would perform certain service or offer certain sacrifices, if God would deliver him from some misfortune or give him success in some enterprise (Gen. 28: 20-22; Judges 11:30-31; 1 Sam. 1:11). So if Job should vow to God to offer certain sacrifices upon condition that God restored him from his sickness, then if he turned from his sin, Eliphaz believed that God would restore him and he would pay his vows. The custom of making vows was so widespread in ancient times that there is no special significance in the reference here.

There is a somewhat mysterious reference in Job 3:8 where Job says of the day of his birth: "Let them curse it that curse the day, who are ready (Margin, 'skilful') to rouse up leviathan." Leviathan was a poetic name for the crocodile or possibly for some sea-monster. It seems to have been thought that eclipses were produced by such a monster swallowing up the sun or the moon. Job thought that if sorcerers who were skilful in rousing up leviathan should practice their art, leviathan would swallow the sun and so blot out the day.

In the last of Job's speeches he said: "If I have beheld the sun (Margin, 'light') when it shined, or the moon walking in brightness, and my heart hath been secretly enticed, and my mouth hath kissed my hand, this also were an inquity to be punished by the judges, for I should have denied the God that is above" (Job 31:26-28). The reference is to worship of the sun and moon. The worshiper kissed his hand and perhaps extended his hand toward the sun or the moon as though he would kiss them (compare I Kings 19:18; Hos. 13:2). The worship of the host of heaven was practised in the northern kingdom before its fall (II Kings 17:16) and later in Judah in the reign of Manasseh (II Kings 21:3, 5; 23:4-5). It is not necessary, however, to conclude that the author of the book was guilty of an anachronism in putting these words into the mouth of Job. The worship of the heavenly bodies was imported from the east. It may have been practised in the land of Uz in Job's time. At any rate he may have been familiar with it.

(3) THE FUTURE LIFE.

The conception of Sheol in the book of Job is the same which we have seen in earlier books and in those of this time. Death is like sleep and those in Sheol have a sleepy existence. It was only because of his great losses and suffering that Job longed to go there. He said: "Now should I have lain down and been quiet. I should have slept. Then had I been at rest, with kings and counsellors of the earth who built up waste places for themselves, or with princes that had gold, who filled their homes with silver. . . . There the wicked cease from troubling, and there the weary are at rest. There the prisoners are at ease together. They hear not the voice of the taskmaster. The small and the great are there, and the servant is free from his master" (Job 3:14-15, 17-19). Job longed for death that he might go to Sheol (Job 3:20-22). Later he said: "Are not my days few? Cease then and let me alone that I may take comfort a little, before I go, whence I shall not return, even to the land of darkness and of the shadow of death, the land dark as midnight, the land of the shadow of death without any order, and where the light is as midnight" (Job 10:20-22).

Job felt that there would be no return from Sheol, for he said: "When a few years are come, I shall go the way whence I shall not return" (Job 16:22). The familiar picture of Sheol is seen in Job 17:13-16. "If I look for Sheol as my house, if I have spread my couch in the darkness, if I have said to corruption, Thou are my father; to the worm, Thou are my mother and my sister, where then is my hope? And as for my hope, who shall see it? It shall go down to the bars of Sheol, when once there is rest in the dust." Sheol is the abode both of those who were prosperous and those who had adversity in this life. "One dieth in his full strength, being wholly at ease and quiet. His pails are full of milk and the marrow of his bones is moistened. And another dieth in bitterness of soul, and never tasteth of good. They lie down alike in the dust and the worm covereth them" (Job 21:23-26).

Again Job said: "They that are deceased (Margin, 'the shades') tremble beneath the waters and the inhabitants thereof. Sheol is naked before God and Abaddon hath no covering" (Job. 26:5-6). "I know that thou wilt bring me to death and to the house appointed for all living" (Job 30:23). Of adultery he said: "It is a fire that consumeth unto destruction (Margin, 'Abaddon')" (Job 31:12; cp. Prov. 7:27). In his great chapter on the search for wisdom the author of this book says: "Destruction (Margin, 'Abaddon') and Death say, We have heard a rumor thereof with our ears" (Job 28:22). In one of his challenging questions Jehovah speaking from the whirlwind asks Job: "Have the gates of death been revealed unto thee, or hast thou seen the gates of the shadow of death?" (Job 38:17).

It is a remarkable fact that none of these references to Sheol are found in the speeches of the three friends or of Elihu. Yet there is no reason to doubt that their conception of that dark and dreary region was the same as Job's. Eliphaz refers to death (Job. 5:20) and the grave (Job 5:26). Bildad refers to death as the king of terrors (Job 18:13-14). Zophar makes an incidental allusion to Sheol (Job 11:8). Elihu refers several times to the pit which is another name for Sheol (Job 33:18, 22, 24, 28, 30). The last of these references might seem to relate to a return from Sheol, a resurrection. Elihu was speaking of God's merciful dealings with man. "He keepeth back his soul from the pit and his life from perishing by the sword" (Job 33:18). "God is gracious unto him and saith, Deliver him from going down to the pit" (Job 33: 24). "He hath redeemed my soul from going into the pit, and my life shall behold the light" (Job 33:28). Then Elihu said: "Lo all these things doth God work twice, yea thrice, with a man, to bring back his soul from the pit, that he may be enlightened with the light of the living" (Job 33:29-30). In the light of his earlier references it is clear that Elihu did not speak of man being brought back from Sheol after he had entered it, after death, but of his being brought back from that land to whose borders he was drawing near (Job 33:22), God let him come near to death but he did not let him die.

As in the writings of Isaiah so also in the book of Job, together with those passages which give the gloomy and hopeless picture of Sheol, there are others which present at least the faint foregleams of a glorious resurrction (Isa. 25:8; 26:19). We cannot tell whether such passages are a true picture of the hope of Job or whether the author has put into Job's mouth the expression of the resurrection hope of his own time. The former hypothesis is preferable. It is quite conceivable that although in Job's time traditional theology had no hope of a resurrection, the intense struggle in Job's soul, made more bitter by the arguments of his friends, led him to a position far in advance of his time. As Hosea's tragic experience under the divine guidance gave him a new conception of the love of God, so Job's tragic experience under God's guidance may have brought him to the hope of the resurrection.

The first faint gleam of this hope came to Job near the end of the first round of speeches. Although Eliphaz at first spoke graciously (chapters 4 and 5), Bildad (chapter 8) and now Zophar (chapter 11) intimated with increasing clearness that Job must have been a great sinner or he would not have such great misfortunes. In opposition to them Job insisted that he was not a great sinner. Yet he could offer no explanation of his sufferings which did not impugn the justice of God. He knew that he did not deserve his sufferings. Yet his disease was hurrying him on to death. How could he explain it? He knew that he was not a great sinner Yet he held back from charging God with injustice in his dealings with him. At last it began to dawn on him that there would be a solution of his problem if there were a life to come in which the wrongs of this life are righted.

The hint of this solution came to Job from looking at a tree which had been cut down and from whose stump a new sprout came up. He said: "There is hope of a tree, if it be cut down, that it will sprout again, and that the tender branch, thereof will not cease. Though the root thereof wax old in the earth and the stock thereof die in the ground; yet through the scent of water it will bud and put forth boughs like a plant. But man dieth and is laid low; yea man giveth up the ghost and where is he? As the waters fail from the sea and the river wasteth and drieth up; so man lieth down and riseth not. Till the heavens be no more, they shall not awake, nor be roused out of their sleep" (Job 14:7-12).

This seems a long way from the hope of a resurrection. In fact on the face of it and looked at unsympathetically it is a distinct denial of the resurrection. Yet man sometimes comes to the firmest faith through the most positive denial. Job said that there was hope for a tree if it was cut down but no hope for a man if he died. The very act of expressing this contrast showed him how impossible it was. He began to question and contradict his own denial. He began timidly to ask himself: "If there is hope for a tree, is it possible that there is also hope for a man?"

This drawing from nature a lesson for man reminds us of our Lord's wonderful teaching, "Consider the lilies of the field, how they grow; they toil not, neither do they spin: yet I say unto you that even Solomon in all his glory was not arrayed like one of these. But if God doth so clothe the grass of the field, which to-day is and tomorrow is cast into the oven, shall he not much more clothe you, O ye of little faith?" (Matt. 6:28-30). Job had not come to this position. He did not say: "If there is hope for a tree, much more must there be hope for a man"; but he was on the way to that thought. Our Lord said: "Are not two sparrows sold for a penny? And not one of them shall fall on the ground without your Father: but the very hairs of your head are all numbered. Fear not therefore; ye are of more value than many sparrows" (Matt. 10:29-31). Job likewise would come to see that a man is of more value in the sight of God than many trees.

The longing in Job's heart that he might have as much hope as a tree led him immediately to cry out to God: "Oh that thou wouldest hide me in Sheol, that thou wouldest keep me secret until thy wrath be past, that thou wouldest appoint me a set time, and remember me! If a man die, shall he live again? All the days of my warfare would I wait till my release should come. Thou wouldest call and I would answer thee. Thou wouldest have a desire to the work of thy hands" (Job 14:13-15).

Job felt that his death was imminent. Yet even if he died, he prayed that God would hide him somewhere in Sheol until God's wrath was past and then remember him. If only he could look forward to such a blessed issue he could endure all his sufferings and even death itself. The word for "warfare" is used here in the sense of a period of military service as in Job 7:1 and Isa. 40:2. Job felt that his period of suffering was such a time of service and he hoped that some day he would be discharged. If so, he would wait patiently for his release. This period of warfare would not end with death. It would continue in Sheol until God's wrath was spent. Peake well says: "The time of his waiting seems to include both the rest of his life on earth and his time in Sheol, till he returns to full life again (Commentary on Job 14:14). This is evident from Job's prayer that God would hide him in

Sheol until his wrath was past and from his tremendous question, "If a man die, shall he live again?" Job had not reached the point yet when he believed in a resurrection from the dead. It was only a hypothesis thus far; but it was a hypothesis which would solve his problem and he was drawn to it powerfully.

Job came to an assured belief in the resurrection during the second round of speeches. Eliphaz and Bildad had spoken. In answer to the latter Job said near the end of his speech: "But as for me, I know that my Redeemer liveth, and at last he will stand up upon the earth: and after my skin, even this body is destroyed, then without my flesh (Margin, 'from my flesh') shall I see God; whom I, even I, shall see on my side, and mine eyes shall behold, and not as a stranger. My heart is consumed within me" (Job 19:25-27).

The Messianic aspect of this great passage will be considered in another connection. We deal here only with its conception of the future life. Job's family had been killed. His three friends had turned again him. Yet he felt sure that he had a Redeemer, a next-of-kin (Num. 35:9-28; Ruth 2:1, 20; 3:12-13; 4:4-6). This Redeemer, this kinsman was God. Job expressed his conviction that after his death God would stand up upon the earth and that he should see him. The line rendered "Without my flesh shall I see God," is ambiguous. The word translated "without" means literally "from." Like the English word the meaning might be either (1) that Job shall see God looking from his flesh, in a new resurrection body or (2) that being out of, separated from his flesh, he shall see God. While the decision between these two is not easy, the first agrees better with the context and with Job's thought in 14:7-15. God was to stand up upon the earth apparently in such form that physical eyes could see him. If Job was to see him he must do so with physical eyes. The reference to his eyes beholding God favors this interpretation. Although nothing is said of the resurrection body and of course we should not read into the passage the fully developed New Testament doctrine, we are justified in concluding that we have here the earliest hint of a bodily resurrection. Hosea referred to the resurrection of the nation from the exile (Hos. 6:2; 13:14) as did Isaiah (Isa. 25:8; 26:19) and later Ezekiel (Ezek. 37:1-14). Job's resurrection, on the other hand, was an individual matter, although to the author of the book it may also have suggested the national resurrection. Job had come now to an assured faith in a life after death. It was but a momentary flash of prophetic insight which did not come to him again. Yet there is no reason to doubt its genuineness.

(4) THE MESSIANIC HOPE.

In the strict sense of the word there is no prediction of the Messiah in the book of Job. The Messiah was the king of the Davidic line (p. 233). Since Job, his three friends and Elihu were not Israelites, they may have known nothing whatever of the Messianic hope; or, if they knew of the existence of this hope in Israel, they may not have believed in it. At any rate there is no reference to the Messianic king either by them or in any other part of the book. The author writing in the reign of Manasseh must have known of this hope which had been cherished so long in Israel and was so prominent in the writings of the eighth-century prophets; but it would have been an anachronism if he had introduced it into the story of Job.

In the broader sense, however, this book has an important and very profound Messianic element; for it is correct to call any passage of the Old Testament Messianic which looks forward to Christ, His work or His times. This is true of certain important passages in the book of Job. They are unique among all the Messianic passages of the Old Testament because they do not foreshadow Christ from the human side but from the divine. They are the very passages we have already mentioned as suggesting a distinction in God which faintly foreshadowed the New Testament distinction in the persons of the Godhead (Job 9:32-33; 16-19-21; 19:25-27). To them we must add the closely related words of Elihu in Job 33:23-24.

Without anticipating the interpretation of these passages, attention should be drawn to the resemblance between them and the conception of the Angel of Jehovah (pp. 26-27, 56-57, 161-164, 209-212, 283). This Angel was a theophany, a temporary manifestation of God which foreshadowed the incarnation. The Messianic passages in Job also look forward to a manifestation of God. Indeed Elihu uses the term angel in this connection (Job 33:23). While, however, the Angel of Jehovah speaks and acts as God—is addressed and treated as God —there is no mention of his relation to the divine nature. This is taken for granted. The distinction is only between God and God manifest. It scarcely suggests the distinctions between the persons of the Trinity although, as we know from the New Testament, the second person of the Trinity is God manifest. In Job, on the other hand, the distinction is between God and God, between God who afflicts Job and God who is on his side and will vindicate him. This is much more suggestive of the distinctions in the persons of the Trinity as we shall see in considering the language used.

Comparison may also be made with Solomon's personification of Wisdom. Wisdom says: "Jehovah possessed me in the beginning of his way before his works of old. I was set up from everlasting from the beginning before the earth was ... Then I was by him as a master workman; and I was daily his delight, rejoicing always before him, rejoicing in his habitable earth, and my delight was with the sons of men" (Prov. 8:22-23, 30-31). This conception of Wisdom personified as being with God before all creation, His master workman in the work of creation, foreshadowed the relation between the Father and the Son and prepared for the New Testament doctrine of the Logos (pp. 272-273). Yet it differs from Job's conception since Wisdom is represented as being with God but is not distinctly identified with God. Job's conception may be considered more primitive, because he does not speak of his coming Vindicator as distinct from God but as God himself.

The first relevant passage is Job 9:32-33 where Job says of God: "He is not a man as I am that I should answer him, that we should come together in judgment. There is no umpire betwixt us, that might lay his hand upon us both." Taken by itself, so far is this from being a Messianic prediction that it is a distinct denial of the Messianic hope. Job says plainly that God is not a man and that there is no umpire or mediator between God and man. This is entirely negative. Its value, however, comes from the fact that Job was beginning to see the elements of the problem. He felt that his greatest need was common standing-ground with God. If God were only a man like him, they could settle the matter face to face. Since this was not so, the next best thing was an umpire, a mediator, who could act as a go-between for them, laying his hand upon them both. Here again he expressed his denial. There was no mediator. This is where this passage leaves us in black despair.

Yet there was something hopeful about it. It was something to recognize the conditions of the problem, even though Job felt that those conditions were contrary to fact. Having given his denial definite shape in a speech, he began to doubt his own words. It was too terrible to be true. It could not be true. God must be human. There must be an umpire between God and man. So easily does denial pass over into affirmation, skepticism into faith, blindness into vision. Job had made a great advance when he spoke on the subject again. He said: "Even now, behold, my witness is in heaven, and he that voucheth for me is on high. My friends scoff at me, but mine eye poureth out tears unto God, that he would maintain the right of a man with God, and of a son of man with his neighbor" (Job 16:19-21).

This is a virtual denial of what he had said before. Job, it is true, uses a different word. Before he said: "There is no umpire betwixt us." Now he says: "Behold my witness is in heaven and he that voucheth for me is on high." This witness is God himself, for it is he who would maintain the right of a man with God. Before, he thought God was not human. Now he pleads with God as his truest friend. There may be no umpire between God and man; but there is something better. An umpire is entirely impartial and neutral; but the one that Job sees is called a witness and one that vouches for him. The two words occur together in Gen. 31:47. When Jacob fled from his uncle, Laban, taking a large part of Laban's flocks and herds, his uncle pursued him. At Laban's suggestion they set up a heap of stones. Laban called it Jegarsahadutha which, in Aramaic, Laban's language, means the heap of witness, and Jacob called it Galeed, which has the same meaning in Hebrew. The word for witness in Job 16:19 is the one that Jacob used and the word rendered "he that voucheth for me" in Job 16:19 is the one rendered witness in Laban's name of the heap of stones. Indeed this Aramaic word for witness occurs only in these two places. Evidently Job expected God as his witness to do for him what Laban and Jacob expected from the heap of stones. Laban said: "This heap be witness, and the pillar be witness, that I will not pass over this heap to thee, and that thou shalt not pass over this heap and this pillar unto me for harm" (Gen. 31:52). The heap would protect Laban from Jacob. So Job believed that God would protect him from God. God would maintain his right with God.

Having made such a confession, Job easily passed to the passionate conviction which he expressed in Job 19:25-27: "But as for me, I know that my Redeemer liveth, and at last he will stand up upon the earth; and after my skin, even this body, is destroyed, then without my flesh (Margin, 'from my flesh') shall I see God: whom I, even I, shall see on my side, and mine eyes shall behold, and not as a stranger."

We have already considered this passage as teaching the resurrection. Here we have to do with its Messianic aspect. The idea of the resurrection and that of the Messiah are brought together here as in Hos. 6:2. Several things must be noted to understand the full force of the passage. The subject of the first verb is emphatic. Job's friends and perhaps even Elihu did not believe that Job would ever be vindicated. In contrast with them he said: "But as for me, I know that my Redeemer liveth." The verb is in the perfect tense expressing the idea that Job came to know it through his past experience. The word for Redeemer is rendered Vindicator in the margin. It is the same word which is used repeatedly as a title of God, especially in the latter part of Isaiah (Isa. 41:14; 43:14; 44:6, 24; 47:4; 48:17; 49:7, 26; 54:5, 8; 59:20; 60:16; 63:16). We should not think from the fact that Christ is said in the New Testament to redeem us (Luke 24:21; Gal. 3:13; 4:5; Tit. 2:14; I Pet. 1:18) that Job referred directly to Christ. It is clear from the next verse that he referred to God as his Redeemer, his Vindicator.

This word is used in the Mosaic legislation for the next-of-kin whose duty it was, if his near relative died, to purchase his property and marry his widow. Boaz did this for Elimelech (Ruth 2:20; 3:9, 12; 4:1, 3, 6, 8, 14; cp. Jer. 32:6-15). The children of such a marriage were counted the children of the dead man. In them the next-of-kin was considered to have redeemed his brother from death. It was also his duty to redeem the person of his relative if he was sold into slavery (Lev. 25:48-49). Furthermore if he was killed by accident or intention, it was his part to pursue the manslayer and take his life unless the manslayer succeeded in reaching one of the cities of refuge before he overtook him. In this connection he was called the avenger of blood, the word for avenger being the same as that for Redeemer here (Num. 35:12, 19, 21, 24, 25, 27; Deut. 19:6, 12; Josh. 20:3, 5, 9; II Sam. 14:11).

Job had no next-of-kin among men. His children had died. His wife urged him to curse God and die. His three friends turned against him and charged him with sin. In his agony he turned to God as his Redeemer, his kinsman, his Vindicator. We should not draw the parallel too literally. He did not think of God as the avenger of blood. Job was expecting death through the ravages of disease but not by violence. The word is used here much as in Prov. 23:10-11. "Remove not the ancient landmark and enter not into the fields of the fatherless, for their Redeemer is strong. He will plead their cause against thee" (cp. Ps. 119:154). Job had insisted that he was righteous. He longed to have his protestations of righteousness recorded in a book and even graven in the rock forever (Job 19:23-24) so that after his death his fellow men might read them. Suddenly there flashed on him a vision of something infinitely better than any such self vindication. God would be living after he was dead. God would be his Vindicator.

Such a God is the human, the compassionate God for whom he longed (Job 9:32). Job would need no umpire, no mediator between himself and such a God (Job 9:33). He could meet him face to face (verses 26-27). He had already called God his witness in heaven and the one that vouched for him on high (Job 16:19). This witness in heaven would maintain Job's right with God and with his neighbor (Job 16:21). Here he sees something better still. This witness, this sponsor, this redeemer, this vindicator will stand up upon the earth after Job's death.

Verse 26 is difficult of translation. Its disjointed character may be due to the intense emotion of Job. It may be rendered literally: "And after my skin—they have struck this away, then from my flesh I shall see God." The sufferer apparently did not finish his first sentence. Perhaps he was going to say: "After my skin is destroyed, I shall see God." All he said was, "After my skin." Then pointing to himself, he added: "They have struck this away." The subject is probably impersonal, meaning "This is struck away." Some think he was referring to his skin which was almost ready to fall off. The context, however, favors the thought of his whole body which under the ravages of his disease was almost ready to disintegrate.

In the last part of the verse Job said: "Then from my flesh I shall see God." As we have seen in another connection, the Hebrew is ambiguous. It may mean "from my flesh" as though Job would be in the flesh and looking out from it he would see God; or it may mean "out of my flesh, without my flesh, separated from my flesh I shall see God." In the former case the sight of God would be physical sight and in the latter spiritual sight. The verb used here is the one which generally refers to spiritual sight; and if this verse stood alone, we might conclude that this is the meaning here. The same verb occurs in the beginning of verse 27. But the context and what Job said in 14:13-15 favors the idea of physical sight and hence of a bodily resurrection. Job said that God would stand up upon the earth. This clearly implies a physical appearance of God, a theophany. If God were in physical form Job could see him only with physical sight. Accordingly in the second line of verse 27 he uses the general word to see, used both of physical and spiritual sight. As if to make clear that he means physical sight, he refers to his eyes saying "and mine eyes shall behold." In Job 14:13-15 the sufferer prayed that God would hide him in Sheol and then raise him from the dead. So here he expressed his faith in such a resurrection. God would appear in human form. Job also would have new flesh, a new body. Then he would see God face to face.

In verse 27, as in verse 25, the subject of the verb is emphatic. "Whom I, even I, shall see." Job was rejoicing that his vision of God would not be through an umpire, an intermediary (Job 9:33) but direct and personal. The Hebrew which is rendered in the text "on my side" and in the margin "for myself" means literally "for me." Exactly the same Hebrew is translated "with me" in Gen. 31:42, "for me" in Ps. 56:9 and "on my side" in Ps. 118:6. The rendering "on my side" is preferable here. Job felt that God had been against him; but looking far into the future he now expressed the belief that after his death and resurrection he would see God standing on the earth, no longer hostile but on his side. Similarly in the next line he said that in that blessed time his eyes would behold God and not as a stranger. God had seemed as an alien, a stranger to him, unfriendly and even unhuman. It would not always be so. God would at last be human, his witness in heaven, his sponsor on high, his ever-living Vindicator. Best of all he would see him with his own eyes, standing upon the earth after his death, on his side, not as a stranger. This was enough. Job felt as David did when he exclaimed: "As for me, I shall behold thy face in righteousness. I shall be satisfied, when I awake, with beholding thy form" (Ps. 17:15; cp. p. 246).

Such was Job's great hope. His understanding of its meaning was vague and shadowy. God was his hope, the God who would stand on the earth in the future. He was looking in the direction of Christ and the figure which he saw was none other than Christ, although he could not discern him clearly or describe him accurately. Whatever Job meant by his words, the inspiring Spirit meant Christ. The Christian church has not erred through all the ages when in the light of the fulfilment they recognize here a picture of our Incarnate Redeemer.

Elihu probably referred to Job's great hope when he said: "If there be with him an angel, an interpreter, one among a thousand, to show unto man what is right for him, then God is gracious unto him and saith, Deliver him from going down to the pit. I have found a ransom" (Job 33:23-24). Elihu did not use Job's words. He did not speak of an umpire, a witness, a sponsor, a Vindicator. Yet the function which he assigned to the angel, the in-

terpreter is similar. The umpire would lay his hand upon
God and Job to bring them together in judgment (Job
9:32-33). The witness and sponsor would maintain Job's
right with God and his neighbor (Job 16:19-21). The
Vindicator would be on Job's side pleading for him with
God (Job 19:25-27). Job's idea was that he needed such
a person, not to show him what was right for him, but to
show God his righteousness. Elihu had a different idea
of the mediator. If there were an angel who would show
man that which was right for him and if (it is implied)
man should heed the message of the angel who interpreted God's will to him, then God would forgive man and
deliver him from death. Elihu implied that if Job should
repent, God would save him from dying. Job believed
that he was righteous. He did not need to repent. His
death seemed sure to come. Yet after death he would
come back from Sheol and clothed in human form he
would see God standing on earth, his Vindicator, on his
side, not a stranger.

(5) Satan.

We should be careful not to read the fully developed
New Testament doctrine of Satan into the book of Job.
The term means an adversary and is used of human adversaries (I Sam. 29:4; II Sam. 19:22; I Kings 5:4;
11:14, 23, 25). When Balaam went with the princes of
Moab, the angel of Jehovah stood in his way as an adversary (Num. 22:22, 32). The term came to be applied
in particular to one of the angels of God whose duty it
was to act as prosecutor before God against man. In the
zealous performance of his duty he went about looking for

human sin and when he found it he reported it to God. This is the situation in the prologue of this book.

"Now it came to pass on the day when the sons of God came to present themselves before Jehovah, that Satan also came among them. And Jehovah said unto Satan, Whence comest thou? Then Satan answered Jehovah and said, From going to and fro in the earth, and from walking up and down in it. And Jehovah said unto Satan, Hast thou considered my servant Job, for there is none like him in the earth, a perfect and an upright man, one that feareth God and turneth away from evil? Then Satan answered Jehovah and said, Doth Job fear God for nought? Hast not thou made a hedge about him, and about his house, and about all that he hath on every side? Thou hast blessed the work of his hands, and his substance is increased in the land. But put forth thy hand now and touch all that he hath and he will renounce thee to thy face. And Jehovah said unto Satan, Behold, all that he hath is in thy power; only upon himself put not forth thy hand. So Satan went forth from the presence of Jehovah" (Job 1:6-12). Although it is not said that Satan brought about the loss of Job's family and property, that is clearly implied.

"Again it came to pass on the day when the sons of God came to present themselves before Jehovah, that Satan came also among them to present himself before Jehovah. And Jehovah said unto Satan. From whence comest thou? And Satan answered Jehovah and said, From going to and fro in the earth, and from walking up and down in it. And Jehovah said unto Satan, Hast thou considered my servant Job, for there is ñone like him in the earth, a perfect and an upright man, one that feareth God and turneth away from evil? And he still holdeth fast his integrity, although thou movedst me against him, to destroy him without cause. And Satan answered Jehovah and said, Skin for skin, yea all that a man hath will he give for his life. But put forth thy hand now and touch his bone and his flesh, and he will renounce thee to thy face. And Jehovah said unto Satan, Behold he is in thy hand; only spare his life. So Satan went forth from the presence of Jehovah, and smote Job with sore boils from the sole of his foot unto his crown" (Job 2:1-7).

It is clear from these passages that Satan was not omnipotent. Indeed he had no power at all except that which God gave him. Like any other angel he had to present himself before God to hear and to obey his will. He could make suggestions but the power was with God alone. When God placed all that Job had in Satan's power, he could cause Job to lose his children and his property; but he could not touch his body, for God commanded, "Only upon himself put not forth thy hand" (Job 1:12). When later God enlarged his permission to Satan, the adversary brought a terrible disease on Job; but he could not cause his death, for God said, "Only spare his life" (Job 2:6). Satan is not mentioned again in the book. We do not know how much of Job's later affliction at the hands of his wife and of his friends was Satan's work. But if Satan caused it, he did so because God permitted him.

The attitude of Satan was a cynical one. While Jehovah drew his attention to the unique integrity and piety of Job (Job 1:8; 2:3), Satan did not believe that Job's piety was unselfish. He thought that Job served God because of the prosperity and protection which God gave him. When Satan's first attempt to turn Job from his piety by taking away his children and his property failed, he still believed that Job's piety was selfish. He claimed that the test had not gone far enough. If only his body were touched, his essential selfishness would be revealed and he would forsake his piety. The attitude of Satan toward God if not hostile was at least unfriendly. He disagreed with God about the integrity and piety of Job. He desired to see Job's integrity and piety broken down and God's faith in Job proven false. He went as far as he could to accomplish these ends.

In this cynical attitude of Satan we can see the germ of the development of the later doctrine, in which Satan is represented as the enemy of God and man. Satan did not tempt Job to sin except in the sense that the losses and the bodily suffering which he brought upon him were themselves the most powerful temptations. So far as the book tells us, Satan never suggested to Job that he should renounce God. Yet the evil thoughts which Job sometimes expressed to his friends, charging God with injustice, the sin for which at last he abhorred himself and repented in dust and ashes (Job 42:6), were directly due to Satan's act in bringing these afflictions upon him. Satan is represented in the book as obeying God, as one of his angels. Yet he obeyed him not with a spirit of genuine understanding. He did not desire that which God desired. God desired righteousness in man and rejoiced in it whenever he found it. Satan desired sin in man and rejoiced in it whenever he found it. Thus in reality he was working against God and man.

A close parallel to the representation of Satan in the book of Job is found in the prophecy of Micaiah to Ahab: "I saw Jehovah sitting on his throne and all the host of heaven standing by him on his right hand and on his left. And Jehovah said, Who shall entice Ahab, that he may go up and fall at Ramoth-gilead? And one said on this manner; and another said on that manner. And there came forth a spirit and stood before Jehovah and said, I will entice him. And Jehovah said unto him, Wherewith? And he said, I will go forth and will be a lying spirit in the mouth of all his prophets. And he said, Thou shall entice him, and shalt prevail also; go forth and do so" (I Kgs. 22:19-22; II Chron. 18:18-21). The spirit mentioned here so closely resembles the Satan of the book of Job that they are doubtless the same. Both are attendants upon the throne of God. Both work to bring about the downfall of a man. God permits both of them to do this evil work. Yet there is a marked difference between the two stories. Ahab was a very wicked man. Therefore God desired his downfall and called for a volunteer to accomplish it (cp pp. 293-295). Job was a very righteous man. God did not desire his downfall and permitted Satan to afflict him only that his character might be developed under suffering.

The conception of Satan in Zechariah's vision somewhat resembles that in the book of Job. "He showed me Joshua the high priest standing before the angel of Jehovah, and Satan standing at his right hand to be his adversary. And Jehovah said unto Satan, Jehovah rebuke thee, O Satan; yea Jehovah that hath chosen Jerusalem rebuke thee. Is not this a brand plucked out of the fire? Now Joshua was clothed with filthy garments and was standing before the angel. And he answered and spake unto those that stood before him saying, Take the filthy garments from off him. And unto him he said, Behold I have caused thine iniquity to pass from thee and I will clothe thee with rich apparel" (Zech. 3:1-4). Here as in Job, Satan is the accuser of man, the prosecutor. As such he stands at the right hand of the accused person (cp. Ps. 109:6). His hostility to God, or rather God's hostility to him, however, comes out more clearly than in Job. God rebukes Satan for bringing charges against Joshua the high priest, and thus against the people whom he represented. Having brought his people out of the exile as a brand is plucked from the fire, he will not hear charges against them. Accordingly he commands that the filthy garments which symbolize the sin of Joshua and his people be taken from him and that he be clothed in rich apparel.

The reference to Satan in I Chron. 21:1 should not be regarded as indicative of the doctrine of Satan in David's time but in the time of the Chronicler. The prophetic historian said: "Again the anger of Jehovah was kindled against Israel and he moved David against them, saying, Go, number Israel and Judah" (II Sam. 24:1). The Chronicler records the same event in these words: "Satan stood up against Israel and moved David to number Israel" (I Chron. 21:1). This was the Chronicler's interpretation of the event. God moved David to number Israel by permitting Satan to do it. Since Satan here is the tempter, the conception should be ascribed to the

Chronicler's time rather than to David's (cp. p. 249-250).

Although in the light of the New Testament we can recognize in the evil intelligence who tempted Eve (Gen. 3:1-6) Satan himself, this was not clear in Old Testament days (cp. p. 21). They are never identified in the Hebrew scriptures. Indeed the doctrine of Satan was but imperfectly developed even at the end of the older revelation. Yet in the Satan of the book of Job who goes to and fro in the earth and walks up and down in it, looking for some man against whom he can bring charges of sin, we can recognize our "adversary, the devil," who "as a roaring lion, walketh about, seeking whom he may devour" (I Pet. 5:8).

(6) ANGELS.

Angels are called by different designations in this book. In the prologue (Job 1:6; 2:1) and once in the address of Jehovah from the whirlwind (Job 38:7) they are called the sons of God. Many scholars think that this title refers to the angels in Gen. 6:2; but such an interpretation would represent the angels as having sexual relation with women, an idea never found elsewhere in scripture and contrary to our Lord's statement that the angels neither marry nor are given in marriage (Mt. 22:30; Mk. 12:25; Luke 20:35-36). The sons of God in Gen. 6:2 were not the angels but the descendants of the godly Sethite line who intermarried with the daughters of men, the women of the wicked Cainite line. The result of this mingling of the godly seed with the wicked was the corruption of all flesh which made the flood necessary. The worshippers of God are called elsewhere his sons (Deut. 14:1; 32:5, 19; Ps. 73:15; Isa. 43:6; Hos. 1:10). The only place outside the book of Job where the angels are called sons of God, or rather where one angel is called a son of God, is Dan. 3:25. Nebuchadnezzar saw four men in the fiery furnace and he said: "The aspect of the fourth is like a son of the gods."

"Now it came to pass on the day when the sons of God came to present themselves before Jehovah that Satan came also among them" (Job 1:6; cp. 2:1). This repeated statement represents the angels as attendants upon the throne of God, messengers who went abroad to do his work and carry out his will. From time to time they presented themselves before Jehovah to report on that which they had seen and done. Satan came among them and was apparently one of them. He had his special work to do for God, to discover and report on any delinquencies, any sin among men. We may infer from this that other angels had their particular work to do; but since the special theme of the book has to do with what Satan did with Job and that which resulted from it, nothing is said in the prologue concerning the duties or the work of other angels.

This is the first time in scripture that a distinction is made between the angels or the name of an angel is given. The earlier distinction between the Angel of Jehovah and other angels is properly not a distinction between different angels, for the Angel of Jehovah is not a permanent being who is always an angel, but a designation of Jehovah when he manifests himself temporarily in the form of an angel. Thus Satan was the first angel mentioned by name in the Old Testament. Later two angels are named in the

book of Daniel. One was Gabriel (Dan. 8:16; 9:21)
who interpreted Daniel's visions to him and may perhaps
be identified with the angel who had the same function
in relation to Zechariah (Zech. 1:9, 13, 14, 19; 2:3; 4:1,
4, 5; 5:5, 10; 6:4). The other is Michael (Dan. 10:13,
21; 12:1) who is called an archangel in Jude 9.

The assembling of the angels in the presence of Jehovah (Job 1:6; 2:1) resembles Micaiah's vision. He
said: "I saw Jehovah sitting on his throne, and all the
host of heaven standing by him on his right hand and on
his left" (I Kgs. 22:19; II Chron. 18:18). The host of
heaven are not called angels in this account. One of them
is called a spirit. Yet they were evidently angels like the
sons of God in Job. We are also reminded of Isaiah's
vision. He said, "I saw the Lord sitting upon a throne,
high and lifted up; and his train filled the temple. Above
him stood the seraphim: each one had six wings; with
twain he covered his face and with twain he covered his
feet, and with twain he did fly. And one cried unto another and said, Holy, holy, holy is Jehovah of hosts; the
whole earth is full of his glory" (Isa. 6:1-3). These
seraphim, however, seem to be a special order of angels.
It was not their function to carry out the distant behests
of God but to guard his holy presence and give him constant praise. A closer parallel to the assembly of the sons
of God in Job is found in Daniel's vision. He said: "I
beheld till thrones were placed, and one that was ancient
of days did sit: his raiment was white as snow, and the
hair of his head like pure wool; his throne was fiery
flames, and the wheels thereof burning fire. A fiery
stream issued and came forth from before him: thousands

of thousands ministered unto him, and ten thousand times ten thousand stood before him" (Dan. 7:9-10).

In his address from the whirlwind Jehovah challenged Job to tell whereupon the foundations of the earth were fastened and who laid the corner-stone thereof, "when the morning stars sang together, and all the sons of God shouted for joy" (Job. 38:7). In this beautiful passage the morning stars are thought of as part of the heavenly host (cp Isa. 40:26) and associated with the angels in praising God for his works of creation. The angels are said to have been in existence before the foundations of the earth. Indeed there is nothing said either in the Old Testament or the New about their being created. It is, however, a sure inference that they are not eternal and self-existent like God but are creatures of his omnipotent hand.

Eliphaz referred twice to the angels as the holy ones. He said to Job: "Call now; is there any that will answer thee? And to which of the holy ones wilt thou turn?" (Job 5:1). His idea apparently was that it would be futile for Job to appeal to the angels against God. His wiser course was to appeal directly to God himself without the use of a mediator (Job 5:8). Eliphaz said of God: "Behold he putteth no trust in his holy ones. Yea the heavens are not clean in his sight" (Job 15:15). This is in a hyperbolic passage concerning the intense purity of God. In saying that God puts no trust in his angels Eliphaz went too far. The angels are by no means sinless beings, as Eliphaz had already said (Job 4:18). Yet they are properly termed God's holy ones and God uses them to carry out his will. The angels are referred to as the holy ones elsewhere in the Old Testament (Ps. 89:5, 7; Dan. 4:13, 17, 23; Zech. 14:5). In the New Testament they are called the holy angels (Mk. 8:38; Luke 9:26).

Eliphaz also referred to the angels by the usual name, saying of God: "Behold he putteth no trust in his servants, and his angels he chargeth with folly" (Job 4:18). God's servants are the angels as the last half of the verse shows. Hence the first line is identical in meaning with the first line of Job 15:15. While God recognizes the imperfection of the angels he does put trust in them. The word rendered folly at the end of the verse occurs nowhere else in the Hebrew scriptures. It is probably related to an Ethiopic verb which means to wander and thus should be translated error.

The last reference to an angel in this book is in the words of Elihu: "If there be with him an angel, an interpreter, one among a thousand, to show unto man what is right for him, then God is gracious unto him and saith, Deliver him from going down to the pit, I have found a ransom" (Job 33:22-23). As we have already seen, Elihu probably referred to Job's hope of an umpire (Job 9:33), a witness, a sponsor (Job 16:19) and a Vindicator (Job 19:25). In his opinion the obstacle to reconciliation was in man and not in God. Man needed an angel to come to him from God, one who would interpret God's will to him and show him his duty. This function of the angel, interpreting God's will, reminds us of the way Gabriel interpreted the revelations of God to Daniel (Dan. 8:15-27; 9:20-27) and the way the angel that talked with Zechariah interpreted his visions (Zech. 1:7-21; 2:1-5; 4:1-14; 5:1-11; 6:1-8). Elihu was right in thinking that if man could have such an angel to interpret his duty to him and if man should heed the lessons of the angel, God would graciously forgive and deliver him.

(7) THE AFFLICTIONS OF THE RIGHTEOUS.

The purpose of Satan in the afflictions of Job is clear. When Jehovah drew his attention to the righteousness and piety of Job he asked: "Doth Job fear God for nought? Hast not thou made a hedge about him and about his house and about all that he hath on every side? Thou hast blessed the work of his hands and his substance is increased in the land. But put forth thy hand now and touch all that he hath, and he will renounce thee to thy face" (Job 1:9-11). Satan's evident purpose was to prove that Job's righteousness and piety were selfish. When the first experiment failed from Satan's standpoint, he said: "Skin for skin, yea all that a man hath will he give for his life. But put forth thy hand now and touch his bone and his flesh and he will renounce thee to thy face" (Job 2:4-5). Satan's persistent desire and purpose were to prove Job a sinner, to make him sin by renouncing God to his face.

The book does not state why God permitted Satan to make these two attempts to prove Job a sinner, to make him sin. The general tenor of Jehovah's address from the whirlwind is that God is sovereign and that man cannot fully understand his ways. It seems to be implied in the prologue that God rejoiced in Job's righteousness and piety. This is seen from his words to Satan: "He still holdeth fast his integrity, although thou movedst me against him, to destroy him without cause" (Job 2:3)

Evidently God hoped that Job would hold fast his integrity in the second trial as he had done in the first. In a sense the story of the book is a contest between God and Satan in which God desired Job's righteousness and Satan desired his sin. Yet in this contest God permitted Satan to afflict Job in a way which might result in sin and thus in a triumph for Satan. We do not know why God permitted this. It is the same question as, Why does God permit sin and trouble in the world? The nearest approach we can get to an answer is that God knows that character can be strengthened only by testing. There is always the possibility that man will fail under the test but there is also the possibility that he will resist the temptation and become stronger. The latter possibility cannot be had without the former. In God's infinite wisdom the hazard is worthwhile.

Neither Job, his three friends nor Elihu knew anything about the scene in heaven in the prologue. They discussed the problem of Job's afflictions from the standpoint of their earthly experience and their views about God. The three friends held the common view that when a man suffers it is proof positive that he is a sinner, that righteousness is always rewarded and sin is always punished in this life. This view seemed the necessary result of their scant knowledge of the future life. Since God was just, rewards and punishments had to come soon. If the state of the righteous and the wicked is the same in the future life, it must be different in this life. This view underlies much of the Old Testament. It inspired the protest against vicarious suffering (Gen. 18:23-25; Jer. 31:29; Ezek. 18:2) and the emphasis of Jeremiah and Ezekiel

upon individual responsibility before God (Jer. 31:29-30;
Ezek. 18). It was also the common view in our Lord's
time. It inspired the question of the disciples: "Who
sinned, this man or his parents, that he should be born
blind?" (John 9:2). It called forth Christ's answer to
those who told him of the Galileans whose blood Pilate
mingled with their sacrifices. "He answered and said
unto them, Think ye that these Galileans were sinners
above all the Galileans, because they have suffered these
things? I tell you, Nay: but except ye repent, ye shall
all in like manner perish. Or those eighteen upon whom
the tower in Siloam fell and killed them, think ye that
they were offenders above all the men that dwell in
Jerusalem? I tell you, Nay: but except ye repent, ye
shall all likewise perish" (Luke 13:2-5). The view of
Elihu was essentially the same as that of the friends. Job
himself probably held the same view before his sufferings.
He was forced by his experience to abandon it although
he had nothing constructive to put in its place until he
heard God's voice and his eyes saw him.

Eliphaz, the oldest and most thoughtful of the friends,
approached the subject with sympathy and tact. He did
not at first charge Job with sin. Yet his doctrine is clear
when he says: "Is not thy fear of God thy confidence and
the integrity of thy ways thy hope? Remember, I pray
thee, who ever perished being innocent? Or where were
the upright cut off? According as I have seen, they that
plow iniquity and sow trouble reap the same. By the
breath of God they perish, and by the blast of his anger
are they consumed" (Job 4:6-9). Apparently Eliphaz
was willing thus far to give Job the benefit of the doubt.

Perhaps his sufferings were the common lot of man. "Affliction cometh not forth from the dust, neither doth trouble spring out of the ground; but man is born unto trouble as the sparks fly upward" (Job 5:6-7).

Eliphaz showed his breadth by recognizing that affliction is often a blessed thing, the disciplinary method of God to turn a man from his sin. "Behold, happy is the man whom God correcteth: therefore despise not thou the chastening of the Almighty. For he maketh sore and bindeth up. He woundeth and his hands make whole. He will deliver thee in six troubles; yea in seven there shall no evil touch thee. In famine he will redeem thee from death, and in war from the power of the sword. Thou shalt be hid from the scourge of the tongue, neither shalt thou be afraid of destruction when it cometh. At destruction and dearth thou shalt laugh, neither shalt thou be afraid of the beasts of the earth. For thou shalt be in league with the stones of the field, and the beasts of the field shall be at peace with thee" (Job 5:17-23).

These were fine words and Job would have done well to heed them. Unfortunately the ideal of righteousness and piety in that time was not very high. Job was a righteous man. He feared God and turned away from evil (Job 1:18; 2:3). But he was not perfect in the sense of being incapable of moral improvement. He could not appreciate the subtler sins which are discernible to the Christian under the guidance of the Holy Spirit. Hence he could not appreciate that perhaps God sent his affliction to purge him from these subtler sins. Eliphaz also had no appreciation of this. He undoubtedly meant that Job must have been guilty of some flagrant sin and that God sent these afflictions to punish him. If he would learn the lesson and repent, all would be well.

In his reply to Eliphaz, Job complained of his misery and he longed for death. But in answer to the hints of Eliphaz that he must have been guilty of flagrant sin, he made a firm denial. He said: "I have not denied the words of the Holy One" (Job 6:10). He demanded: "Cause me to understand wherein I have erred" (Job 6:24). "My cause is righteous. Is there injustice on my tongue?" (Job 6:29-30). At the end of his speech he acknowledged the possibility of his having sinned; but he pled with God: "If I have sinned what do I unto thee, O thou watcher of men? Why hast thou set me as a mark for thee so that I am a burden to myself? And why dost thou not pardon my transgression and take away mine iniquity?" (Job 7:20-21).

Bildad and Zophar taking the hint from Eliphaz come out more clearly in their charge of sin. Thus Bildad says: "If thou wert pure and upright, surely now he would awake for thee and make the habitation of thy righteousness prosperous. . . . Behold God will not cast away a perfect man, neither will he uphold the evildoers" (Job 8:6, 20). Job replies that it is impossible for man to be just with God. "How can man be just with God? If he be pleased to contend with him, he cannot answer him one of a thousand. . . . It is all one; therefore I say, he destroyeth the perfect and the wicked. . . . If I wash myself with snow water and make my hands never so clean, yet wilt thou plunge me in the ditch and mine own clothes shall abhor me" (Job 9:2-3, 22, 30-31). He says to God: "Thou knowest that I am not wicked" (Job

10:7). Zophar says to Job bluntly: "Know therefore that God exacteth of thee less than thine iniquity deserveth. . . . If iniquity be in thy hand put it far away and let not unrighteousness dwell in thy tents" (Job 11:6, 14). Again Job replies: "I know that I am righteous" (Job 13:18).

The second round of speeches follows similar lines. Eliphaz comes out plainly against Job. "Yea thou doest away with fear and hinderest devotion before God. For thine iniquity teacheth thy mouth and thou choosest the tongue of the crafty. Thine own mouth condemneth thee and not I. Yea thine own lips testify against thee" (Job 15:4-6). Job says: "There is no violence in my hands and my prayer is pure" (Job 16:17). Bildad describes the misfortunes of the wicked (Job 18). Job appeals to his friends for pity (Job 19:21) and expresses his faith in his ultimate vindication (Job 19:25-27). Zophar speaks of the prosperity of the wicked as short (Job 20) and Job in direct contradiction declares that the wicked prosper (Job 21:7-16).

In his third speech Eliphaz, doubtless angered by Job's repeated claim of righteousness, charges the sufferer with specific sins. "Is not thy wickedness great? Neither is there any end to thine iniquities. For thou hast taken pledges of thy brother for nought and stripped the naked of their clothing. Thou hast not given water to the weary to drink, and thou hast withholden bread from the hungry. . . . Thou hast sent widows away empty and the arms of the fatherless have been broken. Therefore snares are round about thee and sudden fear troubleth thee. . . . Wilt thou keep the old way which wicked men have trodden, who were snatched away before their time, whose foundation was poured out as a stream? . . . If thou return to the Almighty, thou shalt be built up, if thou put away unrighteousness far from thy tents" (Job 22:5-7, 9-10, 15-16, 23). These charges must have been based on the imagination of Eliphaz. If Job had really been guilty of such sins of omission and commission, he would not have been called perfect and upright, one that feared God and turned away from evil (Job 1:1, 8; 2:3). Following his doctrine that the sufferer must be a sinner, Eliphaz inferred that Job must have been guilty of such sins.

In his answer Job recognizes that his trouble may be God's testing of him. "When he hath tried me, I shall come forth as gold. My foot hath held fast to his steps. His way have I kept and turned not aside. I have not gone back from the commandment of his lips. I have treasured up the words of his mouth more than my necessary food" (Job 23:10-12). Bildad's short third speech contains nothing new. He merely echoes Job's question: "How can man be just with God?" (Job 25:4; cp. 9:2). Job still clings to his integrity saying: "Till I die I will not put away mine integrity from me. My righteousness I hold fast and will not let it go. My heart shall not reproach me so long as I live" (Job 27:5-6). In Job 27:7-23, which is probably part of the lost third speech of Zophar, he describes the evil fate of the wicked.

After the three friends had ceased speaking Job longed for his former days of prosperity and fellowship with God when he did many deeds of kindness and justice (Job 29:12-17; 30:25). He called down curses on him-

self if he had been guilty of such sins as those with which
Eliphaz charged him (Job 31:5-40; cp. 22:6-9). Elihu
made no original contribution to the problem. He emphasized the idea which Eliphaz had already mentioned
that suffering may be God's method of turning a man
from his sin and applied this especially to physical disease
such as that of Job (Job 33:19-28; cp. 5:17-27). If man
repents he is restored. He charged Job with sin (Job
34:5-9) and said: "He addeth rebellion unto his sin. He
clappeth his hands among us and multiplieth his words
against God" (Job 34:37). Even kings are punished for
their sins; but if they repent they are restored (Job 36:7-
12). To Job he says: "Yea he would have allured thee
out of distress into a broad place where there is no strait-
ness" (Job 36:16). At the end of his speeches Elihu
returns to the thought which Job and his friends had also
emphasized that God and his ways are beyond human
comprehension. Yet he contradicted Job's statements that
God was unjust and urged the sufferer to submit piously
to the divine judgment (Job 37:23-24).

Although the address of Jehovah from the whirlwind
does not even mention the problem of Job's sufferings
which he and the friends had been discussing, it is in the
deepest sense an answer to Job. The reason that neither
Job nor the friends could solve this problem was their
ignorance of many of the conditions. The friends did not
know enough about God and his ways to be justified in
concluding that suffering in this life is proof of sin. Job
did not know enough to conclude that God had dealt unjustly with him. His greatest need was a vision of the
majesty and wisdom of God. This would humble him and

make him trust even if he could not know. Therefore Jehovah in a series of ironic questions inquires whether Job understands the divine works of creation and providence (chapters 38-39).

The best possible answer God could give Job was to turn his attention away from the immediate problem of his sufferings to something vastly larger, to give him a new world-view. Moulton well says: "The divine intervention brings out that the good and the great, all that men instinctively admire in the universe, is just as inexplicable as evil. Now this is distinctly a contribution towards the solution of the problem; in philosophic terms, it has included the matter under discussion in a wider category, and this represents a stage of philosophic advance" (Literary Study of the Bible, p. 35). So Jesus turned Nicodemus away from the question he had come to ask, telling him that spiritual truth can be seen only by those who are born anew (John 3:1-3). With Nicodemus as with Job this indirect answer was the best possible answer. If Job would look at his problem in the light of this larger world-view, he would see it in its true proportion and setting even if he could not solve it.

God called Job's attention to the fact that man is not the only being on the earth for whom he cares. He causes it to rain on a land where no man is, on the wilderness wherein there is no man (Job 38:26). He provides for the raven his prey when his young ones cry unto God (Job 38:41). He has many creatures, like the lion (Job 38:39-40), the wild-goat (Job 39:1-4), the wild ass (Job 39:5-8), the wild ox (Job 39:9-12), the ostrich (Job 39:13-18), the horse (Job 39:19-25), the hawk (Job 39:26) and the eagle (Job 39:27-30). Job cannot solve his problem by thinking of himself alone. He must think of himself as a member of society, a part of God's world.

Job was humbled and silenced by Jehovah's address from the whirlwind (Job 40:3-5). Even further to humble him God drew his attention to two of his largest creatures, behemoth (the hippopotamus) and leviathan (the crocodile). Of the former God said: "Behold now behemoth which I made as well as thee. . . . He is the chief of the ways of God. He only that made him giveth him his sword" (Job 40:15, 19). If Job cannot control leviathan how much less can he contend with the God who made leviathan. "None is so fierce that he dare stir him up. Who then is he that can stand before me? Who hath first given unto me that I should repay him? Whatsoever is under the whole heaven is mine" (Job 41:10-11).

At last Job confessed: "Therefore have I uttered that which I understood not, things too wonderful for me, which I knew not. . . . I had heard of thee by the hearing of the ear, but now mine eye seeth thee. Wherefore I abhor myself and repent in dust and ashes" (Job 42:3, 5-6). This repentance of Job was not for sins he had committed before his afflictions, sins which were the cause of those afflictions, but for the sin of charging God with injustice, a sin of which he had been guilty in the argument with the friends (Job 9:17, 22, 30-31; 10:3; 16:9, 12-14; 19:6-12; 27:2; 30:18-23). This sin was due to ignorance. His knowledge of God at that time came from mere hearsay evidence. Now that he saw God in his majesty and wisdom, he saw also his own sin and abhorred himself in dust and ashes. But if Job was guilty of this sin, the three friends had committed a vastly greater offense. They had not spoken of God the thing that was right as Job in the main had (Job 42:7-8). They clung to their outworn theory that suffering was always penal, when the fact of Job's previous integrity should have taught them better. In their narrow attempt to honor God, they had dishonored him far more than Job had. God forgave them when they offered sacrifices and Job prayed for them. As for Job, Jehovah turned his captivity when he prayed for his friends (Job 42:10).

Most commentators have overlooked the significance of this turning-point in Job's fortunes. God did not forgive Job until Job forgave his friends. We might almost say that God could not forgive Job until the true spirit of forgiveness was in Job's heart. It was not that Job's forgiveness of his friends was the price he paid to God for his own forgiveness. Rather Job's forgiving spirit toward his friends was the necessary condition of his heart so that he could receive and appreciate the forgiving love of God. All hatred and malice were gone from his heart when he could pray for his enemies. He loved his enemies and prayed for them that persecuted him. So he became a true child of God who makes his sun to rise on the evil and the good and sends his rain on the just and the unjust (Matt. 5:44-45). He could have prayed: "Forgive us our debts as we also have forgiven our debtors." This was the climax of the development of Job's character. His afflictions had done the work which God meant them to do. God had tried him and he came forth as gold (Job 23:10).

Some writers regard the happy ending of the story of Job as inconsistent with a high view of character and rewards. They fail to see that it was not in the restoration of Job's former external prosperity that his real reward consisted. He had never asked for this. What he longed for supremely was that he might see God and that he might be vindicated from the unjust charges of the friends. His real reward consisted in the divine forgiveness and approval. He had proven that he served God for nought, without hope of reward. His affliction having now accomplished its work, there was no reason that it should continue longer. It was safe for God to give property and prosperity to such a man, for he had proven that he appreciated their true function, not as supplying the motive for righteousness but as the incidental results of righteousness. Job was like those of later time to whom Christ said: "Seek ye first his kingdom and his righteousness; and all these things shall be added unto you" (Matt. 6:33). We should not seek God's kingdom and his righteousness in order to get temporal blessings. If, however, forgetting all earthly rewards we seek God's kingdom and righteousness, we will get them and also the earthly rewards. "So Jehovah blessed the latter end of Job more than his beginning" (Job 42:12). His godliness was seen to be profitable for all things, temporal as well as spiritual (I Tim. 4:8).

(8) MORALITY.

It is difficult to determine whether the book of Job indicates the morality of the time when it was written or of the time when Job lived. If, however, it represents the morality of Job's time, it also is indicative of the moral standards of the author of the book, standards which he wished the people of his time to accept for their own. For he chose this story and gave it its form of prose and poetry, because he thought it appropriate and necessary for his time. We cannot tell how far the morality of the writer's time is reflected in his book. If we are right in placing the book in the time of Manasseh, its morality may be compared with that reflected in the writings of the eighth-century prophets and especially with the latter part of Isaiah which probably was written then.

The most important moral matter in this book is found in the character of Job himself, who was one of the noblest figures in the whole range of scripture. The author says of him that he "was perfect and upright, and one that feared God and turned away from evil" (Job 1:1). He was not only righteous and pious himself but as a true father he was anxious that his children should be the same. Therefore when his sons and daughters feasted he "sent and sanctified them, and rose up early in the morning, and offered burnt-offerings according to the number of them all: for Job said, It may be that my sons have sinned and renounced God in their hearts. Thus did Job continually" (Job 1:5). He was not perfect in the sense that his character could not be improved; but his moral character was mature and his piety was genuine. Not only was he upright but, when evil presented itself to him, he turned away from it.

The testimony of Jehovah to the character of Job is identical with that of the author. "Jehovah said unto Satan, Hast thou considered my servant Job? For there

is none like him in the earth, a perfect and an upright
man, one that feareth God and turneth away from evil"
(Job 1:8).   Evidently Job was quite exceptional in his
integrity and piety.   Yet we should not conclude that the
moral standards of his contemporaries were low.   Whatever may be said concerning the mistaken theory maintained by the friends and by Elihu, they were also men
with high moral standards.   We know nothing of their
conduct except in their attitude towards Job but they were
strict moralists.   Satan suspected Job of serving God for
his selfish advantage; but God trusted him so much that
he was willing to let Satan take away his property and
his children, believing that he would remain true to God
and duty.   The issue showed that God's confidence was
not misplaced.   When the news of repeated disasters came
to him, "Job arose and rent his robe, and shaved his head,
and fell down upon the ground and worshipped: and he
said, Naked came I out of my mother's womb and naked
shall I return thither: Jehovah gave and Jehovah hath
taken away; blessed be the name of Jehovah.   In all this
Job sinned not, nor charged God foolishly (Margin, 'attributed folly to God')" (Job 1:20-22).   Not only was
Job innocent of any sin of commission in this first great
trial but he showed an exemplary piety which has been a
model for all ages.

Jehovah still trusted Job and drew Satan's attention to
the fact that he still held fast his integrity in spite of his
losses (Job 2:3).   Satan, always cynical, felt that the trial
had not gone far enough.   If Job's body were smitten, he
would renounce God to his face.   When with God's consent Satan smote Job with sore boils from the sole of his

foot unto his crown, he made no complaint but took his place outside the town among the ashes where the victims of leprosy were required to stay. When his wife advised him to renounce God and die, he replied, "Thou speakest as one of the foolish women speaketh. What? Shall we receive good at the hand of God, and shall we not receive evil? In all this did not Job sin with his lips" (Job 2:10). So far we can see no fault in him. If there were evil thoughts in his mind, he at least restrained his lips from uttering them.

Job's greatest trial began with the arrival of his friends. He knew as well as they that leprosy was regarded as the sure proof of sin. Their very silence accused him. No wonder he opened his mouth and cursed the day of his birth. This was the first evidence of any defect in him; but we should remember that he did it under great provocation. Furthermore cursing the day of his birth fell far short of cursing God who made him, although to us it seems to imply it. Jeremiah in his sufferings also cursed the day he was born (Jer. 20:14-18). Indeed our judgment on this as well as on Job's complaints against God in the course of his speeches must always take into account the moral standards of his time and the severe physical and mental trials he was enduring. He did not come through his long second trial morally unscathed. Otherwise there would have been nothing for him to repent of. He charged God with dealing unjustly with him (Job 9:17, 22, 30-31; 10:3; 16:9, 12-14; 19:6-12; 27:2; 30:18-23). This was not worthy of the man who had said to his wife, "Shall we receive good at the hand of God, and shall we not receive evil?" (Job 2:10). He repented of it in

dust and ashes. He showed the genuineness of his repentance and his magnanimity by praying for his friends
whose attacks upon him were the hardest trial he had to
bear except the sense of God's displeasure.

In his protestations of righteousness Job gave a beautiful picture of the noble life he had lived in his days of
prosperity. He said: "I delivered the poor that cried, the
fatherless also that had none to help him. The blessing
of him that was ready to perish came upon me, and I
caused the widow's heart to sing for joy. . . . I was
eyes to the blind and feet was I to the lame. I was a
father to the needy and the cause of him that I knew not
I searched out" (Job 29:12-13, 15-16). He could honestly
exclaim: "Did not I weep for him that was in trouble?
Was not my soul grieved for the needy?" (Job 30:25).
His righteousness was not one of deeds merely but of
thought, for he said: "I made a covenant with mine eyes.
How then should I look upon a virgin?" (Job 31:1; cp.
Matt. 5:27-29). He recognized his servants as his
brothers and sisters, saying, "If I have despised the cause
of my man-servant or of my maid-servant, when they
contended with me, what then shall I do when God riseth
up? And when he visiteth, what shall I answer him? Did
not he that made me in the womb make him? And did not
one fashion us in the womb?" (Job 31:13-15). This was
a noble pattern of the relation of employer to employee,
the recognition that God takes account of such things, that
all are brothers and sisters in his sight. Although rich
Job did not make gold his hope nor his confidence. He
did not even rejoice because his wealth was great (Job
31:24-25). Nor did he rejoice in the destruction of his

enemy (Job 31:29-30). In this respect his righteousness exceeded that of the authors of the imprecatory Psalms and even that of Jeremiah (Jer. 11:20; 15:15; 17:18; 18:19-23). The author of the book did well to present such a noble pattern to the people of his time. Even Christians can learn much from him.

The sins with which Eliphaz unjustly charged Job were doubtless common in that day. He said: "Thou hast taken pledges of thy brother for nought and stripped the naked of their clothing. Thou hast not given water to the weary to drink, and thou hast withholden bread from the hungry. . . . Thou hast sent widows away empty and the arms of the fatherless have been broken" (Job 22:6-7, 9). Similarly the offenses of which Job declared himself innocent (Job 31:1, 13-15, 24-25, 29-30) were doubtless common. They are the offenses which were specially abhorrent to the inhabitants of the Arabian desert where Job lived and not those of the settled life of Palestine in the reign of Manasseh. Quite another set of offenses is condemned in the books of Amos, Hosea, Isaiah and Micah.

BIBLIOGRAPHY

The selective bibliography that follows is limited to works in English and is weighted toward those that are more contemporary and more conservative. Works that cover the entire span of Old Testament theology, and those that deal with the Old Testament alone, have also been preferred.

Since Raven's *History of the Religion of Israel* appeared in 1933, the primary conservative works in the field have been by Vos (1948), Payne (1962), and Kaiser (1978). Also conservative and valuable are those by Watts (1947), Lehman (1971), and Purkiser (1977). Raven's volume was preceded by such evangelical works as those of Hengstenberg (1871–1872), Foster (1890) and Girdlestone (1909).

Both Payne and Kaiser see a common theme running throughout the Old Testament and tying it together: for Payne it is God's covenant, for Kaiser His promise.

Probably the most popular Old Testament theologies today are those of Eichrodt (1961–1967) and von Rad (1962–1965). Still two of the best all-around works in the field are Oehler's (1883) and Heinisch's (1950).

An analysis of the state of the discipline can be found in Hasel (1975). (For an evaluation of biblical theology in general, Verhoef [1970], Robertson [1971], and Hasel [1979] may be consulted.) Dentan (1963) relates the history of the field, while Laurin (1970) discusses some of the leading Old Testament theologians.

More complete bibliographies can be found in many of the books listed below. Among the best are those of Dentan (1963), Harrington (1973), and Kaiser (1978). Payne's bibliography is annotated.

Baab, Otto J. *The Theology of the Old Testament.* New York: Abingdon-Cokesbury, 1949.

Botterweck, G. Johannes, and Ringgren, Helmer, eds. *Theological Dictionary of the Old Testament.* Translated by John T. Willis et al. Rev. ed. 3 vols. to date. Grand Rapids: Eerdmans, 1977–.

Bromiley, Geoffrey W. "Biblical Theology." In *Baker's Dictionary of Theology,* edited by Everett F. Harrison. Grand Rapids: Baker, 1960. Pp. 95–97.

Burney, C. F. *Outlines of Old Testament Theology.* London: Rivingtons, 1899.

Burrows, Millar. *An Outline of Biblical Theology.* Philadelphia: Westminster, 1946.

Childs, Brevard S. *Biblical Theology in Crisis.* Philadelphia: Westminster, 1970.

Clements, Ronald E. *Old Testament Theology: A Fresh Approach.* Greenwood, S.C.: Attic, 1978.

Davidson, A. B. *The Theology of the Old Testament.* Edited by S. D. F. Salmond. New York: Scribner, 1904.

Dentan, Robert C. *Preface to Old Testament Theology.* Rev. ed. New York: Seabury, 1963.

Eichrodt, Walther. *Theology of the Old Testament.* Translated by J. A. Baker. 2 vols. Philadelphia: Westminster, 1961–1967.

Foster, Robert V. *Old Testament Studies: An Outline of Old Testament Theology.* Chicago: Revell, 1890.

Fritsch, Charles T. "Biblical Typology," part 1: "New Trends in Old Testament Theology." *Bibliotheca Sacra* 103 (1946): 293–305.

Gelin, Albert. *The Key Concepts of the Old Testament.* Translated by George Lamb. New York: Sheed and Ward, 1955.

Girdlestone, Robert B. *Old Testament Theology and Modern Ideas.* London: Longmans and Green, 1909.

Harrington, Wilfrid J. *The Path of Biblical Theology.* Dublin: Gill and Macmillan, 1973.

Hasel, Gerhard F. "The Future of Biblical Theology." In *Perspectives on Evangelical Theology: Papers from the Thirtieth Annual Meeting of the Evangelical Theological Society,* edited by Kenneth S. Kantzer and Stanley N. Gundry. Grand Rapids: Baker, 1979.

_____. *Old Testament Theology: Basic Issues in the Current Debate.* Rev. ed. Grand Rapids: Eerdmans, 1975.

Heinisch, Paul. *Theology of the Old Testament.* Translated by William Heidt. Collegeville, Minn.; Liturgical, 1950.

Hengstenberg, Ernst W. *History of the Kingdom of God Under the Old Testament.* Translated by Theodore Meyer and James Martin. 2 vols. Edinburgh: Clark, 1871–1872.

Jacob, Edmond. *Theology of the Old Testament*. Translated by Arthur W. Heathcote and Philip A. Allcock. New York: Harper, 1958.

Kaiser, Walter C., Jr. *Toward an Old Testament Theology*. Grand Rapids: Zondervan, 1978.

Kaufmann, Yehezkel. *The Religion of Israel, from Its Beginnings to the Babylonian Exile*. Edited and translated by Moshe Greenberg. Chicago: University of Chicago, 1960.

Knight, George A. F. *A Christian Theology of the Old Testament*. Richmond: John Knox, 1959.

Köhler, Ludwig Hugo. *Old Testament Theology*. Translated by A. S. Todd. Philadelphia: Westminster, 1957.

Laurin, Robert B. *Contemporary Old Testament Theologians*. Valley Forge, Pa.: Judson, 1970.

Lehman, Chester K. *Biblical Theology*. Vol. 1: *Old Testament*. Scottsdale, Pa.: Herald, 1971.

Léon-Dufour, Xavier, ed. *Dictionary of Biblical Theology*. Translation edited by P. Joseph Cahill. New York: Desclee, 1967.

McKenzie, John L. *A Theology of the Old Testament*. Garden City, N.Y.: Doubleday, 1974.

Martens, Elmer A. "Tackling Old Testament Theology." *Journal of the Evangelical Theological Society* 20 (1977): 123–32.

Muilenburg, James. *The Way of Israel: Biblical Faith and Ethics*. New York: Harper, 1961.

Oehler, Gustav Friedrich. *Theology of the Old Testament*. Translated by Ellen D. Smith and Sophia

Taylor. Revised by George E. Day. New York: Funk and Wagnalls, 1883.

Oesterley, W. O. E., and Robinson, Theodore H. *Hebrew Religion: Its Origin and Development.* 2d ed. New York: Macmillan, 1937.

Olbricht, Thomas H. "The Theology of the Old Testament." In *The World and Literature of the Old Testament,* edited by John T. Willis. The Living Word Commentary on the Old Testament, vol. 1. Austin, Tex.: Sweet, 1979. Pp. 296–345.

Payne, J. Barton. *The Theology of the Older Testament.* Grand Rapids: Zondervan, 1962.

Pfeiffer, Robert H. *Religion in the Old Testament: The History of a Spiritual Triumph.* Edited by Charles Conrad Forman. New York: Harper, 1961.

Purkiser, W. T. "Old Testament Foundations." In Purkiser, W. T.; Taylor, Richard S.; and Taylor, Willard H. *God, Man, and Salvation: A Biblical Theology.* Kansas City: Beacon Hill, 1977. Pp. 29–199.

Rad, Gerhard von. *Old Testament Theology.* Translated by D. M. G. Stalker. 2 vols. New York: Harper, 1962–1965.

Ringgren, Helmer. *Israelite Religion.* Translated by David E. Green. Philadelphia: Fortress, 1966.

Robertson, O. Palmer. "The Outlook for Biblical Theology." In *Toward a Theology for the Future,* edited by David F. Wells and Clark H. Pinnock. Carol Stream, Ill.: Creation, 1971. Pp. 65–91.

Robinson, H. Wheeler. *The Religious Ideas of the Old Testament.* New York: Scribner, 1913.

Rowley, H. H. *The Faith of Israel: Aspects of Old Testament Thought.* Philadelphia: Westminster, 1957.

Schofield, John N. *Introducing Old Testament Theology.* Philadelphia: Westminster, 1964.

Schultz, Hermann. *Old Testament Theology: The Religion of Revelation in Its Pre-Christian Stage of Development.* Translated by J. A. Paterson. 2 vols. Edinburgh: Clark, 1892.

Snaith, Norman H. *The Distinctive Ideas of the Old Testament.* Philadelphia: Westminster, 1946.

Stendahl, Krister, and Betz, Otto. "Biblical Theology." In *The Interpreter's Dictionary of the Bible,* edited by George Arthur Buttrick, vol. 1. Nashville: Abingdon, 1962. Pp. 418–37.

Terrien, Samuel L. *The Elusive Presence: Toward a New Biblical Theology.* San Francisco: Harper and Row, 1978.

Verhoef, Pieter A. "Some Thoughts on the Present-Day Situation in Biblical Theology." *The Westminster Theological Journal* 33 (1970): 1–19.

Vos, Geerhardus. *Biblical Theology: Old and New Testaments.* Grand Rapids: Eerdmans, 1948. "Biblical Theology—Old Testament," pp. 11–318.

Vriezen, Theodorus C. *An Outline of Old Testament Theology.* Translated by S. Neuijen. 2d ed. Newton, Mass.: Branford, 1970.

Watts, J. Wash. *A Survey of Old Testament Teaching.* 2 vols. Nashville: Broadman, 1947.

Weidner, Revere Franklin. *Biblical Theology of the Old Testament, Based on Oehler.* 2d ed. New York: Revell, 1896.

Wright, G. Ernest. *God Who Acts: Biblical Theology as Recital*. Chicago: Regnery, 1952.

_____. *The Old Testament and Theology*. New York: Harper and Row, 1969.

Young, Edward J. *The Study of Old Testament Theology Today*. Westwood, N.J.: Revell, 1959.

Young, G. Douglas. "Old Testament Theology: A Method and a Conclusion." In *Papers Read at the Eighth Annual Meeting of the Evangelical Theological Society, December 29–30, 1955, Grand Rapids, Michigan*, edited by John F. Walvoord. Evangelical Theological Society, 1956. Pp. 76–82.

Youngblood, Ronald. *The Heart of the Old Testament*. Grand Rapids: Baker, 1971.

TOPICAL INDEX

afflictions of the righteous, 623-34
angels, 26-27, 159-60, 618-23. *See also* Jehovah, Angel of
animals, clean and unclean, 111-12
ark of the covenant, 165-66
Ashtaroth, 181-84. *See also* worship, idol
atonement, day of, 98-101
Baalim, 181-84, 279-80. *See also* worship, idol
ceremonial uncleanness
  mosaic period, 112-16
  Solomon–Amos, 288-89
ceremonies, religious (sacrifices)
  Amos, 318-21
  Davidic reign, 214-22
  Hosea, 342-45
  Isaiah, 372-77
  Job, 592-95
  Micah, 490-97
  Moses–David, 164-86
  patriarchal period, 29-33
  Solomon–Amos, 283-89
  Solomon's reign, 262-68
Chemosh, 184-85. *See also* worship, idol
circumcision
  Davidic reign, 221
  mosaic period, 116-18
  Moses–David, 175-76
  patriarchal period, 32-33

covenant
  mosaic, 59-66
  with Abraham, 33-35, 60
  with Noah, 20-21, 60
creation, 52-54
  of man, 12-13, 17, 126-28
Dagon, 160, 185. *See also* worship, idol
faith,
  Isaiah, 468-74
feasts (holy times)
  Solomon–Amos, 287-88
  of tabernacles, 92, 101-103
  of unleavened bread, 92-96. *See also* passover
  of weeks, 92, 96-98
God
  attributes of, 209
  conception of
    before Abraham, 12-15
    Amos, 313-18
    Davidic reign, 206-14
    Hosea, 335
    Isaiah, 359-72
    Job, 584-92
    Micah, 487-90
    mosaic period, 45-59
    Moses–David, 158-64
    patriarchal period, 24-29
    Solomon–Amos, 282-83
    Solomon's reign, 257-61
  names of
    before Abraham, 14
    mosaic period, 45-50

SCRIPTURE INDEX